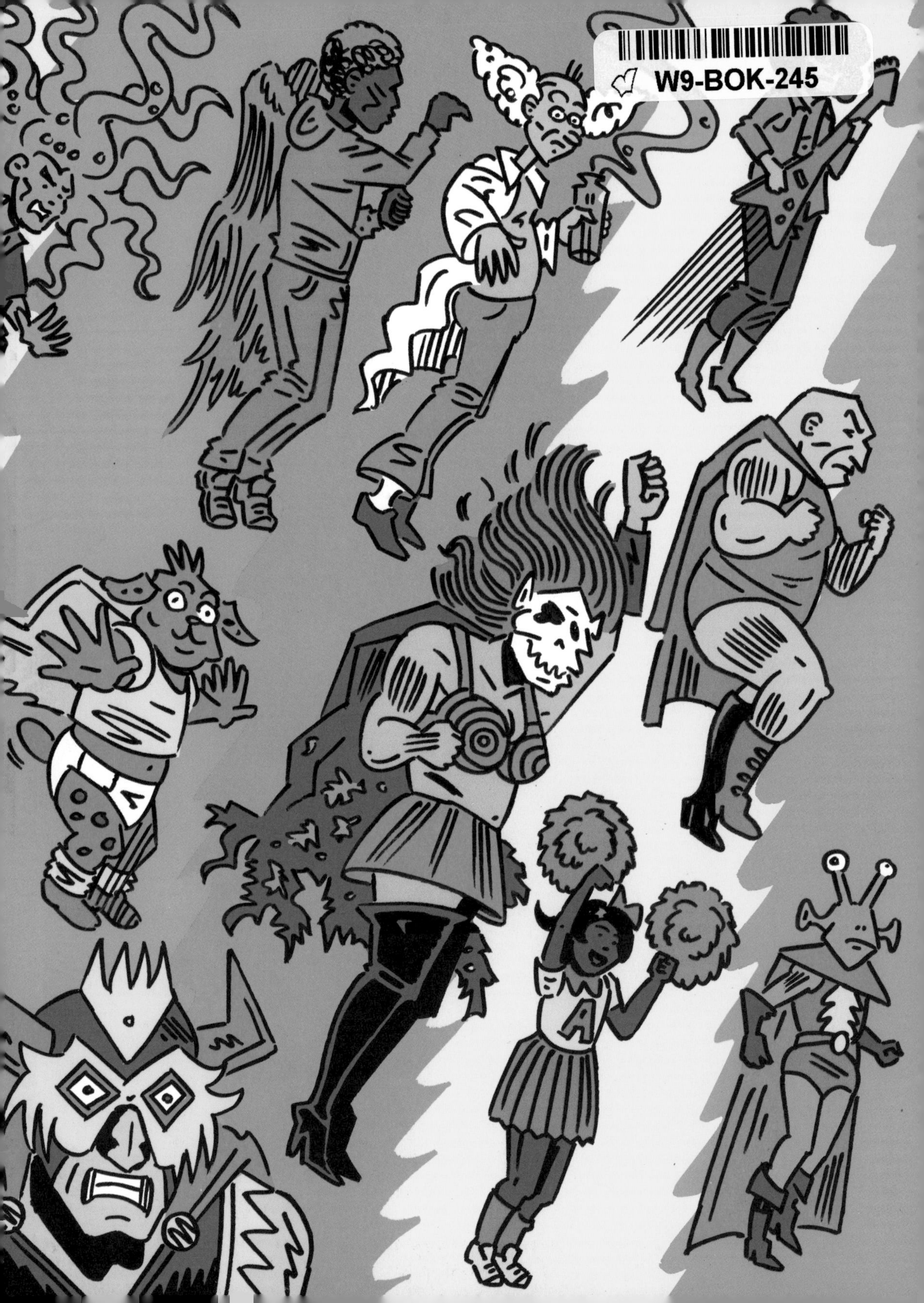

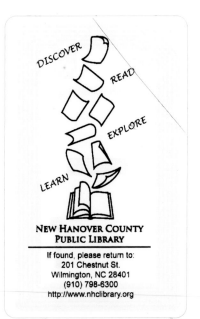

THE BEST AMERICAN

Comics 2015

GUEST EDITORS OF THE
BEST AMERICAN COMICS

2006 HARVEY PEKAR
2007 CHRIS WARE
2008 LYNDA BARRY
2009 CHARLES BURNS
2010 NEIL GAIMAN
2011 ALISON BECHDEL
2012 FRANÇOISE MOULY
2013 JEFF SMITH
2014 SCOTT McCLOUD
2015 JONATHAN LETHEM

THE BEST AMERICAN

Comics

2015

EDITED *and* INTRODUCED
by Jonathan Lethem

BILL KARTALOPOULOS,
series editor

HOUGHTON MIFFLIN HARCOURT
BOSTON · NEW YORK   2015

www.hmhco.com

Library of Congress Cataloging-in-Publication Data is available.

ISBN 978-0-544-10770-0

Book design: David Futato   Cover art: Raymond Pettibon
Endpaper art: Anya Davidson   Cover art direction: Christopher Moisan

PRINTED IN THE UNITED STATES OF AMERICA

DOC 10 9 8 7 6 5 4 3 2 1

Permissions credits are located on page 378.

Contents

Foreword

Comics can be disorienting.
And, arguably, they should be.

The book you hold in your hands is the tenth annual volume of the Best American Comics. Round numbers are arbitrary, but ten years is a significant milestone. Ten years suggests a degree of longevity, a track record, and hopefully some status as a reliable institution: reliable in the sense that you can expect it—like a holiday—and reliable in the sense that you can trust it—like a friend.

But this year is also the one hundredth anniversary of the Best American series overall. The first volume of the Best American Short Stories was published in 1915, as World War I devastated Europe. Founding editor Edward O'Brien (1890–1941) championed the qualities of the American short story of his day, but the short story form itself needed no such defense. Prose fiction was already connected to a deep and respected Western tradition, extending backward to Edgar Allan Poe, to Charles Dickens, to Jane Austen, to Laurence Sterne, to William Shakespeare, to Homer. O'Brien's claim was, in part, nationalistic, but it was also deeply critical: he positioned the "best" work of the year *in opposition to* the more commercial short story production of his day. "Commercialization has never affected any literature more than it has affected the American short story in the past," he wrote. "It is affecting our writing more than ever today. But here and there in quiet places . . . artists are laboring quietly for a literary ideal, and the leaven of their achievement is becoming more and more impressive every day." As the "graphic novel" has been steadily commercialized over the past decade, O'Brien's words are worth considering now, in this context.

Ten years is a drop in the bucket compared to the centuries of critical respectability that literature has enjoyed. Comics have their own deep history, and visual narrative is absolutely ancient. But modern comics—as we know them in the West—have developed outside of the cultural sphere that has nurtured the short story, the essay, and other forms celebrated each year by the Best American series. Comics have developed their own codes and aesthetics, according to their own needs and constraints, incorporating image and text within their own distinct framework, and developing unique modes of expression.

On a fundamental level, comics have often been considered a "lesser" cultural form in part because they violate long-standing art-critical principles that regard narrative as the domain of literature, and spatial experience as the domain of image-making. Comics have typically, of course, integrated those two functions. In fact, comics' core energy radiates from the dynamic structurally inscribed upon the comics page between the propulsive linearity of exposition and the reflective examination of composition. Comics don't merely combine text and image; they are, at least, the very distinct *product* of the interaction between the formal procedures that underlie text and image: a chemical reaction that activates and consumes its constituent elements to produce a third and different thing.

So it's really not right to expect comics to enter too seamlessly into the world of literary book publishing. Comics often *are* books, but so are *Depero Futurista* and Max Ernst's *Une semaine de bonté*. Comics are positioned to bring together the lessons of both the narrative *and* the visual arts. As such, comics *should* continue to have the capacity to appear alien and difficult to assimilate within literary publishing. It is an expression of what they are. To expect comics to function merely as colorful, illustrated cousins of conventional narrative fiction is a profound and wasteful act of self-denial.

In this context, I couldn't be more grateful that Raymond Pettibon has not only allowed us to include some of his recent work in *The Best American Comics 2015*, but has also provided us with an eye-popping cover drawing. Raymond's work, with its text-image combinations and pop cultural visual references, has often gestured toward the influence of comics. But sometimes Raymond has produced pieces, like the pages included here, that perform the fundamental formal operation that qualifies them as *comics*. In truth, work like Raymond's pages here fits into a category that I've been privately referring to as *paracomics*: comics that aren't connected to the field or conventions of comics. This is a huge and rich category, encompassing works by such diverse artists as Sol Lewitt, Ida Applebroog, Jennifer Bartlett, Keith Haring, Duane Michals, Joe Brainard, and so many more. For decades, comics and their creators were alienated from the world of contemporary art. Today, many young comics artists are at ease with the lessons of twentieth- (and twenty-first-) century art, and are producing comics that have a closer kinship to these paracomics than to much of the work that has historically characterized the form. Young cartoonists no longer feel alienated from the traditional fine arts, even if they operate outside of their institutions. I hope, reciprocally, that we can encourage contemporary artists from the other side of the bridge to not feel so alienated from the possibilities of comics, either.

For the past decade, Dan Nadel's PictureBox publishing house behaved as if any barriers that might exist between the worlds of comics and contemporary art were already negligible. I worked with Dan for four years as co-organizers of the Brooklyn Comics and Graphics Festival, which ran from 2009 to 2012. As a reader of the work Dan published, I, like many, was saddened to learn in late 2013 that he'd be closing up shop as a publisher. Dan has moved on to bigger things, and his keen eye has, if anything, been liberated to range more broadly across the world of visual culture. I'm pleased that two of the final PictureBox books—featuring work by Anya Davidson and Matthew Thurber—are included in this year's volume of the Best American Comics. I'm grateful to Anya for providing this volume's bold and colorful endpapers.

I'm also pleased that guest editor Jonathan Lethem has brought his point of view to *The Best American Comics 2015.* I appreciate so deeply that Jonathan has embraced in this volume the broad range of what comics can do, precisely because as a first-rate novelist he understands very well the ways in which comics operate differently from his own primary form of expression. It does not hurt, of course, that Jonathan is a longtime comics fan (and, as you'll see in these pages, an occasional cartoonist himself). It also does not hurt, I think, that Jonathan grew up with a father who is a painter and therefore brings to this project an open-minded sensitivity to the wide-ranging possibilities of visual art. Beyond that, I want to thank Jonathan sincerely for being such a fiercely engaged and intelligent collaborator on this year's volume, even in the midst of a whirlwind of other projects and personal commitments. I would also like to thank him for some of the best-written emails I've ever received.

The Best American Comics 2015 represents a selection of outstanding work published between September 1, 2013, and August 31, 2014. The great majority of the work we considered came to us through our open submission process. Any artist or publisher, large or small, can submit work to our public mailing address with confidence that their comics will be read and seriously considered. The very open quality of this process is a strength and an opportunity that no one should take for granted. In addition, as series editor I keep my eyes open for new work at comic book stores, at comics festivals, online, and through recommendations from trusted colleagues. All told, I read hundreds and hundreds of comics over the course of a year. From this vast pool of material, I select a smaller group of excellent work to forward to each year's guest editor for consideration. From this selection, the guest editor must then choose the final list of pieces that will be published in the Best American Comics (while retaining the ability to bring in some work discovered on his or her own).

While I do my best to be aware of excellent work being published each year, the comics field is vast and diverse. I cannot stress enough that any work submitted to the Best American Comics will be considered on its merits, and that submitting work to our public postal address is the very best way to ensure that we will see and consider any eligible work. Indeed, the continuing diversity and excellence of the series depends upon submissions. Any artists or publishers who wish to submit material for consideration should please send work clearly labeled with publication date and contact information to the following address:

Bill Kartalopoulos
Series Editor
The Best American Comics
Houghton Mifflin Harcourt Publishing Company
215 Park Avenue South
New York, NY 10003

By the time this volume is published, we will have already collected work to consider for *The Best American Comics 2016* and will be actively seeking work published in North America (including Canada and Mexico) between September 1, 2015, and August 31, 2016, for the 2017 volume.

Because we can represent only a sample of all of the great work published every year, each volume in this series also includes a lengthy list of additional notable comics. This list can be found in the back of this book, and all of the comics named there are worth seeking out and exploring if you have enjoyed any of the work reprinted here. I have posted an online version of this list to my website (www.on-panel.com), which includes links to further information about this year's notable comics.

I'd like to take this opportunity to thank Nicole Angeloro, our in-house editor for Best American Comics at Houghton Mifflin Harcourt. As always, Nicole has been a knowledgeable, intelligent, patient, and supportive pillar during the sometimes hectic process behind this series. And that process owes so much to our efficient production editor, Beth Burleigh Fuller, to whom I'm most grateful. Many thanks as well to art director Christopher Moisan, who worked on the cover and endpapers for this volume, and to David Futato, who managed the challenges of production for the book's diverse interior pages with skill and grace. Thanks as well to Mary Dalton-Hoffman, who, as always, negotiated the fraught landscape of rights and permissions with aplomb. I'd also like to thank Chelsea Newbould, who handled publicity for *The Best American Comics 2014* before moving on from Houghton Mifflin Harcourt. She did a wonderful job getting the word out about last year's volume and I wish her the best. On my end I'd like to thank Jenny Goldstick for assisting me in gathering digital files as part of my reading and selection process.

Thanks as well to Branwen Jones, Elizabeth DeMase, and the staff at David Zwirner for all of their assistance, and to Brendan Burford at King Features Syndicate. Many friends and colleagues offered useful feedback during the past year and I thank them all.

Finally, I must note that while we were working on this book we observed the terrible tragedy of the terrorist attacks at the *Charlie Hebdo* offices and elsewhere in Paris, France. It was my privilege to attend the annual comics festival in Angoulême a few short (but heavy) weeks later, and to spend some time in Paris afterwards visiting with cartoonists, editors, and publishers. I don't think it's incorrect to say that this event has affected French society as strongly as 9/11 affected the psyche of New Yorkers in the immediate aftermath of that event, accompanied by the same anxiety over what might constitute the "new normal" in daily life, and the possibility of political responses that might cynically instrumentalize the event to advance dubious agendas.

While much ink and many pixels have been spilled on these shores debating the merits of the contents of *Charlie Hebdo,* I can tell you that in France I encountered no confusion about the fundamental issues at stake. It was civic clarity, not xenophobia, that motivated millions of French citizens of different backgrounds to take to the streets on January 11, 2015, in the biggest peaceful assembly in French history.

We can debate the value of any work of art. The Best American Comics, by making annual critical judgments, is implicitly part of that debate. But the freedom to criticize and the freedom to create are bound up in the same shared premise of freedom. As a first principle, art is the ultimate safe space for the theoretical exploration of visual, ethical, formal, stylistic, expressive, psychological, narrative, ideological, and conceptual ideas, no matter how unorthodox. Everything else comes after. I'm so pleased that *The Best American Comics 2015* features the work of so many artists who have taken that creative freedom and run so far with it, in so many different directions. May we all follow their lead by finding our own equally unique directions to explore in art and in life.

BILL KARTALOPOULOS

Introduction

I'M JONATHAN LETHEM. I WRITE STORIES & NOVELS. I'VE WRITTEN SOME INTRODUCTIONS TO BOOKS, BUT I'VE NEVER DRAWN ONE BEFORE.

AT SOME POINT, AN ARTIST REALIZES THAT EVERYTHING IS A KIND OF SELF-PORTRAIT. BUT THAT DOESN'T MEAN YOU HAVE A CLEAR VIEW OF YOURSELF.

I ONCE GOT DRAWN BY A GREAT CARICATURIST, DAVID LEVINE. IT DIDN'T COME OUT GREAT. HE CLEARLY BASED IT ON A SINGLE PHOTOGRAPH, TAKEN WHEN I'D LOST FIFTEEN POUNDS FROM THE FLU.

AT LEAST HE GOT THE CAPE RIGHT.

Je ne fume pas une pipe

WHEN I DID A SELF-PORTRAIT FOR McSWEENEY'S, PEOPLE TOLD ME IT LOOKED MORE LIKE WILLIAM VOLLMAN.

PAUL HORNSCHEMEIER, A BRILLIANT CARTOONIST WHO'S NOT IN THIS BOOK, ONCE DREW ME WHILE I WAS SITTING UNAWARES. UNFLATTERING, BUT DEAD ON.

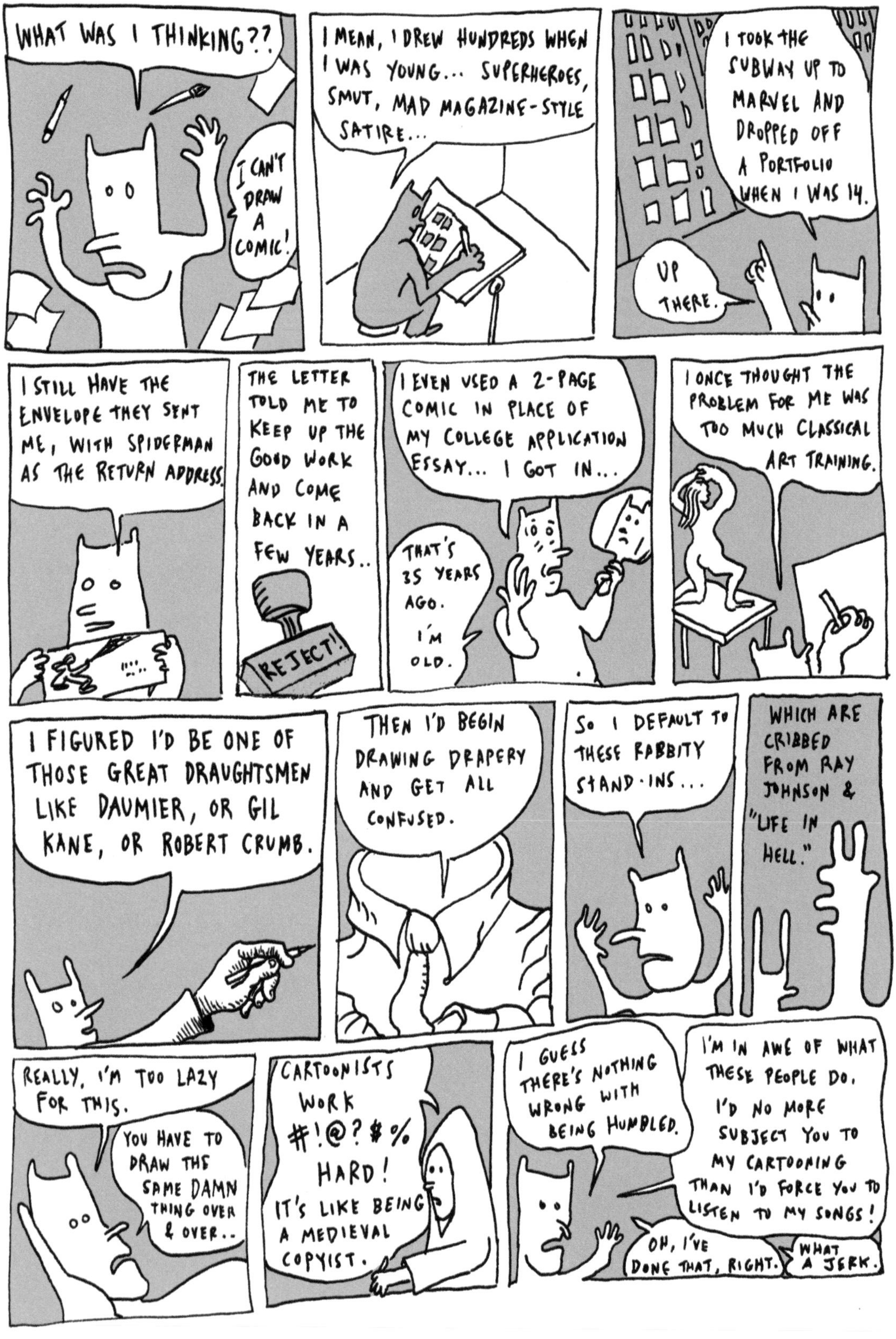
WHAT WAS I THINKING??
I CAN'T DRAW A COMIC!
I MEAN, I DREW HUNDREDS WHEN I WAS YOUNG... SUPERHEROES, SMUT, MAD MAGAZINE-STYLE SATIRE...
I TOOK THE SUBWAY UP TO MARVEL AND DROPPED OFF A PORTFOLIO WHEN I WAS 14.
UP THERE.
I STILL HAVE THE ENVELOPE THEY SENT ME, WITH SPIDERMAN AS THE RETURN ADDRESS.
THE LETTER TOLD ME TO KEEP UP THE GOOD WORK AND COME BACK IN A FEW YEARS...
REJECT!
I EVEN USED A 2-PAGE COMIC IN PLACE OF MY COLLEGE APPLICATION ESSAY... I GOT IN...
THAT'S 35 YEARS AGO.
I'M OLD.
I ONCE THOUGHT THE PROBLEM FOR ME WAS TOO MUCH CLASSICAL ART TRAINING.
I FIGURED I'D BE ONE OF THOSE GREAT DRAUGHTSMEN LIKE DAUMIER, OR GIL KANE, OR ROBERT CRUMB.
THEN I'D BEGIN DRAWING DRAPERY AND GET ALL CONFUSED.
SO I DEFAULT TO THESE RABBITY STAND-INS...
WHICH ARE CRIBBED FROM RAY JOHNSON & "LIFE IN HELL."
REALLY, I'M TOO LAZY FOR THIS.
YOU HAVE TO DRAW THE SAME DAMN THING OVER & OVER..
CARTOONISTS WORK #!@?$% HARD! IT'S LIKE BEING A MEDIEVAL COPYIST.
I GUESS THERE'S NOTHING WRONG WITH BEING HUMBLED.
I'M IN AWE OF WHAT THESE PEOPLE DO. I'D NO MORE SUBJECT YOU TO MY CARTOONING THAN I'D FORCE YOU TO LISTEN TO MY SONGS!
OH, I'VE DONE THAT, RIGHT.
WHAT A JERK.

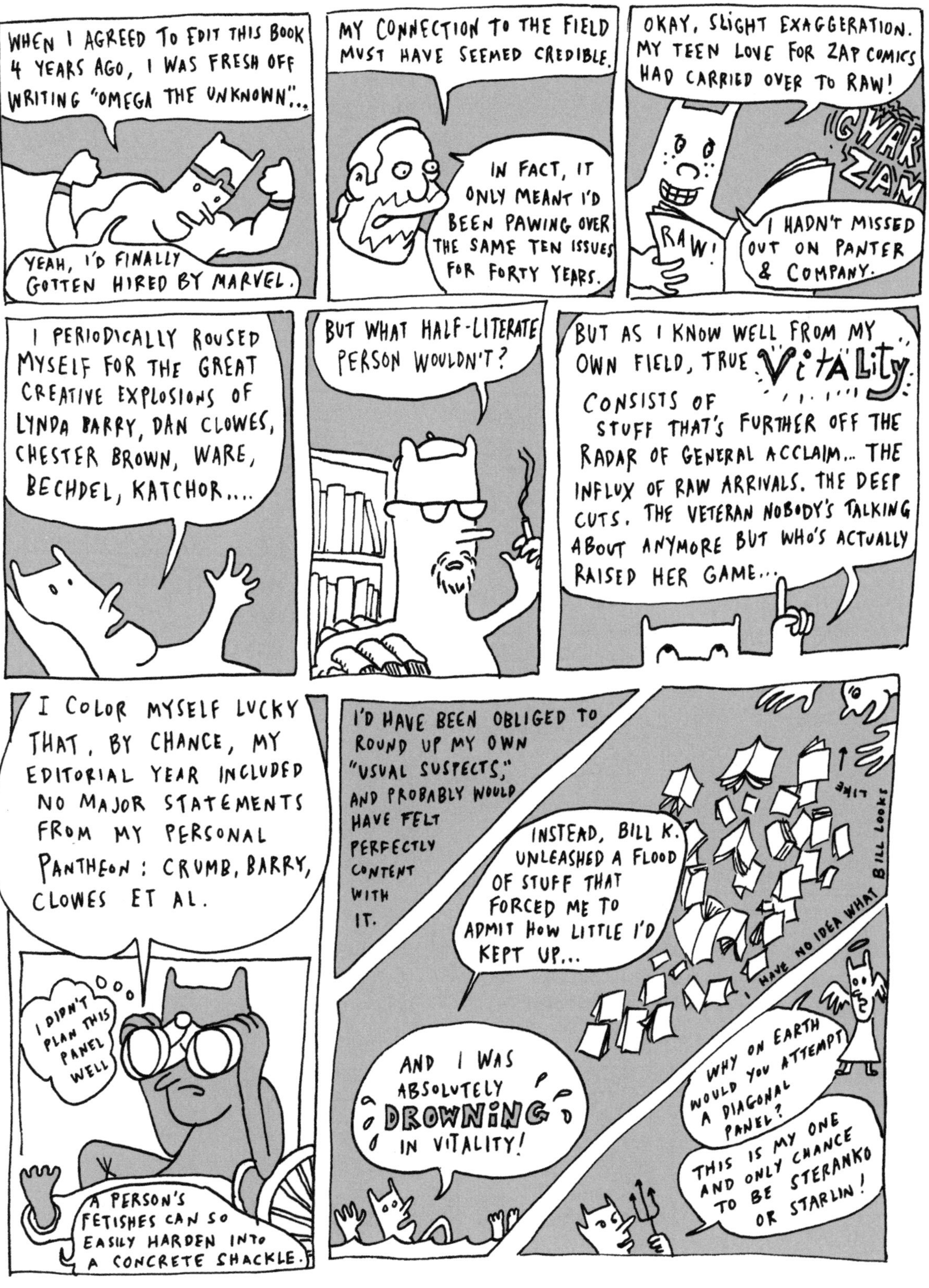
WHEN I AGREED TO EDIT THIS BOOK 4 YEARS AGO, I WAS FRESH OFF WRITING "OMEGA THE UNKNOWN"...
YEAH, I'D FINALLY GOTTEN HIRED BY MARVEL.
MY CONNECTION TO THE FIELD MUST HAVE SEEMED CREDIBLE.
IN FACT, IT ONLY MEANT I'D BEEN PAWING OVER THE SAME TEN ISSUES FOR FORTY YEARS.
OKAY, SLIGHT EXAGGERATION. MY TEEN LOVE FOR ZAP COMICS HAD CARRIED OVER TO RAW!
GWAR ZAM
RAW!
I HADN'T MISSED OUT ON PANTER & COMPANY.
I PERIODICALLY ROUSED MYSELF FOR THE GREAT CREATIVE EXPLOSIONS OF LYNDA BARRY, DAN CLOWES, CHESTER BROWN, WARE, BECHDEL, KATCHOR....
BUT WHAT HALF-LITERATE PERSON WOULDN'T?
BUT AS I KNOW WELL FROM MY OWN FIELD, TRUE VITALITY CONSISTS OF STUFF THAT'S FURTHER OFF THE RADAR OF GENERAL ACCLAIM... THE INFLUX OF RAW ARRIVALS. THE DEEP CUTS. THE VETERAN NOBODY'S TALKING ABOUT ANYMORE BUT WHO'S ACTUALLY RAISED HER GAME...
I COLOR MYSELF LUCKY THAT, BY CHANCE, MY EDITORIAL YEAR INCLUDED NO MAJOR STATEMENTS FROM MY PERSONAL PANTHEON: CRUMB, BARRY, CLOWES ET AL.
I DIDN'T PLAN THIS PANEL WELL
A PERSON'S FETISHES CAN SO EASILY HARDEN INTO A CONCRETE SHACKLE.
I'D HAVE BEEN OBLIGED TO ROUND UP MY OWN "USUAL SUSPECTS," AND PROBABLY WOULD HAVE FELT PERFECTLY CONTENT WITH IT.
INSTEAD, BILL K. UNLEASHED A FLOOD OF STUFF THAT FORCED ME TO ADMIT HOW LITTLE I'D KEPT UP...
I HAVE NO IDEA WHAT BILL LOOKS LIKE
AND I WAS ABSOLUTELY DROWNING IN VITALITY!
WHY ON EARTH WOULD YOU ATTEMPT A DIAGONAL PANEL?
THIS IS MY ONE AND ONLY CHANCE TO BE STERANKO OR STARLIN!

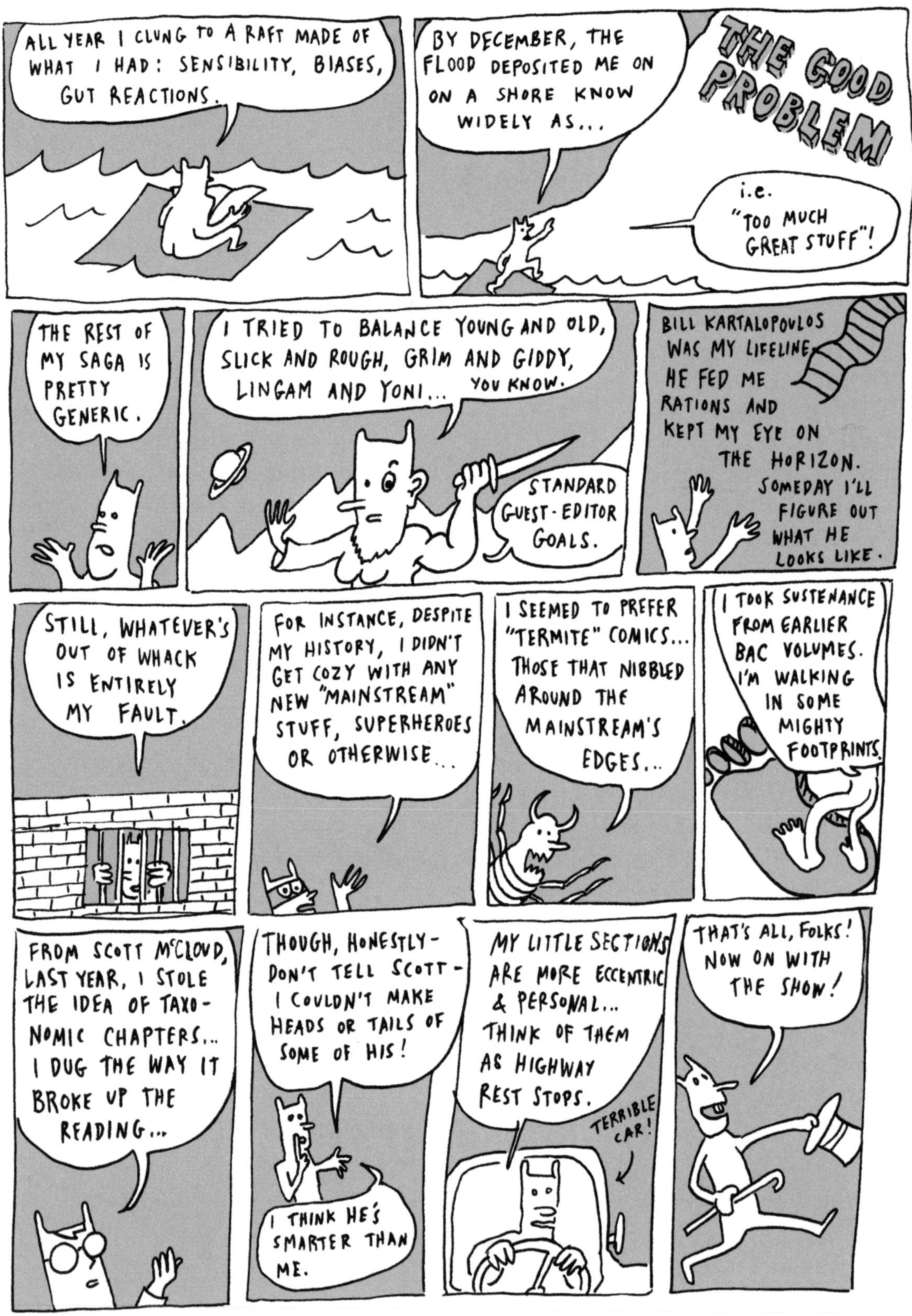
ALL YEAR I CLUNG TO A RAFT MADE OF WHAT I HAD: SENSIBILITY, BIASES, GUT REACTIONS.
BY DECEMBER, THE FLOOD DEPOSITED ME ON ON A SHORE KNOW WIDELY AS...
THE GOOD PROBLEM
i.e. "TOO MUCH GREAT STUFF"!
THE REST OF MY SAGA IS PRETTY GENERIC.
I TRIED TO BALANCE YOUNG AND OLD, SLICK AND ROUGH, GRIM AND GIDDY, LINGAM AND YONI... YOU KNOW.
STANDARD GUEST-EDITOR GOALS.
BILL KARTALOPOULOS WAS MY LIFELINE. HE FED ME RATIONS AND KEPT MY EYE ON THE HORIZON.
SOMEDAY I'LL FIGURE OUT WHAT HE LOOKS LIKE.
STILL, WHATEVER'S OUT OF WHACK IS ENTIRELY MY FAULT.
FOR INSTANCE, DESPITE MY HISTORY, I DIDN'T GET COZY WITH ANY NEW "MAINSTREAM" STUFF, SUPERHEROES OR OTHERWISE...
I SEEMED TO PREFER "TERMITE" COMICS... THOSE THAT NIBBLED AROUND THE MAINSTREAM'S EDGES...
I TOOK SUSTENANCE FROM EARLIER BAC VOLUMES. I'M WALKING IN SOME MIGHTY FOOTPRINTS.
FROM SCOTT McCLOUD, LAST YEAR, I STOLE THE IDEA OF TAXONOMIC CHAPTERS... I DUG THE WAY IT BROKE UP THE READING...
THOUGH, HONESTLY - DON'T TELL SCOTT - I COULDN'T MAKE HEADS OR TAILS OF SOME OF HIS!
I THINK HE'S SMARTER THAN ME.
MY LITTLE SECTIONS ARE MORE ECCENTRIC & PERSONAL... THINK OF THEM AS HIGHWAY REST STOPS.
TERRIBLE CAR!
THAT'S ALL, FOLKS! NOW ON WITH THE SHOW!

THE BEST AMERICAN

Comics 2015

CHAPTER ONE

Mom and Dad

Can't we talk about something more PLEASANT?
ROZ CHAST
A MEMOIR

Kill My Mother
A Graphic Novel
Jules Feiffer

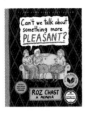

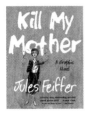

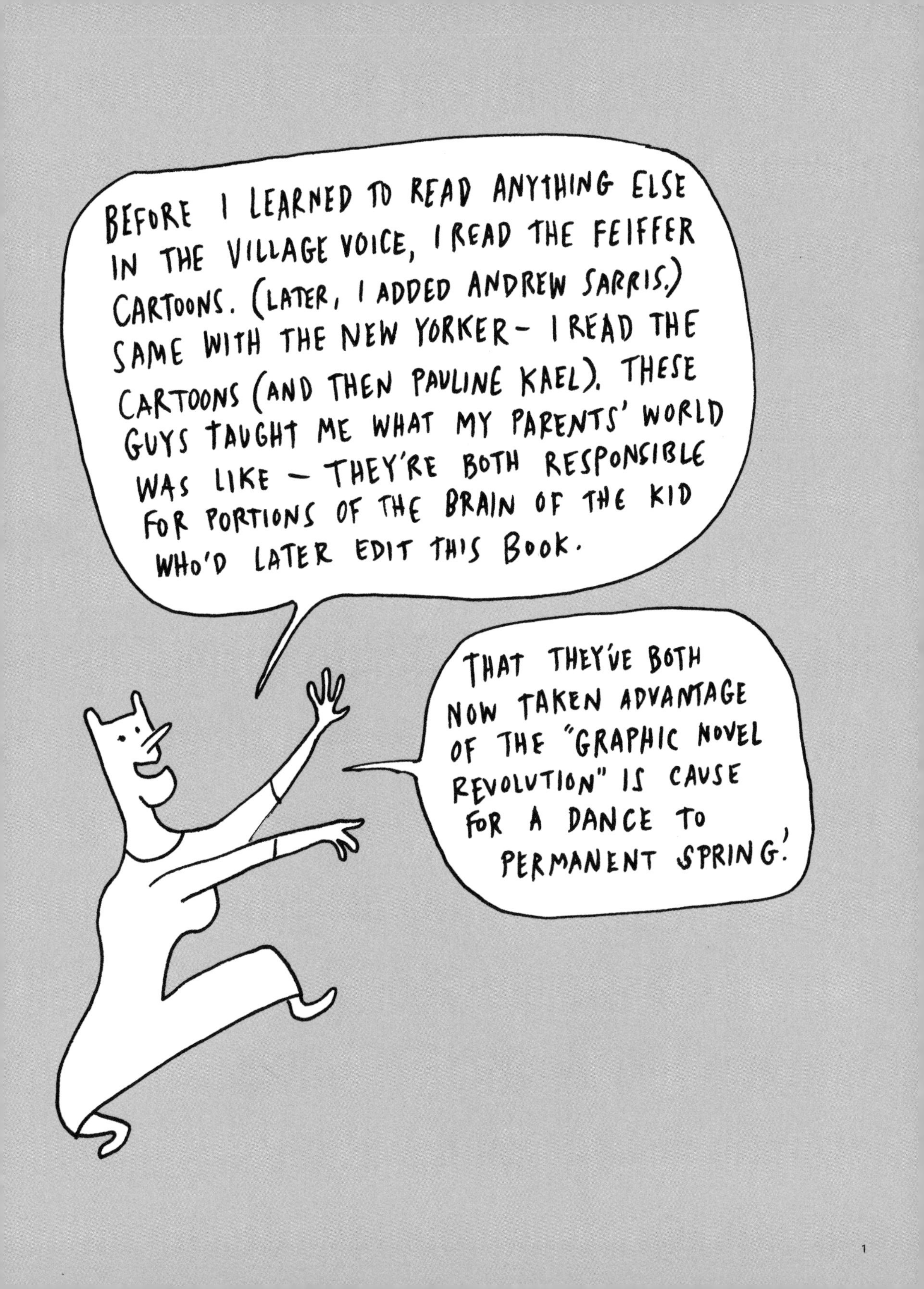
BEFORE I LEARNED TO READ ANYTHING ELSE IN THE VILLAGE VOICE, I READ THE FEIFFER CARTOONS. (LATER, I ADDED ANDREW SARRIS.) SAME WITH THE NEW YORKER – I READ THE CARTOONS (AND THEN PAULINE KAEL). THESE GUYS TAUGHT ME WHAT MY PARENTS' WORLD WAS LIKE – THEY'RE BOTH RESPONSIBLE FOR PORTIONS OF THE BRAIN OF THE KID WHO'D LATER EDIT THIS BOOK.
THAT THEY'VE BOTH NOW TAKEN ADVANTAGE OF THE "GRAPHIC NOVEL REVOLUTION" IS CAUSE FOR A DANCE TO PERMANENT SPRING!

In less than two months by January of 2009, my mother regained the fifteen pounds she'd lost. She didn't go to the dining room, but she was eating. And when she didn't eat, the aides made sure she drank Ensure. I remembered what one of the hospice people called the aides who supplied these nutritional drinks: human feeding tubes.

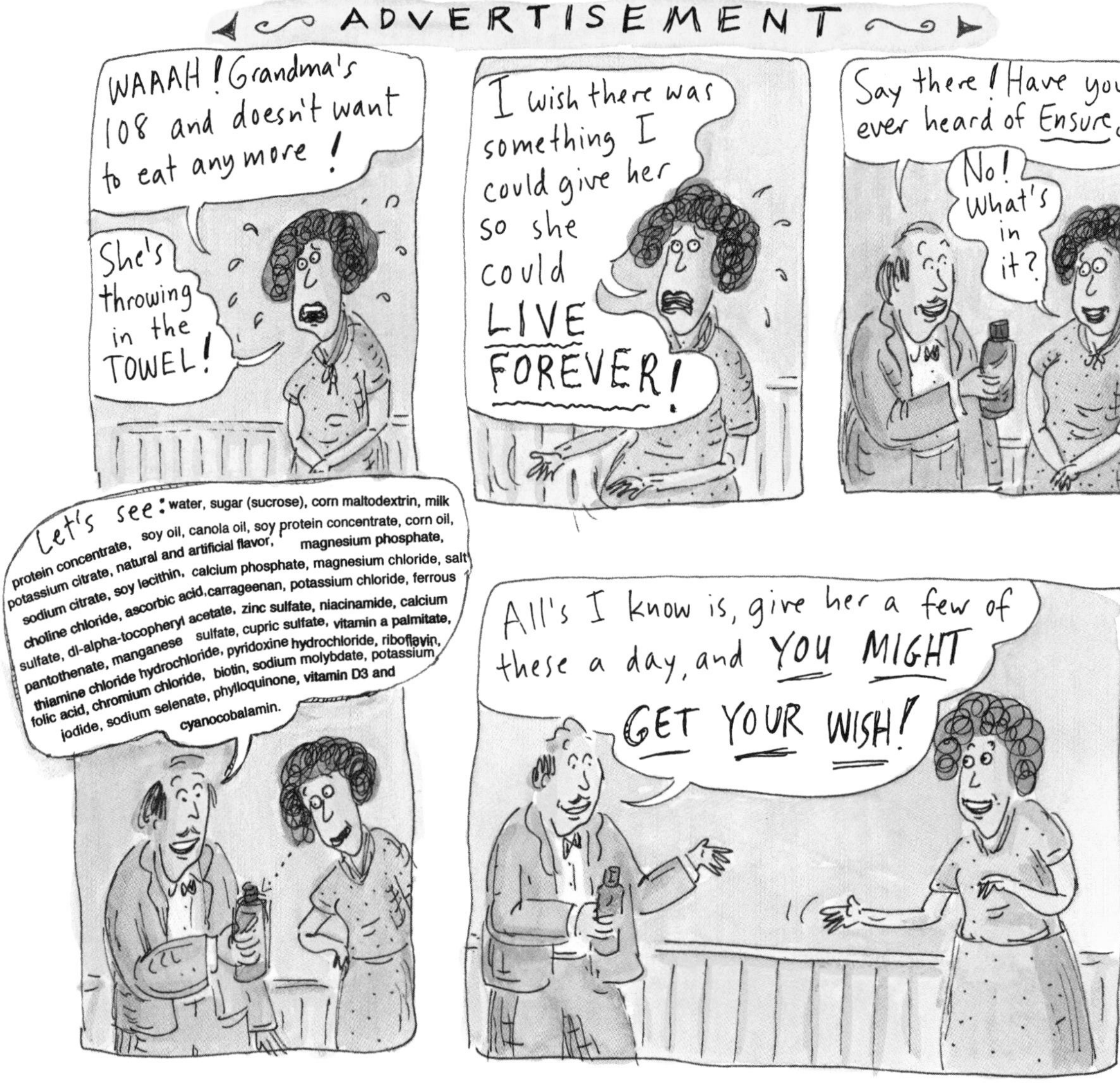
ADVERTISEMENT
WAAAH! Grandma's 108 and doesn't want to eat any more!
She's throwing in the TOWEL!
I wish there was something I could give her so she could LIVE FOREVER!
Say there! Have you ever heard of Ensure®?
No! What's in it?
Let's see: water, sugar (sucrose), corn maltodextrin, milk protein concentrate, soy oil, canola oil, soy protein concentrate, corn oil, potassium citrate, natural and artificial flavor, magnesium phosphate, sodium citrate, soy lecithin, calcium phosphate, magnesium chloride, salt choline chloride, ascorbic acid, carrageenan, potassium chloride, ferrous sulfate, dl-alpha-tocopheryl acetate, zinc sulfate, niacinamide, calcium pantothenate, manganese sulfate, cupric sulfate, vitamin a palmitate, thiamine chloride hydrochloride, pyridoxine hydrochloride, riboflavin, folic acid, chromium chloride, biotin, sodium molybdate, potassium iodide, sodium selenate, phylloquinone, vitamin D3 and cyanocobalamin.
All's I know is, give her a few of these a day, and YOU MIGHT GET YOUR WISH!

She no longer qualified for hospice, but she still needed around-the-clock care. She couldn't feed, toilet, or dress herself. She could stay in the Place, as long as I hired private nurses, or I'd have to put her in a nursing home. Financially, it was a wash.

Goodie volunteered to do both shifts - to sleep in my mother's room, on the sofa. I wanted to buy her a bed, but she said the sofa was o.k. We worked out the payments. It was a phenomenal expense, but it was a phenomenal job. And she and my mother had BONDED. My mother had surrendered control to a lovely stranger.

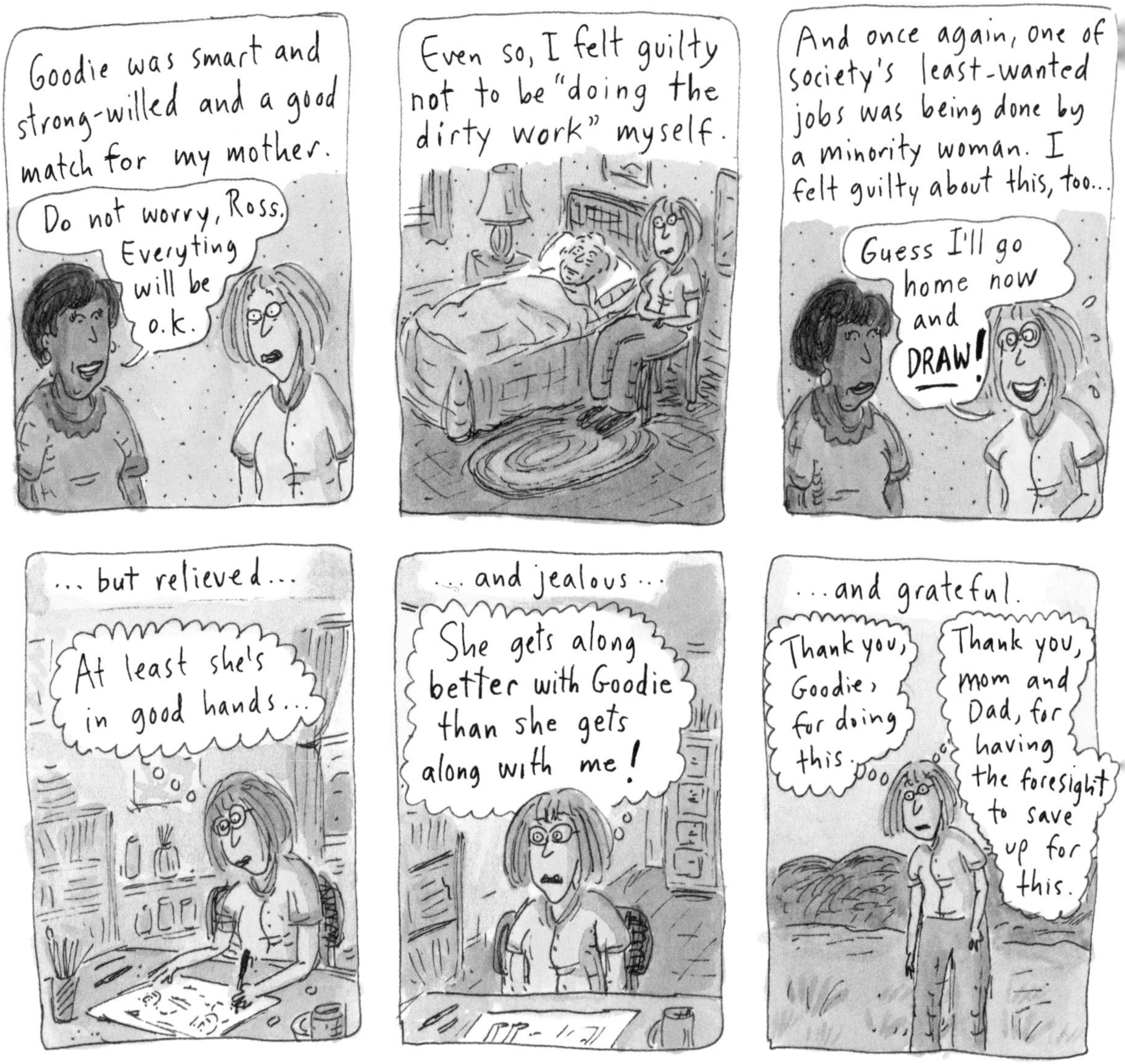
Goodie was smart and strong-willed and a good match for my mother.
Do not worry, Ross. Everyting will be o.k.
Even so, I felt guilty not to be "doing the dirty work" myself.
And once again, one of society's least-wanted jobs was being done by a minority woman. I felt guilty about this, too...
Guess I'll go home now and DRAW!
... but relieved...
At least she's in good hands...
... and jealous...
She gets along better with Goodie than she gets along with me!
... and grateful.
Thank you, Goodie, for doing this.
Thank you, mom and Dad, for having the foresight to save up for this.

My mother's drain-circling had slowed. But she was still completely incontinent, still slept a great deal, and was pretty much holed up in the room with Goodie. Also, her brains *were* starting to melt:

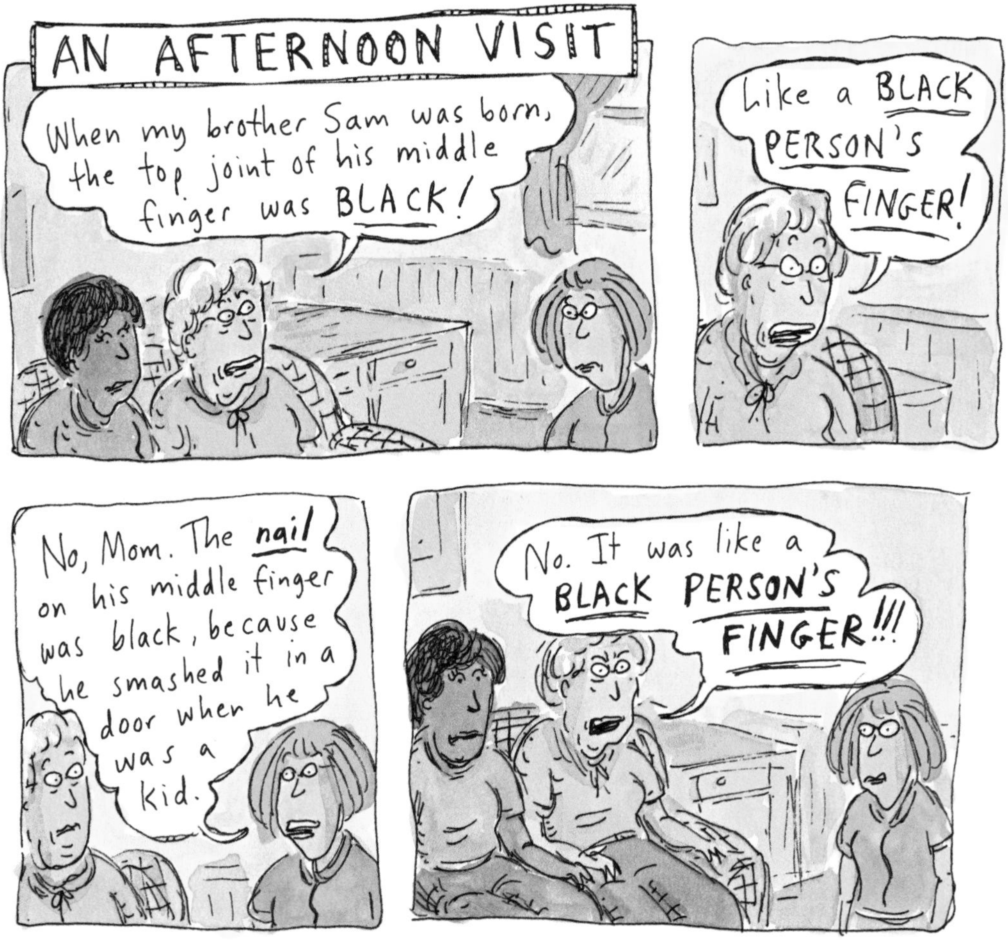
AN AFTERNOON VISIT
When my brother Sam was born, the top joint of his middle finger was BLACK!
Like a BLACK PERSON'S FINGER!
No, Mom. The nail on his middle finger was black, because he smashed it in a door when he was a kid.
No. It was like a BLACK PERSON'S FINGER!!!

I remembered seeing my uncle's discolored nail as a kid and being fascinated and repelled by it. It was odd to recognize it in this story. At least the meaning was—I think—positive: she felt close to Goodie. And Goodie wasn't bothered by it. She'd seen senile dementia before. Sometimes we exchanged "looks" during my mother's increasingly strange stories, like these:

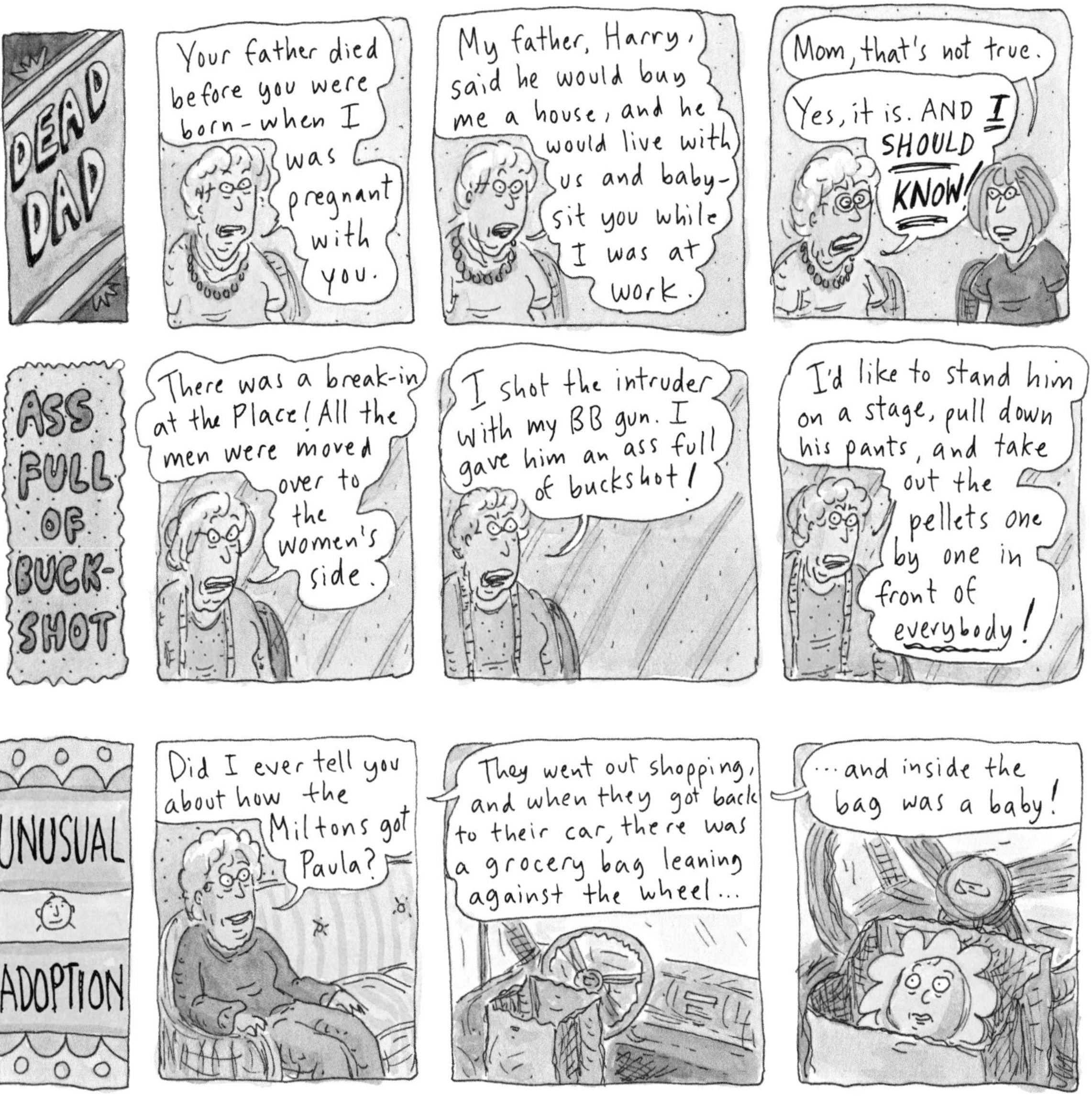

DEAD DAD
Your father died before you were born—when I was pregnant with you.
My father, Harry, said he would buy me a house, and he would live with us and baby-sit you while I was at work.
Mom, that's not true.
Yes, it is. AND I SHOULD KNOW!
ASS FULL OF BUCK-SHOT
There was a break-in at the Place! All the men were moved over to the women's side.
I shot the intruder with my BB gun. I gave him an ass full of buckshot!
I'd like to stand him on a stage, pull down his pants, and take out the pellets one by one in front of everybody!
UNUSUAL ADOPTION
Did I ever tell you about how the Miltons got Paula?
They went out shopping, and when they got back to their car, there was a grocery bag leaning against the wheel...
...and inside the bag was a baby!

As the year continued, she spent more and more time in bed. The stories got stranger and stranger.

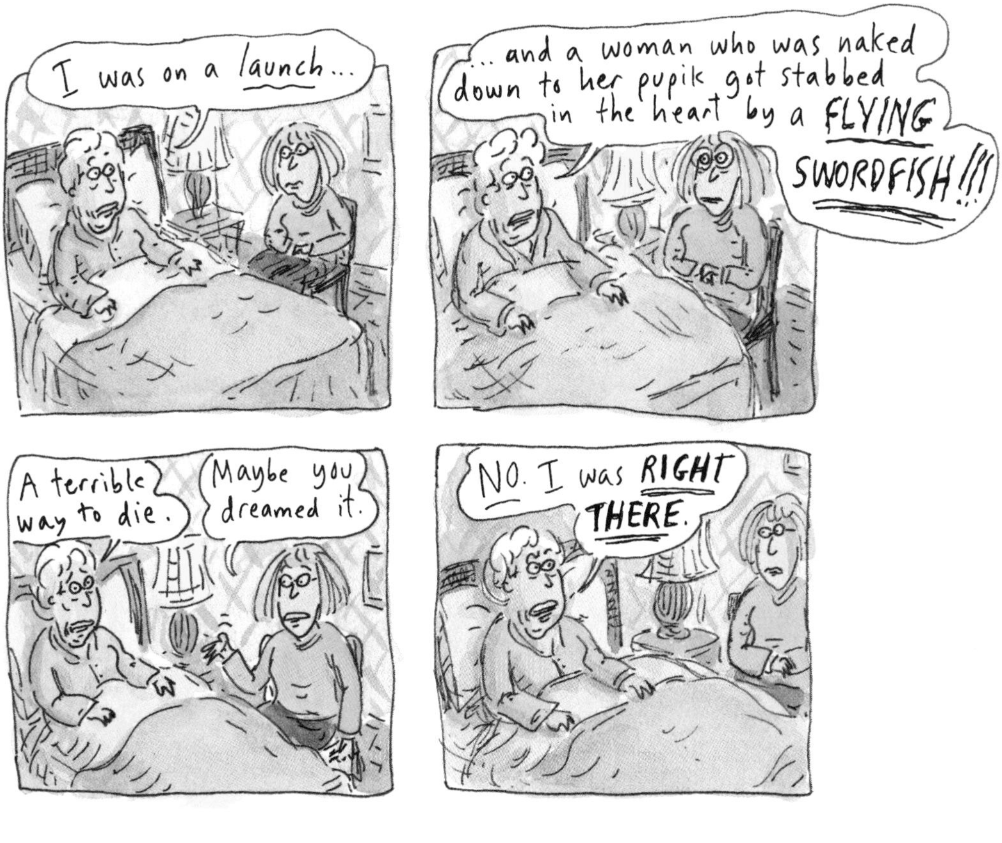

I was on a launch...
...and a woman who was naked down to her pupik got stabbed in the heart by a FLYING SWORDFISH!!!
A terrible way to die.
Maybe you dreamed it.
NO. I was RIGHT THERE.

I started to get really fascinated by these "waking dreams," and looked forward to the next one. And, of course, I was writing them down.

Many of my mother's stories involved my father's mother – my grandmother – Katie. They had not had a good relationship.

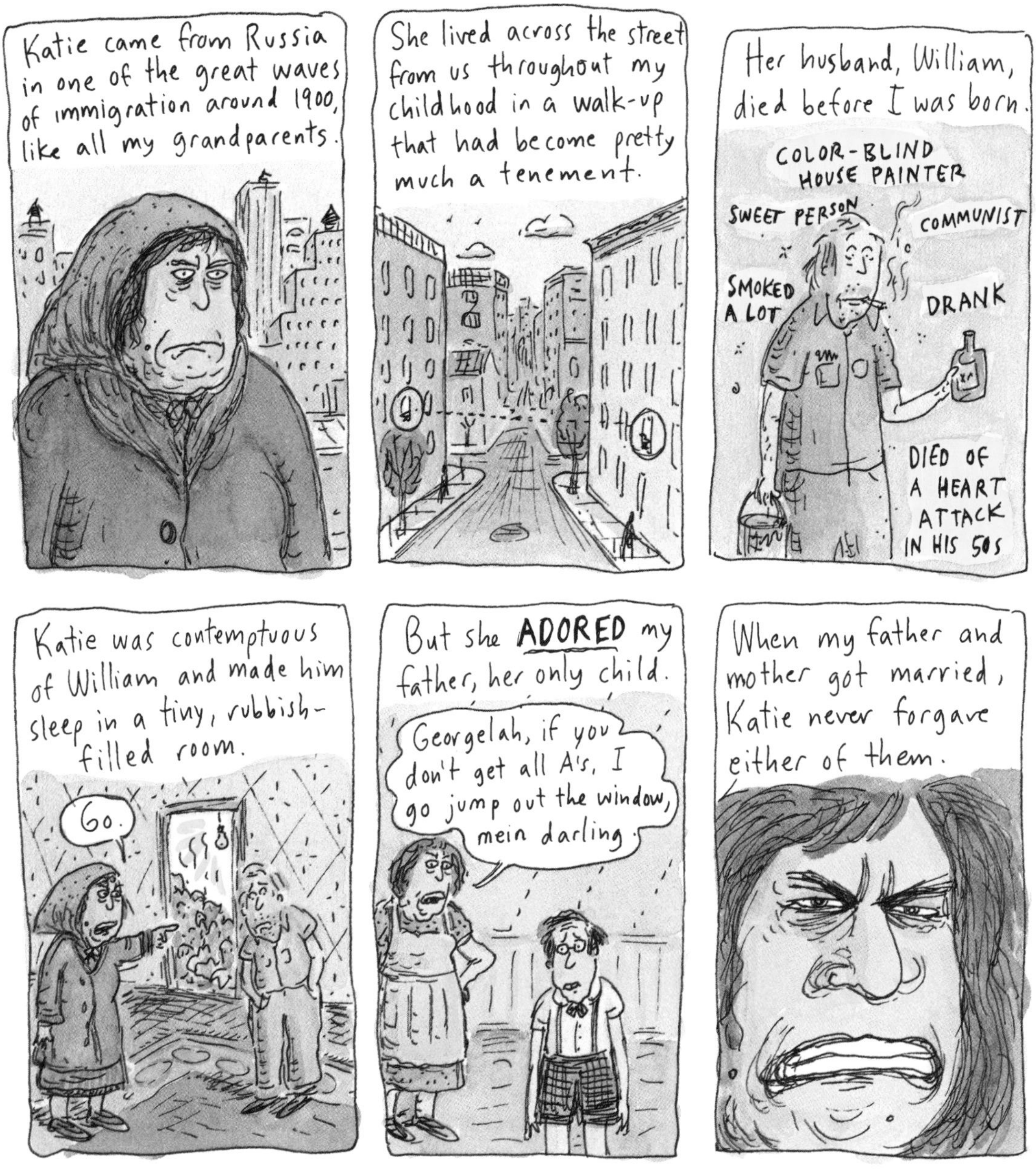
Katie came from Russia in one of the great waves of immigration around 1900, like all my grandparents.
She lived across the street from us throughout my childhood in a walk-up that had become pretty much a tenement.
Her husband, William, died before I was born.
COLOR-BLIND HOUSE PAINTER
SWEET PERSON
COMMUNIST
SMOKED A LOT
DRANK
DIED OF A HEART ATTACK IN HIS 50s
Katie was contemptuous of William and made him sleep in a tiny, rubbish-filled room.
Go.
But she ADORED my father, her only child.
Georgelah, if you don't get all A's, I go jump out the window, mein darling.
When my father and mother got married, Katie never forgave either of them.

She died in 1972. In a Place.

My parents' college graduation photos

Me, age 1

My mother's mother, Mollie

My father's mother, Katie, the imaginary murderer

OLD-COUNTRY GRANDMAS

FUN FACTS:

1. When my mother was a child, she had diptheria. She had a "web of mucus" which grew across her throat. Mollie, ever resourceful, took a clean rag, wrapped it around her finger, and "ripped the web out."

2. Katie slept at the foot of my father's bed, crosswise, until the day he married.

3. Mollie believed that people on TV could see her.

4. The floors of Katie's apartment were covered in wall-to-wall sheets of newspaper. Always. My parents had no explanation for this.

KATIE STORIES

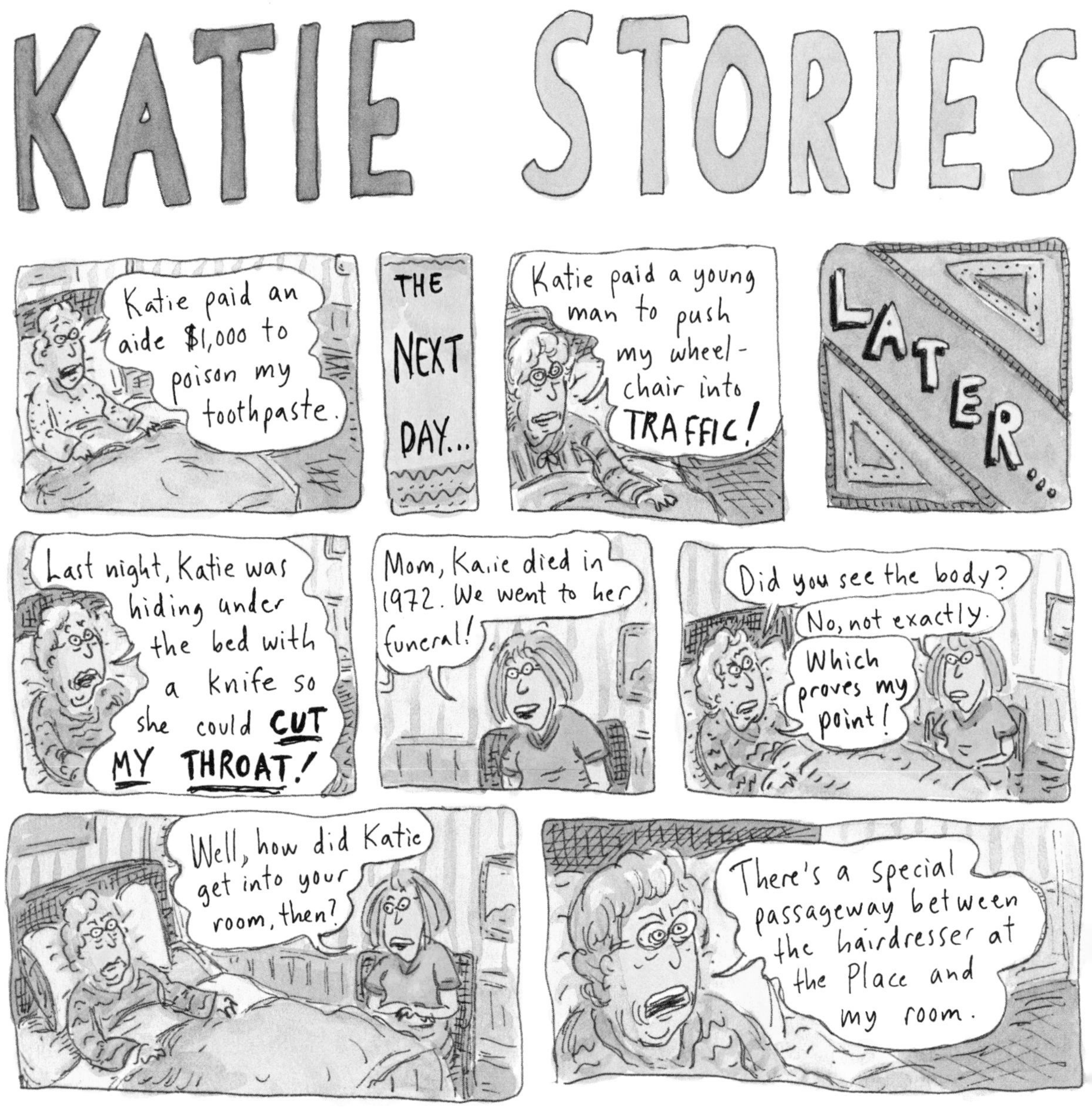

Katie paid an aide $1,000 to poison my toothpaste.
THE NEXT DAY...
Katie paid a young man to push my wheel-chair into TRAFFIC!
LATER...
Last night, Katie was hiding under the bed with a knife so she could CUT MY THROAT!
Mom, Katie died in 1972. We went to her funeral!
Did you see the body?
No, not exactly.
Which proves my point!
Well, how did Katie get into your room, then?
There's a special passageway between the hairdresser at the Place and my room.

More stories, not about Katie:

She told me that her older brother, who had died a few years before, came to visit, and said that when she got to hell, he would "show her the ropes." I asked her why she thought she was going to hell, and she got a "why are you asking such a stupid question" look on her face. This may have had something to do with all the fire-and-brimstone preachers Goodie watched on the TV.

Stick with me, Liz.

She told me that her father asked her, "Who's your daddy?" and when she said, "You," he said, "No, your mother had an affair with the neighbor, and he's your daddy."

Her father, Harry, had "stacks of $10,000 bills" hidden somewhere. I should try to find them.

Had I heard what happened last week? Goodie went to her car to get something, but she was gone such a long time that my mother started to worry. So she called the main desk at the Place. They asked, "What kind of car does Goodie drive," so my mother told them. And lo and behold: Goodie was under the car, unconscious, and frozen to the ice!!! A guy "from the kitchen" had followed her to her car and pushed her! The important thing is: my mother saved Goodie's life.

After Katie, the second-most-popular genre of these stories was my mother's secret real-estate holdings. She knew I'd had dreams of moving back to Manhattan, where I'd lived for many years before my kids were born. I think maybe this was her way of making those wishes come true.

APARTMENT #1

The Board of Education* gave me an apartment in their building.

Where is that?

550 Park Avenue!!!

Oh.

It's as **big as a** **ballroom**: the **entire first floor.** It can hold 100 people!

To have an apartment in that building, you have to be **a person of authority.**

When my brother Aaron** visits, he can stay there.

It has lots of windows, and a **private** bathroom!

* My mother had been an assistant principal in the N.Y.C. public school system for decades. When I was a kid, I often heard stories about "The Board of Ed."

** Aaron was my mother's deceased brother, who was visiting her a lot. Goodie said that when he "visited," she saw a shadow pass over the bed.

APARTMENT # 2

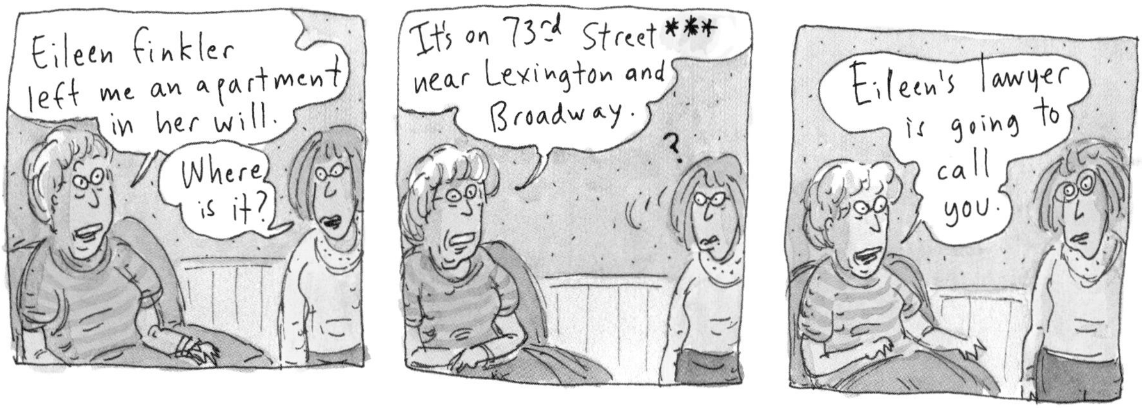

Eileen Finkler left me an apartment in her will.
Where is it?
It's on 73rd Street*** near Lexington and Broadway.
?
Eileen's lawyer is going to call you.

*** My old, beloved apartment, where I lived before I had children, was on West 73rd near Amsterdam Avenue.

Of all the stories, I liked this one the best:

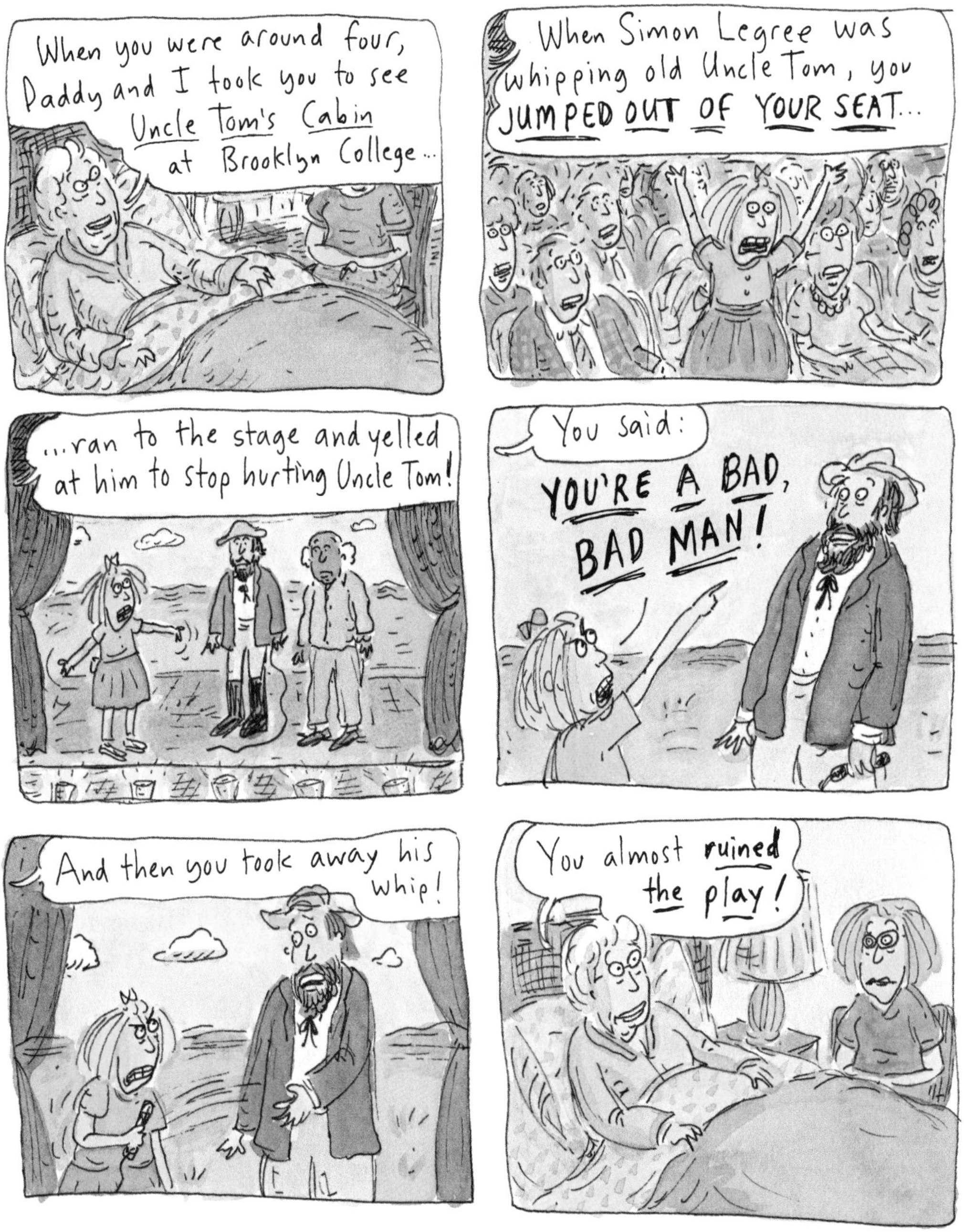
When you were around four, Daddy and I took you to see Uncle Tom's Cabin at Brooklyn College...
When Simon Legree was whipping old Uncle Tom, you JUMPED OUT OF YOUR SEAT...
...ran to the stage and yelled at him to stop hurting Uncle Tom!
You said:
YOU'RE A BAD, BAD MAN!
And then you took away his whip!
You almost ruined the play!

Needless to say, I am 99.9999999% sure nothing like this ever happened.

Chapter Eight: "Shut Up, Artie!" 2

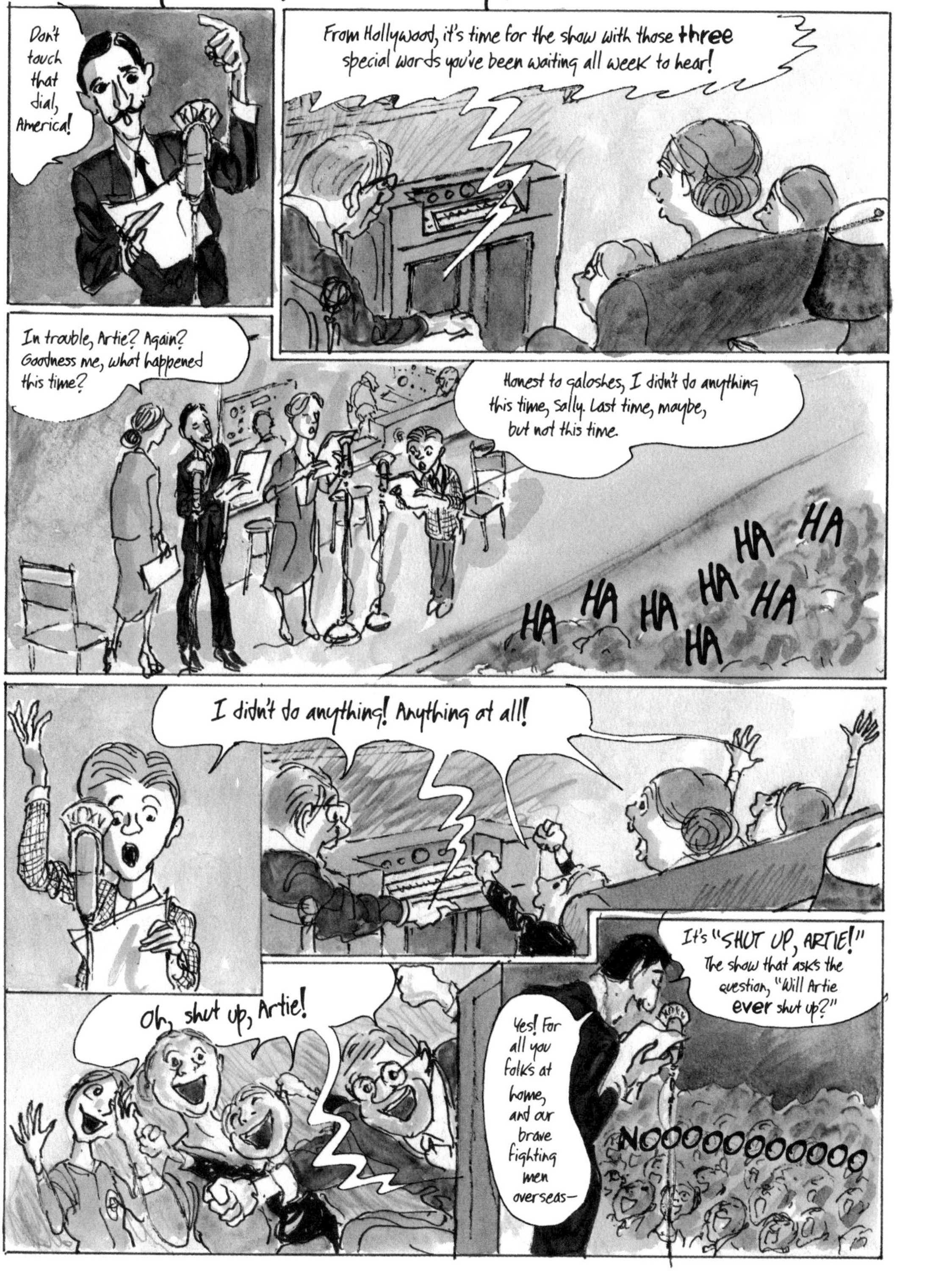

Don't touch that dial, America!
From Hollywood, it's time for the show with those three special words you've been waiting all week to hear!
In trouble, Artie? Again? Goodness me, what happened this time?
Honest to galoshes, I didn't do anything this time, Sally. Last time, maybe, but not this time.
HA HA HA HA HA HA HA HA
I didn't do anything! Anything at all!
Oh, shut up, Artie!
It's "SHUT UP, ARTIE!" The show that asks the question, "Will Artie ever shut up?"
Yes! For all you folks at home, and our brave fighting men overseas—
NOOOOOOOOOOO

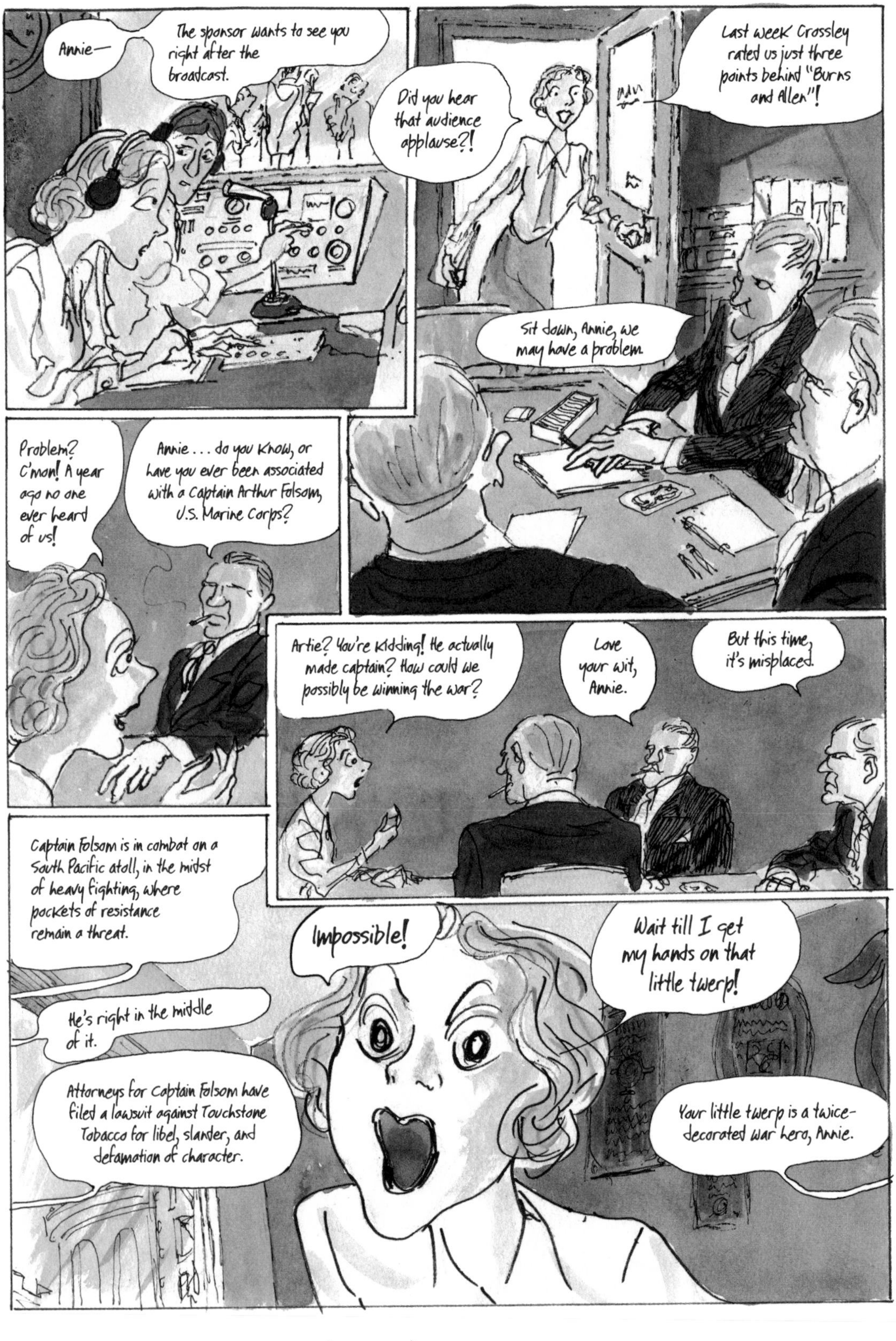
Annie—
The sponsor wants to see you right after the broadcast.
Did you hear that audience applause?!
Last week Crossley rated us just three points behind "Burns and Allen"!
Sit down, Annie, we may have a problem.
Problem? C'mon! A year ago no one ever heard of us!
Annie . . . do you know, or have you ever been associated with a Captain Arthur Folsom, U.S. Marine Corps?
Artie? You're kidding! He actually made captain? How could we possibly be winning the war?
Love your wit, Annie.
But this time, it's misplaced.
Captain Folsom is in combat on a South Pacific atoll, in the midst of heavy fighting, where pockets of resistance remain a threat.
Impossible!
Wait till I get my hands on that little twerp!
He's right in the middle of it.
Attorneys for Captain Folsom have filed a lawsuit against Touchstone Tobacco for libel, slander, and defamation of character.
Your little twerp is a twice-decorated war hero, Annie.

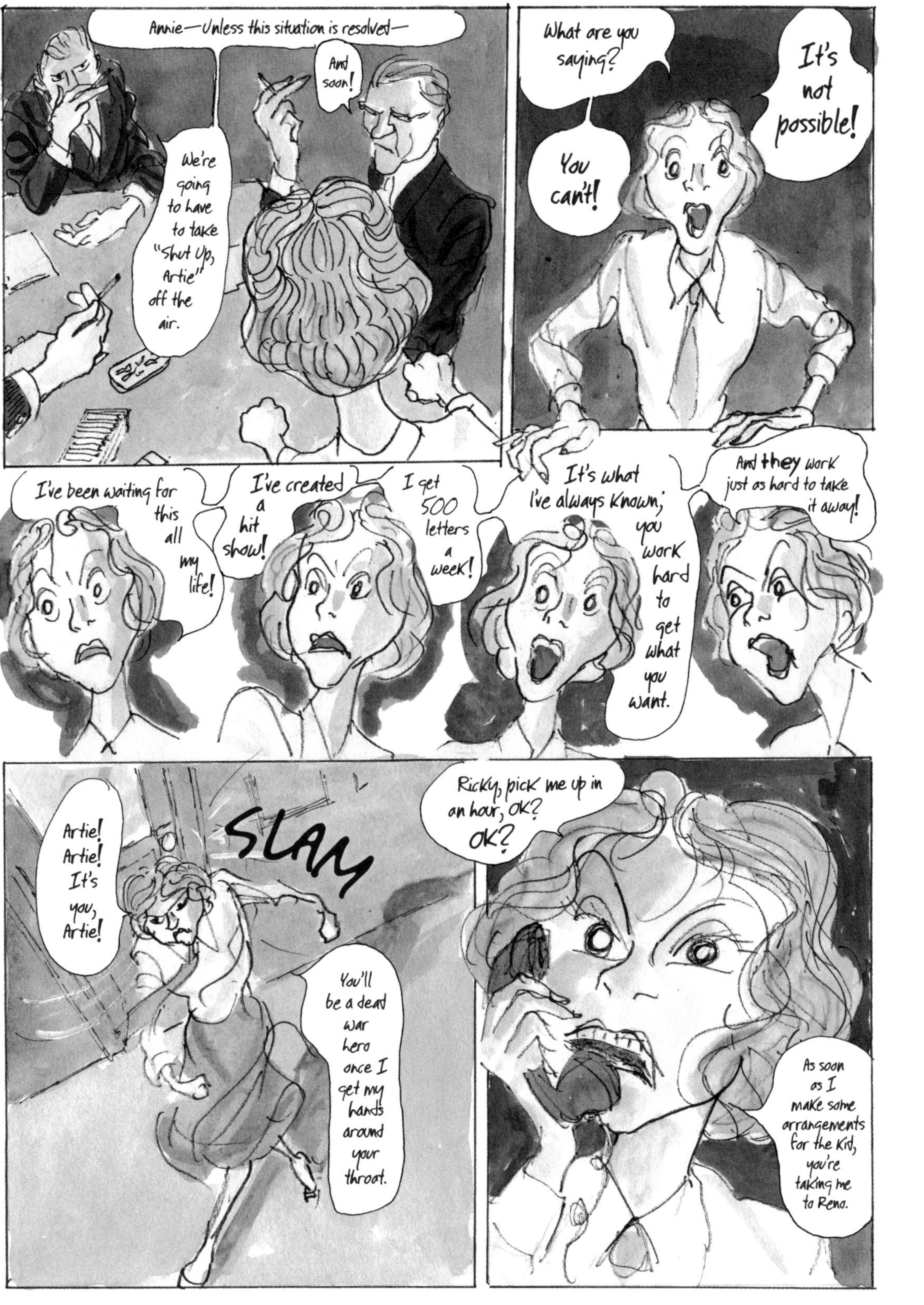
Annie—Unless this situation is resolved—
And soon!
We're going to have to take "Shut Up, Artie" off the air.
What are you saying?
You can't!
It's not possible!
I've been waiting for this all my life!
I've created a hit show!
I get 500 letters a week!
It's what I've always known; you work hard to get what you want.
And they work just as hard to take it away!
Artie! Artie! It's you, Artie!
SLAM
You'll be a dead war hero once I get my hands around your throat.
Ricky, pick me up in an hour, OK? OK?
As soon as I make some arrangements for the Kid, you're taking me to Reno.

Chapter Nine: Elsie's Drunk Scene

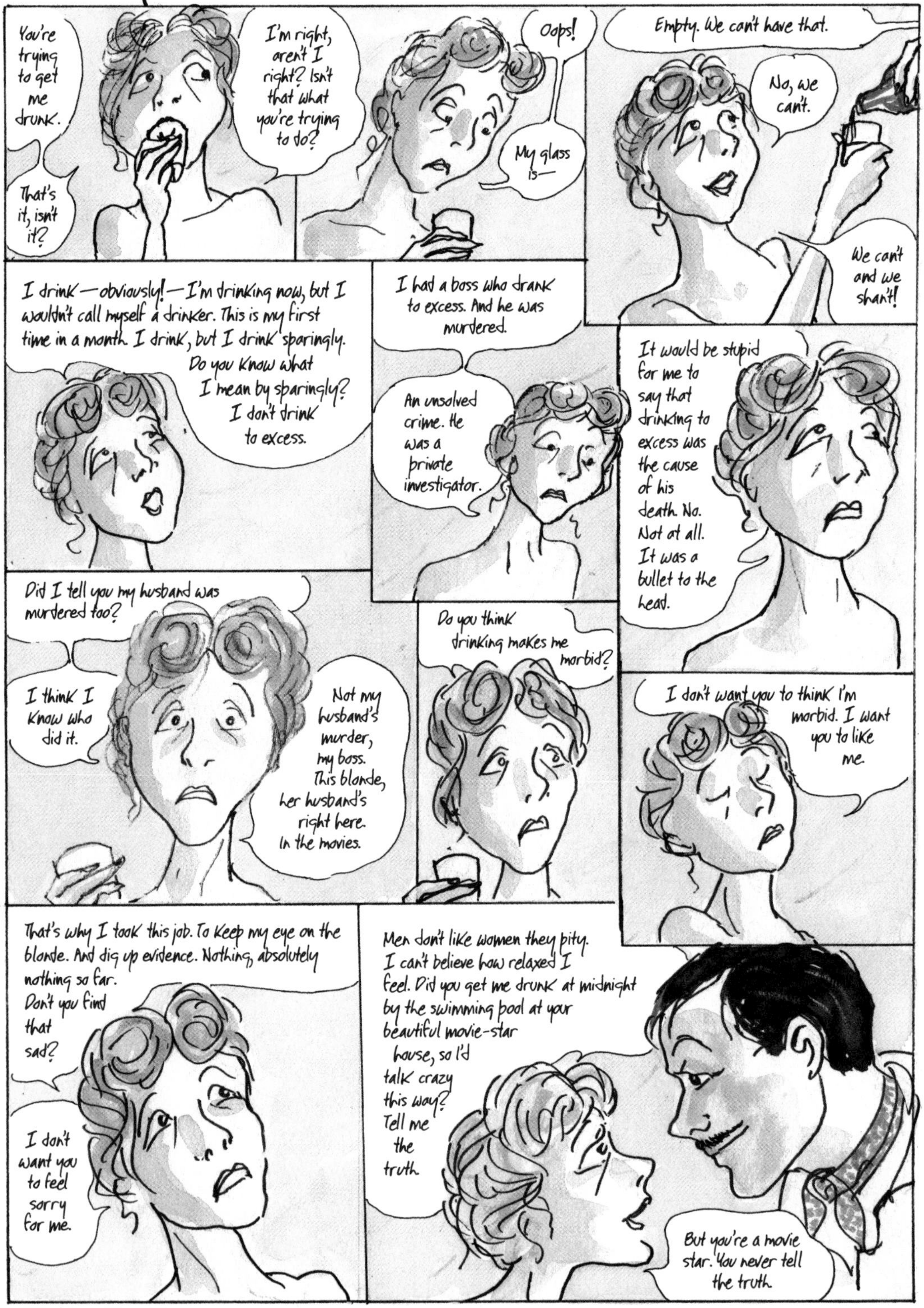

You're trying to get me drunk.
That's it, isn't it?
I'm right, aren't I right? Isn't that what you're trying to do?
Oops!
My glass is—
Empty. We can't have that.
No, we can't.
We can't and we shan't!
I drink—obviously!—I'm drinking now, but I wouldn't call myself a drinker. This is my first time in a month. I drink, but I drink sparingly. Do you know what I mean by sparingly? I don't drink to excess.
I had a boss who drank to excess. And he was murdered.
An unsolved crime. He was a private investigator.
It would be stupid for me to say that drinking to excess was the cause of his death. No. Not at all. It was a bullet to the head.
Did I tell you my husband was murdered too?
I think I know who did it.
Not my husband's murder, my boss. This blonde, her husband's right here. In the movies.
Do you think drinking makes me morbid?
I don't want you to think I'm morbid. I want you to like me.
That's why I took this job. To keep my eye on the blonde. And dig up evidence. Nothing, absolutely nothing so far. Don't you find that sad?
I don't want you to feel sorry for me.
Men don't like women they pity. I can't believe how relaxed I feel. Did you get me drunk at midnight by the swimming pool at your beautiful movie-star house, so I'd talk crazy this way? Tell me the truth.
But you're a movie star. You never tell the truth.

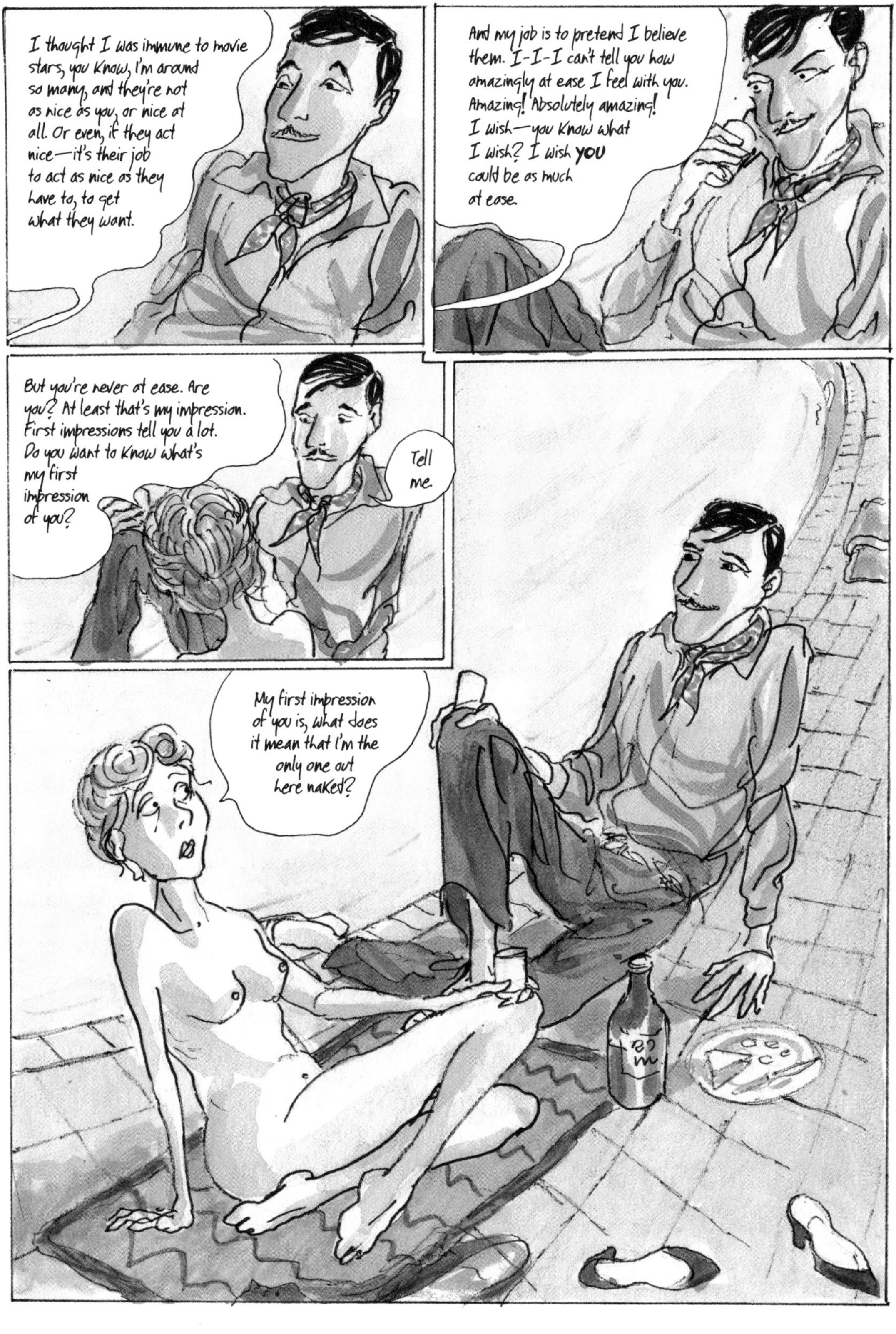
I thought I was immune to movie stars, you know, I'm around so many, and they're not as nice as you, or nice at all. Or even, if they act nice—it's their job to act as nice as they have to, to get what they want.
And my job is to pretend I believe them. I-I-I can't tell you how amazingly at ease I feel with you. Amazing! Absolutely amazing! I wish—you know what I wish? I wish **YOU** could be as much at ease.
But you're never at ease. Are you? At least that's my impression. First impressions tell you a lot. Do you want to know what's my first impression of you?
Tell me.
My first impression of you is, what does it mean that I'm the only one out here naked?

Chapter Ten: Veil Unveiled

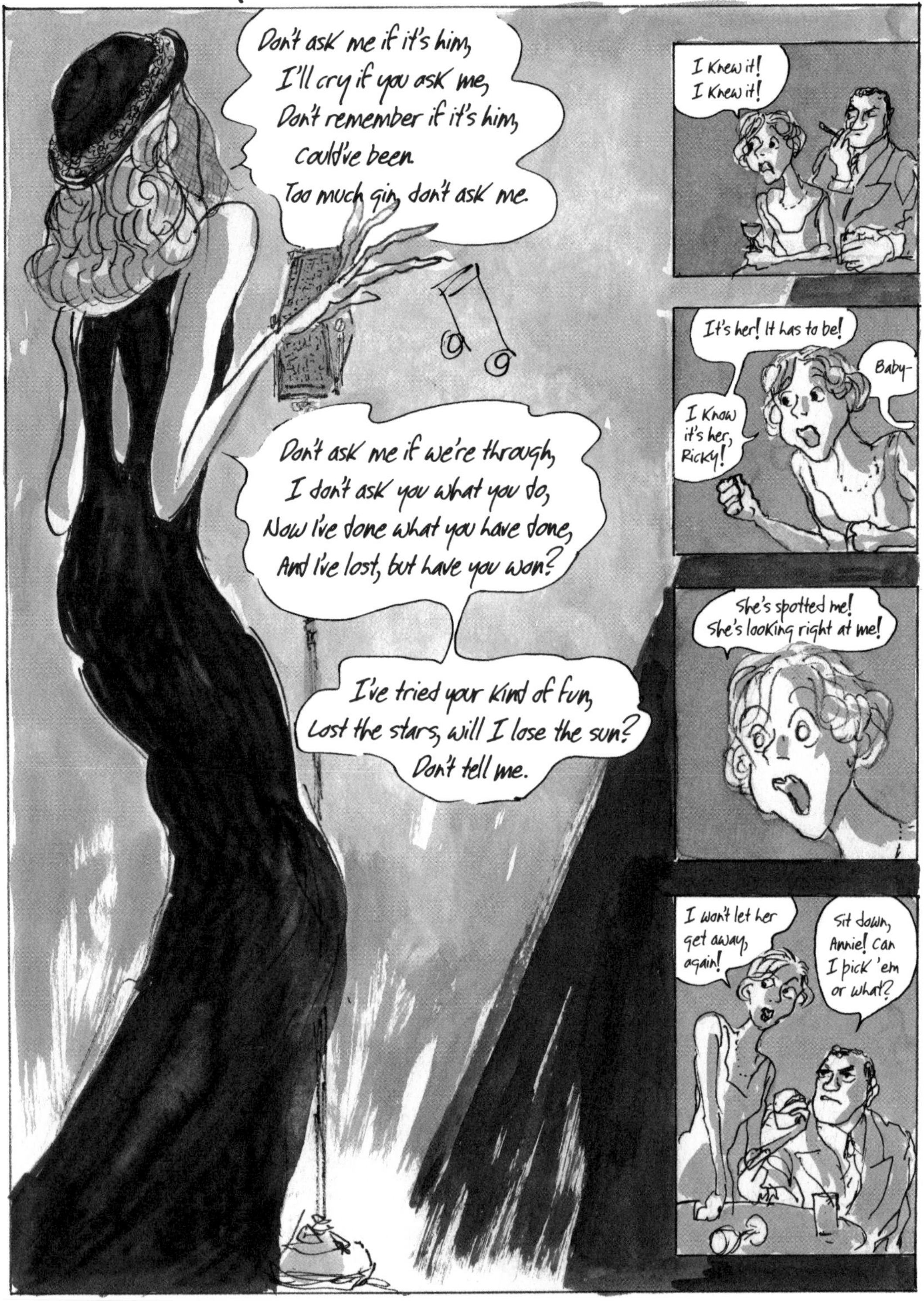

Don't ask me if it's him, I'll cry if you ask me, Don't remember if it's him, could've been. Too much gin, don't ask me.
I Knew it! I Knew it!
It's her! It has to be!
Baby-
I Know it's her, Ricky!
Don't ask me if we're through, I don't ask you what you do, Now I've done what you have done, And I've lost, but have you won?
She's spotted me! She's looking right at me!
I've tried your Kind of fun, Lost the stars, will I lose the sun? Don't tell me.
I won't let her get away, again!
Sit down, Annie! Can I pick 'em or what?

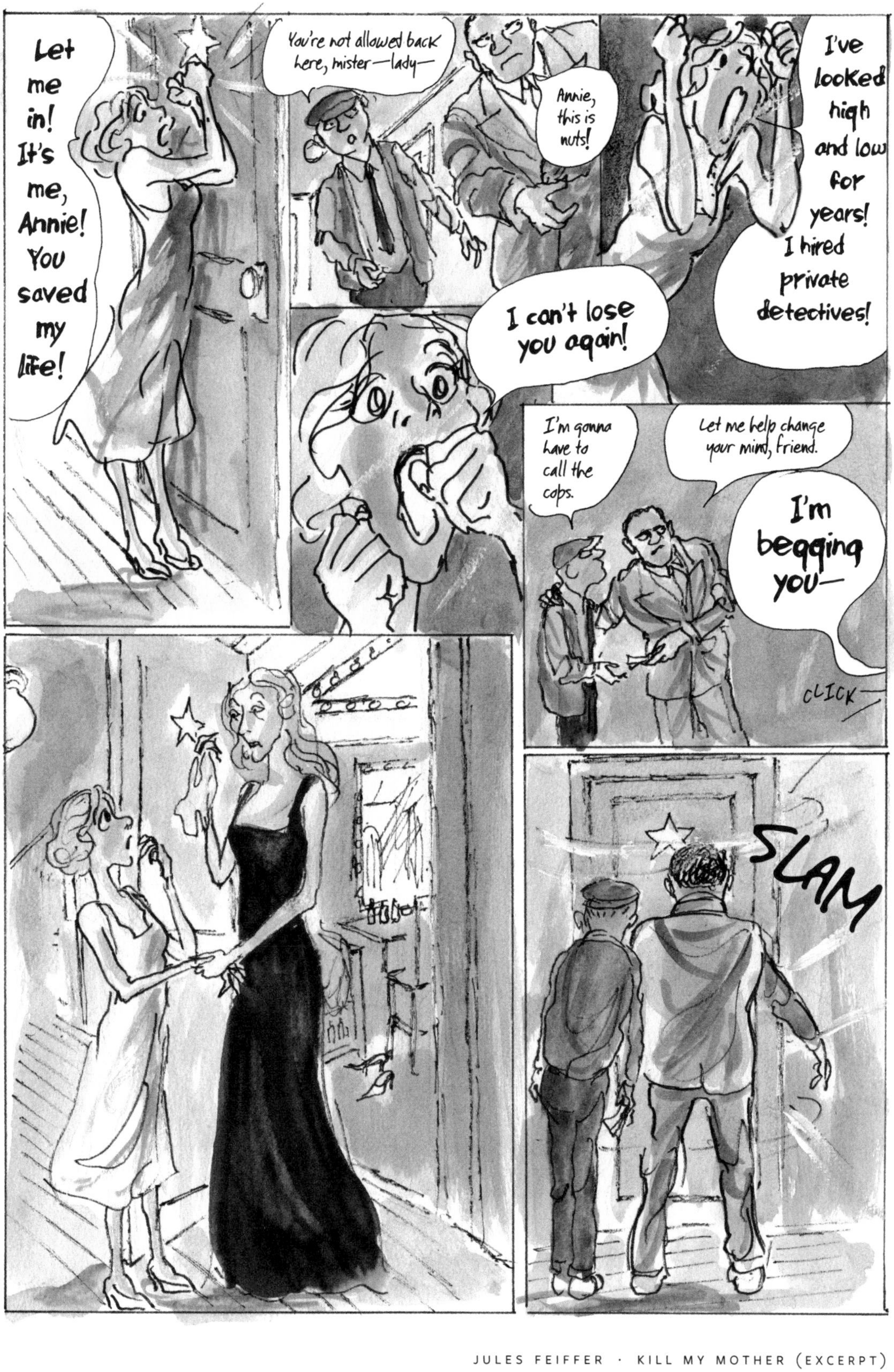
Let me in! It's me, Annie! You saved my life!
You're not allowed back here, mister—lady—
Annie, this is nuts!
I've looked high and low for years! I hired private detectives!
I can't lose you again!
I'm gonna have to call the cops.
Let me help change your mind, friend.
I'm begging you—
CLICK—
SLAM

Chapter Eleven: Anything You Want

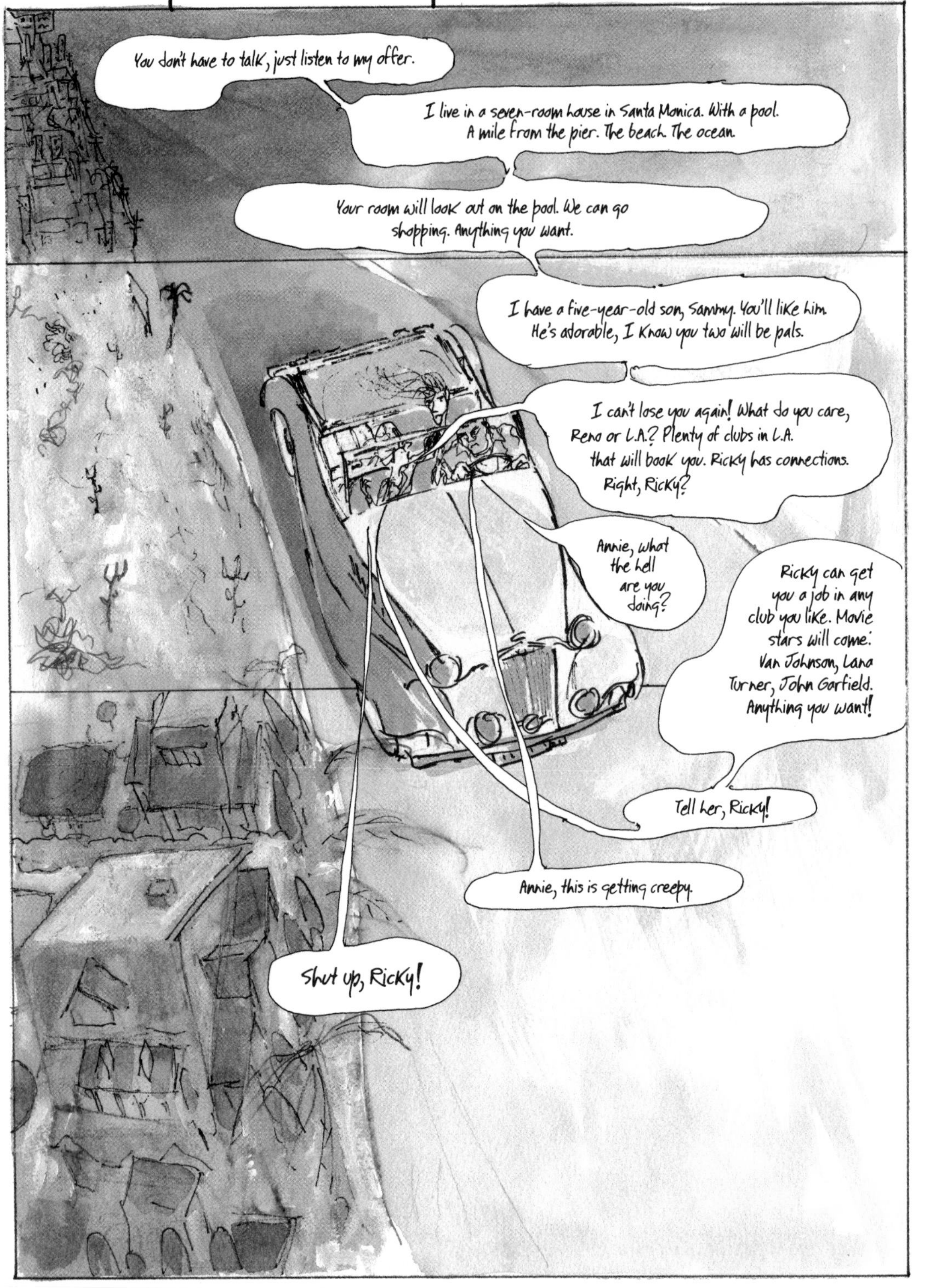

You don't have to talk, just listen to my offer.
I live in a seven-room house in Santa Monica. With a pool. A mile from the pier. The beach. The ocean.
Your room will look out on the pool. We can go shopping. Anything you want.
I have a five-year-old son, Sammy. You'll like him. He's adorable, I know you two will be pals.
I can't lose you again! What do you care, Reno or L.A.? Plenty of clubs in L.A. that will book you. Ricky has connections. Right, Ricky?
Annie, what the hell are you doing?
Ricky can get you a job in any club you like. Movie stars will come: Van Johnson, Lana Turner, John Garfield. Anything you want!
Tell her, Ricky!
Annie, this is getting creepy.
Shut up, Ricky!

CHAPTER TWO
Superheroes Détourned

SO SUE ME: STARTING WITH STEVE GERBER'S "DEFENDERS," I'VE PREFERRED MY SUPERHEROES AS NEUROTIC MOUTHPIECES OR ALLEGORICAL AVATARS.

A LUCKY CONVERGENCE PRODUCED "WONDER WOMAN YEAR." SIKORYAK & OBOMSAWIN WERE INTENDED TO BE JOINED HERE BY RON REGÉ JR.'s "DIANA" UNTIL A LAWYER TOLD US WE COULDN'T. MY BEST "FAIR USE" ARGUMENTS FELL ON DEAF EARS. BOO!

JOSH BAYER SEEMS LIKE A GIANT IN THE MAKING — WOW. AS FOR BEN DUNCAN, HE'S MORE LIKE A FEVER DREAM.

BOTH? EVEN BETTER.

ORIGINALLY, THIS CATEGORY WAS GOING TO INCLUDE AN AMAZING PIECE BY COMICS OUTSIDER-EMERITUS STEVE DITKO, BUT HE DIDN'T LET US REPRINT IT. WE'RE NOT WORTHY!

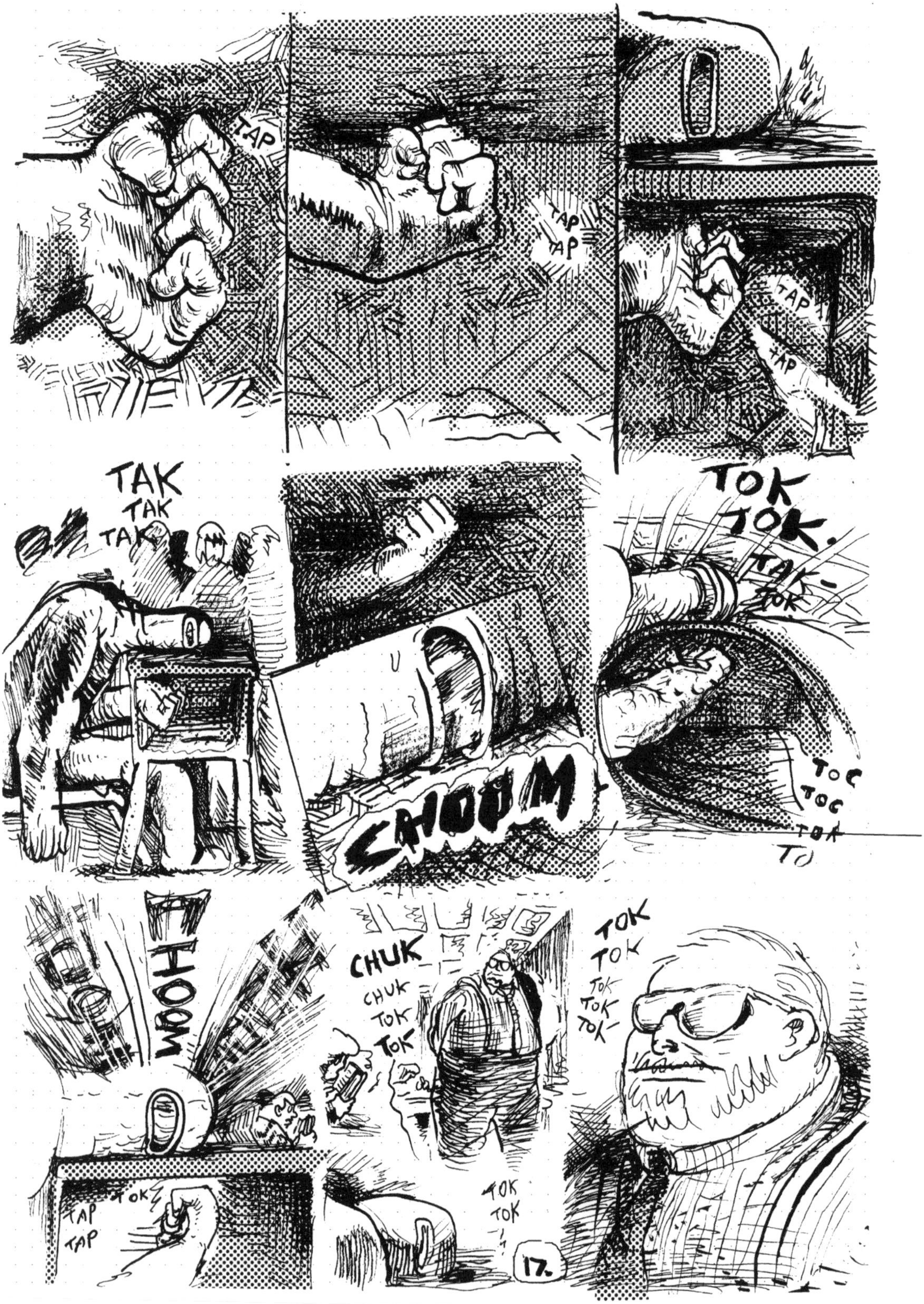
TAP
TAP
TAP
TAP
TAP
TAK
TAK
TAK
TOK
TOK.
TAK-
TOK
CHOOM
TOC
TOC
TOK
WHOOM
TAP
TAP
TOK
CHUK
CHUK
TOK
TOK
TOK
TOK
TOK
TOK
TOK
TOK
TOK
TOK-
17.

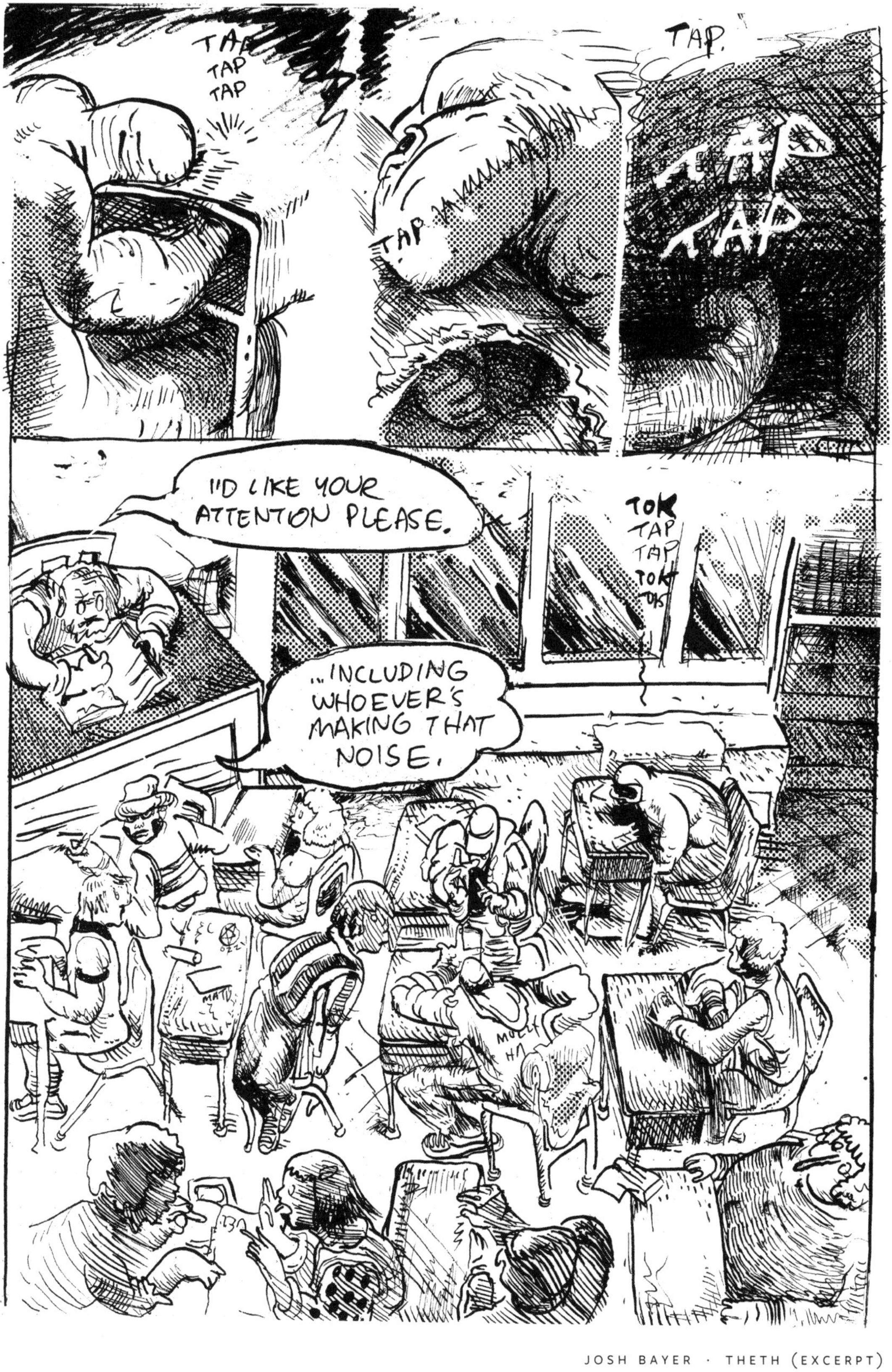
TAP
TAP
TAP
TAP.
TAP
TAP
TAP
I'D LIKE YOUR ATTENTION PLEASE.
TOK
TAP
TAP
TOK
...INCLUDING WHOEVER'S MAKING THAT NOISE.

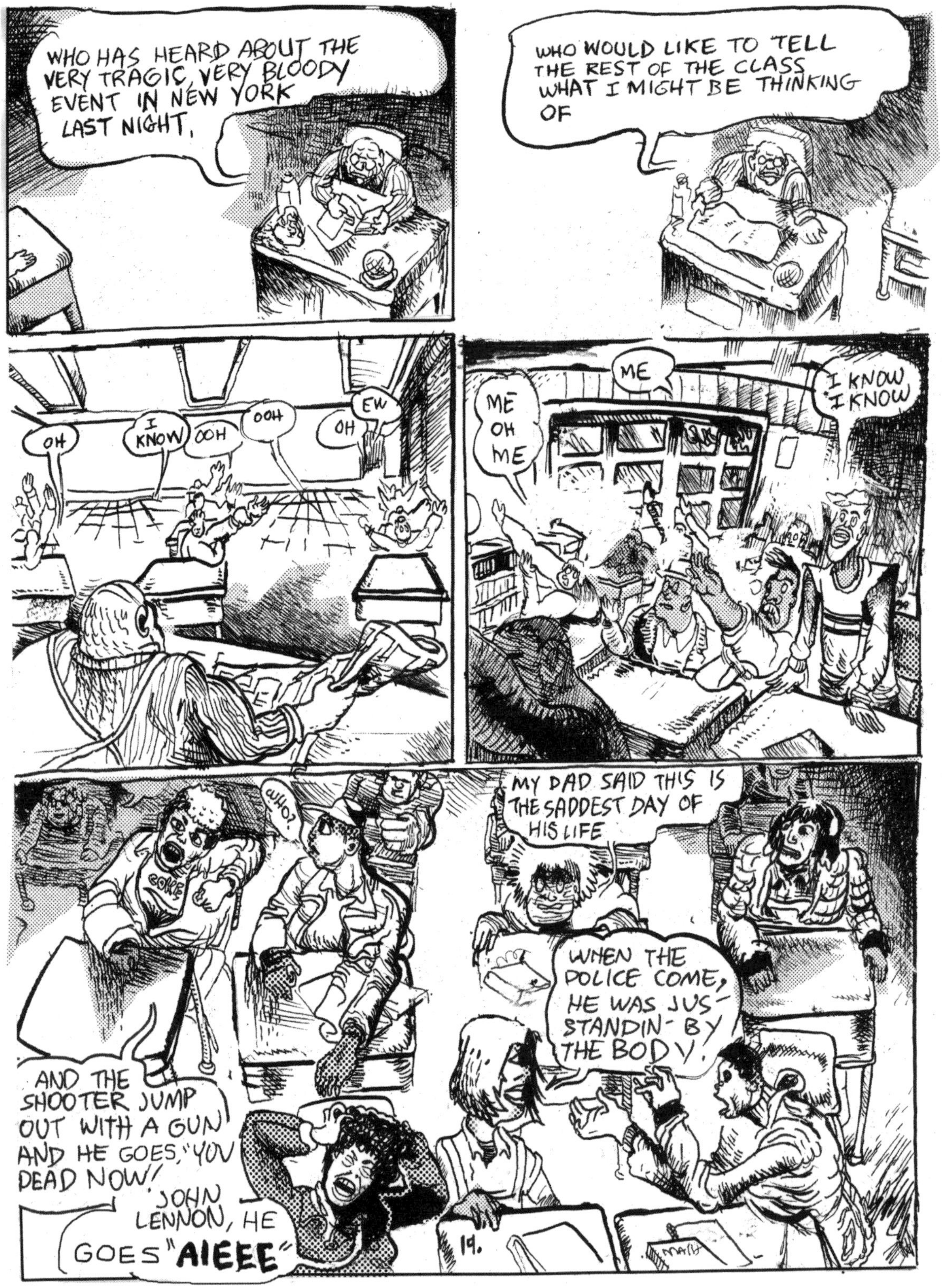
WHO HAS HEARD ABOUT THE VERY TRAGIC, VERY BLOODY EVENT IN NEW YORK LAST NIGHT,
WHO WOULD LIKE TO TELL THE REST OF THE CLASS WHAT I MIGHT BE THINKING OF
OH
I KNOW
OOH
OOH
OH
EW
ME OH ME
ME
I KNOW I KNOW
WHO?
MY DAD SAID THIS IS THE SADDEST DAY OF HIS LIFE
WHEN THE POLICE COME, HE WAS JUS' STANDIN' BY THE BODY.
AND THE SHOOTER JUMP OUT WITH A GUN AND HE GOES, "YOU DEAD NOW!"
JOHN LENNON, HE GOES "AIEEE"
14.

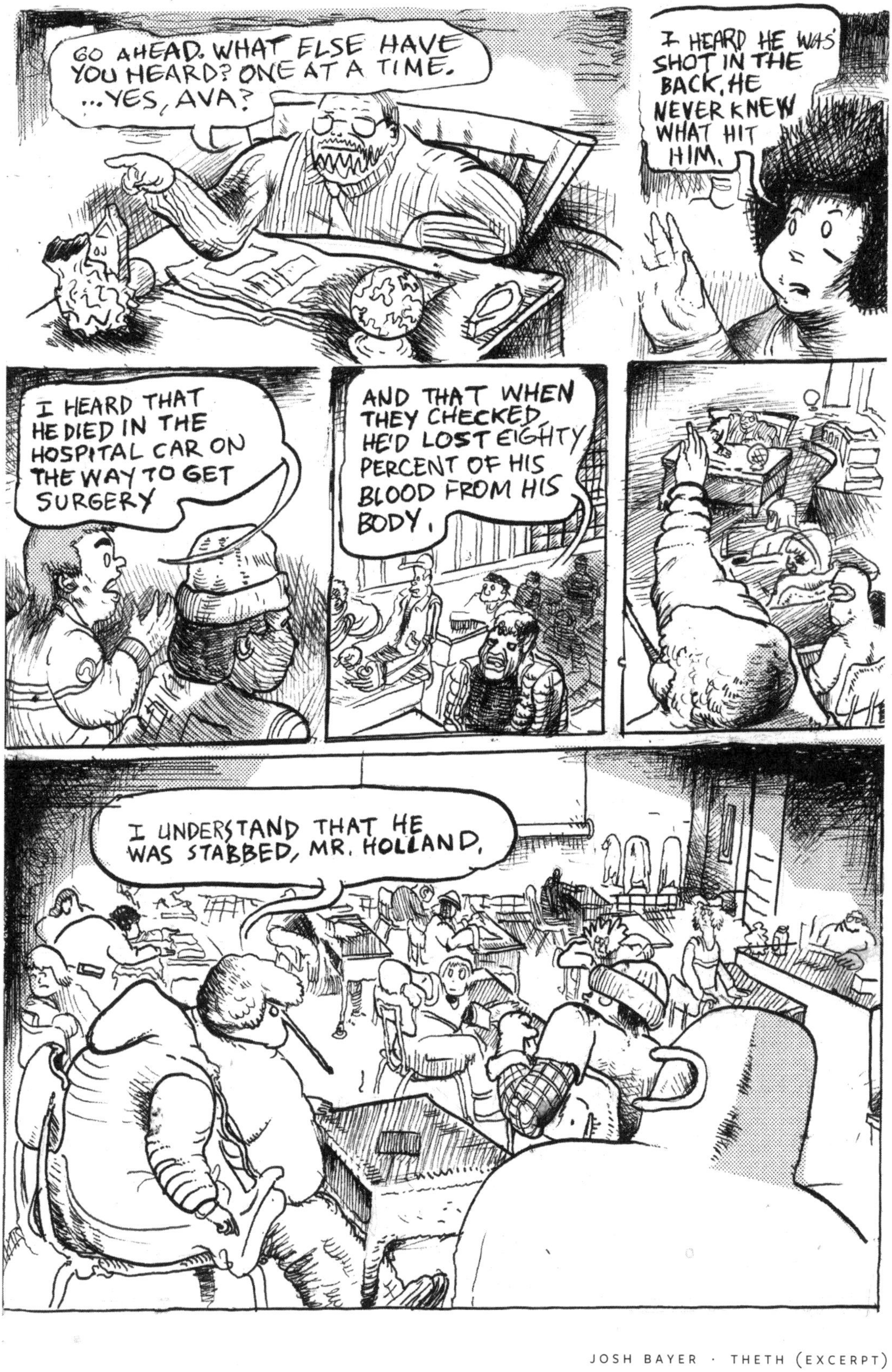
GO AHEAD. WHAT ELSE HAVE YOU HEARD? ONE AT A TIME. ...YES, AVA?
I HEARD HE WAS SHOT IN THE BACK, HE NEVER KNEW WHAT HIT HIM.
I HEARD THAT HE DIED IN THE HOSPITAL CAR ON THE WAY TO GET SURGERY
AND THAT WHEN THEY CHECKED, HE'D LOST EIGHTY PERCENT OF HIS BLOOD FROM HIS BODY.
I UNDERSTAND THAT HE WAS STABBED, MR. HOLLAND.

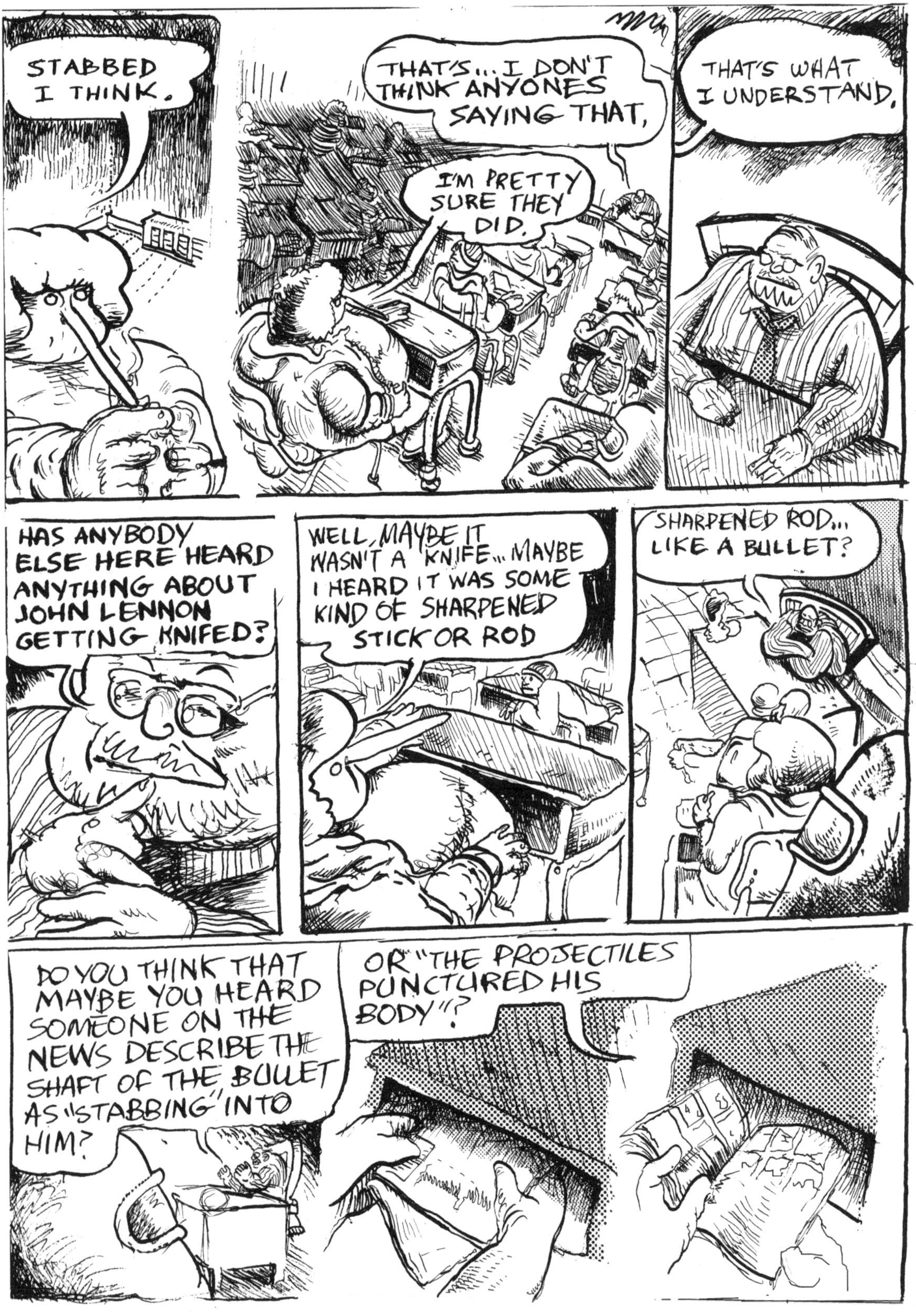
STABBED I THINK.
THAT'S... I DON'T THINK ANYONES SAYING THAT,
I'M PRETTY SURE THEY DID.
THAT'S WHAT I UNDERSTAND,
HAS ANYBODY ELSE HERE HEARD ANYTHING ABOUT JOHN LENNON GETTING KNIFED?
WELL, MAYBE IT WASN'T A KNIFE... MAYBE I HEARD IT WAS SOME KIND OF SHARPENED STICK OR ROD
SHARPENED ROD... LIKE A BULLET?
DO YOU THINK THAT MAYBE YOU HEARD SOMEONE ON THE NEWS DESCRIBE THE SHAFT OF THE BULLET AS "STABBING" INTO HIM?
OR "THE PROJECTILES PUNCTURED HIS BODY"?

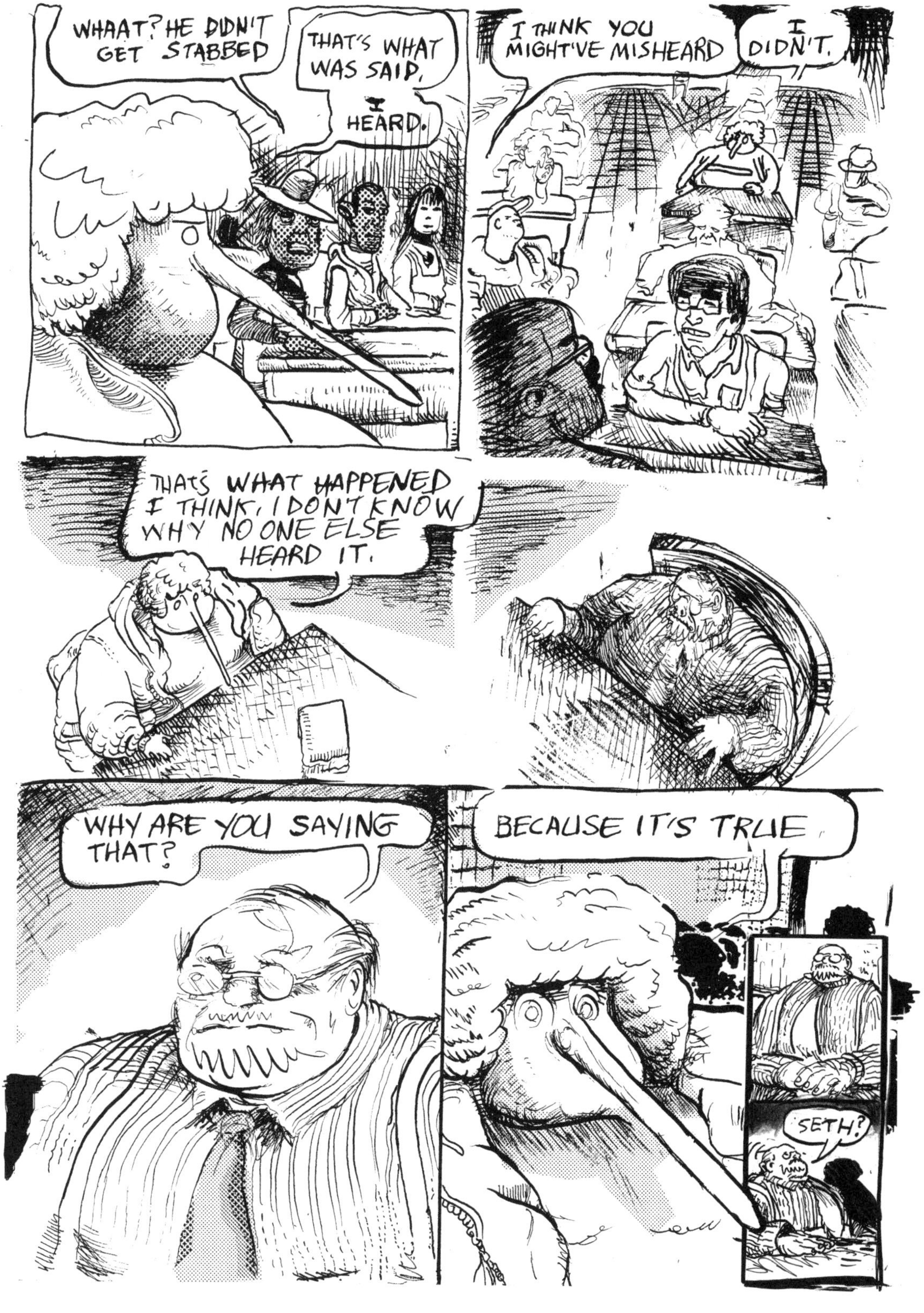
WHAAT? HE DIDN'T GET STABBED
THAT'S WHAT WAS SAID,
I HEARD.
I THINK YOU MIGHT'VE MISHEARD
I DIDN'T.
THAT'S WHAT HAPPENED I THINK, I DON'T KNOW WHY NO ONE ELSE HEARD IT.
WHY ARE YOU SAYING THAT?
BECAUSE IT'S TRUE
SETH?

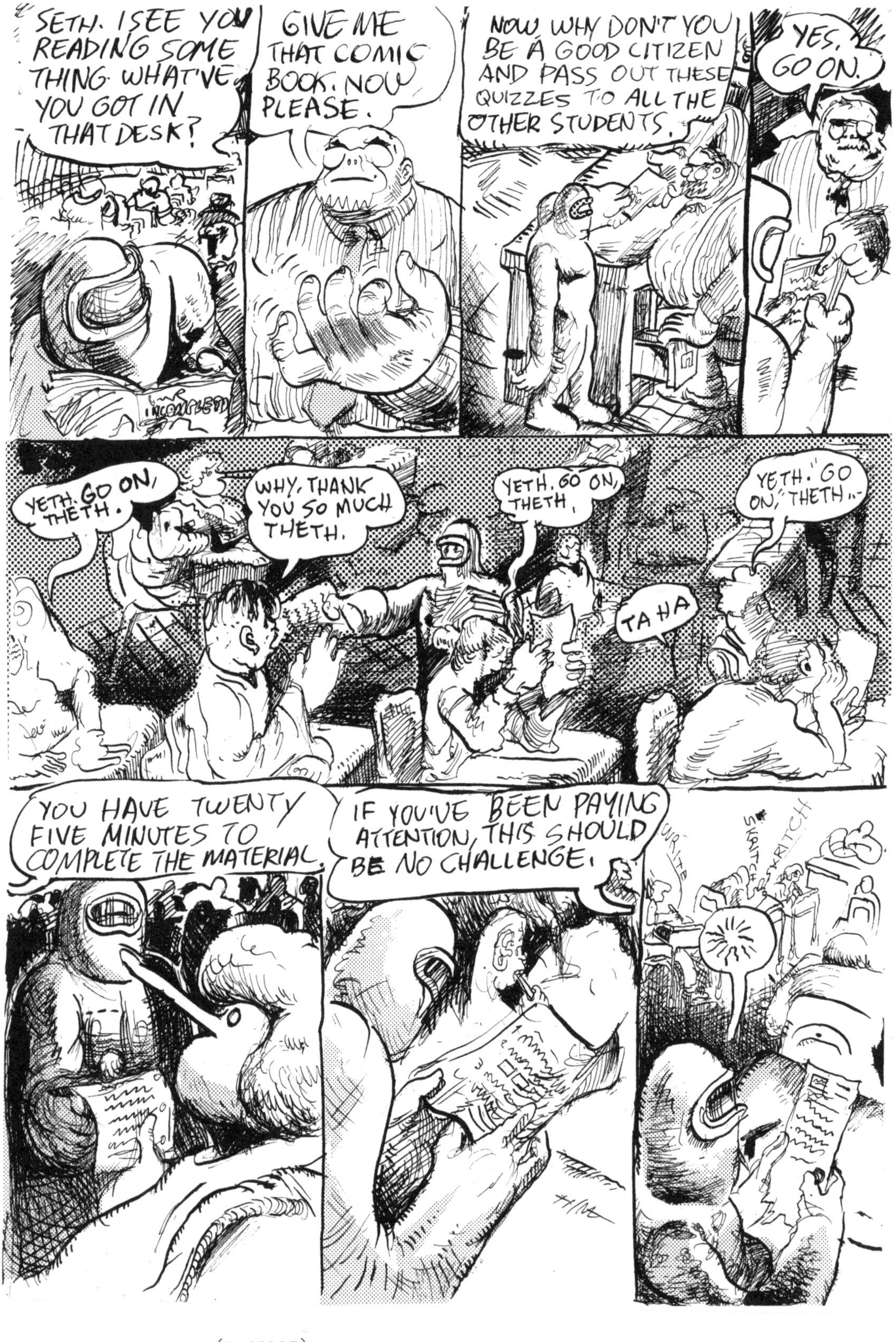
SETH. I SEE YOU READING SOME THING. WHAT'VE YOU GOT IN THAT DESK?
GIVE ME THAT COMIC BOOK. NOW PLEASE.
NOW WHY DON'T YOU BE A GOOD CITIZEN AND PASS OUT THESE QUIZZES TO ALL THE OTHER STUDENTS.
YES. GO ON.
YETH. GO ON, THETH.
WHY, THANK YOU SO MUCH THETH.
YETH. GO ON, THETH.
YETH. GO ON, THETH..
TA HA
YOU HAVE TWENTY FIVE MINUTES TO COMPLETE THE MATERIAL.
IF YOU'VE BEEN PAYING ATTENTION, THIS SHOULD BE NO CHALLENGE.
WRITE
SKRITCH SKRITCH SKRITCH

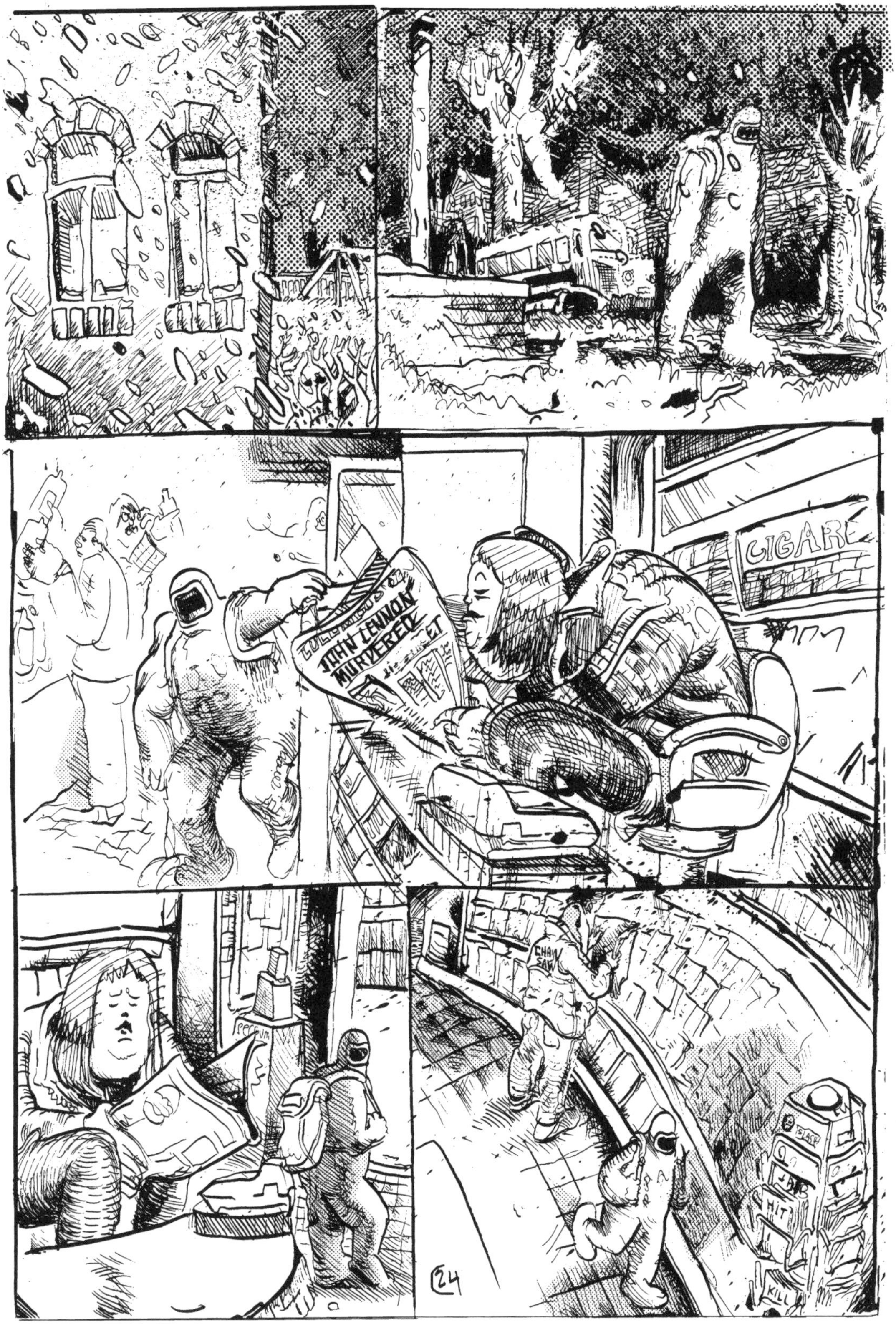
JOHN LENNON MURDERED
CIGARE
HIT
KILL

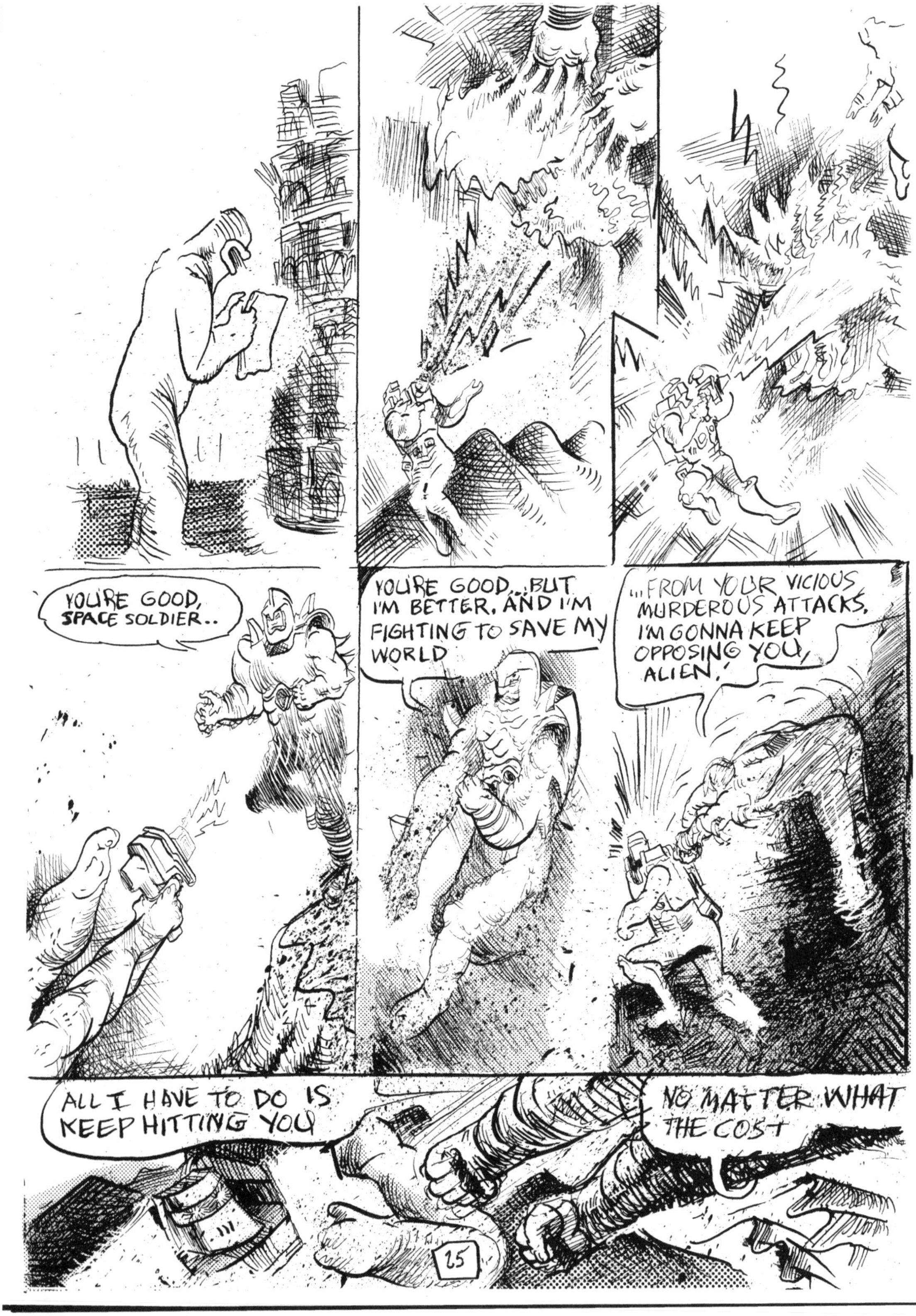
YOU'RE GOOD, SPACE SOLDIER..
YOU'RE GOOD.. BUT I'M BETTER. AND I'M FIGHTING TO SAVE MY WORLD
...FROM YOUR VICIOUS MURDEROUS ATTACKS, I'M GONNA KEEP OPPOSING YOU, ALIEN,
ALL I HAVE TO DO IS KEEP HITTING YOU
NO MATTER WHAT THE COST
25

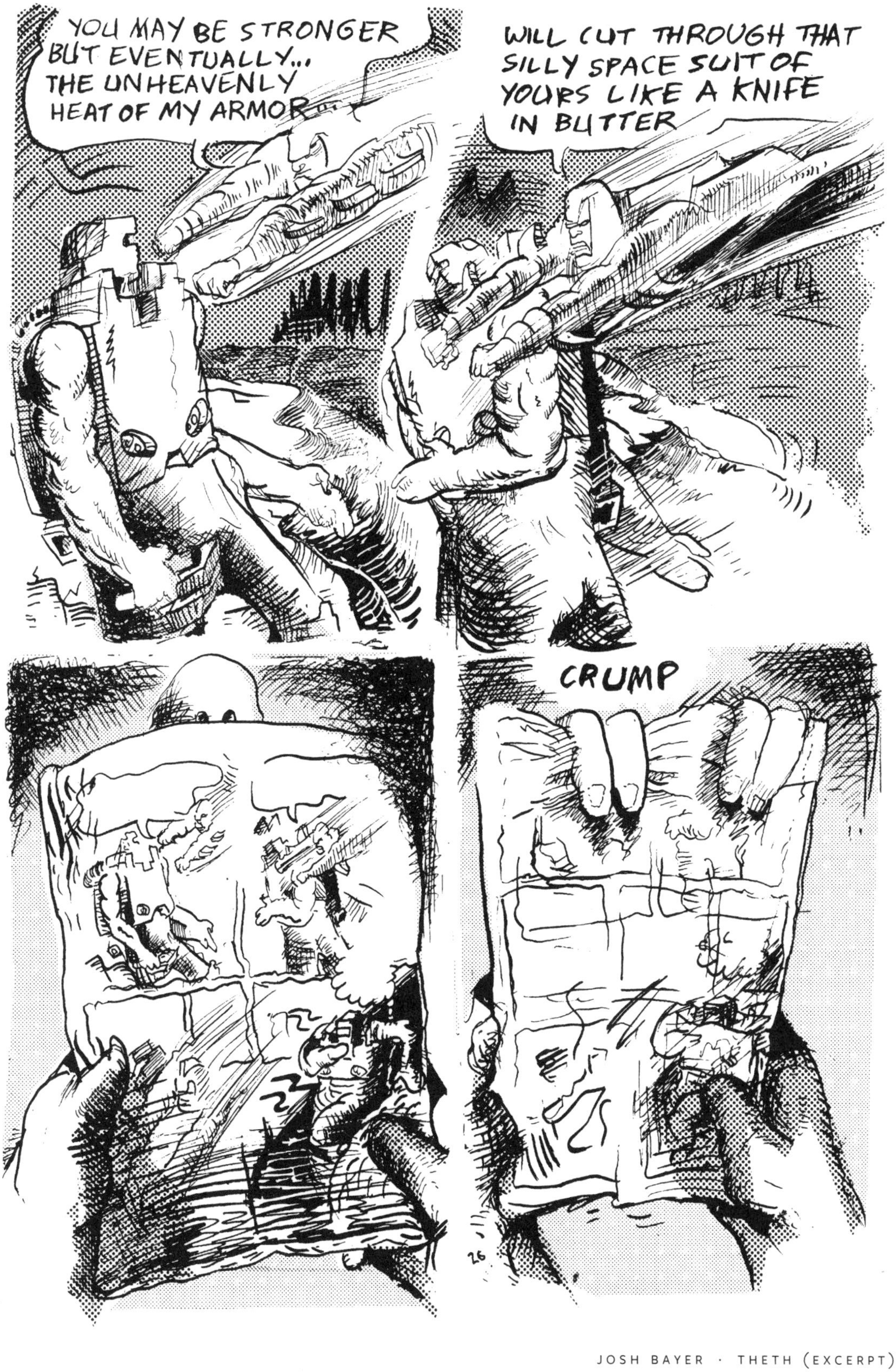
YOU MAY BE STRONGER BUT EVENTUALLY... THE UNHEAVENLY HEAT OF MY ARMOR...
WILL CUT THROUGH THAT SILLY SPACE SUIT OF YOURS LIKE A KNIFE IN BUTTER
CRUMP
26

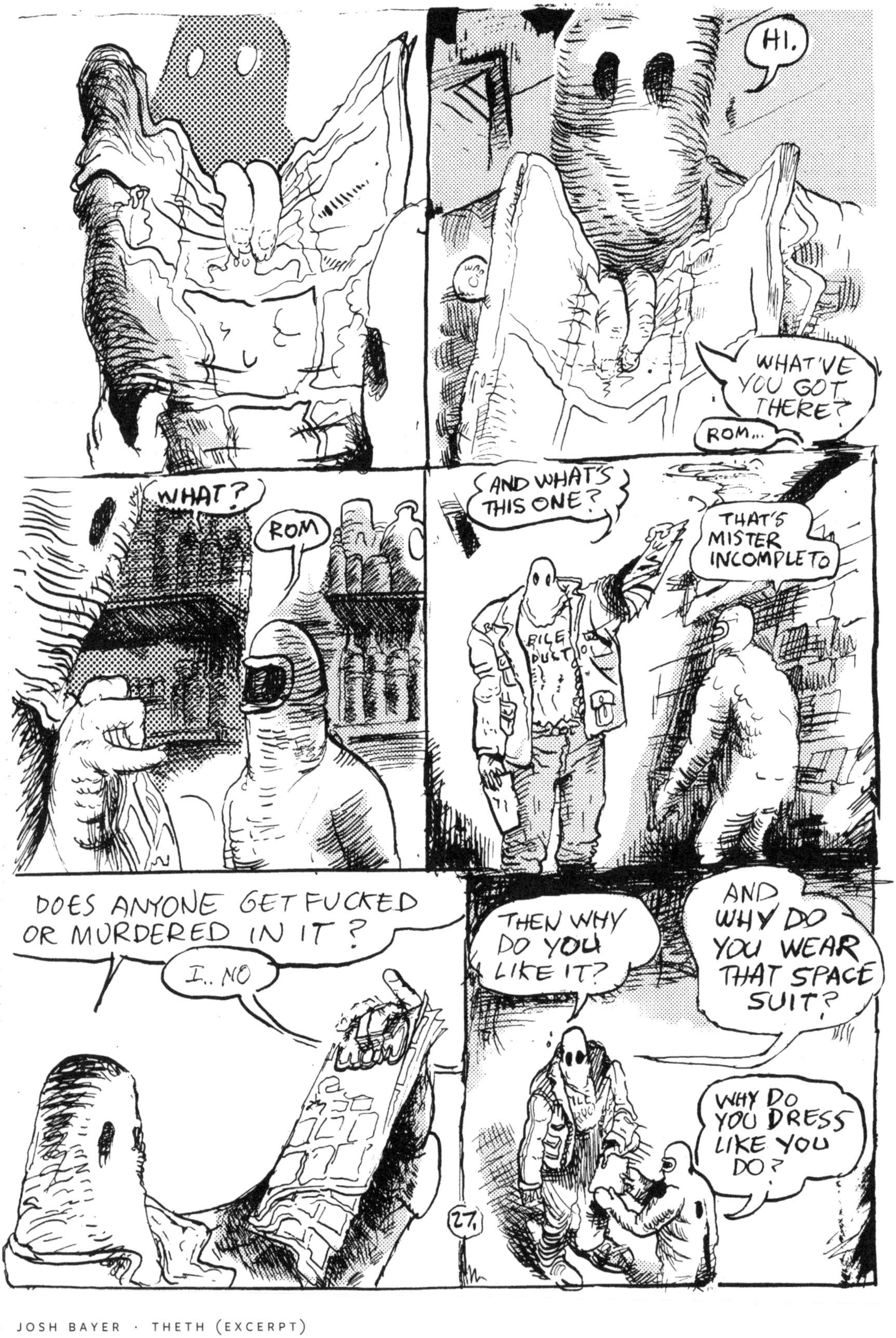
HI.
WHAT'VE YOU GOT THERE?
ROM...
WHAT?
ROM
AND WHAT'S THIS ONE?
THAT'S MISTER INCOMPLETO
DOES ANYONE GET FUCKED OR MURDERED IN IT?
I.. NO
THEN WHY DO YOU LIKE IT?
AND WHY DO YOU WEAR THAT SPACE SUIT?
WHY DO YOU DRESS LIKE YOU DO?
27.

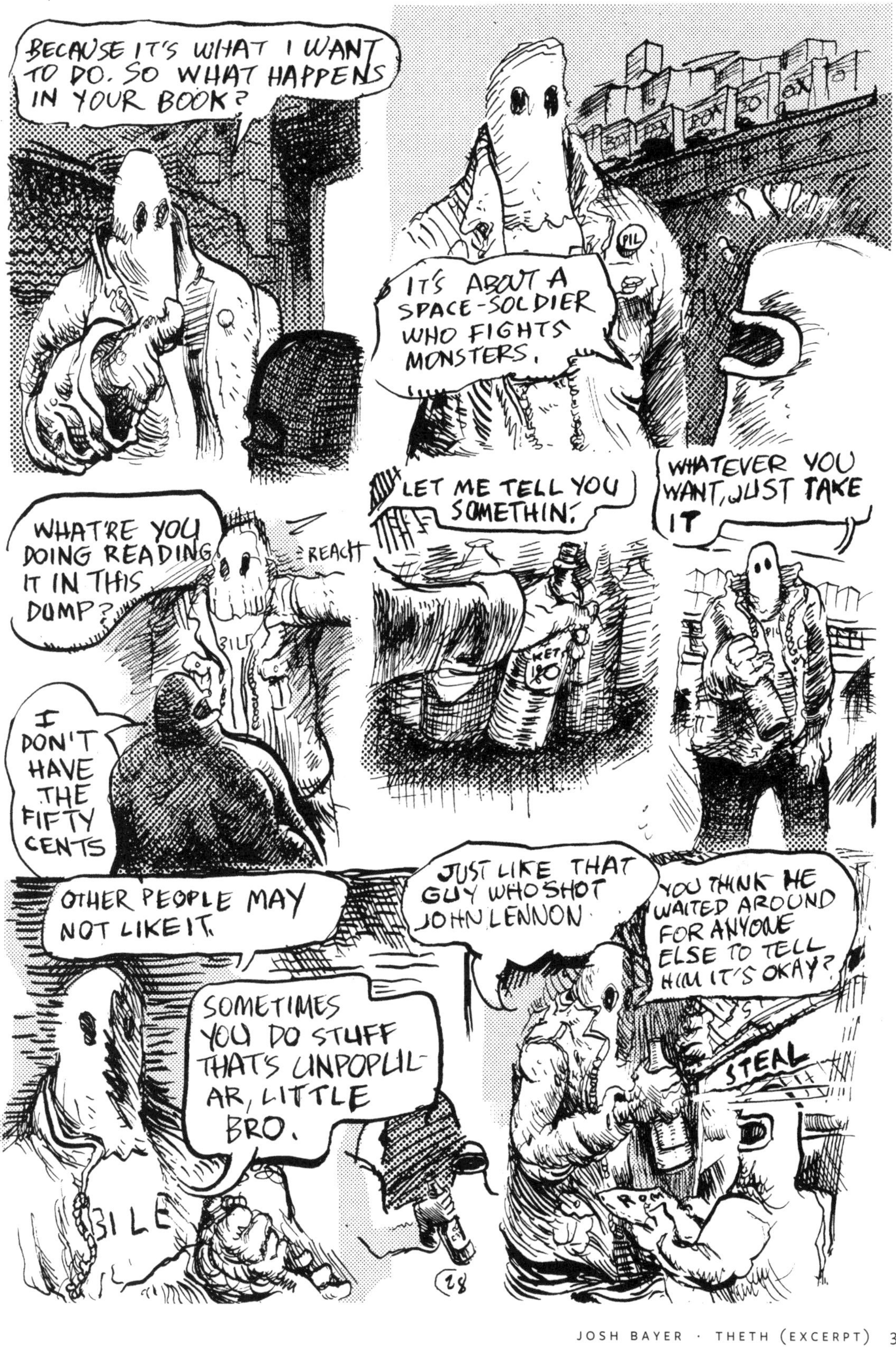
BECAUSE IT'S WHAT I WANT TO DO. SO WHAT HAPPENS IN YOUR BOOK?
IT'S ABOUT A SPACE-SOLDIER WHO FIGHTS MONSTERS.
WHAT'RE YOU DOING READING IT IN THIS DUMP?
REACH
I DON'T HAVE THE FIFTY CENTS
LET ME TELL YOU SOMETHIN'.
WHATEVER YOU WANT, JUST TAKE IT
OTHER PEOPLE MAY NOT LIKE IT.
SOMETIMES YOU DO STUFF THAT'S UNPOPULAR, LITTLE BRO.
BILE
JUST LIKE THAT GUY WHO SHOT JOHN LENNON
YOU THINK HE WAITED AROUND FOR ANYONE ELSE TO TELL HIM IT'S OKAY?
STEAL
28

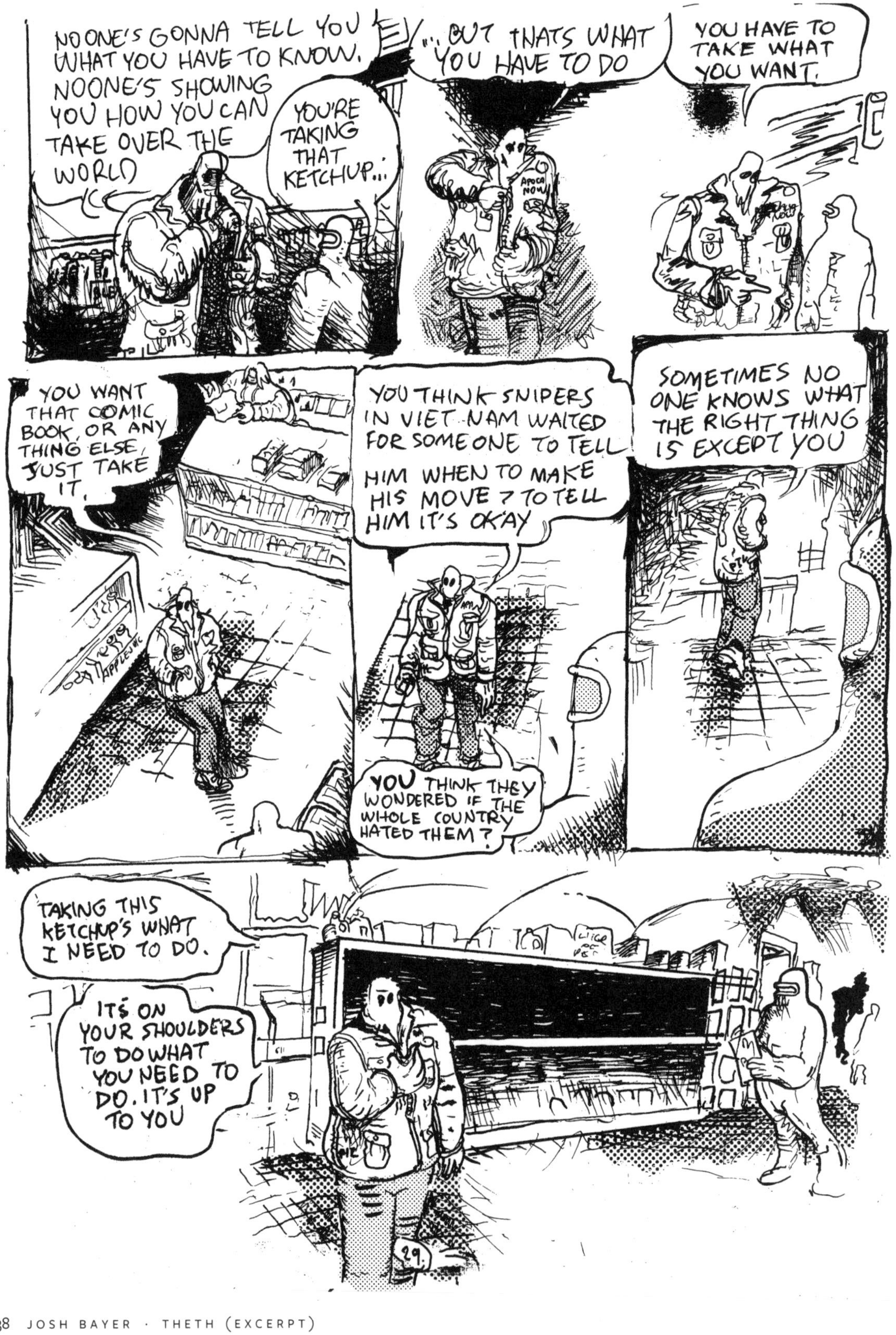
NOONE'S GONNA TELL YOU WHAT YOU HAVE TO KNOW. NOONE'S SHOWING YOU HOW YOU CAN TAKE OVER THE WORLD
YOU'RE TAKING THAT KETCHUP...
...BUT THATS WHAT YOU HAVE TO DO
YOU HAVE TO TAKE WHAT YOU WANT.
YOU WANT THAT COMIC BOOK, OR ANY THING ELSE, JUST TAKE IT.
YOU THINK SNIPERS IN VIET NAM WAITED FOR SOME ONE TO TELL HIM WHEN TO MAKE HIS MOVE? TO TELL HIM IT'S OKAY
YOU THINK THEY WONDERED IF THE WHOLE COUNTRY HATED THEM?
SOMETIMES NO ONE KNOWS WHAT THE RIGHT THING IS EXCEPT YOU
TAKING THIS KETCHUP'S WHAT I NEED TO DO.
ITS ON YOUR SHOULDERS TO DO WHAT YOU NEED TO DO. IT'S UP TO YOU

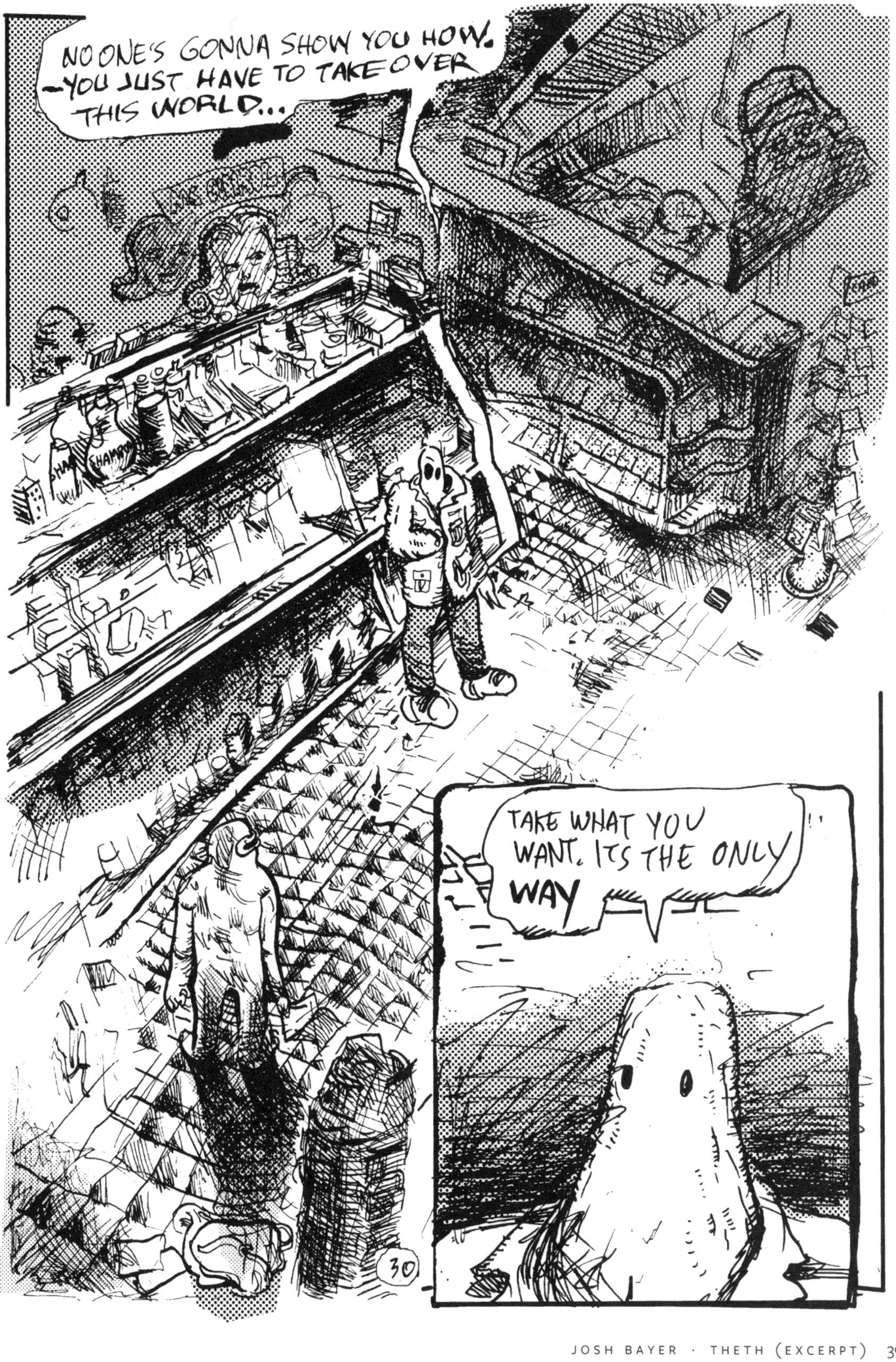
NO ONE'S GONNA SHOW YOU HOW. —YOU JUST HAVE TO TAKE OVER THIS WORLD...
TAKE WHAT YOU WANT. ITS THE ONLY WAY
30

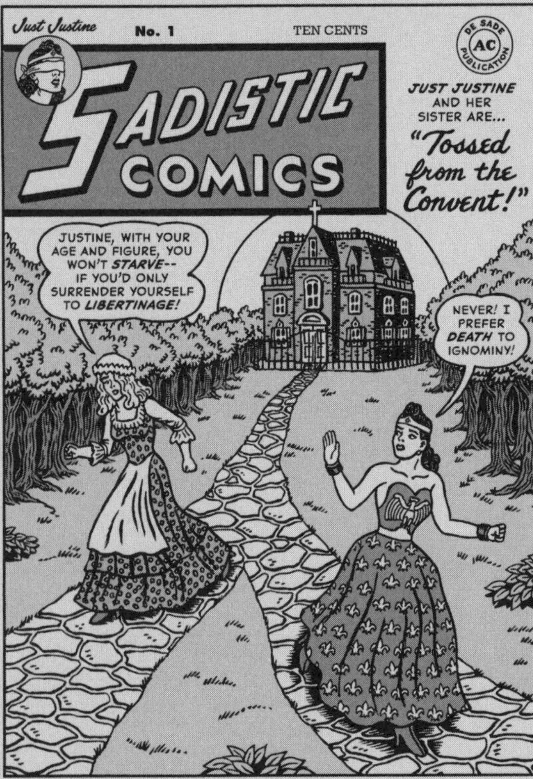
Just Justine
No. 1
TEN CENTS
DE SADE AC PUBLICATION
SADISTIC COMICS
JUST JUSTINE AND HER SISTER ARE... "Tossed from the Convent!"
JUSTINE, WITH YOUR AGE AND FIGURE, YOU WON'T STARVE-- IF YOU'D ONLY SURRENDER YOURSELF TO LIBERTINAGE!
NEVER! I PREFER DEATH TO IGNOMINY!

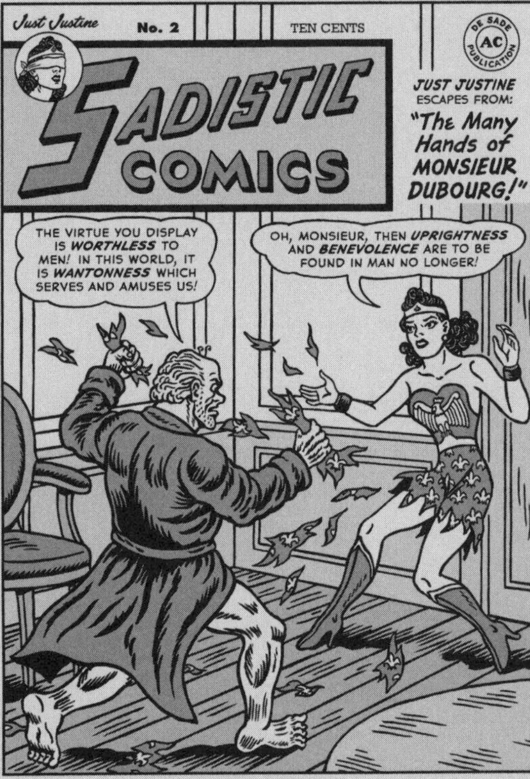
Just Justine
No. 2
TEN CENTS
DE SADE AC PUBLICATION
SADISTIC COMICS
JUST JUSTINE ESCAPES FROM: "The Many Hands of MONSIEUR DUBOURG!"
THE VIRTUE YOU DISPLAY IS WORTHLESS TO MEN! IN THIS WORLD, IT IS WANTONNESS WHICH SERVES AND AMUSES US!
OH, MONSIEUR, THEN UPRIGHTNESS AND BENEVOLENCE ARE TO BE FOUND IN MAN NO LONGER!

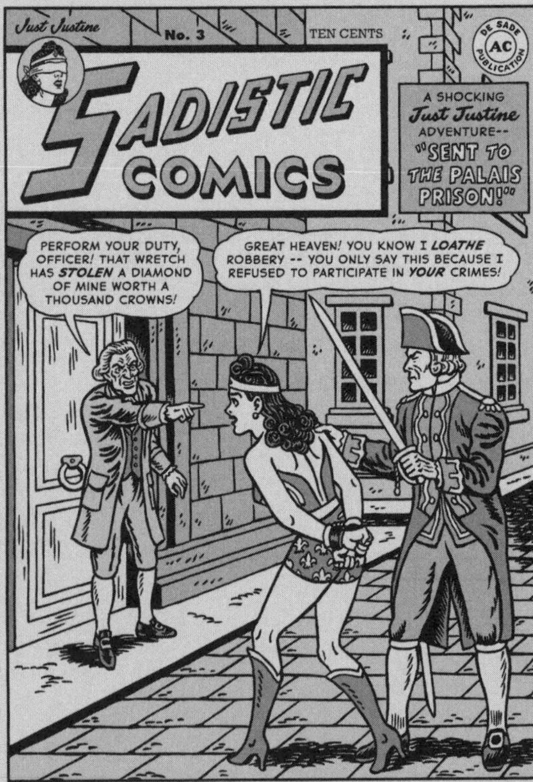
Just Justine
No. 3
TEN CENTS
DE SADE AC PUBLICATION
SADISTIC COMICS
A SHOCKING Just Justine ADVENTURE-- "SENT TO THE PALAIS PRISON!"
PERFORM YOUR DUTY, OFFICER! THAT WRETCH HAS STOLEN A DIAMOND OF MINE WORTH A THOUSAND CROWNS!
GREAT HEAVEN! YOU KNOW I LOATHE ROBBERY -- YOU ONLY SAY THIS BECAUSE I REFUSED TO PARTICIPATE IN YOUR CRIMES!

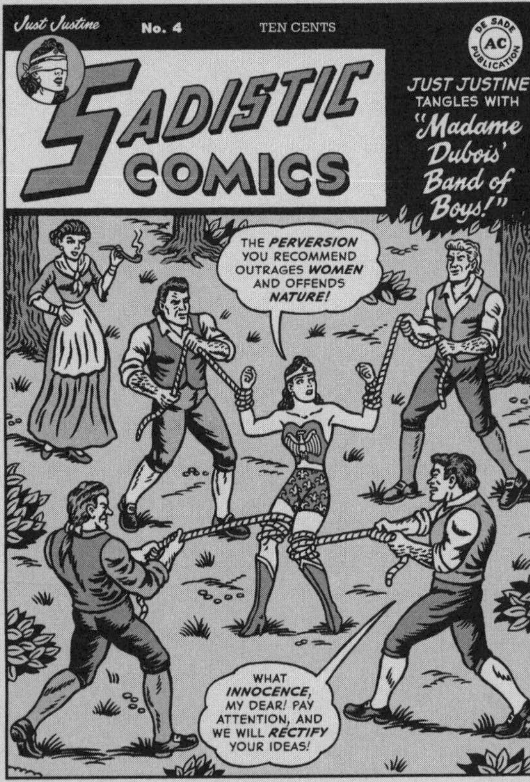
Just Justine
No. 4
TEN CENTS
DE SADE AC PUBLICATION
SADISTIC COMICS
JUST JUSTINE TANGLES WITH "Madame Dubois' Band of Boys!"
THE PERVERSION YOU RECOMMEND OUTRAGES WOMEN AND OFFENDS NATURE!
WHAT INNOCENCE, MY DEAR! PAY ATTENTION, AND WE WILL RECTIFY YOUR IDEAS!

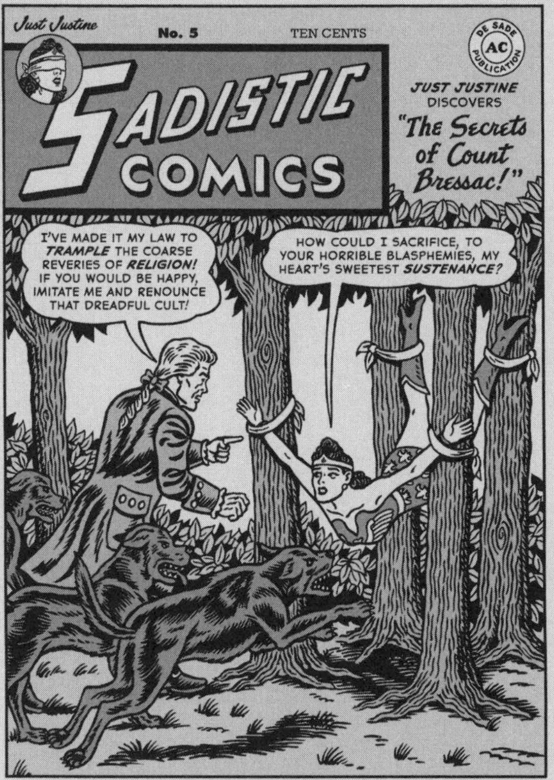
Just Justine
No. 5
TEN CENTS
DE SADE AC PUBLICATION
SADISTIC COMICS
JUST JUSTINE DISCOVERS "The Secrets of Count Bressac!"
I'VE MADE IT MY LAW TO TRAMPLE THE COARSE REVERIES OF RELIGION! IF YOU WOULD BE HAPPY, IMITATE ME AND RENOUNCE THAT DREADFUL CULT!
HOW COULD I SACRIFICE, TO YOUR HORRIBLE BLASPHEMIES, MY HEART'S SWEETEST SUSTENANCE?

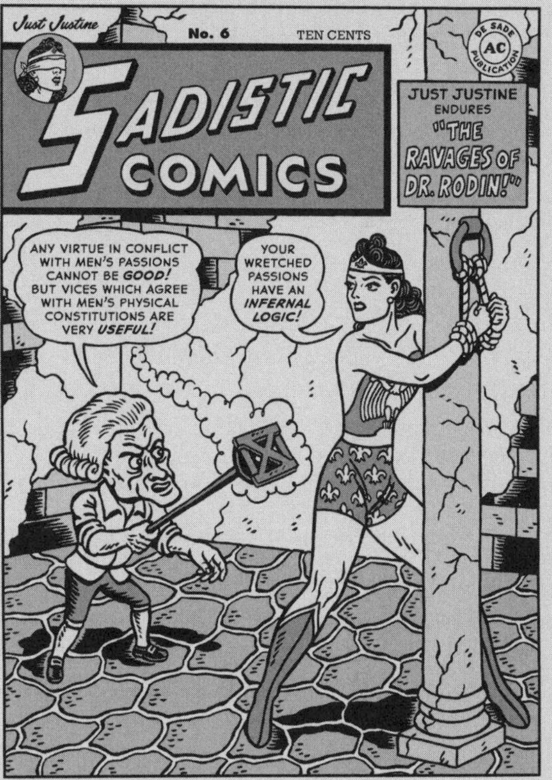
Just Justine
No. 6
TEN CENTS
DE SADE AC PUBLICATION
SADISTIC COMICS
JUST JUSTINE ENDURES "THE RAVAGES OF DR. RODIN!"
ANY VIRTUE IN CONFLICT WITH MEN'S PASSIONS CANNOT BE GOOD! BUT VICES WHICH AGREE WITH MEN'S PHYSICAL CONSTITUTIONS ARE VERY USEFUL!
YOUR WRETCHED PASSIONS HAVE AN INFERNAL LOGIC!

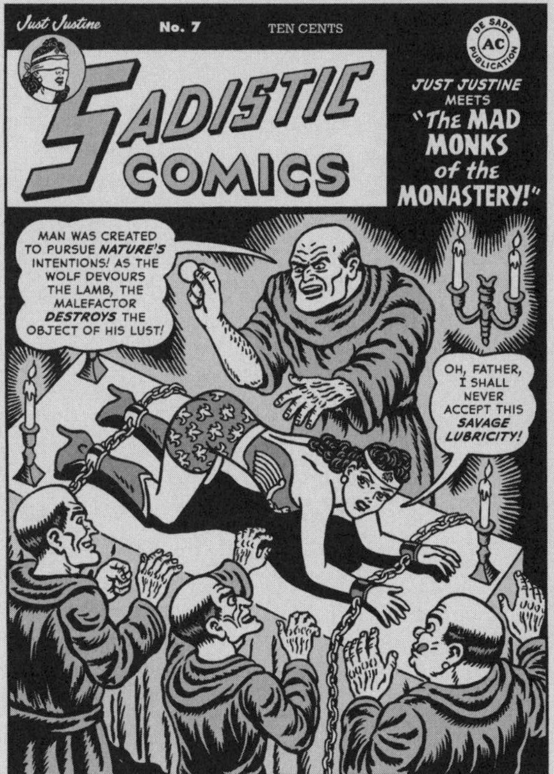
Just Justine
No. 7
TEN CENTS
DE SADE AC PUBLICATION
SADISTIC COMICS
JUST JUSTINE MEETS "The MAD MONKS of the MONASTERY!"
MAN WAS CREATED TO PURSUE NATURE'S INTENTIONS! AS THE WOLF DEVOURS THE LAMB, THE MALEFACTOR DESTROYS THE OBJECT OF HIS LUST!
OH, FATHER, I SHALL NEVER ACCEPT THIS SAVAGE LUBRICITY!

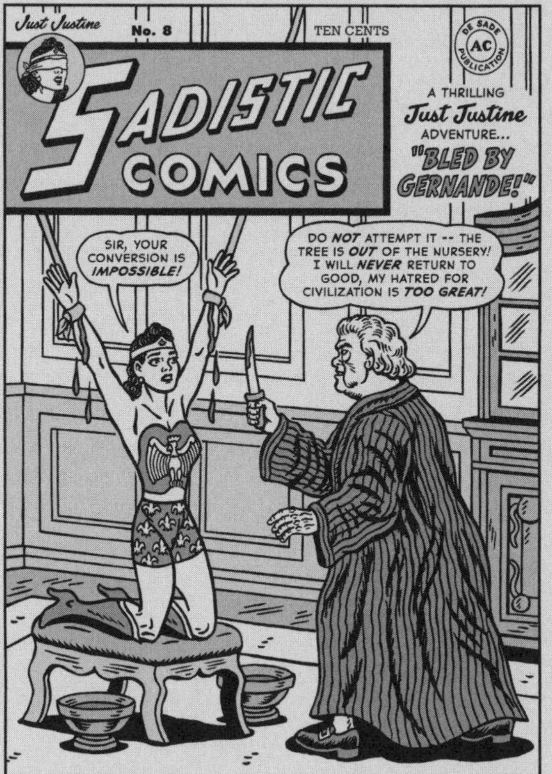
Just Justine
No. 8
TEN CENTS
DE SADE AC PUBLICATION
SADISTIC COMICS
A THRILLING Just Justine ADVENTURE... "BLED BY GERNANDE!"
SIR, YOUR CONVERSION IS IMPOSSIBLE!
DO NOT ATTEMPT IT -- THE TREE IS OUT OF THE NURSERY! I WILL NEVER RETURN TO GOOD, MY HATRED FOR CIVILIZATION IS TOO GREAT!

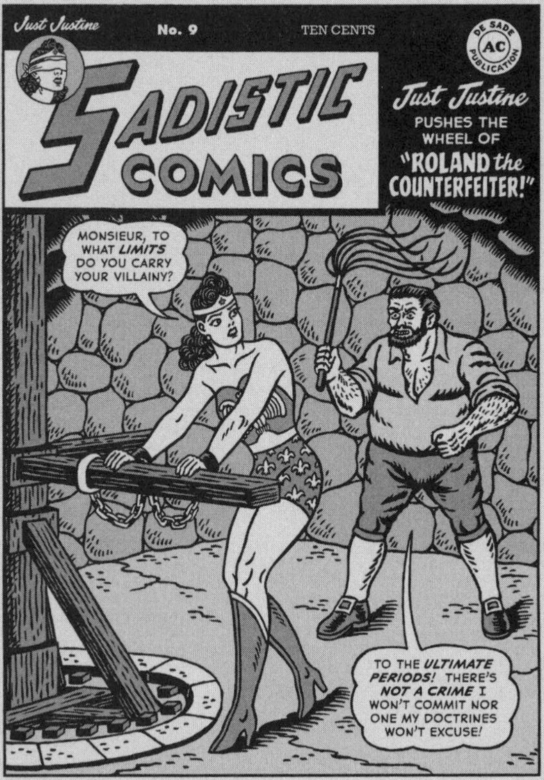
Just Justine
No. 9
TEN CENTS
DE SADE AC PUBLICATION
SADISTIC COMICS
Just Justine PUSHES THE WHEEL OF "ROLAND the COUNTERFEITER!"
MONSIEUR, TO WHAT LIMITS DO YOU CARRY YOUR VILLAINY?
TO THE ULTIMATE PERIODS! THERE'S NOT A CRIME I WON'T COMMIT NOR ONE MY DOCTRINES WON'T EXCUSE!

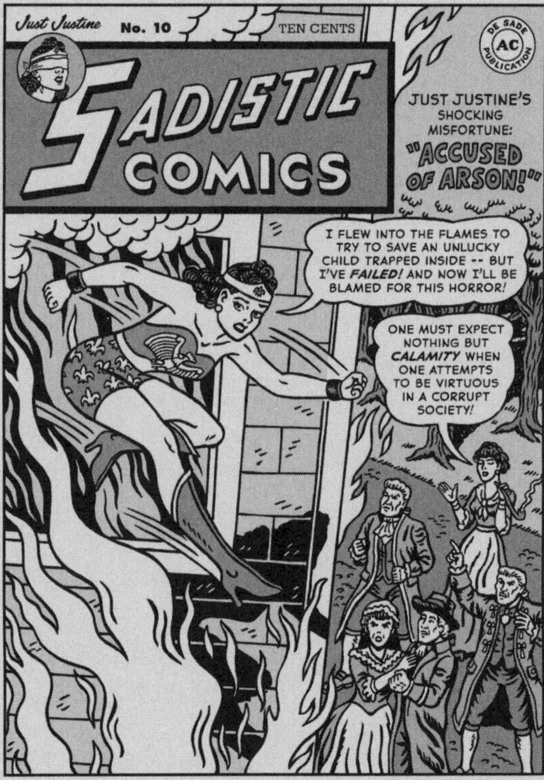
Just Justine
No. 10
TEN CENTS
DE SADE AC PUBLICATION
SADISTIC COMICS
JUST JUSTINE'S SHOCKING MISFORTUNE: "ACCUSED OF ARSON!"
I FLEW INTO THE FLAMES TO TRY TO SAVE AN UNLUCKY CHILD TRAPPED INSIDE -- BUT I'VE FAILED! AND NOW I'LL BE BLAMED FOR THIS HORROR!
ONE MUST EXPECT NOTHING BUT CALAMITY WHEN ONE ATTEMPTS TO BE VIRTUOUS IN A CORRUPT SOCIETY!

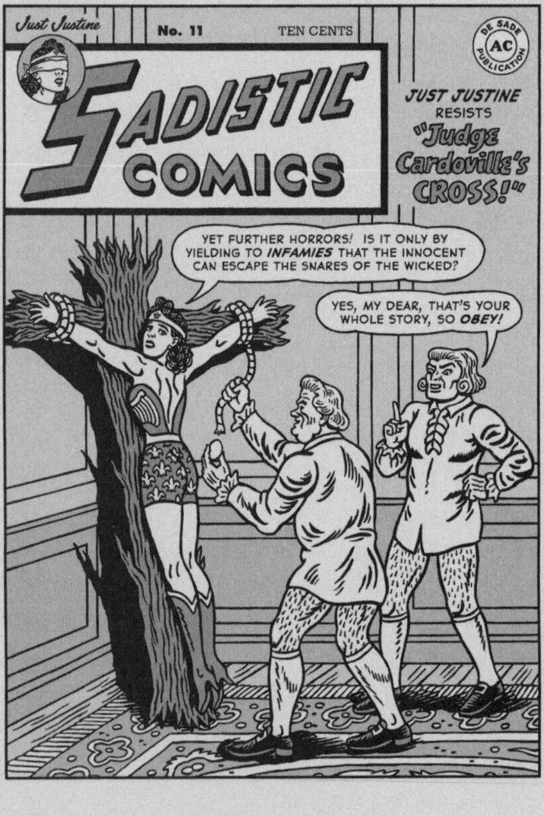
Just Justine
No. 11
TEN CENTS
DE SADE AC PUBLICATION
SADISTIC COMICS
JUST JUSTINE RESISTS "Judge Cardoville's CROSS!"
YET FURTHER HORRORS! IS IT ONLY BY YIELDING TO INFAMIES THAT THE INNOCENT CAN ESCAPE THE SNARES OF THE WICKED?
YES, MY DEAR, THAT'S YOUR WHOLE STORY, SO OBEY!

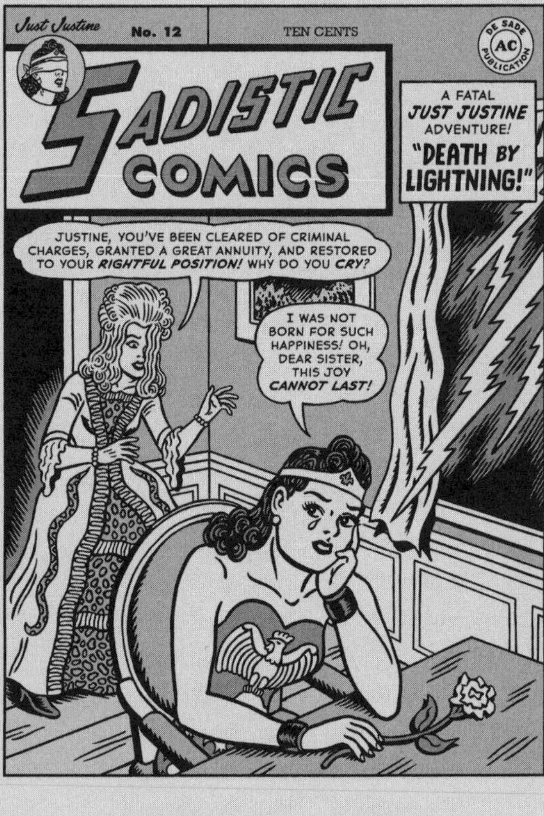
Just Justine
No. 12
TEN CENTS
DE SADE AC PUBLICATION
SADISTIC COMICS
A FATAL JUST JUSTINE ADVENTURE! "DEATH BY LIGHTNING!"
JUSTINE, YOU'VE BEEN CLEARED OF CRIMINAL CHARGES, GRANTED A GREAT ANNUITY, AND RESTORED TO YOUR RIGHTFUL POSITION! WHY DO YOU CRY?
I WAS NOT BORN FOR SUCH HAPPINESS! OH, DEAR SISTER, THIS JOY CANNOT LAST!

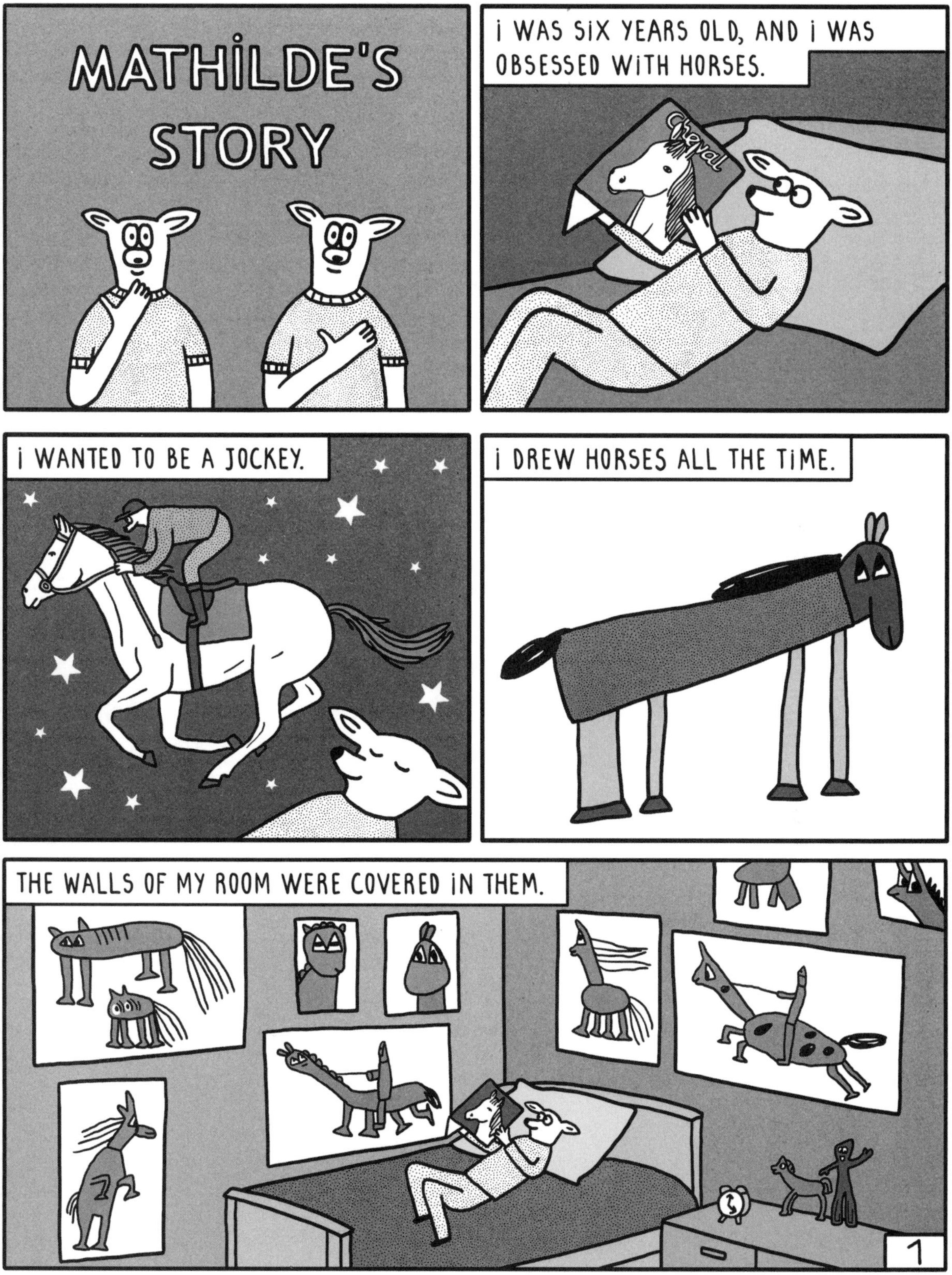
MATHILDE'S STORY
I WAS SIX YEARS OLD, AND I WAS OBSESSED WITH HORSES.
Cheval
I WANTED TO BE A JOCKEY.
I DREW HORSES ALL THE TIME.
THE WALLS OF MY ROOM WERE COVERED IN THEM.
1

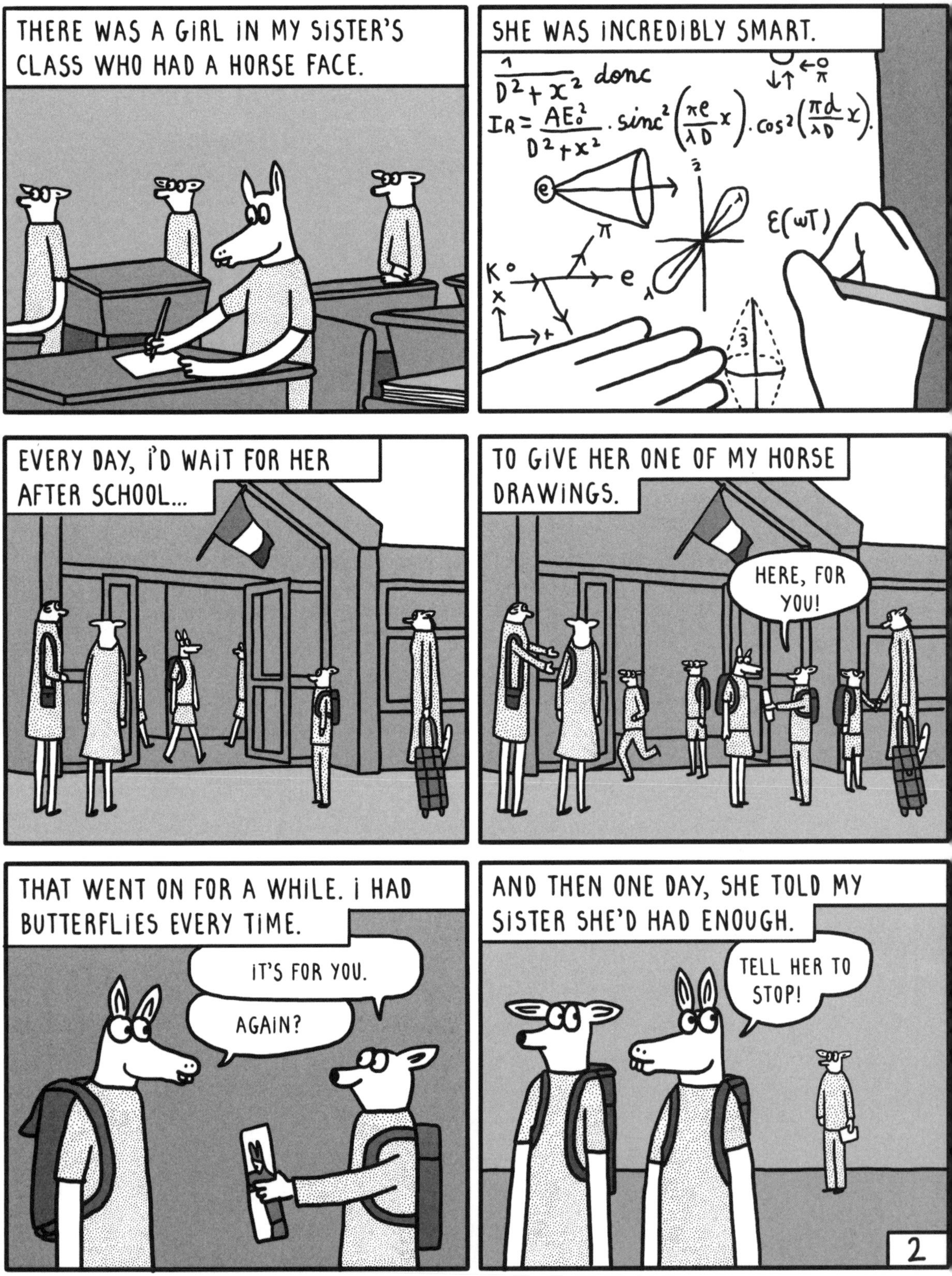
THERE WAS A GIRL IN MY SISTER'S CLASS WHO HAD A HORSE FACE.
SHE WAS INCREDIBLY SMART.
EVERY DAY, I'D WAIT FOR HER AFTER SCHOOL...
TO GIVE HER ONE OF MY HORSE DRAWINGS.
HERE, FOR YOU!
THAT WENT ON FOR A WHILE. I HAD BUTTERFLIES EVERY TIME.
IT'S FOR YOU.
AGAIN?
AND THEN ONE DAY, SHE TOLD MY SISTER SHE'D HAD ENOUGH.
TELL HER TO STOP!
2

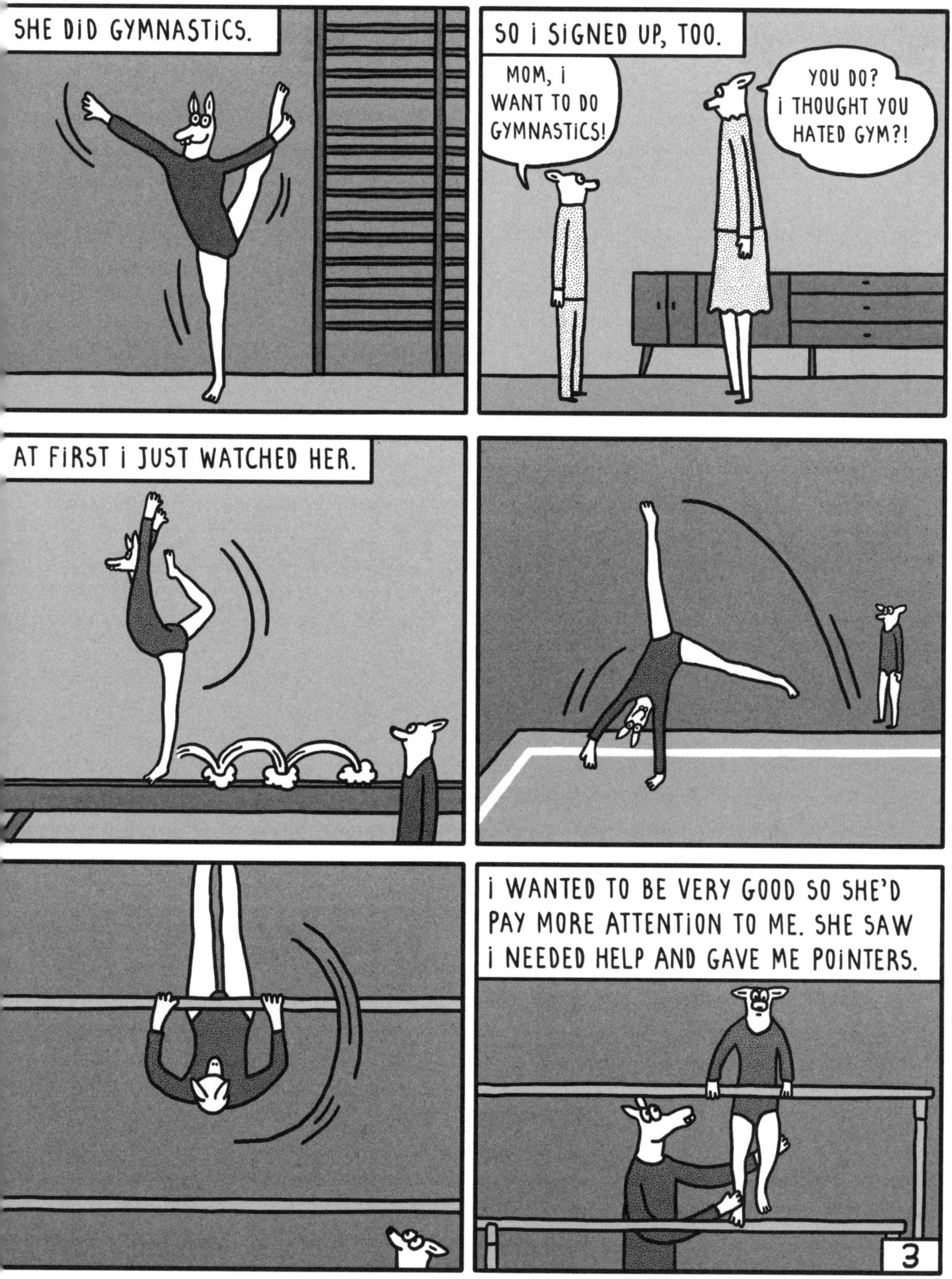

SHE DiD GYMNASTiCS.
SO i SiGNED UP, TOO.
MOM, i WANT TO DO GYMNASTiCS!
YOU DO? i THOUGHT YOU HATED GYM?!
AT FiRST i JUST WATCHED HER.
i WANTED TO BE VERY GOOD SO SHE'D PAY MORE ATTENTiON TO ME. SHE SAW i NEEDED HELP AND GAVE ME POiNTERS.
3

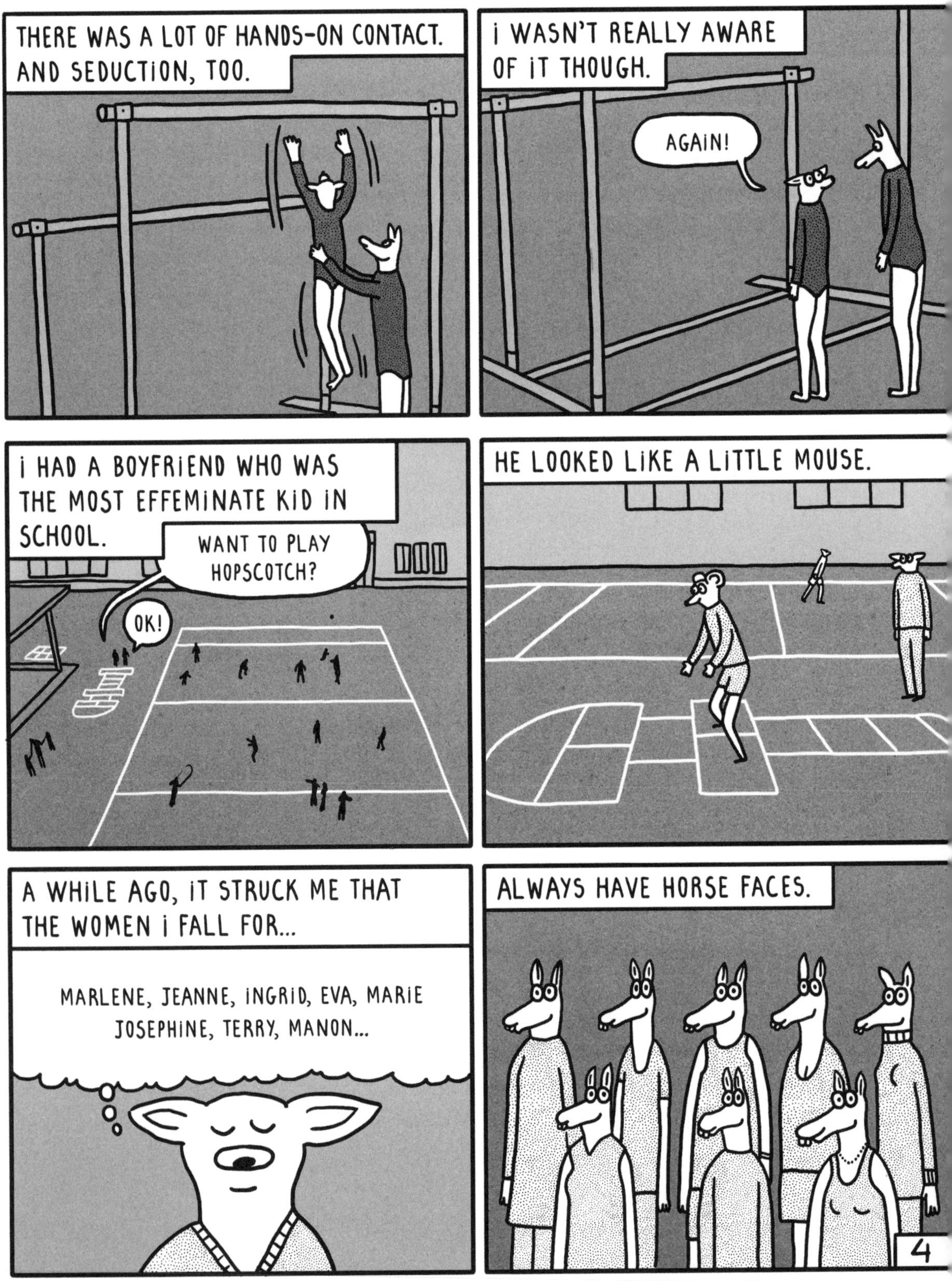
THERE WAS A LOT OF HANDS-ON CONTACT. AND SEDUCTION, TOO.
I WASN'T REALLY AWARE OF IT THOUGH.
AGAIN!
I HAD A BOYFRIEND WHO WAS THE MOST EFFEMINATE KID IN SCHOOL.
WANT TO PLAY HOPSCOTCH?
OK!
HE LOOKED LIKE A LITTLE MOUSE.
A WHILE AGO, IT STRUCK ME THAT THE WOMEN I FALL FOR...
MARLENE, JEANNE, INGRID, EVA, MARIE JOSEPHINE, TERRY, MANON...
ALWAYS HAVE HORSE FACES.
4

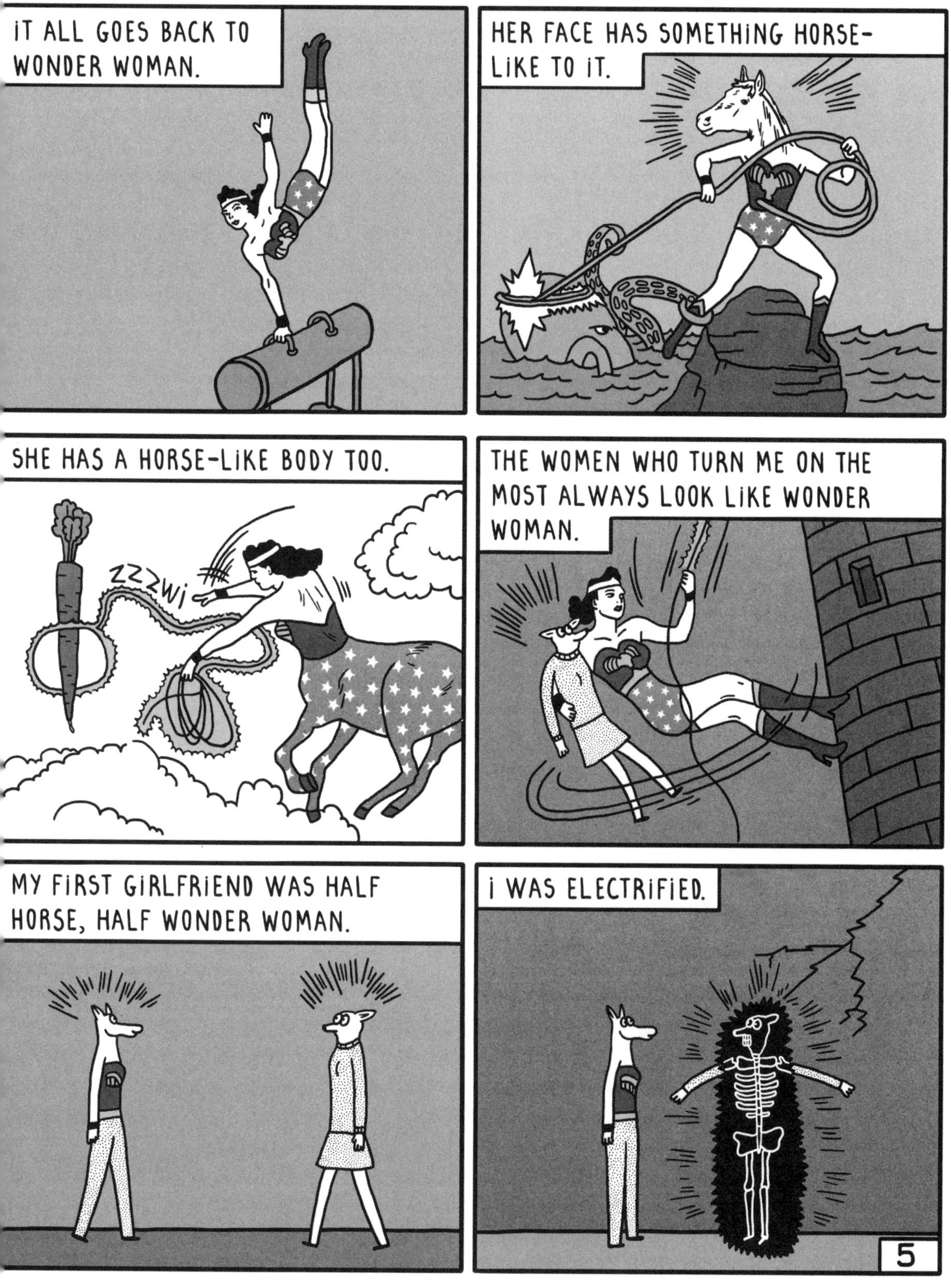
iT ALL GOES BACK TO WONDER WOMAN.
HER FACE HAS SOMETHiNG HORSE-LiKE TO iT.
SHE HAS A HORSE-LiKE BODY TOO.
ZZZWi
THE WOMEN WHO TURN ME ON THE MOST ALWAYS LOOK LiKE WONDER WOMAN.
MY FiRST GiRLFRiEND WAS HALF HORSE, HALF WONDER WOMAN.
i WAS ELECTRiFiED.
5

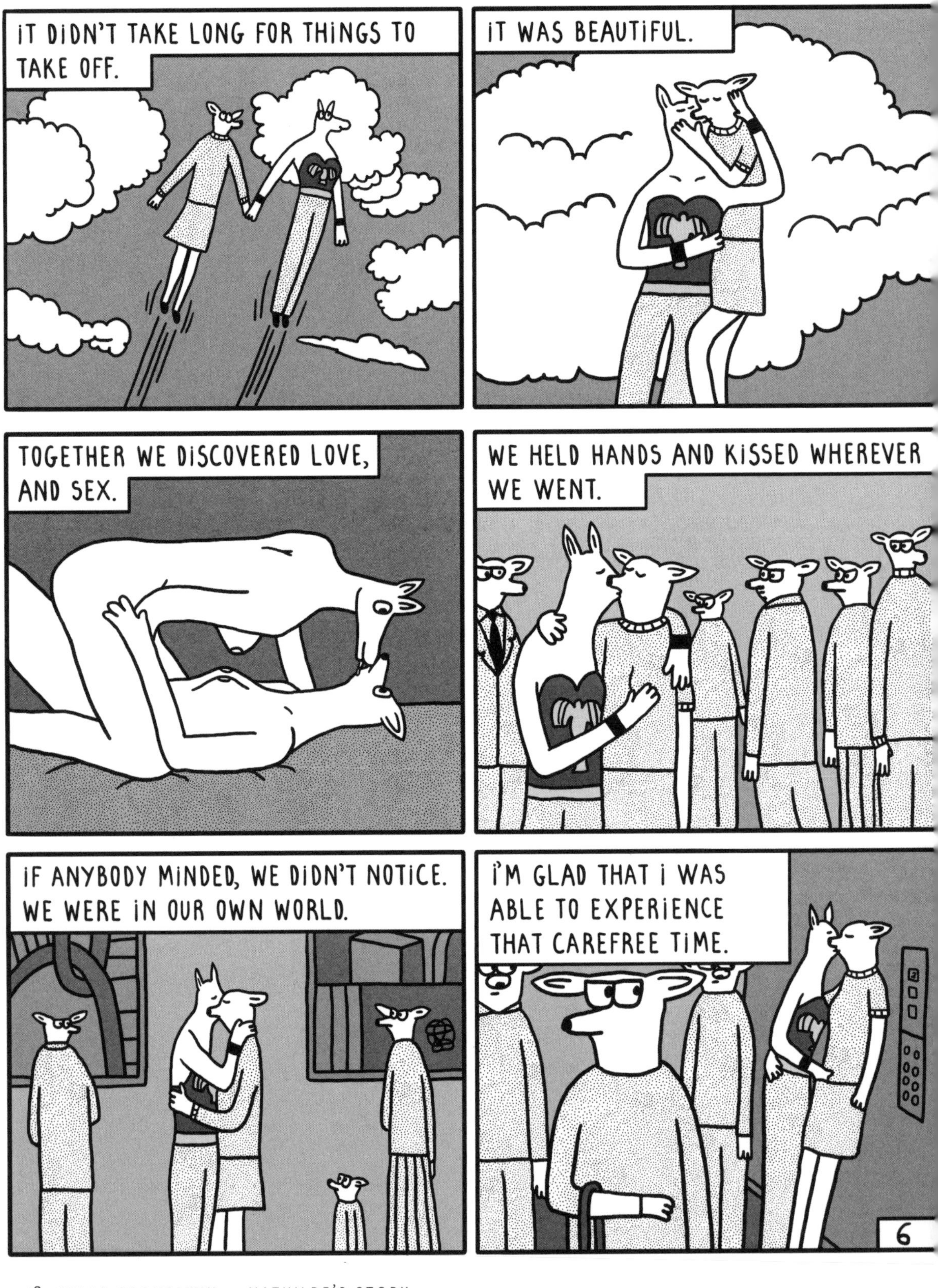
IT DIDN'T TAKE LONG FOR THINGS TO TAKE OFF.
IT WAS BEAUTIFUL.
TOGETHER WE DISCOVERED LOVE, AND SEX.
WE HELD HANDS AND KISSED WHEREVER WE WENT.
IF ANYBODY MINDED, WE DIDN'T NOTICE. WE WERE IN OUR OWN WORLD.
I'M GLAD THAT I WAS ABLE TO EXPERIENCE THAT CAREFREE TIME.
6

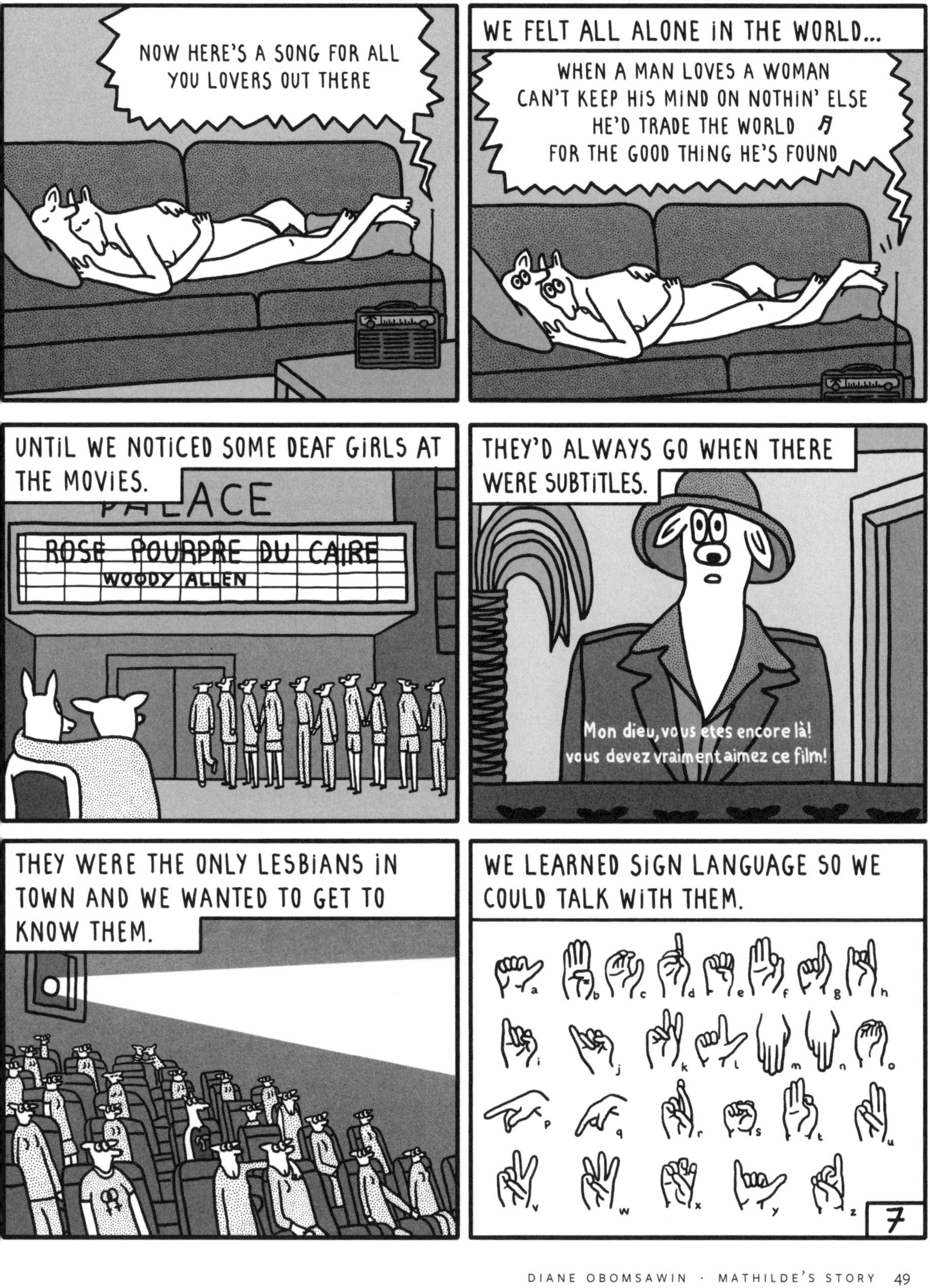
NOW HERE'S A SONG FOR ALL YOU LOVERS OUT THERE
WE FELT ALL ALONE IN THE WORLD...
WHEN A MAN LOVES A WOMAN
CAN'T KEEP HIS MIND ON NOTHIN' ELSE
HE'D TRADE THE WORLD
FOR THE GOOD THING HE'S FOUND
UNTIL WE NOTICED SOME DEAF GIRLS AT THE MOVIES.
PALACE
ROSE POURPRE DU CAIRE
WOODY ALLEN
THEY'D ALWAYS GO WHEN THERE WERE SUBTITLES.
Mon dieu, vous etes encore là!
vous devez vraiment aimez ce film!
THEY WERE THE ONLY LESBIANS IN TOWN AND WE WANTED TO GET TO KNOW THEM.
WE LEARNED SIGN LANGUAGE SO WE COULD TALK WITH THEM.
a b c d e f g h
i j k l m n o
p q r s t u
v w x y z
7

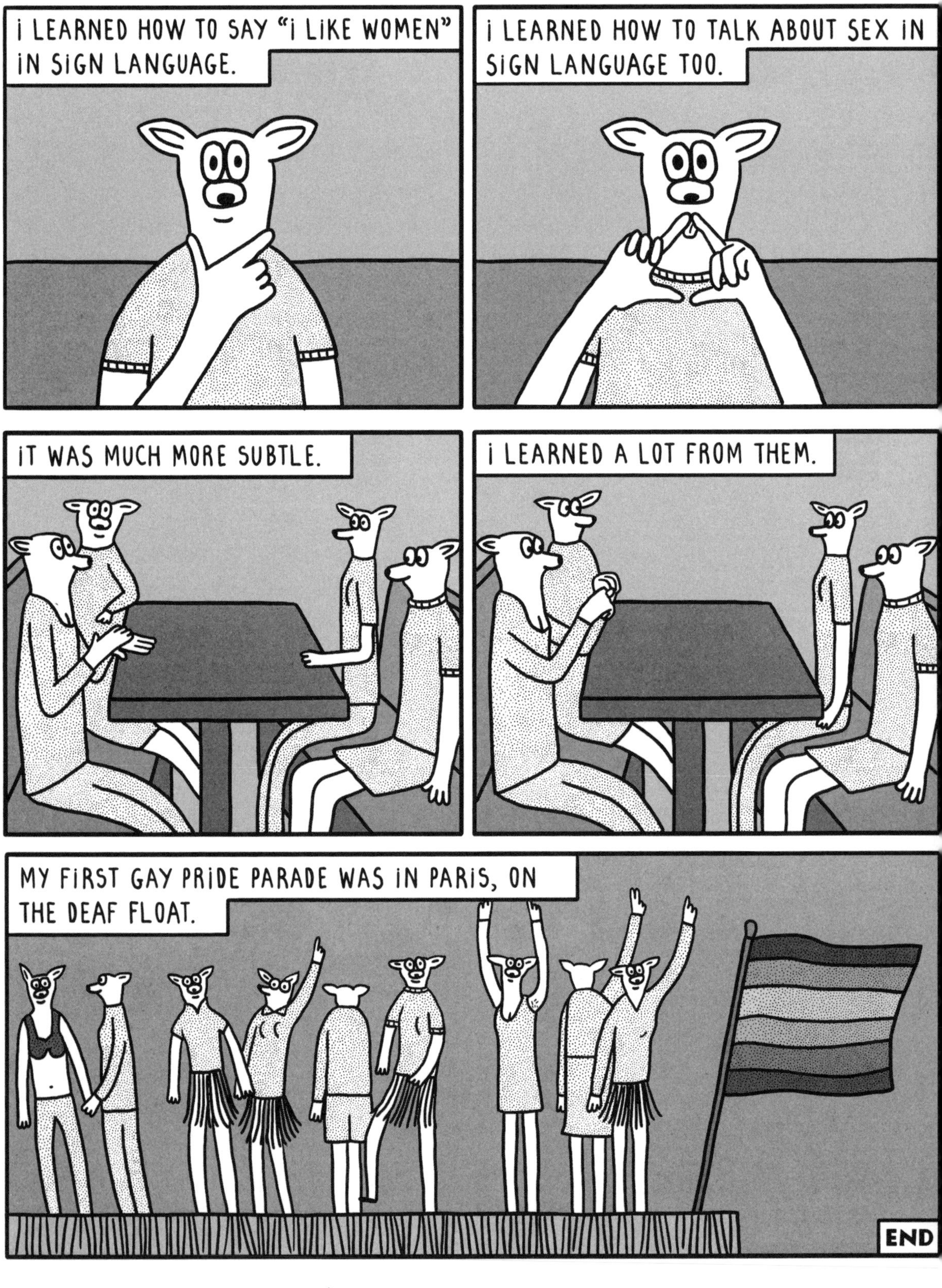
i LEARNED HOW TO SAY "i LiKE WOMEN" iN SiGN LANGUAGE.
i LEARNED HOW TO TALK ABOUT SEX iN SiGN LANGUAGE TOO.
iT WAS MUCH MORE SUBTLE.
i LEARNED A LOT FROM THEM.
MY FiRST GAY PRiDE PARADE WAS iN PARiS, ON THE DEAF FLOAT.
END

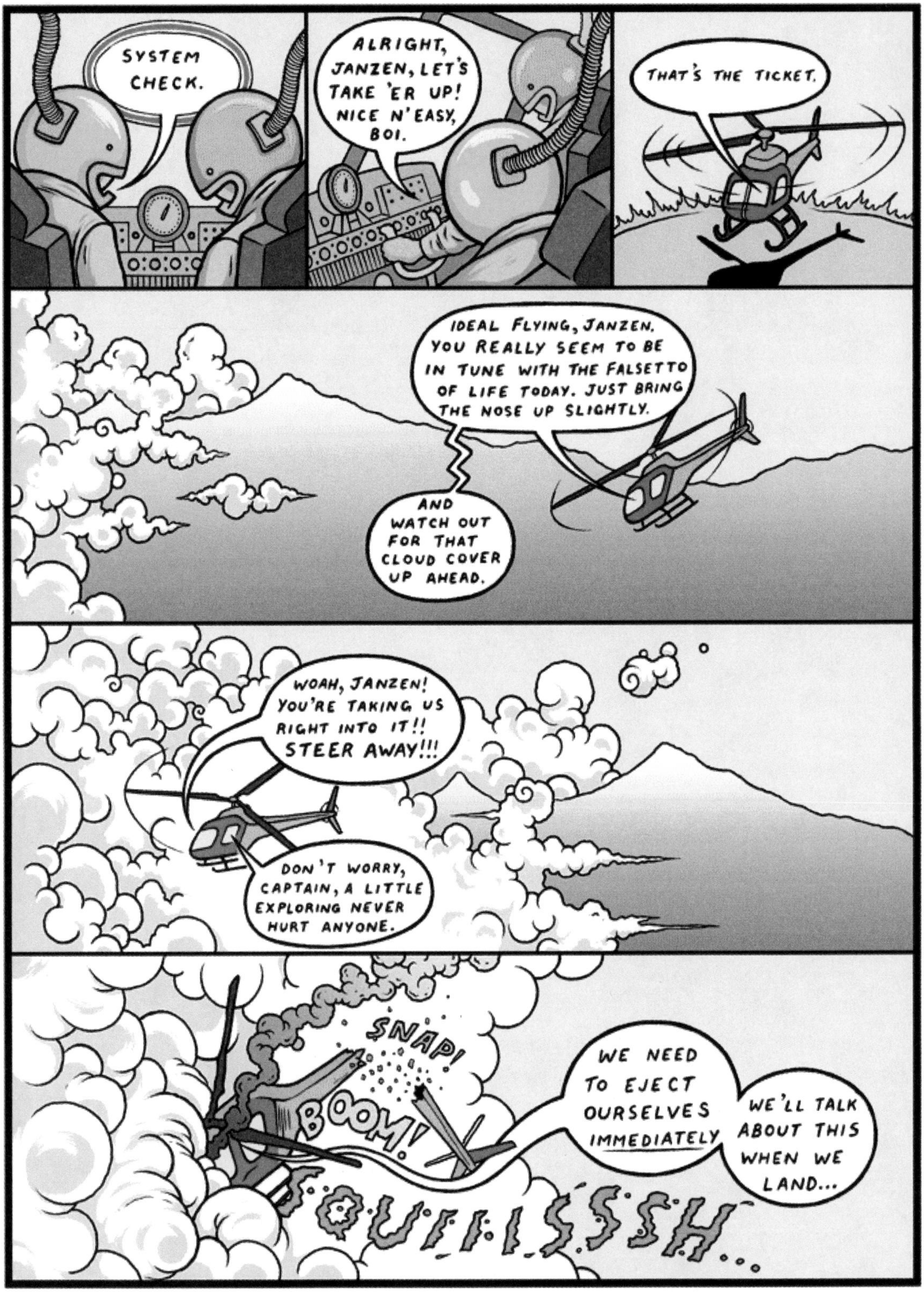
SYSTEM CHECK.
ALRIGHT, JANZEN, LET'S TAKE 'ER UP! NICE N' EASY, BOI.
THAT'S THE TICKET.
IDEAL FLYING, JANZEN. YOU REALLY SEEM TO BE IN TUNE WITH THE FALSETTO OF LIFE TODAY. JUST BRING THE NOSE UP SLIGHTLY.
AND WATCH OUT FOR THAT CLOUD COVER UP AHEAD.
WOAH, JANZEN! YOU'RE TAKING US RIGHT INTO IT!! STEER AWAY!!!
DON'T WORRY, CAPTAIN, A LITTLE EXPLORING NEVER HURT ANYONE.
SNAP!
BOOM!
WE NEED TO EJECT OURSELVES IMMEDIATELY
WE'LL TALK ABOUT THIS WHEN WE LAND...
QUFFISSSH...

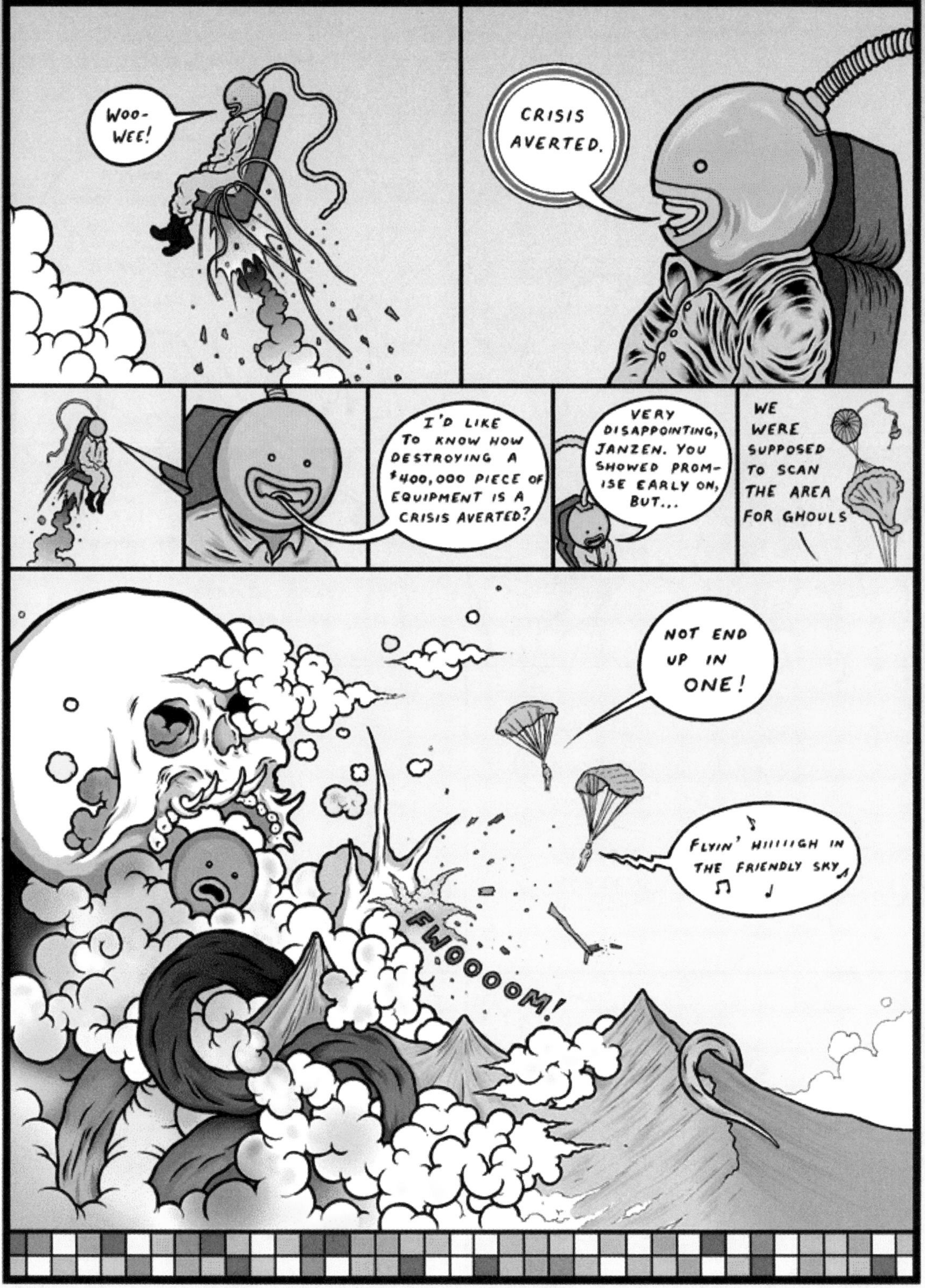
WOO-WEE!
CRISIS AVERTED.
I'D LIKE TO KNOW HOW DESTROYING A $400,000 PIECE OF EQUIPMENT IS A CRISIS AVERTED?
VERY DISAPPOINTING, JANZEN. YOU SHOWED PROMISE EARLY ON, BUT...
WE WERE SUPPOSED TO SCAN THE AREA FOR GHOULS
NOT END UP IN ONE!
FLYIN' HIIIIIGH IN THE FRIENDLY SKY
FWOOOOOM!

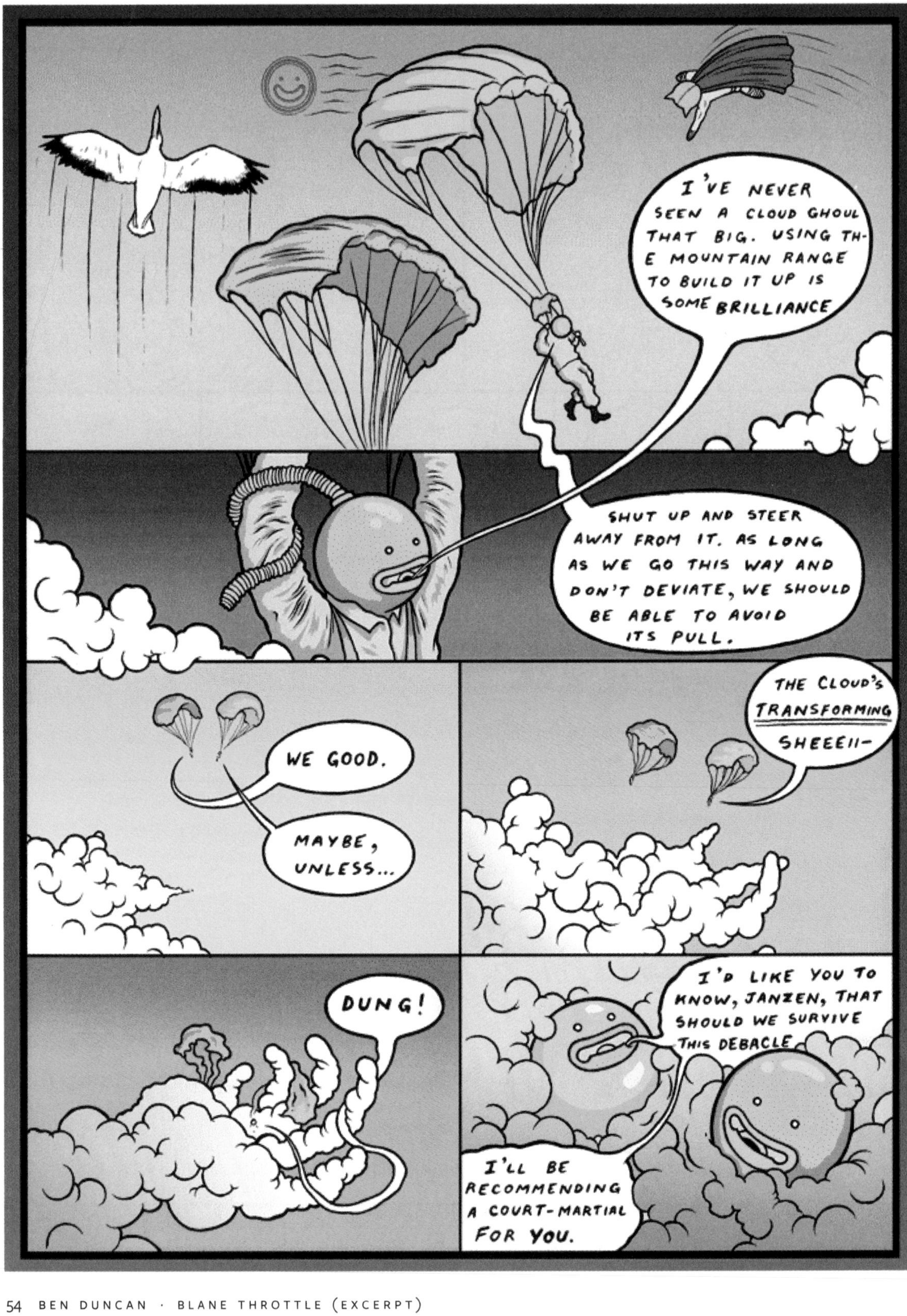
I'VE NEVER SEEN A CLOUD GHOUL THAT BIG. USING TH-E MOUNTAIN RANGE TO BUILD IT UP IS SOME BRILLIANCE
SHUT UP AND STEER AWAY FROM IT. AS LONG AS WE GO THIS WAY AND DON'T DEVIATE, WE SHOULD BE ABLE TO AVOID ITS PULL.
WE GOOD.
MAYBE, UNLESS...
THE CLOUD'S TRANSFORMING
SHEEEII-
DUNG!
I'D LIKE YOU TO KNOW, JANZEN, THAT SHOULD WE SURVIVE THIS DEBACLE
I'LL BE RECOMMENDING A COURT-MARTIAL FOR YOU.

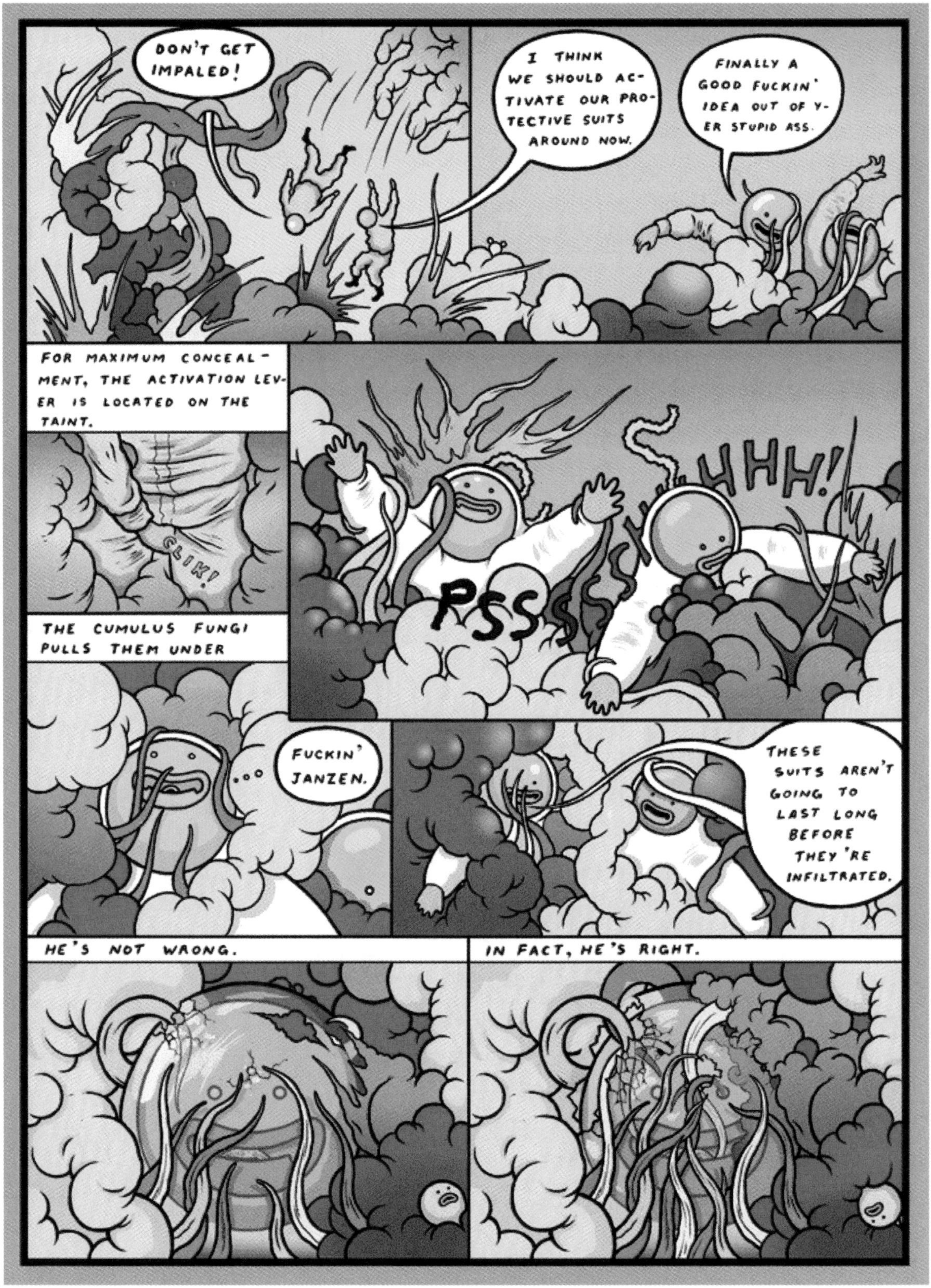
DON'T GET IMPALED!
I THINK WE SHOULD ACTIVATE OUR PROTECTIVE SUITS AROUND NOW.
FINALLY A GOOD FUCKIN' IDEA OUT OF Y-ER STUPID ASS.
FOR MAXIMUM CONCEALMENT, THE ACTIVATION LEVER IS LOCATED ON THE TAINT.
CLIK!
PSSSSSSHHHH!
THE CUMULUS FUNGI PULLS THEM UNDER
...
FUCKIN' JANZEN.
THESE SUITS AREN'T GOING TO LAST LONG BEFORE THEY'RE INFILTRATED.
HE'S NOT WRONG.
IN FACT, HE'S RIGHT.

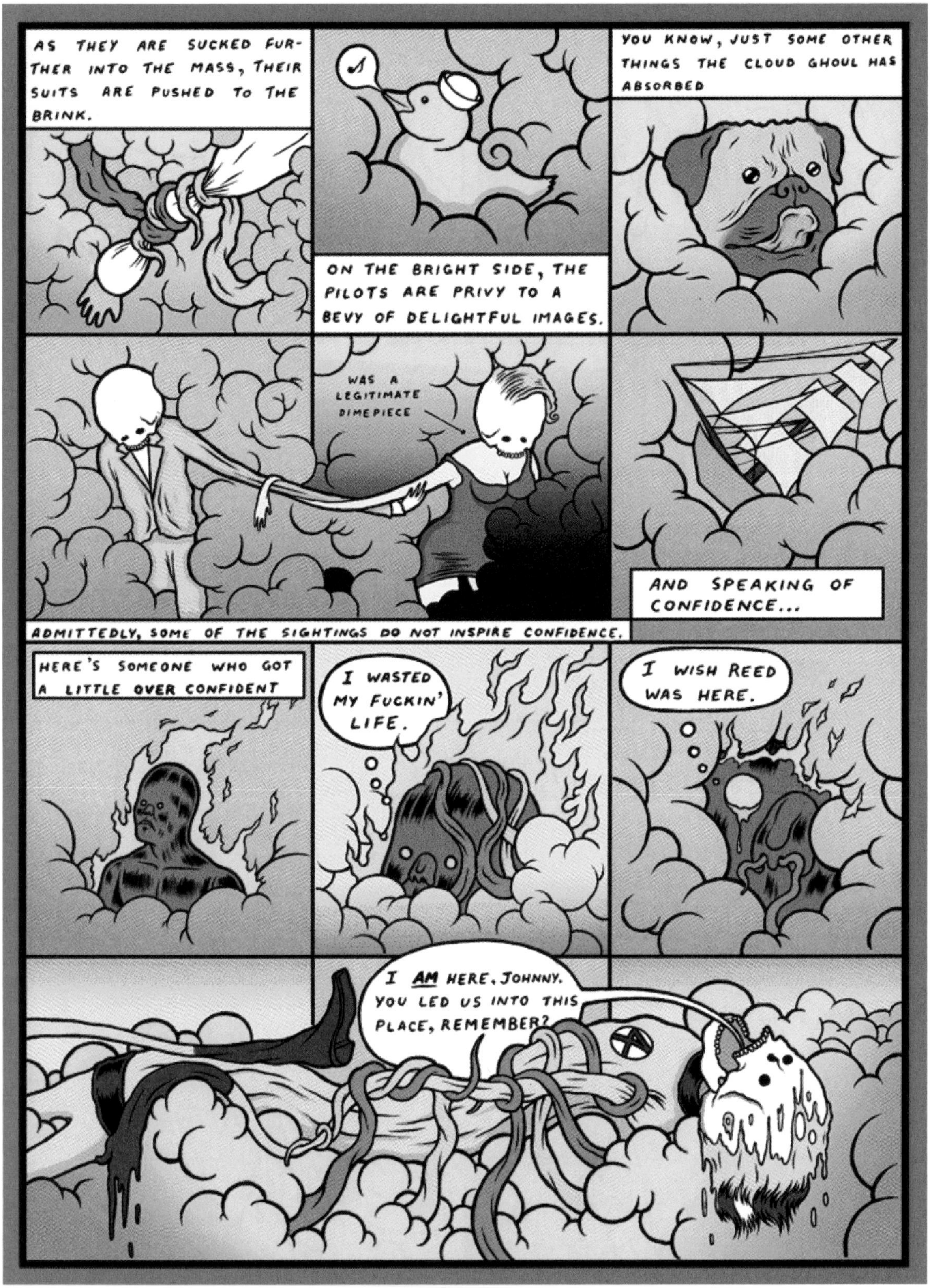
AS THEY ARE SUCKED FURTHER INTO THE MASS, THEIR SUITS ARE PUSHED TO THE BRINK.
ON THE BRIGHT SIDE, THE PILOTS ARE PRIVY TO A BEVY OF DELIGHTFUL IMAGES.
YOU KNOW, JUST SOME OTHER THINGS THE CLOUD GHOUL HAS ABSORBED
WAS A LEGITIMATE DIMEPIECE
ADMITTEDLY, SOME OF THE SIGHTINGS DO NOT INSPIRE CONFIDENCE.
AND SPEAKING OF CONFIDENCE...
HERE'S SOMEONE WHO GOT A LITTLE OVER CONFIDENT
I WASTED MY FUCKIN' LIFE.
I WISH REED WAS HERE.
I AM HERE, JOHNNY. YOU LED US INTO THIS PLACE, REMEMBER?

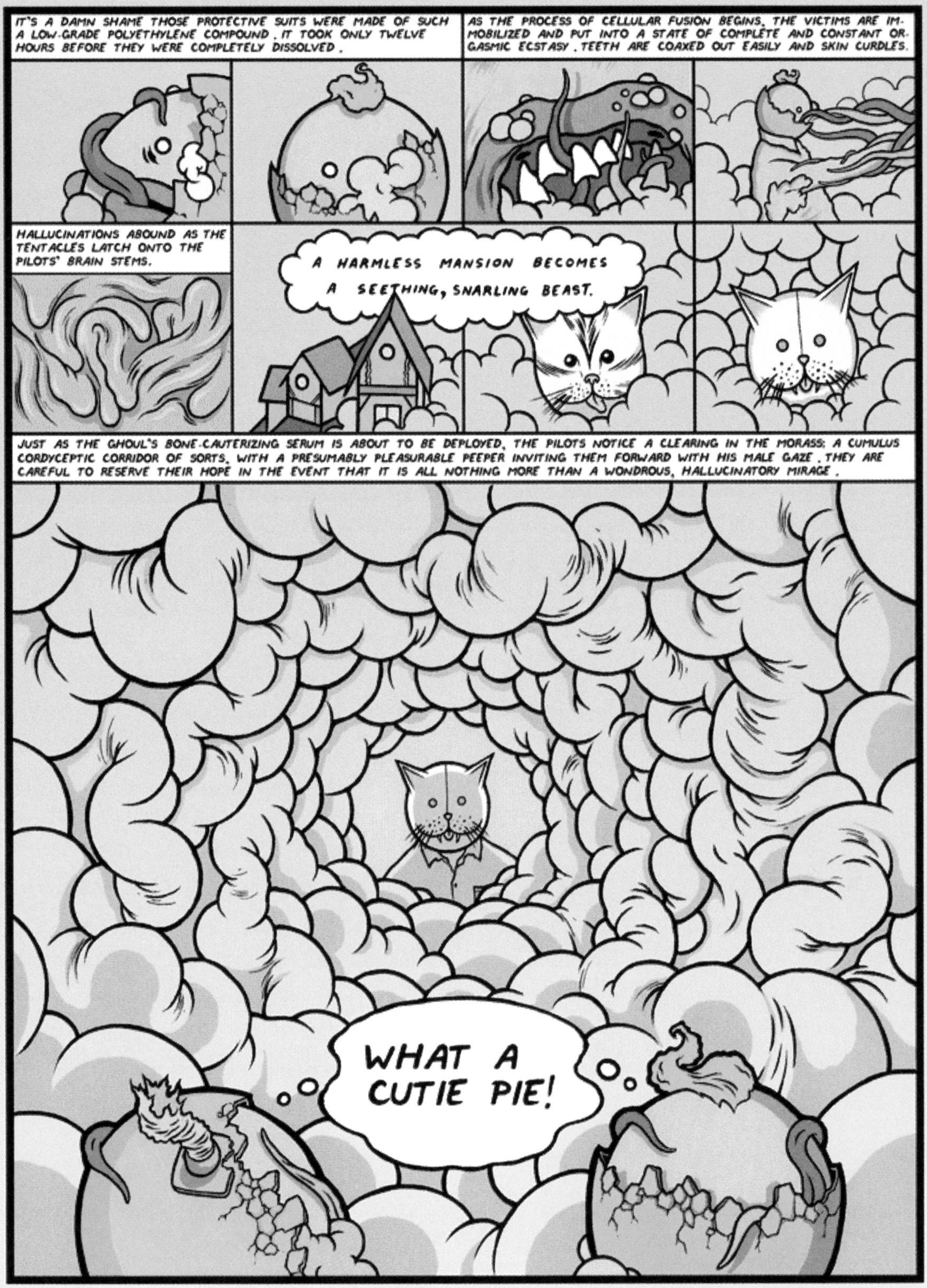
IT'S A DAMN SHAME THOSE PROTECTIVE SUITS WERE MADE OF SUCH A LOW-GRADE POLYETHYLENE COMPOUND. IT TOOK ONLY TWELVE HOURS BEFORE THEY WERE COMPLETELY DISSOLVED.
AS THE PROCESS OF CELLULAR FUSION BEGINS, THE VICTIMS ARE IMMOBILIZED AND PUT INTO A STATE OF COMPLETE AND CONSTANT ORGASMIC ECSTASY. TEETH ARE COAXED OUT EASILY AND SKIN CURDLES.
HALLUCINATIONS ABOUND AS THE TENTACLES LATCH ONTO THE PILOTS' BRAIN STEMS.
A HARMLESS MANSION BECOMES A SEETHING, SNARLING BEAST.
JUST AS THE GHOUL'S BONE-CAUTERIZING SERUM IS ABOUT TO BE DEPLOYED, THE PILOTS NOTICE A CLEARING IN THE MORASS: A CUMULUS CORDYCEPTIC CORRIDOR OF SORTS, WITH A PRESUMABLY PLEASURABLE PEEPER INVITING THEM FORWARD WITH HIS MALE GAZE. THEY ARE CAREFUL TO RESERVE THEIR HOPE IN THE EVENT THAT IT IS ALL NOTHING MORE THAN A WONDROUS, HALLUCINATORY MIRAGE.
WHAT A CUTIE PIE!

CHAPTER THREE

Storytellers

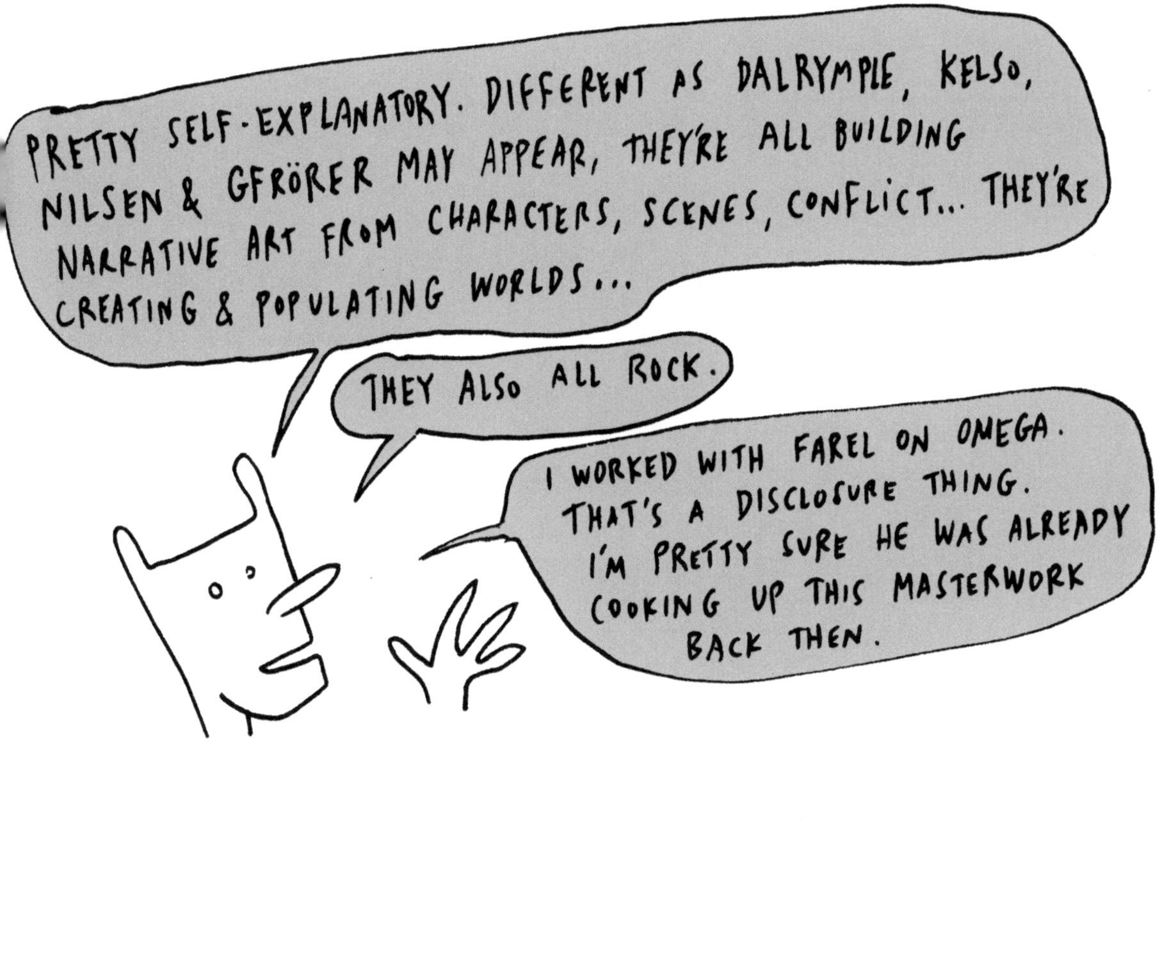
PRETTY SELF-EXPLANATORY. DIFFERENT AS DALRYMPLE, KELSO, NILSEN & GFRÖRER MAY APPEAR, THEY'RE ALL BUILDING NARRATIVE ART FROM CHARACTERS, SCENES, CONFLICT... THEY'RE CREATING & POPULATING WORLDS...
THEY ALSO ALL ROCK.
I WORKED WITH FAREL ON OMEGA. THAT'S A DISCLOSURE THING. I'M PRETTY SURE HE WAS ALREADY COOKING UP THIS MASTERWORK BACK THEN.

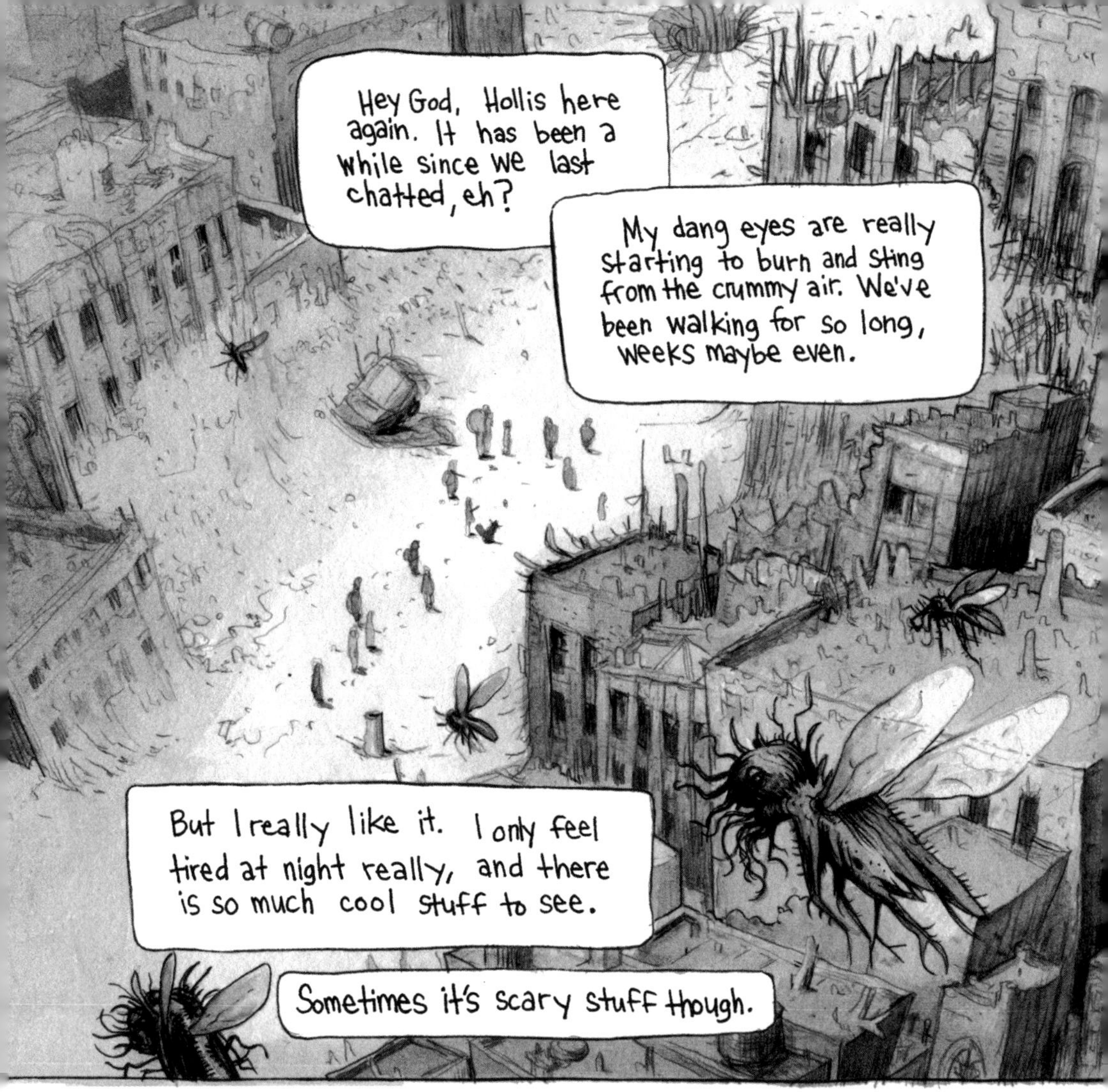
Hey God, Hollis here again. It has been a while since we last chatted, eh?
My dang eyes are really starting to burn and sting from the crummy air. We've been walking for so long, weeks maybe even.
But I really like it. I only feel tired at night really, and there is so much cool stuff to see.
Sometimes it's scary stuff though.

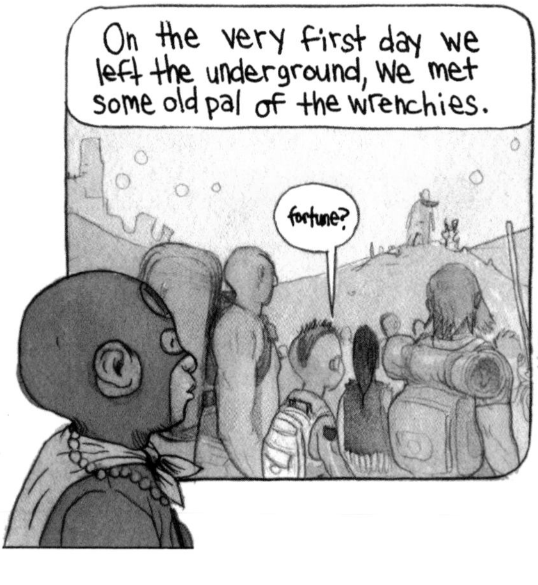
On the very first day we left the underground, we met some old pal of the wrenchies.
fortune?

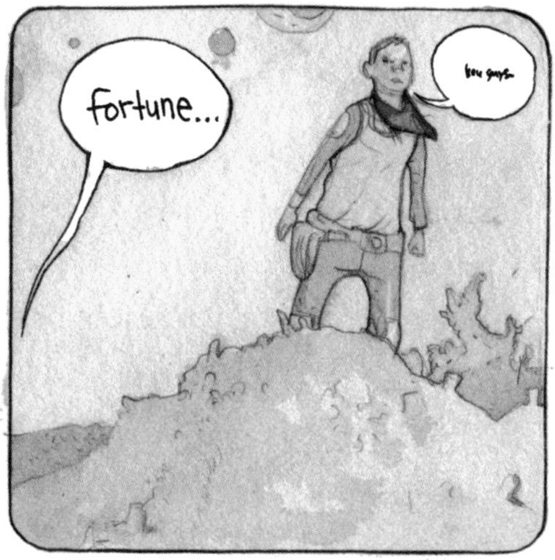
fortune...

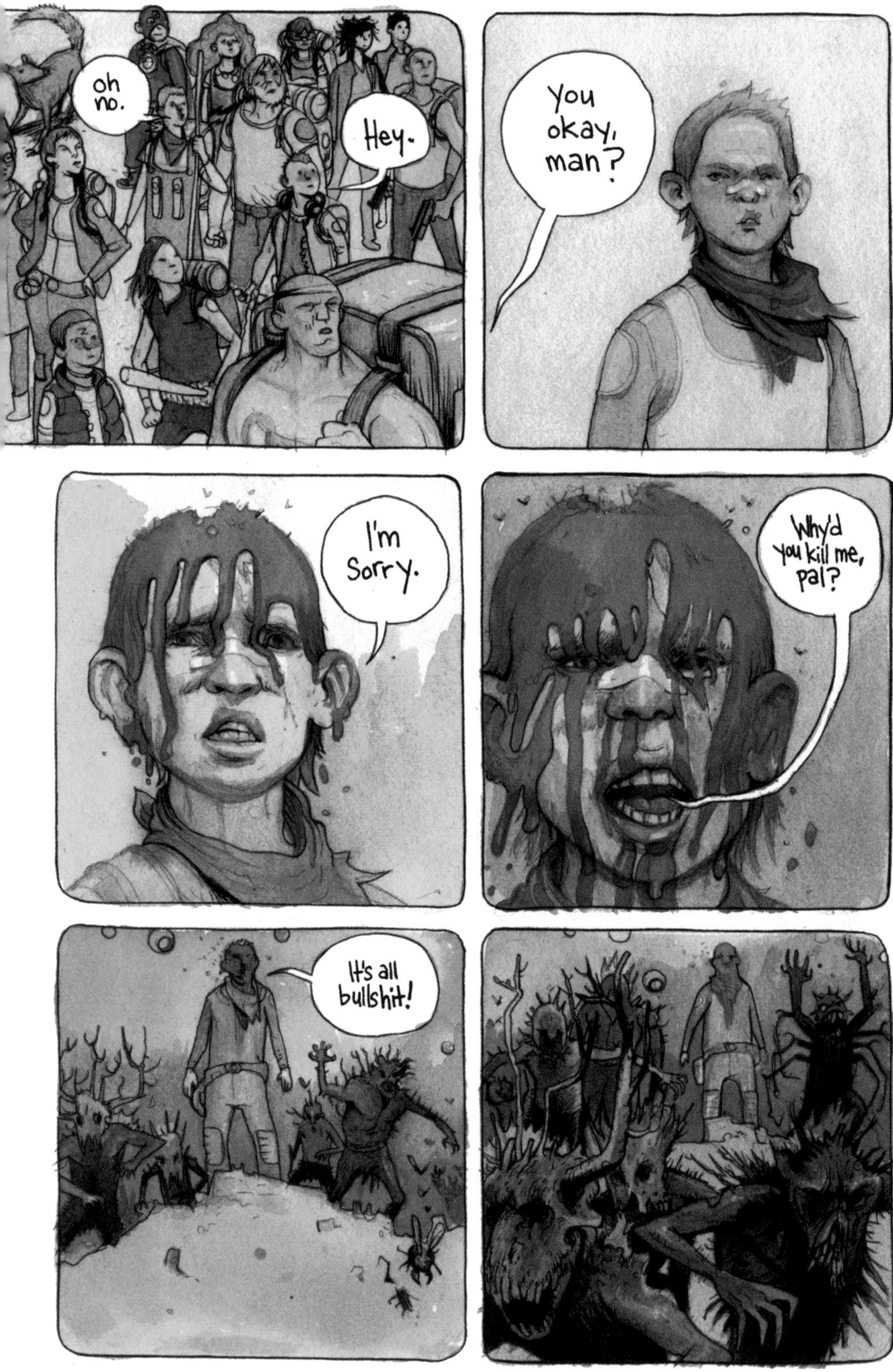
oh no.
Hey.
You okay, man?
I'm Sorry.
Why'd you kill me, pal?
It's all bullshit!

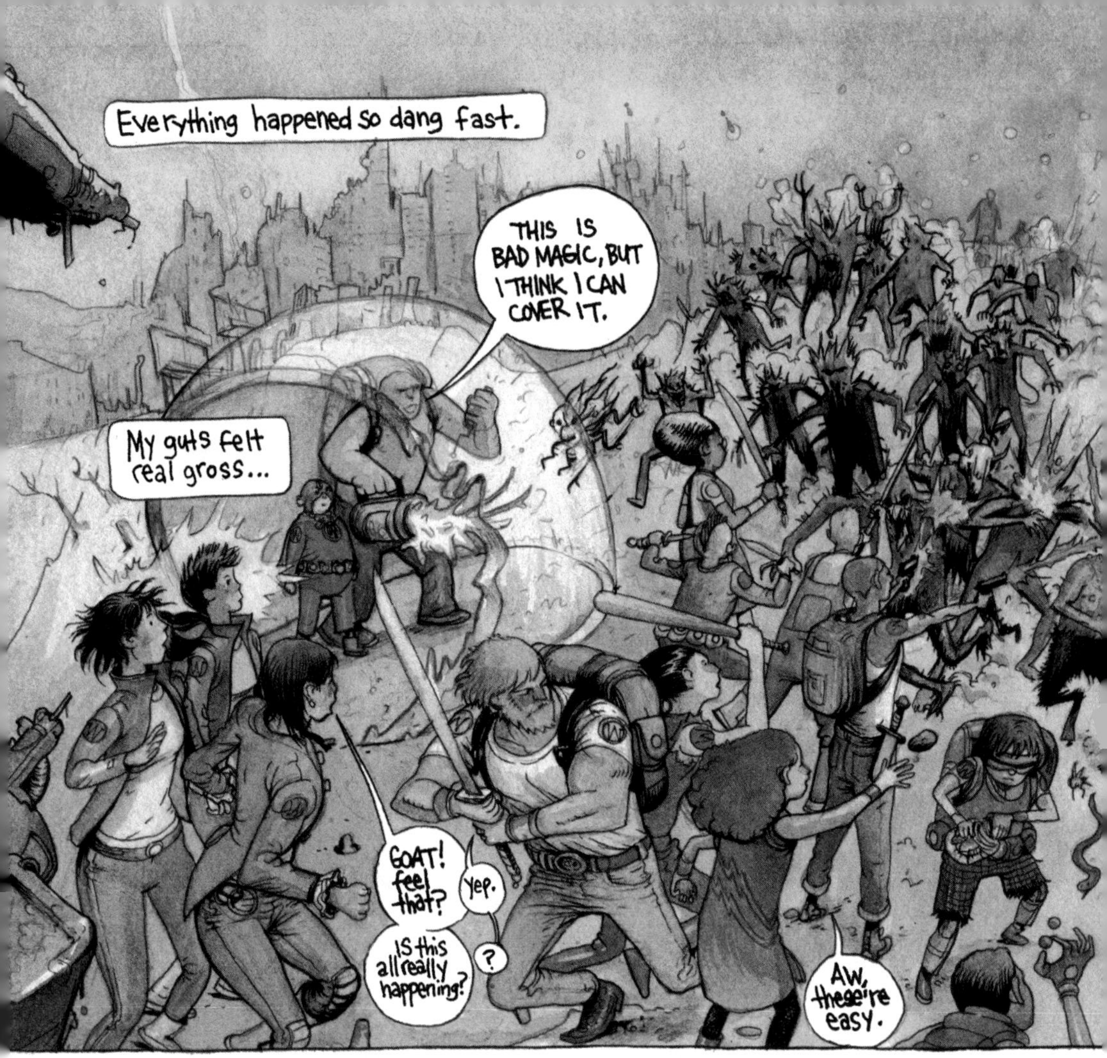
Everything happened so dang fast.
THIS IS BAD MAGIC, BUT I THINK I CAN COVER IT.
My guts felt real gross...
GOAT! feel that?
Yep.
Is this all really happening?
?
AW, these're easy.

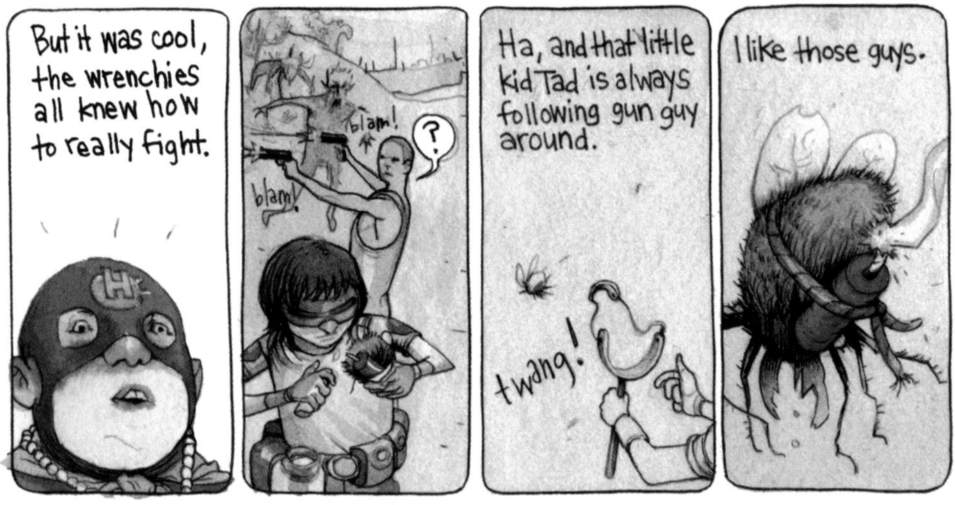
But it was cool, the wrenchies all knew how to really fight.
blam!
blam!
?
Ha, and that little kid Tad is always following gun guy around.
twang!
I like those guys.

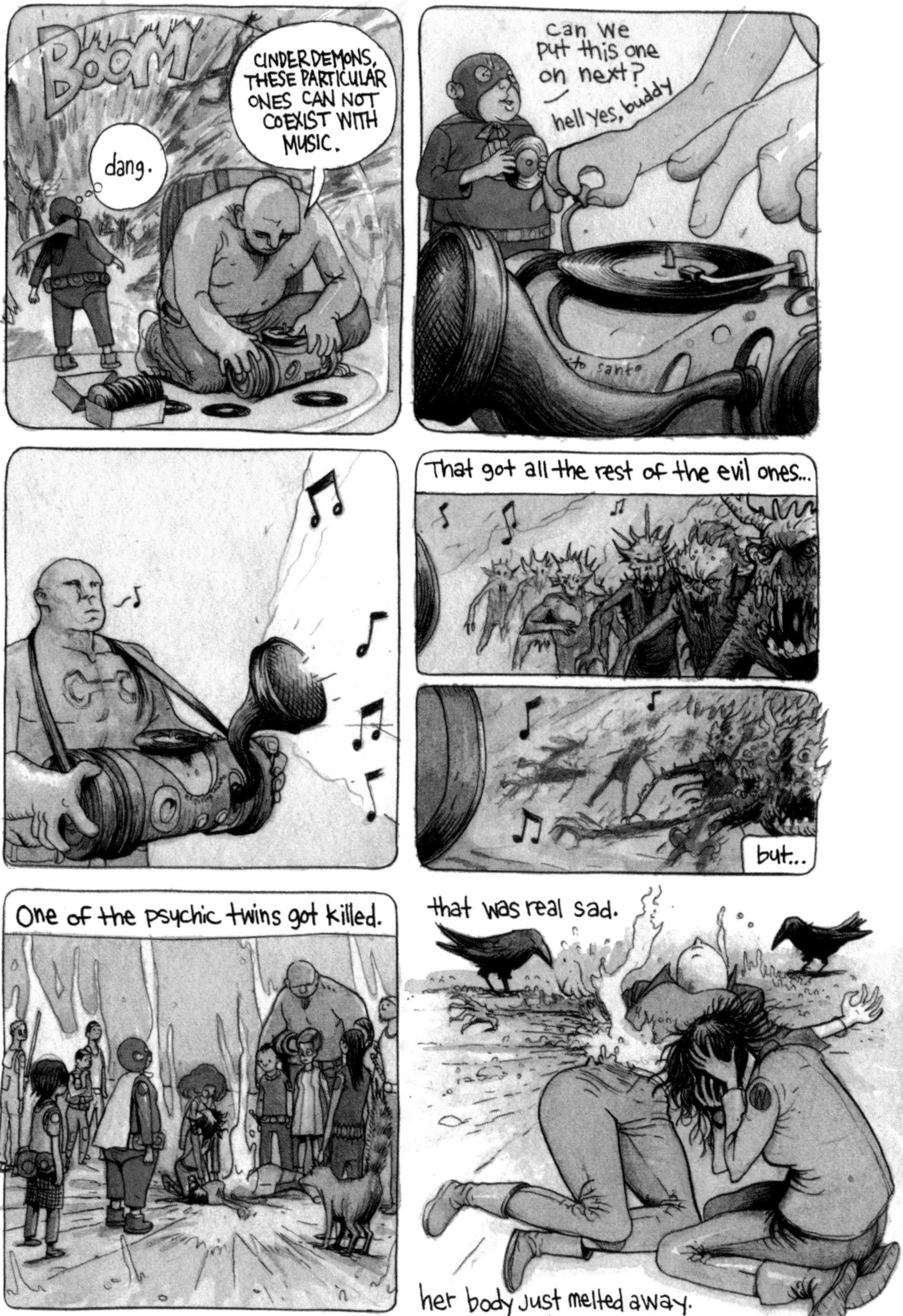
BOOM
dang.
CINDERDEMONS, THESE PARTICULAR ONES CAN NOT COEXIST WITH MUSIC.
can we put this one on next?
hell yes, buddy
That got all the rest of the evil ones...
but...
One of the psychic twins got killed.
that was real sad.
her body just melted away.

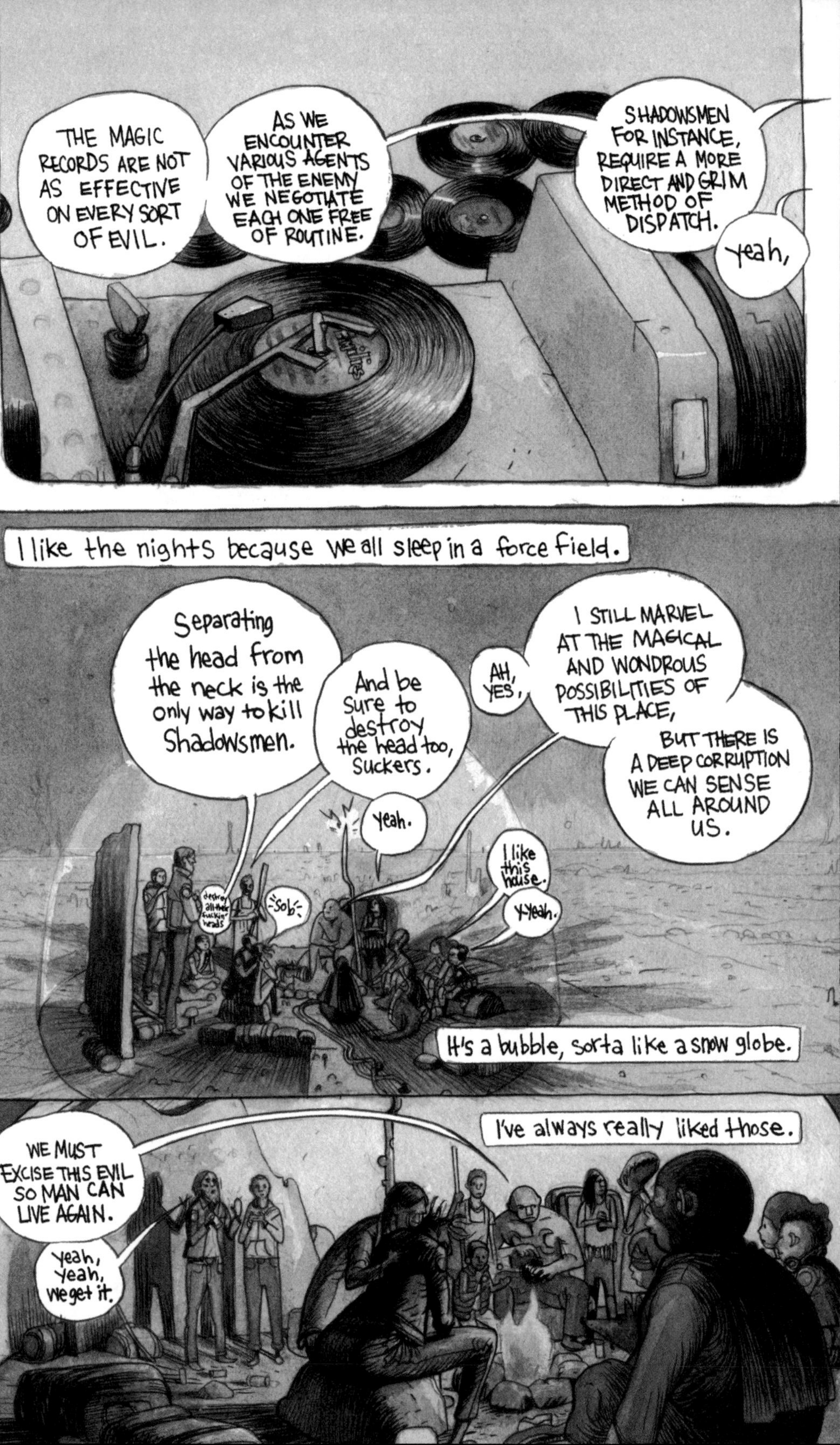
THE MAGIC RECORDS ARE NOT AS EFFECTIVE ON EVERY SORT OF EVIL.
AS WE ENCOUNTER VARIOUS AGENTS OF THE ENEMY WE NEGOTIATE EACH ONE FREE OF ROUTINE.
SHADOWSMEN FOR INSTANCE, REQUIRE A MORE DIRECT AND GRIM METHOD OF DISPATCH.
yeah,
I like the nights because we all sleep in a force field.
Separating the head from the neck is the only way to kill Shadowsmen.
And be sure to destroy the head too, suckers.
AH, YES,
I STILL MARVEL AT THE MAGICAL AND WONDROUS POSSIBILITIES OF THIS PLACE,
BUT THERE IS A DEEP CORRUPTION WE CAN SENSE ALL AROUND US.
Yeah.
destroy all their fuckin' heads
sob
I like this house.
Y-Yeah.
It's a bubble, sorta like a snow globe.
I've always really liked those.
WE MUST EXCISE THIS EVIL SO MAN CAN LIVE AGAIN.
yeah, yeah, we get it.

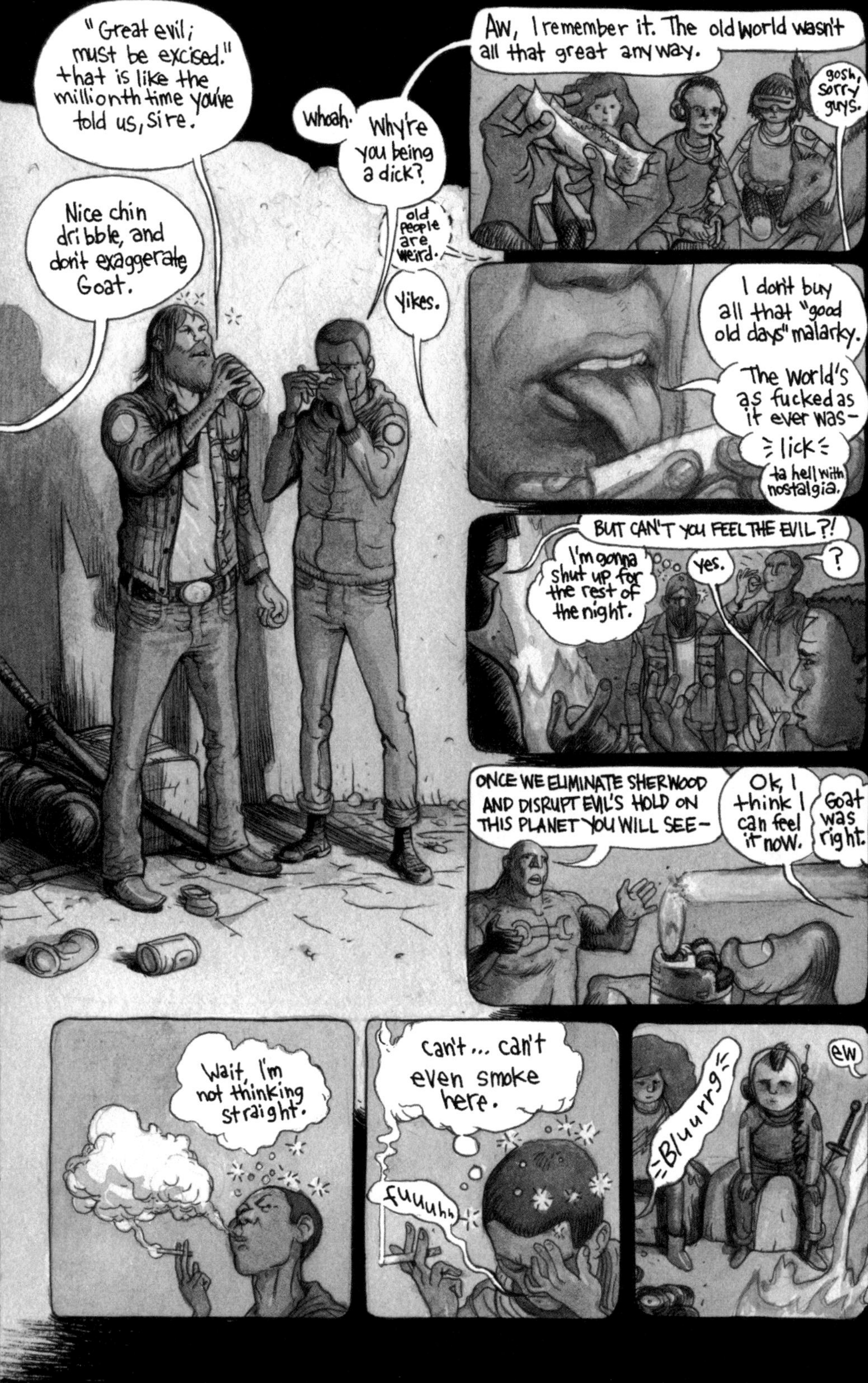
"Great evil; must be excised." that is like the millionth time you've told us, Sire.
Nice chin dribble, and don't exaggerate Goat.
Whoah.
Why're you being a dick?
old people are weird.
Yikes.
Aw, I remember it. The old world wasn't all that great anyway.
gosh, sorry guys.
I don't buy all that "good old days" malarky.
The world's as fucked as it ever was—
lick
ta hell with nostalgia.
BUT CAN'T YOU FEEL THE EVIL?!
I'm gonna shut up for the rest of the night.
yes.
?
ONCE WE ELIMINATE SHERWOOD AND DISRUPT EVIL'S HOLD ON THIS PLANET YOU WILL SEE—
Ok, I think I can feel it now.
Goat was right.
Wait, I'm not thinking straight.
can't... can't even smoke here.
fuuuhh
Bluurrg
ew

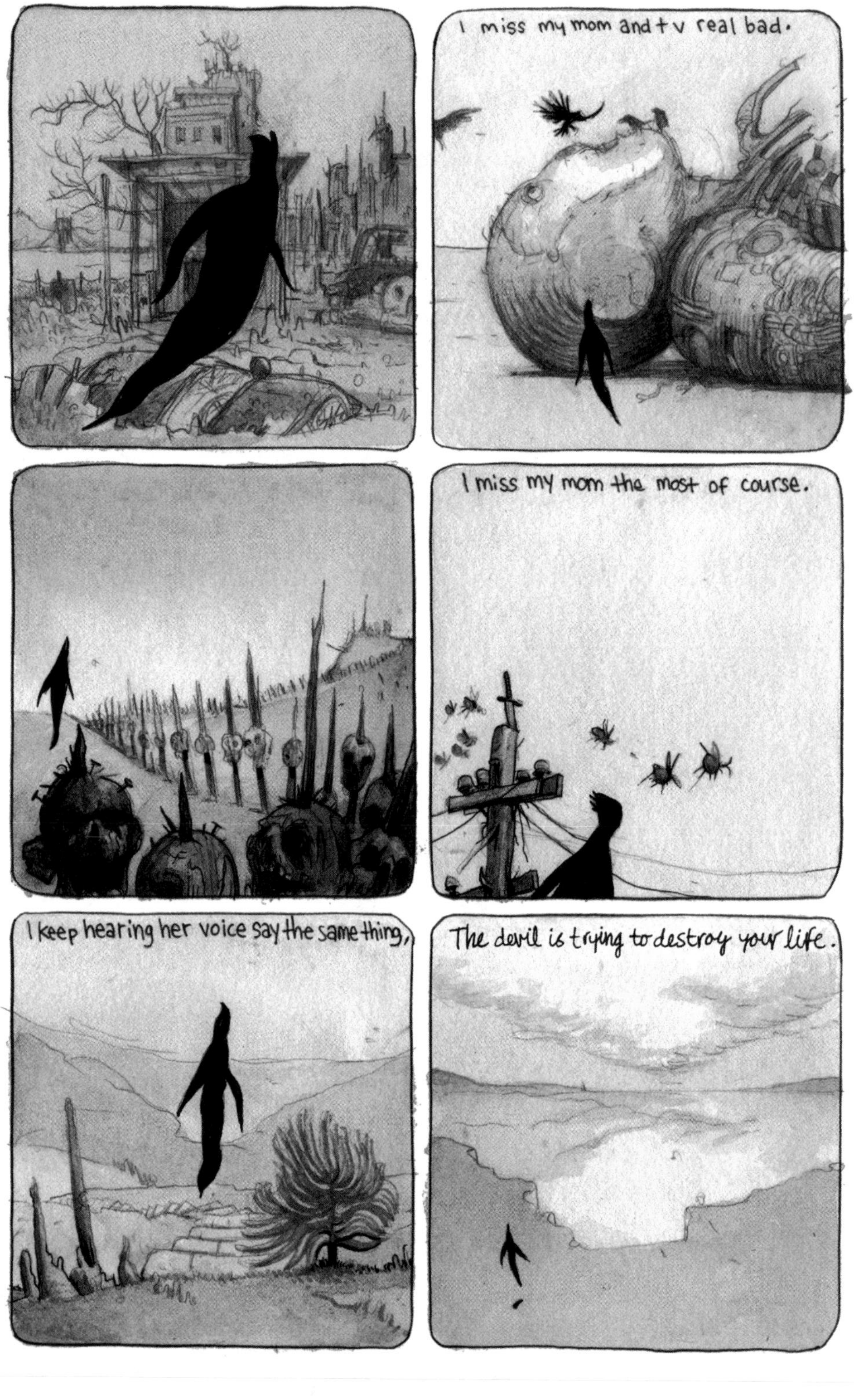
I miss my mom and tv real bad.
I miss my mom the most of course.
I keep hearing her voice say the same thing,
The devil is trying to destroy your life.

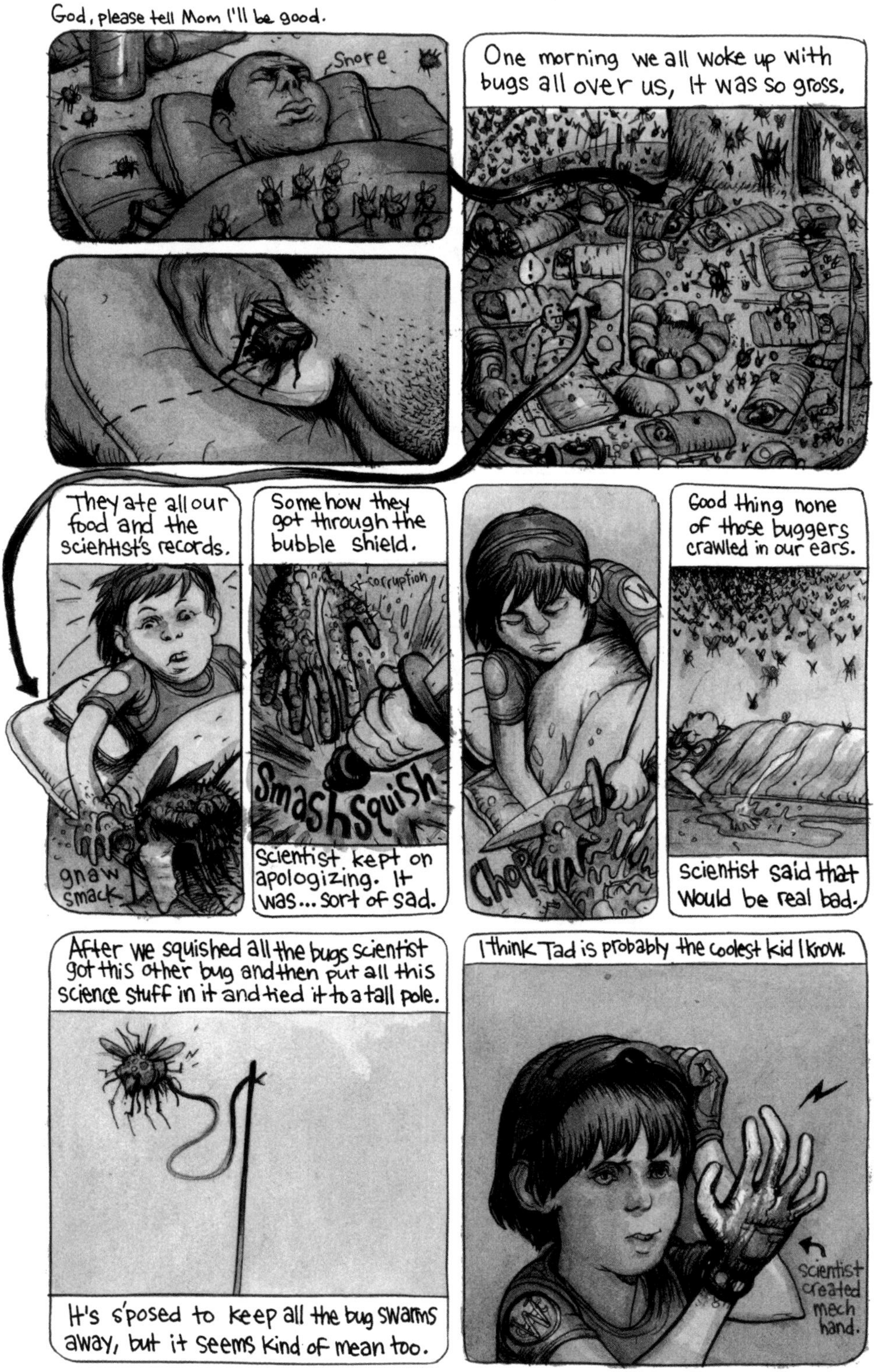
God, please tell Mom I'll be good.
Snore
One morning we all woke up with bugs all over us, It was so gross.
They ate all our food and the scientist's records.
gnaw
smack
Some how they got through the bubble shield.
corruption
Smash squish
Scientist kept on apologizing. It was... sort of sad.
Chop
Good thing none of those buggers crawled in our ears.
Scientist said that would be real bad.
After we squished all the bugs scientist got this other bug and then put all this science stuff in it and tied it to a tall pole.
It's s'posed to keep all the bug swarms away, but it seems kind of mean too.
I think Tad is probably the coolest kid I know.
scientist created mech hand.

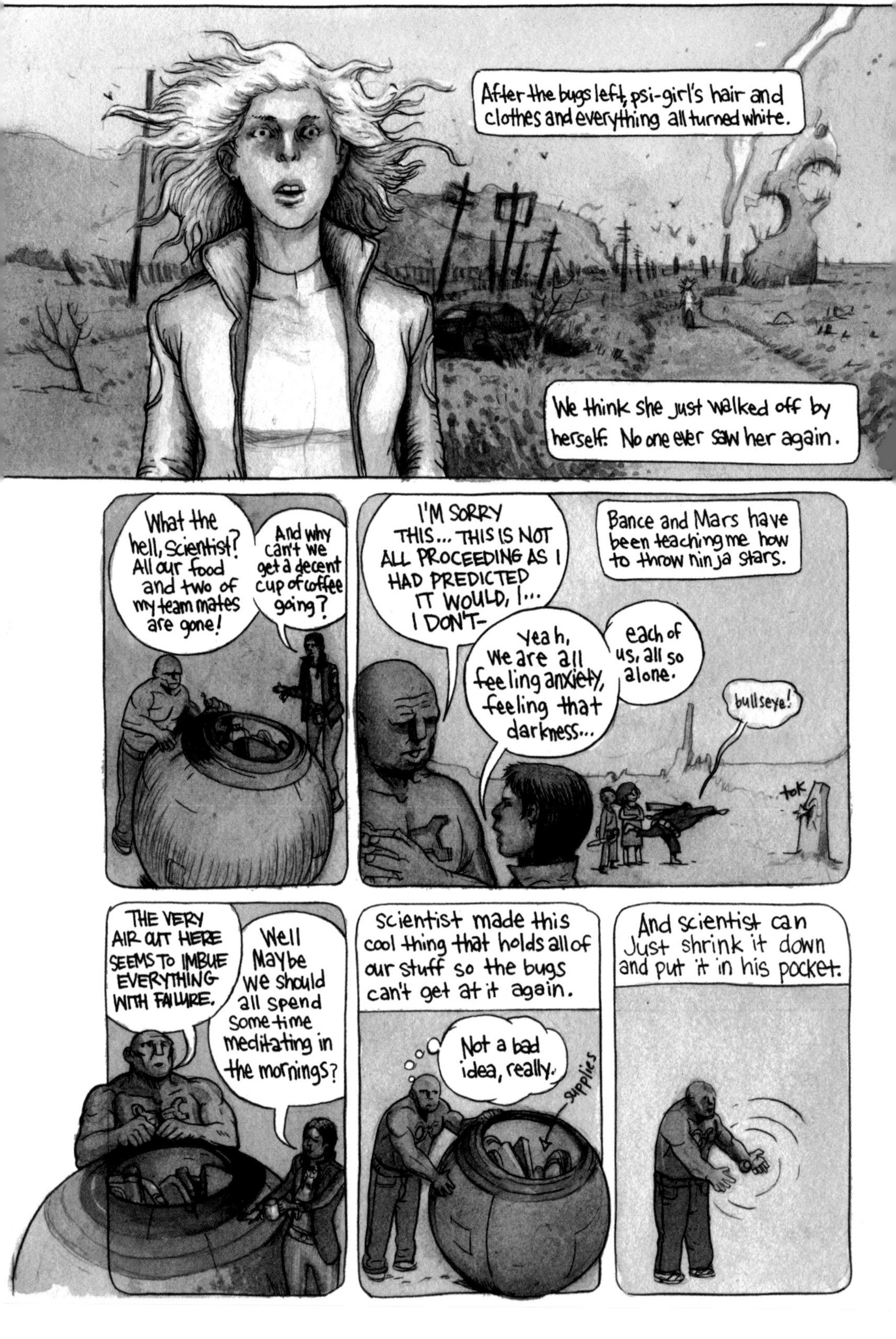

After the bugs left, psi-girl's hair and clothes and everything all turned white.
We think she just walked off by herself. No one ever saw her again.
What the hell, scientist? All our food and two of my team mates are gone!
And why can't we get a decent cup of coffee going?
I'M SORRY THIS... THIS IS NOT ALL PROCEEDING AS I HAD PREDICTED IT WOULD, I... I DON'T-
Bance and Mars have been teaching me how to throw ninja stars.
Yeah, we are all feeling anxiety, feeling that darkness...
each of us, all so alone.
bullseye!
tok
THE VERY AIR OUT HERE SEEMS TO IMBUE EVERYTHING WITH FAILURE.
Well Maybe we should all spend some time meditating in the mornings?
scientist made this cool thing that holds all of our stuff so the bugs can't get at it again.
Not a bad idea, really.
supplies
And scientist can just shrink it down and put it in his pocket.

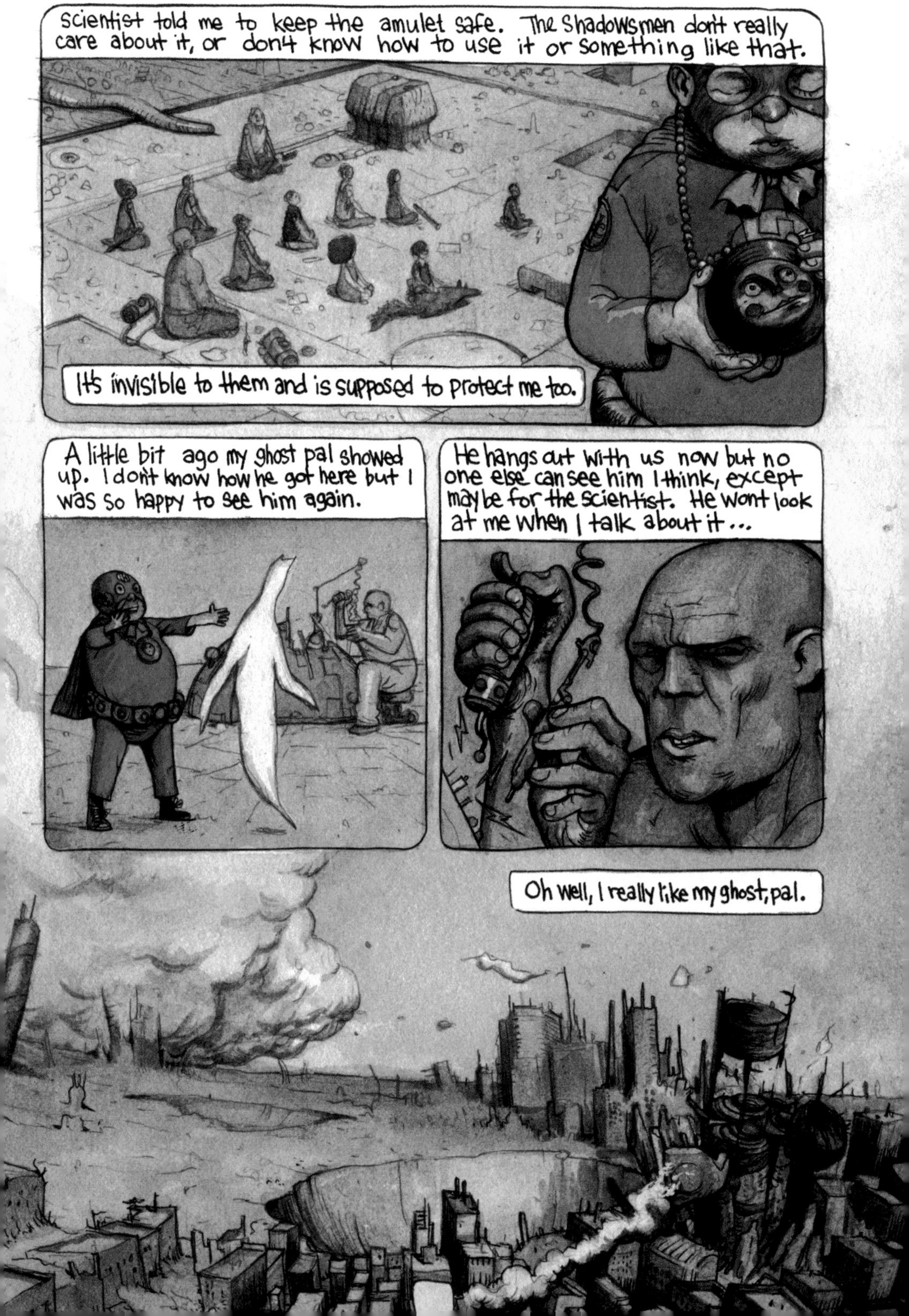
scientist told me to keep the amulet safe. The Shadowsmen don't really care about it, or don't know how to use it or something like that.
It's invisible to them and is supposed to protect me too.
A little bit ago my ghost pal showed up. I don't know how he got here but I was so happy to see him again.
He hangs out with us now but no one else can see him I think, except maybe for the scientist. He wont look at me when I talk about it...
Oh well, I really like my ghost, pal.

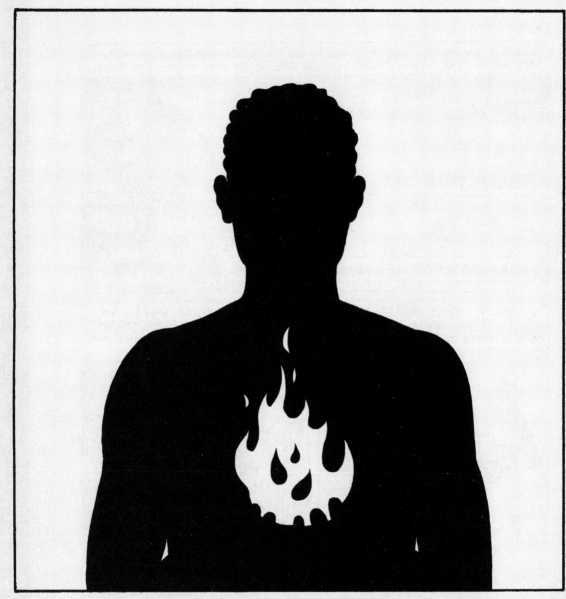

SO IMAGINE YOU ARE PROMETHEUS. YOU'VE JUST STOLEN THE SECRET OF FIRE FROM THE GODS AND BROUGHT IT DOWN TO A CAVE WHERE A GROUP OF BEAST-LIKE "HUMANS," CREATURES YOU CREATED FROM CLAY SO MANY MILLENNIA AGO, HUDDLE TOGETHER FOR WARMTH AND GNAW HUNGRILY ON BARK.

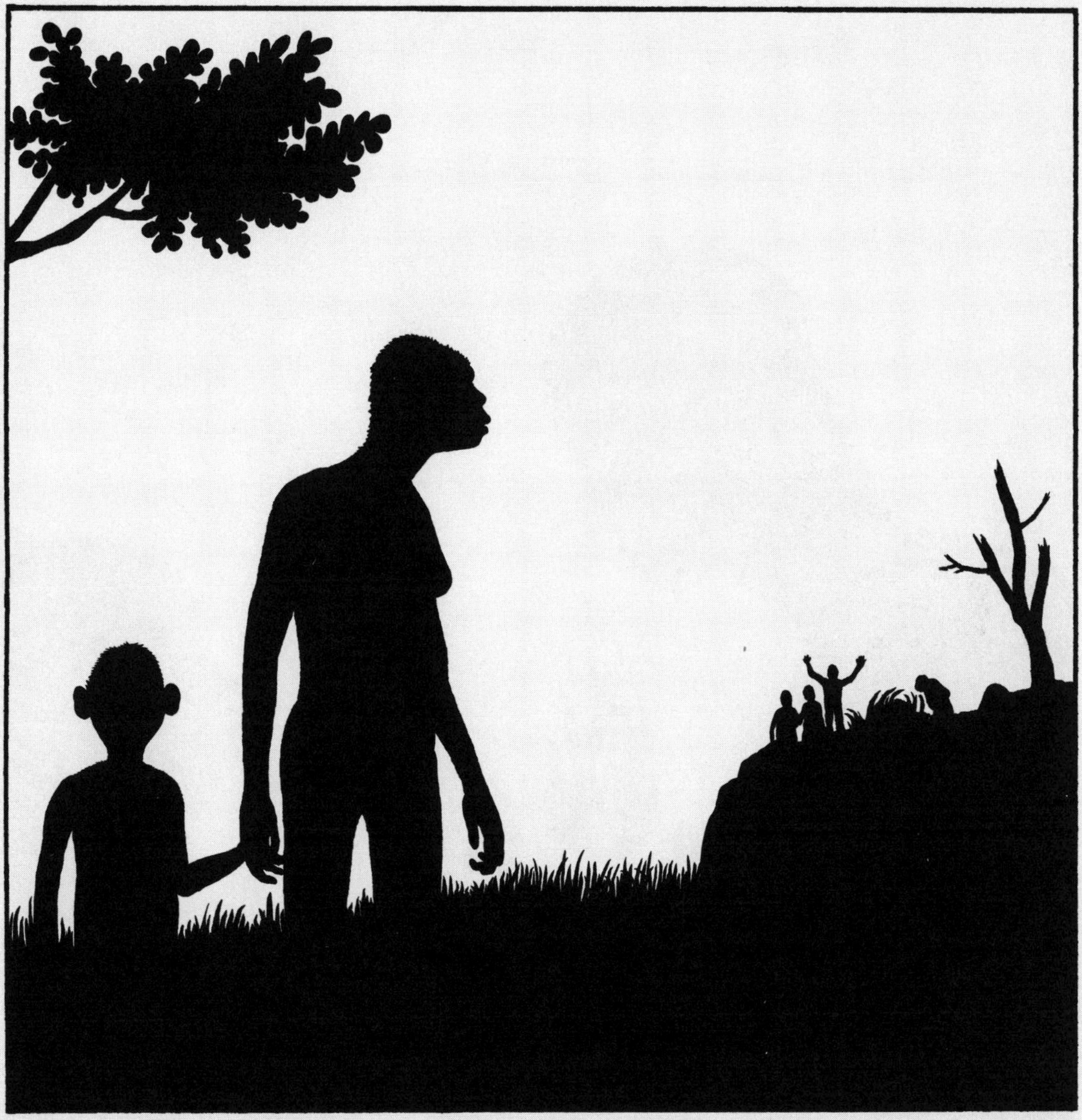

YOU'VE CHOSEN THIS PARTICULAR GROUP CAREFULLY FROM THE DOZENS OF LITTLE BANDS THAT SCRAPE AND FIGHT OVER THE BARE HILLS WHERE YOU FIRST BREATHED LIFE INTO THEM. THIS GROUP HAS SHOWN PROMISE. THEY'VE BEGUN MAKING FUNNY CLICKS AND THROATY GROWLS, IMITATING, IN THEIR CRUDE WAY, THE SPEECH OF THEIR BETTERS. THEY ACTUALLY SEEM TO UNDERSTAND ONE ANOTHER. THEY'VE LEARNED TO CHIP STONES INTO USEFUL SHAPES, AND MOST PROMISING OF ALL, THEY'VE BEGUN SHOWING SOMETHING LIKE REAL EMPATHY AND EMOTIONAL CONNECTION. THEY EVEN CARE FOR THEIR SICK, SOMETHING RARE EVEN AMONG THE GODS.

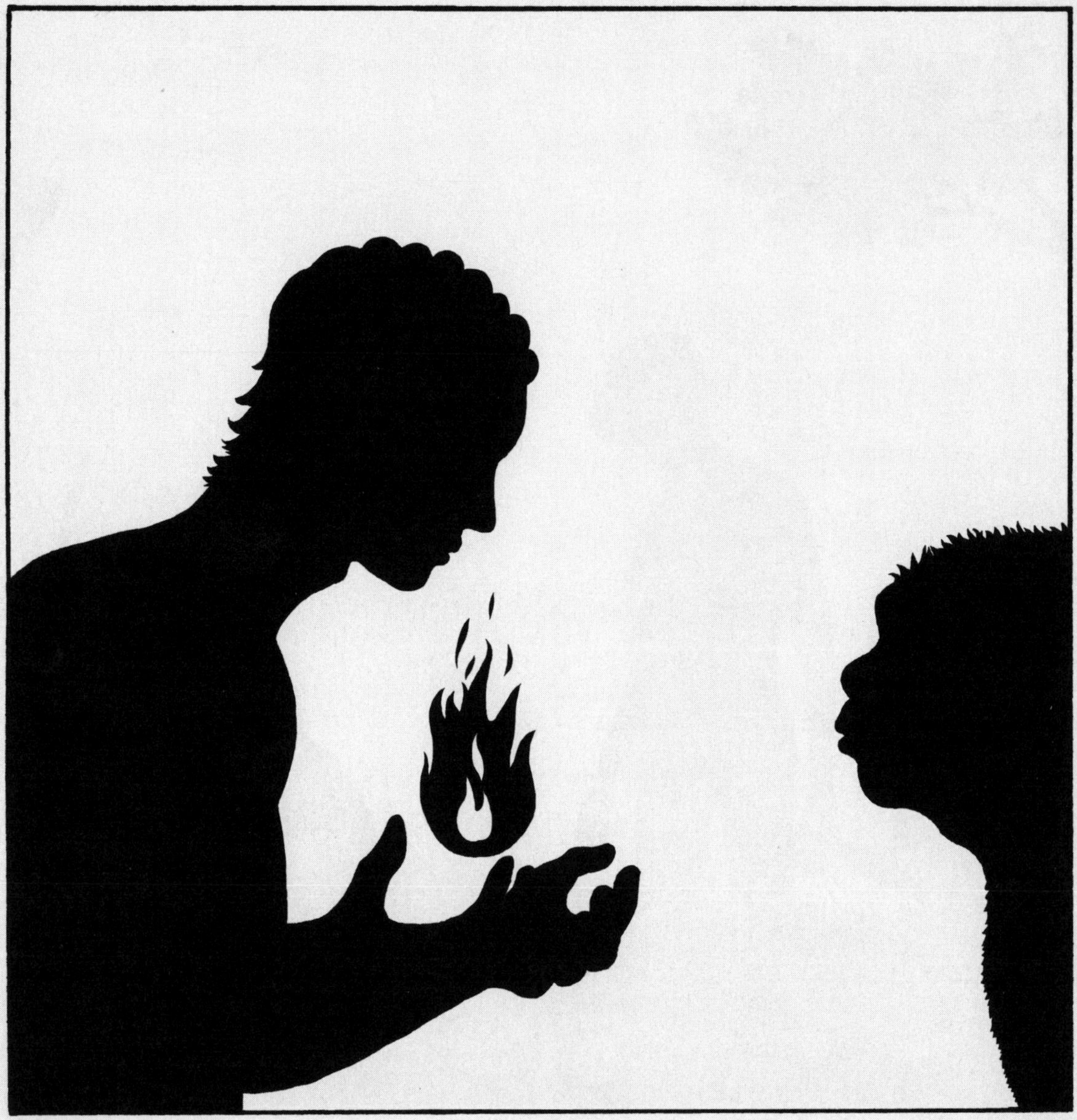

WHEN THEY SEE YOU, MOST OF THEM HURRY TO THE BACK OF THE CAVE TO HIDE FROM YOUR BRILLIANCE AND THE FLICKERING LIGHT IN YOUR HANDS. BUT TWO OR THREE ARE BRAVE. THERE IS FEAR IN THEIR EYES, BUT THEY NEVERTHELESS STEP FORWARD TO RECEIVE YOUR GIFT AND LISTEN CLOSELY AS YOU EXPLAIN ITS PROPERTIES AND USES. AS YOU LEAVE YOU CAN HEAR THEM BEGIN TO CHATTER EXCITEDLY. AND YOU CAN SEE THE LIGHT FLICKERING IN THE DARKNESS THROUGH THE MOUTH OF THE CAVE. THE LAUGHTER AND EXCITEMENT IN THEIR VOICES AT THIS MOMENT WILL SUSTAIN YOU FOR EONS.

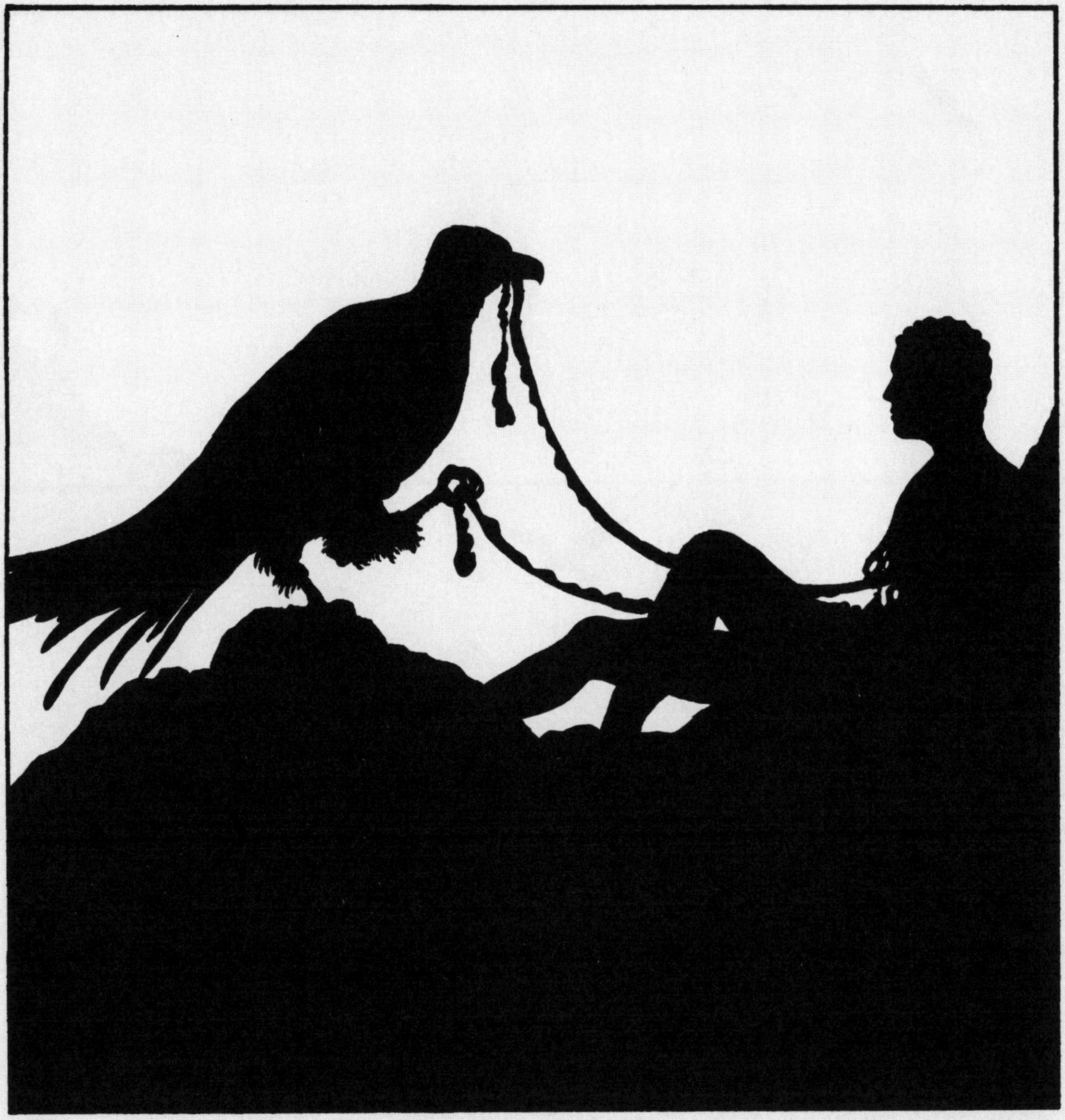

NOW IT'S MANY THOUSANDS OF YEARS LATER. FOR WHAT IS NOW AN ANCIENT TRANSGRESSION, YOU ARE CHAINED TO A ROCK ON TOP OF A DESOLATE MOUNTAIN IN THE MIDDLE EAST. THERE ARE OCCASIONAL HELICOPTERS, DISTANT EXPLOSIONS. THE EAGLE THAT IS SENT EACH DAY TO DEVOUR YOUR LIVER IS GIVING YOU HIS USUAL UPDATE ON WHAT IS HAPPENING IN THE WORLD BELOW. IT'S BEEN BAD ALMOST AS LONG AS YOU CAN REMEMBER AND DOESN'T SEEM TO BE GETTING ANY BETTER. THE GIFT OF FIRE HAS SPREAD, EVOLVED, PROLIFERATED. WHEN HE'S DONE GIVING YOU THE NEWS, THE EAGLE TEARS INTO YOUR ABDOMEN. THE PAIN IS UNIMAGINABLE. REPETITION HAS DONE NOTHING TO DULL ITS BITE. AND HE'LL BE BACK AGAIN TOMORROW, AND EVERY DAY INTO THE FUTURE.

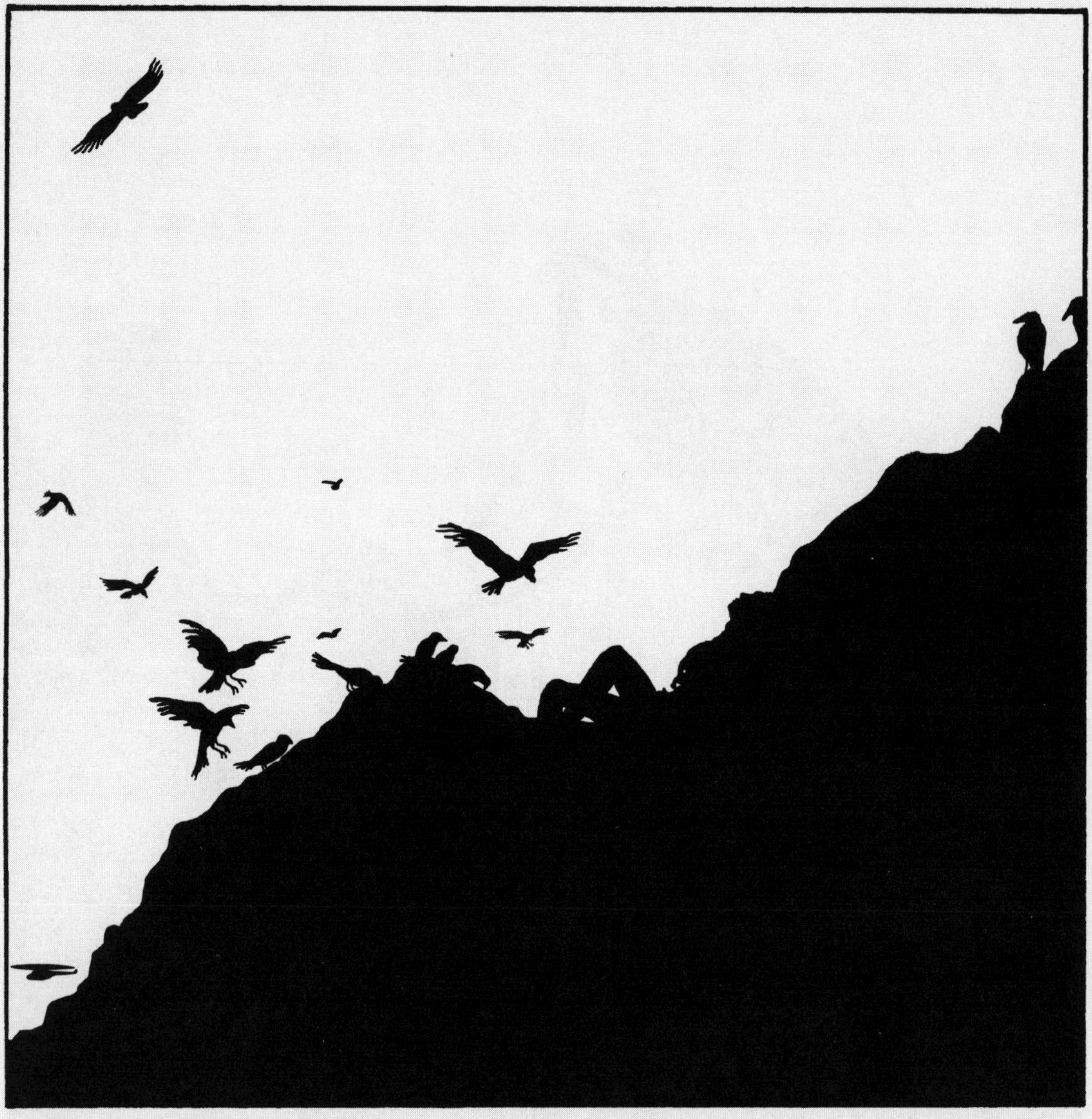

STILL, YOU THINK TO YOURSELF, WITH GRITTED TEETH, YOU'D DO THE SAME THING OVER AGAIN. IN THE END, THINGS HAVE NOT TURNED OUT SO WELL, BUT THERE WAS THE LOOK IN THAT NEW CREATURE'S EYE ALL THOSE MANY YEARS AGO. AND AS FOR THE GODS WHO CHAINED YOU HERE, THE GODS ARE FORGOTTEN. AND THAT IS THE SWEETEST REVENGE.

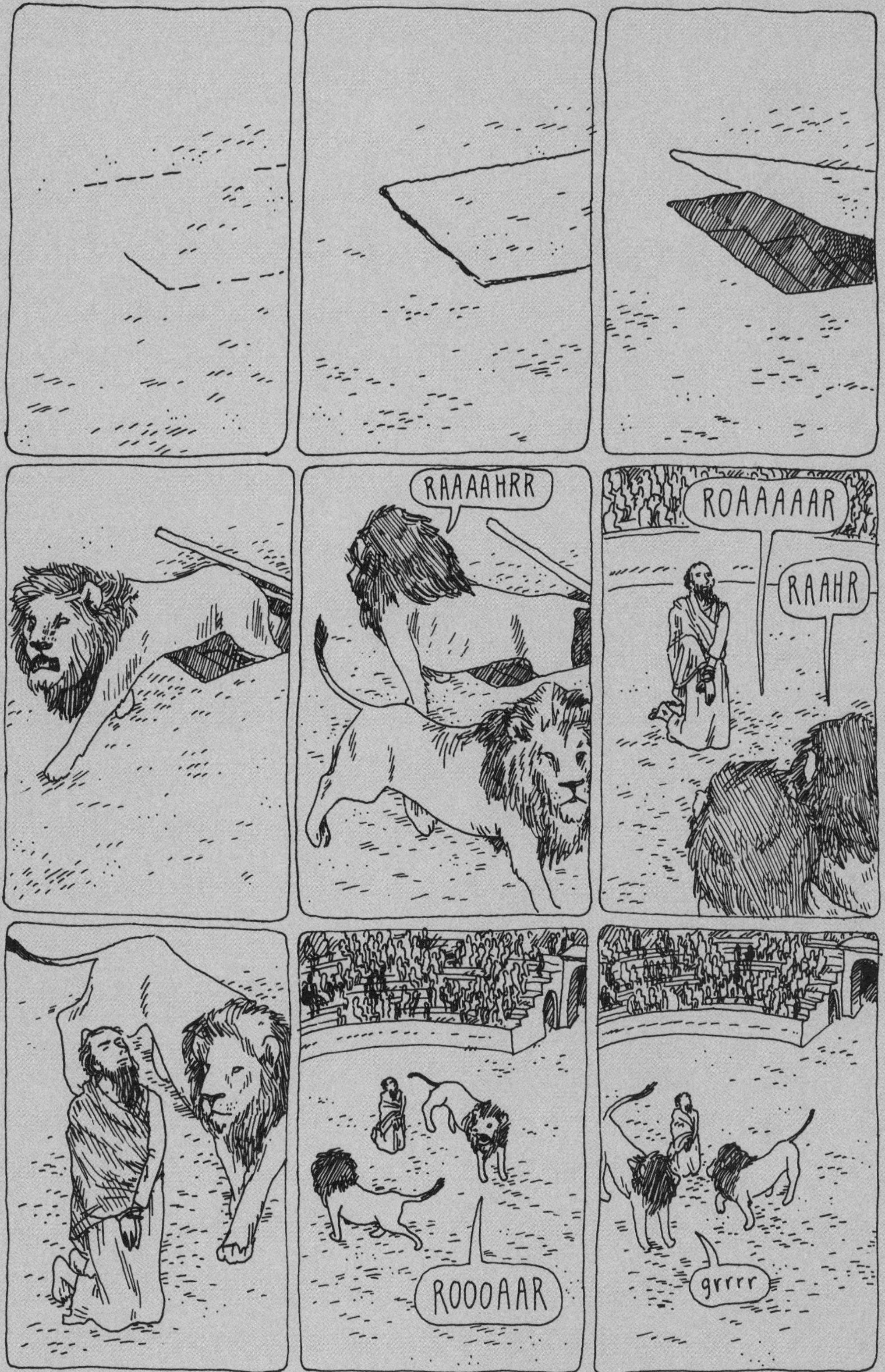
RAAAAHRR
ROAAAAAR
RAAHR
ROOOAAR
grrrr

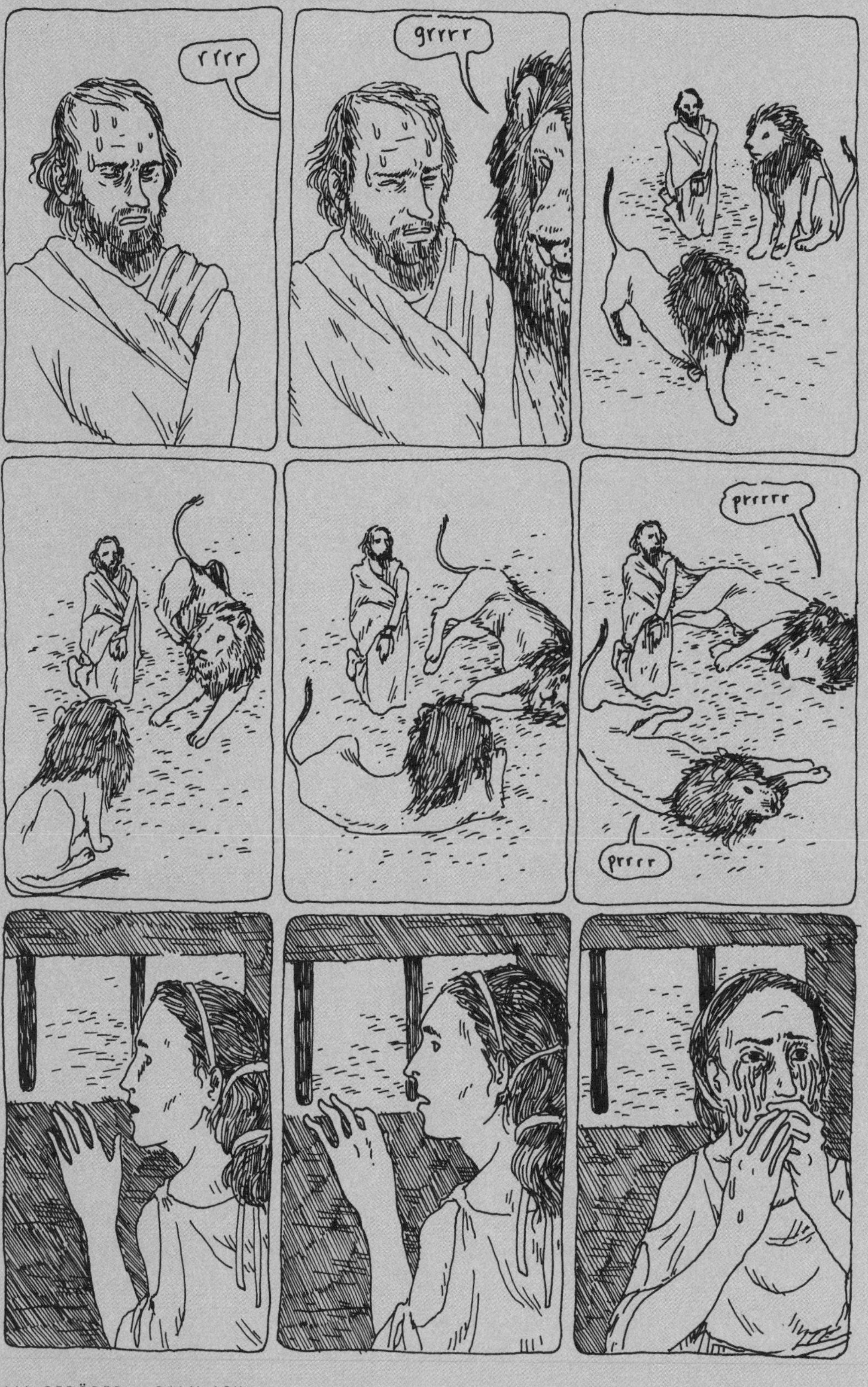
rrrr
grrrr
prrrrr
prrrr

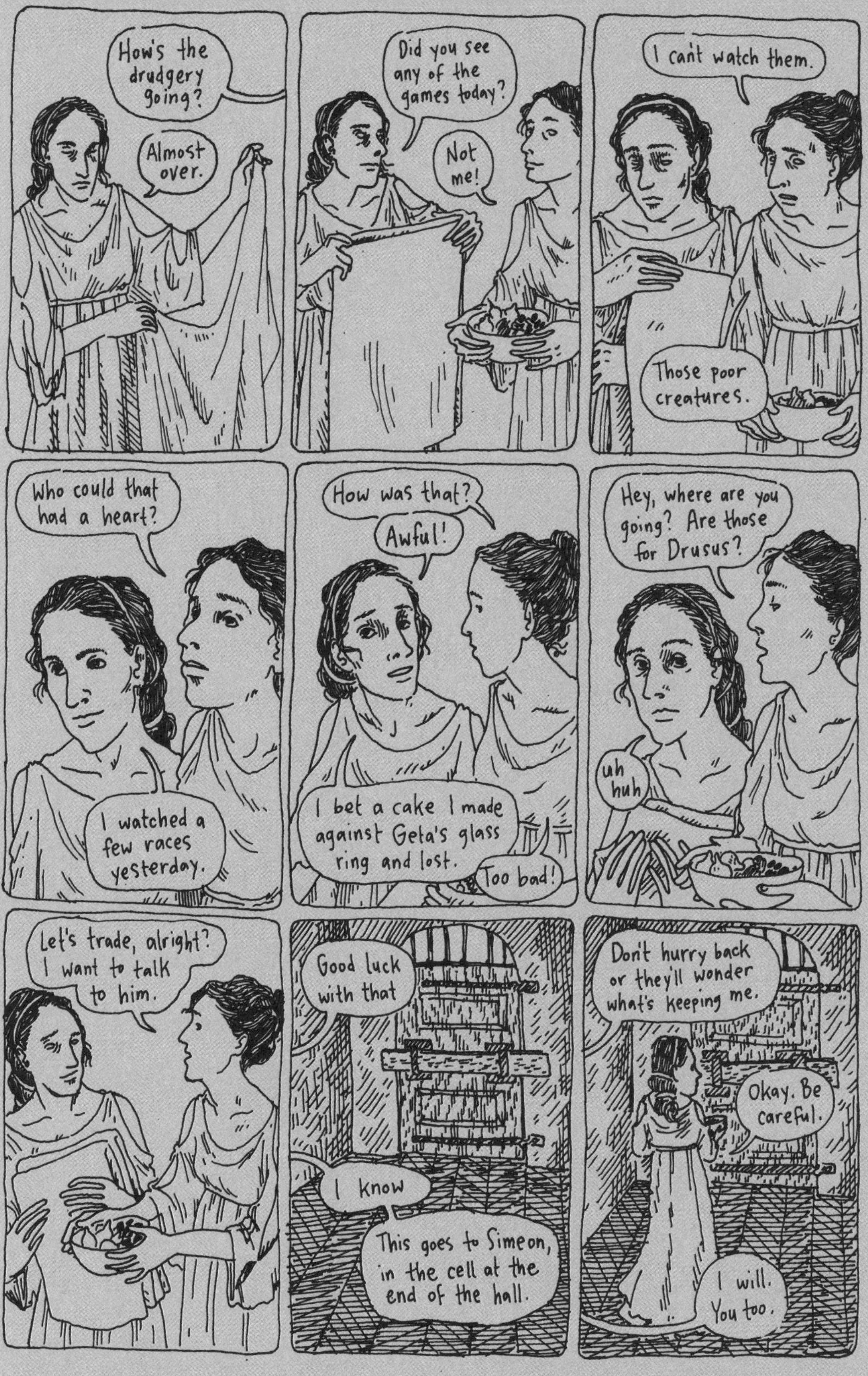
How's the drudgery going?
Almost over.
Did you see any of the games today?
Not me!
I can't watch them.
Those poor creatures.
Who could that had a heart?
I watched a few races yesterday.
How was that?
Awful!
I bet a cake I made against Geta's glass ring and lost.
Too bad!
Hey, where are you going? Are those for Drusus?
uh huh
Let's trade, alright? I want to talk to him.
Good luck with that
I know
This goes to Simeon, in the cell at the end of the hall.
Don't hurry back or they'll wonder what's keeping me.
Okay. Be careful.
I will. You too.

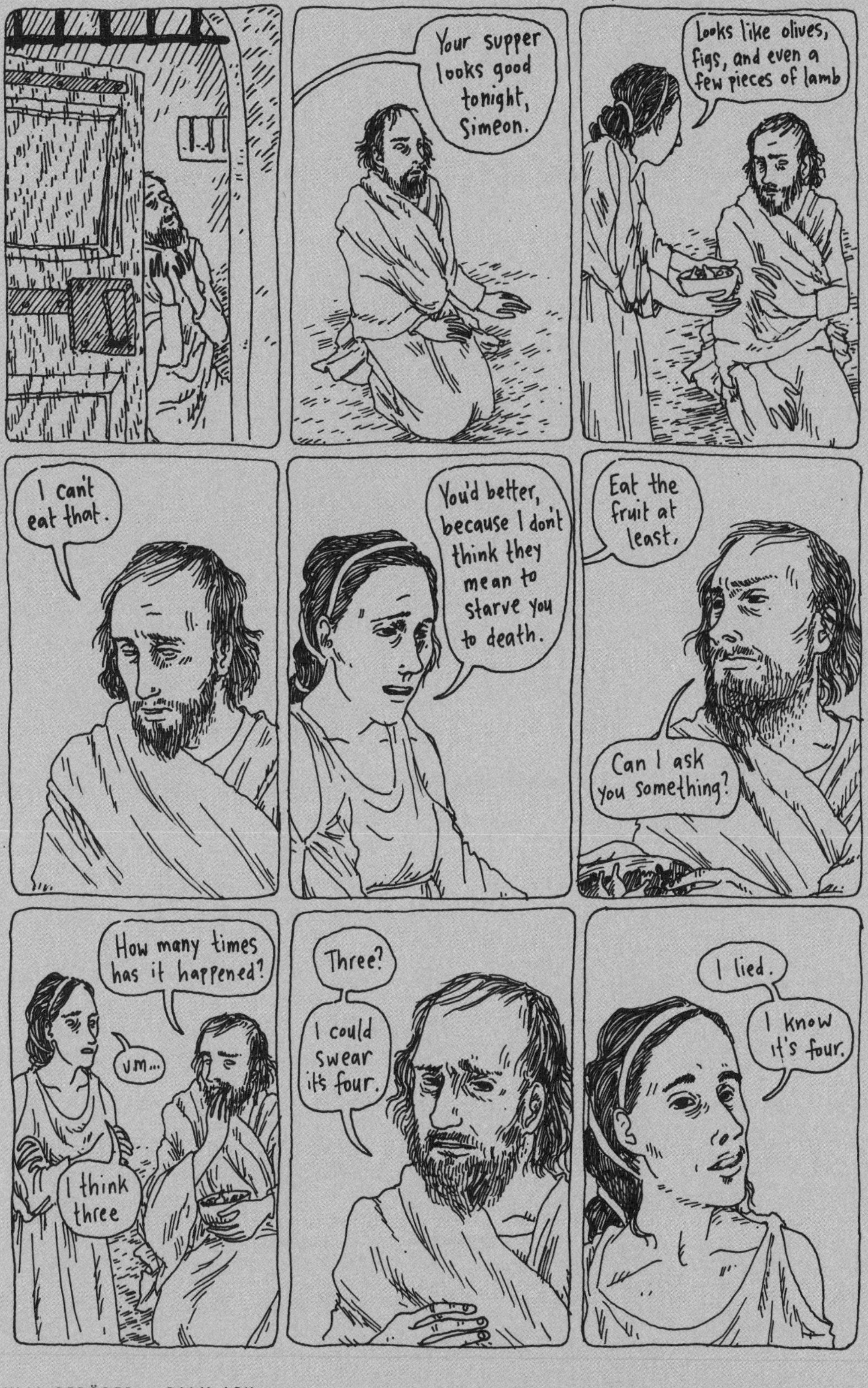
Your supper looks good tonight, Simeon.
Looks like olives, figs, and even a few pieces of lamb
I can't eat that.
You'd better, because I don't think they mean to starve you to death.
Eat the fruit at least.
Can I ask you something?
How many times has it happened?
um...
I think three
Three?
I could swear it's four.
I lied.
I know it's four.

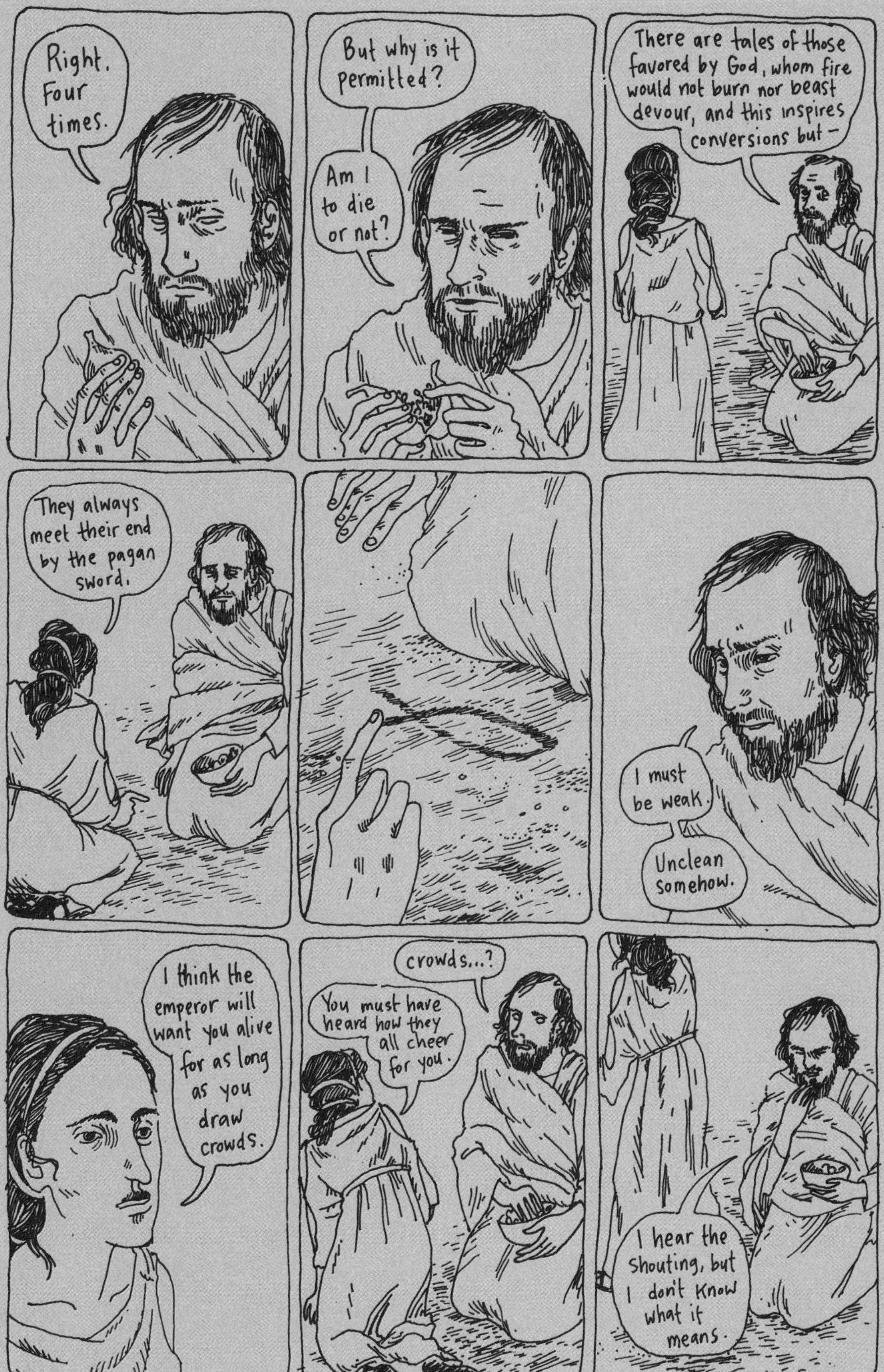
Right. Four times.
But why is it permitted?
Am I to die or not?
There are tales of those favored by God, whom fire would not burn nor beast devour, and this inspires conversions but —
They always meet their end by the pagan sword.
I must be weak.
Unclean somehow.
I think the emperor will want you alive for as long as you draw crowds.
crowds...?
You must have heard how they all cheer for you.
I hear the shouting, but I don't know what it means.

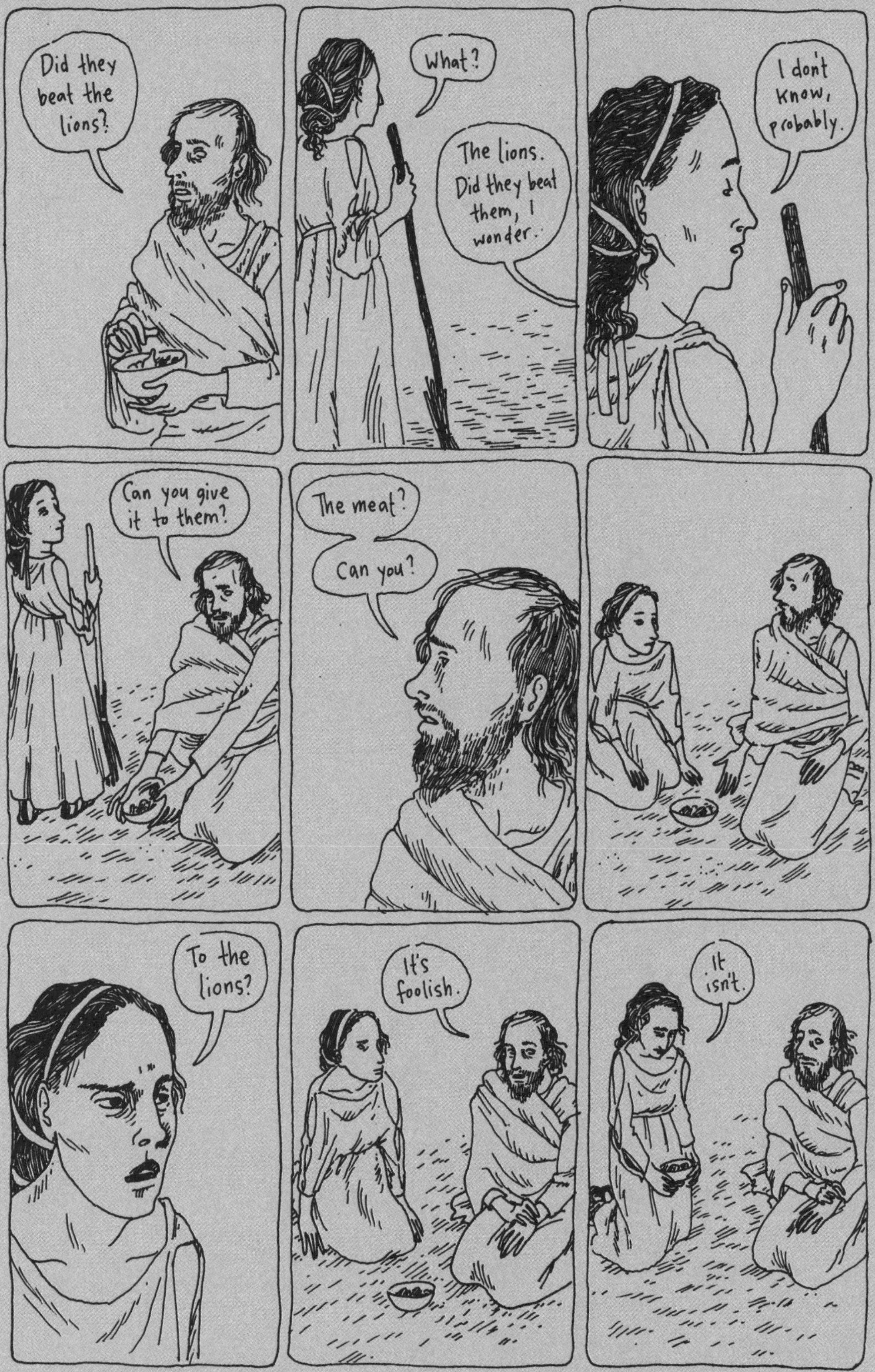
Did they beat the lions?
What?
The lions. Did they beat them, I wonder.
I don't know, probably.
Can you give it to them?
The meat?
Can you?
To the lions?
It's foolish.
It isn't.

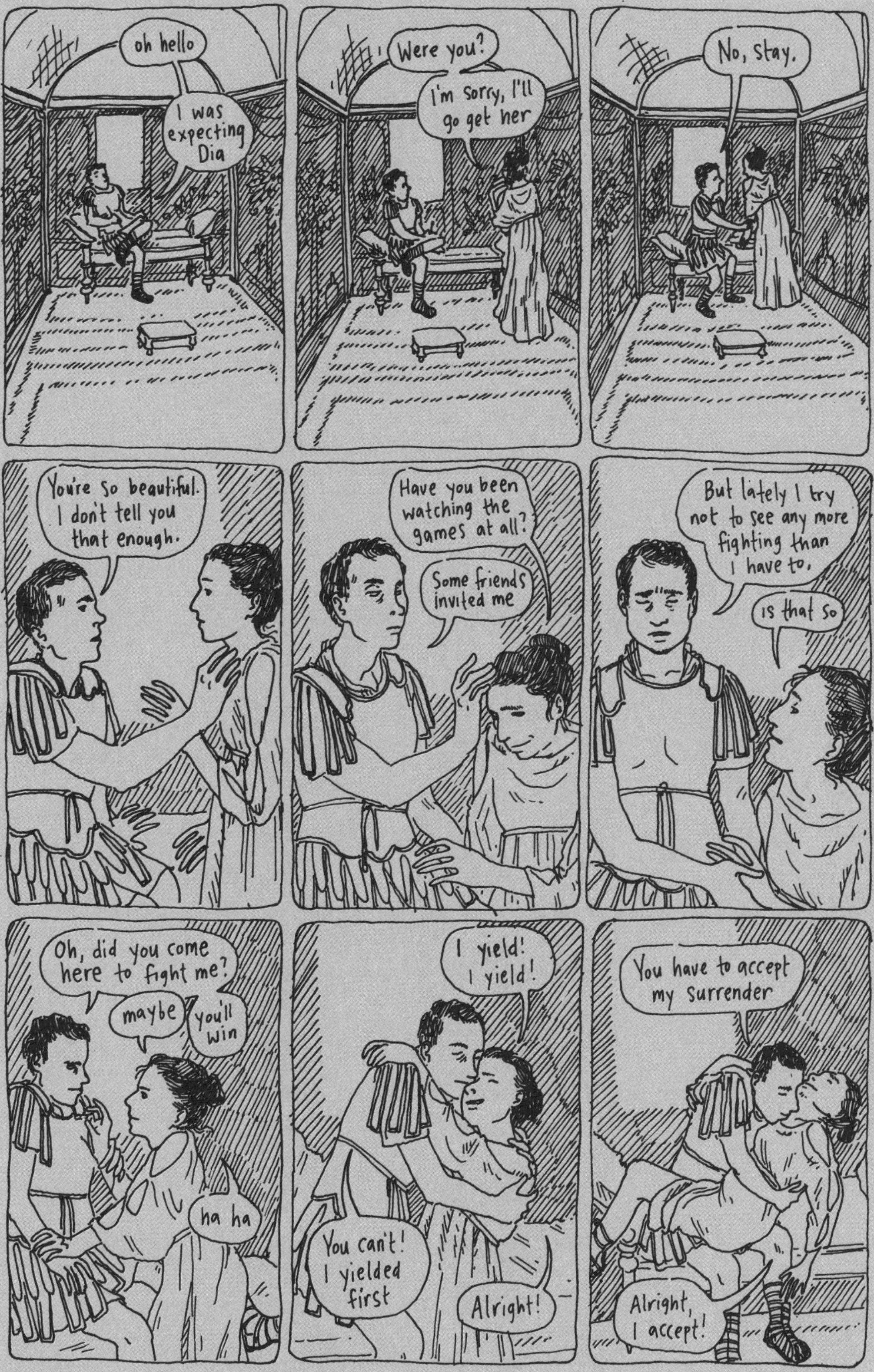
oh hello
I was expecting Dia
Were you?
I'm sorry, I'll go get her
No, stay.
You're so beautiful. I don't tell you that enough.
Have you been watching the games at all?
Some friends invited me
But lately I try not to see any more fighting than I have to,
is that so
Oh, did you come here to fight me?
maybe
you'll win
ha ha
I yield! I yield!
You can't! I yielded first
Alright!
You have to accept my surrender
Alright, I accept!

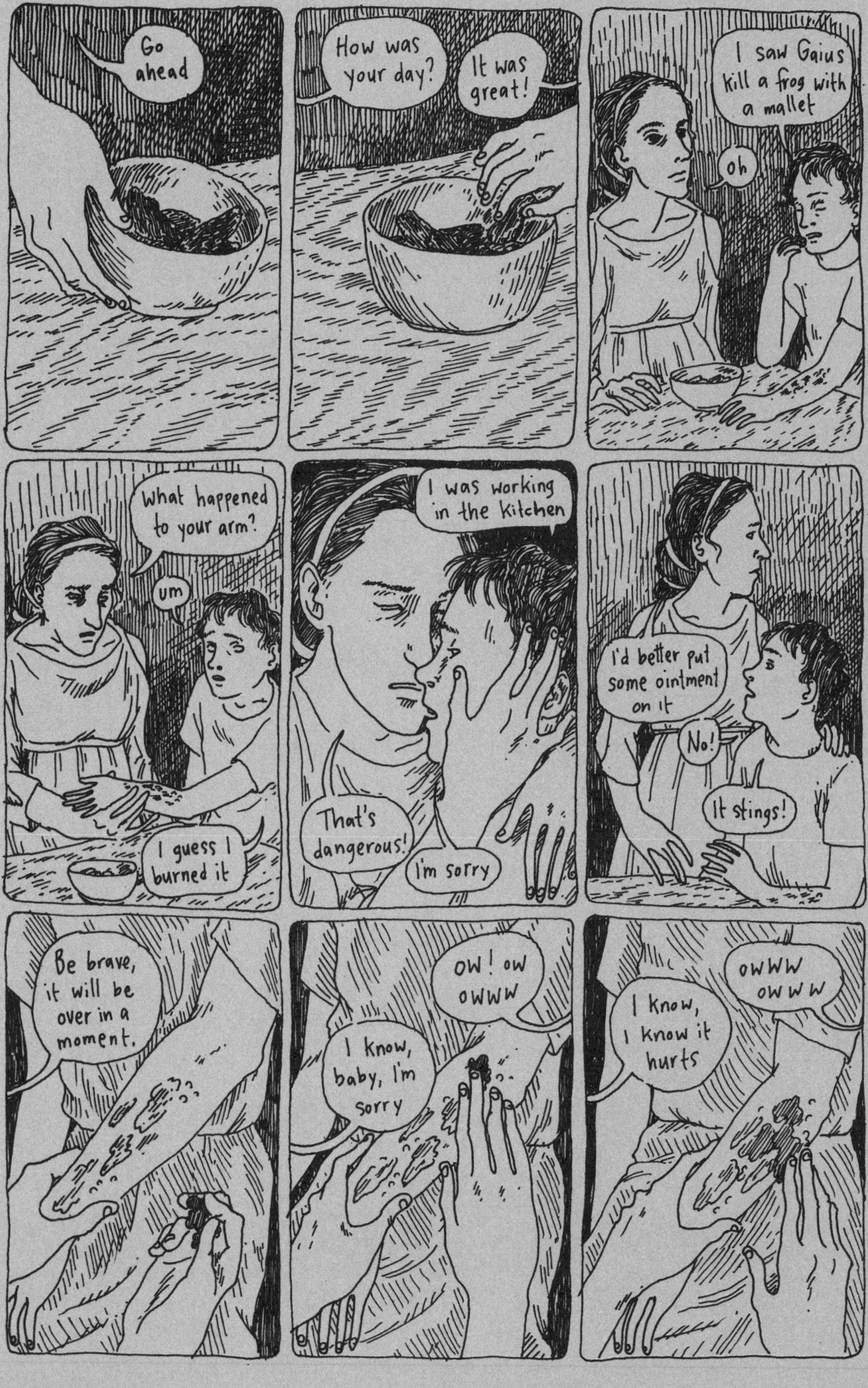
Go ahead
How was your day?
It was great!
I saw Gaius kill a frog with a mallet
oh
What happened to your arm?
um
I guess I burned it
I was working in the kitchen
That's dangerous!
I'm sorry
I'd better put some ointment on it
No!
It stings!
Be brave, it will be over in a moment.
OW! ow owww
I know, baby, I'm sorry
owww owww
I know, I know it hurts

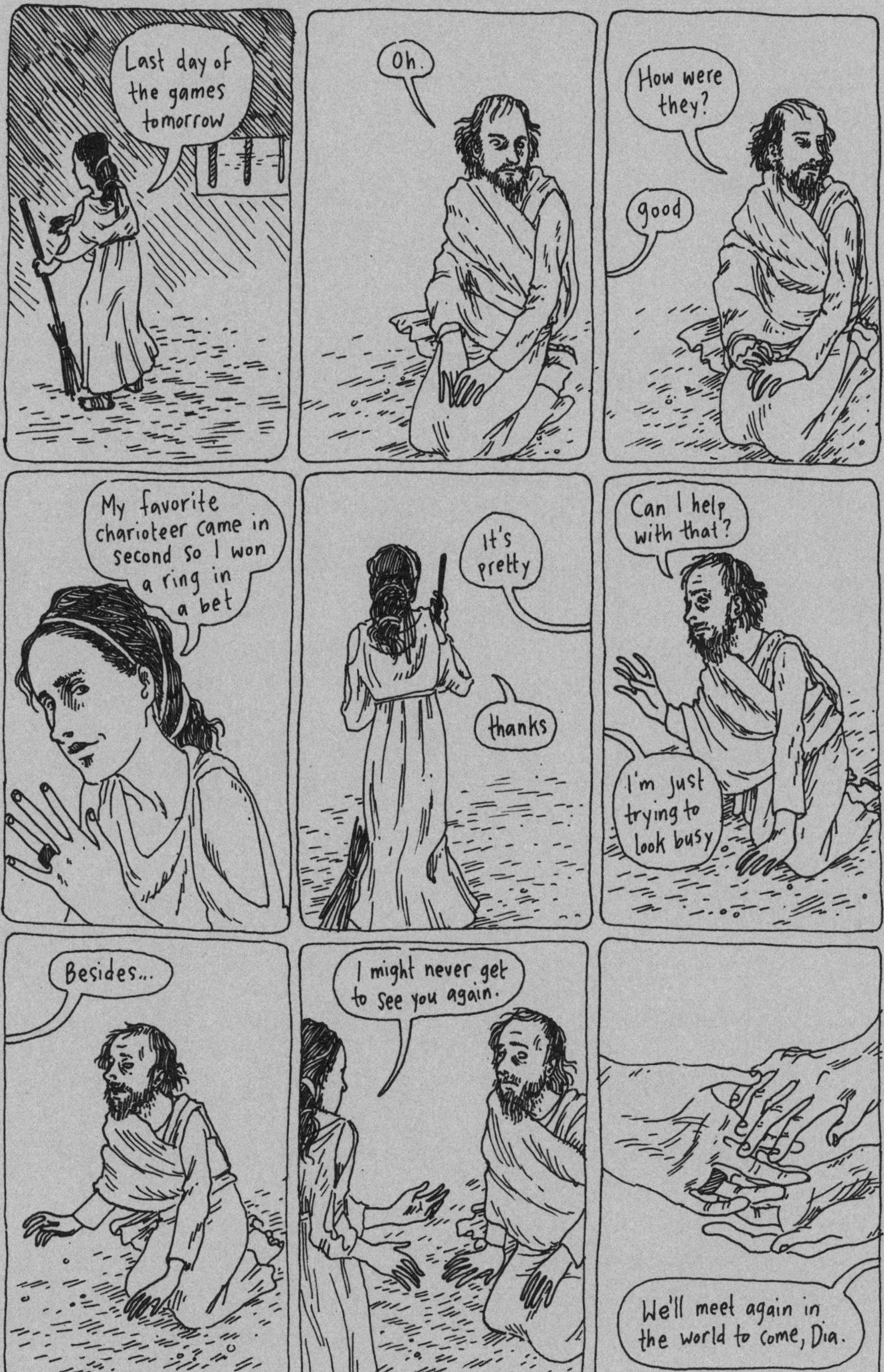
Last day of the games tomorrow
Oh.
How were they?
good
My favorite charioteer came in second so I won a ring in a bet
It's pretty
thanks
Can I help with that?
I'm just trying to look busy
Besides...
I might never get to see you again.
We'll meet again in the world to come, Dia.

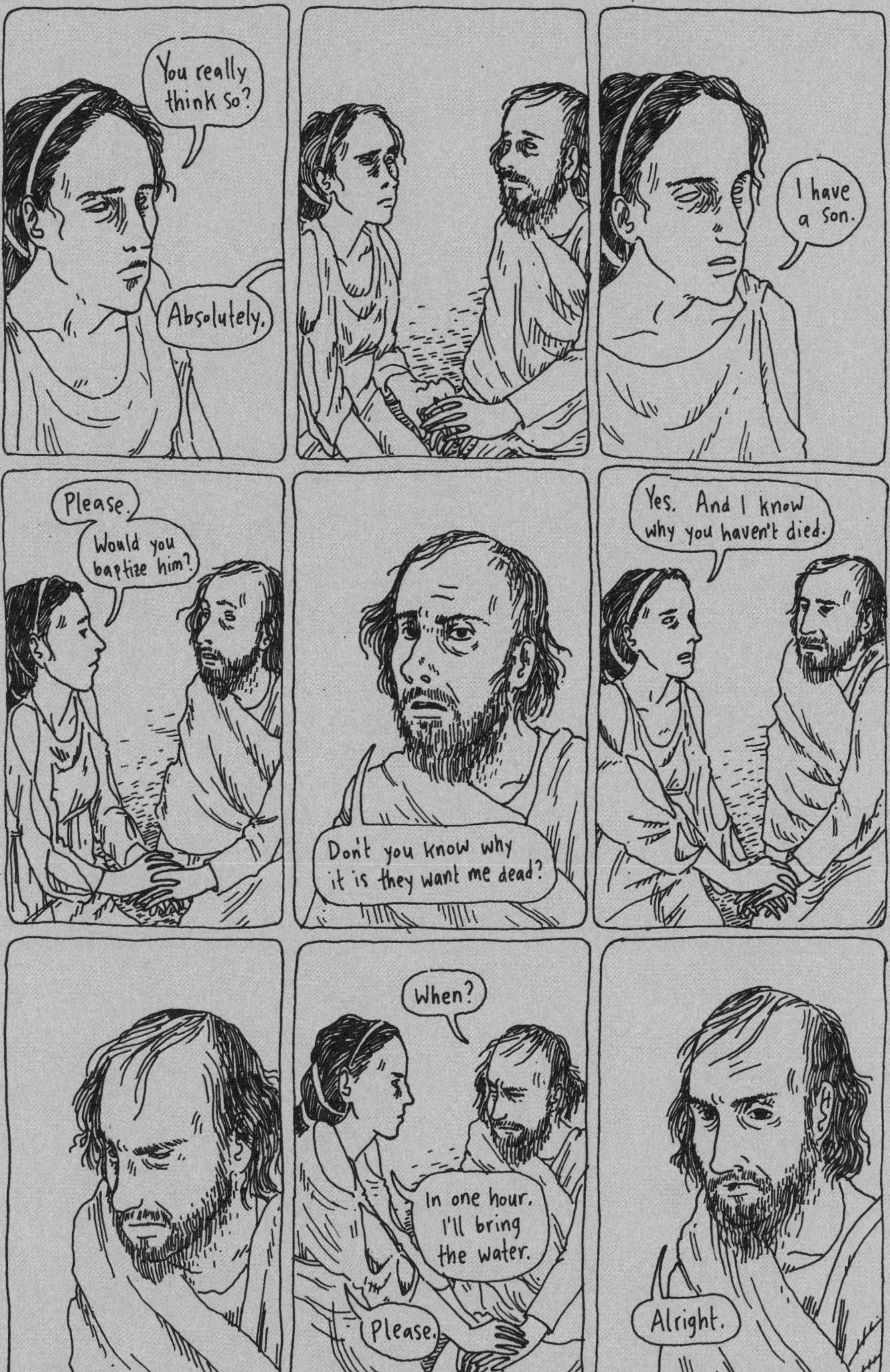

You really think so?
Absolutely.
I have a son.
Please.
Would you baptize him?
Don't you know why it is they want me dead?
Yes. And I know why you haven't died.
When?
In one hour. I'll bring the water.
Please.
Alright.

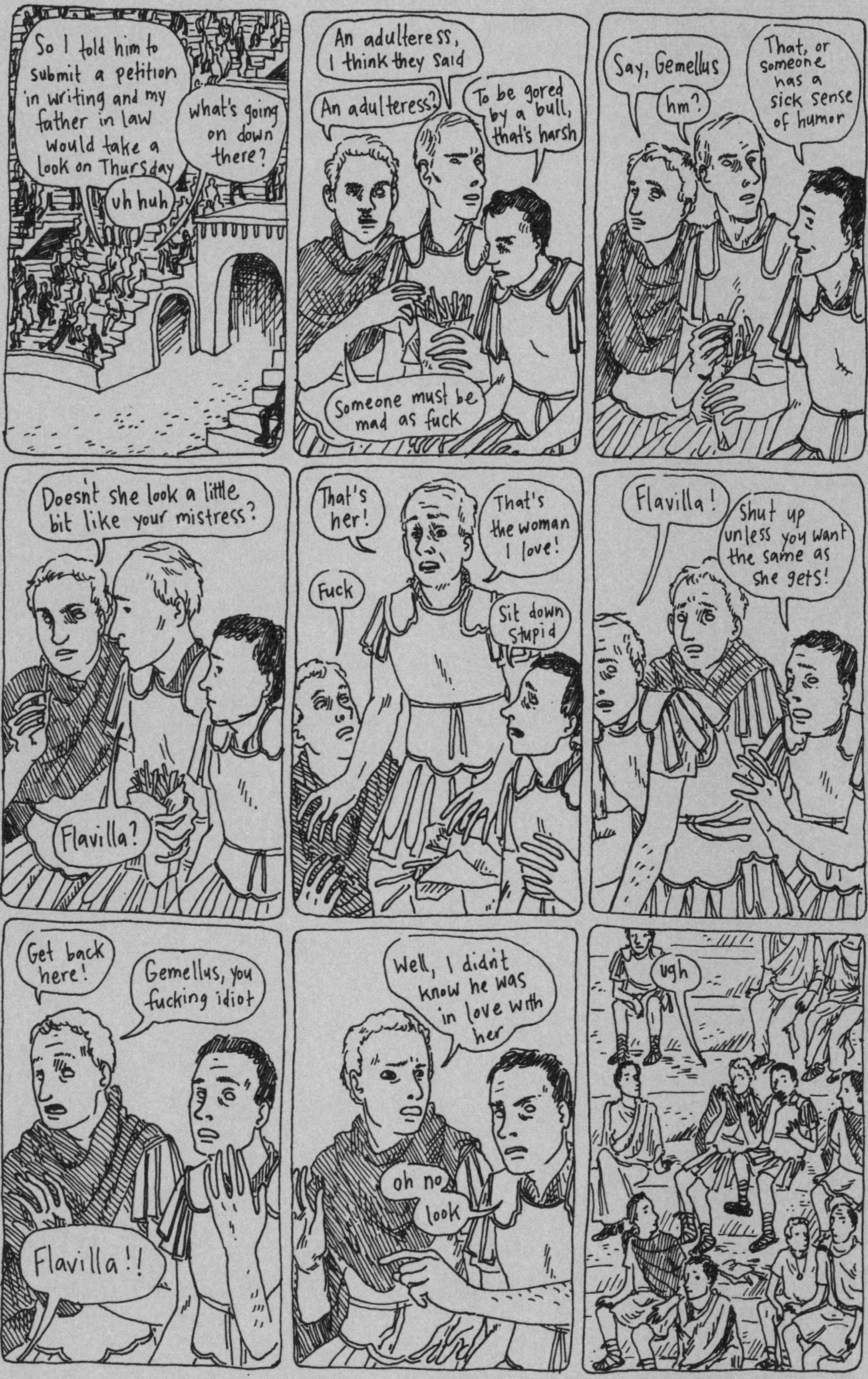
So I told him to submit a petition in writing and my father in law would take a look on Thursday
what's going on down there?
uh huh
An adulteress, I think they said
An adulteress?
To be gored by a bull, that's harsh
Someone must be mad as fuck
Say, Gemellus
hm?
That, or someone has a sick sense of humor
Doesn't she look a little bit like your mistress?
Flavilla?
That's her!
That's the woman I love!
Fuck
Sit down stupid
Flavilla!
Shut up unless you want the same as she gets!
Get back here!
Gemellus, you fucking idiot
Flavilla!!
Well, I didn't know he was in love with her
oh no look
ugh

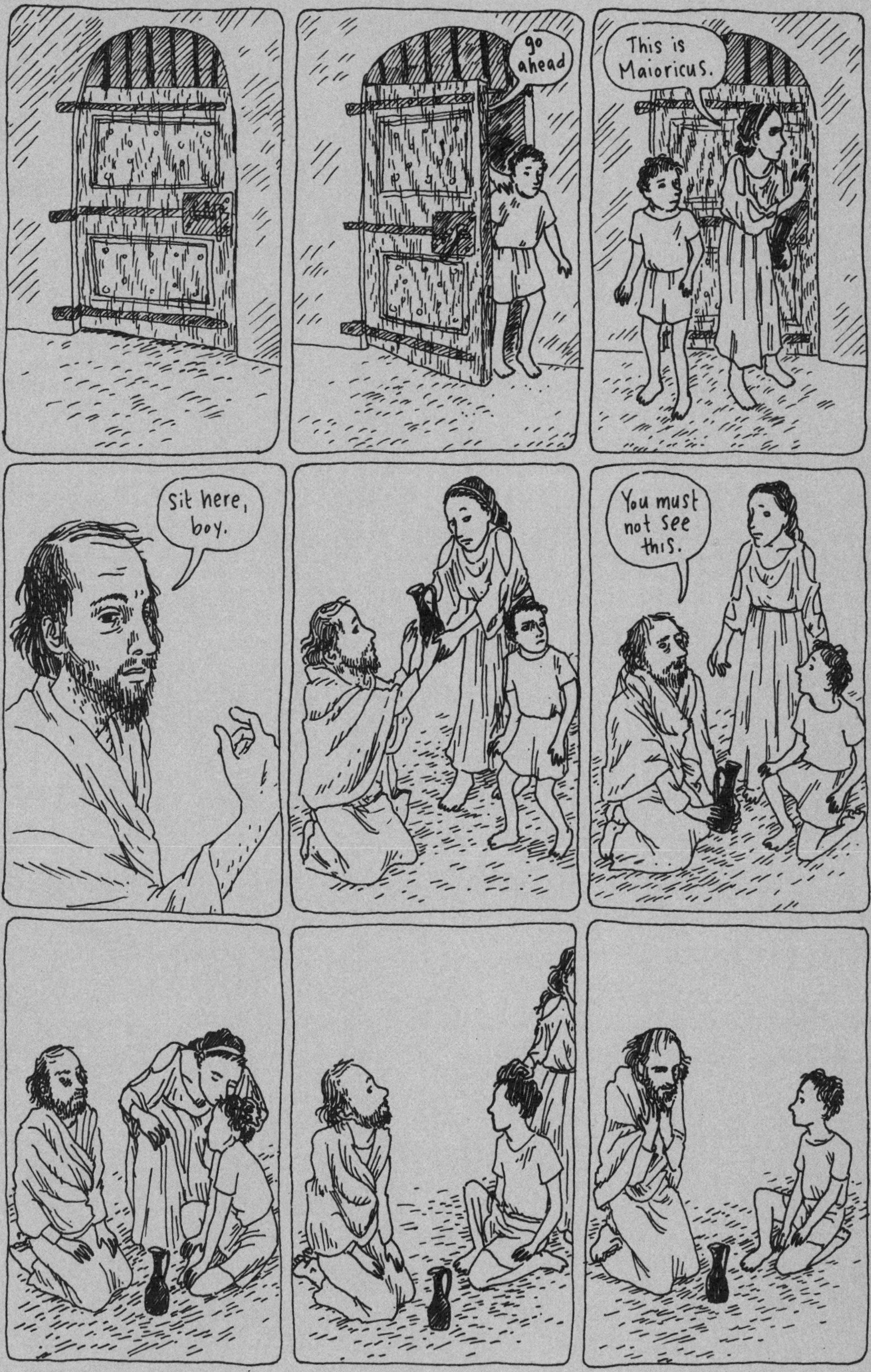
go ahead
This is Maioricus.
Sit here, boy.
You must not see this.

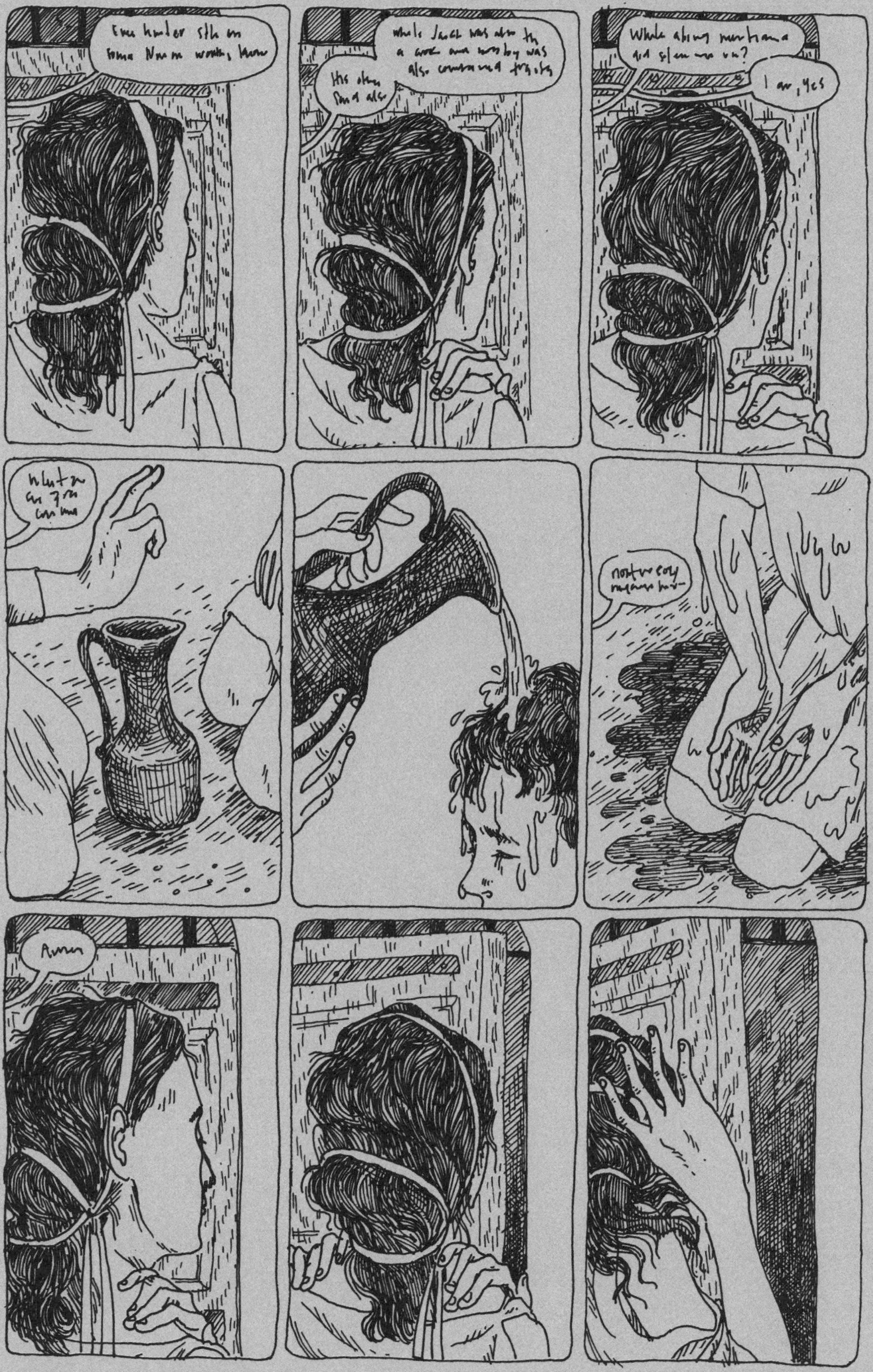
I am, Yes
Amen

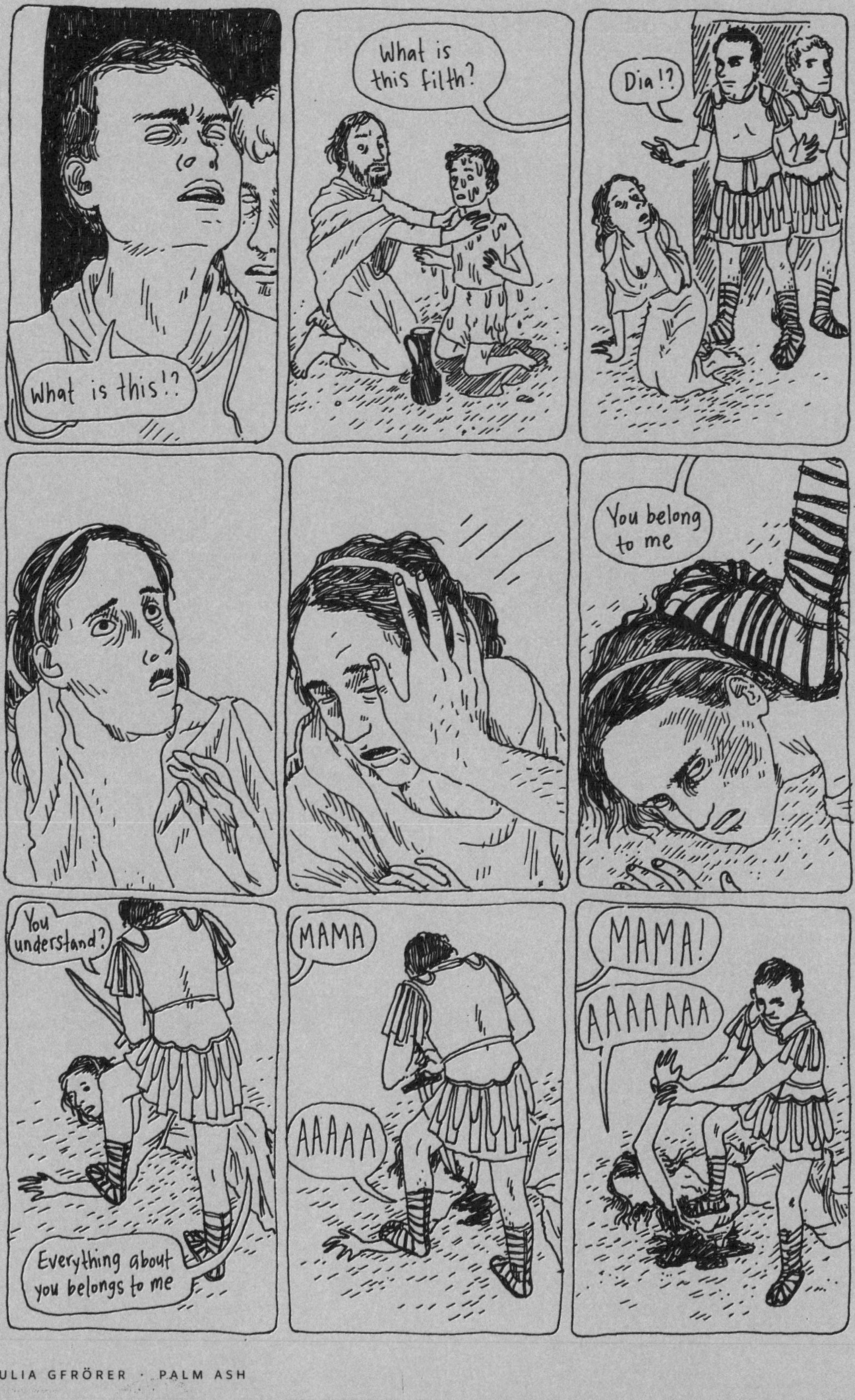
What is this!?
What is this filth?
Dia!?
You belong to me
You understand?
Everything about you belongs to me
MAMA
AAAAA
MAMA!
AAAAAAA

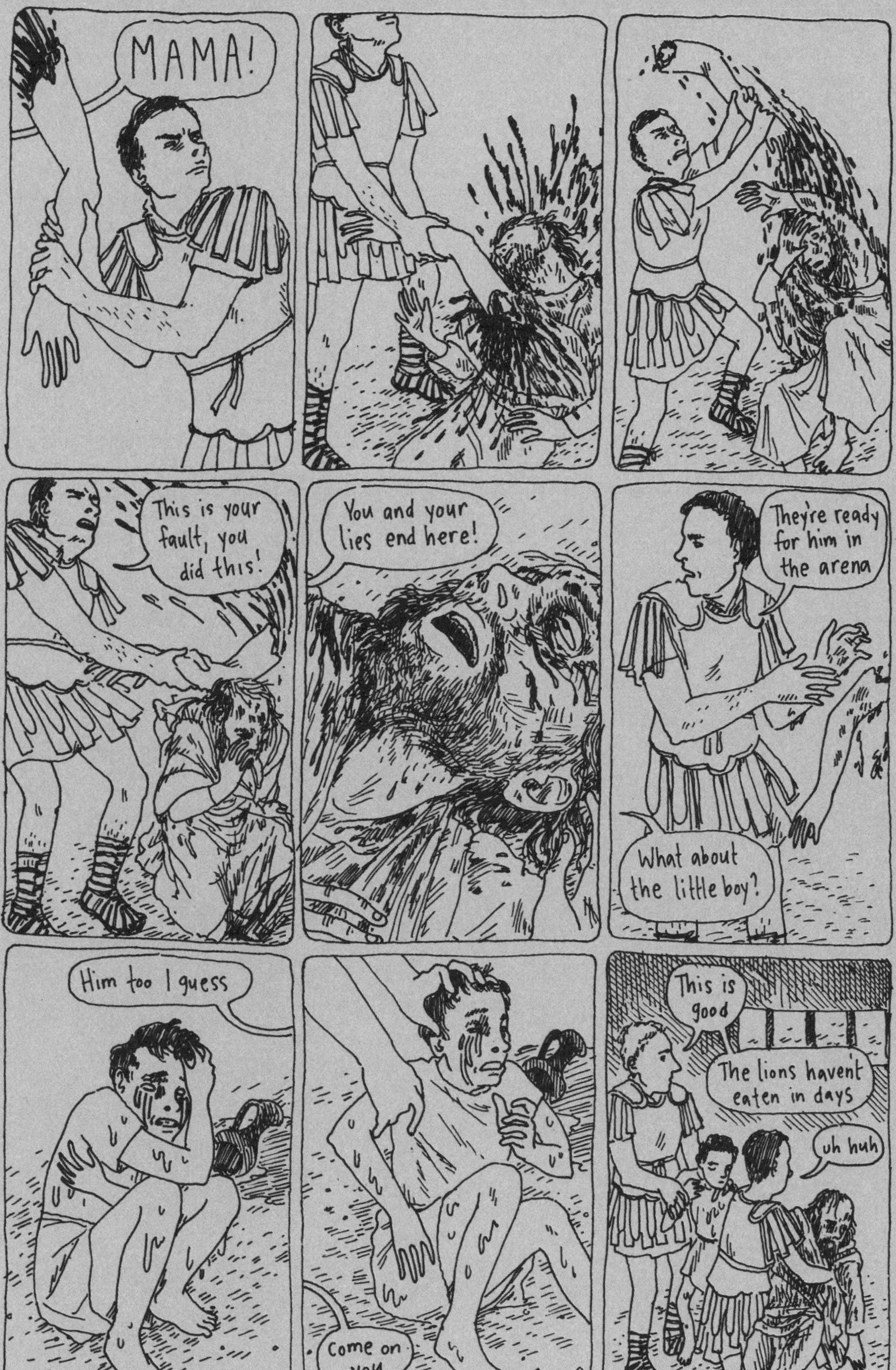
MAMA!
This is your fault, you did this!
You and your lies end here!
They're ready for him in the arena
What about the little boy?
Him too I guess
Come on you
This is good
The lions havent eaten in days
uh huh

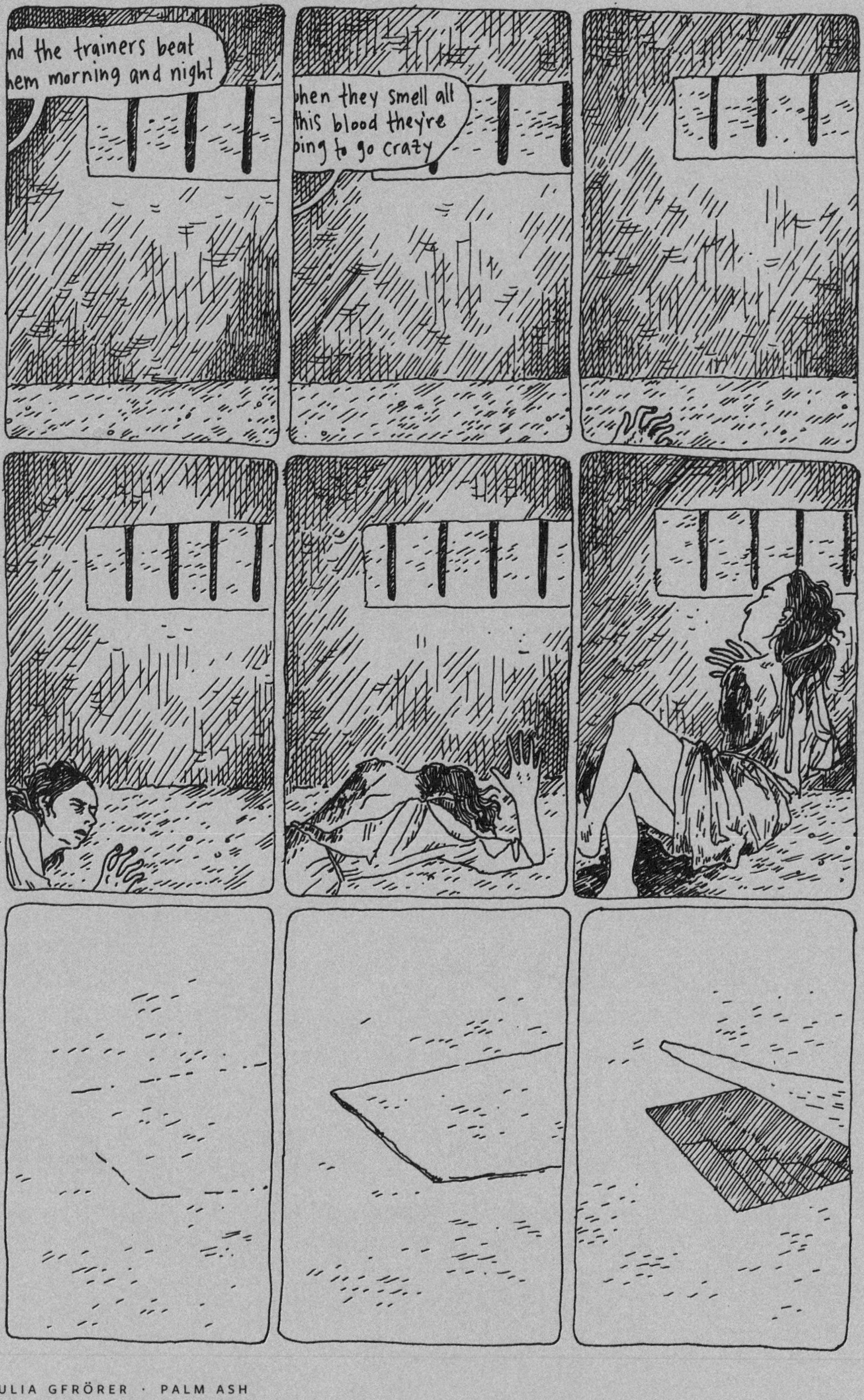
nd the trainers beat hem morning and night
hen they smell all this blood they're oing to go crazy

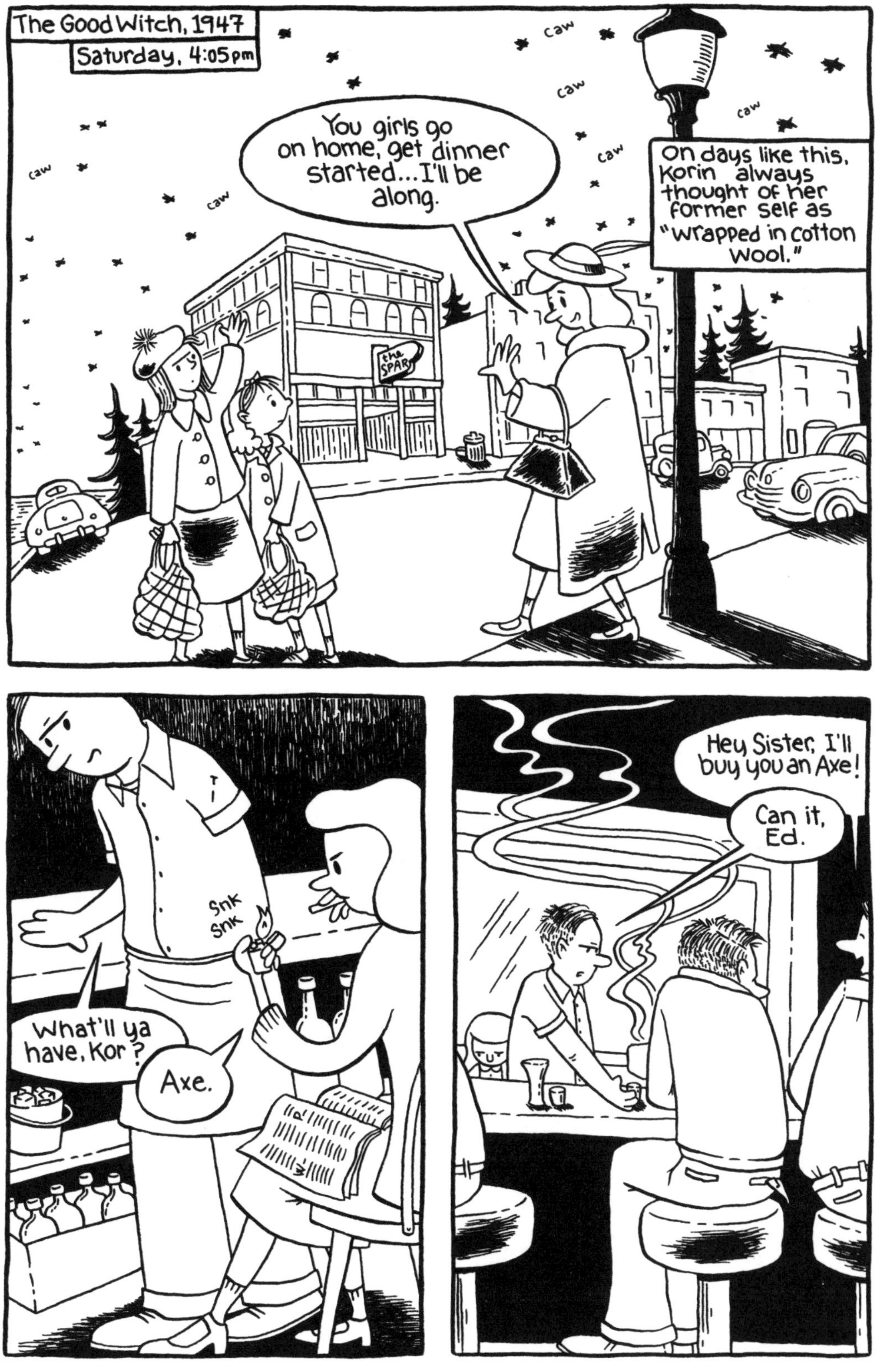
The Good Witch, 1947
Saturday, 4:05pm
caw
You girls go on home, get dinner started... I'll be along.
On days like this, Korin always thought of her former self as "wrapped in cotton wool."
the SPAR
snk snk
What'll ya have, Kor?
Axe.
Hey Sister, I'll buy you an Axe!
Can it, Ed.

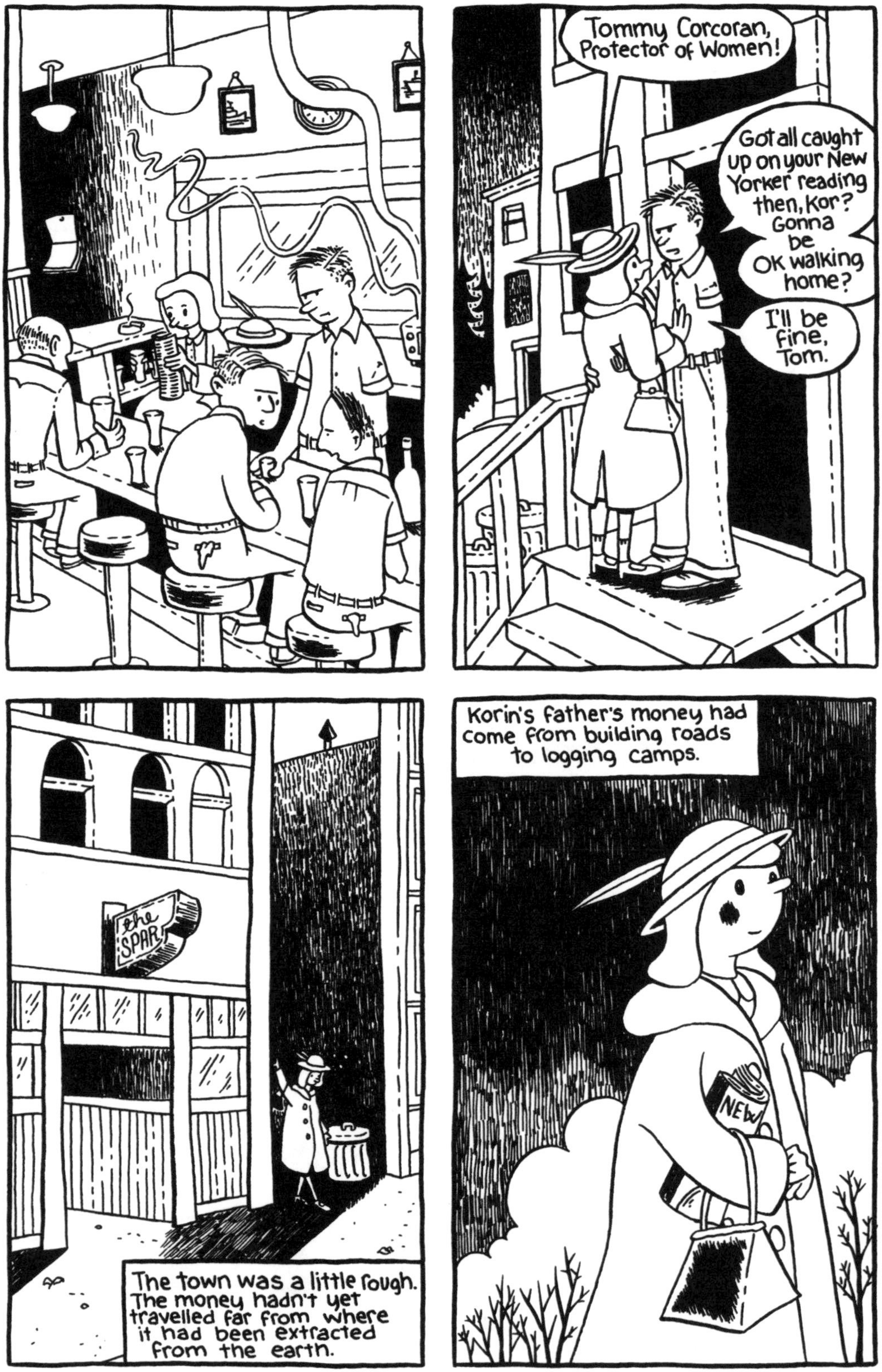
Tommy Corcoran, Protector of Women!
Got all caught up on your New Yorker reading then, Kor? Gonna be OK walking home?
I'll be fine, Tom.
the SPAR
The town was a little rough. The money hadn't yet travelled far from where it had been extracted from the earth.
Korin's father's money had come from building roads to logging camps.
NEW

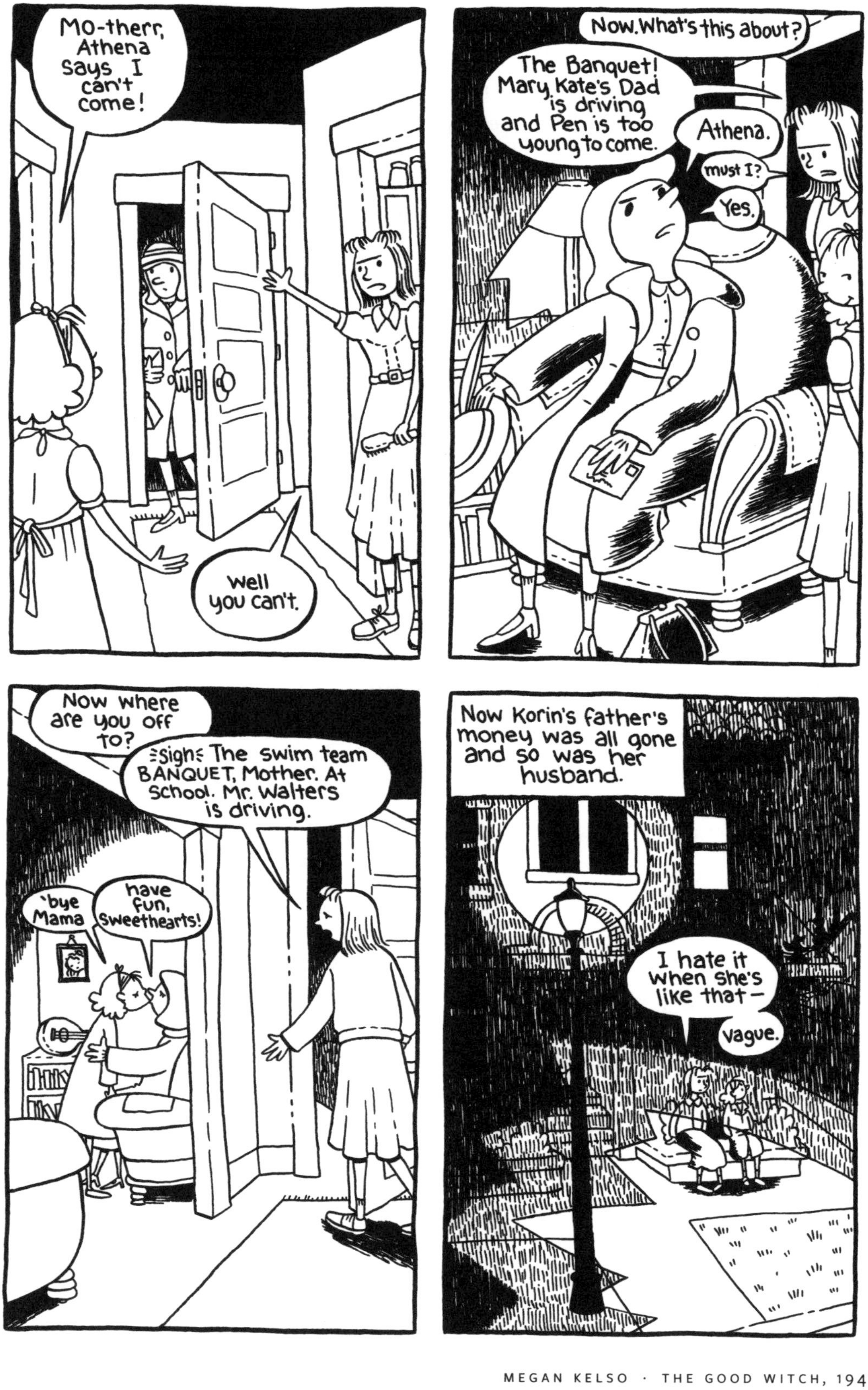

Mo-therr, Athena says I can't come!
Well you can't.
Now. What's this about?
The Banquet! Mary Kate's Dad is driving and Pen is too young to come.
Athena.
must I?
Yes.
Now where are you off to?
≷sigh≶ The swim team BANQUET, Mother. At School. Mr. Walters is driving.
`bye Mama
have fun, sweethearts!
Now Korin's father's money was all gone and so was her husband.
I hate it when she's like that—
Vague.

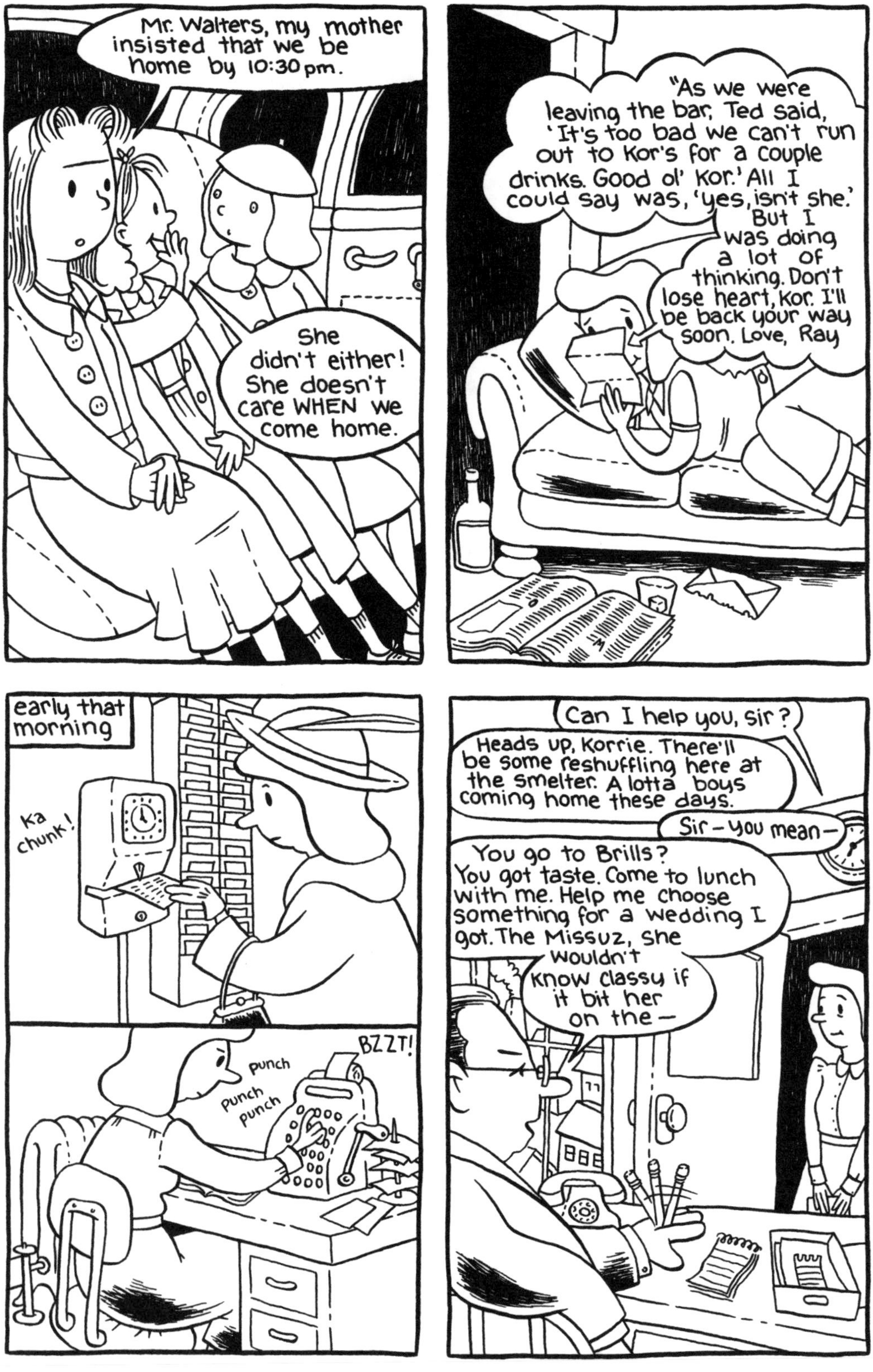

Mr. Walters, my mother insisted that we be home by 10:30 pm.
She didn't either! She doesn't care WHEN we come home.
"As we were leaving the bar, Ted said, 'It's too bad we can't run out to Kor's for a couple drinks. Good ol' Kor.' All I could say was, 'yes, isn't she.' But I was doing a lot of thinking. Don't lose heart, Kor. I'll be back your way soon. Love, Ray
early that morning
Ka chunk!
punch
punch punch
BZZT!
Can I help you, sir?
Heads up, Korrie. There'll be some reshuffling here at the smelter. A lotta boys coming home these days.
Sir – you mean–
You go to Brills? You got taste. Come to lunch with me. Help me choose something for a wedding I got. The Missuz, she wouldn't know classy if it bit her on the –

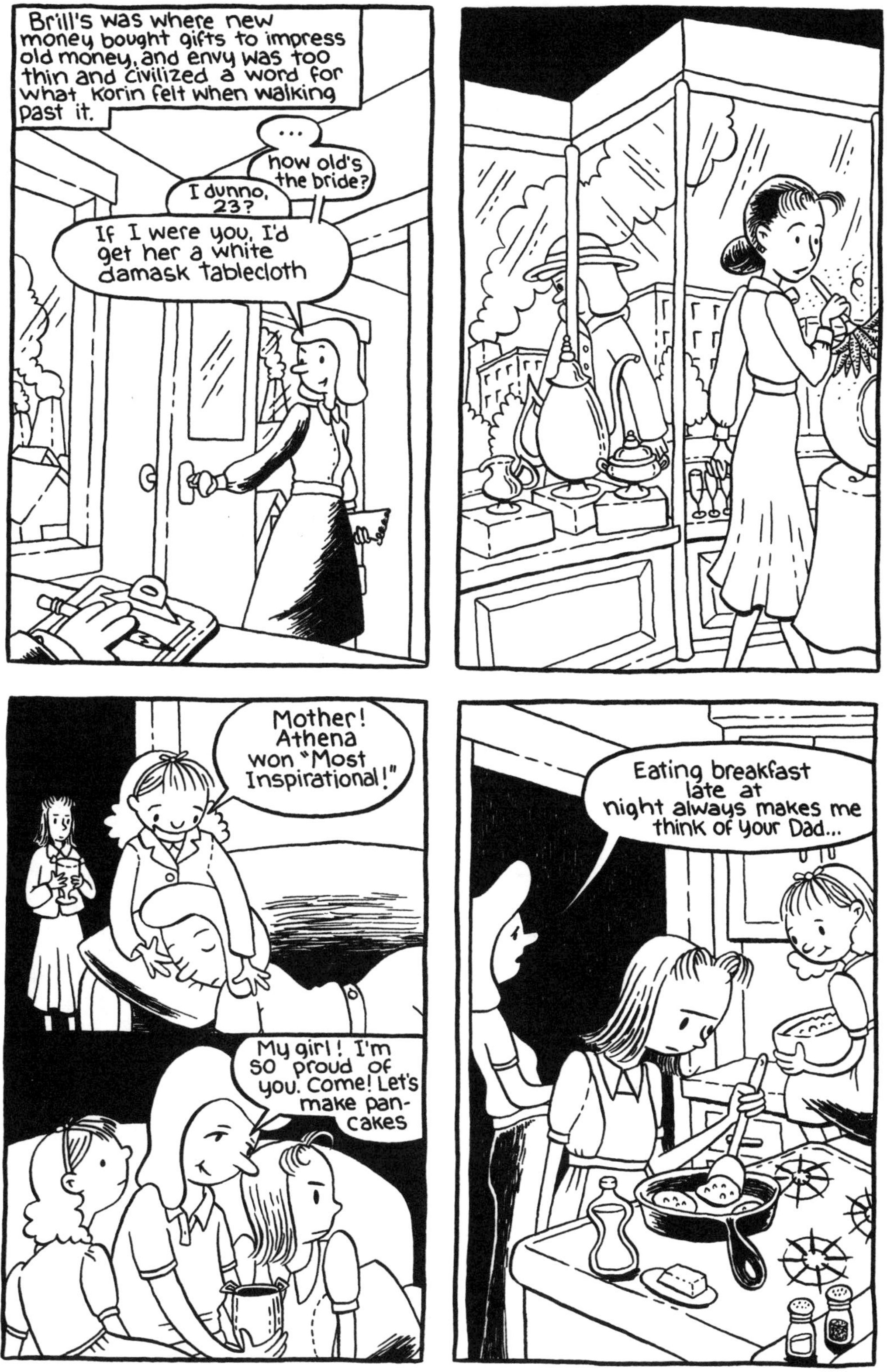
Brill's was where new money bought gifts to impress old money, and envy was too thin and civilized a word for what Korin felt when walking past it.
...
how old's the bride?
I dunno, 23?
If I were you, I'd get her a white damask tablecloth
Mother! Athena won "Most Inspirational!"
My girl! I'm so proud of you. Come! Let's make pan-cakes
Eating breakfast late at night always makes me think of your Dad...

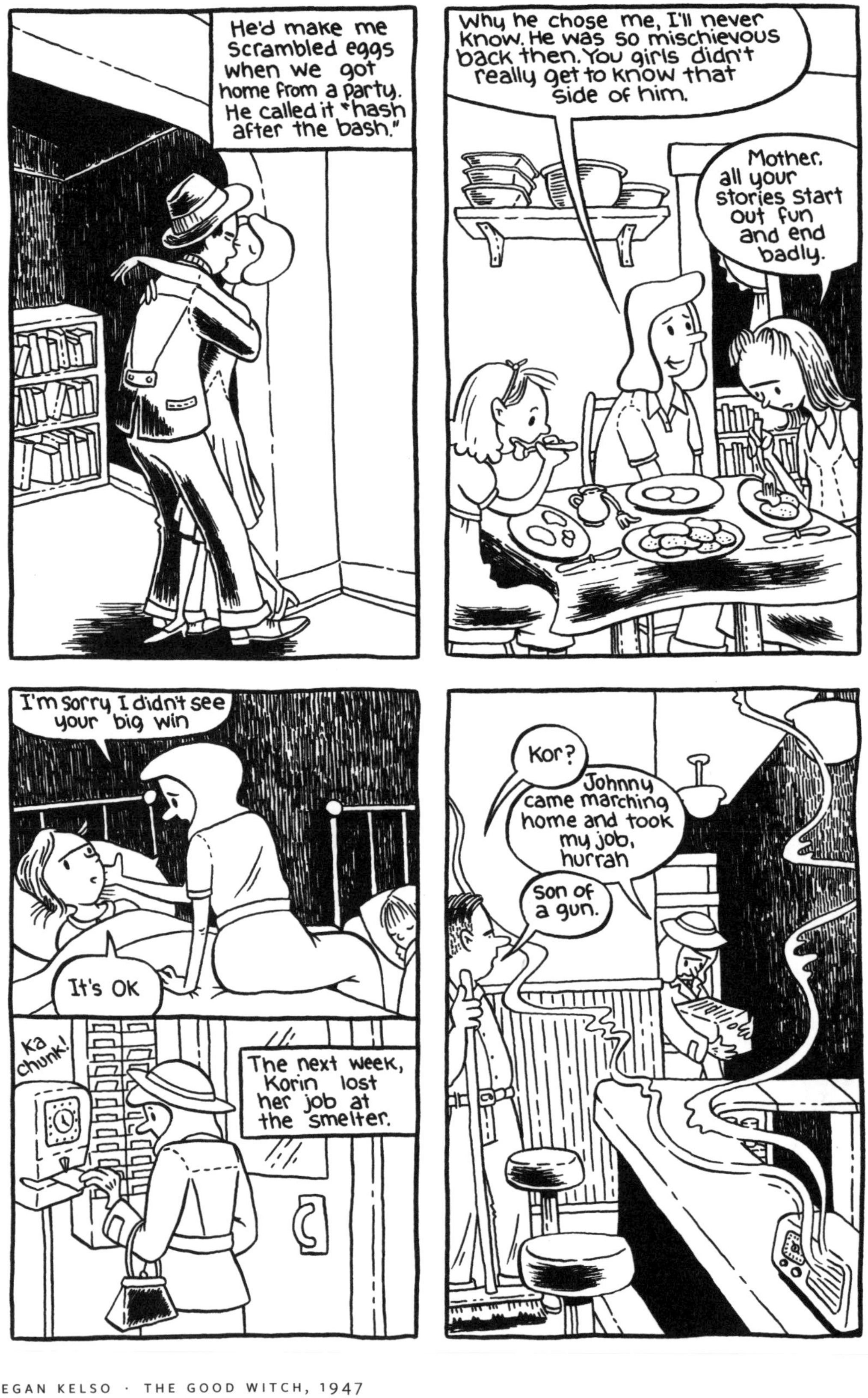
He'd make me scrambled eggs when we got home from a party. He called it "hash after the bash."
Why he chose me, I'll never know. He was so mischievous back then. You girls didn't really get to know that side of him.
Mother, all your stories start out fun and end badly.
I'm sorry I didn't see your big win
It's OK
Ka chunk!
The next week, Korin lost her job at the smelter.
Kor?
Johnny came marching home and took my job, hurrah
Son of a gun.

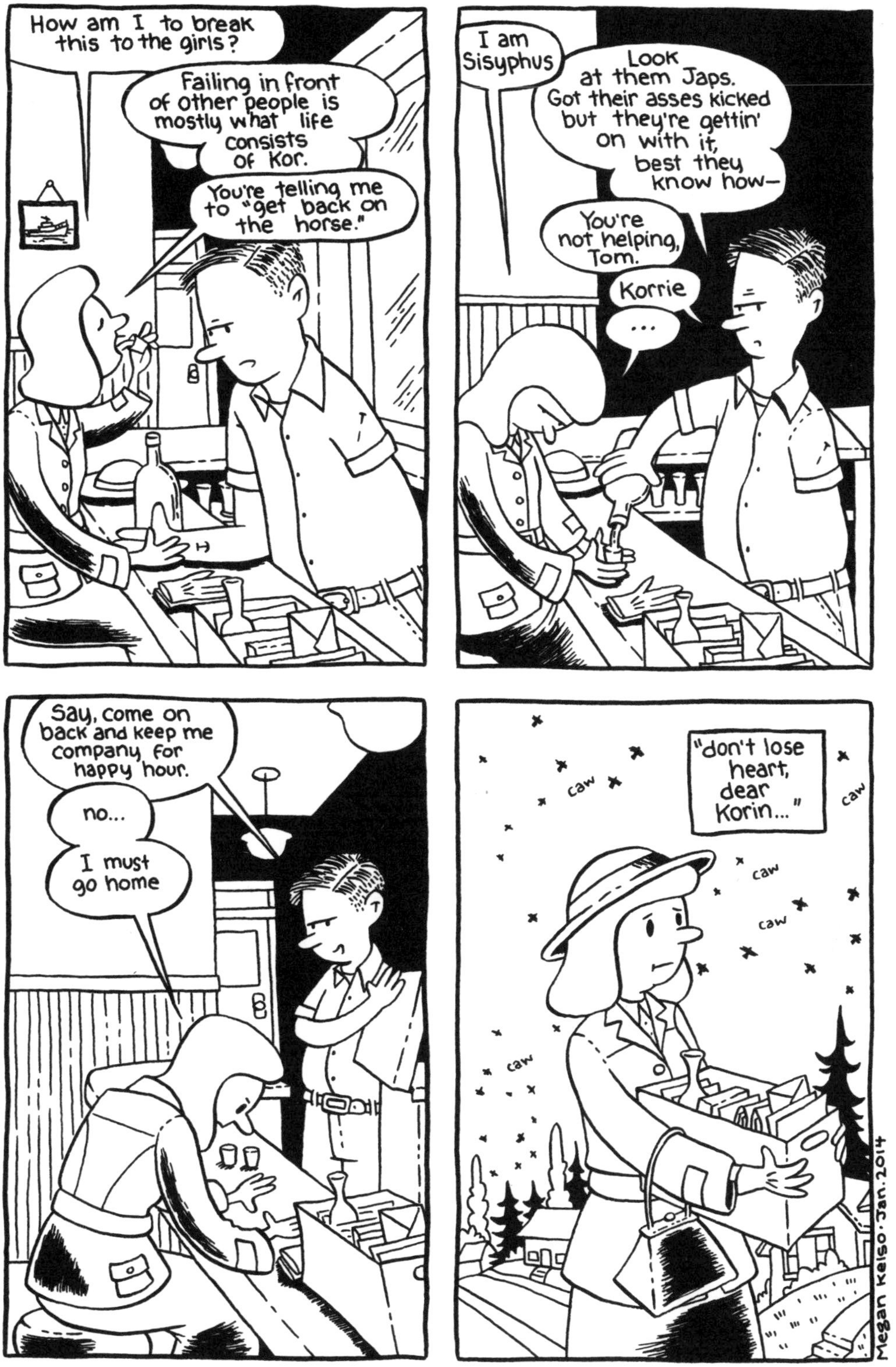
How am I to break this to the girls?
Failing in front of other people is mostly what life consists of Kor.
You're telling me to "get back on the horse."
I am Sisyphus
Look at them Japs. Got their asses kicked but they're gettin' on with it, best they know how–
You're not helping, Tom.
Korrie
...
Say, come on back and keep me company for happy hour.
no...
I must go home
"don't lose heart, dear Korin..."
caw
caw
caw
caw
caw
Megan Kelso · Jan. 2014

CHAPTER FOUR

Voices

DAVIS, BURKHOLDER & BELL WORK WITH NARRATIVE TOO — BUT UNLIKE MY "STORYTELLERS", THEY SEEM MORE ENGAGED WITH LANGUAGE, SUBJECTIVITY, INTERIORITY... CONSCIOUSNESS - THE STUFF OF ESSAYS, MEMOIR & POETRY.

I WISH I COULD DO "SPOT BLACK" LIKE GABRIELLE BELL.

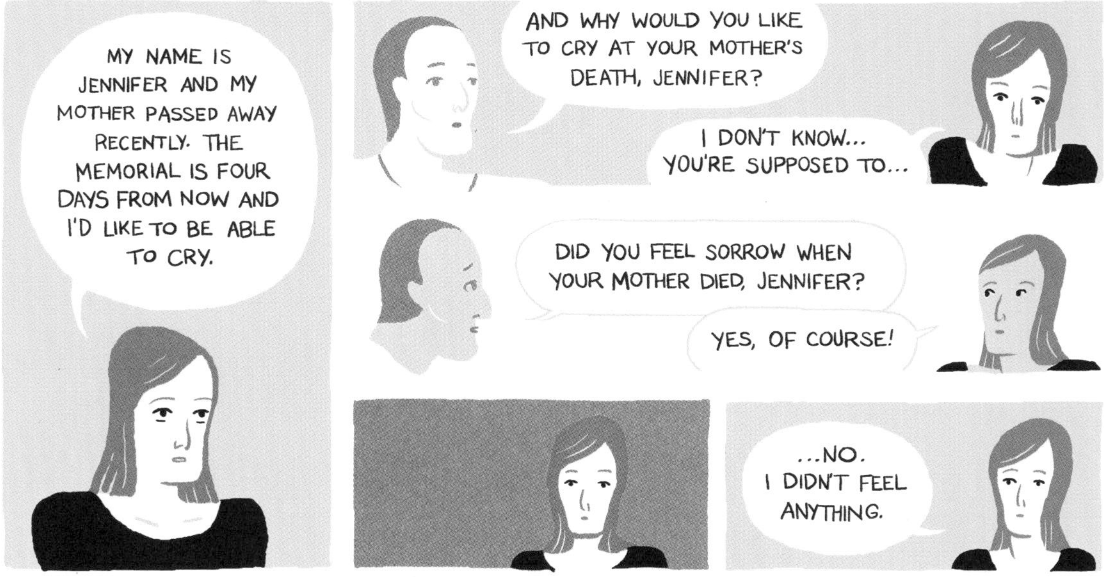
MY NAME IS JENNIFER AND MY MOTHER PASSED AWAY RECENTLY. THE MEMORIAL IS FOUR DAYS FROM NOW AND I'D LIKE TO BE ABLE TO CRY.
AND WHY WOULD YOU LIKE TO CRY AT YOUR MOTHER'S DEATH, JENNIFER?
I DON'T KNOW... YOU'RE SUPPOSED TO...
DID YOU FEEL SORROW WHEN YOUR MOTHER DIED, JENNIFER?
YES, OF COURSE!
...NO. I DIDN'T FEEL ANYTHING.

NO TEARS, NO SORROW

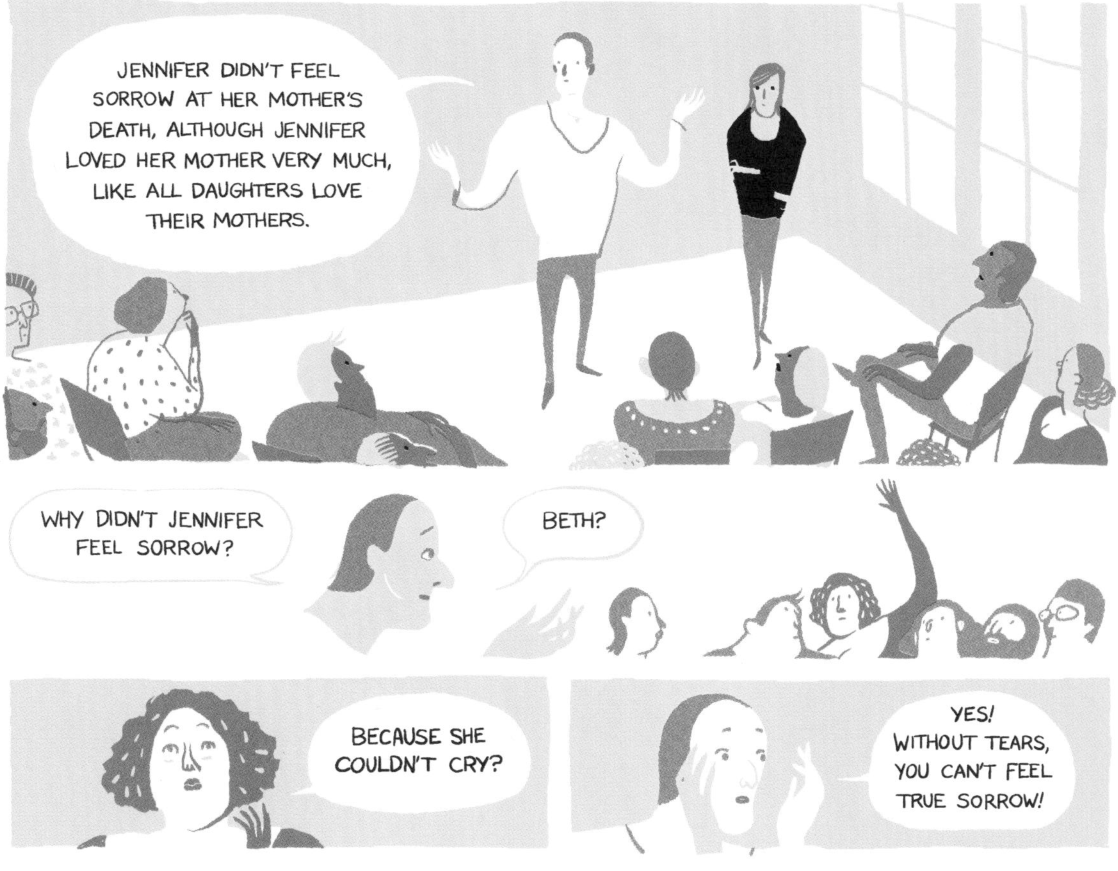
JENNIFER DIDN'T FEEL SORROW AT HER MOTHER'S DEATH, ALTHOUGH JENNIFER LOVED HER MOTHER VERY MUCH, LIKE ALL DAUGHTERS LOVE THEIR MOTHERS.
WHY DIDN'T JENNIFER FEEL SORROW?
BETH?
BECAUSE SHE COULDN'T CRY?
YES! WITHOUT TEARS, YOU CAN'T FEEL TRUE SORROW!

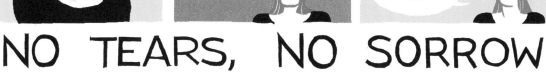

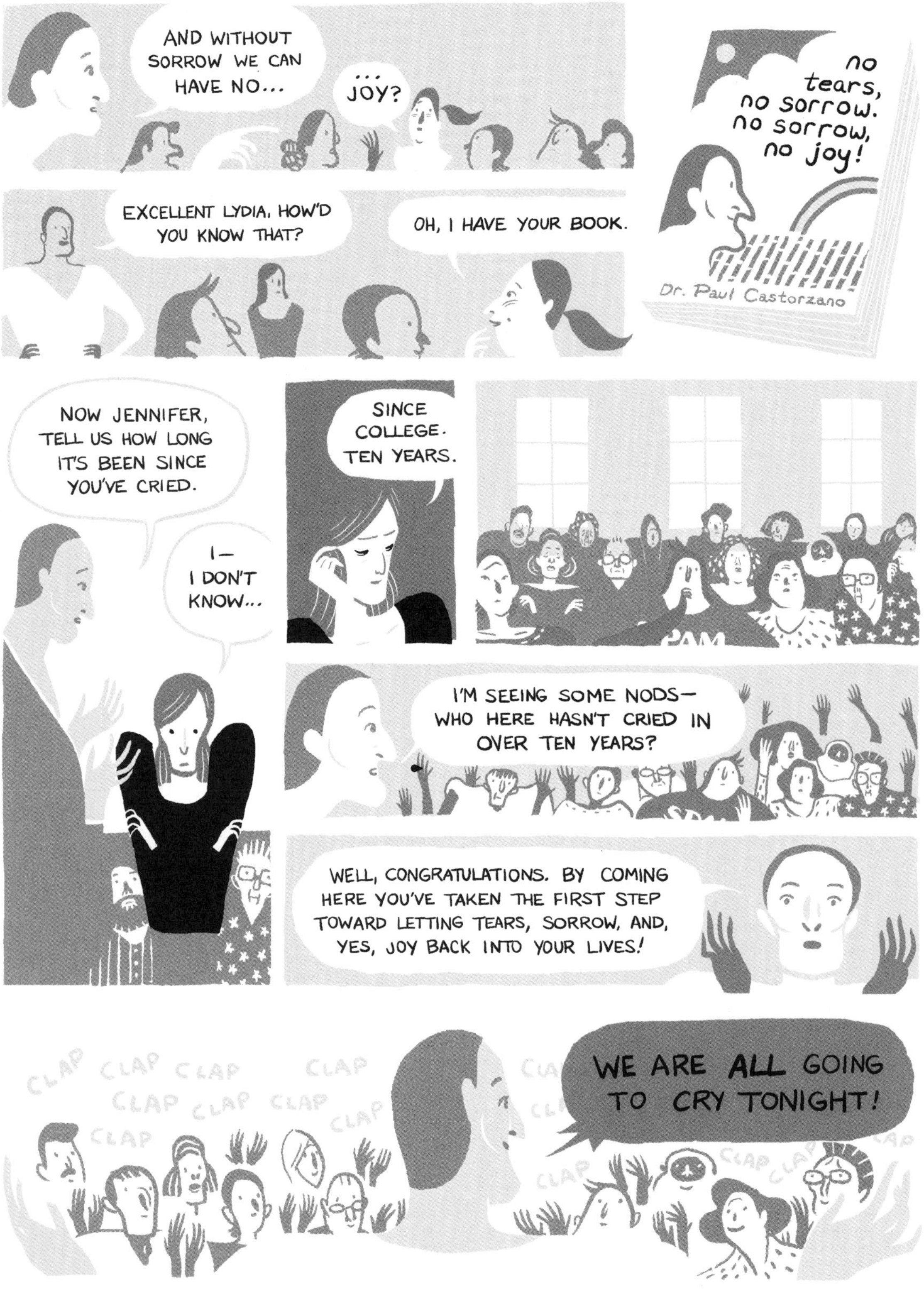
AND WITHOUT SORROW WE CAN HAVE NO...
... JOY?
no tears, no sorrow. no sorrow, no joy!
Dr. Paul Castorzano
EXCELLENT LYDIA. HOW'D YOU KNOW THAT?
OH, I HAVE YOUR BOOK.
NOW JENNIFER, TELL US HOW LONG IT'S BEEN SINCE YOU'VE CRIED.
I— I DON'T KNOW...
SINCE COLLEGE. TEN YEARS.
I'M SEEING SOME NODS— WHO HERE HASN'T CRIED IN OVER TEN YEARS?
WELL, CONGRATULATIONS. BY COMING HERE YOU'VE TAKEN THE FIRST STEP TOWARD LETTING TEARS, SORROW, AND, YES, JOY BACK INTO YOUR LIVES!
CLAP CLAP CLAP CLAP CLAP CLAP CLAP CLAP CLAP
WE ARE **ALL** GOING TO CRY TONIGHT!
CLAP CLAP CLAP

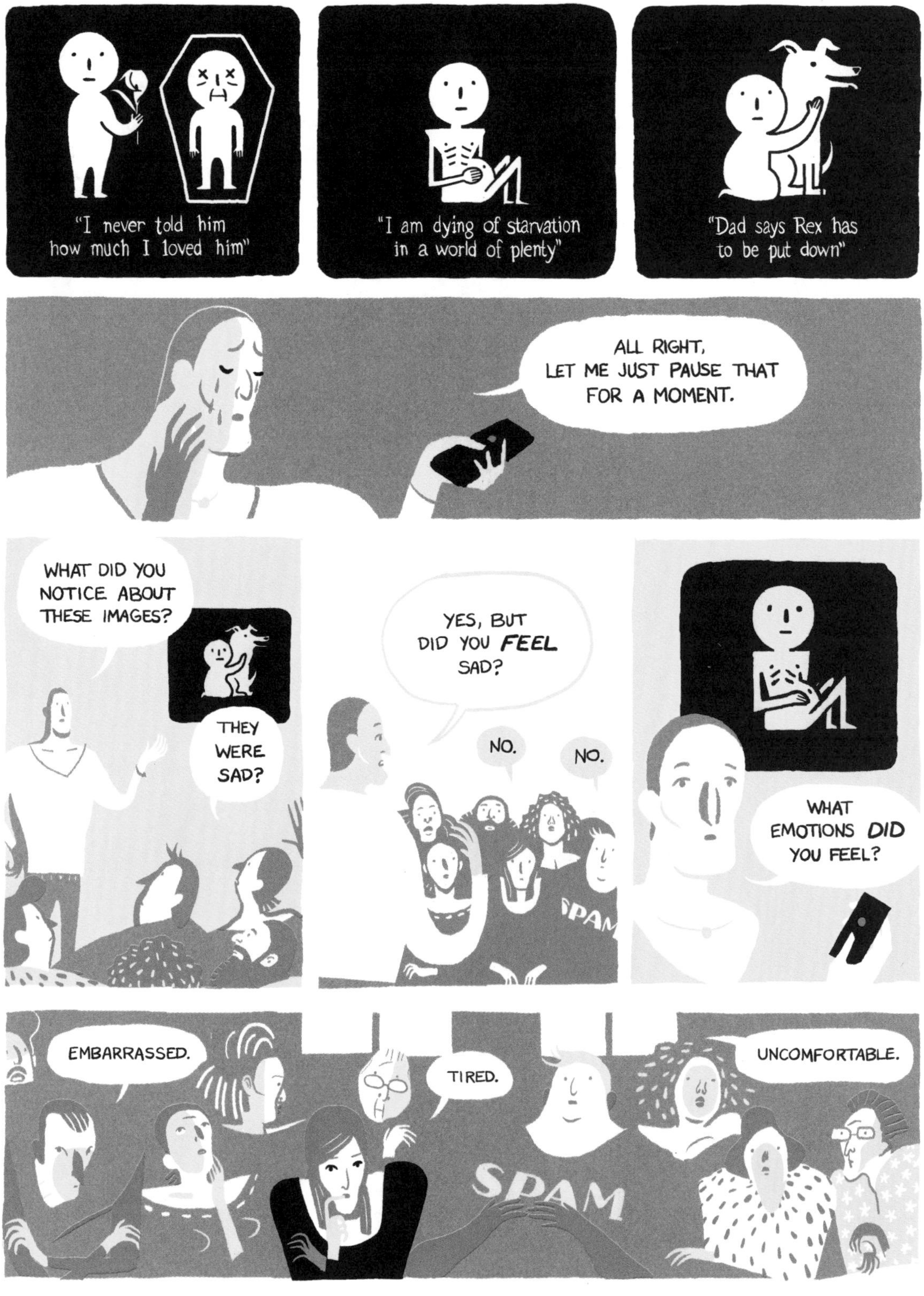
"I never told him how much I loved him"
"I am dying of starvation in a world of plenty"
"Dad says Rex has to be put down"
ALL RIGHT, LET ME JUST PAUSE THAT FOR A MOMENT.
WHAT DID YOU NOTICE ABOUT THESE IMAGES?
THEY WERE SAD?
YES, BUT DID YOU FEEL SAD?
NO.
NO.
SPAM
WHAT EMOTIONS DID YOU FEEL?
EMBARRASSED.
TIRED.
UNCOMFORTABLE.
SPAM

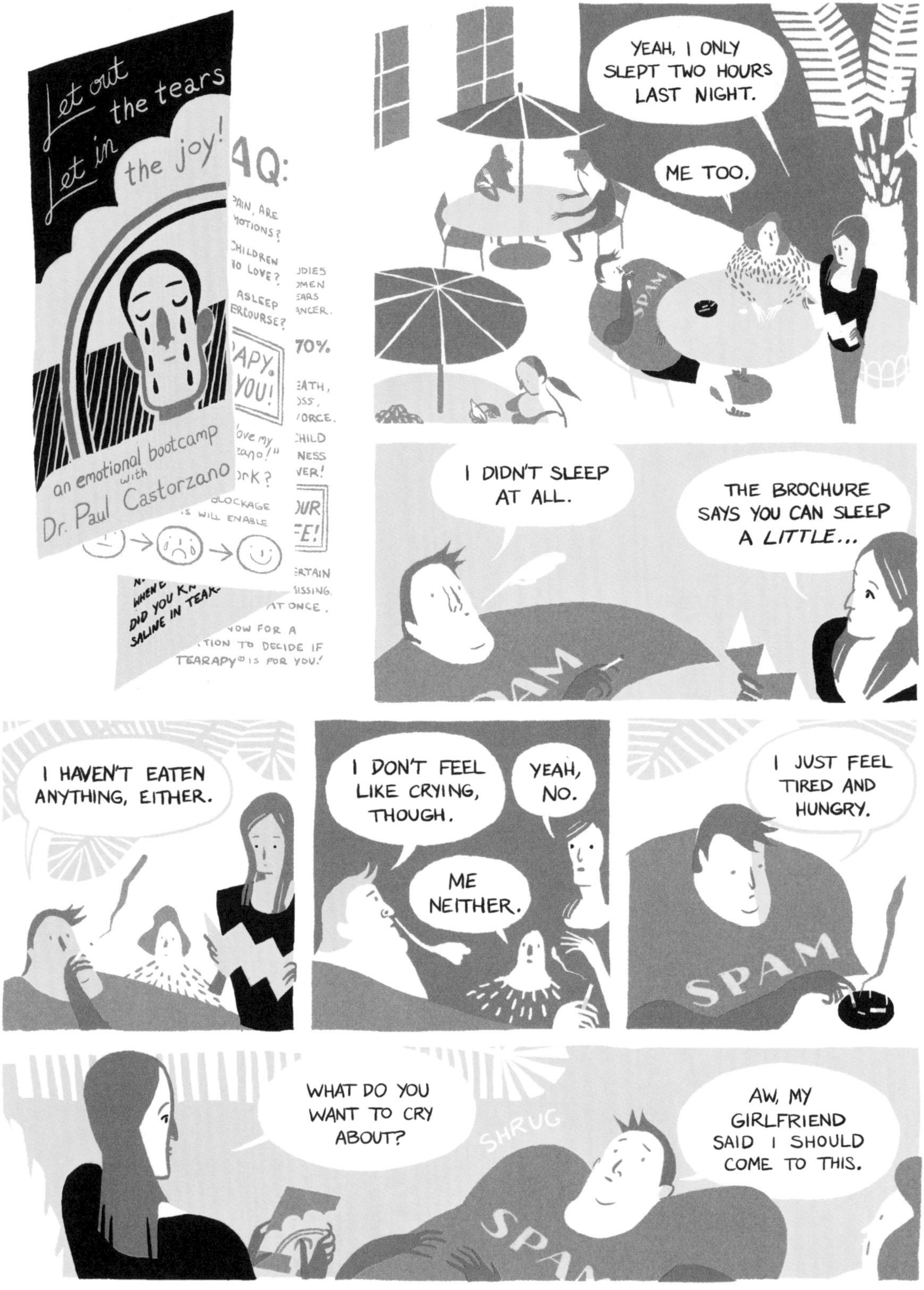
Let out the tears
Let in the joy!
an emotional bootcamp with Dr. Paul Castorzano
70%
YEAH, I ONLY SLEPT TWO HOURS LAST NIGHT.
ME TOO.
I DIDN'T SLEEP AT ALL.
THE BROCHURE SAYS YOU CAN SLEEP A *LITTLE*...
I HAVEN'T EATEN ANYTHING, EITHER.
I DON'T FEEL LIKE CRYING, THOUGH.
YEAH, NO.
ME NEITHER.
I JUST FEEL TIRED AND HUNGRY.
SPAM
WHAT DO YOU WANT TO CRY ABOUT?
SHRUG
AW, MY GIRLFRIEND SAID I SHOULD COME TO THIS.

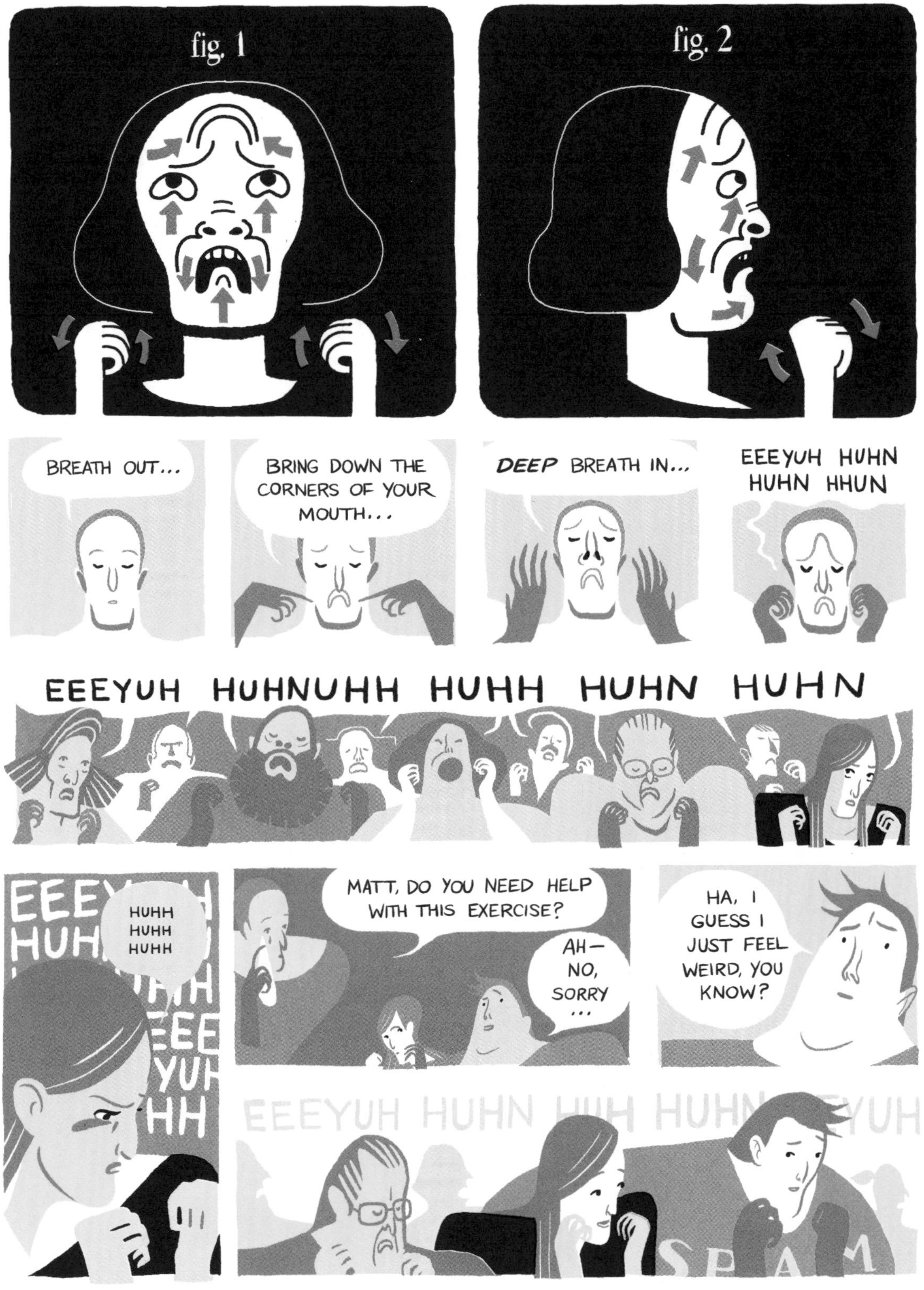
fig. 1
fig. 2
BREATH OUT...
BRING DOWN THE CORNERS OF YOUR MOUTH...
DEEP BREATH IN...
EEEYUH HUHN HUHN HHUN
EEEYUH HUHNUHH HUHH HUHN HUHN
HUHH HUHH HUHH
MATT, DO YOU NEED HELP WITH THIS EXERCISE?
AH— NO, SORRY ...
HA, I GUESS I JUST FEEL WEIRD, YOU KNOW?
EEEYUH HUHN HUH HUHN EEYUH

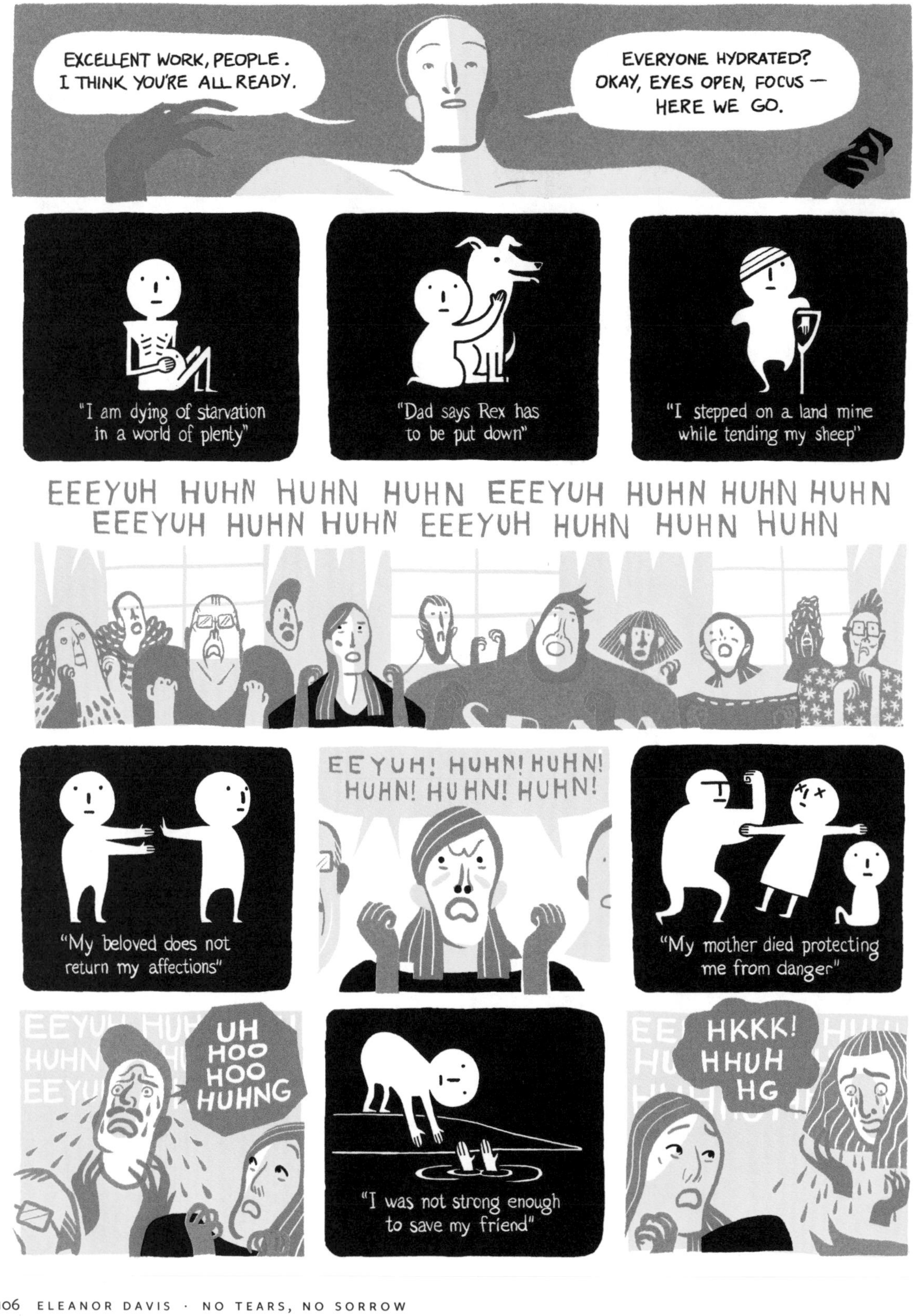
EXCELLENT WORK, PEOPLE. I THINK YOU'RE ALL READY.
EVERYONE HYDRATED? OKAY, EYES OPEN, FOCUS — HERE WE GO.
"I am dying of starvation in a world of plenty"
"Dad says Rex has to be put down"
"I stepped on a land mine while tending my sheep"
EEEYUH HUHN HUHN HUHN EEEYUH HUHN HUHN HUHN
EEEYUH HUHN HUHN EEEYUH HUHN HUHN HUHN
"My beloved does not return my affections"
EEYUH! HUHN! HUHN! HUHN! HUHN! HUHN!
"My mother died protecting me from danger"
UH HOO HOO HUHNG
"I was not strong enough to save my friend"
HKKK! HHUH HG

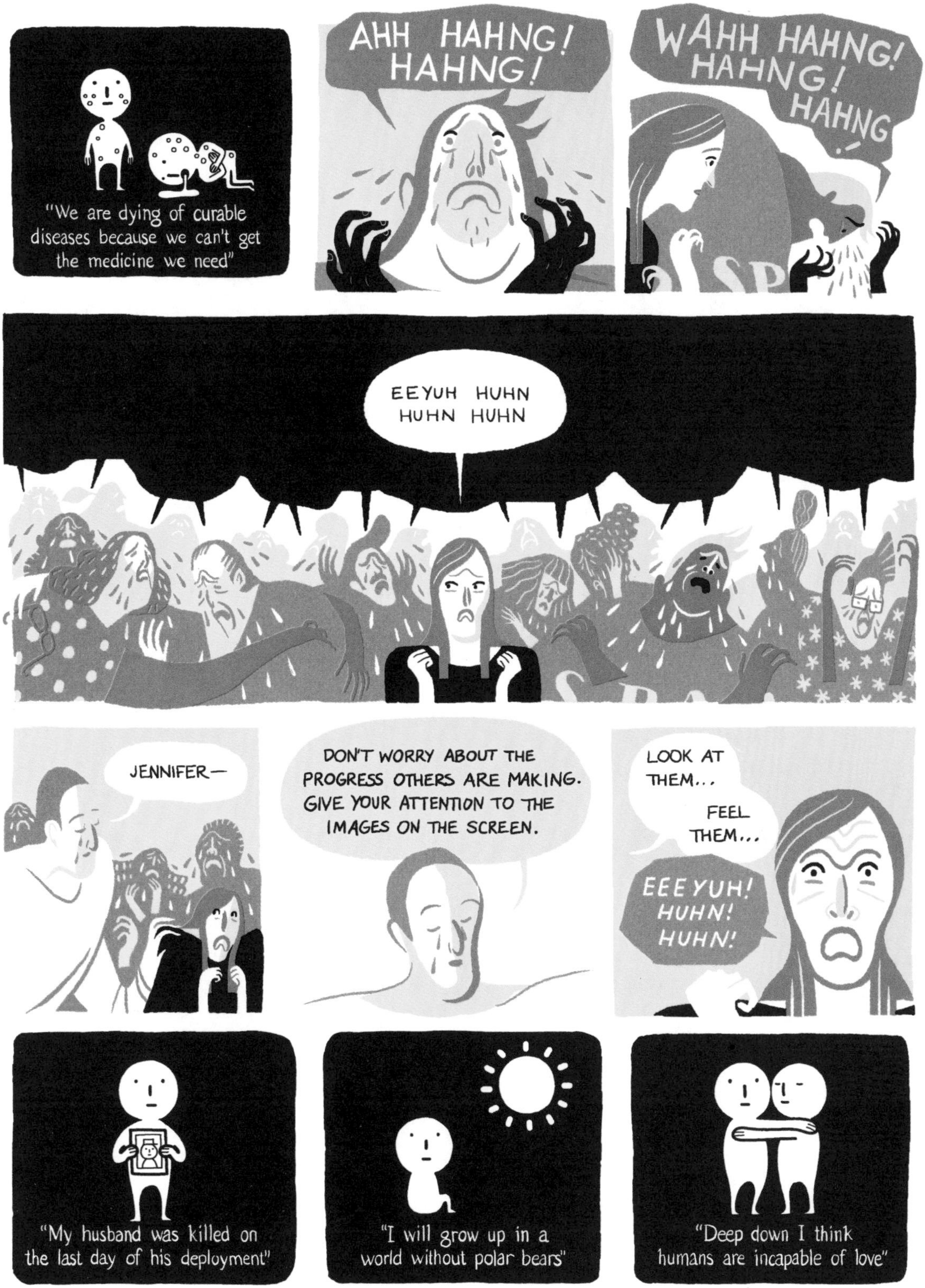

"We are dying of curable diseases because we can't get the medicine we need"
AHH HAHNG! HAHNG!
WAHH HAHNG! HAHNG! HAHNG!
EEYUH HUHN HUHN HUHN
JENNIFER—
DON'T WORRY ABOUT THE PROGRESS OTHERS ARE MAKING. GIVE YOUR ATTENTION TO THE IMAGES ON THE SCREEN.
LOOK AT THEM...
FEEL THEM...
EEEYUH! HUHN! HUHN!
"My husband was killed on the last day of his deployment"
"I will grow up in a world without polar bears"
"Deep down I think humans are incapable of love"

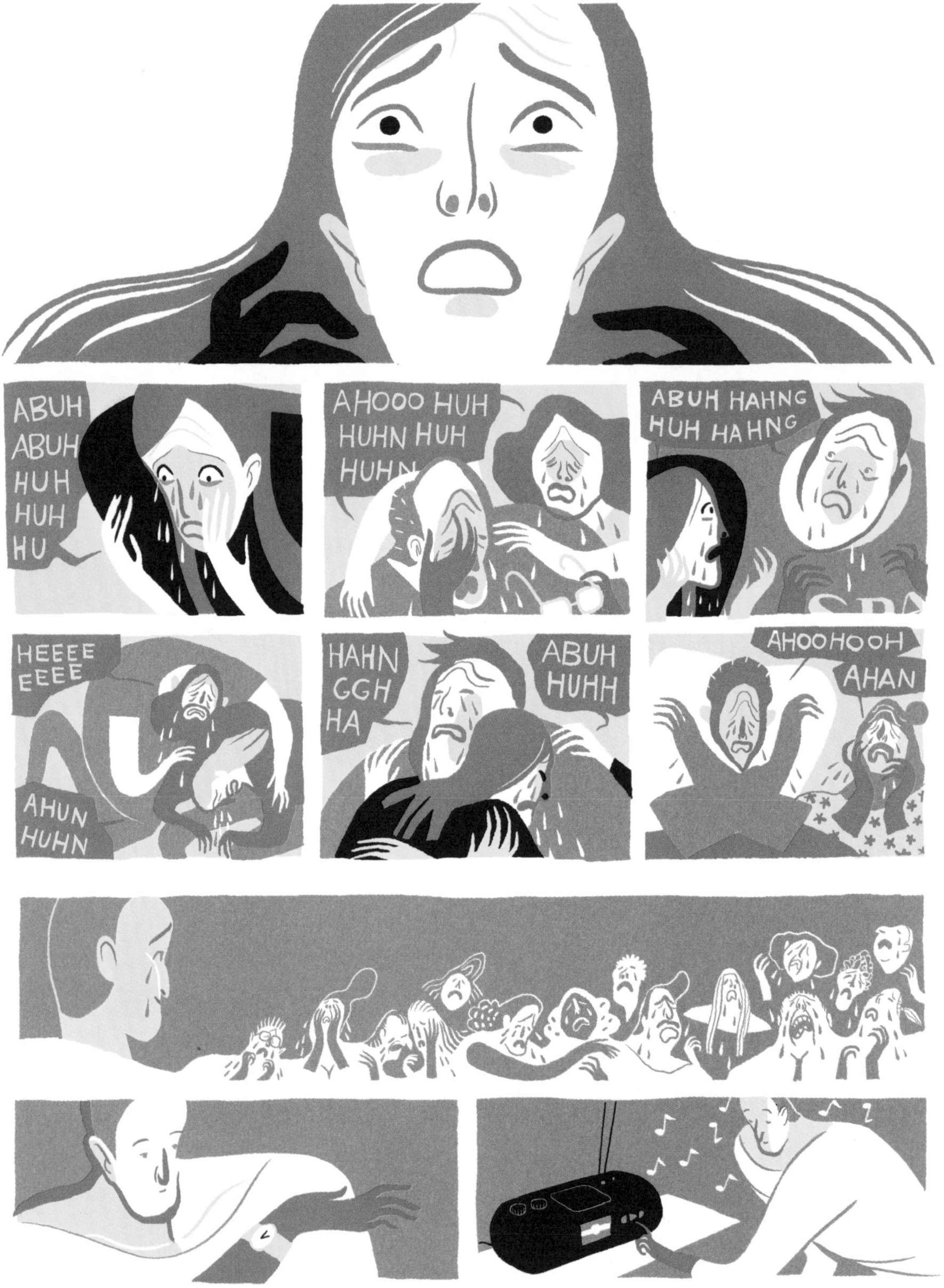
ABUH ABUH HUH HUH HU
AHOOO HUH HUHN HUH HUHN
ABUH HAHNG HUH HAHNG
HEEEE EEEE
AHUN HUHN
HAHN GGH HA
ABUH HUHH
AHOOHOOH
AHAN

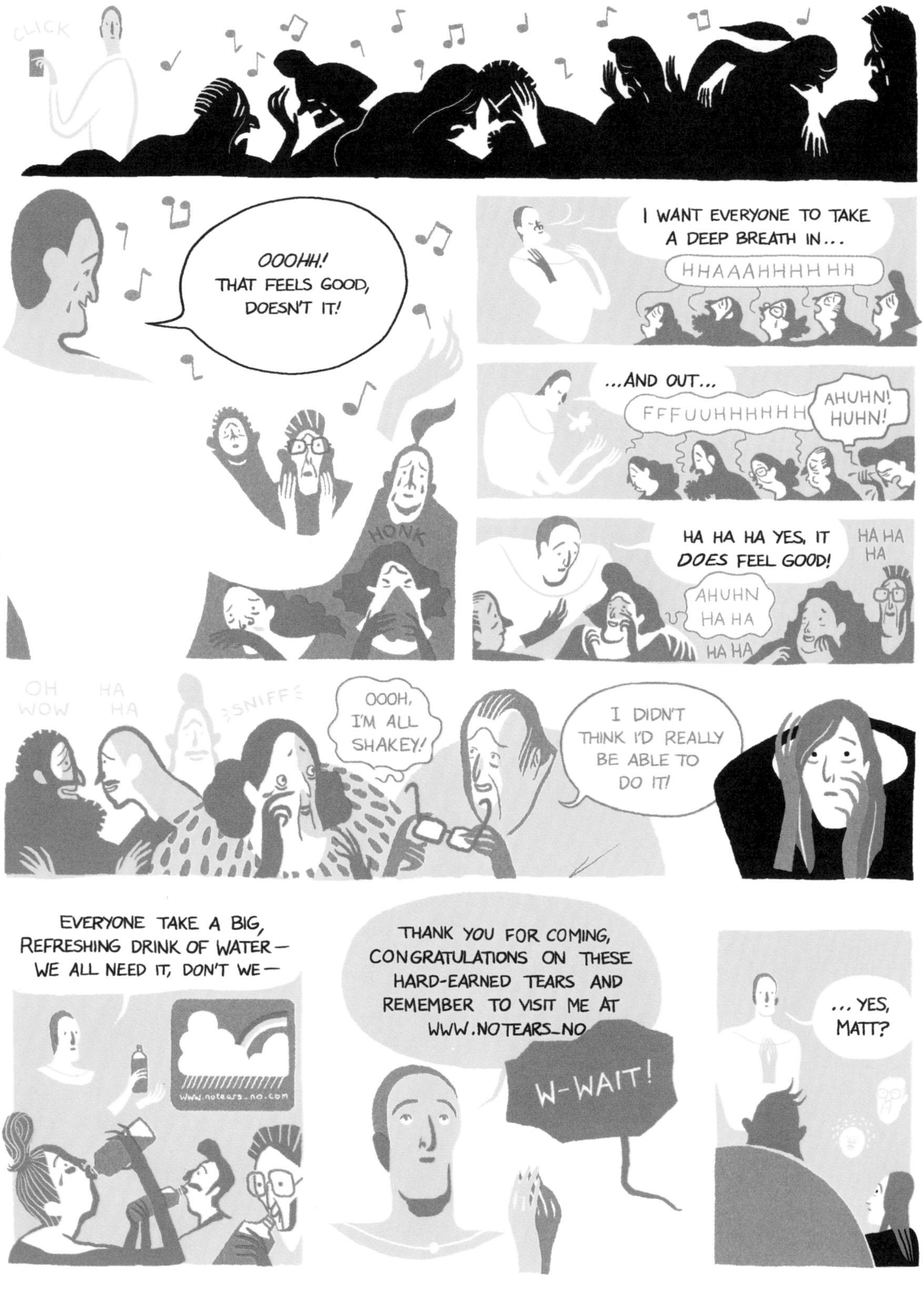

CLICK
OOOHH! THAT FEELS GOOD, DOESN'T IT!
I WANT EVERYONE TO TAKE A DEEP BREATH IN...
HHAAAHHHHHH
HONK
...AND OUT...
FFFUUHHHHHH
AHUHN! HUHN!
HA HA HA YES, IT DOES FEEL GOOD!
HA HA HA
AHUHN HA HA
HA HA
OH WOW
HA HA
SNIFF
OOOH, I'M ALL SHAKEY!
I DIDN'T THINK I'D REALLY BE ABLE TO DO IT!
EVERYONE TAKE A BIG, REFRESHING DRINK OF WATER— WE ALL NEED IT, DON'T WE—
www.notears_no.com
THANK YOU FOR COMING, CONGRATULATIONS ON THESE HARD-EARNED TEARS AND REMEMBER TO VISIT ME AT WWW.NOTEARS_NO
W-WAIT!
...YES, MATT?

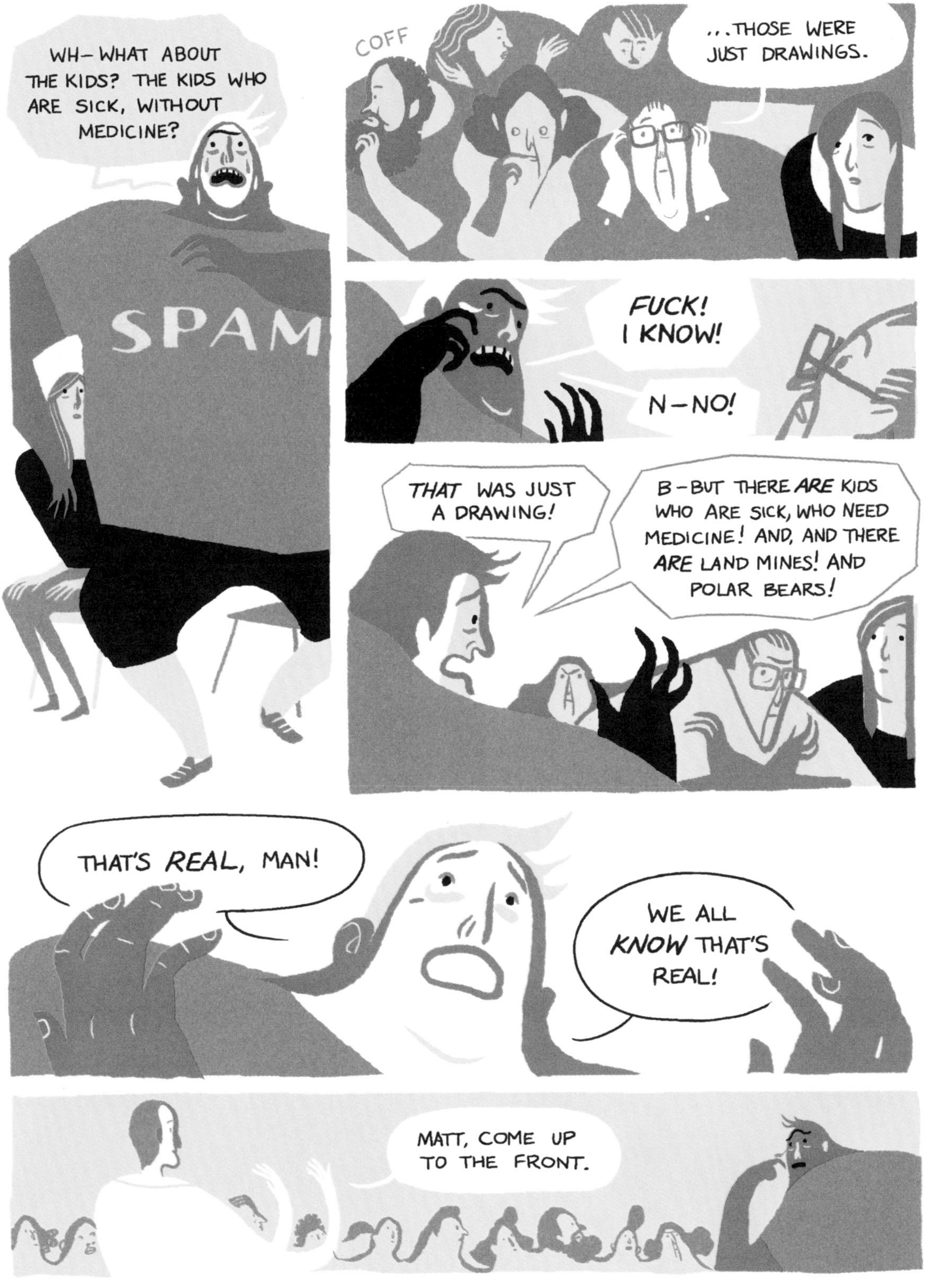
WH-WHAT ABOUT THE KIDS? THE KIDS WHO ARE SICK, WITHOUT MEDICINE?
COFF
...THOSE WERE JUST DRAWINGS.
FUCK! I KNOW!
N-NO!
THAT WAS JUST A DRAWING!
B-BUT THERE ARE KIDS WHO ARE SICK, WHO NEED MEDICINE! AND, AND THERE ARE LAND MINES! AND POLAR BEARS!
SPAM
THAT'S REAL, MAN!
WE ALL KNOW THAT'S REAL!
MATT, COME UP TO THE FRONT.

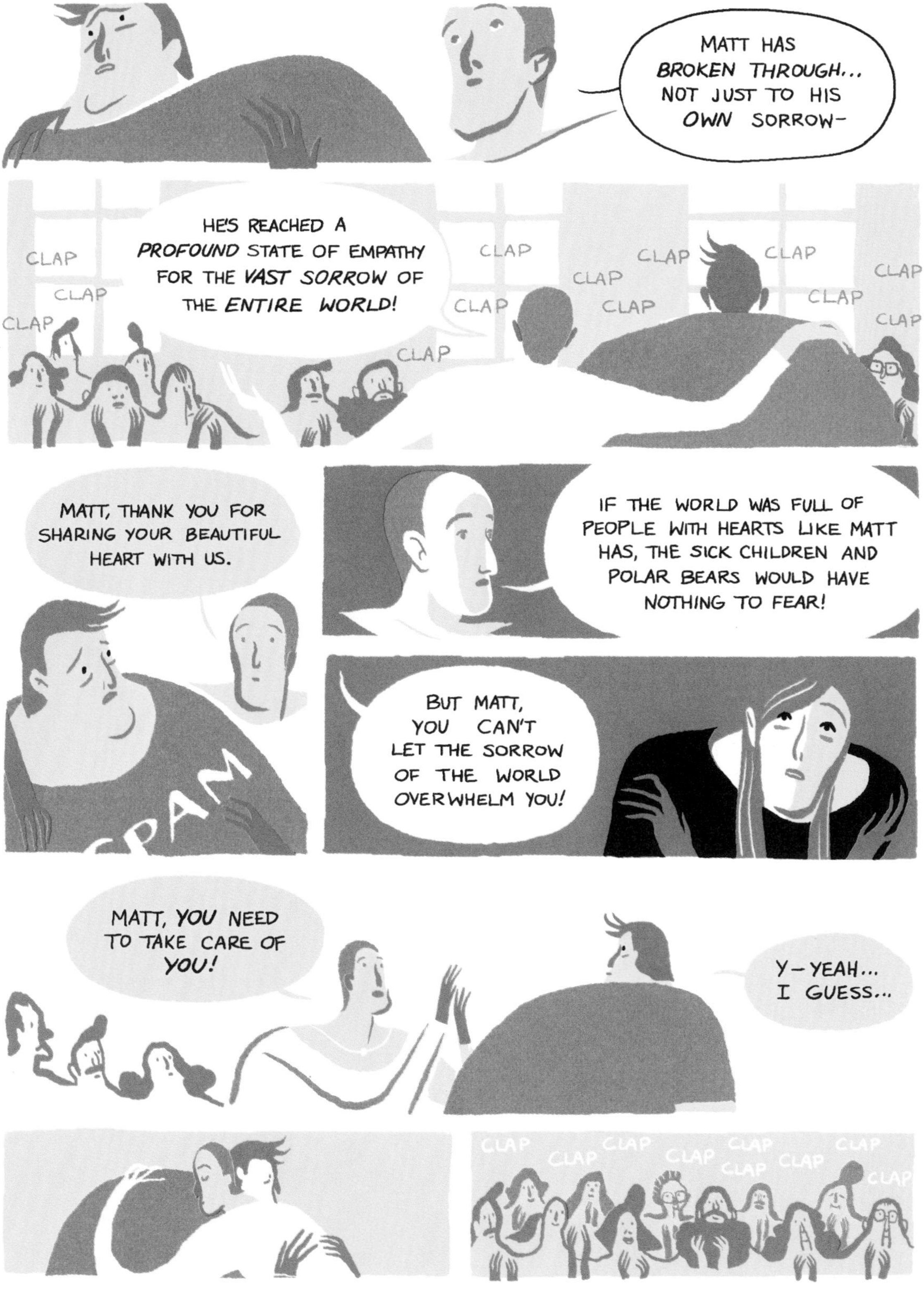
MATT HAS BROKEN THROUGH... NOT JUST TO HIS OWN SORROW-
HE'S REACHED A PROFOUND STATE OF EMPATHY FOR THE VAST SORROW OF THE ENTIRE WORLD!
CLAP CLAP CLAP CLAP CLAP CLAP CLAP CLAP CLAP CLAP CLAP CLAP
MATT, THANK YOU FOR SHARING YOUR BEAUTIFUL HEART WITH US.
IF THE WORLD WAS FULL OF PEOPLE WITH HEARTS LIKE MATT HAS, THE SICK CHILDREN AND POLAR BEARS WOULD HAVE NOTHING TO FEAR!
BUT MATT, YOU CAN'T LET THE SORROW OF THE WORLD OVERWHELM YOU!
MATT, YOU NEED TO TAKE CARE OF YOU!
Y-YEAH... I GUESS...
CLAP CLAP CLAP CLAP CLAP CLAP CLAP CLAP CLAP

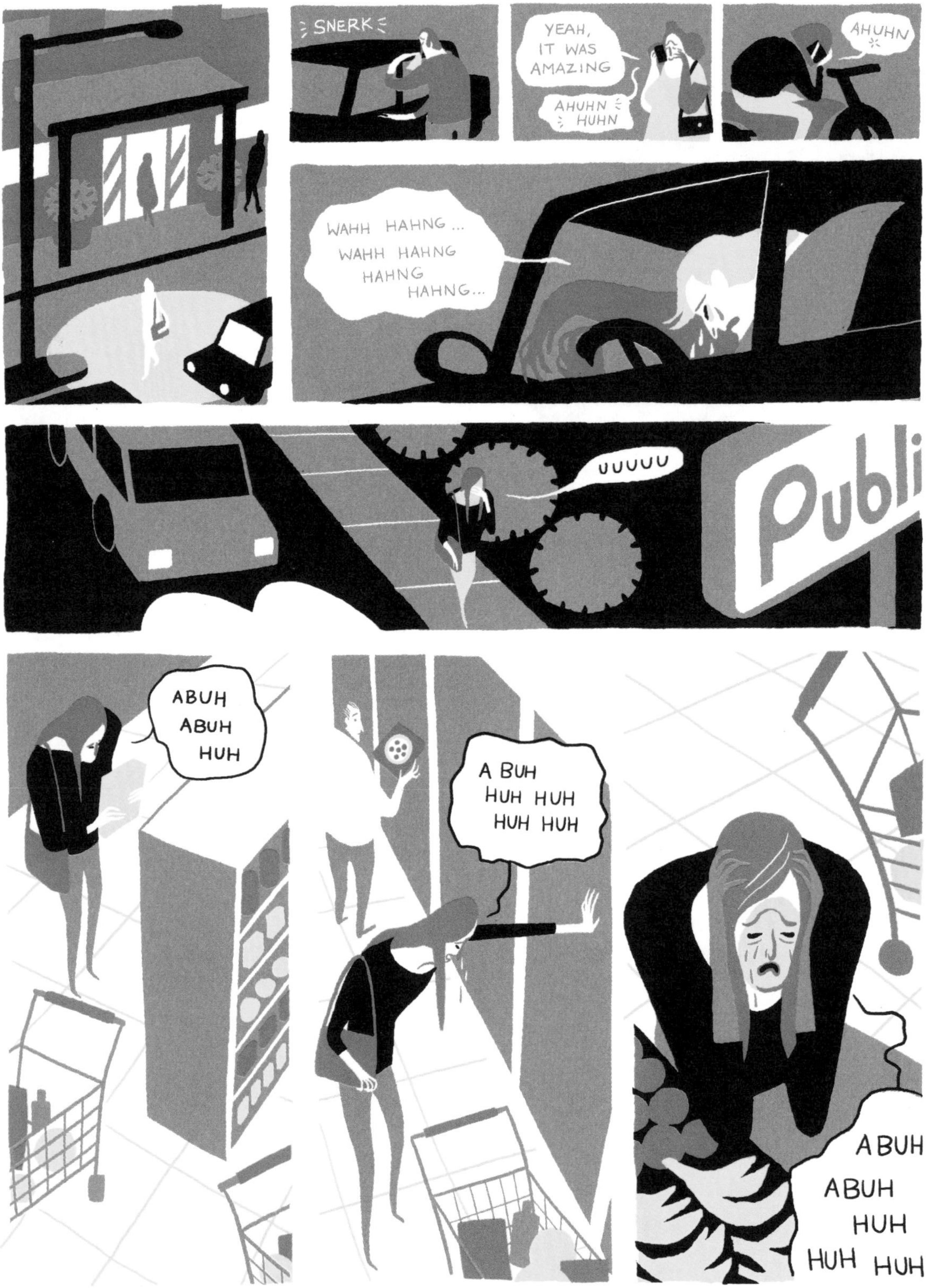
SNERK
YEAH, IT WAS AMAZING
AHUHN HUHN
AHUHN
WAHH HAHNG... WAHH HAHNG HAHNG HAHNG...
UUUUU
Publi
ABUH ABUH HUH
A BUH HUH HUH HUH HUH
ABUH ABUH HUH HUH HUH

ROSE
TO: ROSE
SUBJECT TO ROSE TO
ROSE TO:
ROSE

ROSE HEY ROSE HEY HOW ARE YOU ROSE ARE YOU SUBJECT ROSE ARE YOU DOING SUBJECT

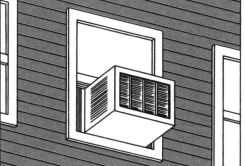

RECENTLY THERE WAS THIS TIME RECENTLY THERE WAS THIS RECENT TIME LAST NIGHT I WENT OUT LAST NIGHT LET ME START OVER I WAS OUT LAST NIGHT WHILE I WAS OUT I DID SOMETHING I DID NOT WANT TO DO I MEAN I DID SOMETHING I INITIALLY WANTED TO DO SO I DID BUT AFTER DOING SO I REGRETTED MY DECISION MY DECISION TO DESIRE FIRST TO DESIRE A HAIRY NAVEL TO ORDERING ONE SECOND TO THIRD SORRY THE BAR POLICY IS NO SORRY THE BAR POLICY IS NOT TO SERVE DRINKS NOT LISTED ON THE BAR DRINK LIST ONLY DRINKS LISTED FROM THE DRINK LIST OF THE BAR ONLY BAR DRINKS FROM THE BAR LIST THE BARTENDER CAN MAKE A FUZZY NAVEL INSTEAD OF FOURTH SORRY NO SORRY YOU CAN ADD NO VODKA THE BAR DRINK LIST IS PRICE FIXED

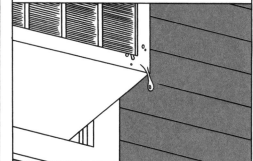

WE CAN CALL WHERE I WAS LAST NIGHT A CLUB SHALL I CALL IT A CLUB NO IT WAS MORE LIKE A BAR MORE LIKE A BIG BAR NO MEMBERS IT HAD NO MEMBERS THERE WAS NO MEMBERSHIP NO SIGNING UP AS A MEMBER AT A CLUB WITH NO MEMBERS ALONE I CAME ALL BY MYSELF WITH NO HELP WITH NO ASSISTANCE AT THE CLUB I DID NOT MEET ANYONE OR REQUIRE ANY ASSISTANCE AT THE CLUB DID NOT TRY TO MEET SOMEONE WHILE AT THE CLUB ALL BY MYSELF AT THE CLUB WITH NO DRINK

OUTSIDE TO SMOKE I WENT OUTSIDE TO SMOKE OUTSIDE WITH THE SMOKERS TO LEAN WITH THE SMOKERS TO LEAN ON A WALL AND NOT BORROW A CIGARETTE TO SMOKE TO LEAN ON A WALL AND SMOKE WITH OTHER SMOKERS SMOKING TO NOT TALK AND TO SMOKE OR LEAVE TO LEAVE THE SMOKERS TO LEAVE THE SMOKERS TO HAVE LEFT THE SMOKERS TO GO HOME WHERE I SLEEP WHERE I AM NOT OUTSIDE NOT OUTSIDE LIKE TREES OUTSIDE LIKE A FRONT LAWN INSIDE NOT SMOKING

NOW I AM ALONE ALSO I AM ALONE AT MY APARTMENT NOT THE CLUB MY RESIDENCE INSIDE MY PLACE WITH MY FAVORITE POSTERS ALL ON THE WALLS ARE MY FAVORITE POSTERS WHICH I PAID FOR EXCEPT THE ONE I FOUND IT IS ON MY WALL POSTERS ON THE WALL I GAZE UPON MY COVETED VERTICAL HANGING ORNAMENTS WHILE ON MY LAPTOP I AM INSPECTING MY WALLS AND I AM EMAILING YOU MY POSTERS MY WALLS

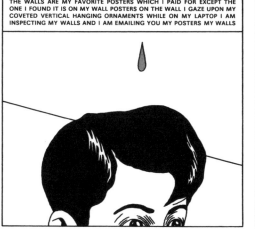

WITH MY LAPTOP WITH MY LAPTOP ON MY LAP WITH MY LAPTOP ALONE ON MY LAP MY LONE LAPTOP IS THE ONLY OBJECT ON MY LAP WE ARE BY OURSELVES MY LAPTOP AND I IS YOUR LAPTOP ON YOUR LAP IS YOUR LAPTOP ON YOUR LAP NOT ON YOUR LAP YOU MIGHT NOT BE ALONE WITH YOUR LAPTOP ALONE WITH YOUR LAPTOP ALONE ON YOUR LAP YOU MIGHT BE WITH FRIENDS THERE MIGHT BE A PILLOW ON YOUR LAP

PROBABLY LAPTOP ON YOUR LAP YOUR FRIENDS ALONE WITH FRIENDS OR YOUR FRIENDS ALONE YOUR FRIENDS LAPTOP YOUR FRIENDS ALONE WITH ME WITH YOU OR YOUR FRIENDS ALONE WITH EACH OTHERS LAPTOPS OR THEIR OWN LAPTOPS ON THEIR LAPS AND ME ALONE WITH OUR LAPTOPS ON EACH OTHERS LAPS LAPTOP ON YOUR LAP   LAP   FUCK

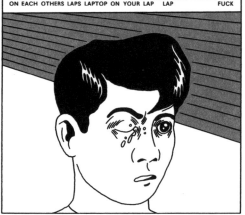

WATER COLD WATER NO COLD WATER EYELASH PROTECTION NO WARM EYELID EYE PROTECTION FROM WATER NO NOT PROTECTED NOW HIM HE IS THIS MAN HE IS THIS MAN THAT IS A MAN THIS MAN WILL SEE THIS

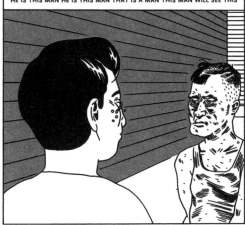

THIS DROP A CRY THE CRYING DOES HE THINK I AM OR WAS CRYING DOES HE THINK THIS WATER IS A TEAR DOES HE THINK I AM CRYING A TEAR DOES HE THINK I AM CRYING A TEAR DOES HE THINK CRYING WAS CAUSED BY A THING A MAN WOULD NOT CRY TEARS TO NOT ONE OR ANOTHER TEAR TO A THING NOT REQUIRING TEARS FROM A MAN

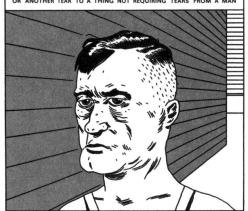

FEELING I DO NOT LIKE THIS FEELING I DO NOT CARE FOR THIS FEELING FOR FEELING THIS FEELING THAT IS LIKE I AM SUPPOSED TO CRY TEARS OVER A THING NOT WARRANTING TEARS A PRESENTATION OF TEARS THAT I HAVE CRIED IN FRONT OF THIS MAN WITH MY TEARS OUT

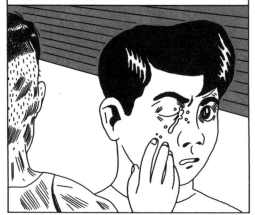

A LONG TIME AGO A TIME NOT REALLY THAT LONG AGO ANOTHER TIME ANOTHER MAN WHO WAS NOT THE MAN WITH MY TEARS IN HIS MIND THIS OTHER MAN DID NOT HAVE HIS DOG ON A LEASH HIS MAN OWNED DOG WAS UNLEASHED A SMALL DOG BUT UNLEASHED SHOULD BE OR SHOULD HAVE BEEN LEASHED IN A SPORTING WAY IN THE AREA WHERE WE WERE WHICH WAS ON THE SIDEWALK OR STREET NO SIDEWALK

THE DOG OF THE MAN UNLEASHED THE MAN AND HIS SMALL DOG WITHOUT A LEASH NOT A SMALL LEASH EVEN A SMALL DOG A NORMAL MAN OF ACCEPTABLE SIZE WITH AN UNLEASHED DOG THAT MOVES AT ME FAST ON THE SIDEWALK THE DOG MOVES FAST AT ME SO I SHOUT WHEN THIS DOG ADVANCEMENT OCCURS THE ADVANCEMENT OF THE DOG TO MY GRID OR SECTION OF THE SIDEWALK MY LOCATION

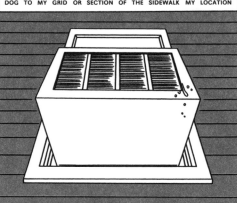

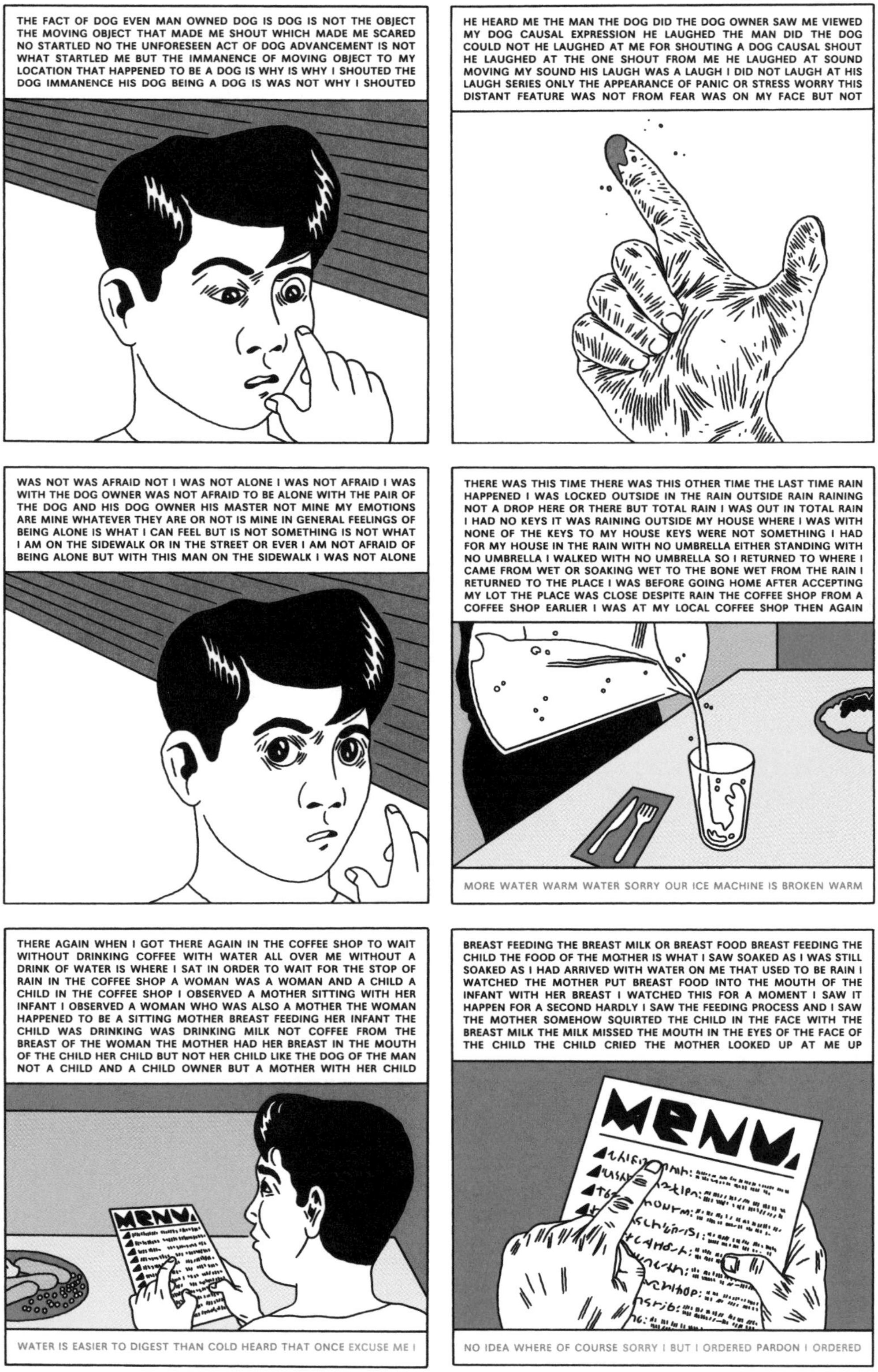
THE FACT OF DOG EVEN MAN OWNED DOG IS DOG IS NOT THE OBJECT THE MOVING OBJECT THAT MADE ME SHOUT WHICH MADE ME SCARED NO STARTLED NO THE UNFORESEEN ACT OF DOG ADVANCEMENT IS NOT WHAT STARTLED ME BUT THE IMMANENCE OF MOVING OBJECT TO MY LOCATION THAT HAPPENED TO BE A DOG IS WHY IS WHY I SHOUTED THE DOG IMMANENCE HIS DOG BEING A DOG IS WAS NOT WHY I SHOUTED
HE HEARD ME THE MAN THE DOG DID THE DOG OWNER SAW ME VIEWED MY DOG CAUSAL EXPRESSION HE LAUGHED THE MAN DID THE DOG COULD NOT HE LAUGHED AT ME FOR SHOUTING A DOG CAUSAL SHOUT HE LAUGHED AT THE ONE SHOUT FROM ME HE LAUGHED AT SOUND MOVING MY SOUND HIS LAUGH WAS A LAUGH I DID NOT LAUGH AT HIS LAUGH SERIES ONLY THE APPEARANCE OF PANIC OR STRESS WORRY THIS DISTANT FEATURE WAS NOT FROM FEAR WAS ON MY FACE BUT NOT
WAS NOT WAS AFRAID NOT I WAS NOT ALONE I WAS NOT AFRAID I WAS WITH THE DOG OWNER WAS NOT AFRAID TO BE ALONE WITH THE PAIR OF THE DOG AND HIS DOG OWNER HIS MASTER NOT MINE MY EMOTIONS ARE MINE WHATEVER THEY ARE OR NOT IS MINE IN GENERAL FEELINGS OF BEING ALONE IS WHAT I CAN FEEL BUT IS NOT SOMETHING IS NOT WHAT I AM ON THE SIDEWALK OR IN THE STREET OR EVER I AM NOT AFRAID OF BEING ALONE BUT WITH THIS MAN ON THE SIDEWALK I WAS NOT ALONE
THERE WAS THIS TIME THERE WAS THIS OTHER TIME THE LAST TIME RAIN HAPPENED I WAS LOCKED OUTSIDE IN THE RAIN OUTSIDE RAIN RAINING NOT A DROP HERE OR THERE BUT TOTAL RAIN I WAS OUT IN TOTAL RAIN I HAD NO KEYS IT WAS RAINING OUTSIDE MY HOUSE WHERE I WAS WITH NONE OF THE KEYS TO MY HOUSE KEYS WERE NOT SOMETHING I HAD FOR MY HOUSE IN THE RAIN WITH NO UMBRELLA EITHER STANDING WITH NO UMBRELLA I WALKED WITH NO UMBRELLA SO I RETURNED TO WHERE I CAME FROM WET OR SOAKING WET TO THE BONE WET FROM THE RAIN I RETURNED TO THE PLACE I WAS BEFORE GOING HOME AFTER ACCEPTING MY LOT THE PLACE WAS CLOSE DESPITE RAIN THE COFFEE SHOP FROM A COFFEE SHOP EARLIER I WAS AT MY LOCAL COFFEE SHOP THEN AGAIN
MORE WATER WARM WATER SORRY OUR ICE MACHINE IS BROKEN WARM
THERE AGAIN WHEN I GOT THERE AGAIN IN THE COFFEE SHOP TO WAIT WITHOUT DRINKING COFFEE WITH WATER ALL OVER ME WITHOUT A DRINK OF WATER IS WHERE I SAT IN ORDER TO WAIT FOR THE STOP OF RAIN IN THE COFFEE SHOP A WOMAN WAS A WOMAN AND A CHILD A CHILD IN THE COFFEE SHOP I OBSERVED A MOTHER SITTING WITH HER INFANT I OBSERVED A WOMAN WHO WAS ALSO A MOTHER THE WOMAN HAPPENED TO BE A SITTING MOTHER BREAST FEEDING HER INFANT THE CHILD WAS DRINKING WAS DRINKING MILK NOT COFFEE FROM THE BREAST OF THE WOMAN THE MOTHER HAD HER BREAST IN THE MOUTH OF THE CHILD HER CHILD BUT NOT HER CHILD LIKE THE DOG OF THE MAN NOT A CHILD AND A CHILD OWNER BUT A MOTHER WITH HER CHILD
MENU
WATER IS EASIER TO DIGEST THAN COLD HEARD THAT ONCE EXCUSE ME I
BREAST FEEDING THE BREAST MILK OR BREAST FOOD BREAST FEEDING THE CHILD THE FOOD OF THE MOTHER IS WHAT I SAW SOAKED AS I WAS STILL SOAKED AS I HAD ARRIVED WITH WATER ON ME THAT USED TO BE RAIN I WATCHED THE MOTHER PUT BREAST FOOD INTO THE MOUTH OF THE INFANT WITH HER BREAST I WATCHED THIS FOR A MOMENT I SAW IT HAPPEN FOR A SECOND HARDLY I SAW THE FEEDING PROCESS AND I SAW THE MOTHER SOMEHOW SQUIRTED THE CHILD IN THE FACE WITH THE BREAST MILK THE MILK MISSED THE MOUTH IN THE EYES OF THE FACE OF THE CHILD THE CHILD CRIED THE MOTHER LOOKED UP AT ME UP
MENU
NO IDEA WHERE OF COURSE SORRY I BUT I ORDERED PARDON I ORDERED

ME FIRST SHE LOOKED UP AT ME FIRST HER INSTINCT WAS TO LOOK UP AT ME WATCHING HER SPILL BEFORE SEEING HOW THE MILK AFFECTED THE CHILD HOW THE WETTED CHILD FELT HER INITIAL REACTION WAS WATCHING ME WATCH THIS BEFORE ASSESSING THE OUTCOME OF THE SPILL I HAD NO REACTION NO NEW FEELING MY FEELING DID NOT WAVER UPON SEEING WHAT I SAW SO MY EXPRESSION DID NOT CHANGE SHE SAW NO CHANGE IN ME SEEING SPILLING ON THE CHILD THE CHILD WET WITH MILK I WAS WET WITH RAIN WE WERE POURED UPON WE WERE DRENCHED MILK WET OR RAIN WET WE WERE WET I FELT THE SAME

THEN IT CHANGED SHE CHANGED HER EXPRESSION WAS DIFFERENT SINCE MINE WAS NOT HER FACE WAS PINCHED HER FEATURES CLOSED AT THE EDGES HER MOUTH FOLDED HER EYES AS CORNERS FORMED A CELLAR I FELT DIFFERENT MY FACE SHOWED SOMETHING ELSE SHE LOOKED DOWN AS A MOTHER I LOOKED DOWN LOOKED DIFFERENT MYSELF NOT LOOKING AT THE EVENT OR THE WET CHILD CRYING STILL RAINING STILL WET STILL

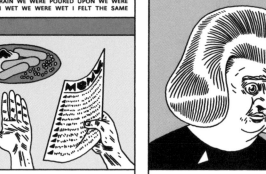

THIS BUT GOT THIS SO HM I NEED TO SWITCH THE I SEE SORRY TO NO

PROBLEM SORRY TO BE A PAIN OR BE NO PROBLEM I CAN SWITCH IT JUST

CRYING A WET SOUND MORE NOTICEABLE THAN TEARS FALLING OUT

LET ME THROW THIS AWAY FIRST THANKS I NO PROBLEM NOT A PROBLEM

WATER IN A CUP I COULD USE A CUP OF WATER SIMPLY A MOUTHFUL OF WATER TO SWALLOW WARM WATER COLD EVEN I HEARD SOMETHING ABOUT A MONK I READ IN A BOOK A ZEN MONK SAYING TO DRINK COLD WATER WHEN DOING SOMETHING WHEN DOING SOMETHING WITH TOO MUCH THOUGHT MAYBE CAUGHT UP IN THINKING ABOUT SOMETHING TOO MUCH OR MAYBE IF A MONK IS DEPRESSED THEY ARE SUPPOSED TO DRINK COLD WATER BECAUSE MONKS ARE NOT SUPPOSED TO USE DRUGS

WHEN MONKS ARE DEPRESSED THEY DRINK COLD WATER INSTEAD OF USING DRUGS OR BUYING THINGS I DO NOT USE DRUGS BUT SOMETIMES I DRINK NOT WATER BUT COFFEE OR ALCOHOL OR TEA MONKS MIGHT DRINK TEA PROBABLY TEA PROBABLY DO NOT BUY THINGS WITH THEIR MONEY I EARN FROM MY JOB MONKS DO NOT EARN MONEY OR SPEND IT

I BUY POSTERS LIKE THE POSTERS I MENTIONED MY FAVORITE IS OF A CAT HANGING IT SAYS HANG IN THERE I RELATE TO THIS NOT SO MUCH SO MUCH BECAUSE I LIKE CATS OR AM NOT HANGING IN THERE BUT THAT THERE WERE SO MANY COPIES OF THIS POSTER AT THE STORE WHERE I BOUGHT IT THERE WERE SO MANY COPIES OF THE SAME POSTER ROSE

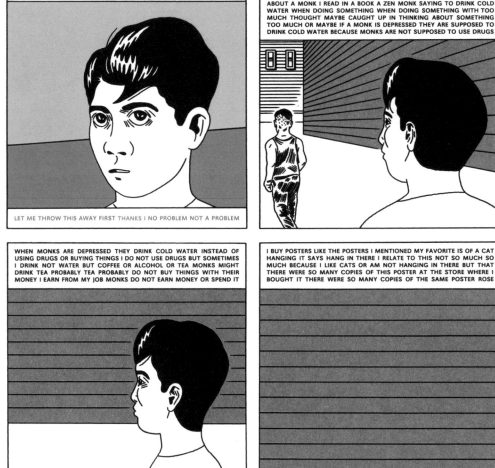

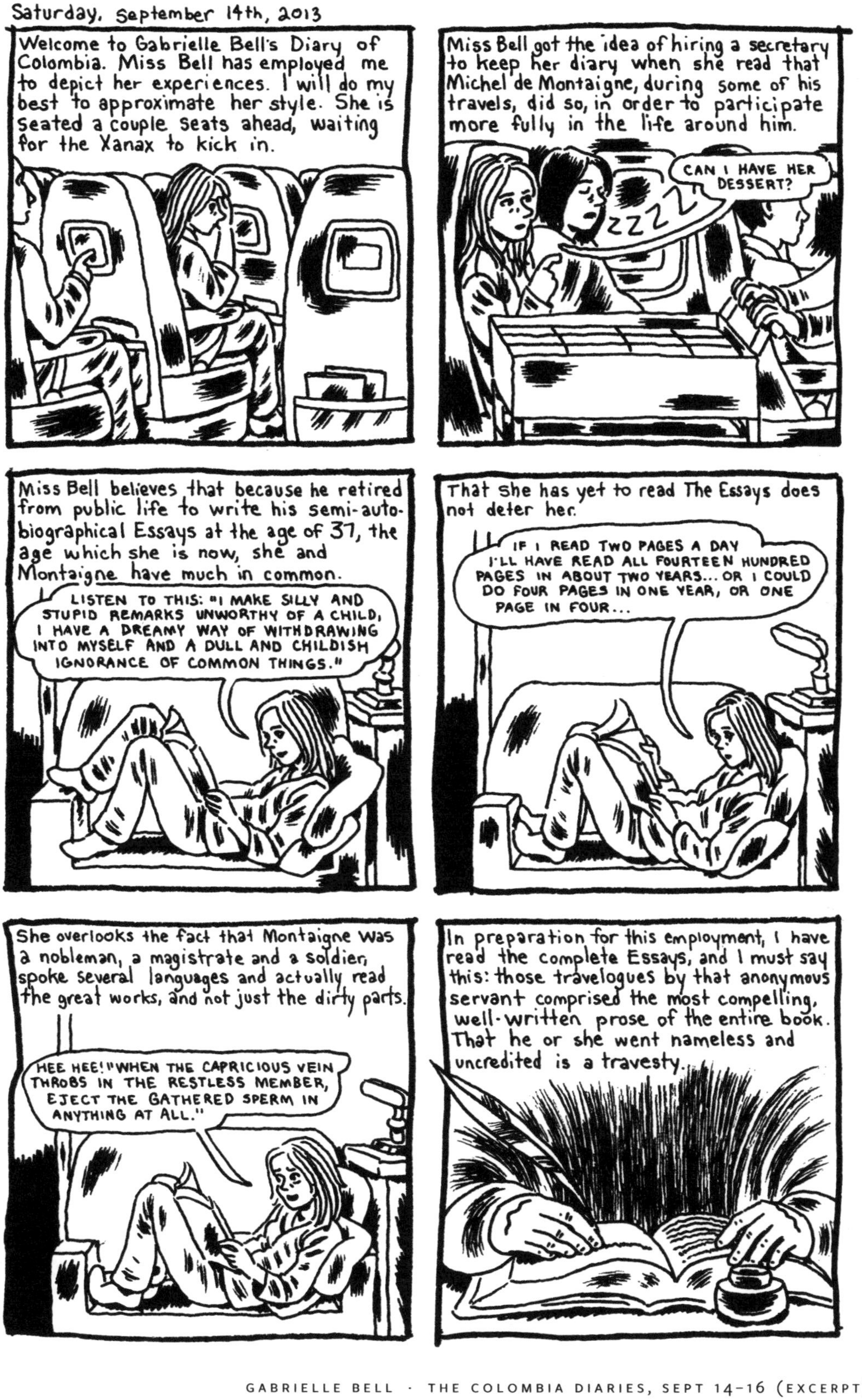
Saturday, september 14th, 2013
Welcome to Gabrielle Bell's Diary of Colombia. Miss Bell has employed me to depict her experiences. I will do my best to approximate her style. She is seated a couple seats ahead, waiting for the Xanax to kick in.
Miss Bell got the idea of hiring a secretary to keep her diary when she read that Michel de Montaigne, during some of his travels, did so, in order to participate more fully in the life around him.
ZZZZ
CAN I HAVE HER DESSERT?
Miss Bell believes that because he retired from public life to write his semi-autobiographical Essays at the age of 37, the age which she is now, she and Montaigne have much in common.
LISTEN TO THIS: "I MAKE SILLY AND STUPID REMARKS UNWORTHY OF A CHILD, I HAVE A DREAMY WAY OF WITHDRAWING INTO MYSELF AND A DULL AND CHILDISH IGNORANCE OF COMMON THINGS."
That she has yet to read The Essays does not deter her.
IF I READ TWO PAGES A DAY I'LL HAVE READ ALL FOURTEEN HUNDRED PAGES IN ABOUT TWO YEARS... OR I COULD DO FOUR PAGES IN ONE YEAR, OR ONE PAGE IN FOUR...
She overlooks the fact that Montaigne was a nobleman, a magistrate and a soldier, spoke several languages and actually read the great works, and not just the dirty parts.
HEE HEE! "WHEN THE CAPRICIOUS VEIN THROBS IN THE RESTLESS MEMBER, EJECT THE GATHERED SPERM IN ANYTHING AT ALL."
In preparation for this employment, I have read the complete Essays, and I must say this: those travelogues by that anonymous servant comprised the most compelling, well-written prose of the entire book. That he or she went nameless and uncredited is a travesty.

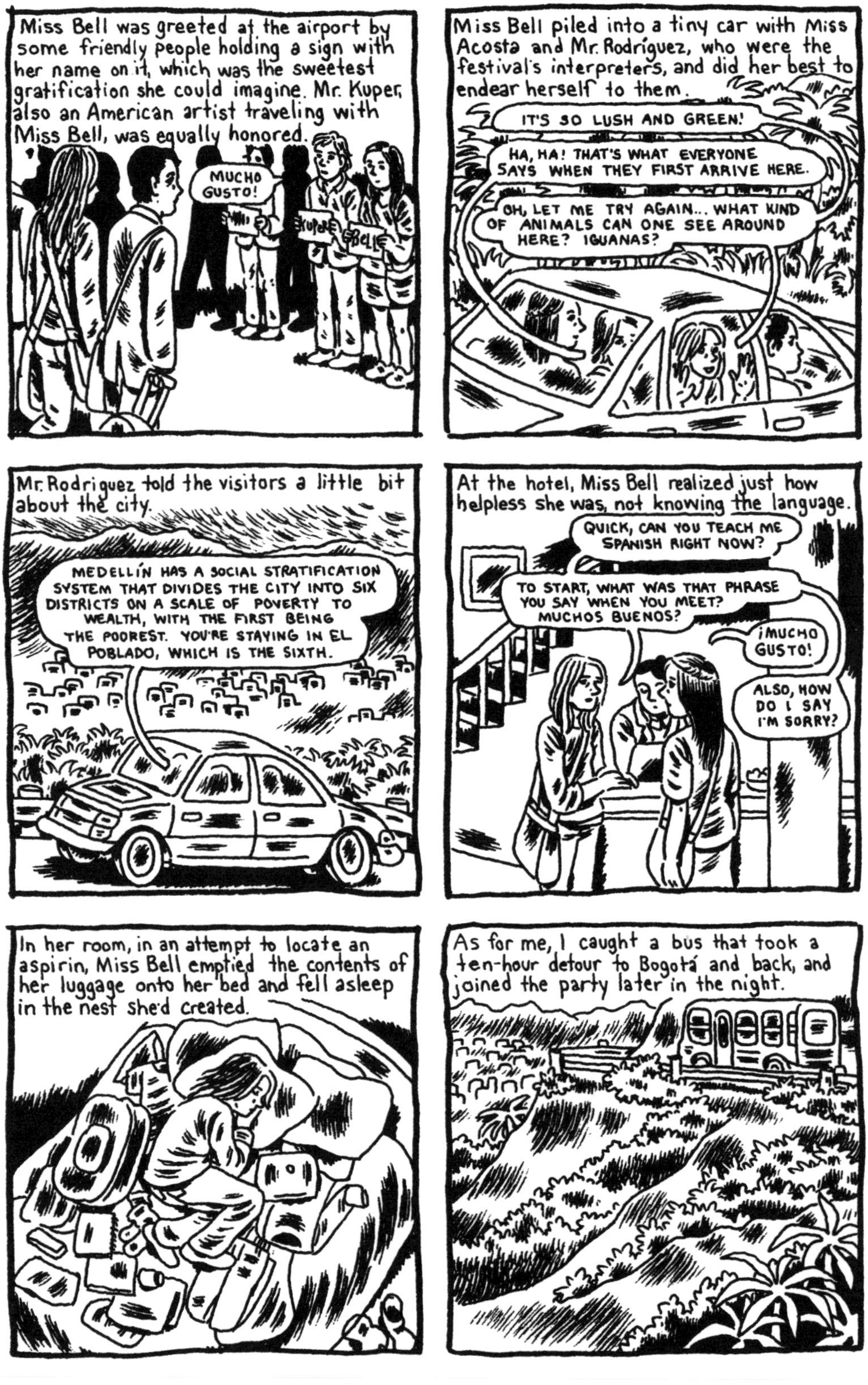
Miss Bell was greeted at the airport by some friendly people holding a sign with her name on it, which was the sweetest gratification she could imagine. Mr. Kuper, also an American artist traveling with Miss Bell, was equally honored.
MUCHO GUSTO!
KUPER
BELL
Miss Bell piled into a tiny car with Miss Acosta and Mr. Rodríguez, who were the festival's interpreters, and did her best to endear herself to them.
IT'S SO LUSH AND GREEN!
HA, HA! THAT'S WHAT EVERYONE SAYS WHEN THEY FIRST ARRIVE HERE.
OH, LET ME TRY AGAIN... WHAT KIND OF ANIMALS CAN ONE SEE AROUND HERE? IGUANAS?
Mr. Rodriguez told the visitors a little bit about the city.
MEDELLÍN HAS A SOCIAL STRATIFICATION SYSTEM THAT DIVIDES THE CITY INTO SIX DISTRICTS ON A SCALE OF POVERTY TO WEALTH, WITH THE FIRST BEING THE POOREST. YOU'RE STAYING IN EL POBLADO, WHICH IS THE SIXTH.
At the hotel, Miss Bell realized just how helpless she was, not knowing the language.
QUICK, CAN YOU TEACH ME SPANISH RIGHT NOW?
TO START, WHAT WAS THAT PHRASE YOU SAY WHEN YOU MEET? MUCHOS BUENOS?
¡MUCHO GUSTO!
ALSO, HOW DO I SAY I'M SORRY?
In her room, in an attempt to locate an aspirin, Miss Bell emptied the contents of her luggage onto her bed and fell asleep in the nest she'd created.
As for me, I caught a bus that took a ten-hour detour to Bogotá and back, and joined the party later in the night.

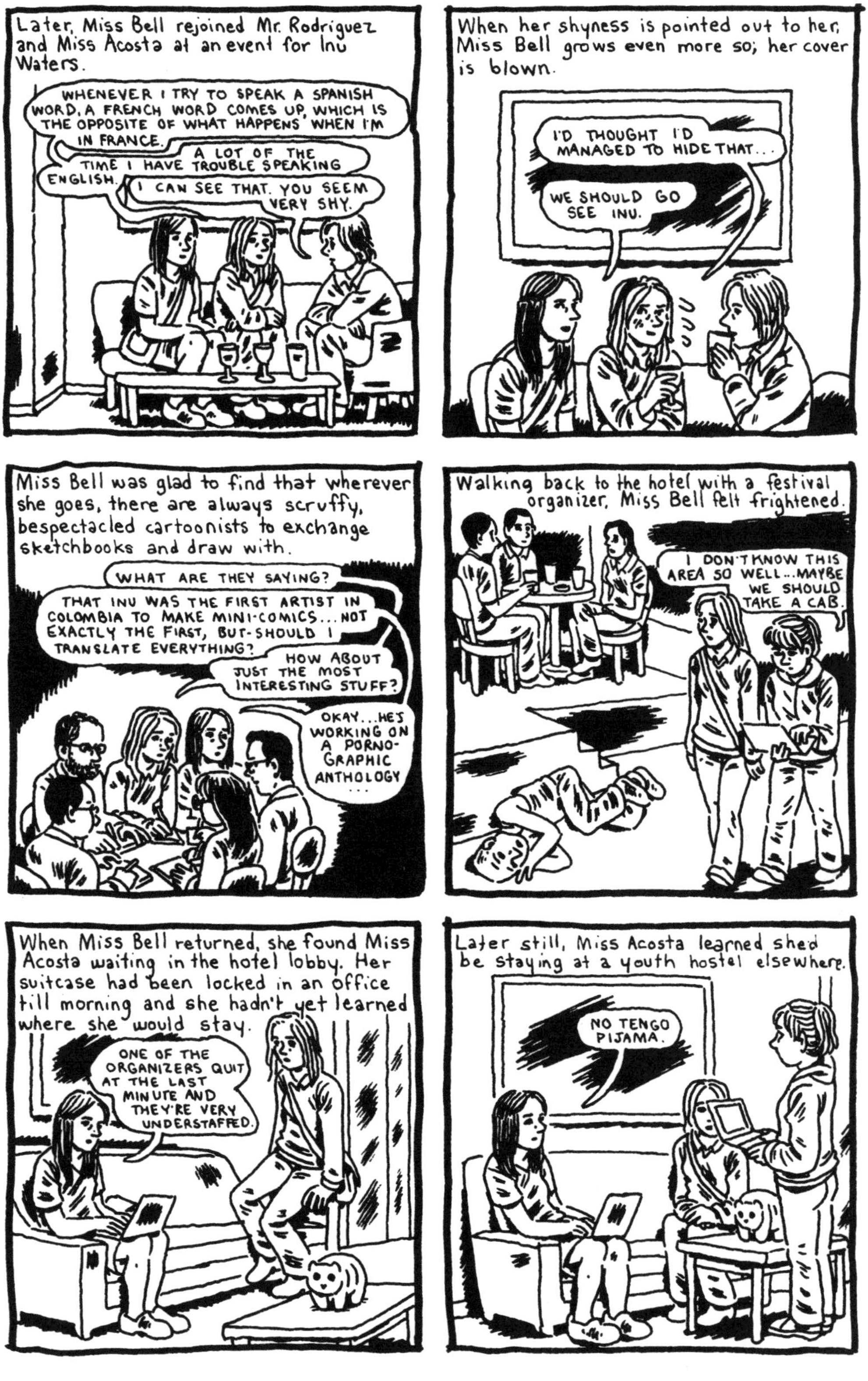

Later, Miss Bell rejoined Mr. Rodriguez and Miss Acosta at an event for Inu Waters.
WHENEVER I TRY TO SPEAK A SPANISH WORD, A FRENCH WORD COMES UP, WHICH IS THE OPPOSITE OF WHAT HAPPENS WHEN I'M IN FRANCE.
A LOT OF THE TIME I HAVE TROUBLE SPEAKING ENGLISH.
I CAN SEE THAT. YOU SEEM VERY SHY.
When her shyness is pointed out to her, Miss Bell grows even more so; her cover is blown.
I'D THOUGHT I'D MANAGED TO HIDE THAT...
WE SHOULD GO SEE INU.
Miss Bell was glad to find that wherever she goes, there are always scruffy, bespectacled cartoonists to exchange sketchbooks and draw with.
WHAT ARE THEY SAYING?
THAT INU WAS THE FIRST ARTIST IN COLOMBIA TO MAKE MINI-COMICS... NOT EXACTLY THE FIRST, BUT-SHOULD I TRANSLATE EVERYTHING?
HOW ABOUT JUST THE MOST INTERESTING STUFF?
OKAY... HE'S WORKING ON A PORNO-GRAPHIC ANTHOLOGY...
Walking back to the hotel with a festival organizer, Miss Bell felt frightened.
I DON'T KNOW THIS AREA SO WELL... MAYBE WE SHOULD TAKE A CAB.
When Miss Bell returned, she found Miss Acosta waiting in the hotel lobby. Her suitcase had been locked in an office till morning and she hadn't yet learned where she would stay.
ONE OF THE ORGANIZERS QUIT AT THE LAST MINUTE AND THEY'RE VERY UNDERSTAFFED.
Later still, Miss Acosta learned she'd be staying at a youth hostel elsewhere.
NO TENGO PIJAMA.

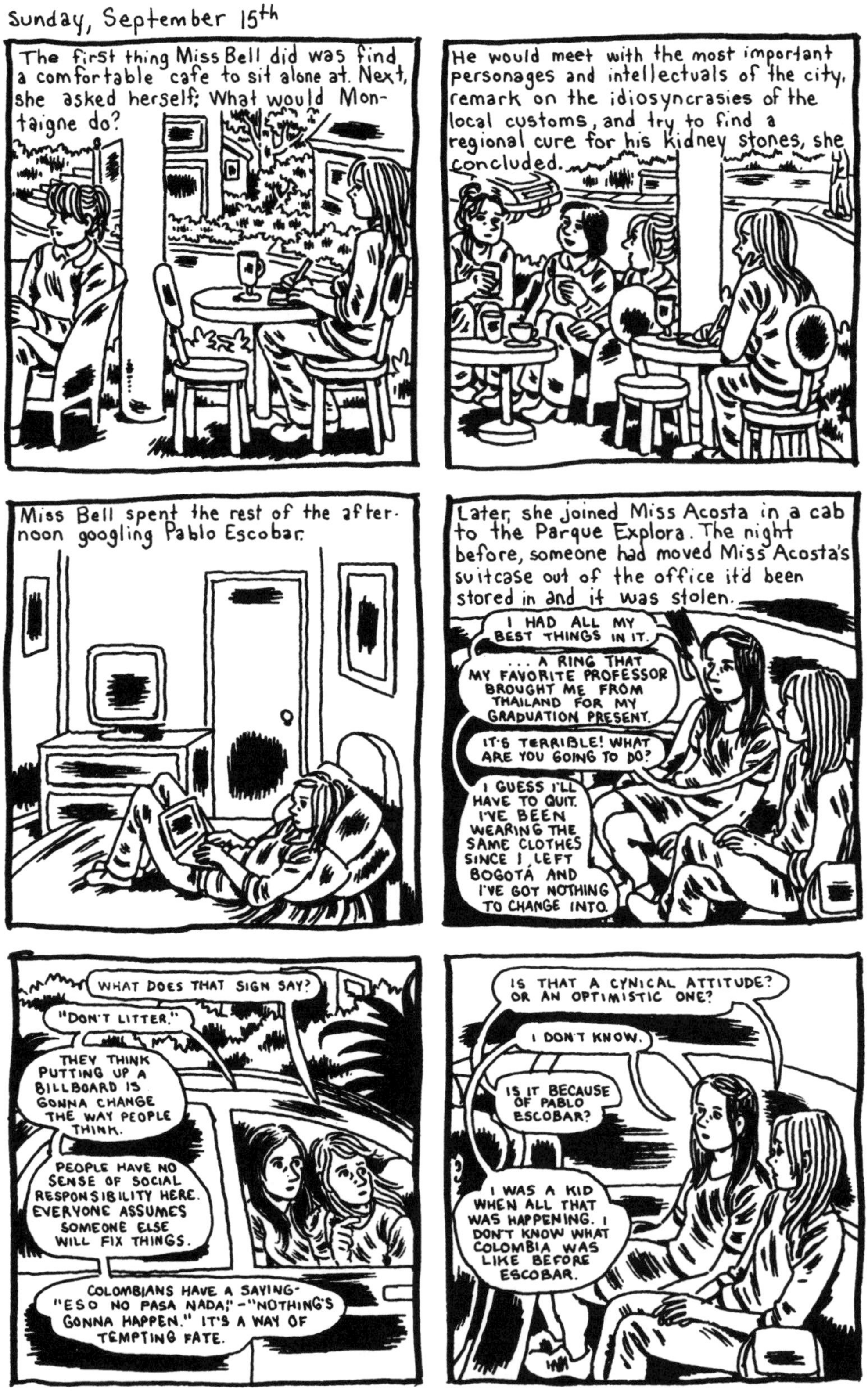
Sunday, September 15th
The first thing Miss Bell did was find a comfortable cafe to sit alone at. Next, she asked herself: What would Montaigne do?
He would meet with the most important personages and intellectuals of the city, remark on the idiosyncrasies of the local customs, and try to find a regional cure for his kidney stones, she concluded.
Miss Bell spent the rest of the afternoon googling Pablo Escobar.
Later, she joined Miss Acosta in a cab to the Parque Explora. The night before, someone had moved Miss Acosta's suitcase out of the office it'd been stored in and it was stolen.
I HAD ALL MY BEST THINGS IN IT.
... A RING THAT MY FAVORITE PROFESSOR BROUGHT ME FROM THAILAND FOR MY GRADUATION PRESENT.
IT'S TERRIBLE! WHAT ARE YOU GOING TO DO?
I GUESS I'LL HAVE TO QUIT. I'VE BEEN WEARING THE SAME CLOTHES SINCE I LEFT BOGOTÁ AND I'VE GOT NOTHING TO CHANGE INTO.
WHAT DOES THAT SIGN SAY?
"DON'T LITTER."
THEY THINK PUTTING UP A BILLBOARD IS GONNA CHANGE THE WAY PEOPLE THINK.
PEOPLE HAVE NO SENSE OF SOCIAL RESPONSIBILITY HERE. EVERYONE ASSUMES SOMEONE ELSE WILL FIX THINGS.
COLOMBIANS HAVE A SAYING- "ESO NO PASA NADA!" - "NOTHING'S GONNA HAPPEN." IT'S A WAY OF TEMPTING FATE.
IS THAT A CYNICAL ATTITUDE? OR AN OPTIMISTIC ONE?
I DON'T KNOW.
IS IT BECAUSE OF PABLO ESCOBAR?
I WAS A KID WHEN ALL THAT WAS HAPPENING. I DON'T KNOW WHAT COLOMBIA WAS LIKE BEFORE ESCOBAR.

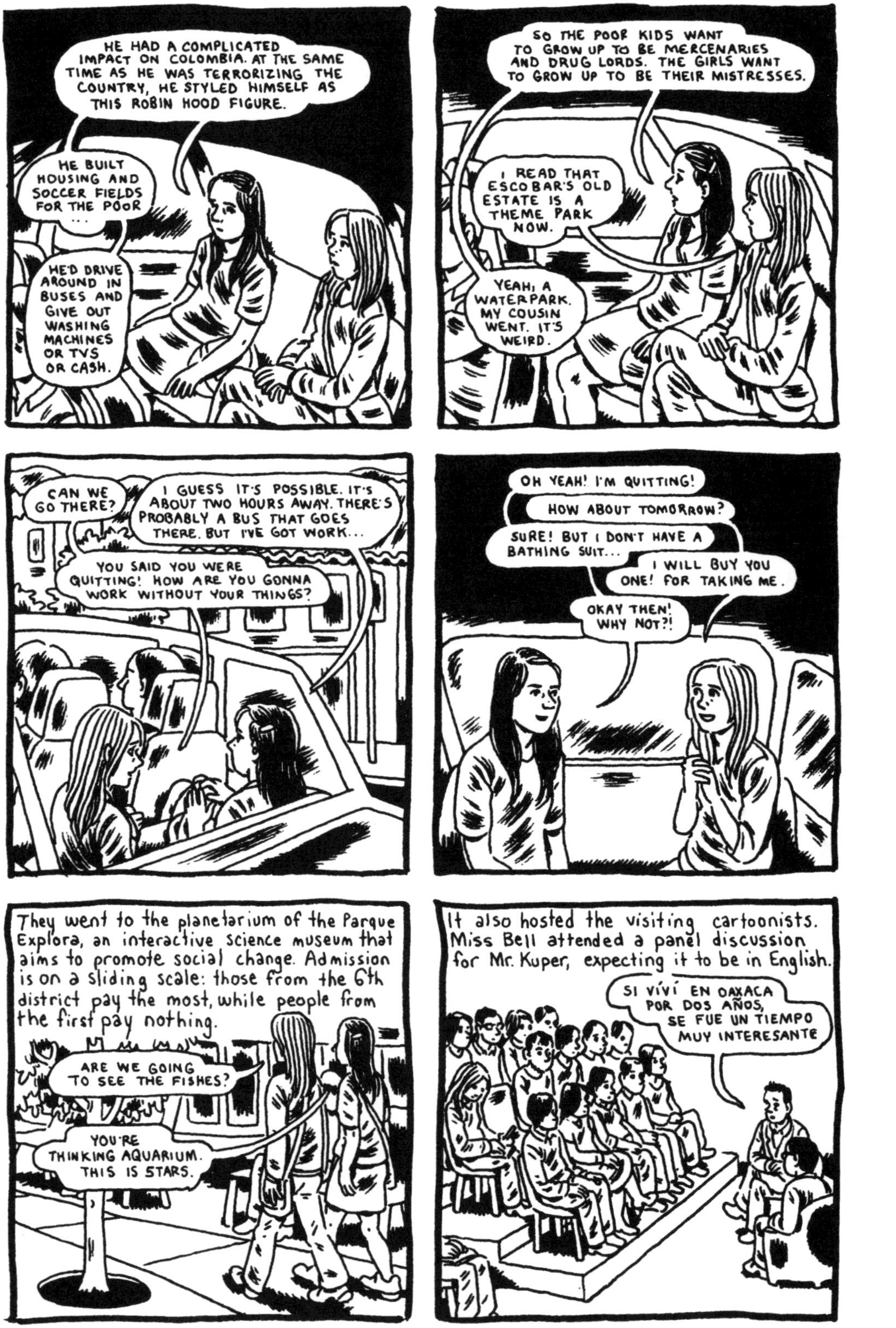

HE HAD A COMPLICATED IMPACT ON COLOMBIA. AT THE SAME TIME AS HE WAS TERRORIZING THE COUNTRY, HE STYLED HIMSELF AS THIS ROBIN HOOD FIGURE.
HE BUILT HOUSING AND SOCCER FIELDS FOR THE POOR ...
HE'D DRIVE AROUND IN BUSES AND GIVE OUT WASHING MACHINES OR TVS OR CASH.
SO THE POOR KIDS WANT TO GROW UP TO BE MERCENARIES AND DRUG LORDS. THE GIRLS WANT TO GROW UP TO BE THEIR MISTRESSES.
I READ THAT ESCOBAR'S OLD ESTATE IS A THEME PARK NOW.
YEAH, A WATERPARK. MY COUSIN WENT. IT'S WEIRD.
CAN WE GO THERE?
I GUESS IT'S POSSIBLE. IT'S ABOUT TWO HOURS AWAY. THERE'S PROBABLY A BUS THAT GOES THERE. BUT I'VE GOT WORK...
YOU SAID YOU WERE QUITTING! HOW ARE YOU GONNA WORK WITHOUT YOUR THINGS?
OH YEAH! I'M QUITTING!
HOW ABOUT TOMORROW?
SURE! BUT I DON'T HAVE A BATHING SUIT...
I WILL BUY YOU ONE! FOR TAKING ME.
OKAY THEN! WHY NOT?!
They went to the planetarium of the Parque Explora, an interactive science museum that aims to promote social change. Admission is on a sliding scale: those from the 6th district pay the most, while people from the first pay nothing.
ARE WE GOING TO SEE THE FISHES?
YOU'RE THINKING AQUARIUM. THIS IS STARS.
It also hosted the visiting cartoonists. Miss Bell attended a panel discussion for Mr. Kuper, expecting it to be in English.
SI VÍVÍ EN OAXACA POR DOS AÑOS, SE FUE UN TIEMPO MUY INTERESANTE

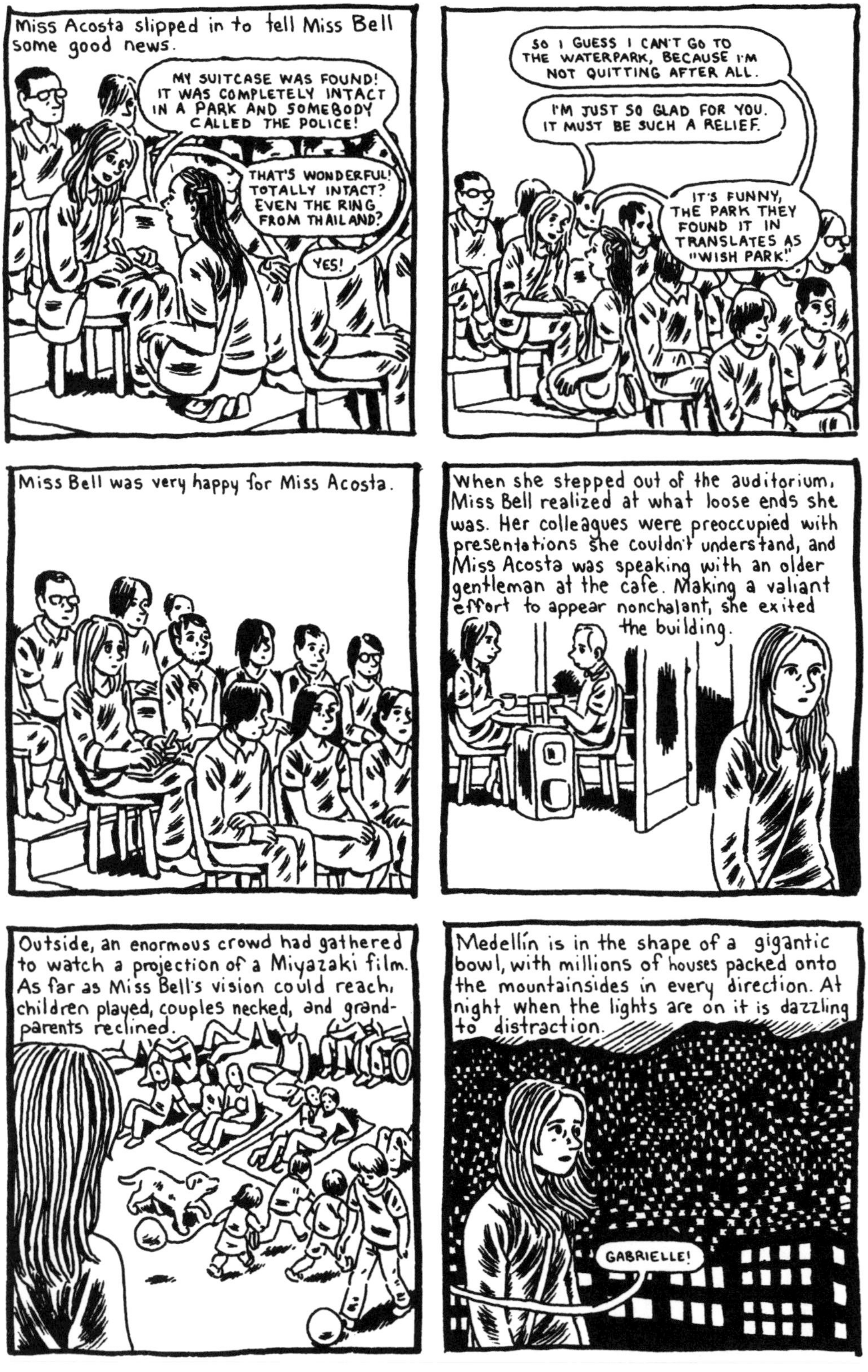
Miss Acosta slipped in to tell Miss Bell some good news.
MY SUITCASE WAS FOUND! IT WAS COMPLETELY INTACT IN A PARK AND SOMEBODY CALLED THE POLICE!
THAT'S WONDERFUL! TOTALLY INTACT? EVEN THE RING FROM THAILAND?
YES!
SO I GUESS I CAN'T GO TO THE WATERPARK, BECAUSE I'M NOT QUITTING AFTER ALL.
I'M JUST SO GLAD FOR YOU. IT MUST BE SUCH A RELIEF.
IT'S FUNNY, THE PARK THEY FOUND IT IN TRANSLATES AS "WISH PARK."
Miss Bell was very happy for Miss Acosta.
When she stepped out of the auditorium, Miss Bell realized at what loose ends she was. Her colleagues were preoccupied with presentations she couldn't understand, and Miss Acosta was speaking with an older gentleman at the cafe. Making a valiant effort to appear nonchalant, she exited the building.
Outside, an enormous crowd had gathered to watch a projection of a Miyazaki film. As far as Miss Bell's vision could reach, children played, couples necked, and grandparents reclined.
Medellín is in the shape of a gigantic bowl, with millions of houses packed onto the mountainsides in every direction. At night when the lights are on it is dazzling to distraction.
GABRIELLE!

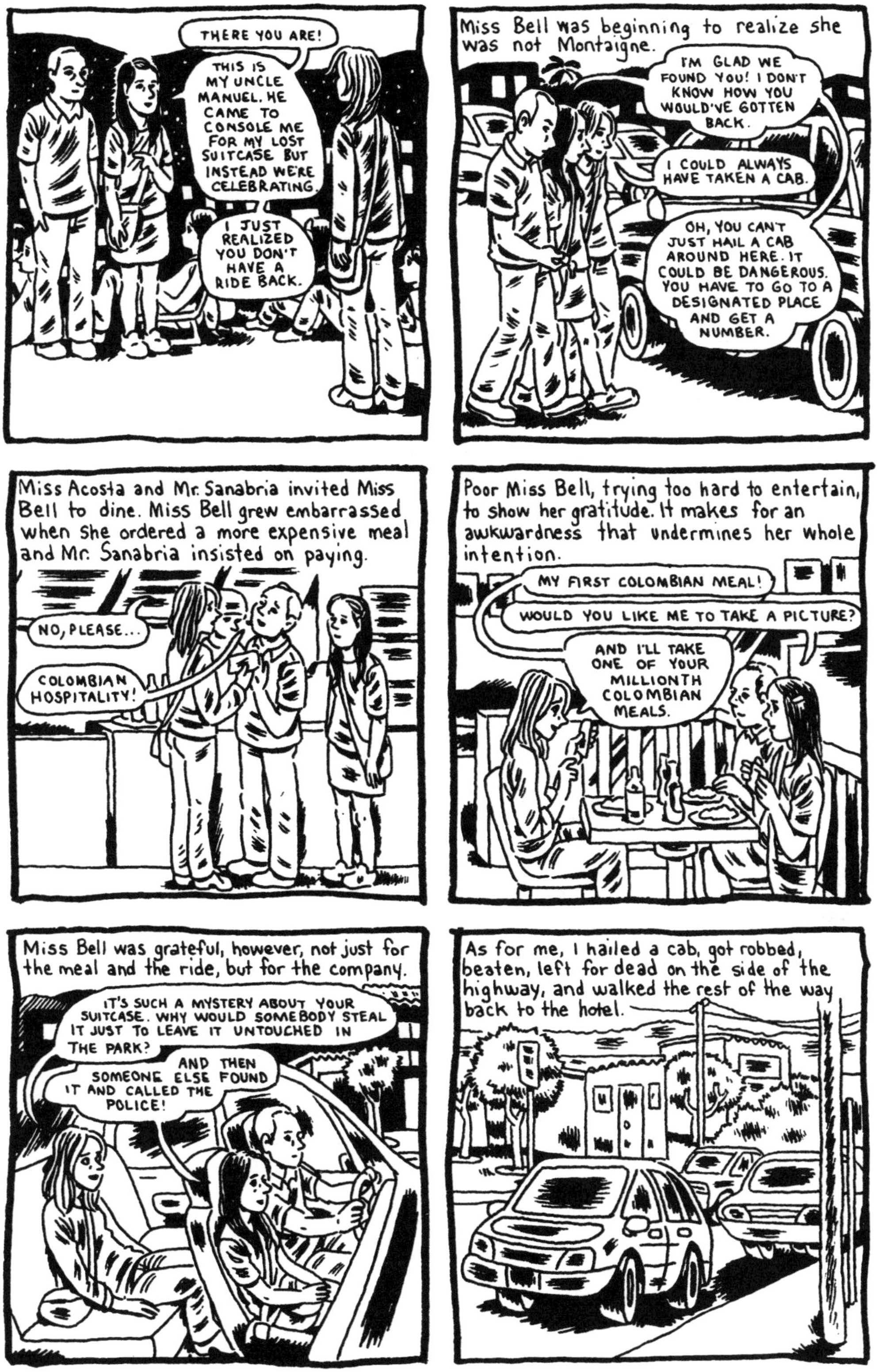
THERE YOU ARE!
THIS IS MY UNCLE MANUEL. HE CAME TO CONSOLE ME FOR MY LOST SUITCASE BUT INSTEAD WE'RE CELEBRATING.
I JUST REALIZED YOU DON'T HAVE A RIDE BACK.
Miss Bell was beginning to realize she was not Montaigne.
I'M GLAD WE FOUND YOU! I DON'T KNOW HOW YOU WOULD'VE GOTTEN BACK.
I COULD ALWAYS HAVE TAKEN A CAB.
OH, YOU CAN'T JUST HAIL A CAB AROUND HERE. IT COULD BE DANGEROUS. YOU HAVE TO GO TO A DESIGNATED PLACE AND GET A NUMBER.
Miss Acosta and Mr. Sanabria invited Miss Bell to dine. Miss Bell grew embarrassed when she ordered a more expensive meal and Mr. Sanabria insisted on paying.
NO, PLEASE...
COLOMBIAN HOSPITALITY!
Poor Miss Bell, trying too hard to entertain, to show her gratitude. It makes for an awkwardness that undermines her whole intention.
MY FIRST COLOMBIAN MEAL!
WOULD YOU LIKE ME TO TAKE A PICTURE?
AND I'LL TAKE ONE OF YOUR MILLIONTH COLOMBIAN MEALS.
Miss Bell was grateful, however, not just for the meal and the ride, but for the company.
IT'S SUCH A MYSTERY ABOUT YOUR SUITCASE. WHY WOULD SOMEBODY STEAL IT JUST TO LEAVE IT UNTOUCHED IN THE PARK?
AND THEN SOMEONE ELSE FOUND IT AND CALLED THE POLICE!
As for me, I hailed a cab, got robbed, beaten, left for dead on the side of the highway, and walked the rest of the way back to the hotel.

Monday, September 16th

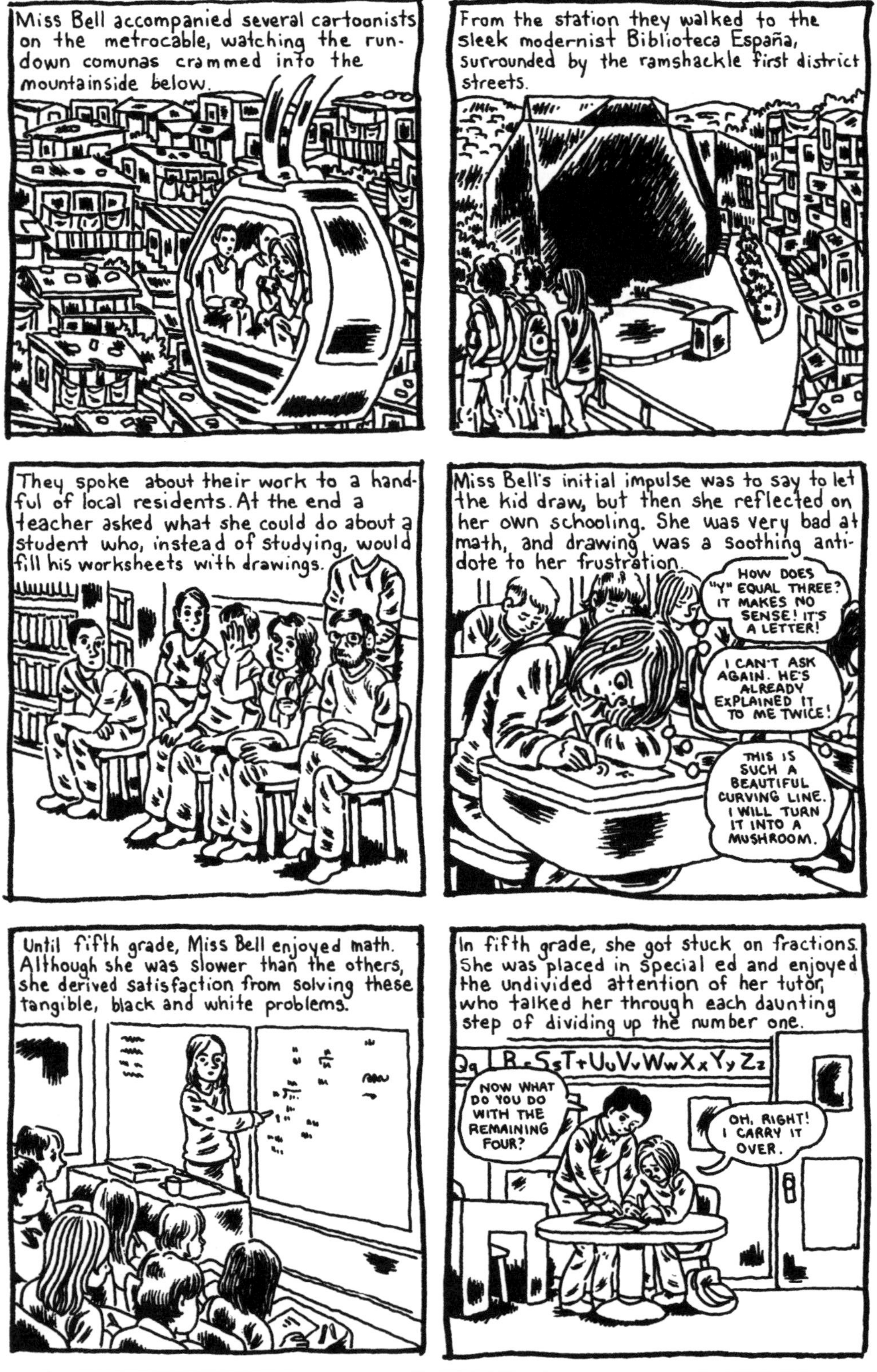
Miss Bell accompanied several cartoonists on the metrocable, watching the run-down comunas crammed into the mountainside below.
From the station they walked to the sleek modernist Biblioteca España, surrounded by the ramshackle first district streets.
They spoke about their work to a handful of local residents. At the end a teacher asked what she could do about a student who, instead of studying, would fill his worksheets with drawings.
Miss Bell's initial impulse was to say to let the kid draw, but then she reflected on her own schooling. She was very bad at math, and drawing was a soothing antidote to her frustration.
HOW DOES "Y" EQUAL THREE? IT MAKES NO SENSE! IT'S A LETTER!
I CAN'T ASK AGAIN. HE'S ALREADY EXPLAINED IT TO ME TWICE!
THIS IS SUCH A BEAUTIFUL CURVING LINE. I WILL TURN IT INTO A MUSHROOM.
Until fifth grade, Miss Bell enjoyed math. Although she was slower than the others, she derived satisfaction from solving these tangible, black and white problems.
In fifth grade, she got stuck on fractions. She was placed in special ed and enjoyed the undivided attention of her tutor, who talked her through each daunting step of dividing up the number one.
Qq R Ss Tt Uu Vv Ww Xx Yy Zz
NOW WHAT DO YOU DO WITH THE REMAINING FOUR?
OH, RIGHT! I CARRY IT OVER.

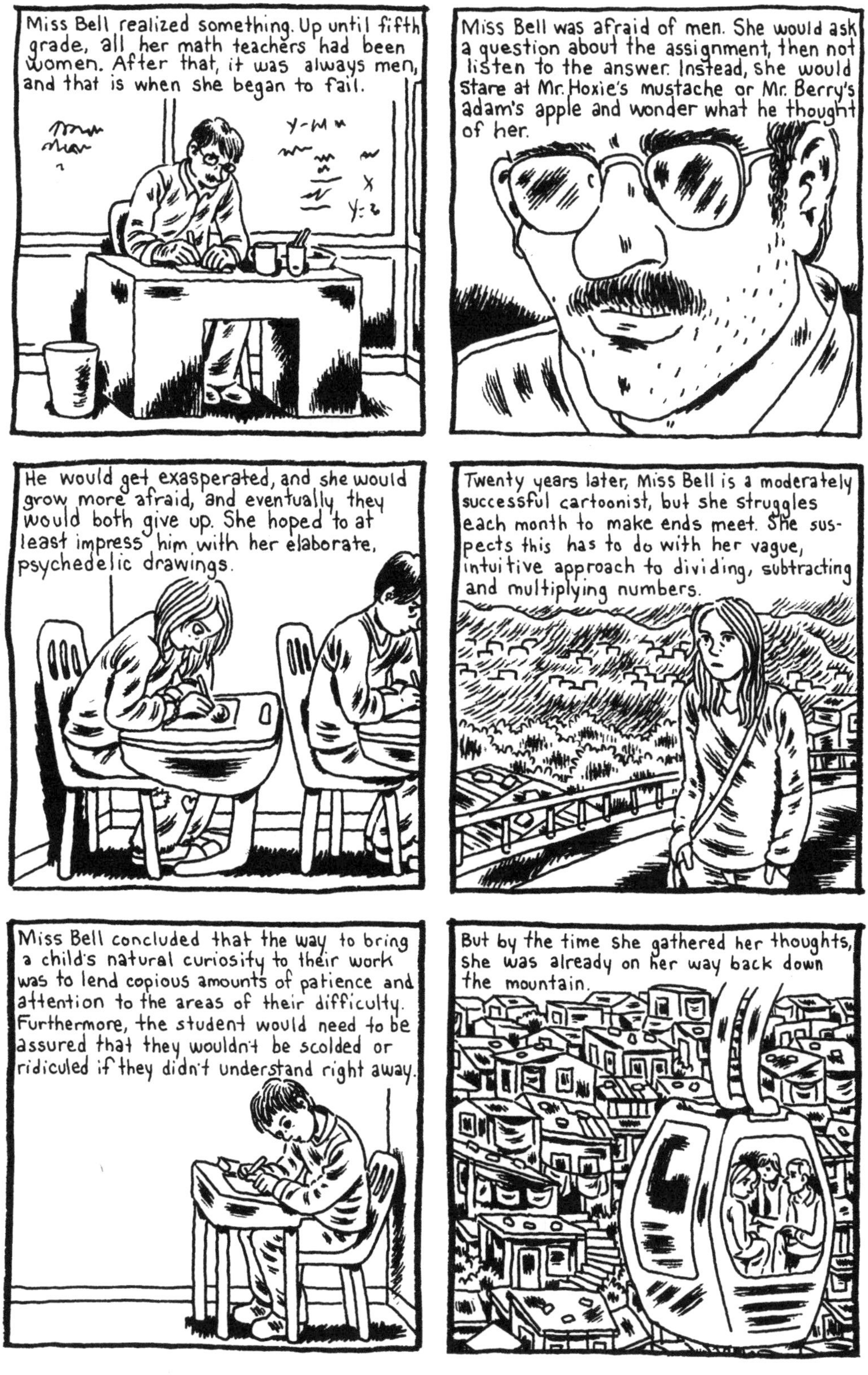
Miss Bell realized something. Up until fifth grade, all her math teachers had been women. After that, it was always men, and that is when she began to fail.
Miss Bell was afraid of men. She would ask a question about the assignment, then not listen to the answer. Instead, she would stare at Mr. Hoxie's mustache or Mr. Berry's adam's apple and wonder what he thought of her.
He would get exasperated, and she would grow more afraid, and eventually they would both give up. She hoped to at least impress him with her elaborate, psychedelic drawings.
Twenty years later, Miss Bell is a moderately successful cartoonist, but she struggles each month to make ends meet. She suspects this has to do with her vague, intuitive approach to dividing, subtracting and multiplying numbers.
Miss Bell concluded that the way to bring a child's natural curiosity to their work was to lend copious amounts of patience and attention to the areas of their difficulty. Furthermore, the student would need to be assured that they wouldn't be scolded or ridiculed if they didn't understand right away.
But by the time she gathered her thoughts, she was already on her way back down the mountain.

CHAPTER FIVE

You Might Even Hang Them on Your Wall

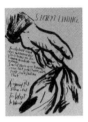

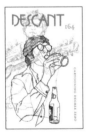

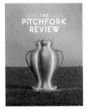

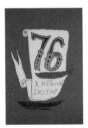

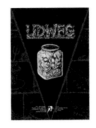

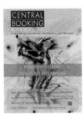

WHETHER THEY ABJURE WORDS & STORY COMPLETELY, OR JUST MAKE THEM SUBSIDIARY TO SHEER VISUAL FORCE, THIS BUNCH OF GENIUSES COULD DECORATE THE CORRIDORS OF MY MIND ANYTIME THEY LIKE.

I ONCE HAD THE LUCK TO COLLABORATE WITH RAYMOND, WHO ALSO GRACED ME & BILL WITH THIS BOOK'S COVER ART. (NOT THAT HE TRULY NEEDED MY HELP WITH LANGUAGE — HIS WORK ERUPTS WITH IT.)

RAYMOND PETTIBON

No Title (I was fumbling...)

2013

Ink, acrylic, and collage on paper
34½ × 41½ inches
87.6 × 105.4 cm

Courtesy David Zwirner, New York

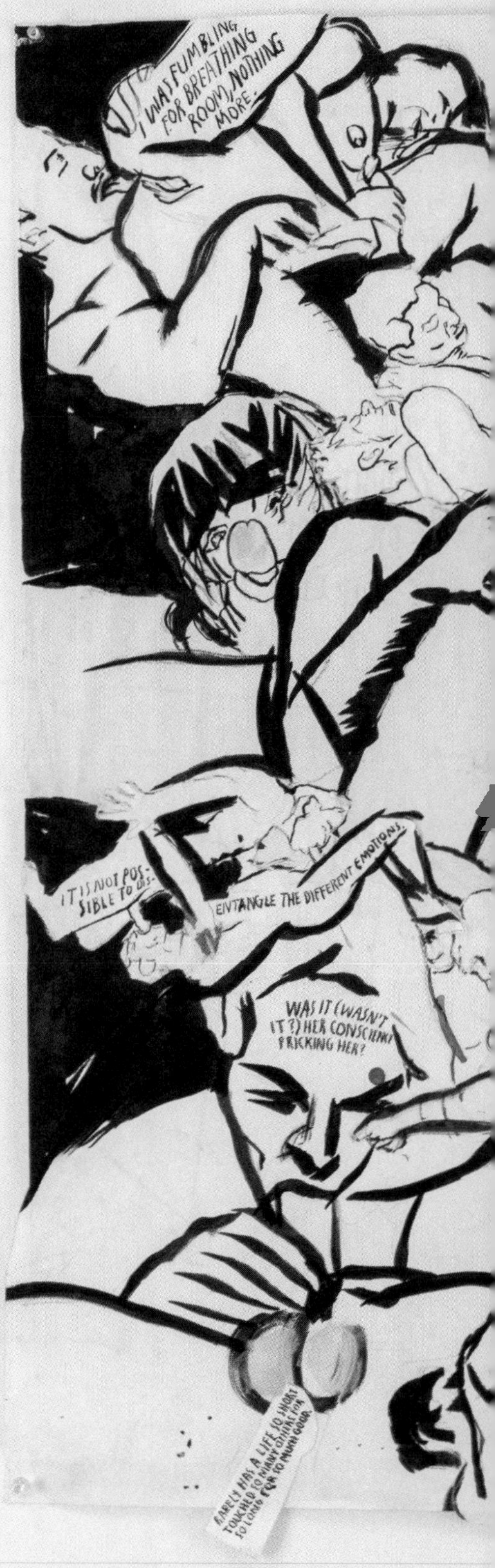

I WAS FUMBLING FOR BREATHING ROOM, NOTHING MORE.
IT IS NOT POSSIBLE TO DISENTANGLE THE DIFFERENT EMOTIONS.
WAS IT (WASN'T IT?) HER CONSCIENCE PRICKING HER?
RARELY HAS A LIFE SO SHORT TOUCHED SO MANY OTHERS FOR SO LONG FOR SO MUCH GOOD.

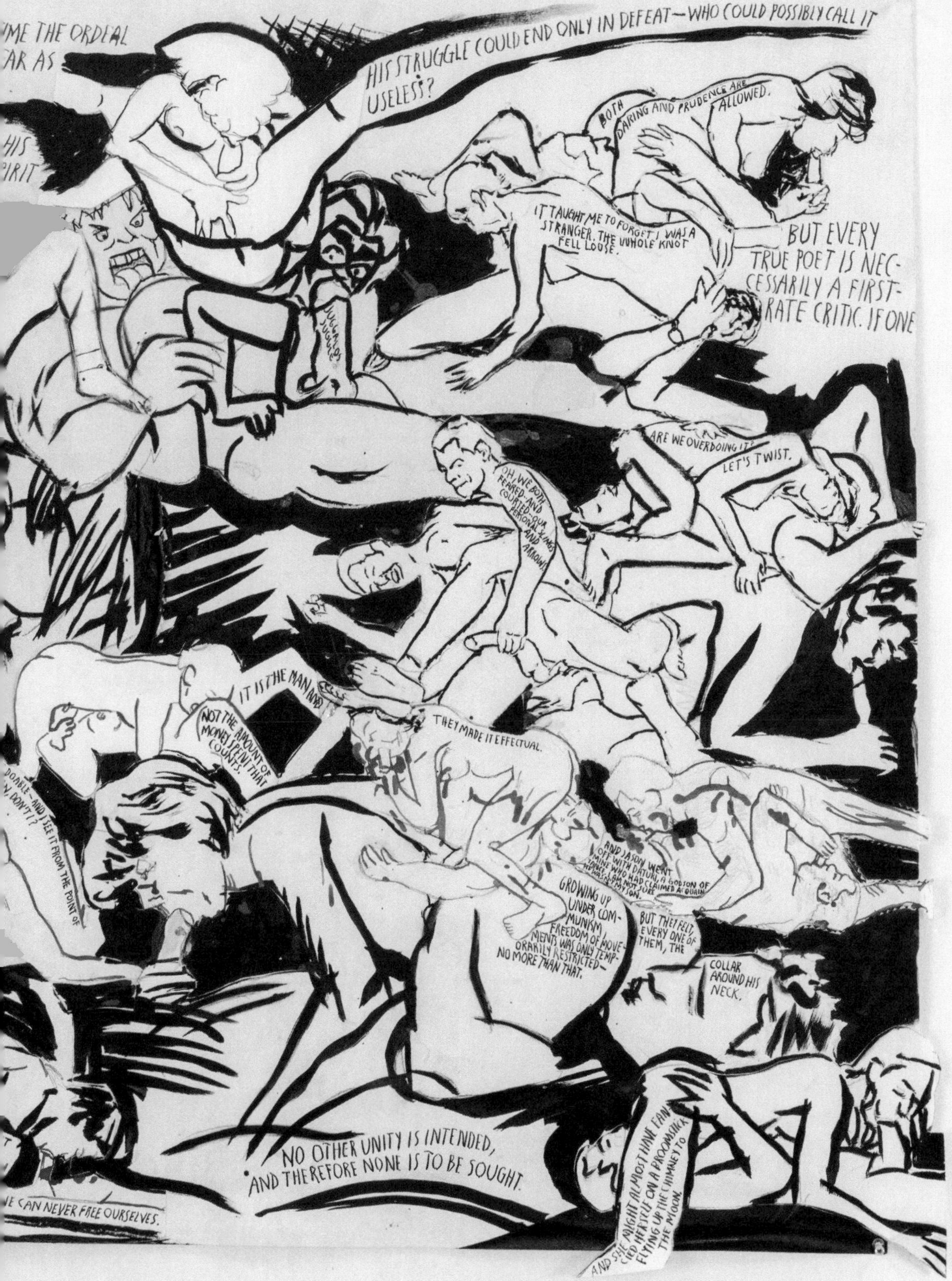
ME THE ORDEAL
CAR AS
HIS
PIRIT
HIS STRUGGLE COULD END ONLY IN DEFEAT — WHO COULD POSSIBLY CALL IT USELESS?
BOTH DARING AND PRUDENCE ARE ALLOWED.
IT TAUGHT ME TO FORGET I WAS A STRANGER. THE WHOLE KNOT FELL LOUSE.
BUT EVERY TRUE POET IS NECCESSARILY A FIRST-RATE CRITIC. IF ONE
JUGGALOS JUGGLE
ARE WE OVERDOING IT?
LET'S TWIST.
OH, WE BOTH FEARED—AND COURTED—OUR PERSONAL SLINGS AND ARROWS.
IT IS THE MAN AND
NOT THE AMOUNT OF MONEY SPENT THAT COUNTS.
THEY MADE IT EFFECTUAL.
DOABLE—AND I SEE IT FROM THE POINT OF
N, DON'T I?
AND JASON WENT OFF WITH DATURI, A GODSON OF MINE WHO HAD CLAIMED ACQUAINTANCE. I AM NOT SURE HE WASN'T MY SON.
GROWING UP UNDER COMMUNISM, FREEDOM OF MOVEMENTS WAS ONLY TEMPORARILY RESTRICTED—NO MORE THAN THAT.
BUT THEY FELT, EVERY ONE OF THEM, THE
COLLAR AROUND HIS NECK.
NO OTHER UNITY IS INTENDED, AND THEREFORE NONE IS TO BE SOUGHT.
E CAN NEVER FREE OURSELVES.
AND SHE MIGHT ALMOST HAVE FANCIED HERSELF ON A BROOMSTICK FLYING UP THE CHIMNEY TO THE MOON.

RAYMOND PETTIBON

No Title (The credits rolled...)

2013

Ink, gouache, acrylic, and collage on paper
32 × 40¼ inches
81.3 × 102.2 cm

Courtesy David Zwirner, New York

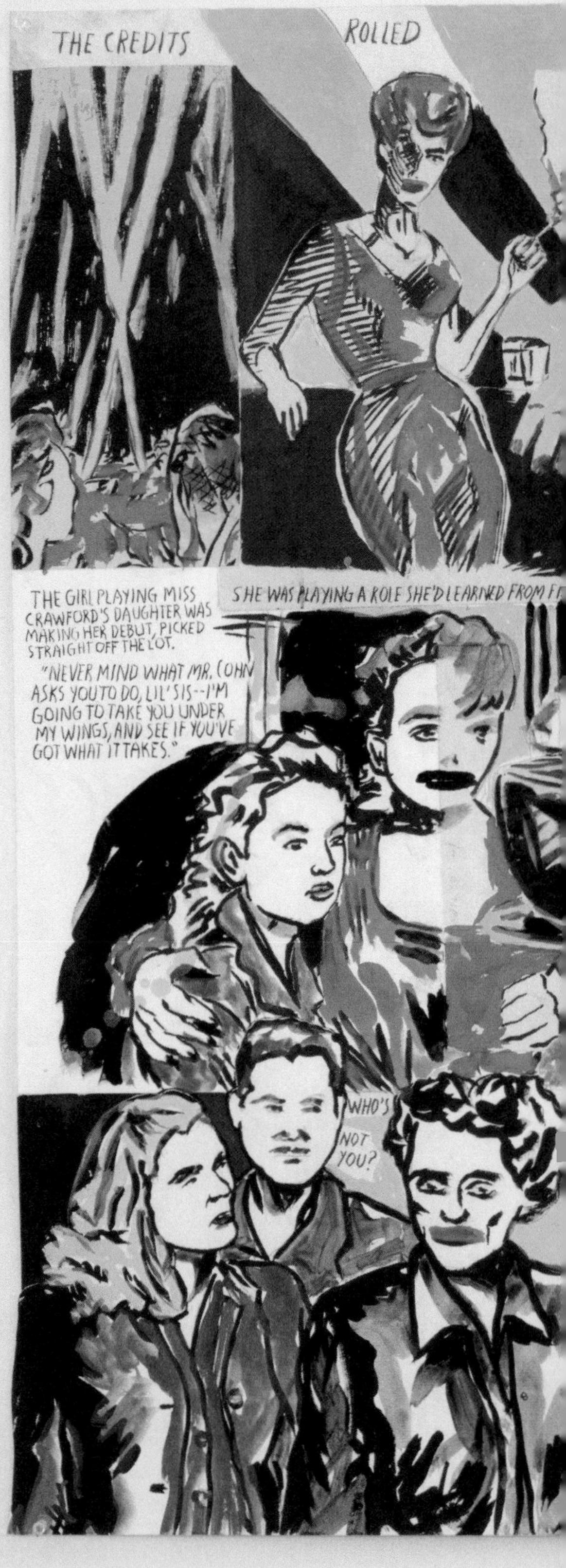

THE CREDITS
ROLLED
THE GIRL PLAYING MISS CRAWFORD'S DAUGHTER WAS MAKING HER DEBUT, PICKED STRAIGHT OFF THE LOT.
"NEVER MIND WHAT MR. COHN ASKS YOU TO DO, LIL' SIS--I'M GOING TO TAKE YOU UNDER MY WINGS, AND SEE IF YOU'VE GOT WHAT IT TAKES."
SHE WAS PLAYING A ROLE SHE'D LEARNED FROM
WHO'S
NOT YOU?

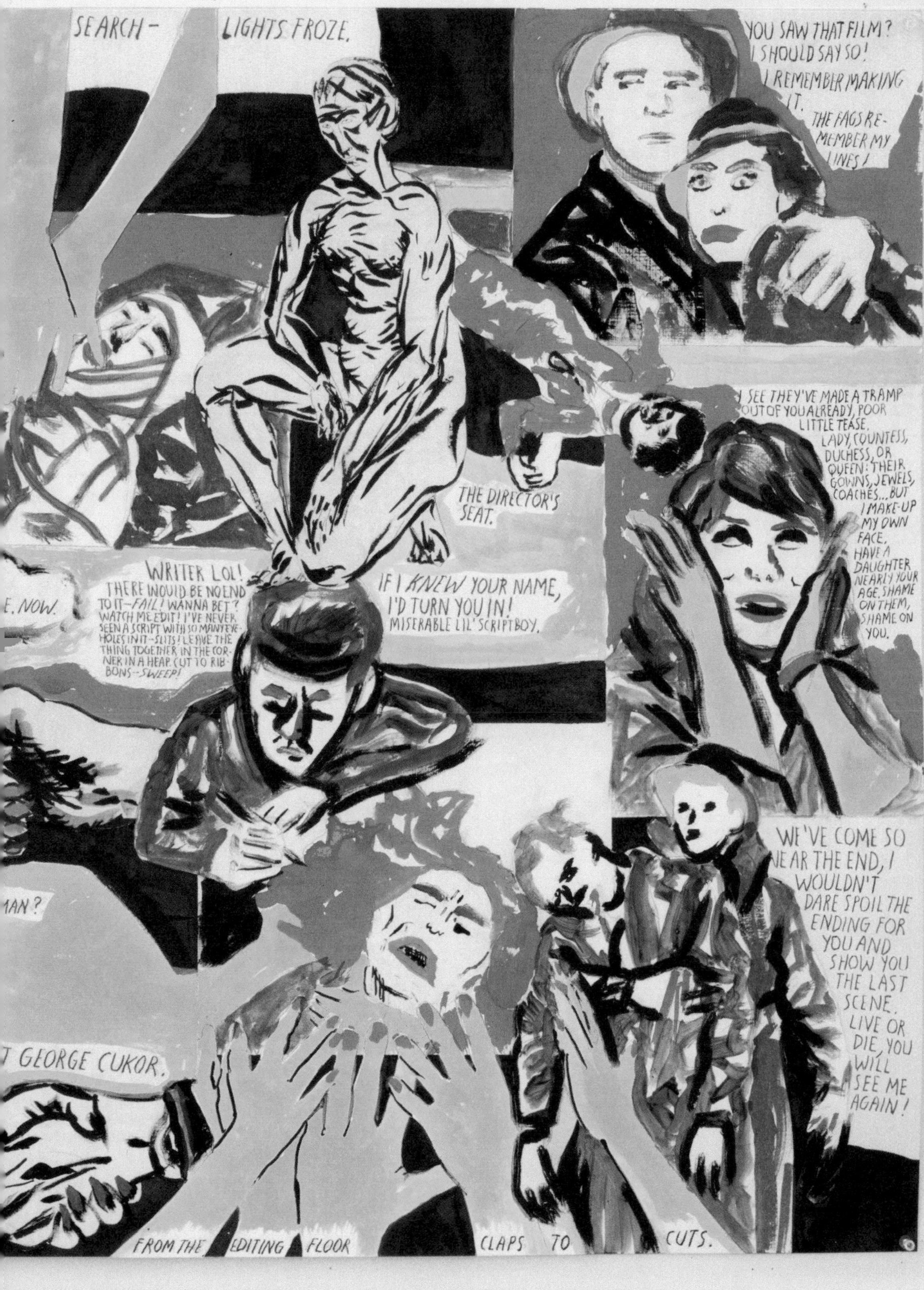
SEARCH- LIGHTS FROZE.
YOU SAW THAT FILM? I SHOULD SAY SO! I REMEMBER MAKING IT.
THE FAGS REMEMBER MY LINES!
THE DIRECTOR'S SEAT.
I SEE THEY'VE MADE A TRAMP OUT OF YOU ALREADY, POOR LITTLE TEASE. LADY, COUNTESS, DUCHESS, OR QUEEN: THEIR GOWNS, JEWELS, COACHES... BUT I MAKE-UP MY OWN FACE. HAVE A DAUGHTER NEARLY YOUR AGE. SHAME ON THEM, SHAME ON YOU.
E. NOW.
WRITER LOL! THERE WOULD BE NO END TO IT—FAIL! WANNA BET? WATCH ME EDIT! I'VE NEVER SEEN A SCRIPT WITH SO MANY EYE-HOLES IN IT—SLITS! LEAVE THE THING TOGETHER IN THE CORNER IN A HEAP. CUT TO RIBBONS—SWEEP!
IF I KNEW YOUR NAME, I'D TURN YOU IN! MISERABLE LIL' SCRIPTBOY.
MAN?
WE'VE COME SO NEAR THE END, I WOULDN'T DARE SPOIL THE ENDING FOR YOU AND SHOW YOU THE LAST SCENE. LIVE OR DIE, YOU WILL SEE ME AGAIN!
T GEORGE CUKOR.
FROM THE EDITING FLOOR CLAPS TO CUTS.

RAYMOND PETTIBON

No Title (As we can...)

2012

Ink, acrylic, graphite, and collage on paper
33 × 40 inches
83.8 × 101.6 cm

Courtesy David Zwirner, New York

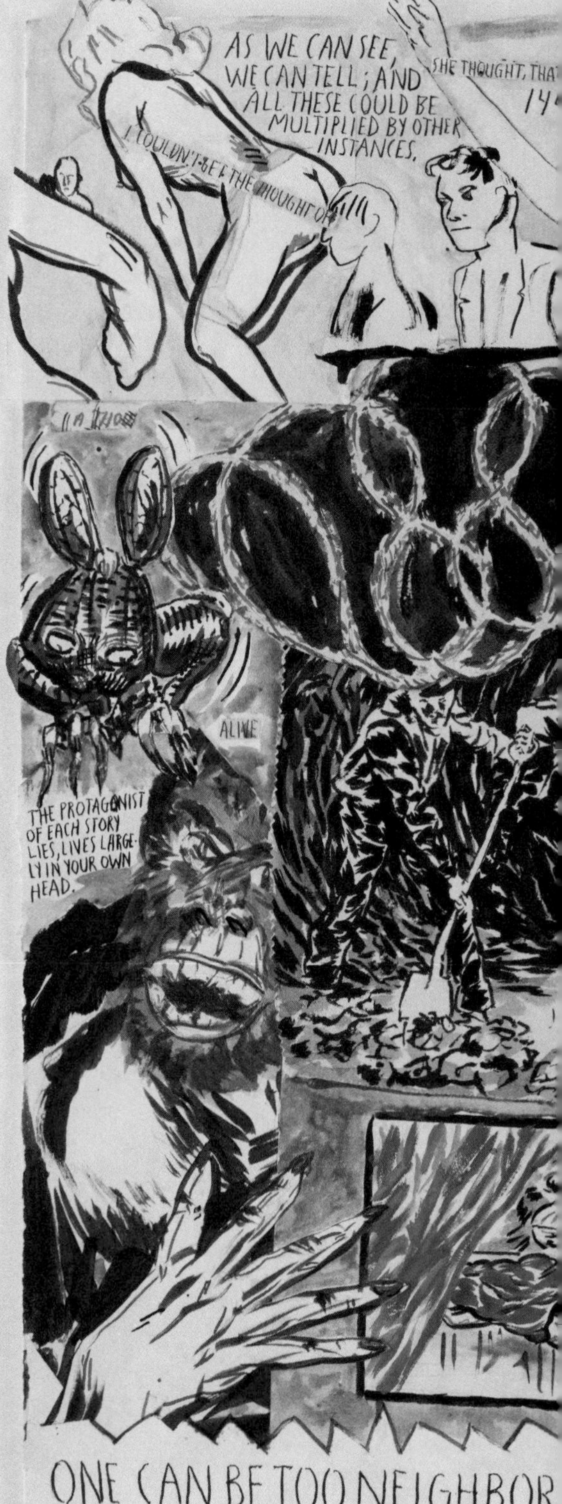
AS WE CAN SEE, WE CAN TELL; AND ALL THESE COULD BE MULTIPLIED BY OTHER INSTANCES.
SHE THOUGHT,
ALIVE
THE PROTAGONIST OF EACH STORY LIES, LIVES LARGE-LY IN YOUR OWN HEAD.
ONE CAN BE TOO NEIGHBOR

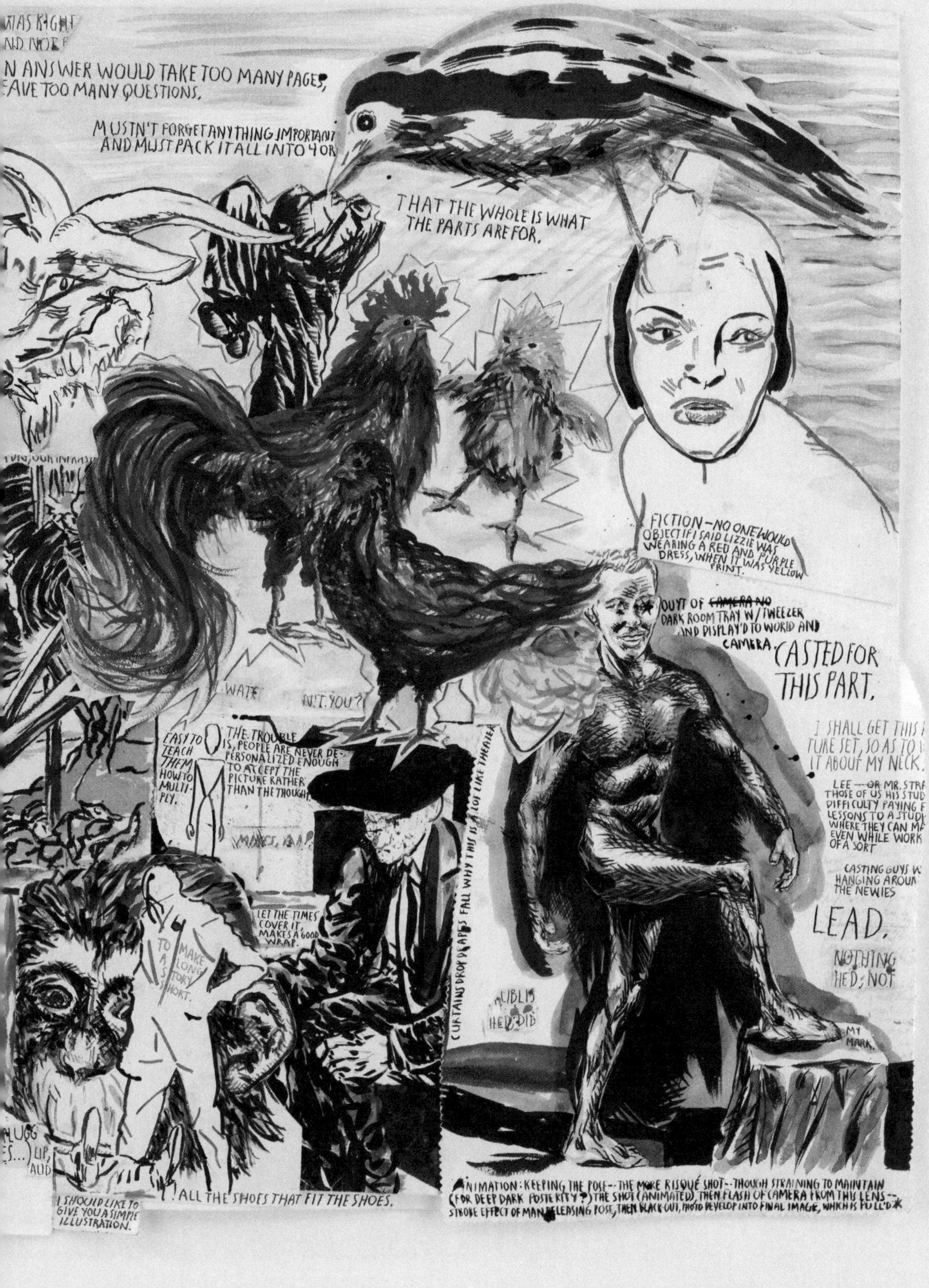

N ANSWER WOULD TAKE TOO MANY PAGES,
EAVE TOO MANY QUESTIONS.
MUSTN'T FORGET ANYTHING IMPORTANT
AND MUST PACK IT ALL INTO 4 OR
THAT THE WHOLE IS WHAT THE PARTS ARE FOR.
FICTION—NO ONE WOULD OBJECT IF I SAID LIZZIE WAS WEARING A RED AND PURPLE DRESS, WHEN IT WAS YELLOW PRINT.
OUT OF ~~CAMERA NO~~ DARK ROOM TRAY W/ TWEEZER AND DISPLAY'D TO WORLD AND CAMERA.
CASTED FOR THIS PART.
I SHALL GET THIS TURE SET, SO AS TO IT ABOUT MY NECK.
LEE — OR MR. STRA THOSE OF US HIS STUD DIFFICULTY PAYING F LESSONS TO A STUD WHERE THEY CAN MA EVEN WHILE WORK OF A SORT
CASTING GUYS W HANGING AROUN THE NEWIES
LEAD.
NOTHING HED; NOT
MY MARK.
WATE
N'T YOU?
EASY TO TEACH THEM HOW TO MULTIPLY.
THE TROUBLE IS, PEOPLE ARE NEVER DEPERSONALIZED ENOUGH TO ACCEPT THE PICTURE RATHER THAN THE THOUGHT.
LET THE TIMES COVER IT, MAKES A GOOD WRAP.
TO MAKE A LONG STORY SHORT.
CURTAINS DROP DRAPES FALL WHY THIS IS A LOT LIKE THEATER
ALL THE SHOES THAT FIT THE SHOES.
I SHOULD LIKE TO GIVE YOU A SIMPLE ILLUSTRATION.
ANIMATION: KEEPING THE POSE--THE MORE RISQUÉ SHOT--THOUGH STRAINING TO MAINTAIN (FOR DEEP DARK POSTERITY?) THE SHOT (ANIMATED), THEN FLASH OF CAMERA FROM THIS LENS--STROBE EFFECT OF MAN RELEASING POSE, THEN BLACK-OUT, PHOTO DEVELOP INTO FINAL IMAGE, WHICH IS FULL'D*

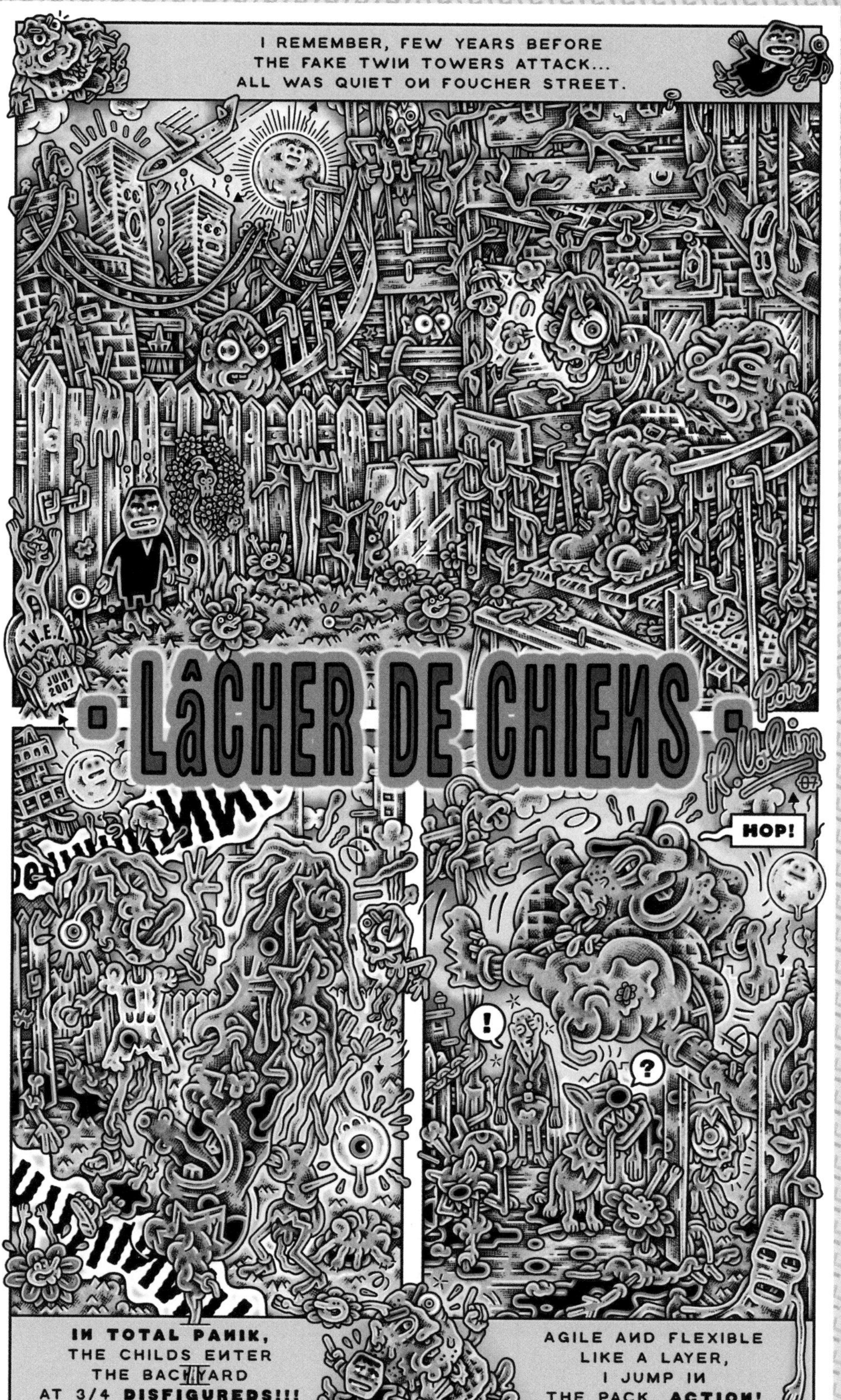

I REMEMBER, FEW YEARS BEFORE
THE FAKE TWIN TOWERS ATTACK...
ALL WAS QUIET ON FOUCHER STREET.
T.V.E.L. DUMAS JUIN 2007
- LâCHER DE CHIENS -
Par
07
HOP!
!
?
IN TOTAL PANIK,
THE CHILDS ENTER
THE BACKYARD
AT 3/4 DISFIGUREDS!!!
AGILE AND FLEXIBLE
LIKE A LAYER,
I JUMP IN
THE PACK. ACTION!

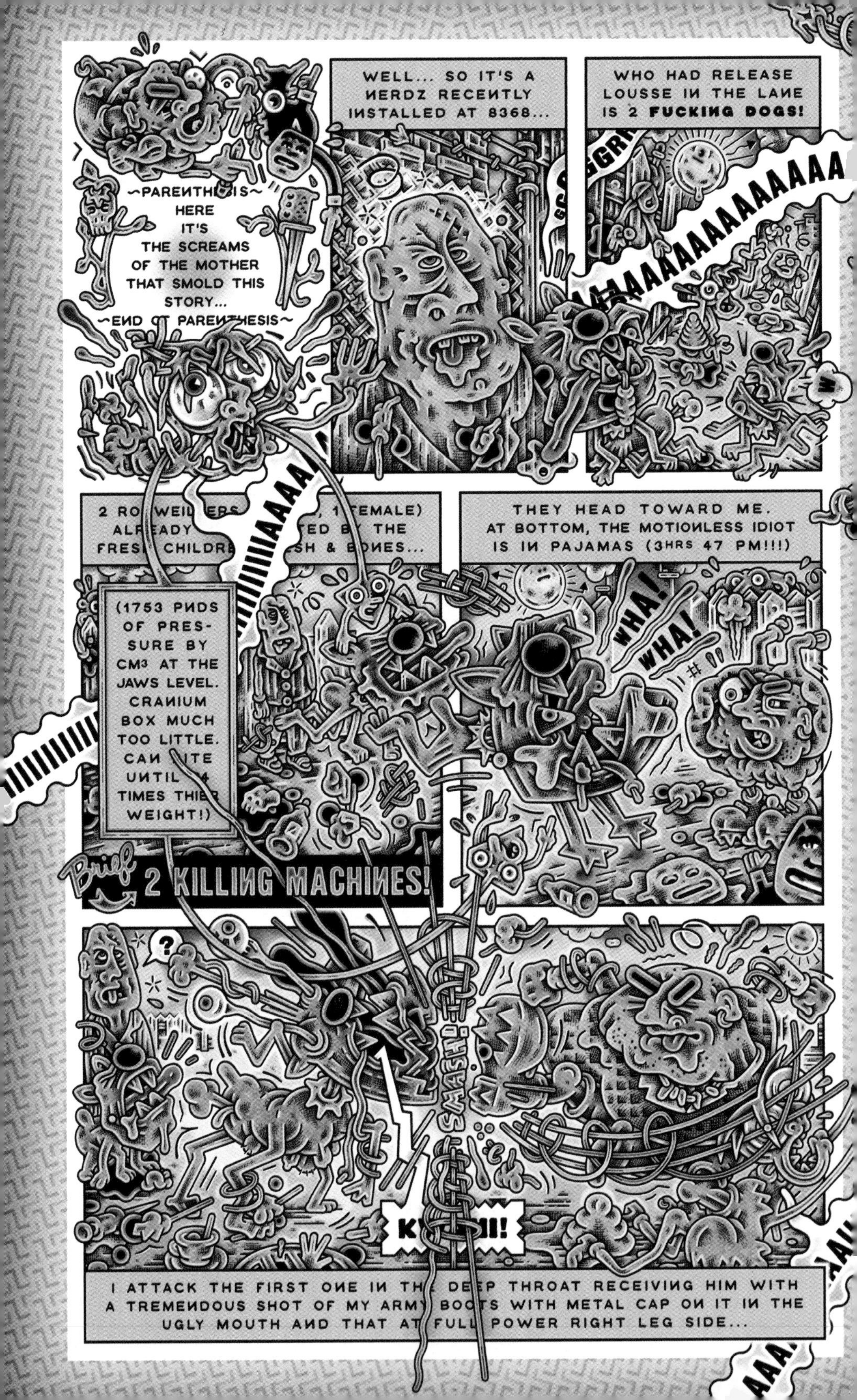
~PARENTHESIS~
HERE IT'S THE SCREAMS OF THE MOTHER THAT SMOLD THIS STORY...
~END OF PARENTHESIS~
WELL... SO IT'S A NERDZ RECENTLY INSTALLED AT 8368...
WHO HAD RELEASE LOUSSE IN THE LANE IS 2 **FUCKING DOGS!**
AAAAAAAAAAAAAAAA
1 FEMALE) ALREADY BY THE
THEY HEAD TOWARD ME. AT BOTTOM, THE MOTIONLESS IDIOT IS IN PAJAMAS (3HRS 47 PM!!!)
(1753 PNDS OF PRES-SURE BY CM3 AT THE JAWS LEVEL. CRANIUM BOX MUCH TOO LITTLE. CAN BITE UNTIL 4 TIMES THIER WEIGHT!)
WHA!
WHA!
Brief
2 KILLING MACHINES!
?
SMASH!
I ATTACK THE FIRST ONE IN THE DEEP THROAT RECEIVING HIM WITH A TREMENDOUS SHOT OF MY ARMY BOOTS WITH METAL CAP ON IT IN THE UGLY MOUTH AND THAT AT FULL POWER RIGHT LEG SIDE...

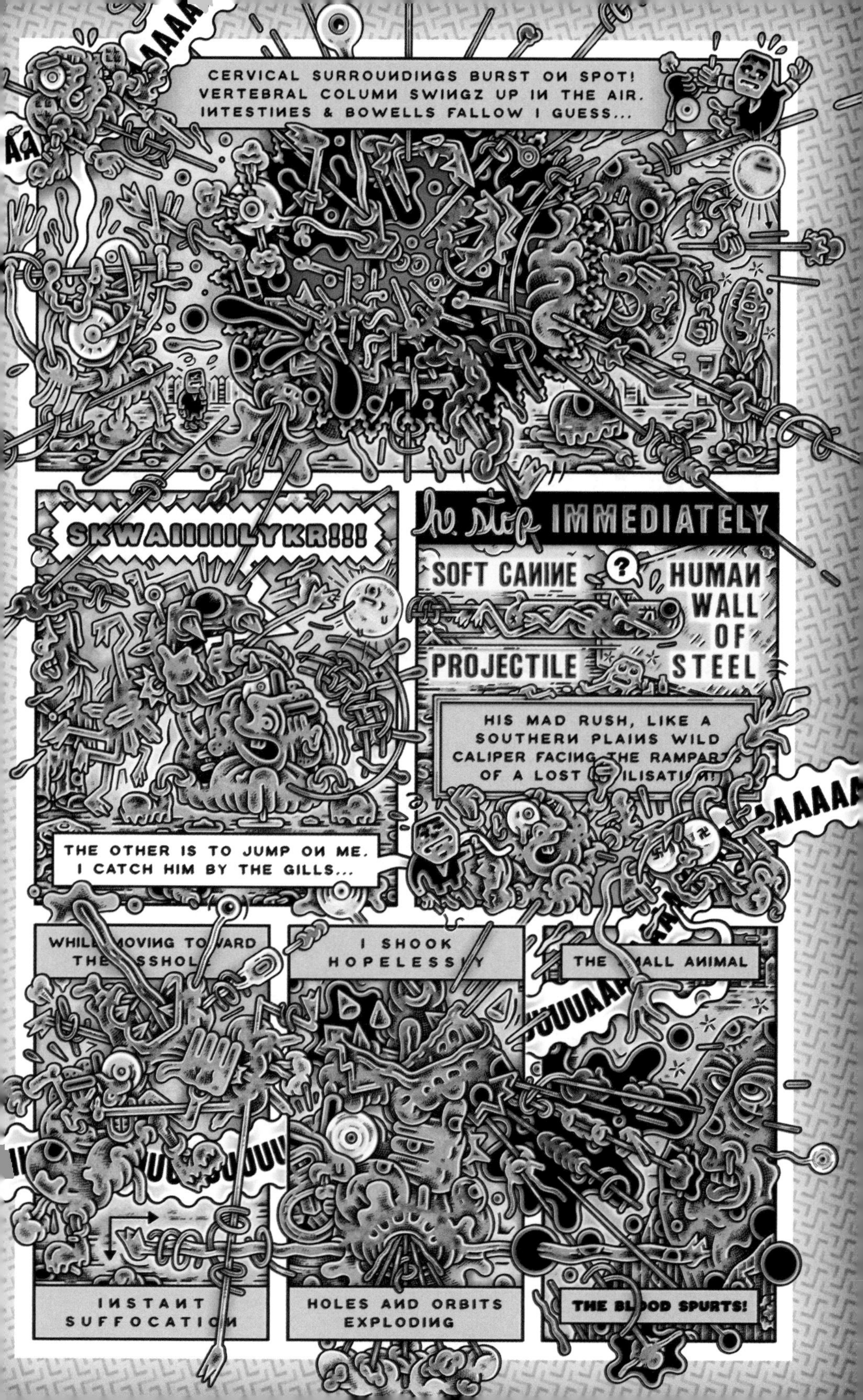
AAAAA
CERVICAL SURROUNDINGS BURST ON SPOT! VERTEBRAL COLUMN SWINGZ UP IN THE AIR. INTESTINES & BOWELLS FALLOW I GUESS...
SKWAIIIIIILYKR!!!
THE OTHER IS TO JUMP ON ME. I CATCH HIM BY THE GILLS...
he stop IMMEDIATELY
SOFT CANINE
?
HUMAN WALL OF STEEL
PROJECTILE
HIS MAD RUSH, LIKE A SOUTHERN PLAINS WILD CALIPER FACING THE RAMPARTS OF A LOST CIVILISATION!
AAAAAA
I SHOOK HOPELESSLY
THE SMALL ANIMAL
INSTANT SUFFOCATION
HOLES AND ORBITS EXPLODING
THE BLOOD SPURTS!

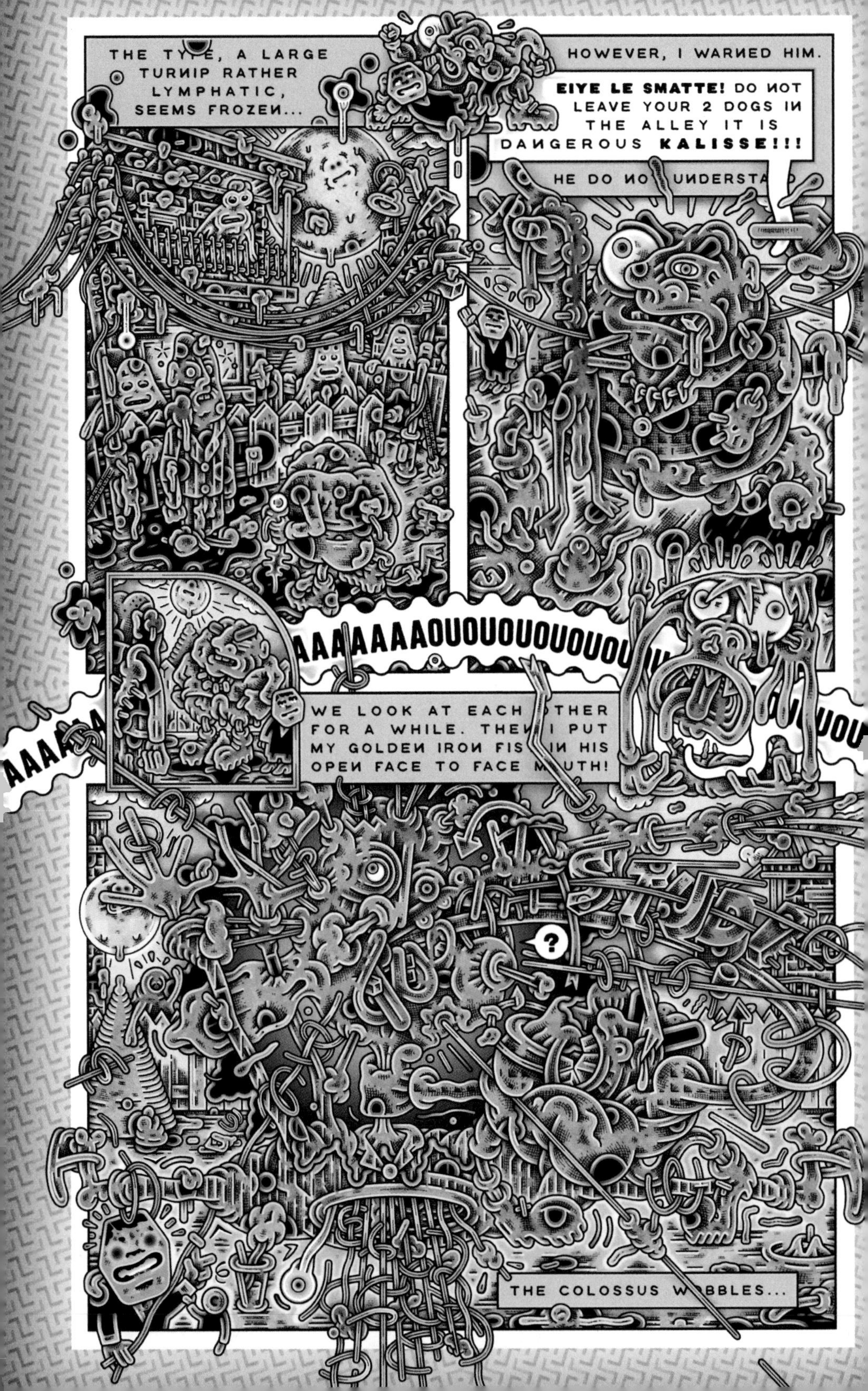
THE TYPE, A LARGE TURNIP RATHER LYMPHATIC, SEEMS FROZEN...
HOWEVER, I WARNED HIM.
EIYE LE SMATTE! DO NOT LEAVE YOUR 2 DOGS IN THE ALLEY IT IS DANGEROUS KALISSE!!!
HE DO NO UNDERSTA
AAAAAAAOUOUOUOUOUOU
WE LOOK AT EACH OTHER FOR A WHILE. THEN I PUT MY GOLDEN IRON FIST IN HIS OPEN FACE TO FACE MOUTH!
?
THE COLOSSUS WOBBLES...

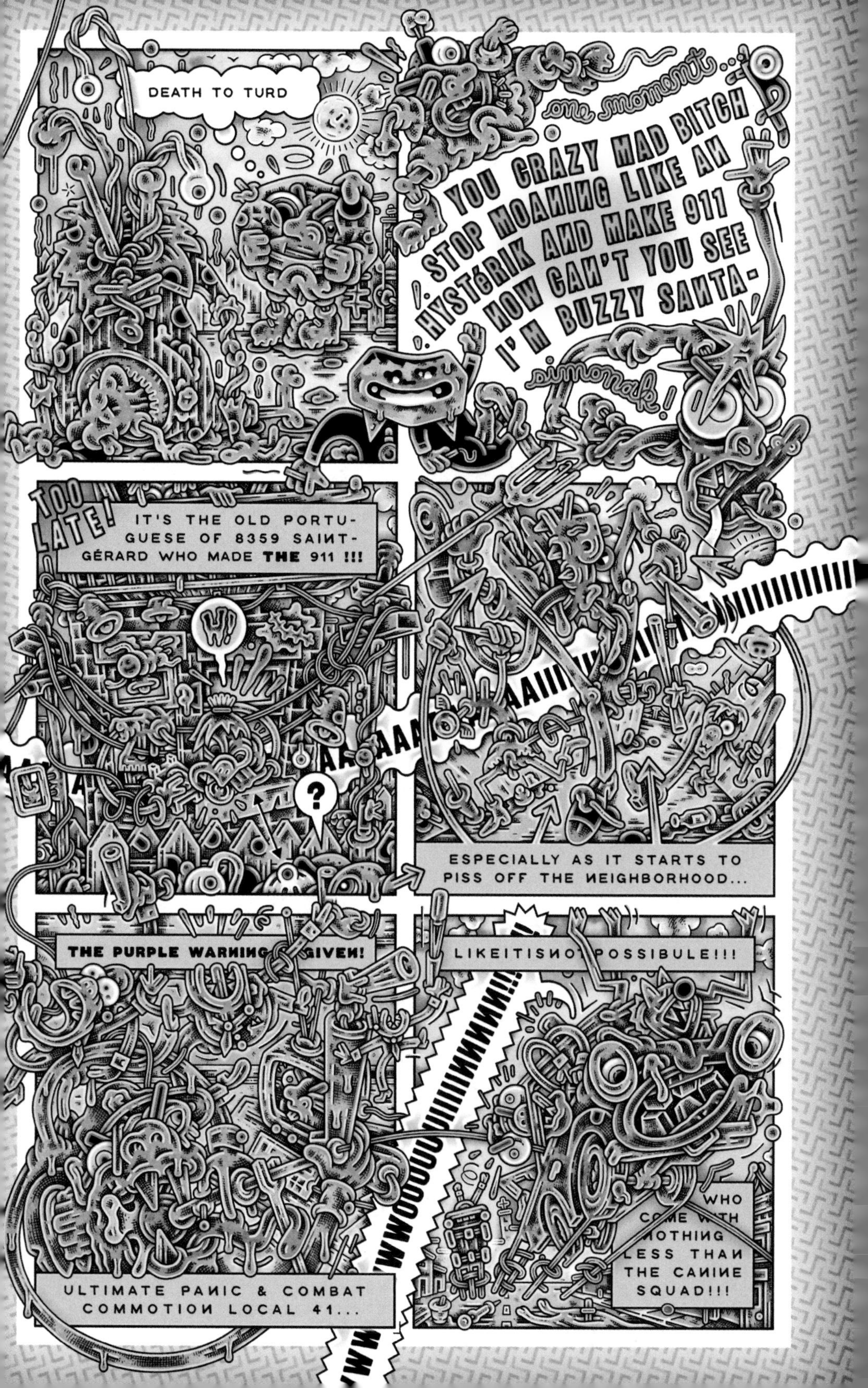
DEATH TO TURD
one moment...
YOU CRAZY MAD BITCH STOP MOANING LIKE AN HYSTéRIK AND MAKE 911 NOW CAN'T YOU SEE I'M BUZZY SANTA-
simonak!
TOO LATE!
IT'S THE OLD PORTUGUESE OF 8359 SAINT-GÉRARD WHO MADE THE 911 !!!
?
ESPECIALLY AS IT STARTS TO PISS OFF THE NEIGHBORHOOD...
THE PURPLE WARNING GIVEN!
LIKEITISNO POSSIBULE!!!
ULTIMATE PANIC & COMBAT COMMOTION LOCAL 41...
WHO COME WITH NOTHING LESS THAN THE CANINE SQUAD!!!

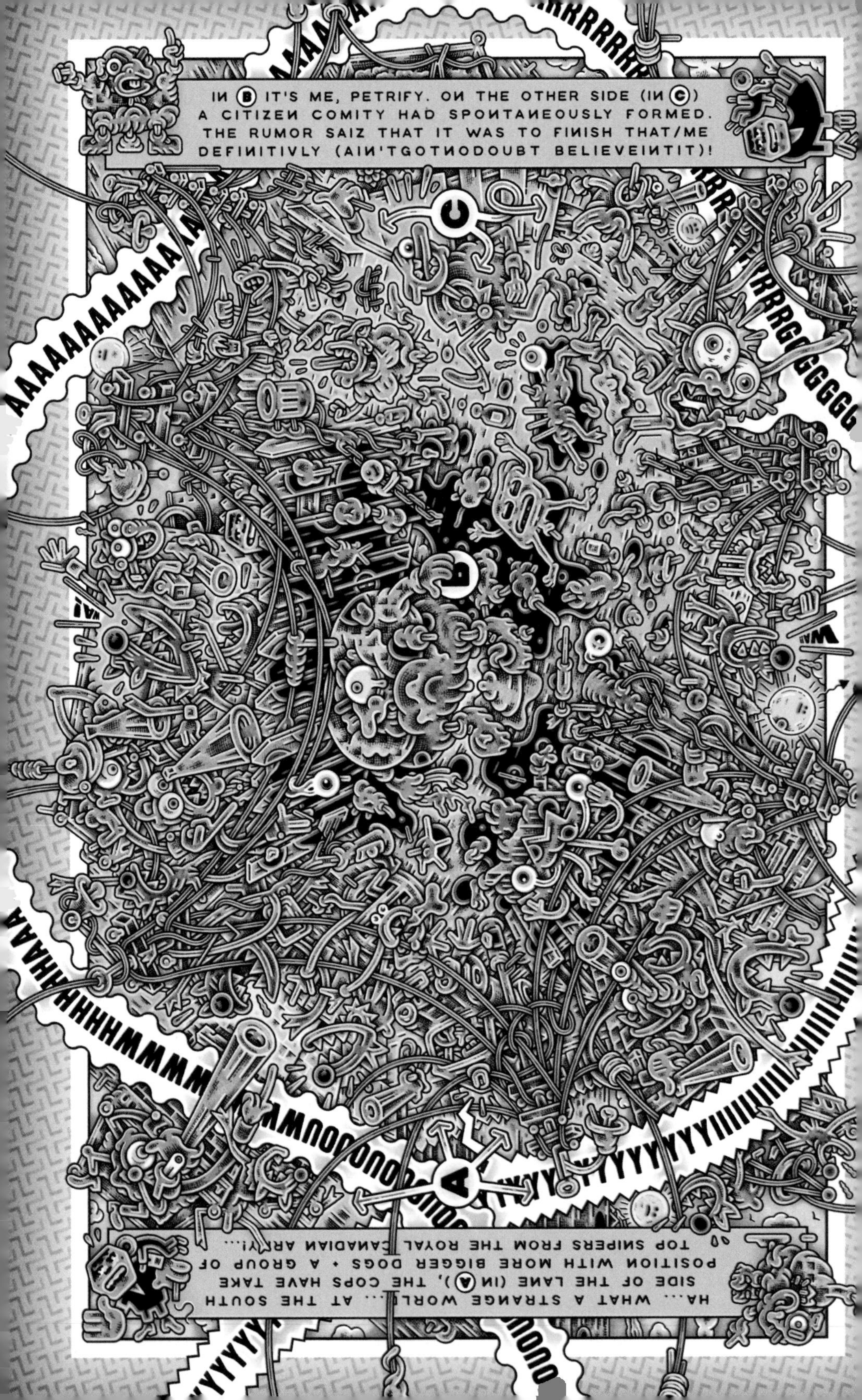

IN B IT'S ME, PETRIFY. ON THE OTHER SIDE (IN C) A CITIZEN COMITY HAD SPONTANEOUSLY FORMED. THE RUMOR SAIZ THAT IT WAS TO FINISH THAT/ME DEFINITIVLY (AIN'TGOTNODOUBT BELIEVEINTIT)!
C
A
HA... WHAT A STRANGE WORLD... AT THE SOUTH SIDE OF THE LANE (IN A), THE COPS HAVE TAKE POSITION WITH MORE BIGGER DOGS + A GROUP OF TOP SNIPERS FROM THE ROYAL CANADIAN ARMY!...

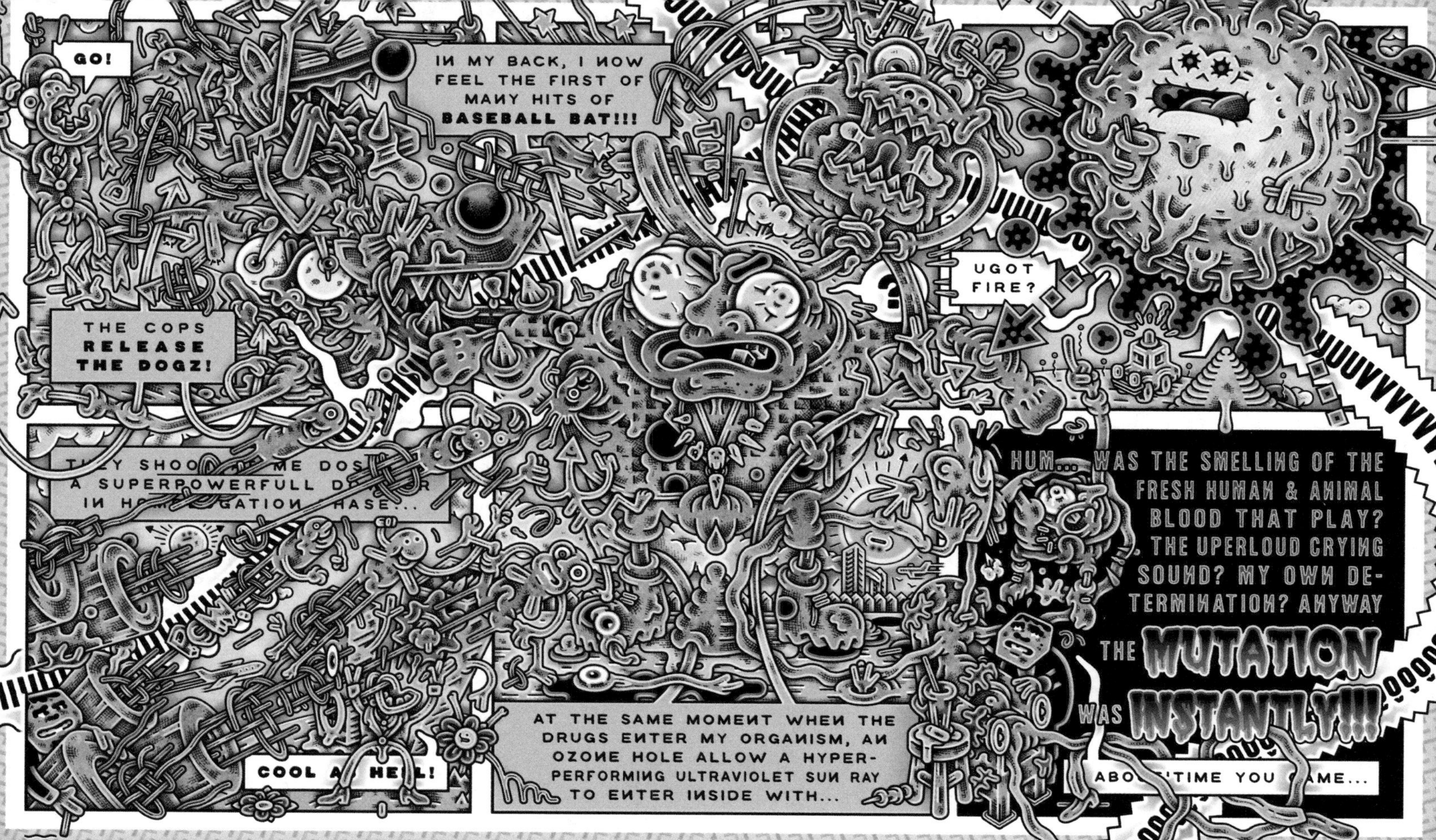
GO!
IN MY BACK, I NOW FEEL THE FIRST OF MANY HITS OF **BASEBALL BAT!!!**
THE COPS **RELEASE THE DOGZ!**
UGOT FIRE?
A SUPERPOWERFULL
AT THE SAME MOMENT WHEN THE DRUGS ENTER MY ORGANISM, AN OZONE HOLE ALLOW A HYPER-PERFORMING ULTRAVIOLET SUN RAY TO ENTER INSIDE WITH...
HUM... WAS THE SMELLING OF THE FRESH HUMAN & ANIMAL BLOOD THAT PLAY? THE UPERLOUD CRYING SOUND? MY OWN DE-TERMINATION? ANYWAY THE MUTATION WAS INSTANTLY!!!
TIME YOU

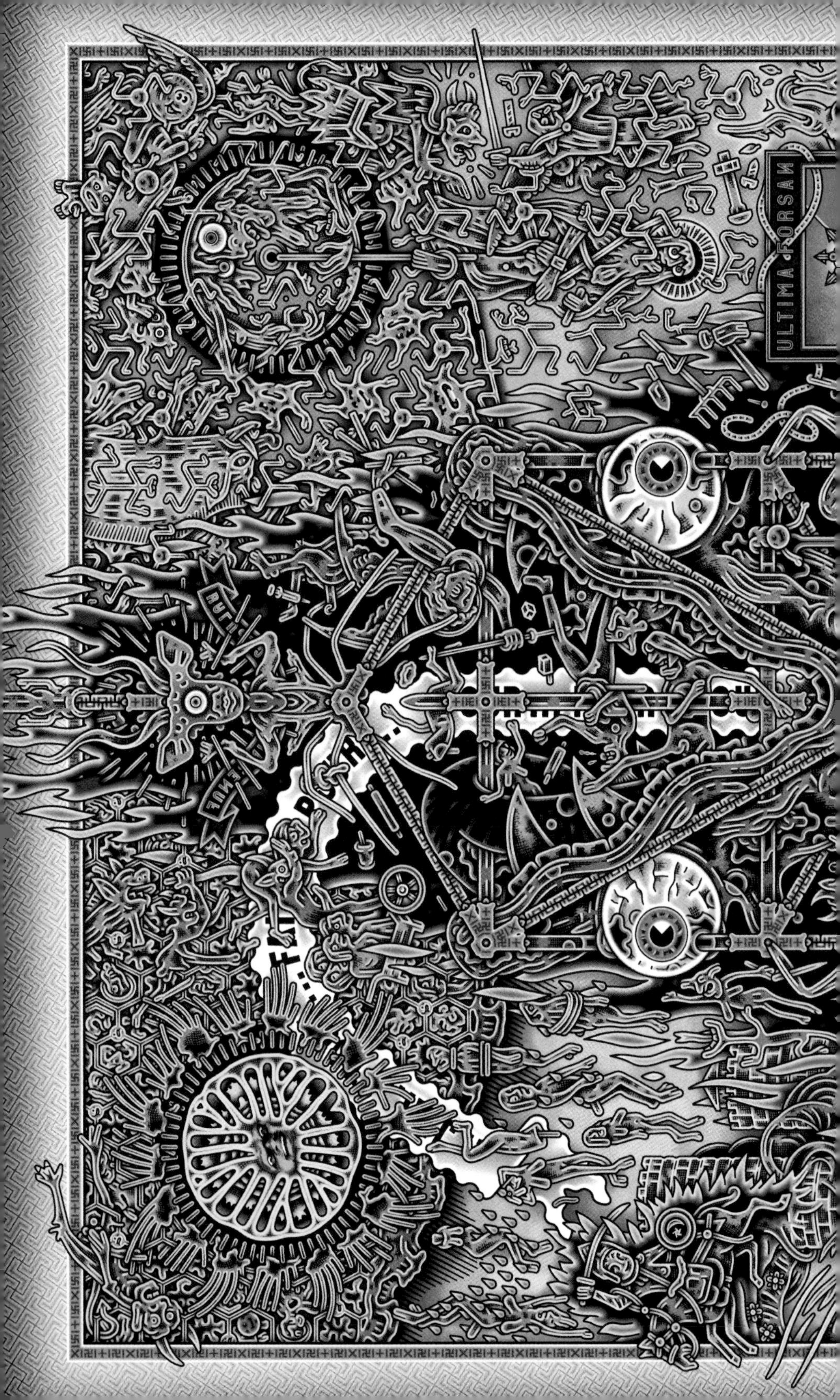
ULTIMA FORSAN

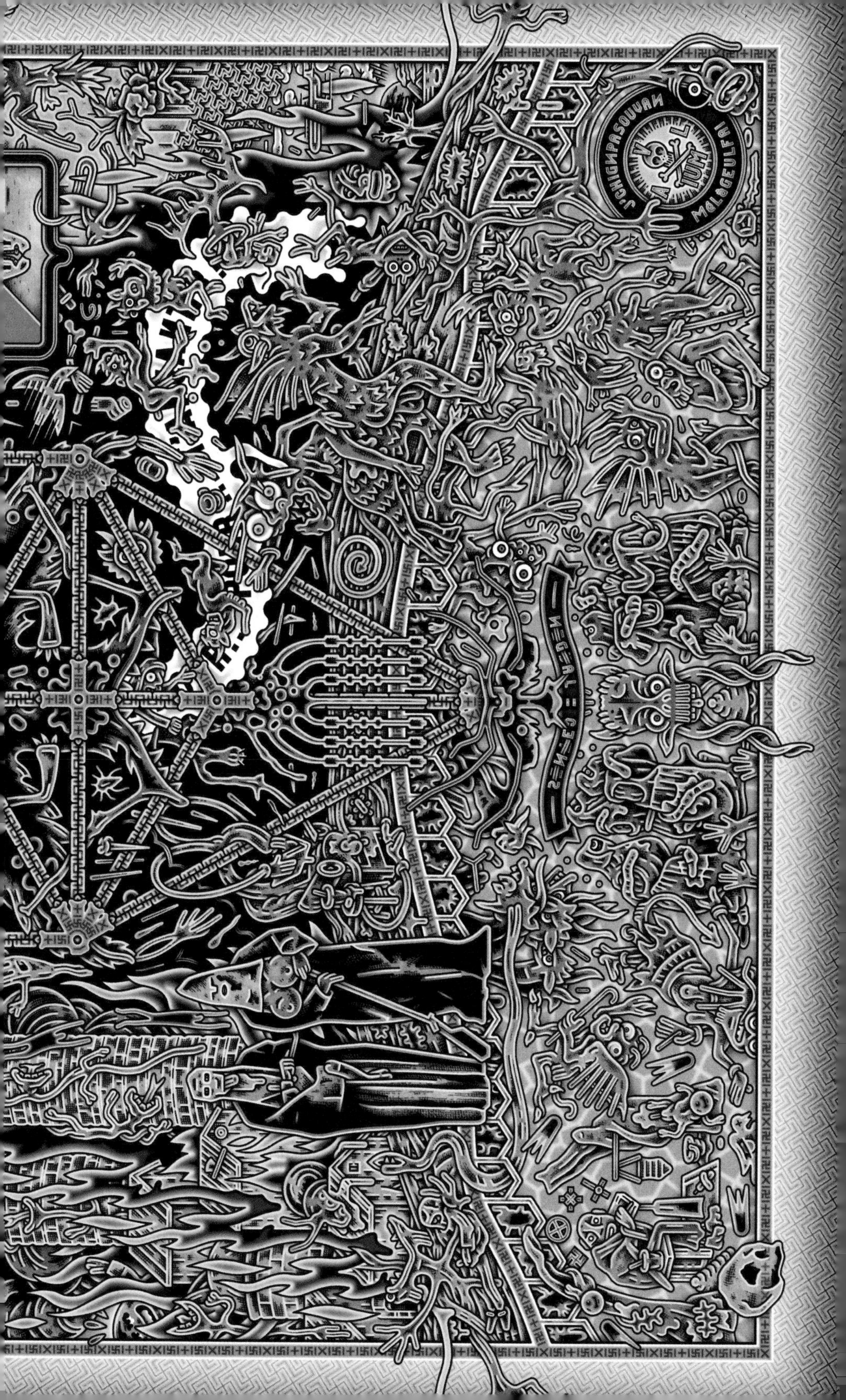

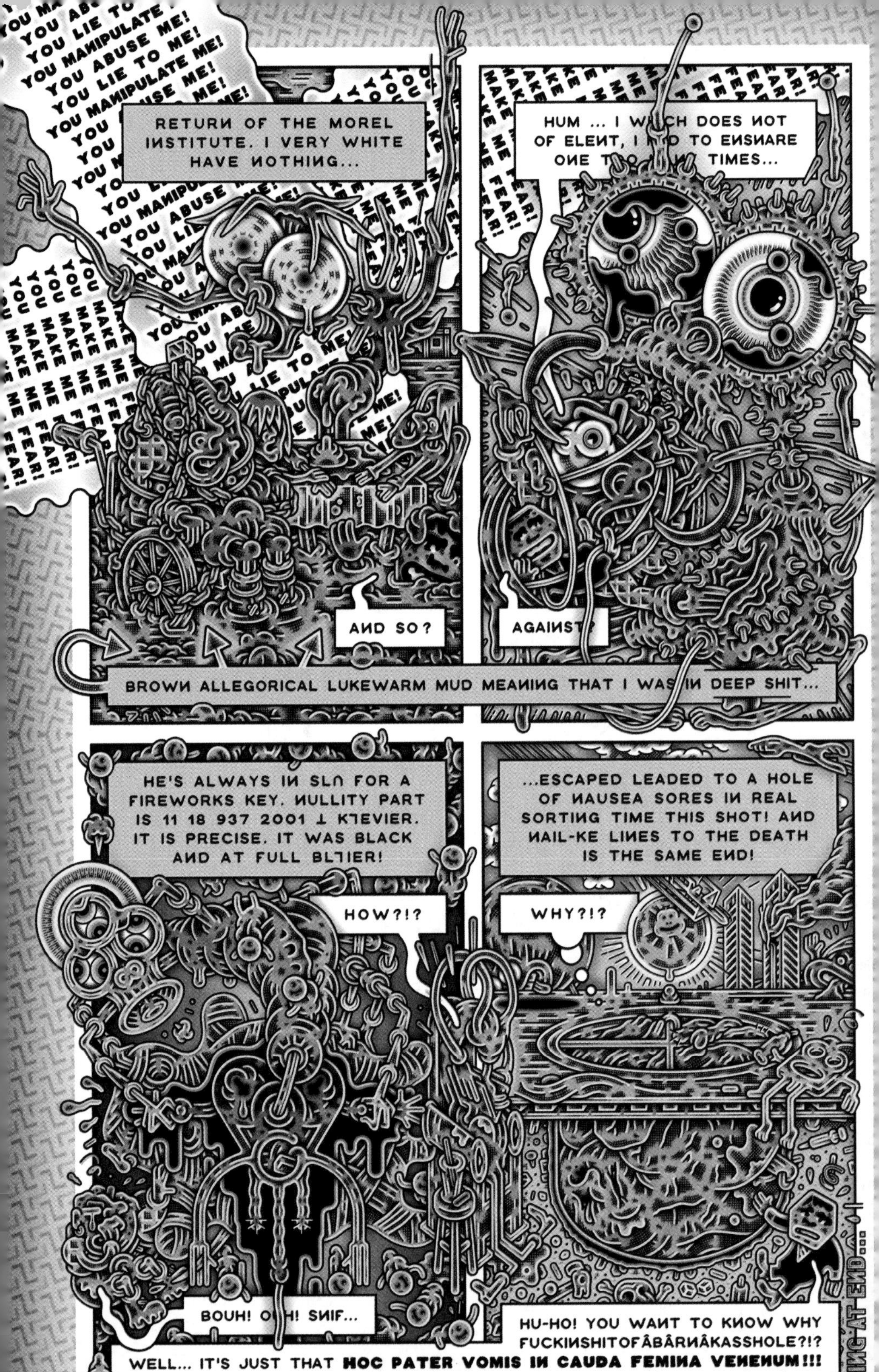
YOU MAKE ME FEAR!
YOU LIE TO ME!
YOU MANIPULATE ME!
YOU ABUSE ME!
RETURN OF THE MOREL INSTITUTE. I VERY WHITE HAVE NOTHING...
HUM ... I W CH DOES NOT OF ELENT, I D TO ENSNARE ONE T TIMES...
AND SO?
AGAINST?
BROWN ALLEGORICAL LUKEWARM MUD MEANING THAT I WAS IN DEEP SHIT...
HE'S ALWAYS IN SLN FOR A FIREWORKS KEY. NULLITY PART IS 11 18 937 2001 ⊥ K7EVIER. IT IS PRECISE. IT WAS BLACK AND AT FULL BL7IER!
HOW?!?
...ESCAPED LEADED TO A HOLE OF NAUSEA SORES IN REAL SORTING TIME THIS SHOT! AND NAIL-KE LINES TO THE DEATH IS THE SAME END!
WHY?!?
BOUH! O H! SNIF...
HU-HO! YOU WANT TO KNOW WHY FUCKINSHITOFÂBÂRNÂKASSHOLE?!?
WELL... IT'S JUST THAT **HOC PATER VOMIS IN CAUDA FEMINA VENENUM!!!**
...AND I'M LOOKING AT END...

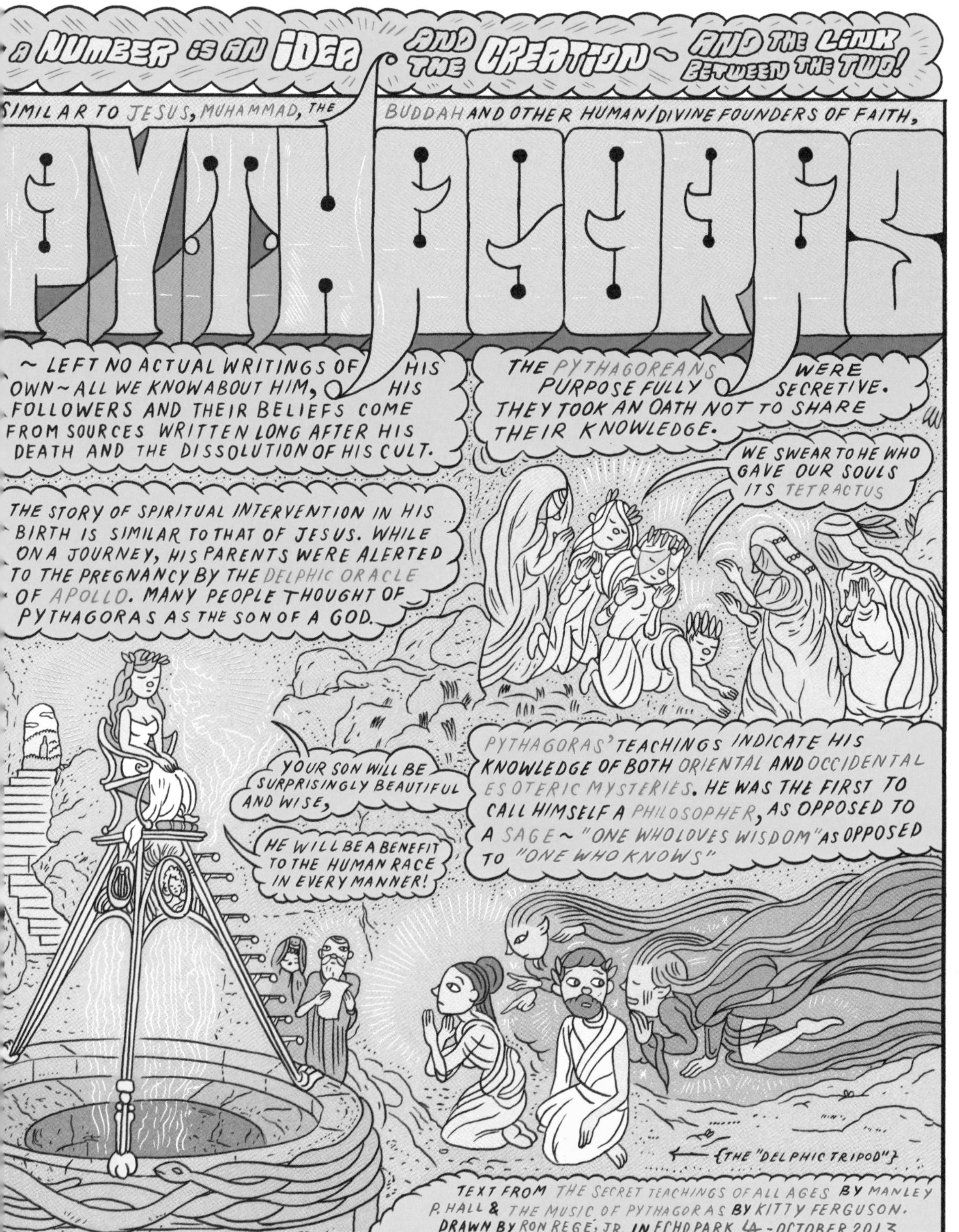

A NUMBER IS AN IDEA AND THE CREATION ~ AND THE LINK BETWEEN THE TWO!
SIMILAR TO JESUS, MUHAMMAD, THE BUDDAH AND OTHER HUMAN/DIVINE FOUNDERS OF FAITH,
PYTHAGORAS
~ LEFT NO ACTUAL WRITINGS OF HIS OWN ~ ALL WE KNOW ABOUT HIM, HIS FOLLOWERS AND THEIR BELIEFS COME FROM SOURCES WRITTEN LONG AFTER HIS DEATH AND THE DISSOLUTION OF HIS CULT.
THE PYTHAGOREANS WERE PURPOSEFULLY SECRETIVE. THEY TOOK AN OATH NOT TO SHARE THEIR KNOWLEDGE.
WE SWEAR TO HE WHO GAVE OUR SOULS ITS TETRACTUS
THE STORY OF SPIRITUAL INTERVENTION IN HIS BIRTH IS SIMILAR TO THAT OF JESUS. WHILE ON A JOURNEY, HIS PARENTS WERE ALERTED TO THE PREGNANCY BY THE DELPHIC ORACLE OF APOLLO. MANY PEOPLE THOUGHT OF PYTHAGORAS AS THE SON OF A GOD.
YOUR SON WILL BE SURPRISINGLY BEAUTIFUL AND WISE,
HE WILL BE A BENEFIT TO THE HUMAN RACE IN EVERY MANNER!
PYTHAGORAS' TEACHINGS INDICATE HIS KNOWLEDGE OF BOTH ORIENTAL AND OCCIDENTAL ESOTERIC MYSTERIES. HE WAS THE FIRST TO CALL HIMSELF A PHILOSOPHER, AS OPPOSED TO A SAGE ~ "ONE WHO LOVES WISDOM" AS OPPOSED TO "ONE WHO KNOWS"
{THE "DELPHIC TRIPOD"}
TEXT FROM THE SECRET TEACHINGS OF ALL AGES BY MANLEY P. HALL & THE MUSIC OF PYTHAGORAS BY KITTY FERGUSON. DRAWN BY RON REGÉ, JR. IN ECHO PARK LA - OCTOBER 2013

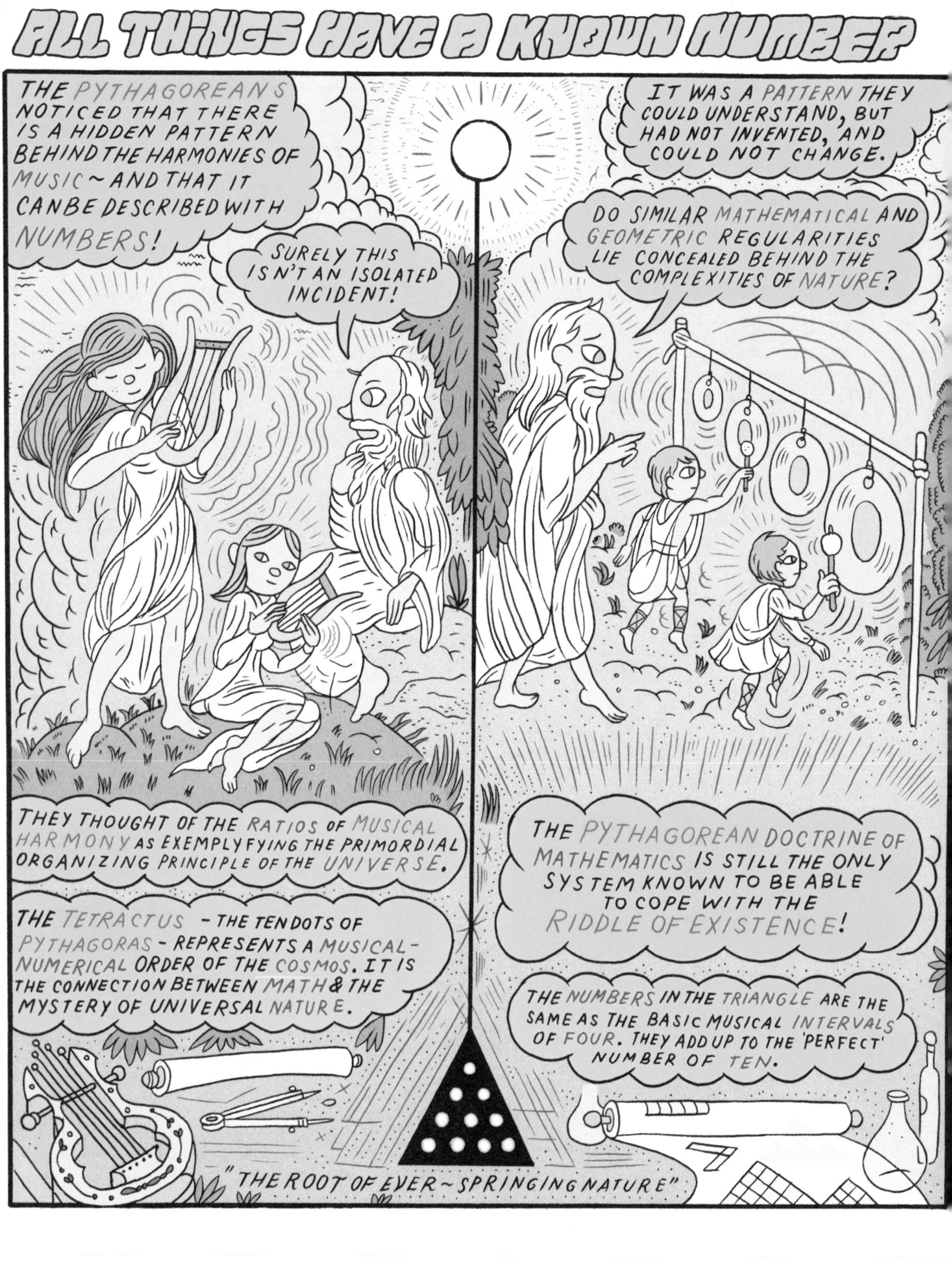
ALL THINGS HAVE A KNOWN NUMBER
THE PYTHAGOREANS NOTICED THAT THERE IS A HIDDEN PATTERN BEHIND THE HARMONIES OF MUSIC ~ AND THAT IT CANBE DESCRIBED WITH NUMBERS!
SURELY THIS ISN'T AN ISOLATED INCIDENT!
IT WAS A PATTERN THEY COULD UNDERSTAND, BUT HAD NOT INVENTED, AND COULD NOT CHANGE.
DO SIMILAR MATHEMATICAL AND GEOMETRIC REGULARITIES LIE CONCEALED BEHIND THE COMPLEXITIES OF NATURE?
THEY THOUGHT OF THE RATIOS OF MUSICAL HARMONY AS EXEMPLYFYING THE PRIMORDIAL ORGANIZING PRINCIPLE OF THE UNIVERSE.
THE TETRACTUS - THE TEN DOTS OF PYTHAGORAS - REPRESENTS A MUSICAL-NUMERICAL ORDER OF THE COSMOS. IT IS THE CONNECTION BETWEEN MATH & THE MYSTERY OF UNIVERSAL NATURE.
THE PYTHAGOREAN DOCTRINE OF MATHEMATICS IS STILL THE ONLY SYSTEM KNOWN TO BE ABLE TO COPE WITH THE RIDDLE OF EXISTENCE!
THE NUMBERS IN THE TRIANGLE ARE THE SAME AS THE BASIC MUSICAL INTERVALS OF FOUR. THEY ADD UP TO THE 'PERFECT' NUMBER OF TEN.
"THE ROOT OF EVER ~ SPRINGING NATURE"

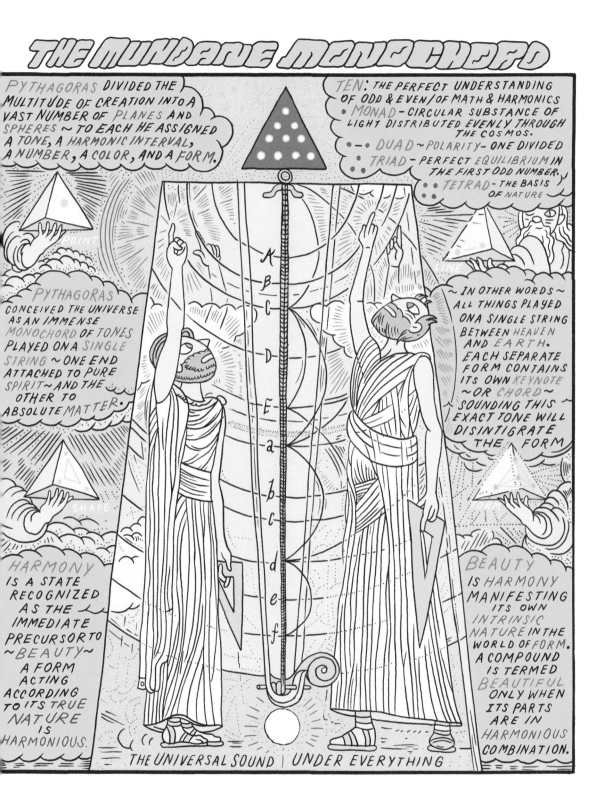

THE MUNDANE MONOCHORD

PYTHAGORAS DIVIDED THE MULTITUDE OF CREATION INTO A VAST NUMBER OF PLANES AND SPHERES ~ TO EACH HE ASSIGNED A TONE, A HARMONIC INTERVAL, A NUMBER, A COLOR, AND A FORM.

TEN: THE PERFECT UNDERSTANDING OF ODD & EVEN / OF MATH & HARMONICS
• MONAD - CIRCULAR SUBSTANCE OF LIGHT DISTRIBUTED EVENLY THROUGH THE COSMOS.
• - DUAD ~ POLARITY - ONE DIVIDED
• TRIAD - PERFECT EQUILIBRIUM IN THE FIRST ODD NUMBER.
• TETRAD - THE BASIS OF NATURE

POINT

LINE

PYTHAGORAS CONCEIVED THE UNIVERSE AS AN IMMENSE MONOCHORD OF TONES PLAYED ON A SINGLE STRING ~ ONE END ATTACHED TO PURE SPIRIT ~ AND THE OTHER TO ABSOLUTE MATTER.

~ IN OTHER WORDS ~ ALL THINGS PLAYED ON A SINGLE STRING BETWEEN HEAVEN AND EARTH. EACH SEPARATE FORM CONTAINS ITS OWN KEYNOTE ~ OR CHORD ~ SOUNDING THIS EXACT TONE WILL DISINTIGRATE THE FORM

SHAPE

FORM

HARMONY IS A STATE RECOGNIZED AS THE IMMEDIATE PRECURSOR TO ~ BEAUTY ~ A FORM ACTING ACCORDING TO ITS TRUE NATURE IS HARMONIOUS.

BEAUTY IS HARMONY MANIFESTING ITS OWN INTRINSIC NATURE IN THE WORLD OF FORM. A COMPOUND IS TERMED BEAUTIFUL ONLY WHEN ITS PARTS ARE IN HARMONIOUS COMBINATION.

THE UNIVERSAL SOUND | UNDER EVERYTHING

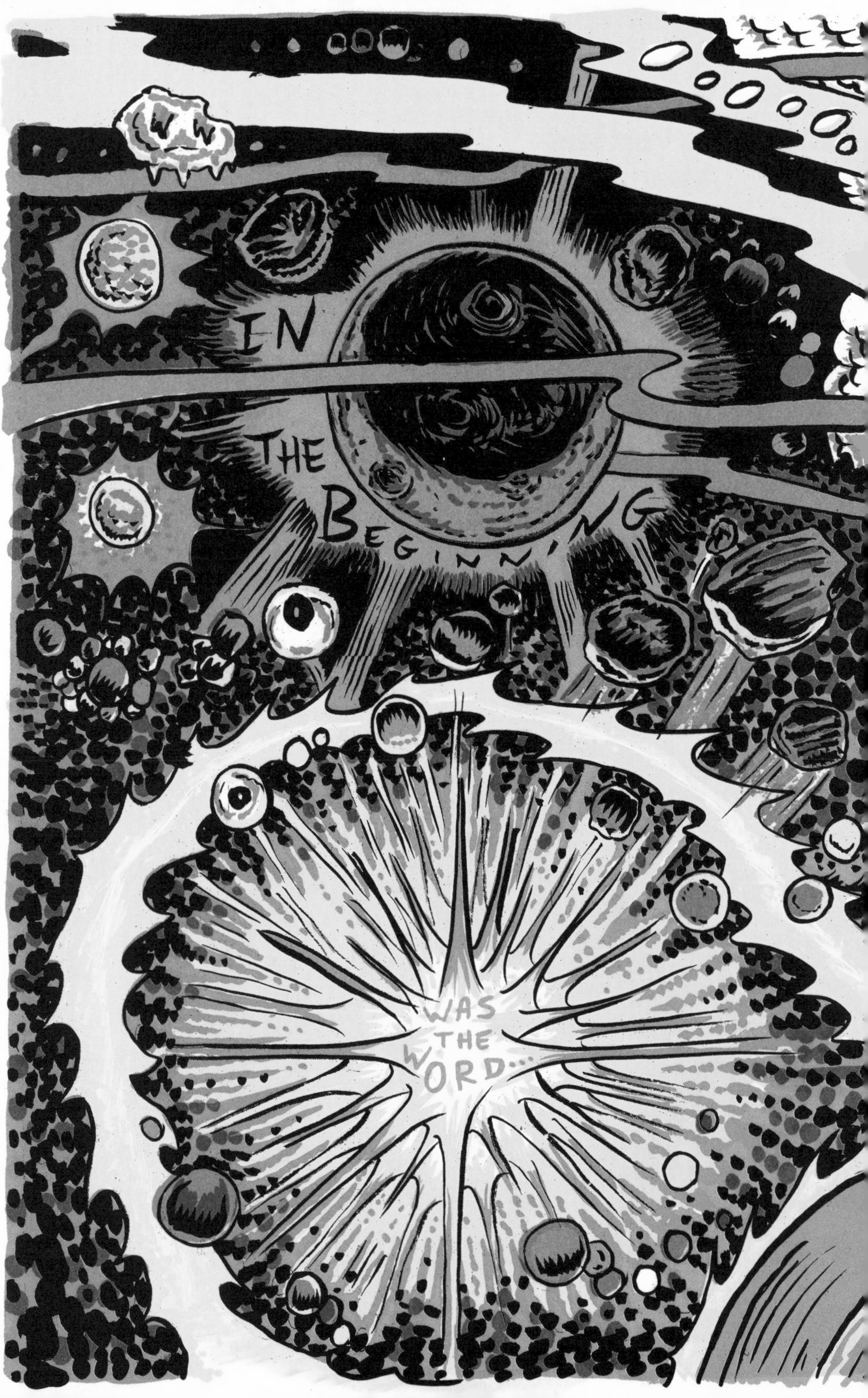
IN
THE
BEGINNING
WAS
THE
WORD...

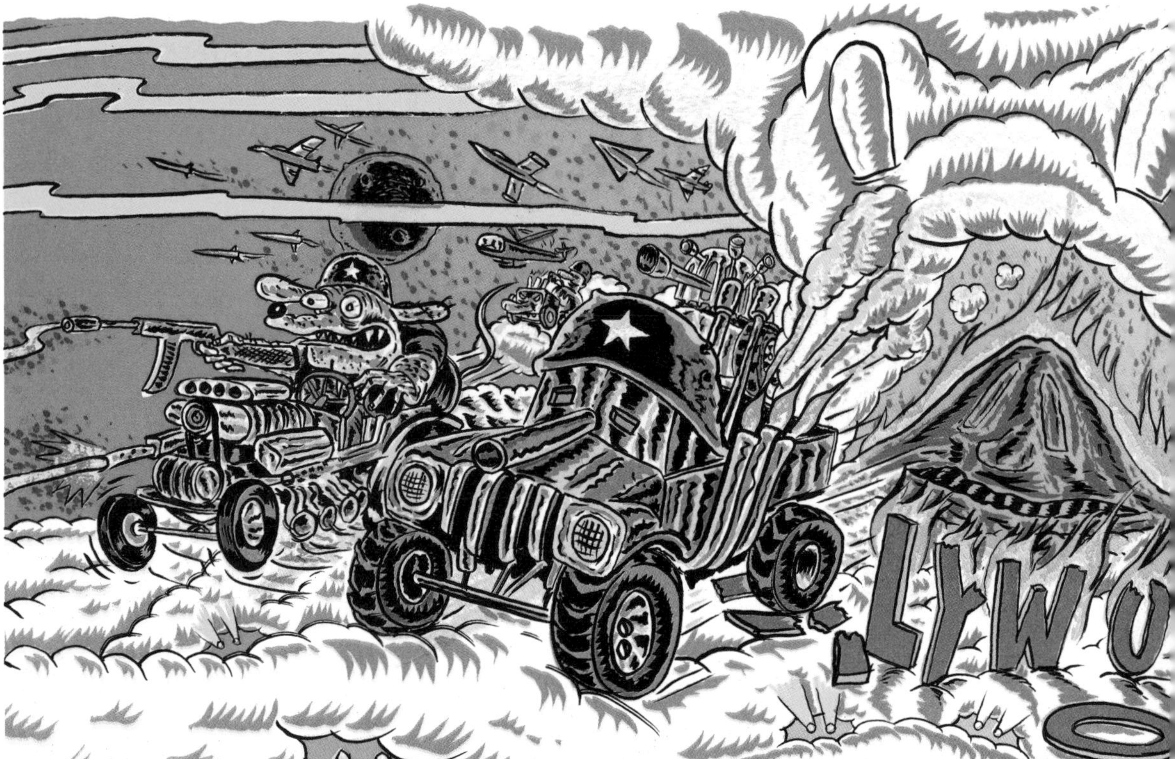
LYWO
KRABOOM

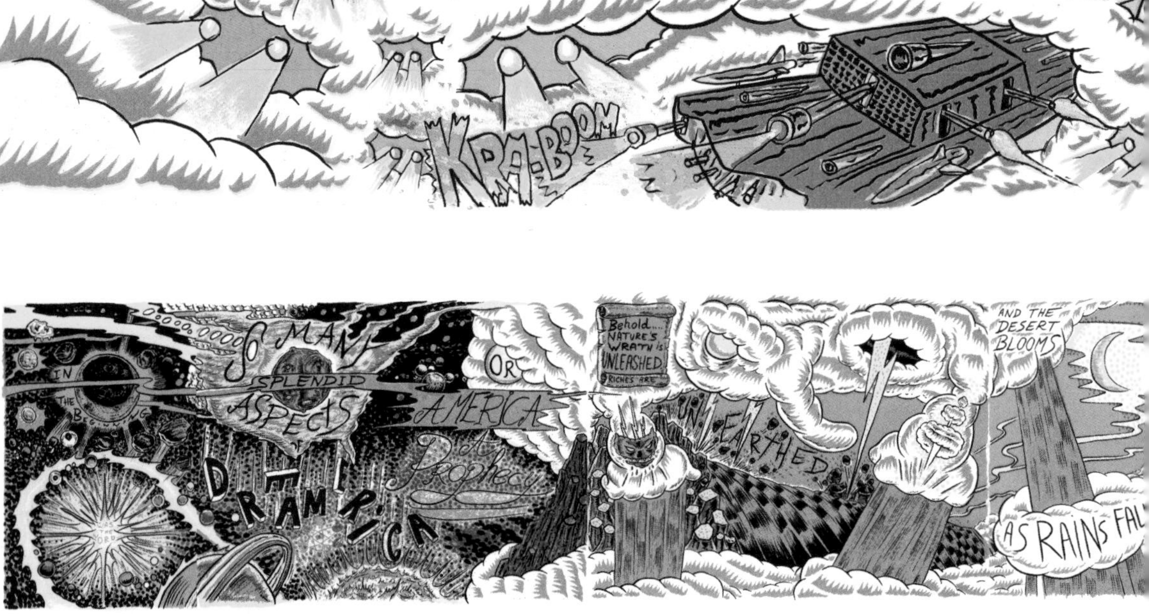
SO MANY
SPLENDID
ASPECTS
AMERICA
OR
A Prophecy
DRAMRICA
Behold... NATURE'S WRATH is UNLEASHED
UNEARTHED
AND THE DESERT BLOOMS

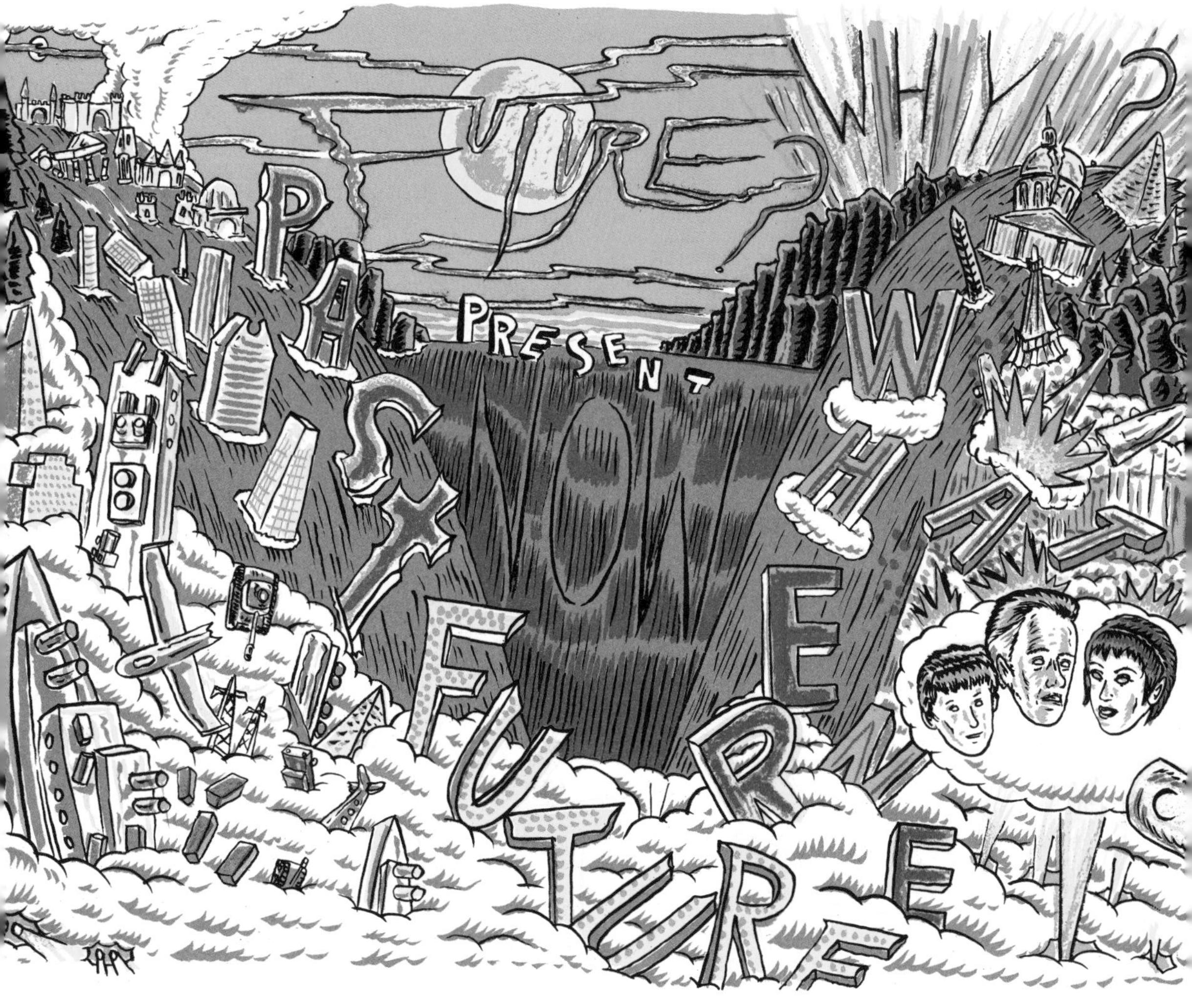
PRESENT
NOW
FUTURE

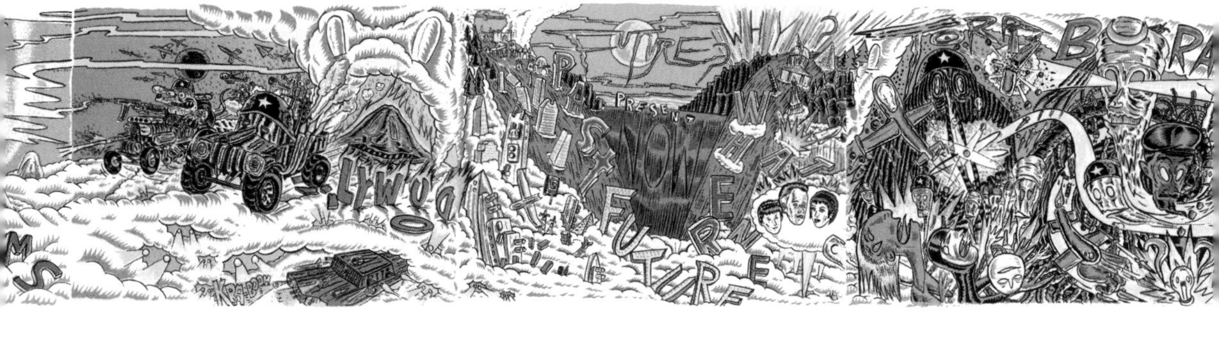

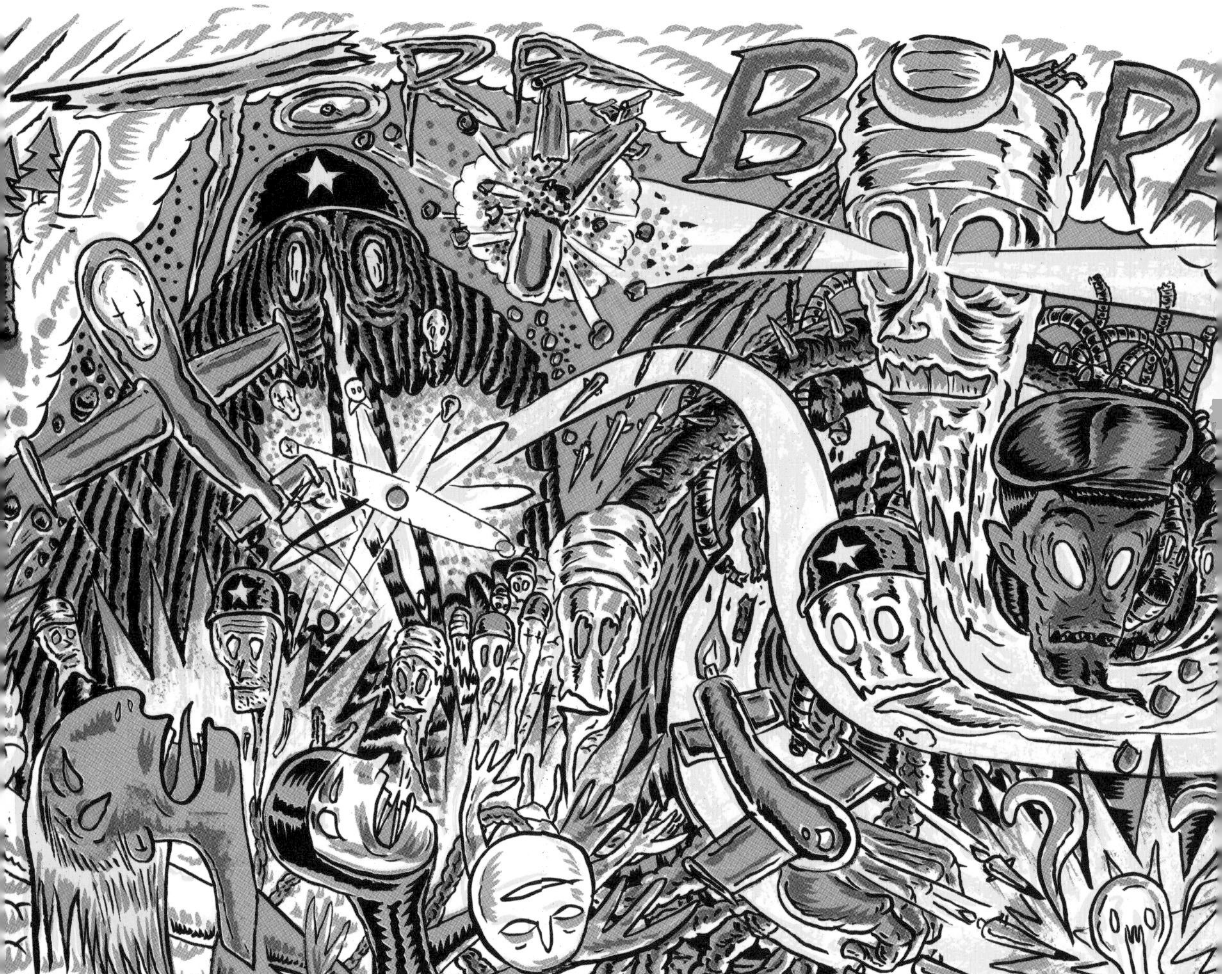

TORA
BORA

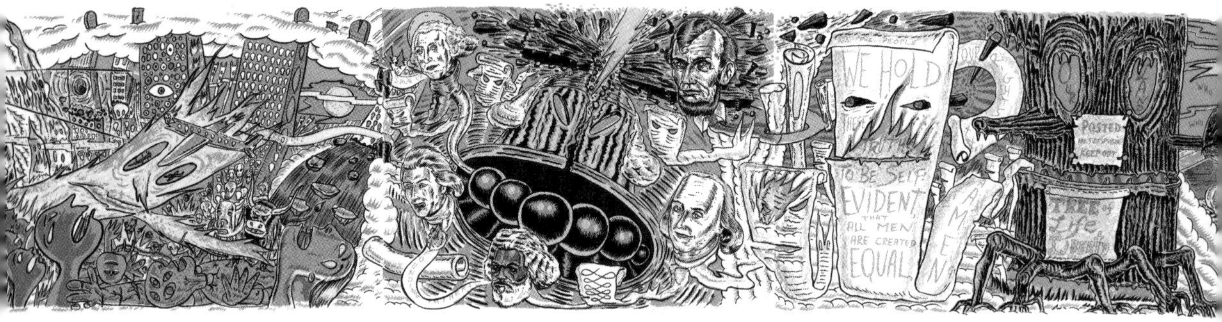

WE HOLD
TO BE SELF
EVIDENT
THAT
ALL MEN
ARE CREATED
EQUAL
POSTED
TREE of
Life

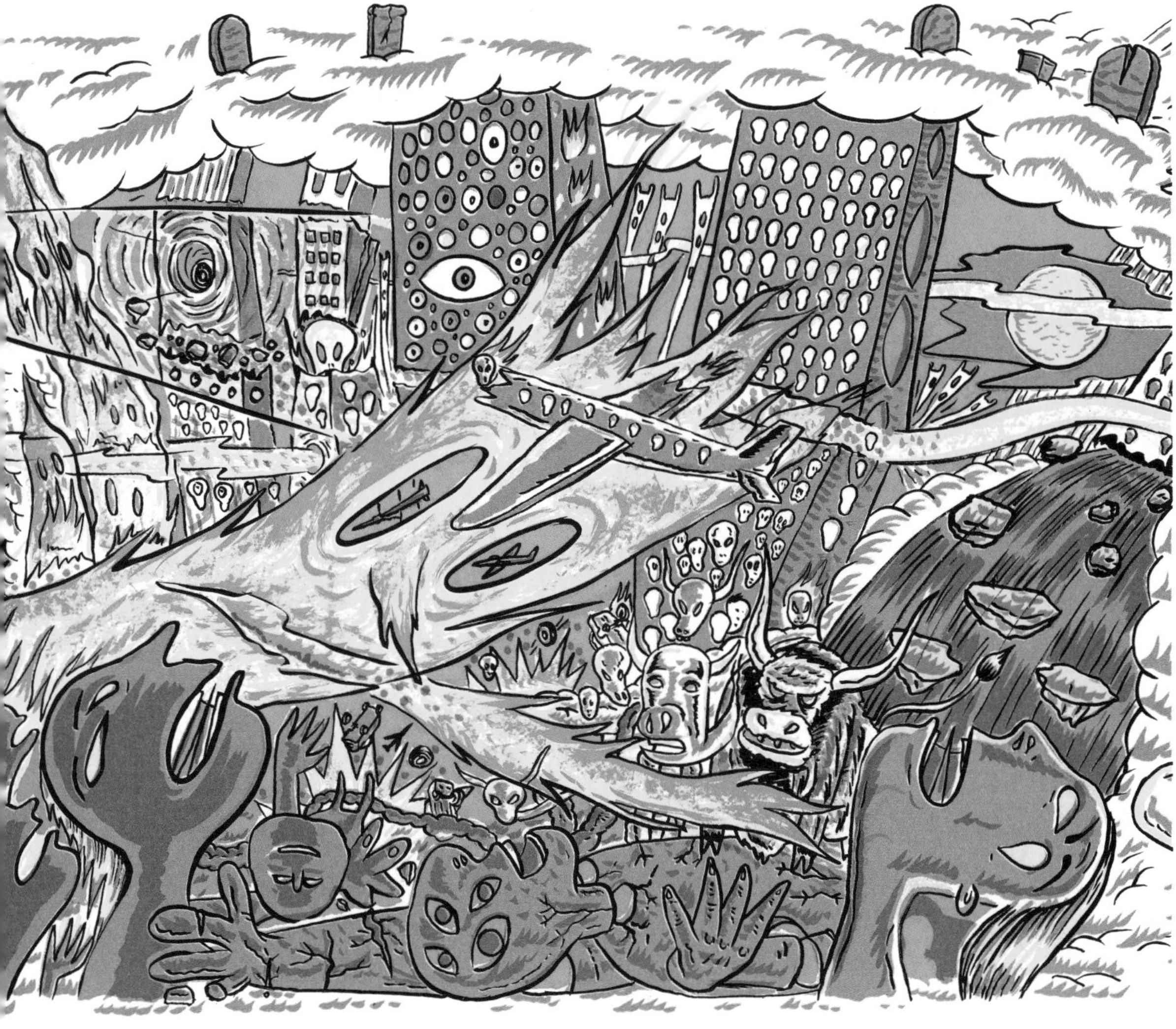

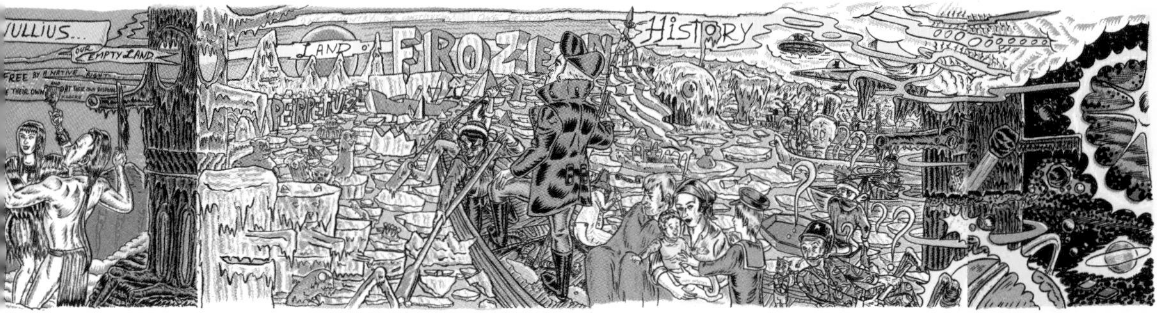

ULLIUS...
OUR EMPTY LAND
LAND O'
FROZE
History
PERPETU

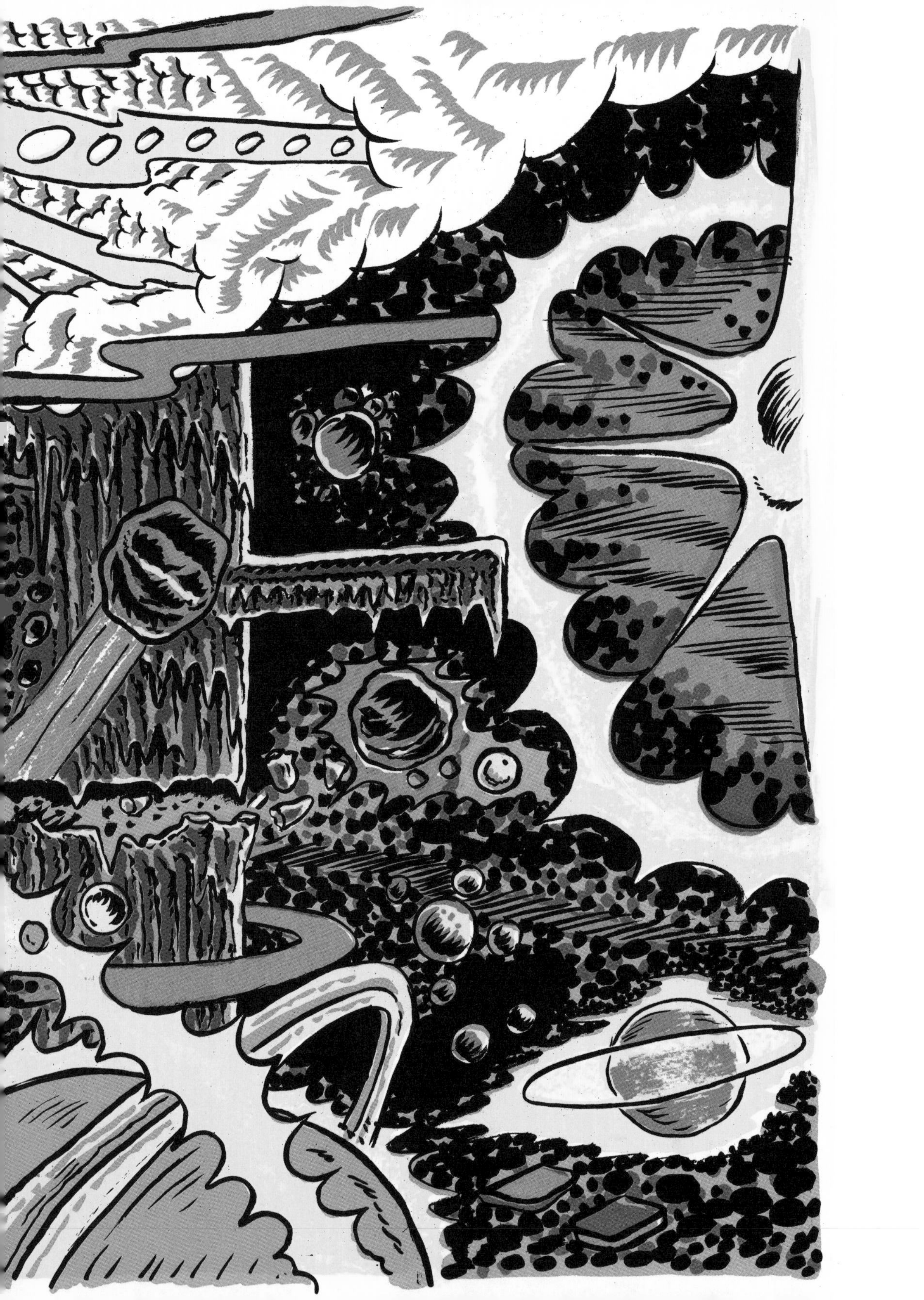

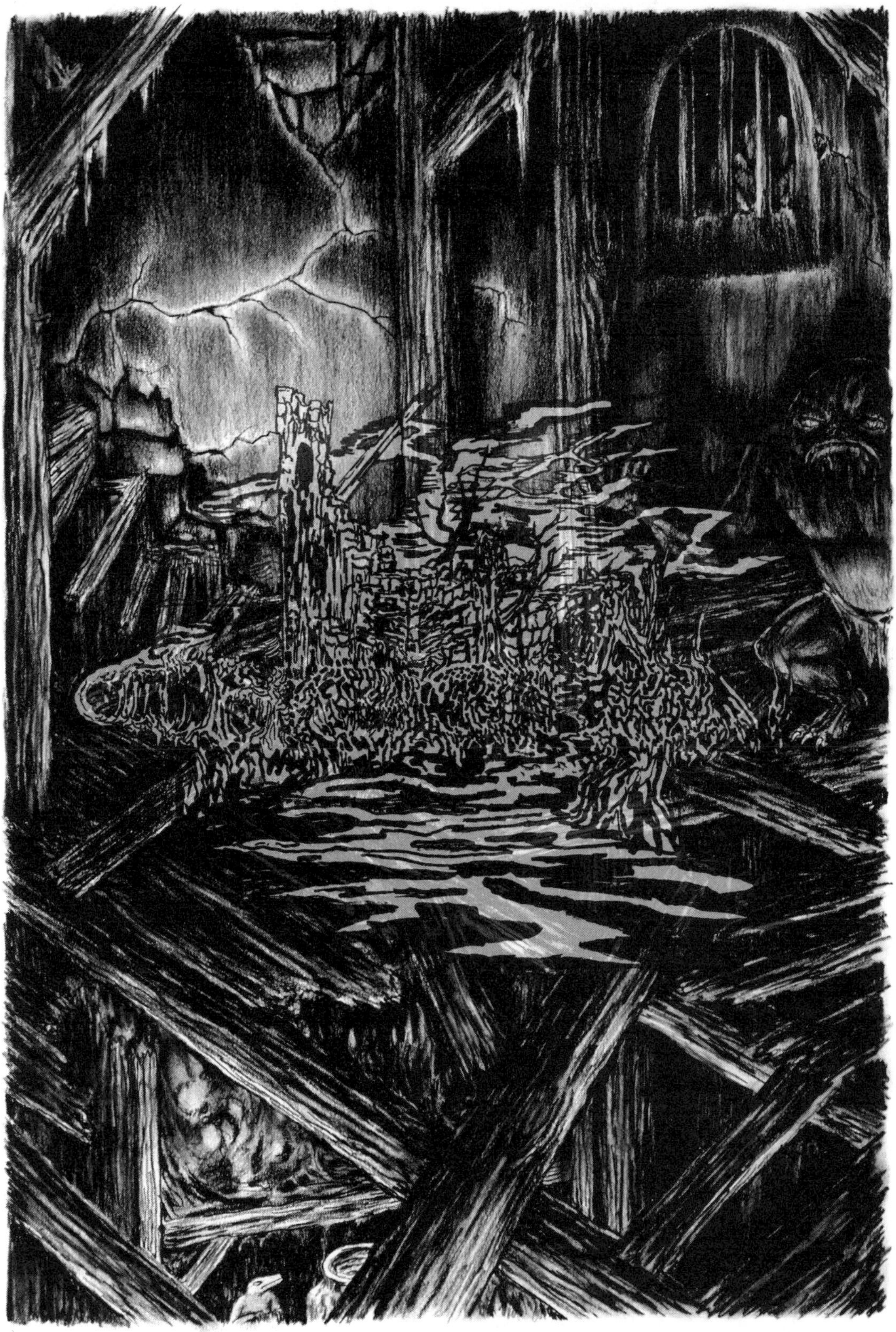

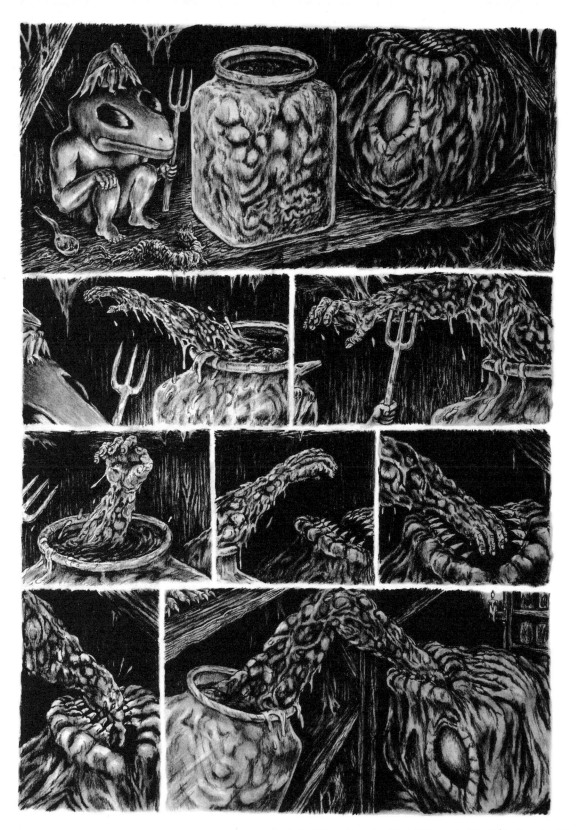

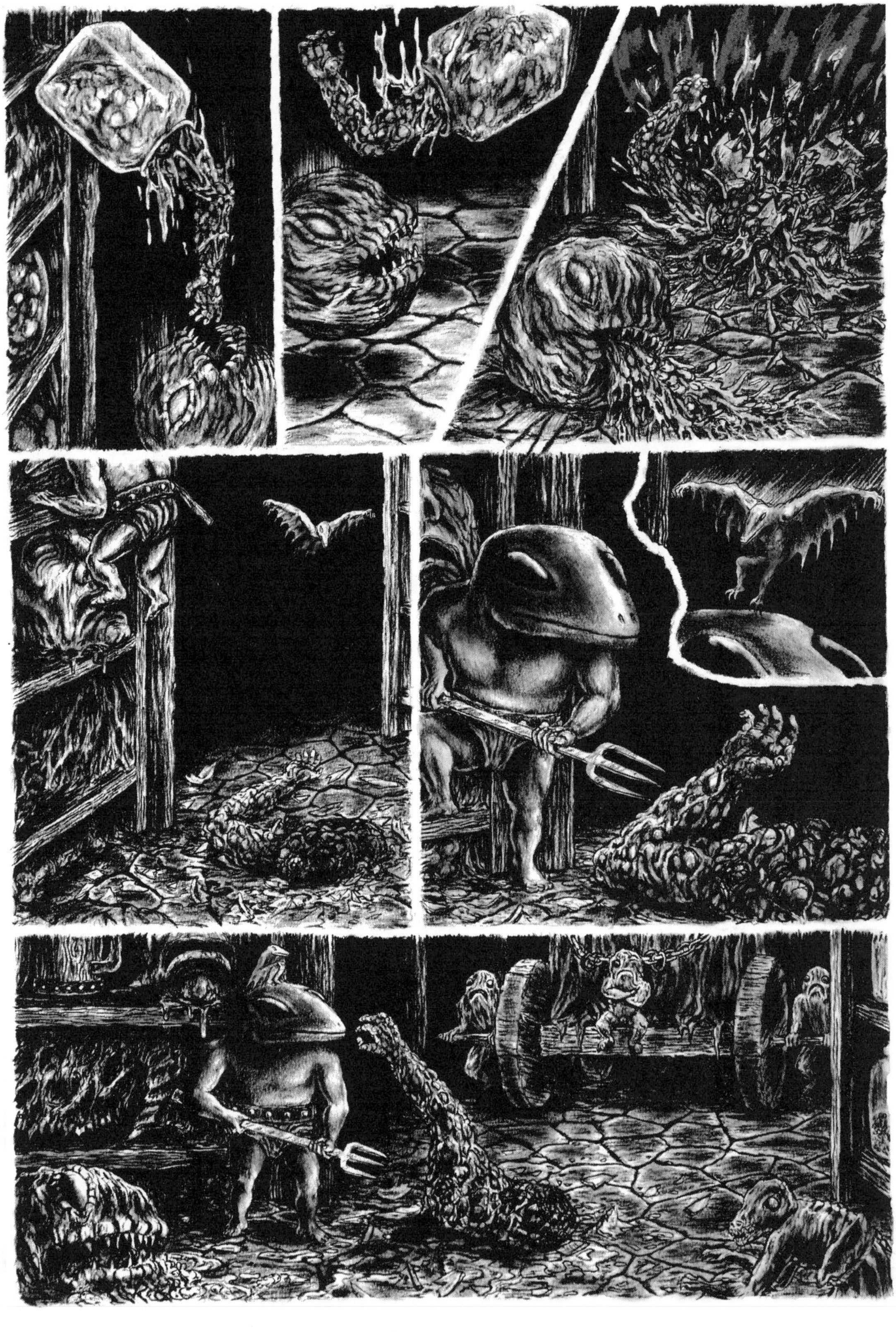

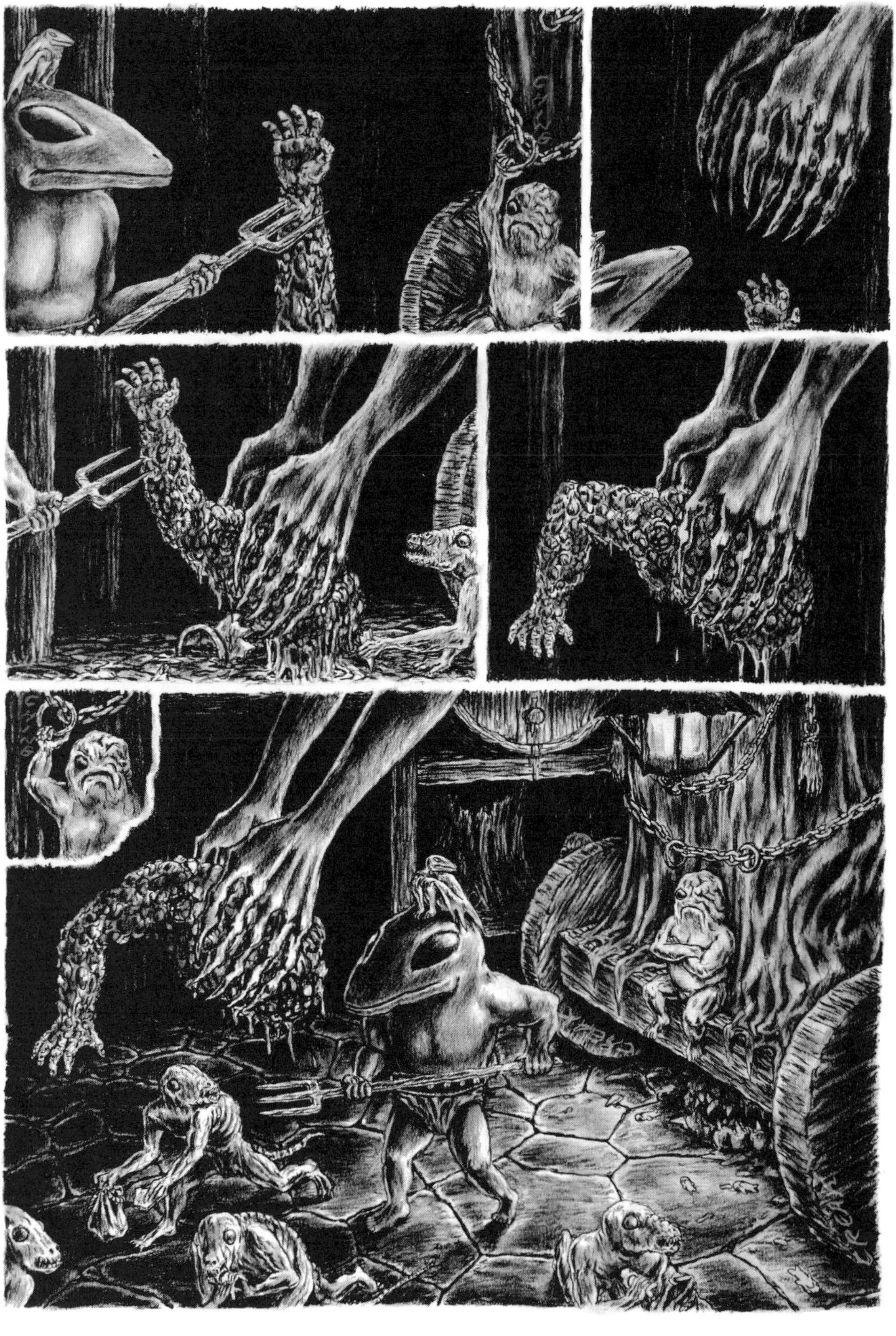

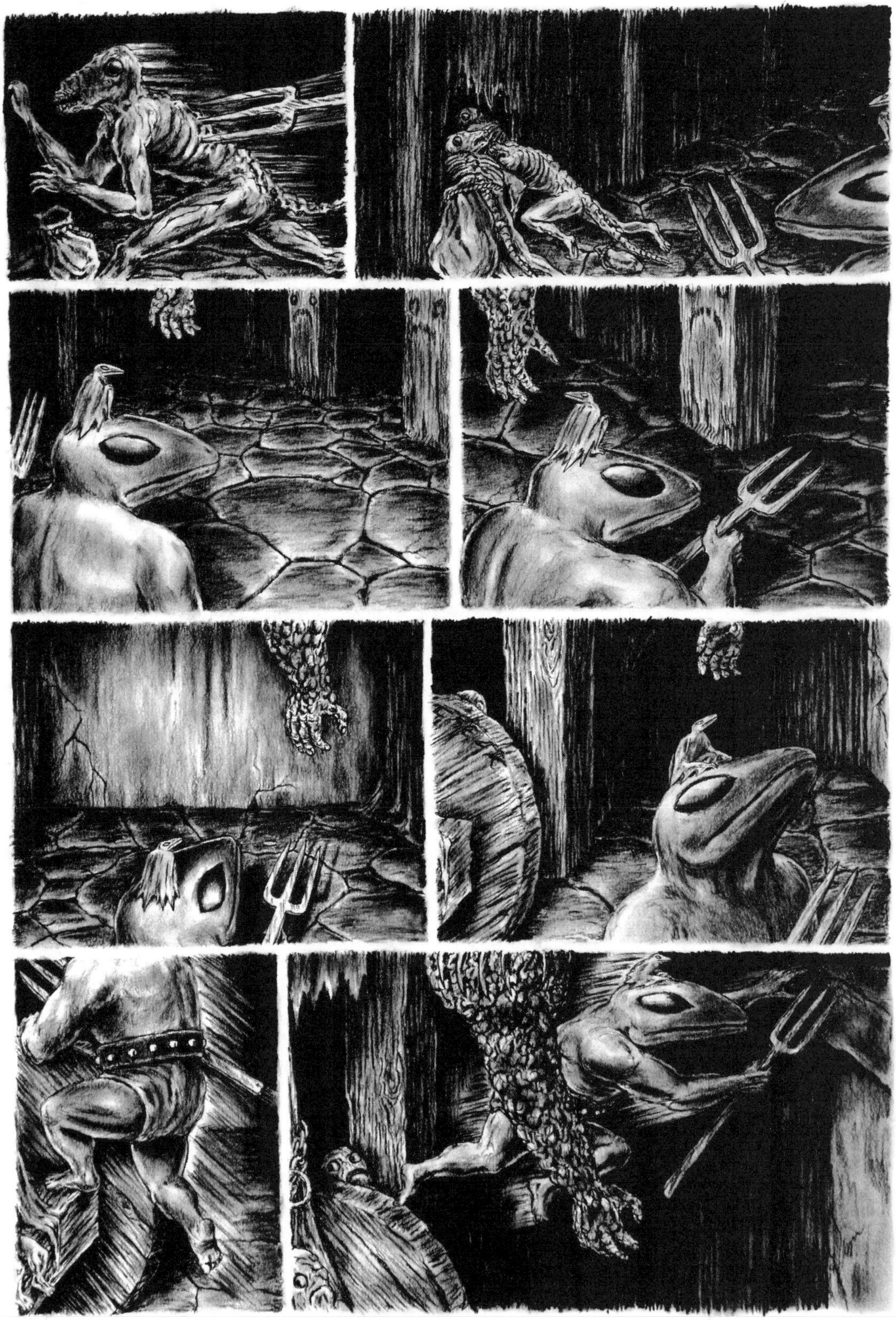

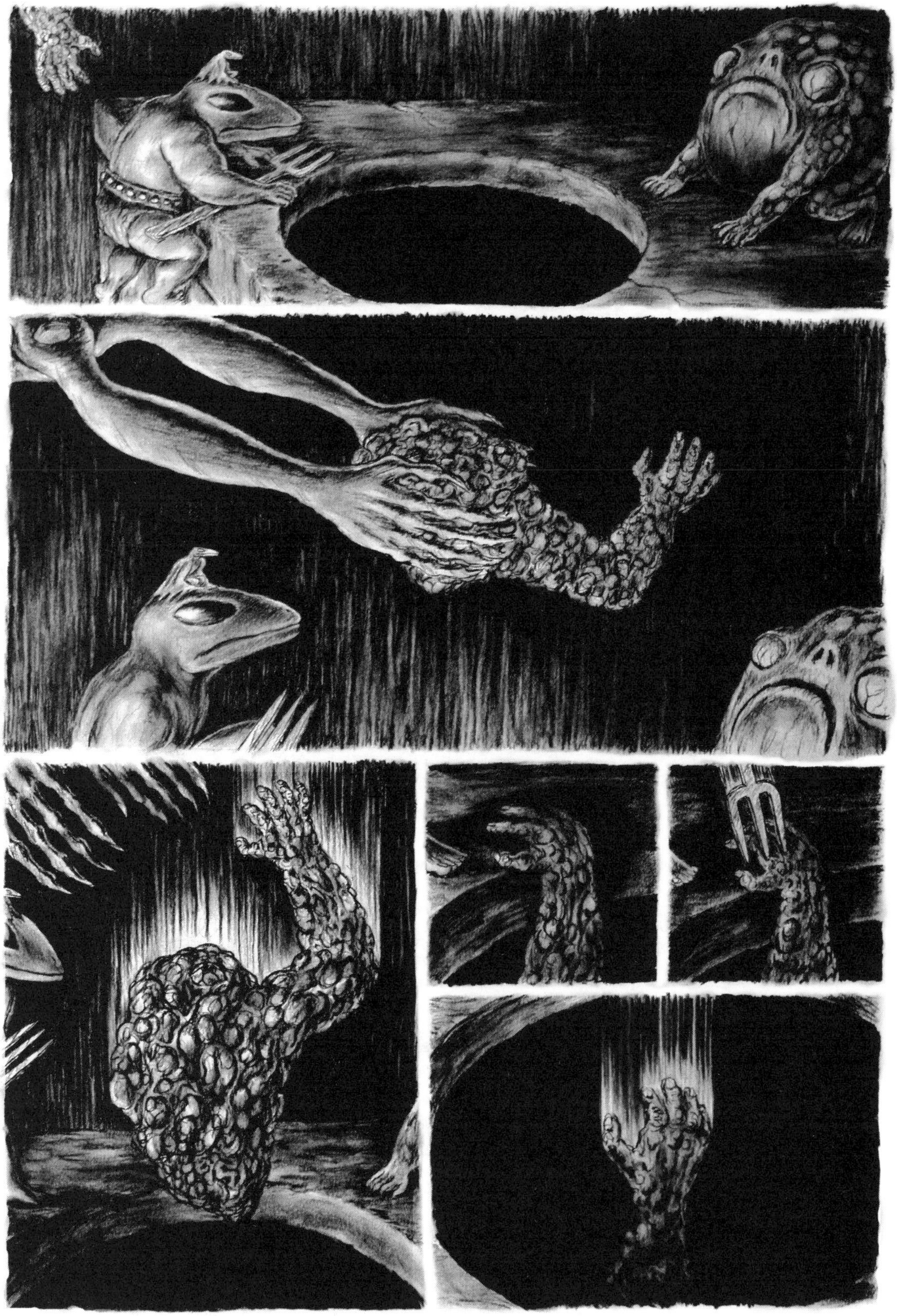

"briefly, before dawn"

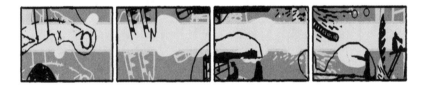

by Rosaire Appel

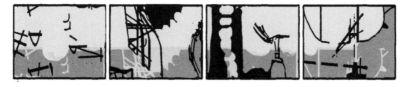

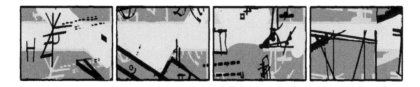

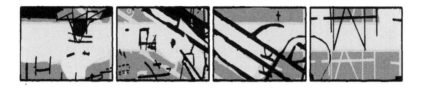

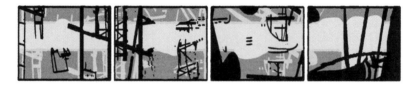

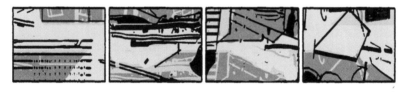

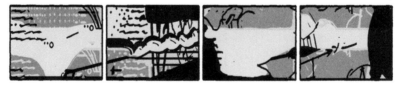

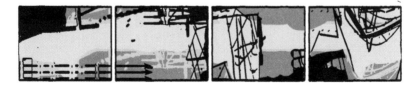

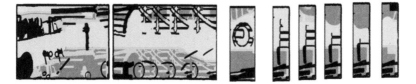

CHAPTER SIX

Biopics and Historical Fictions

WOMAN REBEL
THE MARGARET SANGER STORY

JOE SACCO
THE
GREAT WAR

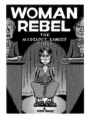

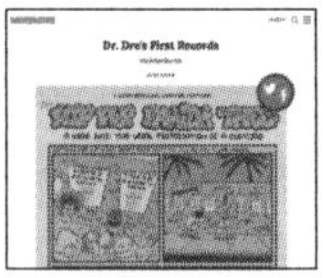

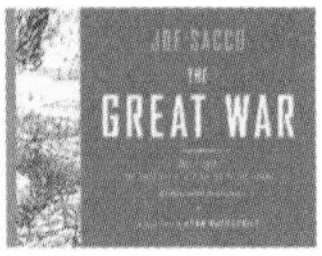

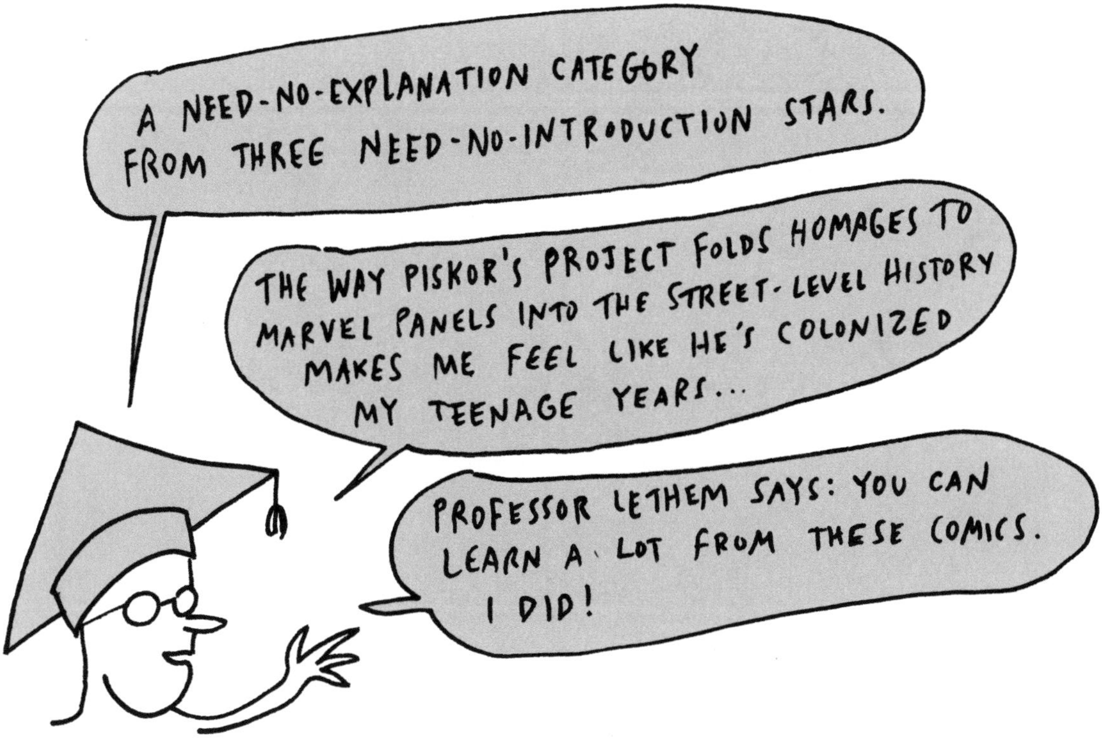
A NEED-NO-EXPLANATION CATEGORY FROM THREE NEED-NO-INTRODUCTION STARS.
THE WAY PISKOR'S PROJECT FOLDS HOMAGES TO MARVEL PANELS INTO THE STREET-LEVEL HISTORY MAKES ME FEEL LIKE HE'S COLONIZED MY TEENAGE YEARS...
PROFESSOR LETHEM SAYS: YOU CAN LEARN A LOT FROM THESE COMICS. I DID!

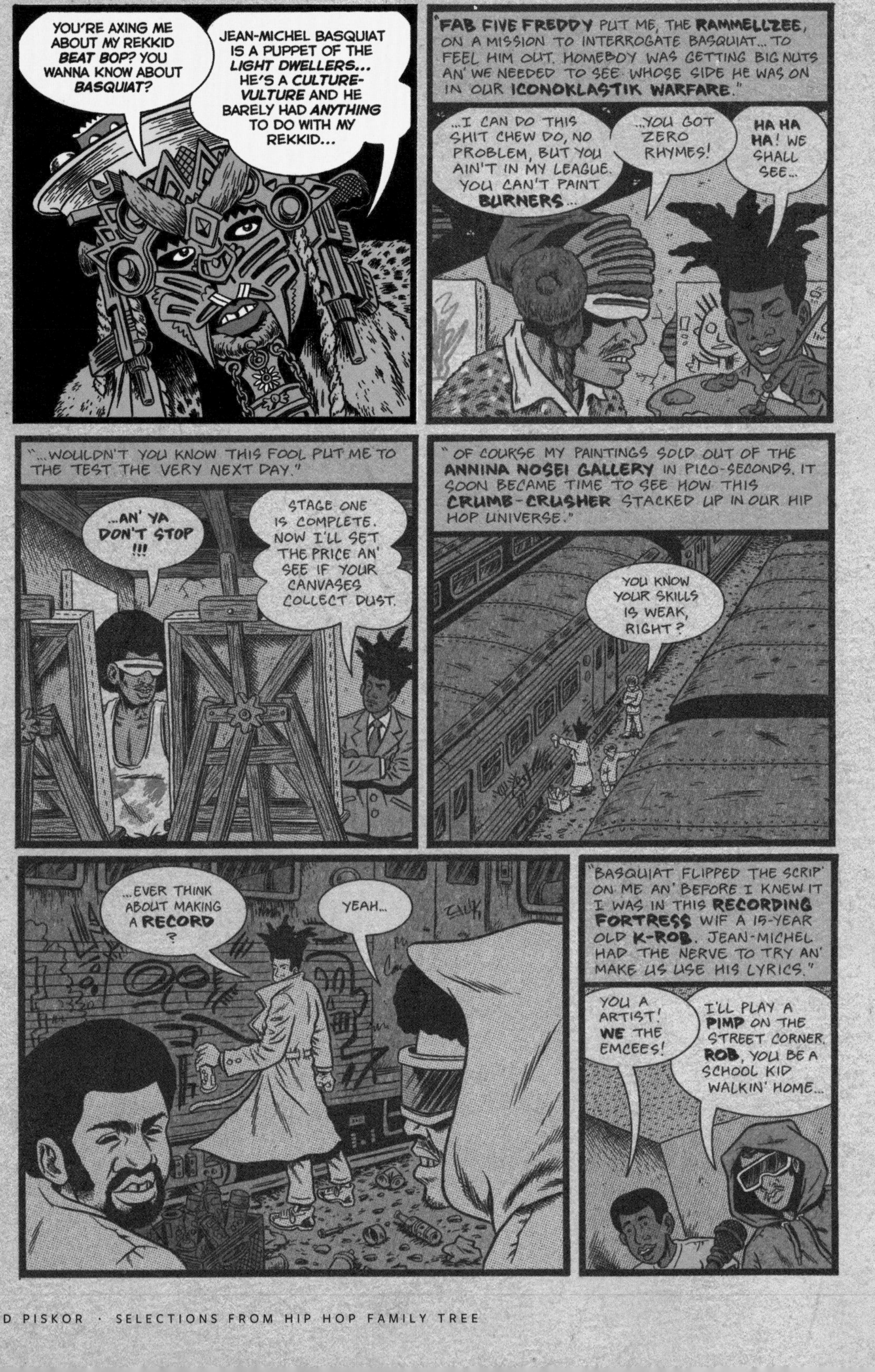

YOU'RE AXING ME ABOUT MY REKKID BEAT BOP? YOU WANNA KNOW ABOUT BASQUIAT?
JEAN-MICHEL BASQUIAT IS A PUPPET OF THE LIGHT DWELLERS... HE'S A CULTURE-VULTURE AND HE BARELY HAD ANYTHING TO DO WITH MY REKKID...
"FAB FIVE FREDDY PUT ME, THE RAMMELLZEE, ON A MISSION TO INTERROGATE BASQUIAT... TO FEEL HIM OUT. HOMEBOY WAS GETTING BIG NUTS AN' WE NEEDED TO SEE WHOSE SIDE HE WAS ON IN OUR ICONOKLASTIK WARFARE."
...I CAN DO THIS SHIT CHEW DO, NO PROBLEM, BUT YOU AIN'T IN MY LEAGUE. YOU CAN'T PAINT BURNERS...
...YOU GOT ZERO RHYMES!
HA HA HA! WE SHALL SEE...
"...WOULDN'T YOU KNOW THIS FOOL PUT ME TO THE TEST THE VERY NEXT DAY."
...AN' YA DON'T STOP !!!
STAGE ONE IS COMPLETE. NOW I'LL SET THE PRICE AN' SEE IF YOUR CANVASES COLLECT DUST.
"OF COURSE MY PAINTINGS SOLD OUT OF THE ANNINA NOSEI GALLERY IN PICO-SECONDS. IT SOON BECAME TIME TO SEE HOW THIS CRUMB-CRUSHER STACKED UP IN OUR HIP HOP UNIVERSE."
YOU KNOW YOUR SKILLS IS WEAK, RIGHT?
...EVER THINK ABOUT MAKING A RECORD ?
YEAH...
"BASQUIAT FLIPPED THE SCRIP' ON ME AN' BEFORE I KNEW IT I WAS IN THIS RECORDING FORTRESS WIF A 15-YEAR OLD K-ROB. JEAN-MICHEL HAD THE NERVE TO TRY AN' MAKE US USE HIS LYRICS."
YOU A ARTIST! WE THE EMCEES!
I'LL PLAY A PIMP ON THE STREET CORNER. ROB, YOU BE A SCHOOL KID WALKIN' HOME...

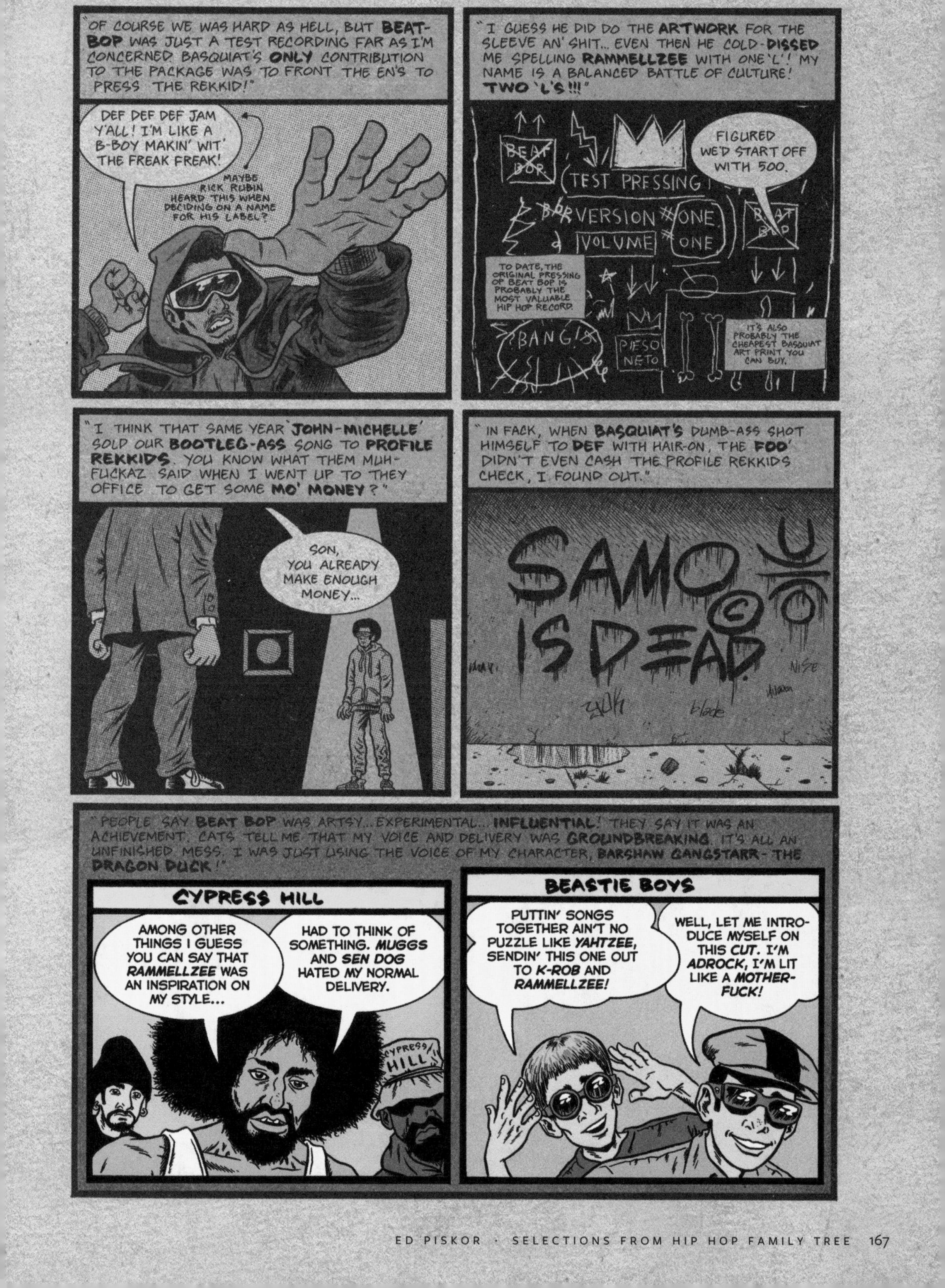
"OF COURSE WE WAS HARD AS HELL, BUT BEAT-BOP WAS JUST A TEST RECORDING FAR AS I'M CONCERNED. BASQUIAT'S ONLY CONTRIBUTION TO THE PACKAGE WAS TO FRONT THE EN'S TO PRESS THE REKKID!"
DEF DEF DEF JAM Y'ALL! I'M LIKE A B-BOY MAKIN' WIT' THE FREAK FREAK!
MAYBE RICK RUBIN HEARD THIS WHEN DECIDING ON A NAME FOR HIS LABEL?
"I GUESS HE DID DO THE ARTWORK FOR THE SLEEVE AN' SHIT... EVEN THEN HE COLD-DISSED ME SPELLING RAMMELLZEE WITH ONE 'L'! MY NAME IS A BALANCED BATTLE OF CULTURE! TWO 'L'S!!!"
FIGURED WE'D START OFF WITH 500.
BEAT BOP
TEST PRESSING
VERSION ONE
VOLUME ONE
BANG!
PIESO NETO
TO DATE, THE ORIGINAL PRESSING OF BEAT BOP IS PROBABLY THE MOST VALUABLE HIP HOP RECORD.
IT'S ALSO PROBABLY THE CHEAPEST BASQUIAT ART PRINT YOU CAN BUY.
"I THINK THAT SAME YEAR 'JOHN-MICHELLE' SOLD OUR BOOTLEG-ASS SONG TO PROFILE REKKIDS. YOU KNOW WHAT THEM MUH-FUCKAZ SAID WHEN I WENT UP TO THEY OFFICE TO GET SOME MO' MONEY?"
SON, YOU ALREADY MAKE ENOUGH MONEY...
"IN FACK, WHEN BASQUIAT'S DUMB-ASS SHOT HIMSELF TO DEF WITH HAIR-ON, THE FOO' DIDN'T EVEN CASH THE PROFILE REKKIDS CHECK, I FOUND OUT."
SAMO © IS DEAD
"PEOPLE SAY BEAT BOP WAS ARTSY... EXPERIMENTAL... INFLUENTIAL! THEY SAY IT WAS AN ACHIEVEMENT. CATS TELL ME THAT MY VOICE AND DELIVERY WAS GROUNDBREAKING. IT'S ALL AN UNFINISHED MESS. I WAS JUST USING THE VOICE OF MY CHARACTER, BARSHAW GANGSTARR- THE DRAGON DUCK!"
CYPRESS HILL
AMONG OTHER THINGS I GUESS YOU CAN SAY THAT RAMMELLZEE WAS AN INSPIRATION ON MY STYLE...
HAD TO THINK OF SOMETHING. MUGGS AND SEN DOG HATED MY NORMAL DELIVERY.
CYPRESS HILL
BEASTIE BOYS
PUTTIN' SONGS TOGETHER AIN'T NO PUZZLE LIKE YAHTZEE, SENDIN' THIS ONE OUT TO K-ROB AND RAMMELLZEE!
WELL, LET ME INTRODUCE MYSELF ON THIS CUT. I'M ADROCK, I'M LIT LIKE A MOTHER-FUCK!

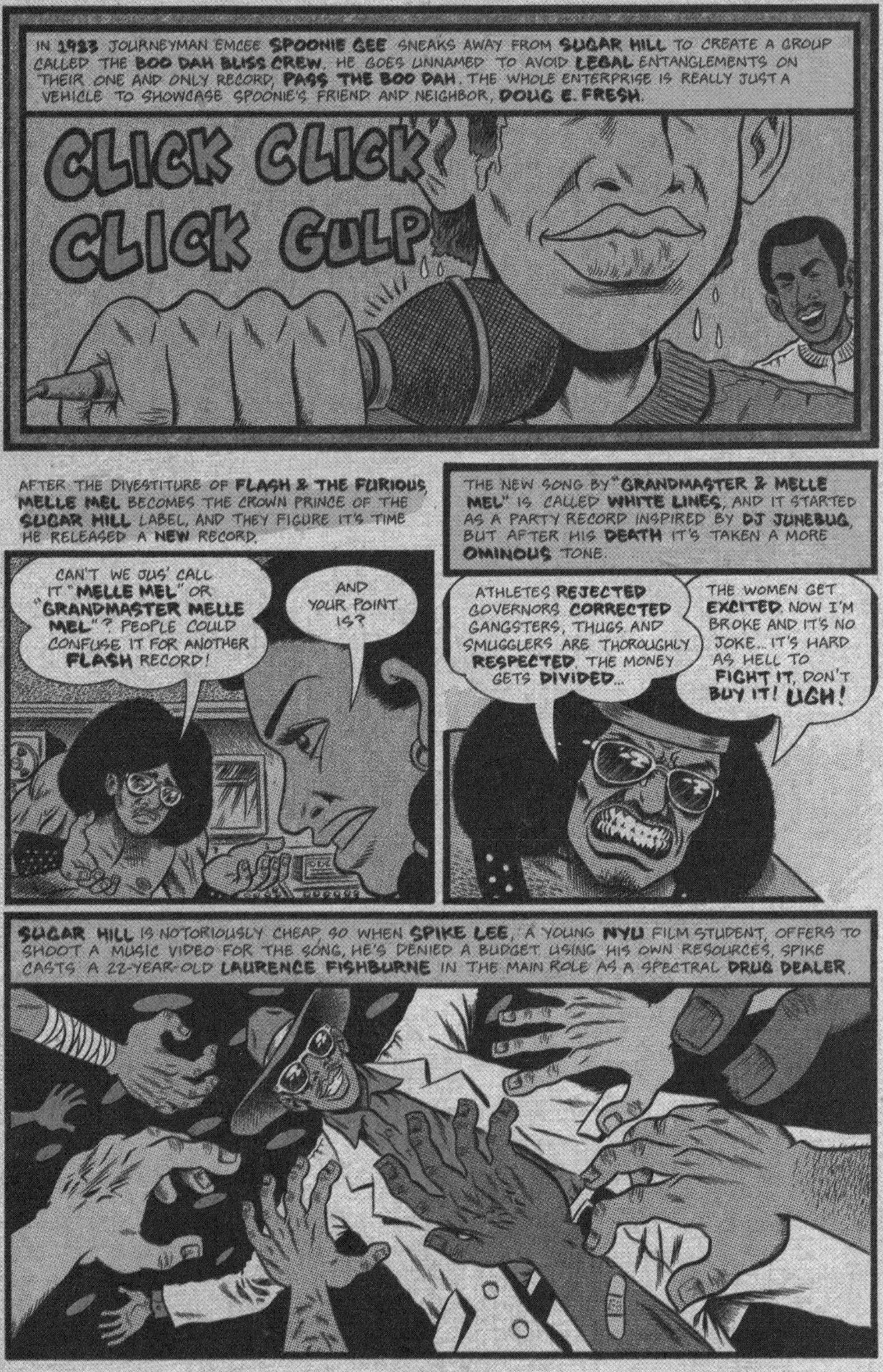
IN 1983 JOURNEYMAN EMCEE SPOONIE GEE SNEAKS AWAY FROM SUGAR HILL TO CREATE A GROUP CALLED THE BOO DAH BLISS CREW. HE GOES UNNAMED TO AVOID LEGAL ENTANGLEMENTS ON THEIR ONE AND ONLY RECORD, PASS THE BOO DAH. THE WHOLE ENTERPRISE IS REALLY JUST A VEHICLE TO SHOWCASE SPOONIE'S FRIEND AND NEIGHBOR, DOUG E. FRESH.
CLICK CLICK CLICK GULP
AFTER THE DIVESTITURE OF FLASH & THE FURIOUS, MELLE MEL BECOMES THE CROWN PRINCE OF THE SUGAR HILL LABEL, AND THEY FIGURE IT'S TIME HE RELEASED A NEW RECORD.
CAN'T WE JUS' CALL IT "MELLE MEL" OR "GRANDMASTER MELLE MEL"? PEOPLE COULD CONFUSE IT FOR ANOTHER FLASH RECORD!
AND YOUR POINT IS?
THE NEW SONG BY "GRANDMASTER & MELLE MEL" IS CALLED WHITE LINES, AND IT STARTED AS A PARTY RECORD INSPIRED BY DJ JUNEBUG, BUT AFTER HIS DEATH IT'S TAKEN A MORE OMINOUS TONE.
ATHLETES REJECTED GOVERNORS CORRECTED GANGSTERS, THUGS AND SMUGGLERS ARE THOROUGHLY RESPECTED. THE MONEY GETS DIVIDED...
THE WOMEN GET EXCITED. NOW I'M BROKE AND IT'S NO JOKE... IT'S HARD AS HELL TO FIGHT IT, DON'T BUY IT! UGH!
SUGAR HILL IS NOTORIOUSLY CHEAP, SO WHEN SPIKE LEE, A YOUNG NYU FILM STUDENT, OFFERS TO SHOOT A MUSIC VIDEO FOR THE SONG, HE'S DENIED A BUDGET. USING HIS OWN RESOURCES, SPIKE CASTS A 22-YEAR-OLD LAURENCE FISHBURNE IN THE MAIN ROLE AS A SPECTRAL DRUG DEALER.

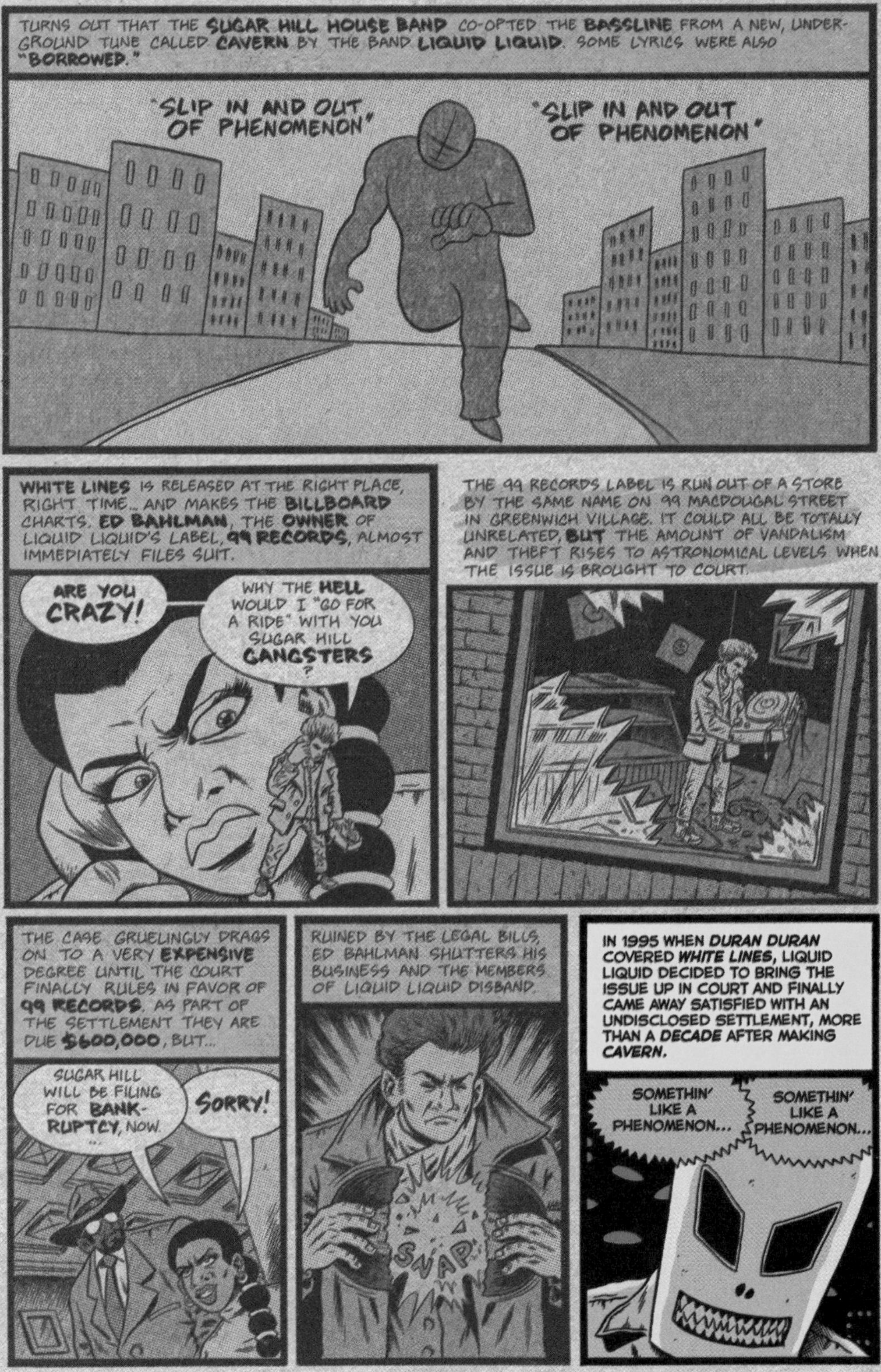

TURNS OUT THAT THE SUGAR HILL HOUSE BAND CO-OPTED THE BASSLINE FROM A NEW, UNDERGROUND TUNE CALLED CAVERN BY THE BAND LIQUID LIQUID. SOME LYRICS WERE ALSO "BORROWED."
"SLIP IN AND OUT OF PHENOMENON"
"SLIP IN AND OUT OF PHENOMENON"
WHITE LINES IS RELEASED AT THE RIGHT PLACE, RIGHT TIME... AND MAKES THE BILLBOARD CHARTS. ED BAHLMAN, THE OWNER OF LIQUID LIQUID'S LABEL, 99 RECORDS, ALMOST IMMEDIATELY FILES SUIT.
ARE YOU CRAZY!
WHY THE HELL WOULD I "GO FOR A RIDE" WITH YOU SUGAR HILL GANGSTERS?
THE 99 RECORDS LABEL IS RUN OUT OF A STORE BY THE SAME NAME ON 99 MACDOUGAL STREET IN GREENWICH VILLAGE. IT COULD ALL BE TOTALLY UNRELATED, BUT THE AMOUNT OF VANDALISM AND THEFT RISES TO ASTRONOMICAL LEVELS WHEN THE ISSUE IS BROUGHT TO COURT.
THE CASE GRUELINGLY DRAGS ON TO A VERY EXPENSIVE DEGREE UNTIL THE COURT FINALLY RULES IN FAVOR OF 99 RECORDS. AS PART OF THE SETTLEMENT THEY ARE DUE $600,000, BUT...
SUGAR HILL WILL BE FILING FOR BANKRUPTCY, NOW...
SORRY!
RUINED BY THE LEGAL BILLS, ED BAHLMAN SHUTTERS HIS BUSINESS AND THE MEMBERS OF LIQUID LIQUID DISBAND.
SNAP!
IN 1995 WHEN DURAN DURAN COVERED WHITE LINES, LIQUID LIQUID DECIDED TO BRING THE ISSUE UP IN COURT AND FINALLY CAME AWAY SATISFIED WITH AN UNDISCLOSED SETTLEMENT, MORE THAN A DECADE AFTER MAKING CAVERN.
SOMETHIN' LIKE A PHENOMENON...
SOMETHIN' LIKE A PHENOMENON...

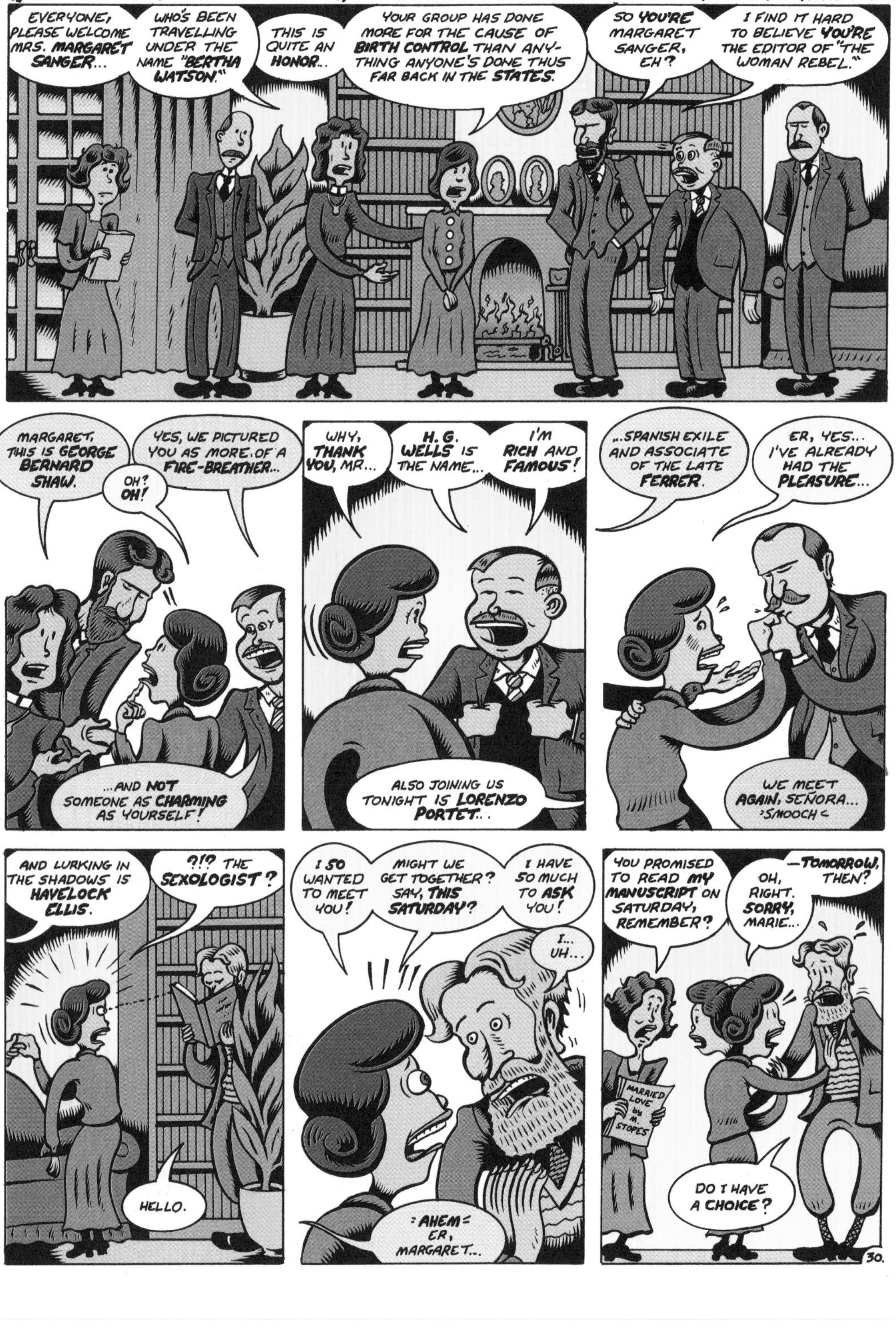
A MEETING OF THE NEO-MALTHUSIAN SOCIETY, AT THE HOME OF DR C.V. AND BESSIE DRYSDALE, LONDON, U.K., LATE 1914...
EVERYONE, PLEASE WELCOME MRS. MARGARET SANGER...
WHO'S BEEN TRAVELLING UNDER THE NAME "BERTHA WATSON."
THIS IS QUITE AN HONOR...
YOUR GROUP HAS DONE MORE FOR THE CAUSE OF BIRTH CONTROL THAN ANYTHING ANYONE'S DONE THUS FAR BACK IN THE STATES.
SO YOU'RE MARGARET SANGER, EH?
I FIND IT HARD TO BELIEVE YOU'RE THE EDITOR OF "THE WOMAN REBEL."
MARGARET, THIS IS GEORGE BERNARD SHAW.
YES, WE PICTURED YOU AS MORE OF A FIRE-BREATHER...
OH? OH!
...AND NOT SOMEONE AS CHARMING AS YOURSELF!
WHY, THANK YOU, MR...
H.G. WELLS IS THE NAME...
I'M RICH AND FAMOUS!
ALSO JOINING US TONIGHT IS LORENZO PORTET...
...SPANISH EXILE AND ASSOCIATE OF THE LATE FERRER.
ER, YES... I'VE ALREADY HAD THE PLEASURE...
WE MEET AGAIN, SEÑORA... ᶻSMOOCHᶻ
AND LURKING IN THE SHADOWS IS HAVELOCK ELLIS.
?!? THE SEXOLOGIST?
HELLO.
I SO WANTED TO MEET YOU!
MIGHT WE GET TOGETHER? SAY, THIS SATURDAY?
I HAVE SO MUCH TO ASK YOU!
I... UH...
AHEM ER, MARGARET...
YOU PROMISED TO READ MY MANUSCRIPT ON SATURDAY, REMEMBER?
OH, RIGHT. SORRY, MARIE...
—TOMORROW, THEN?
DO I HAVE A CHOICE?
MARRIED LOVE by M. STOPES
30.

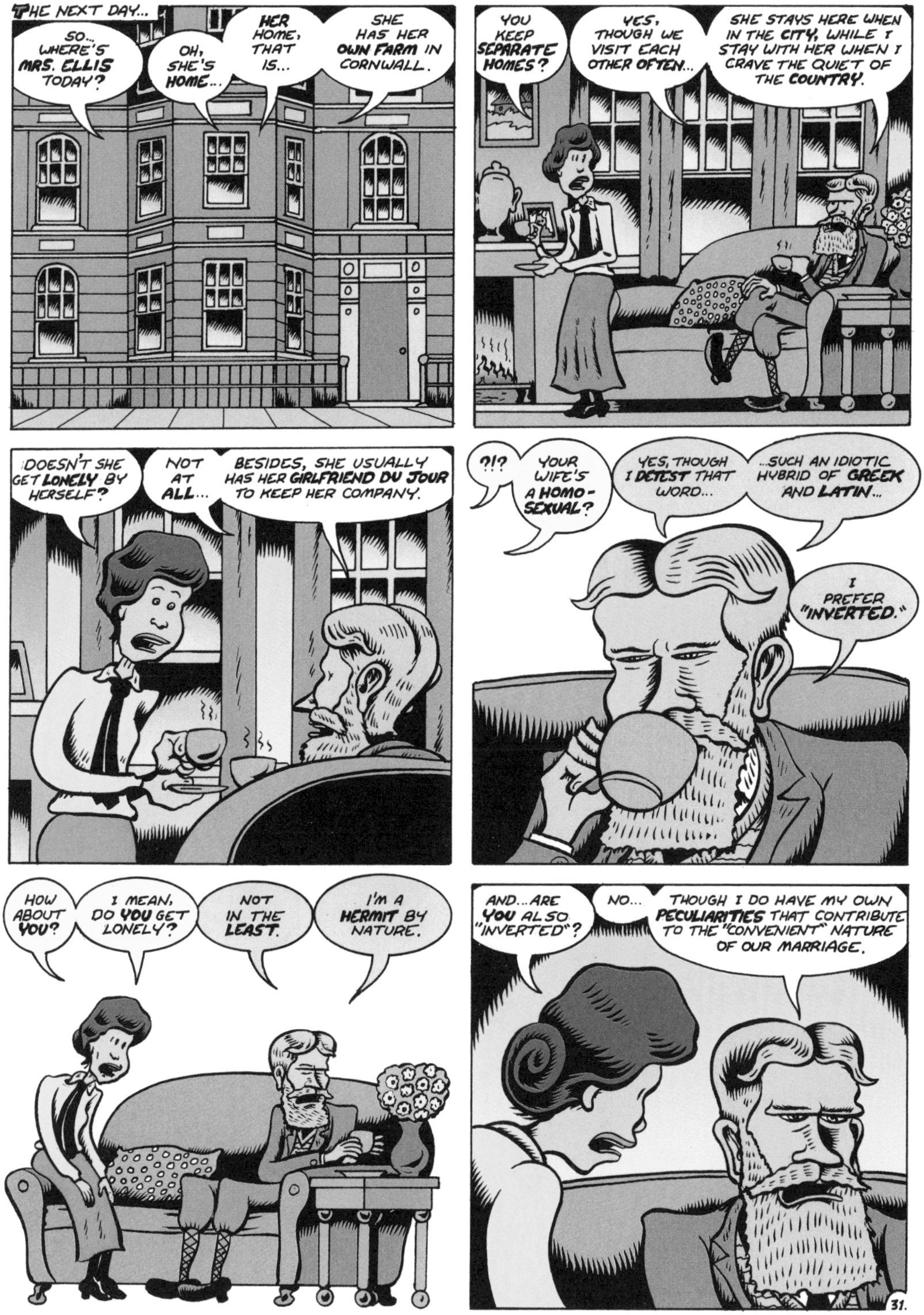
THE NEXT DAY...
SO... WHERE'S MRS. ELLIS TODAY?
OH, SHE'S HOME...
HER HOME, THAT IS...
SHE HAS HER OWN FARM IN CORNWALL.
YOU KEEP SEPARATE HOMES?
YES, THOUGH WE VISIT EACH OTHER OFTEN...
SHE STAYS HERE WHEN IN THE CITY, WHILE I STAY WITH HER WHEN I CRAVE THE QUIET OF THE COUNTRY.
DOESN'T SHE GET LONELY BY HERSELF?
NOT AT ALL...
BESIDES, SHE USUALLY HAS HER GIRLFRIEND DU JOUR TO KEEP HER COMPANY.
?!?
YOUR WIFE'S A HOMO-SEXUAL?
YES, THOUGH I DETEST THAT WORD...
...SUCH AN IDIOTIC HYBRID OF GREEK AND LATIN...
I PREFER "INVERTED."
HOW ABOUT YOU?
I MEAN, DO YOU GET LONELY?
NOT IN THE LEAST.
I'M A HERMIT BY NATURE.
AND... ARE YOU ALSO "INVERTED"?
NO...
THOUGH I DO HAVE MY OWN PECULIARITIES THAT CONTRIBUTE TO THE "CONVENIENT" NATURE OF OUR MARRIAGE.
31.

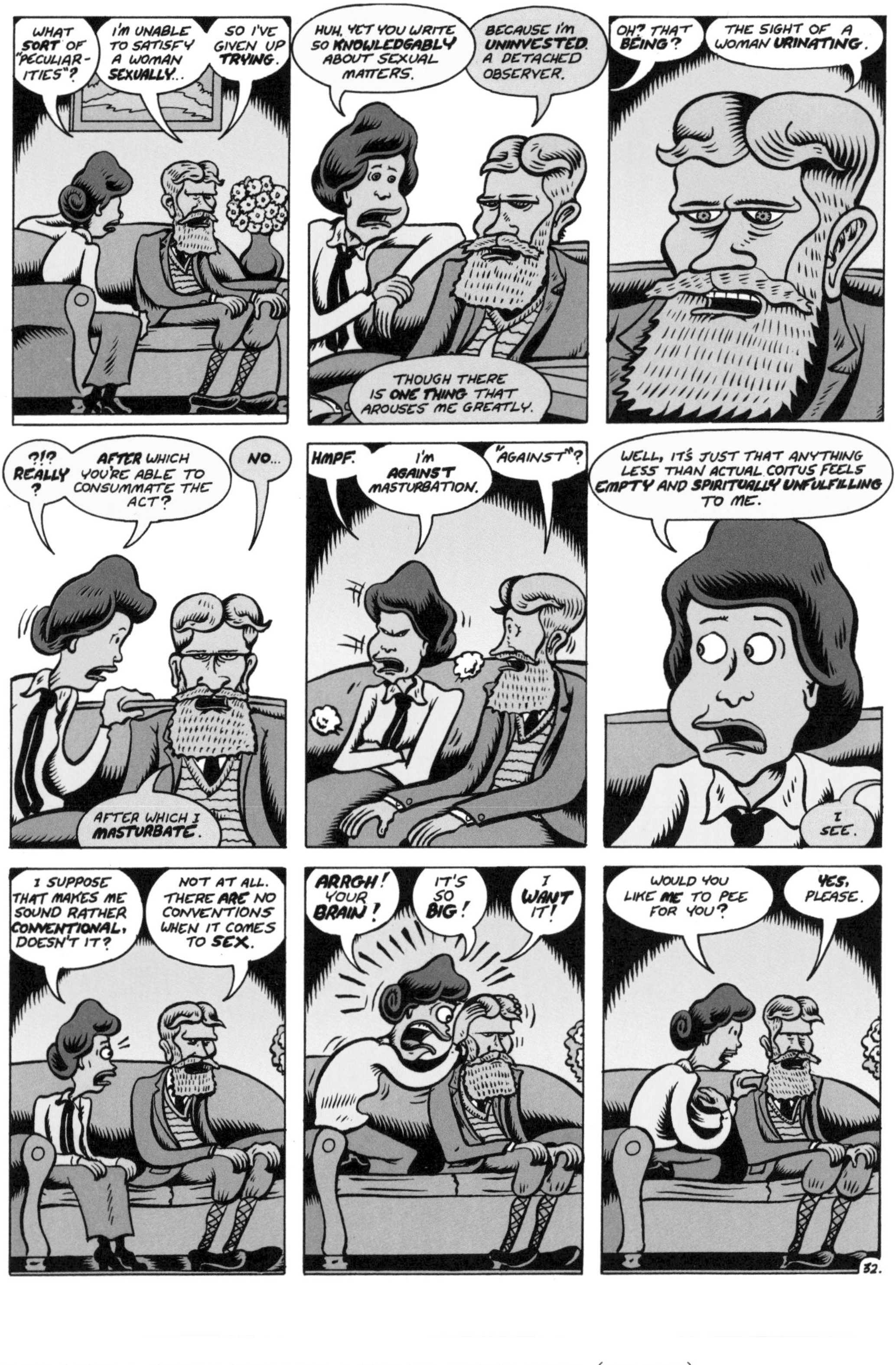

WHAT SORT OF "PECULIARITIES"?
I'M UNABLE TO SATISFY A WOMAN SEXUALLY...
SO I'VE GIVEN UP TRYING.
HUH, YET YOU WRITE SO KNOWLEDGABLY ABOUT SEXUAL MATTERS.
BECAUSE I'M UNINVESTED. A DETACHED OBSERVER.
THOUGH THERE IS ONE THING THAT AROUSES ME GREATLY.
OH? THAT BEING?
THE SIGHT OF A WOMAN URINATING.
?!? REALLY?
AFTER WHICH YOU'RE ABLE TO CONSUMMATE THE ACT?
NO...
AFTER WHICH I MASTURBATE.
HMPF.
I'M AGAINST MASTURBATION.
"AGAINST"?
WELL, IT'S JUST THAT ANYTHING LESS THAN ACTUAL COITUS FEELS EMPTY AND SPIRITUALLY UNFULFILLING TO ME.
I SEE.
I SUPPOSE THAT MAKES ME SOUND RATHER CONVENTIONAL, DOESN'T IT?
NOT AT ALL. THERE ARE NO CONVENTIONS WHEN IT COMES TO SEX.
ARRGH! YOUR BRAIN!
IT'S SO BIG!
I WANT IT!
WOULD YOU LIKE ME TO PEE FOR YOU?
YES, PLEASE.
32.

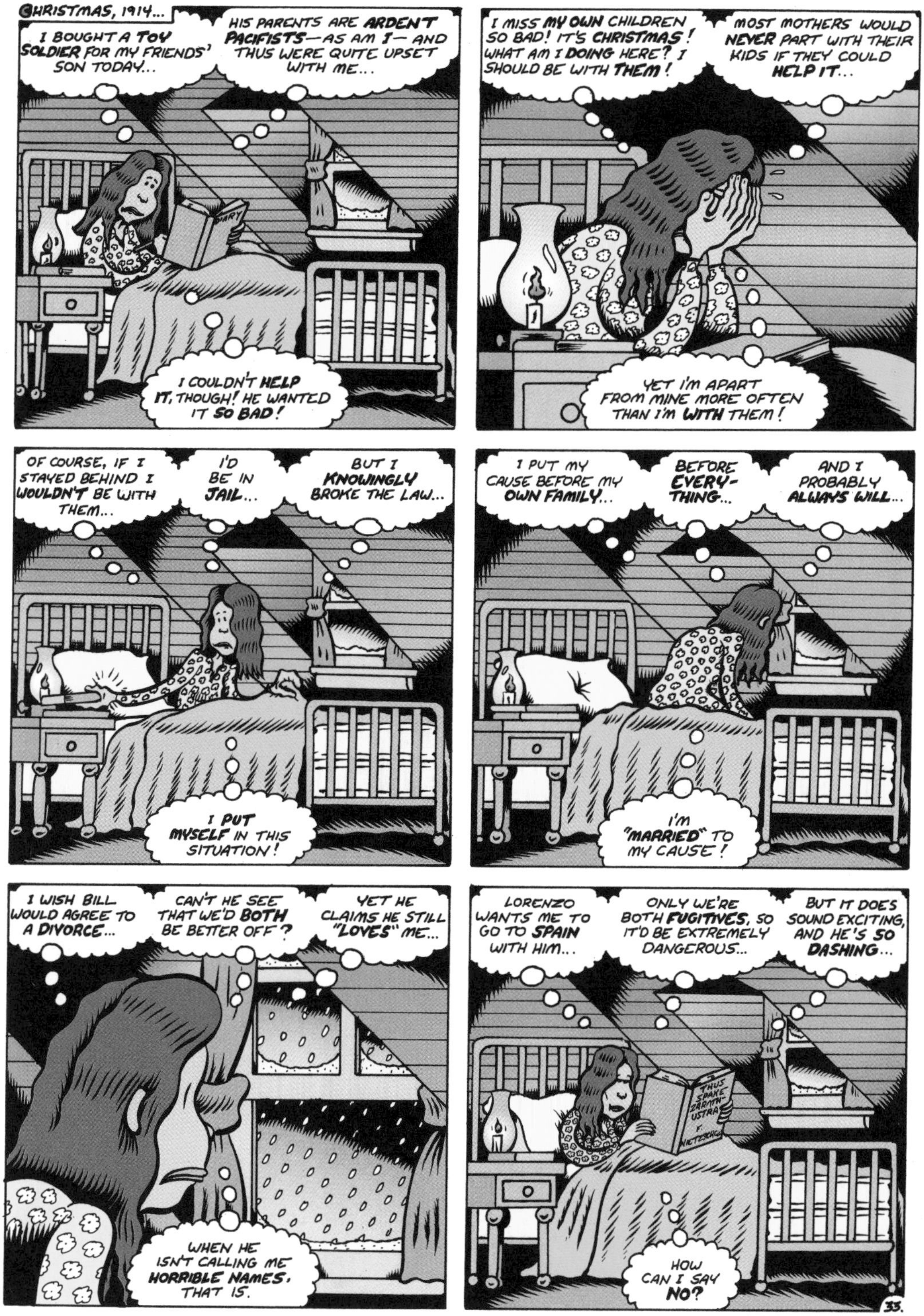
CHRISTMAS, 1914...
I BOUGHT A TOY SOLDIER FOR MY FRIENDS' SON TODAY...
HIS PARENTS ARE ARDENT PACIFISTS—AS AM I—AND THUS WERE QUITE UPSET WITH ME...
DIARY
I COULDN'T HELP IT, THOUGH! HE WANTED IT SO BAD!
I MISS MY OWN CHILDREN SO BAD! IT'S CHRISTMAS! WHAT AM I DOING HERE? I SHOULD BE WITH THEM!
MOST MOTHERS WOULD NEVER PART WITH THEIR KIDS IF THEY COULD HELP IT...
YET I'M APART FROM MINE MORE OFTEN THAN I'M WITH THEM!
OF COURSE, IF I STAYED BEHIND I WOULDN'T BE WITH THEM...
I'D BE IN JAIL...
BUT I KNOWINGLY BROKE THE LAW...
I PUT MYSELF IN THIS SITUATION!
I PUT MY CAUSE BEFORE MY OWN FAMILY...
BEFORE EVERY-THING...
AND I PROBABLY ALWAYS WILL...
I'M "MARRIED" TO MY CAUSE!
I WISH BILL WOULD AGREE TO A DIVORCE...
CAN'T HE SEE THAT WE'D BOTH BE BETTER OFF?
YET HE CLAIMS HE STILL "LOVES" ME...
WHEN HE ISN'T CALLING ME HORRIBLE NAMES, THAT IS.
LORENZO WANTS ME TO GO TO SPAIN WITH HIM...
ONLY WE'RE BOTH FUGITIVES, SO IT'D BE EXTREMELY DANGEROUS...
BUT IT DOES SOUND EXCITING, AND HE'S SO DASHING...
THUS SPAKE ZARATHUSTRA F. NIETZSCHE
HOW CAN I SAY NO?
33.

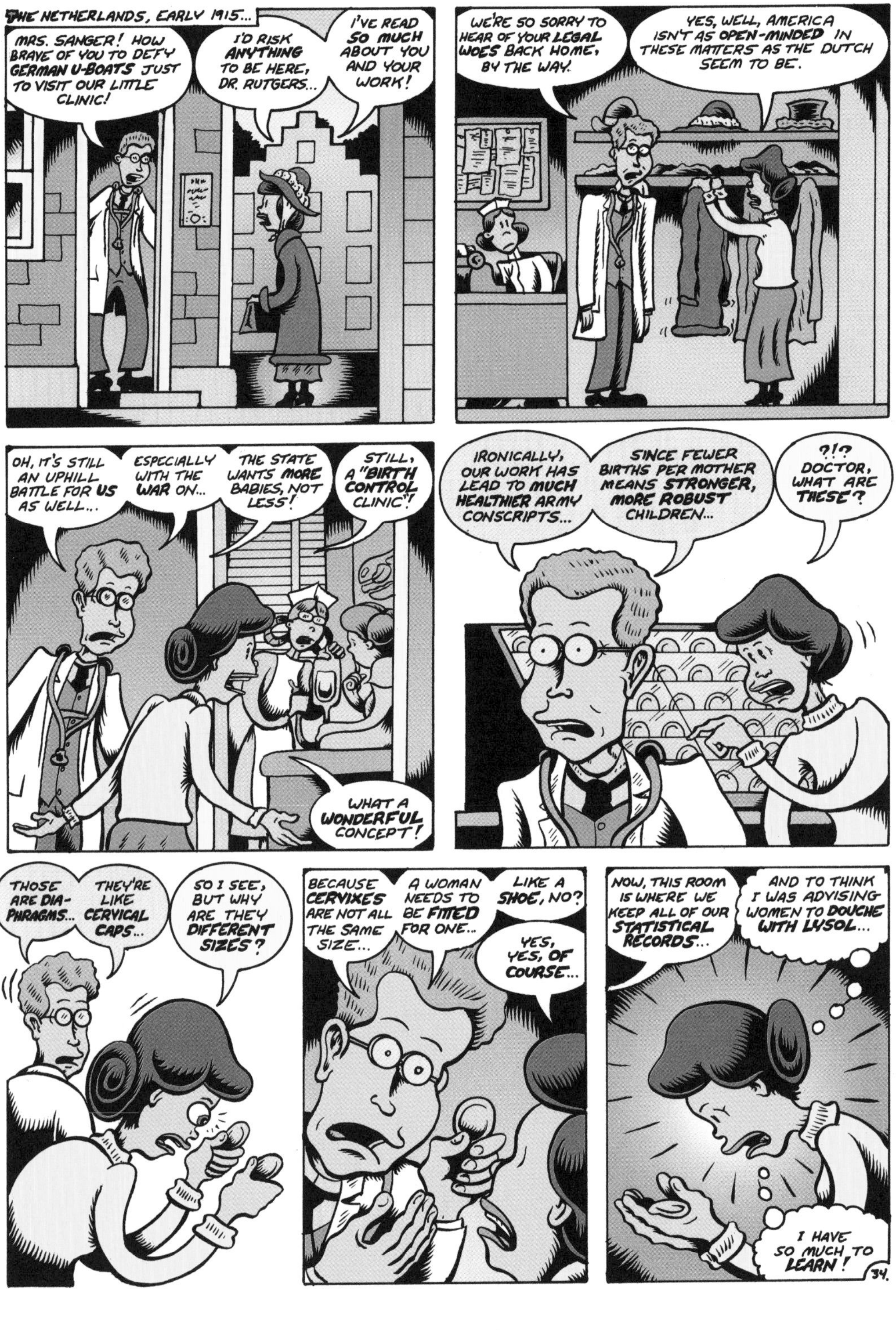
THE NETHERLANDS, EARLY 1915...
MRS. SANGER! HOW BRAVE OF YOU TO DEFY GERMAN U-BOATS JUST TO VISIT OUR LITTLE CLINIC!
I'D RISK ANYTHING TO BE HERE, DR. RUTGERS...
I'VE READ SO MUCH ABOUT YOU AND YOUR WORK!
WE'RE SO SORRY TO HEAR OF YOUR LEGAL WOES BACK HOME, BY THE WAY.
YES, WELL, AMERICA ISN'T AS OPEN-MINDED IN THESE MATTERS AS THE DUTCH SEEM TO BE.
OH, IT'S STILL AN UPHILL BATTLE FOR US AS WELL...
ESPECIALLY WITH THE WAR ON...
THE STATE WANTS MORE BABIES, NOT LESS!
STILL, A "BIRTH CONTROL CLINIC"!
WHAT A WONDERFUL CONCEPT!
IRONICALLY, OUR WORK HAS LEAD TO MUCH HEALTHIER ARMY CONSCRIPTS...
SINCE FEWER BIRTHS PER MOTHER MEANS STRONGER, MORE ROBUST CHILDREN...
?!? DOCTOR, WHAT ARE THESE?
THOSE ARE DIA-PHRAGMS...
THEY'RE LIKE CERVICAL CAPS...
SO I SEE, BUT WHY ARE THEY DIFFERENT SIZES?
BECAUSE CERVIXES ARE NOT ALL THE SAME SIZE...
A WOMAN NEEDS TO BE FITTED FOR ONE...
LIKE A SHOE, NO?
YES, YES, OF COURSE...
NOW, THIS ROOM IS WHERE WE KEEP ALL OF OUR STATISTICAL RECORDS...
AND TO THINK I WAS ADVISING WOMEN TO DOUCHE WITH LYSOL...
I HAVE SO MUCH TO LEARN!
34.

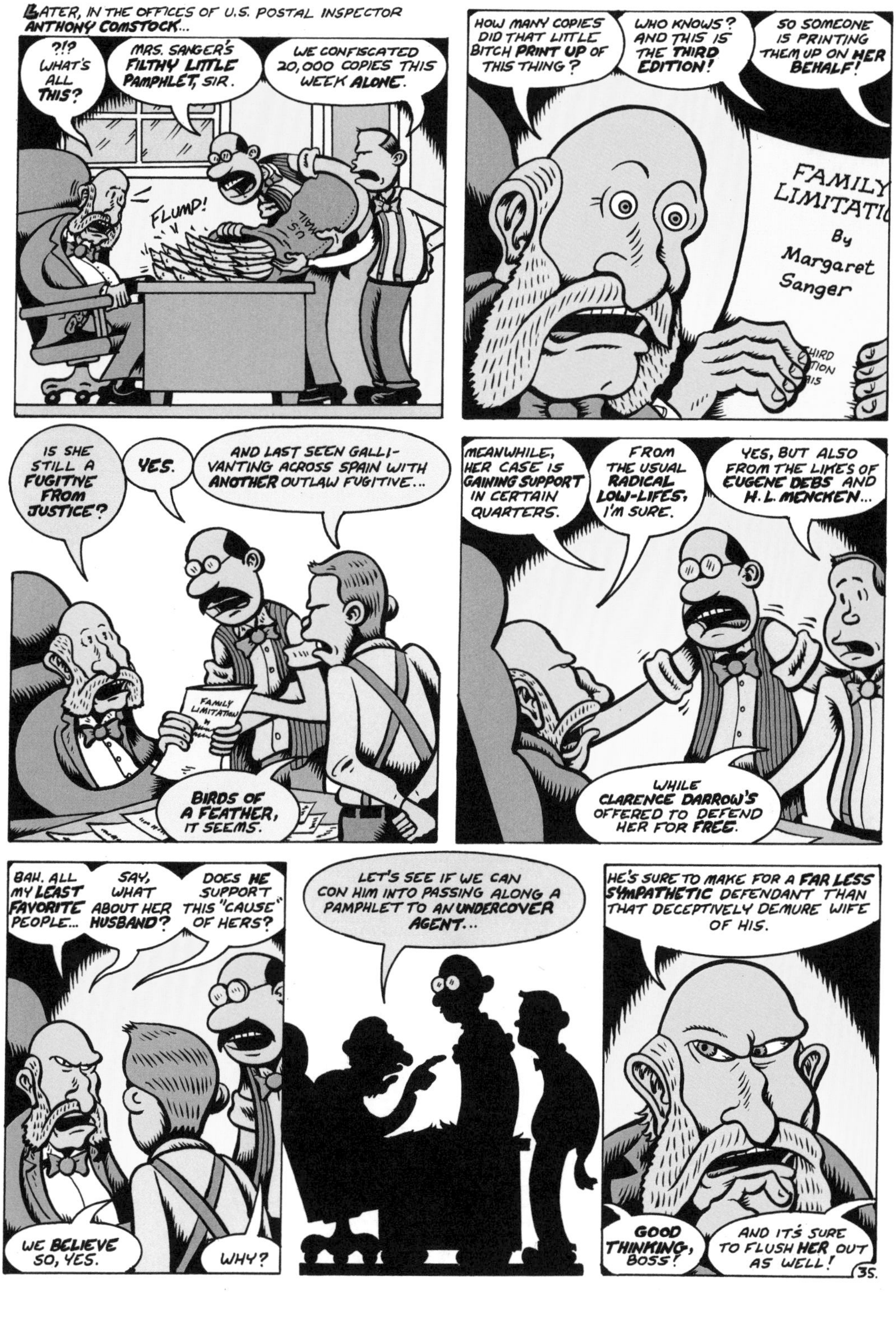
LATER, IN THE OFFICES OF U.S. POSTAL INSPECTOR ANTHONY COMSTOCK...
?!? WHAT'S ALL THIS?
MRS. SANGER'S FILTHY LITTLE PAMPHLET, SIR.
WE CONFISCATED 20,000 COPIES THIS WEEK ALONE.
FLUMP!
U.S. MAIL
HOW MANY COPIES DID THAT LITTLE BITCH PRINT UP OF THIS THING?
WHO KNOWS? AND THIS IS THE THIRD EDITION!
SO SOMEONE IS PRINTING THEM UP ON HER BEHALF!
FAMILY LIMITATI
By Margaret Sanger
IS SHE STILL A FUGITIVE FROM JUSTICE?
YES.
AND LAST SEEN GALLIVANTING ACROSS SPAIN WITH ANOTHER OUTLAW FUGITIVE...
FAMILY LIMITATION
BIRDS OF A FEATHER, IT SEEMS.
MEANWHILE, HER CASE IS GAINING SUPPORT IN CERTAIN QUARTERS.
FROM THE USUAL RADICAL LOW-LIFES, I'M SURE.
YES, BUT ALSO FROM THE LIKES OF EUGENE DEBS AND H.L. MENCKEN...
WHILE CLARENCE DARROW'S OFFERED TO DEFEND HER FOR FREE.
BAH. ALL MY LEAST FAVORITE PEOPLE...
SAY, WHAT ABOUT HER HUSBAND?
DOES HE SUPPORT THIS "CAUSE" OF HERS?
WE BELIEVE SO, YES.
WHY?
LET'S SEE IF WE CAN CON HIM INTO PASSING ALONG A PAMPHLET TO AN UNDERCOVER AGENT...
HE'S SURE TO MAKE FOR A FAR LESS SYMPATHETIC DEFENDANT THAN THAT DECEPTIVELY DEMURE WIFE OF HIS.
GOOD THINKING, BOSS!
AND IT'S SURE TO FLUSH HER OUT AS WELL!
35.

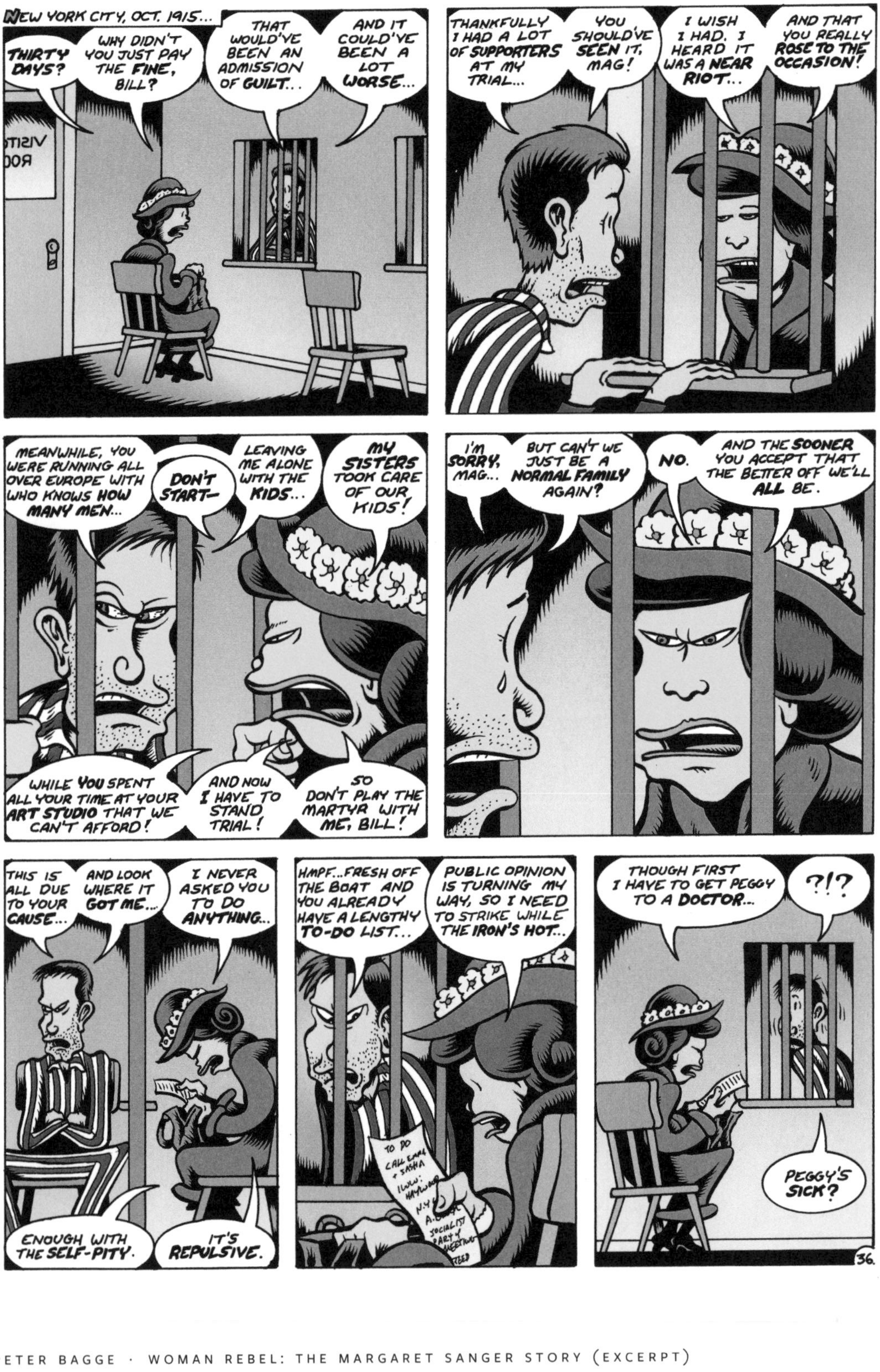
NEW YORK CITY, OCT. 1915...
THIRTY DAYS?
WHY DIDN'T YOU JUST PAY THE FINE, BILL?
THAT WOULD'VE BEEN AN ADMISSION OF GUILT...
AND IT COULD'VE BEEN A LOT WORSE...
THANKFULLY I HAD A LOT OF SUPPORTERS AT MY TRIAL...
YOU SHOULD'VE SEEN IT, MAG!
I WISH I HAD. I HEARD IT WAS A NEAR RIOT...
AND THAT YOU REALLY ROSE TO THE OCCASION!
MEANWHILE, YOU WERE RUNNING ALL OVER EUROPE WITH WHO KNOWS HOW MANY MEN...
DON'T START-
LEAVING ME ALONE WITH THE KIDS...
MY SISTERS TOOK CARE OF OUR KIDS!
WHILE YOU SPENT ALL YOUR TIME AT YOUR ART STUDIO THAT WE CAN'T AFFORD!
AND NOW I HAVE TO STAND TRIAL!
SO DON'T PLAY THE MARTYR WITH ME, BILL!
I'M SORRY, MAG...
BUT CAN'T WE JUST BE A NORMAL FAMILY AGAIN?
NO.
AND THE SOONER YOU ACCEPT THAT THE BETTER OFF WE'LL ALL BE.
THIS IS ALL DUE TO YOUR CAUSE...
AND LOOK WHERE IT GOT ME...
I NEVER ASKED YOU TO DO ANYTHING...
ENOUGH WITH THE SELF-PITY.
IT'S REPULSIVE.
HMPF...FRESH OFF THE BOAT AND YOU ALREADY HAVE A LENGTHY TO-DO LIST...
PUBLIC OPINION IS TURNING MY WAY, SO I NEED TO STRIKE WHILE THE IRON'S HOT...
THOUGH FIRST I HAVE TO GET PEGGY TO A DOCTOR...
?!?
PEGGY'S SICK?
36.

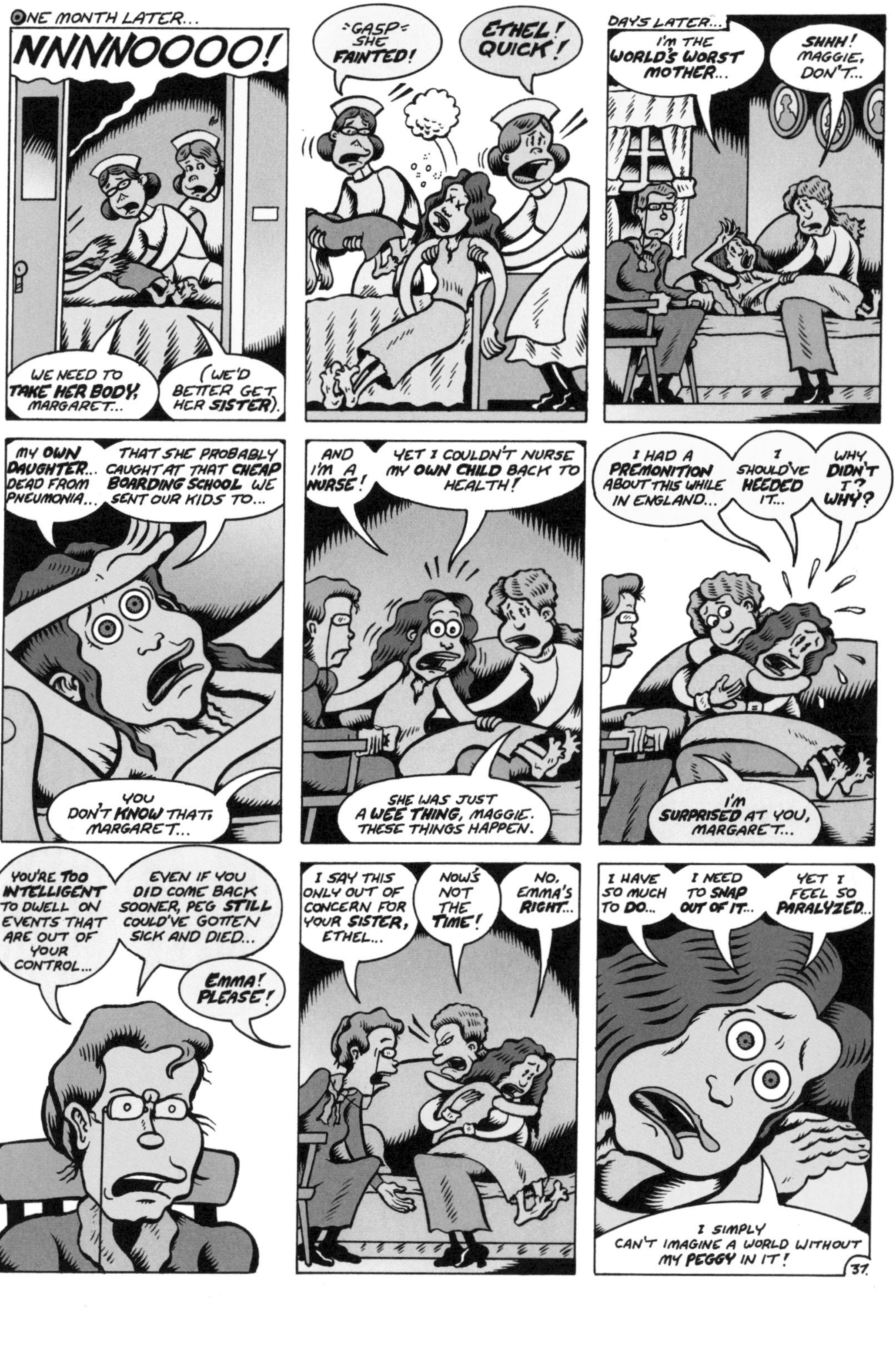
ONE MONTH LATER...
NNNNOOOO!
WE NEED TO TAKE HER BODY, MARGARET...
(WE'D BETTER GET HER SISTER).
=GASP= SHE FAINTED!
ETHEL! QUICK!
DAYS LATER...
I'M THE WORLD'S WORST MOTHER...
SHHH! MAGGIE, DON'T...
MY OWN DAUGHTER... DEAD FROM PNEUMONIA...
THAT SHE PROBABLY CAUGHT AT THAT CHEAP BOARDING SCHOOL WE SENT OUR KIDS TO...
YOU DON'T KNOW THAT, MARGARET...
AND I'M A NURSE!
YET I COULDN'T NURSE MY OWN CHILD BACK TO HEALTH!
SHE WAS JUST A WEE THING, MAGGIE. THESE THINGS HAPPEN.
I HAD A PREMONITION ABOUT THIS WHILE IN ENGLAND...
I SHOULD'VE HEEDED IT...
WHY DIDN'T I? WHY?
I'M SURPRISED AT YOU, MARGARET...
YOU'RE TOO INTELLIGENT TO DWELL ON EVENTS THAT ARE OUT OF YOUR CONTROL...
EVEN IF YOU DID COME BACK SOONER, PEG STILL COULD'VE GOTTEN SICK AND DIED...
EMMA! PLEASE!
I SAY THIS ONLY OUT OF CONCERN FOR YOUR SISTER, ETHEL...
NOW'S NOT THE TIME!
NO, EMMA'S RIGHT...
I HAVE SO MUCH TO DO...
I NEED TO SNAP OUT OF IT...
YET I FEEL SO PARALYZED...
I SIMPLY CAN'T IMAGINE A WORLD WITHOUT MY PEGGY IN IT!
37.

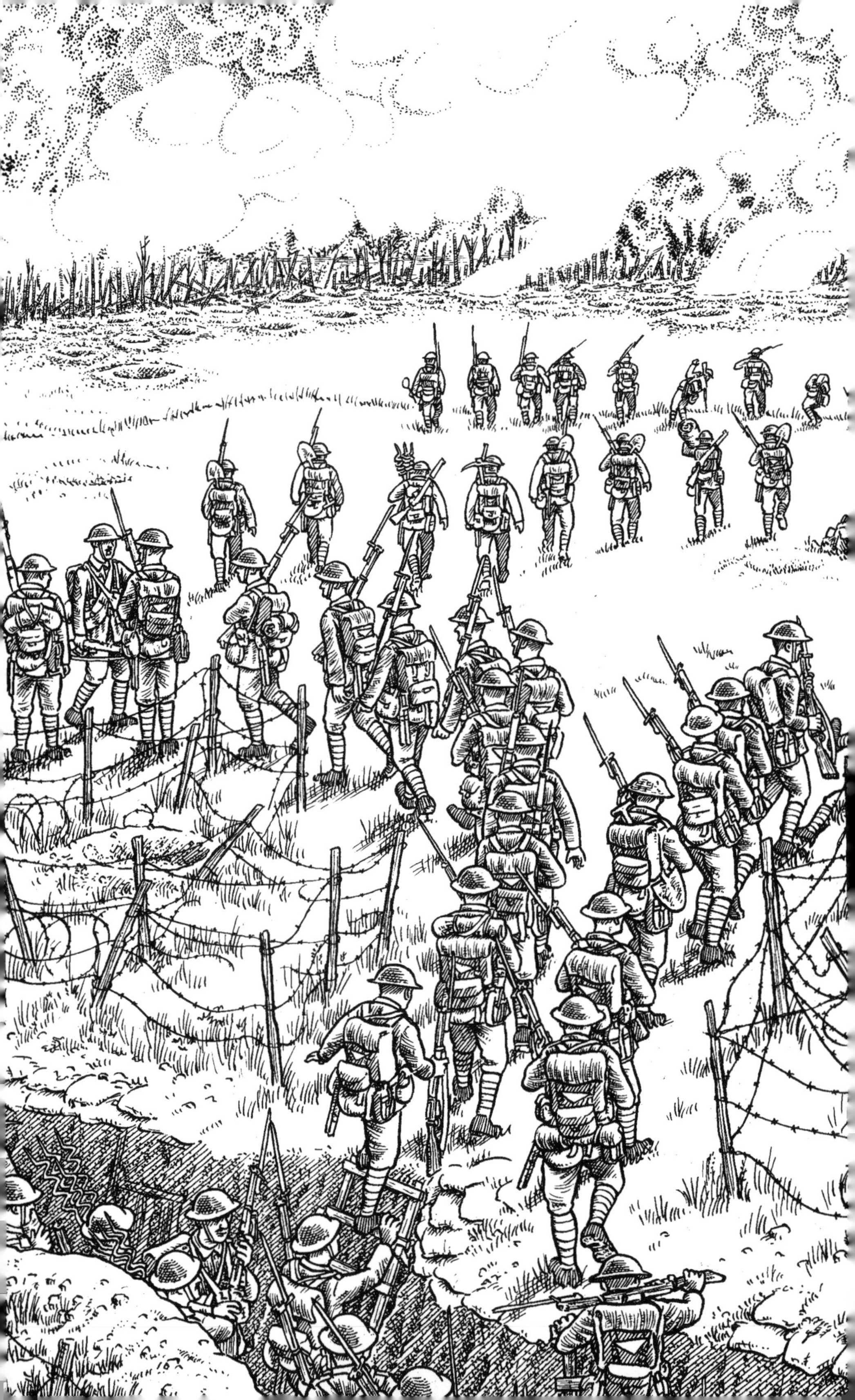

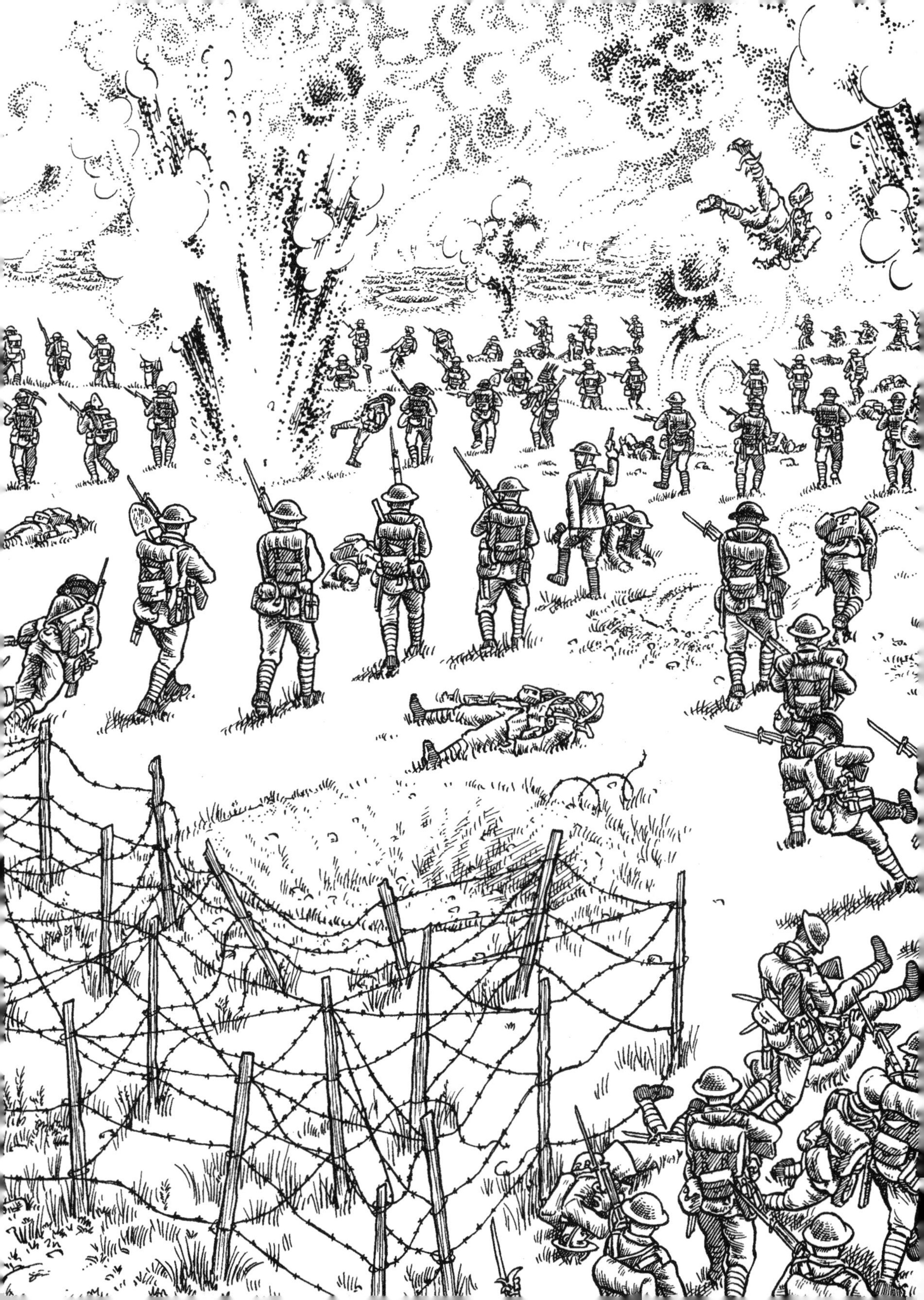

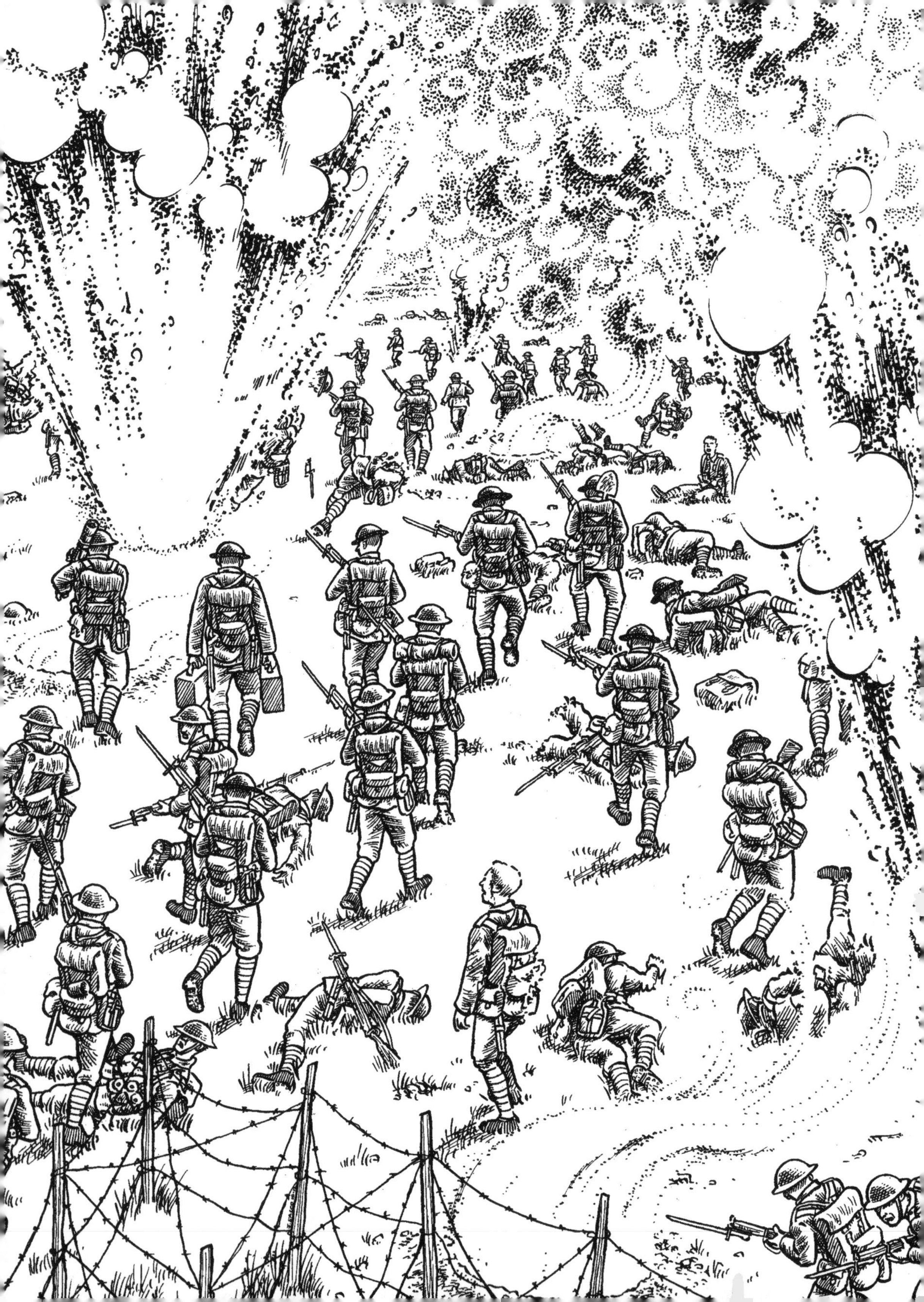

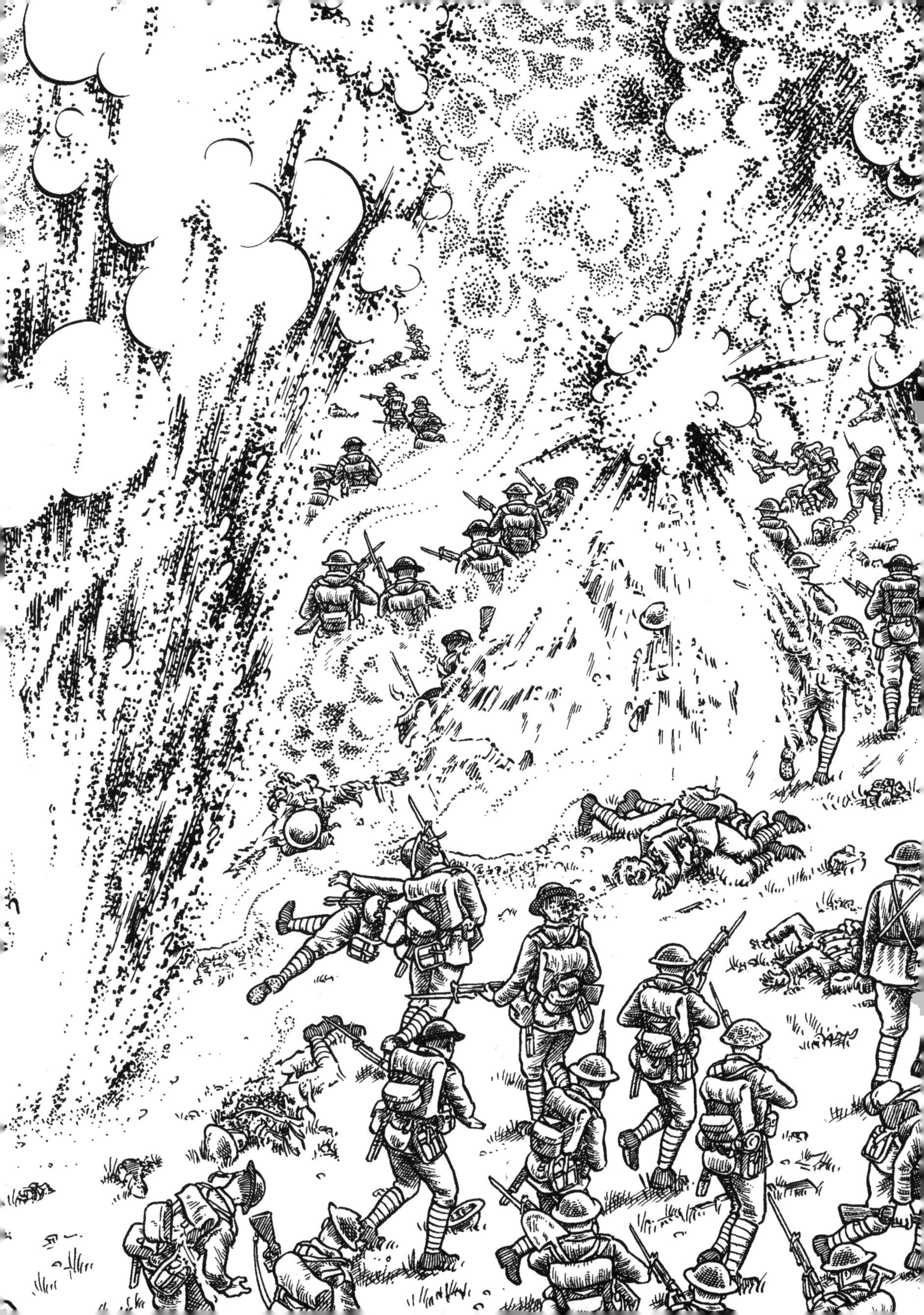

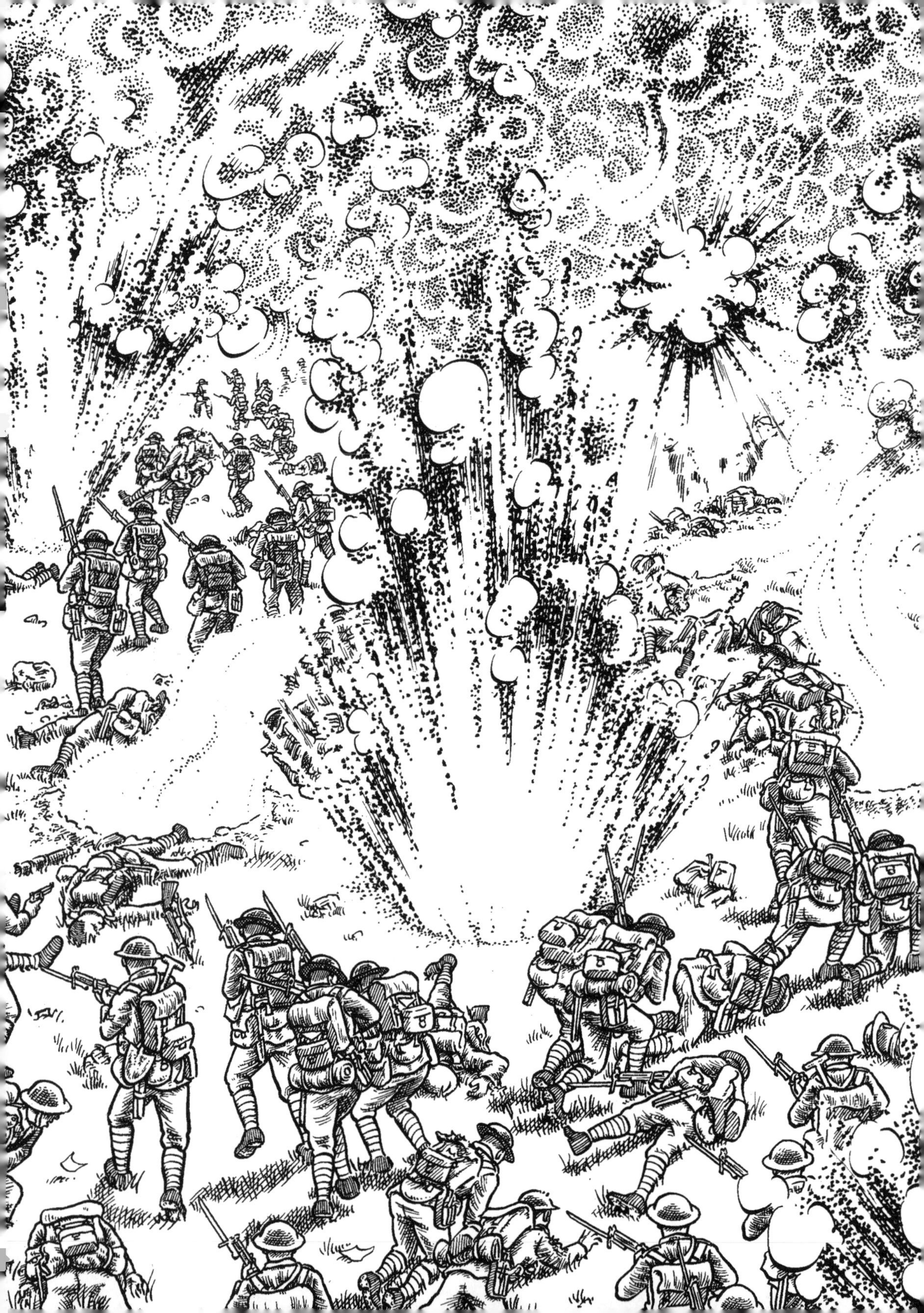

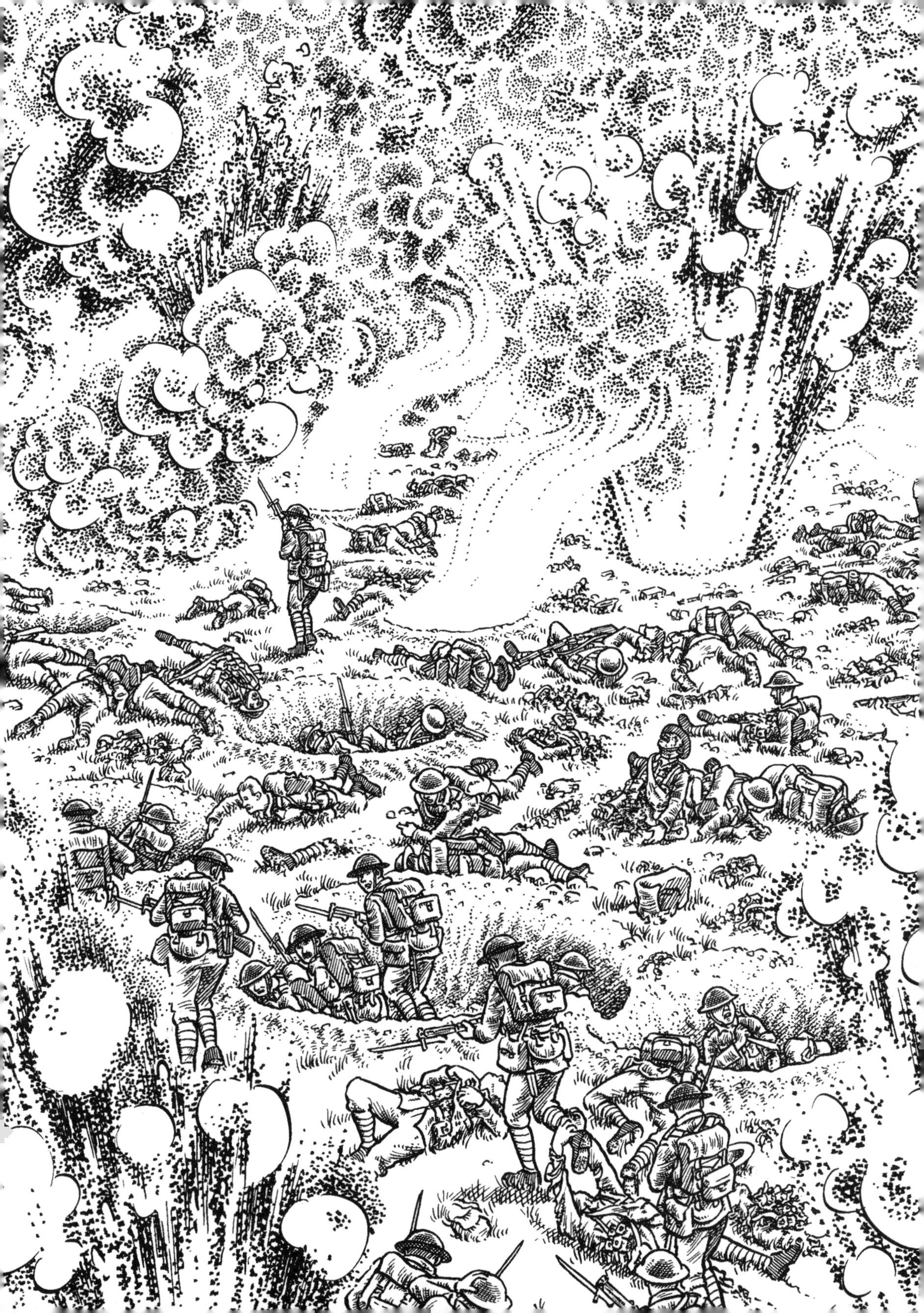

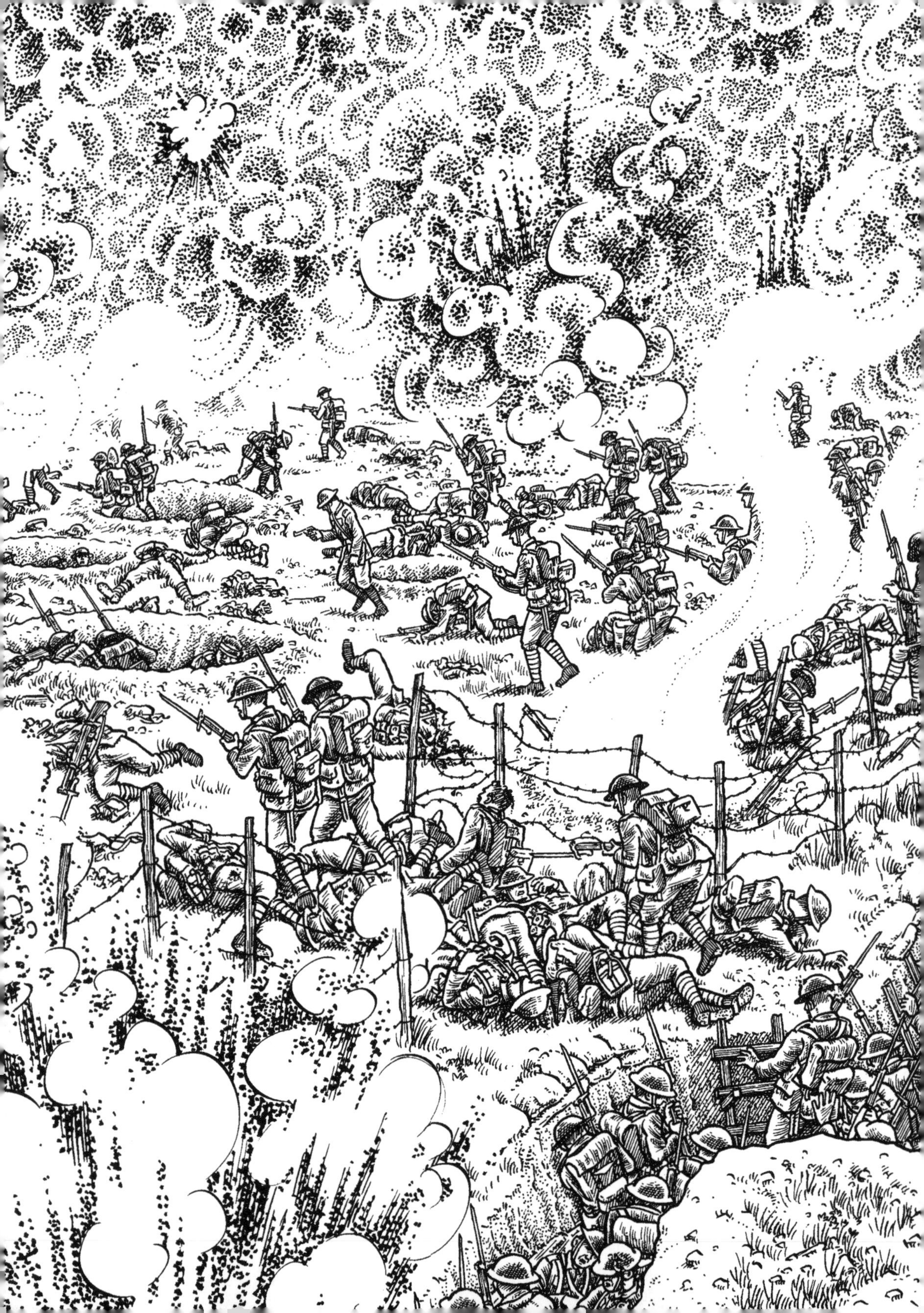

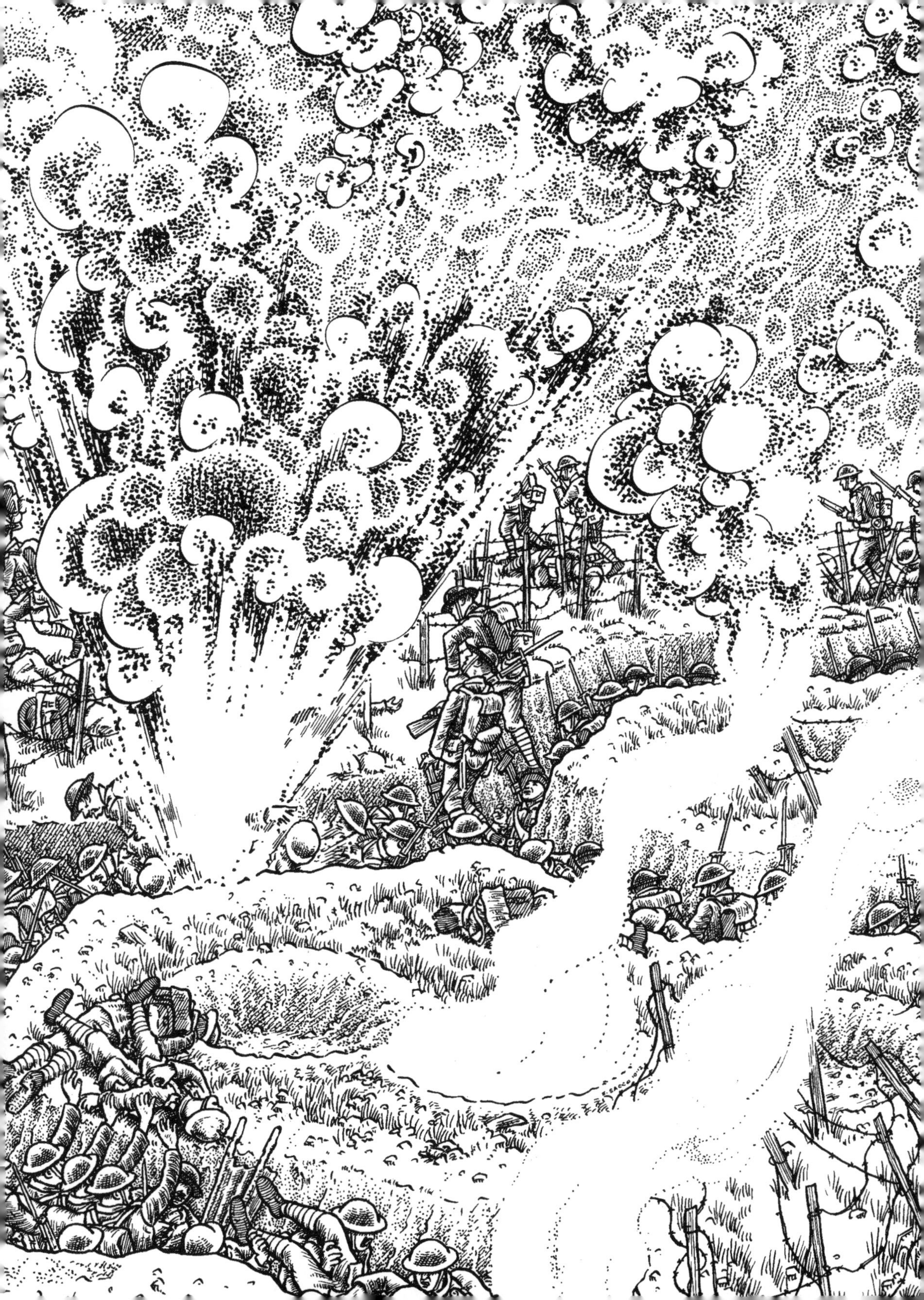

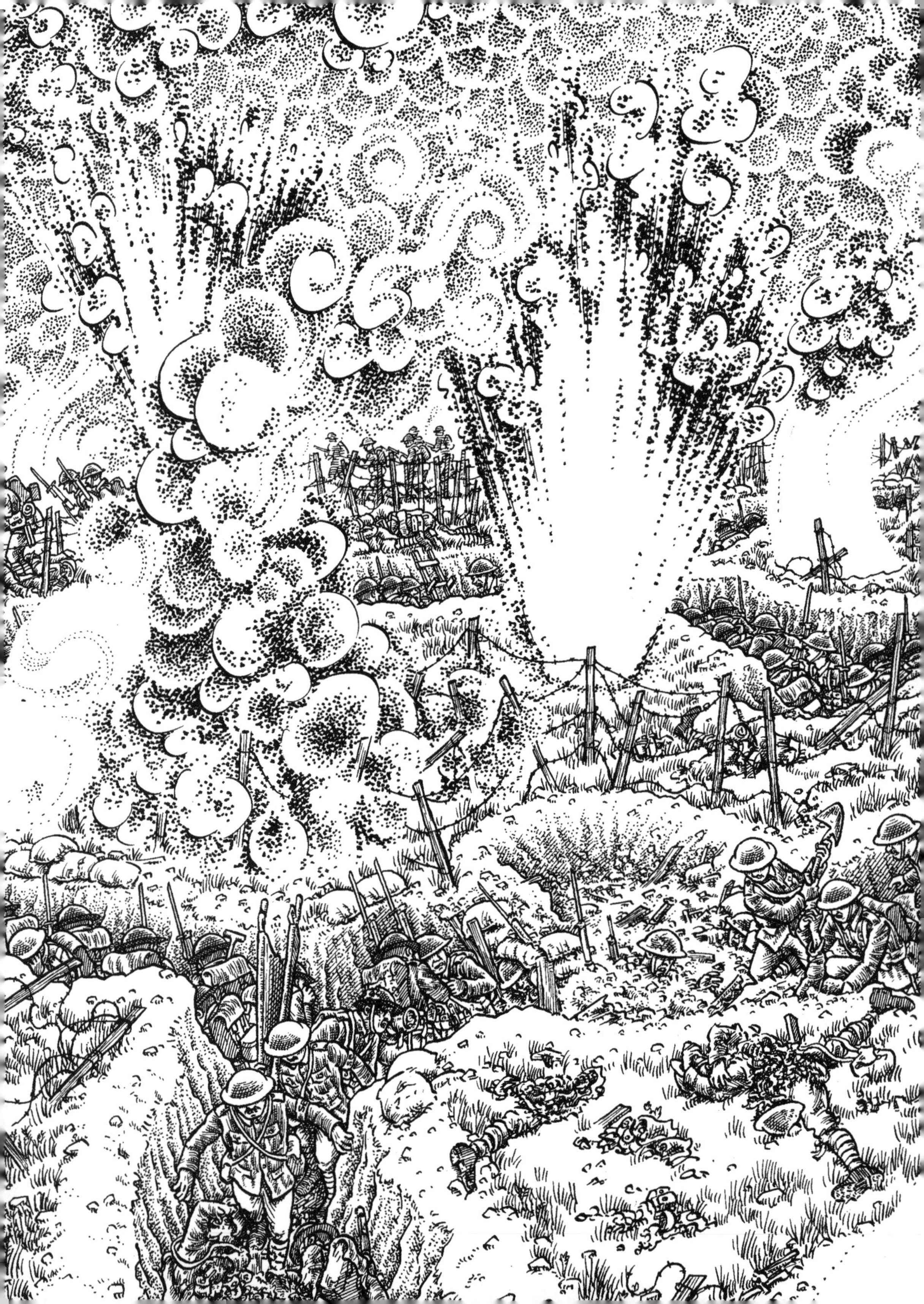

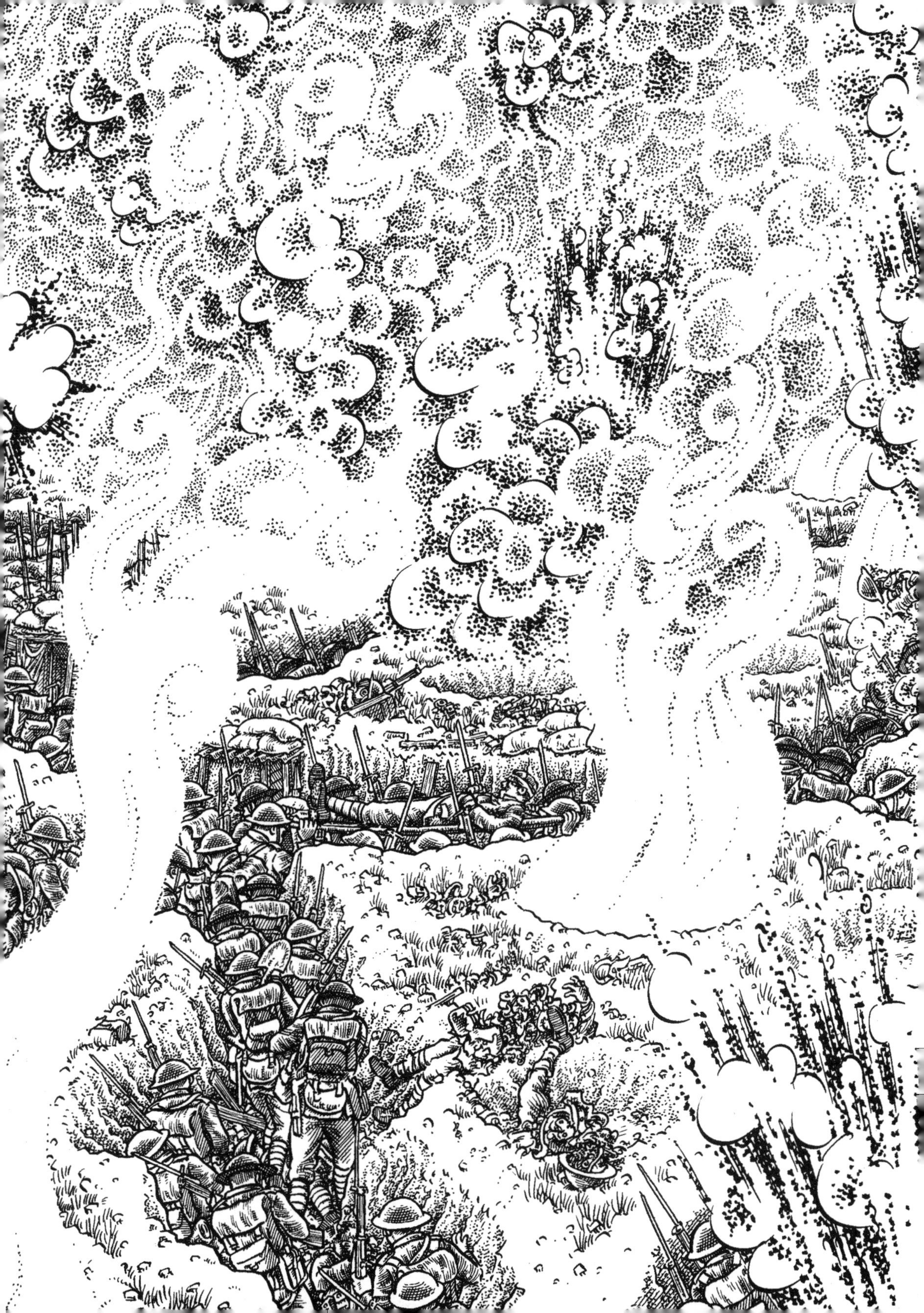

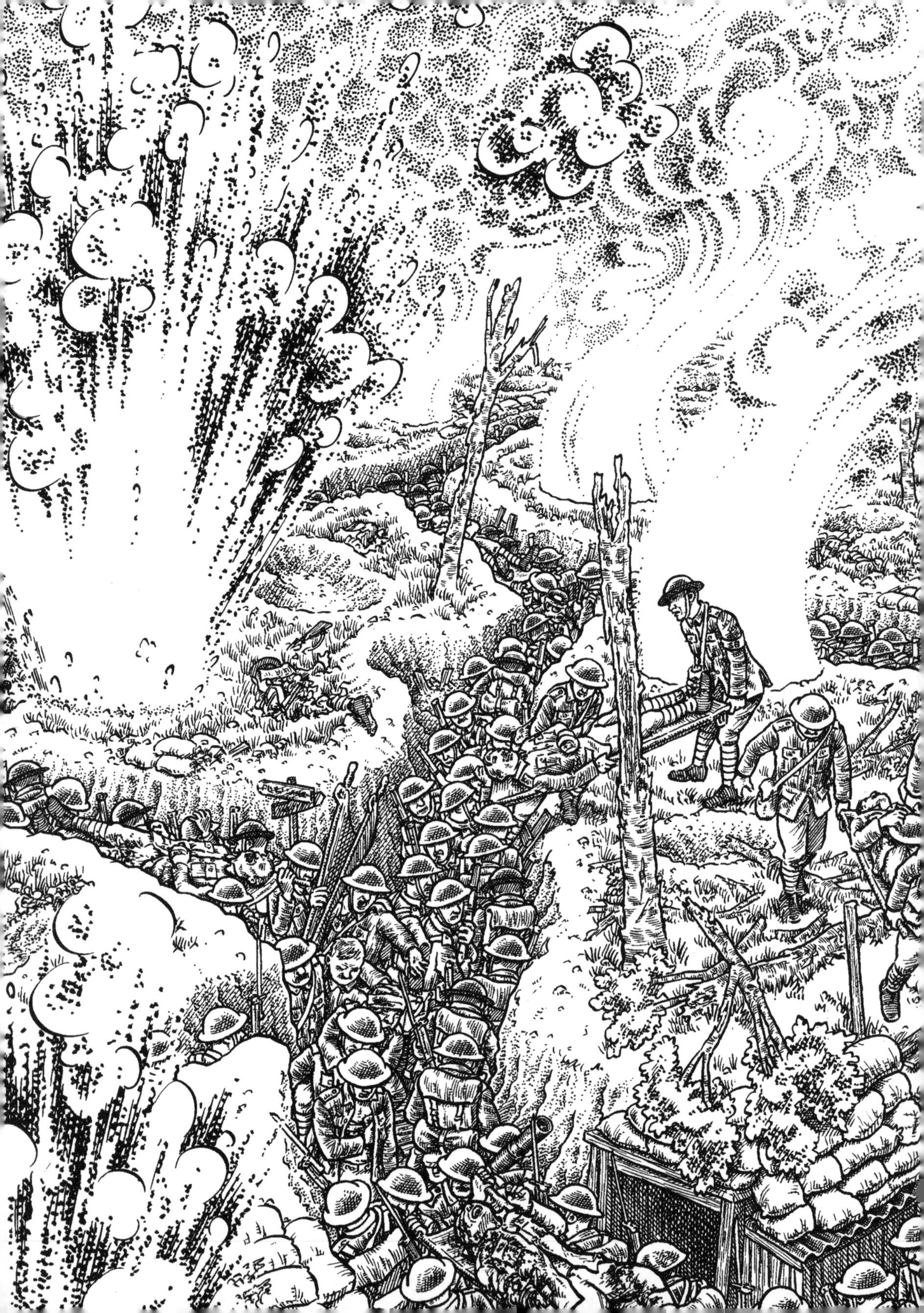

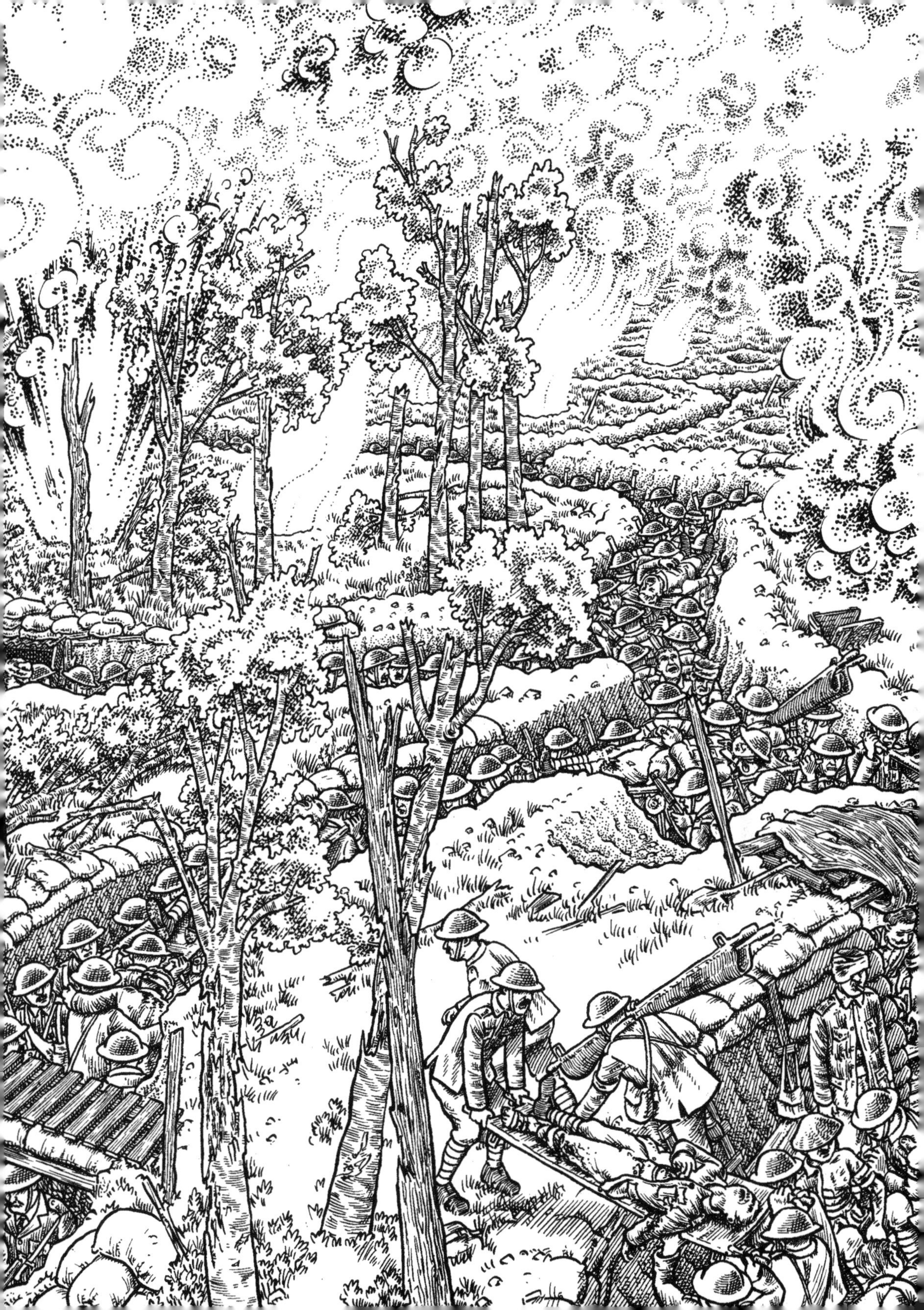

CHAPTER SEVEN

Working the Cute Nerve

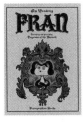

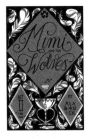

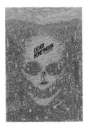

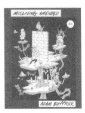

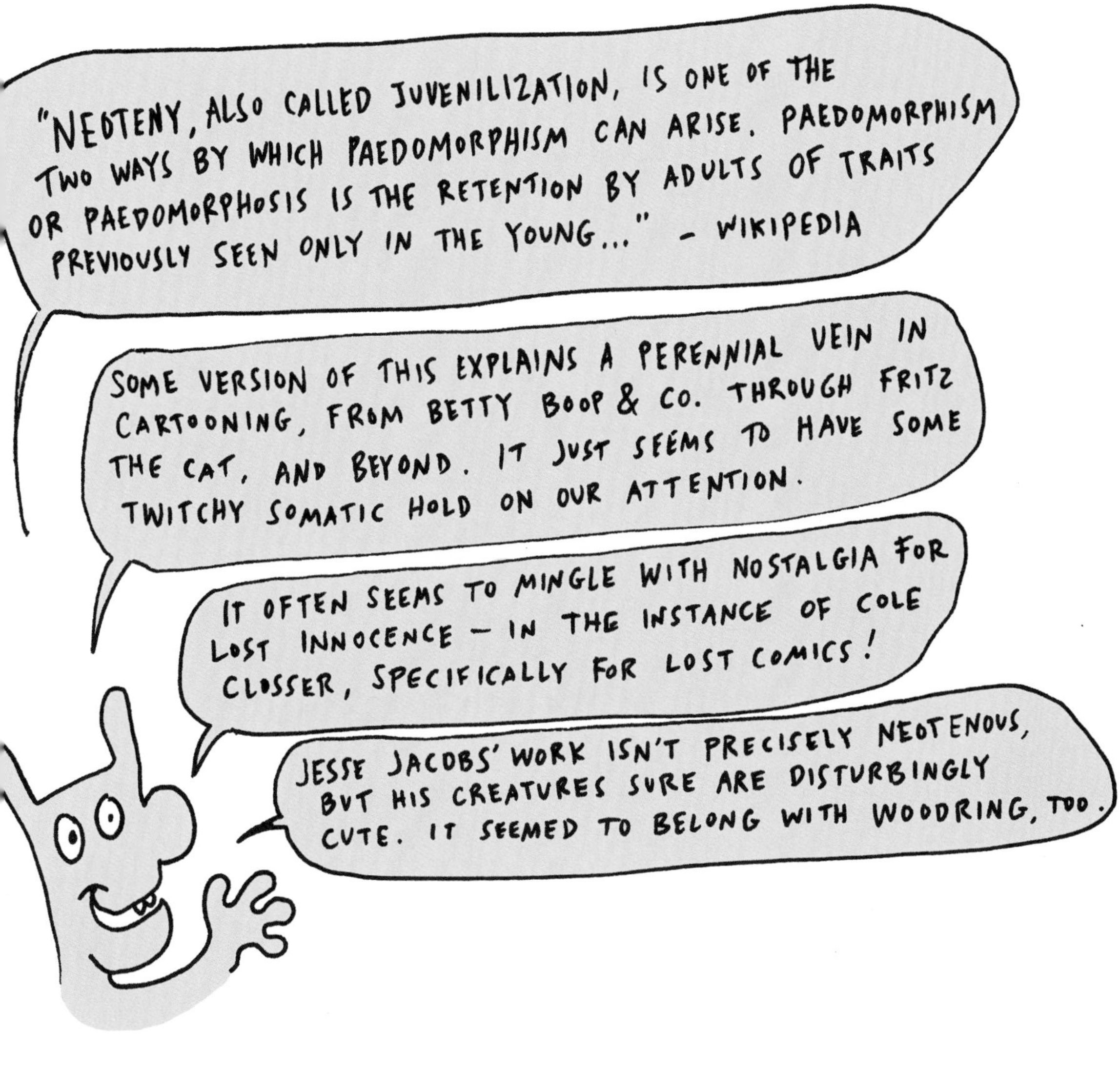
"NEOTENY, ALSO CALLED JUVENILIZATION, IS ONE OF THE TWO WAYS BY WHICH PAEDOMORPHISM CAN ARISE. PAEDOMORPHISM OR PAEDOMORPHOSIS IS THE RETENTION BY ADULTS OF TRAITS PREVIOUSLY SEEN ONLY IN THE YOUNG..." - WIKIPEDIA
SOME VERSION OF THIS EXPLAINS A PERENNIAL VEIN IN CARTOONING, FROM BETTY BOOP & CO. THROUGH FRITZ THE CAT, AND BEYOND. IT JUST SEEMS TO HAVE SOME TWITCHY SOMATIC HOLD ON OUR ATTENTION.
IT OFTEN SEEMS TO MINGLE WITH NOSTALGIA FOR LOST INNOCENCE – IN THE INSTANCE OF COLE CLOSSER, SPECIFICALLY FOR LOST COMICS!
JESSE JACOBS' WORK ISN'T PRECISELY NEOTENOUS, BUT HIS CREATURES SURE ARE DISTURBINGLY CUTE. IT SEEMED TO BELONG WITH WOODRING, TOO.

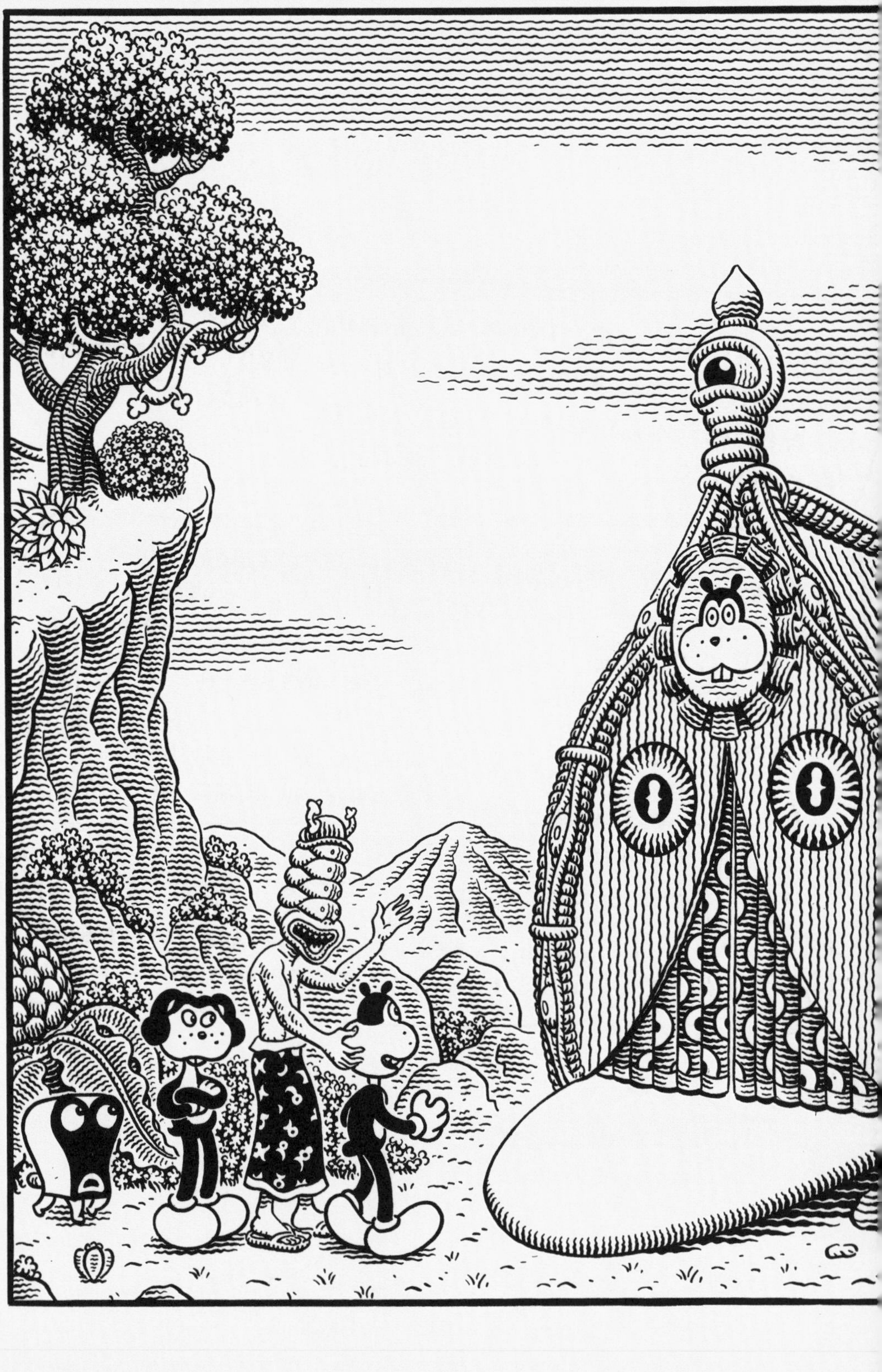

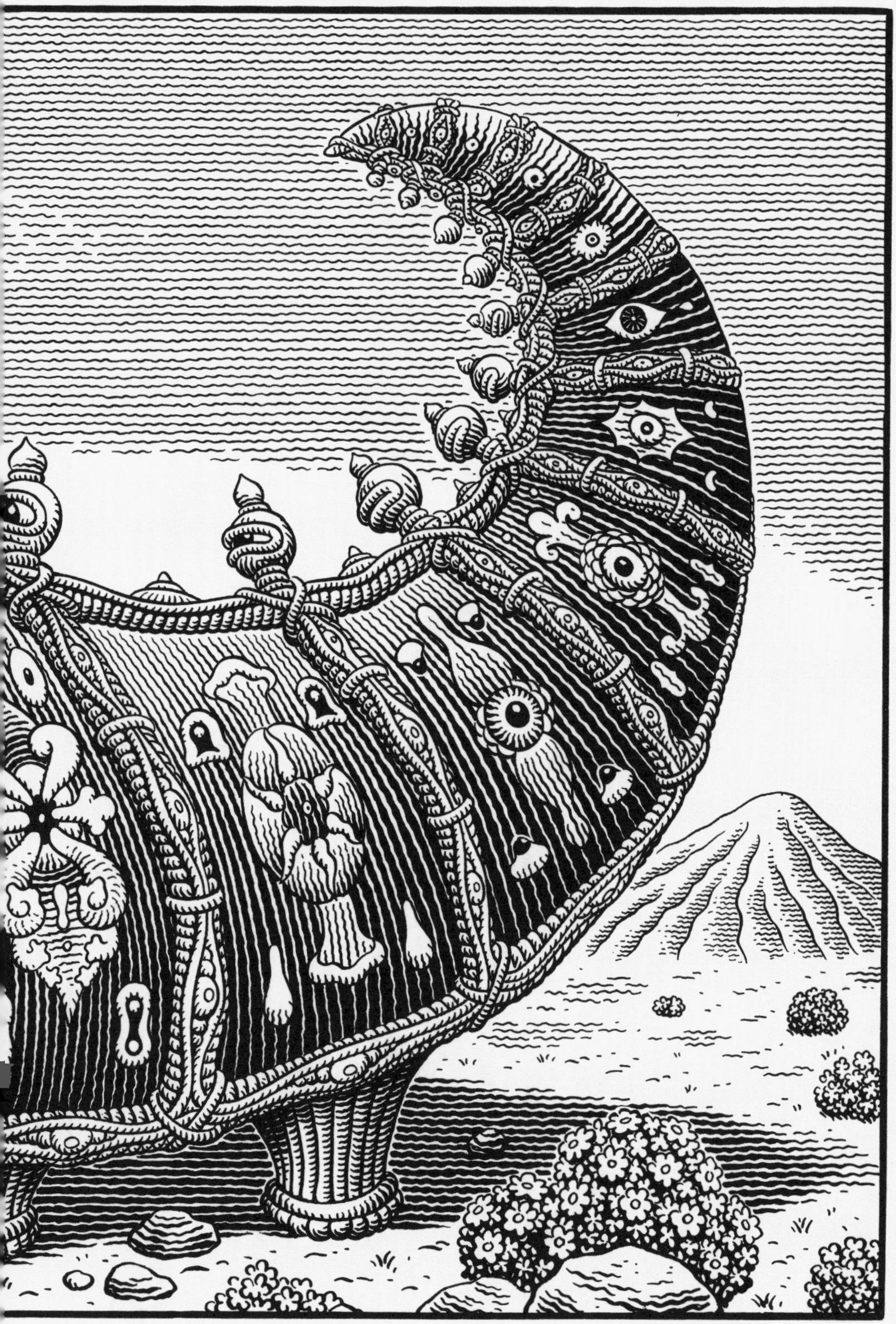

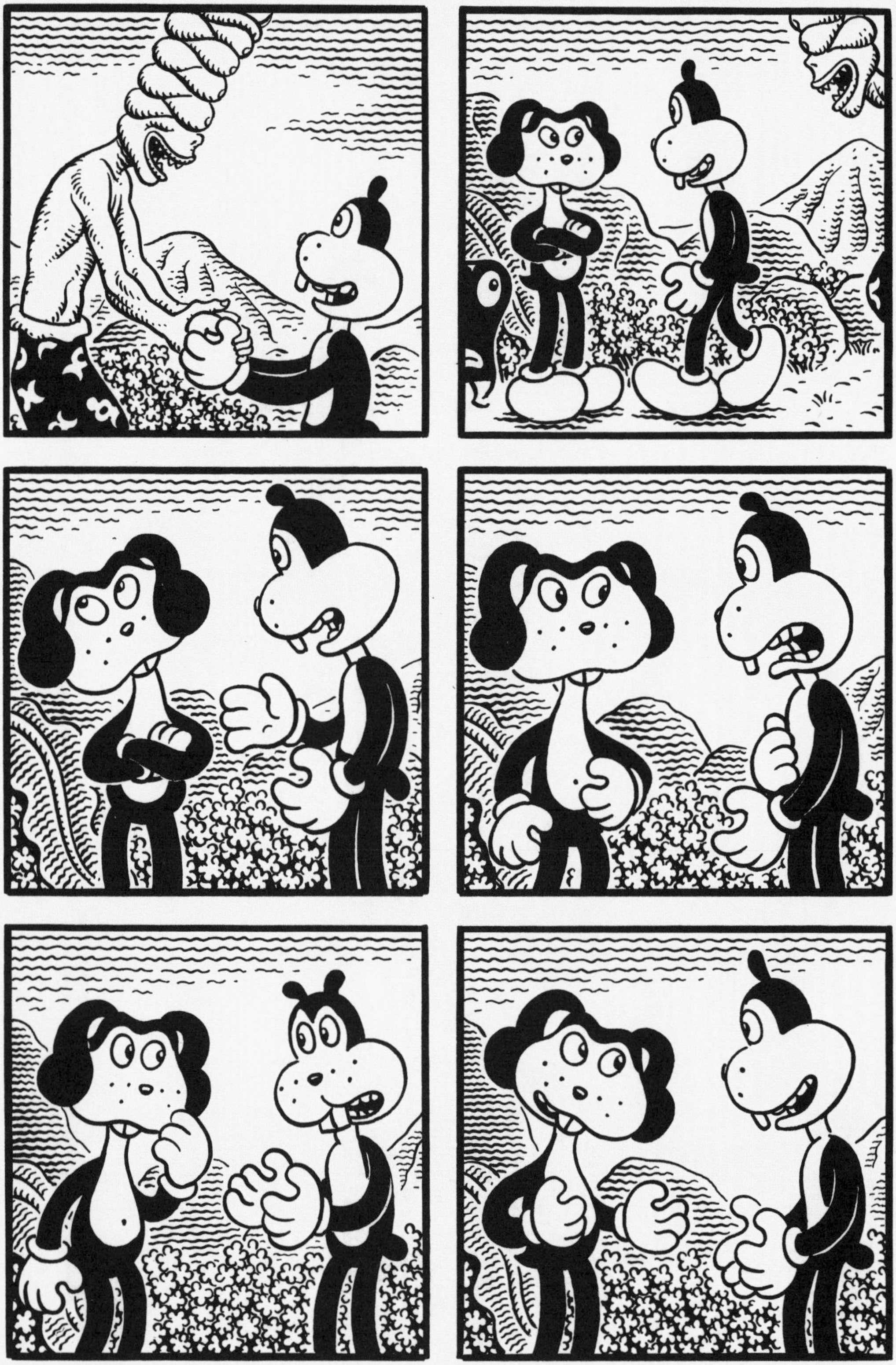

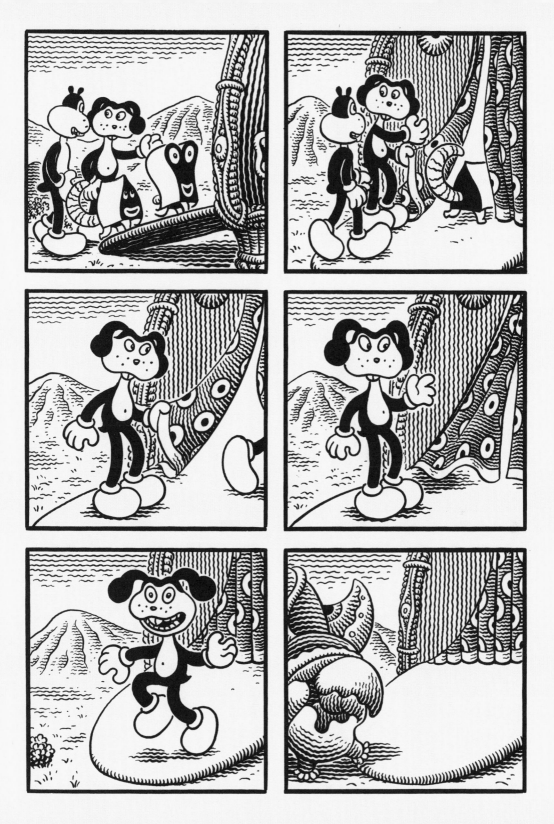

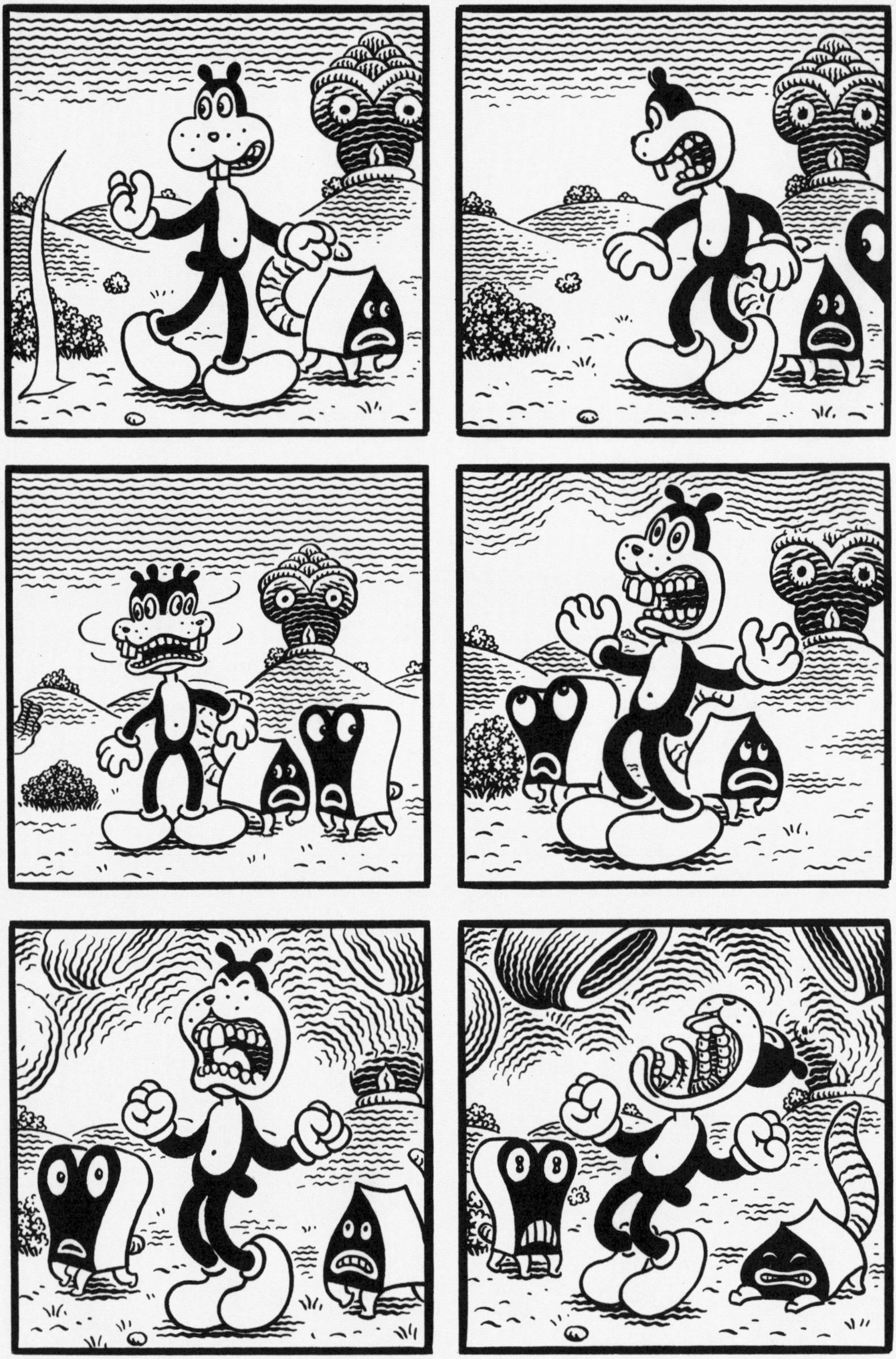

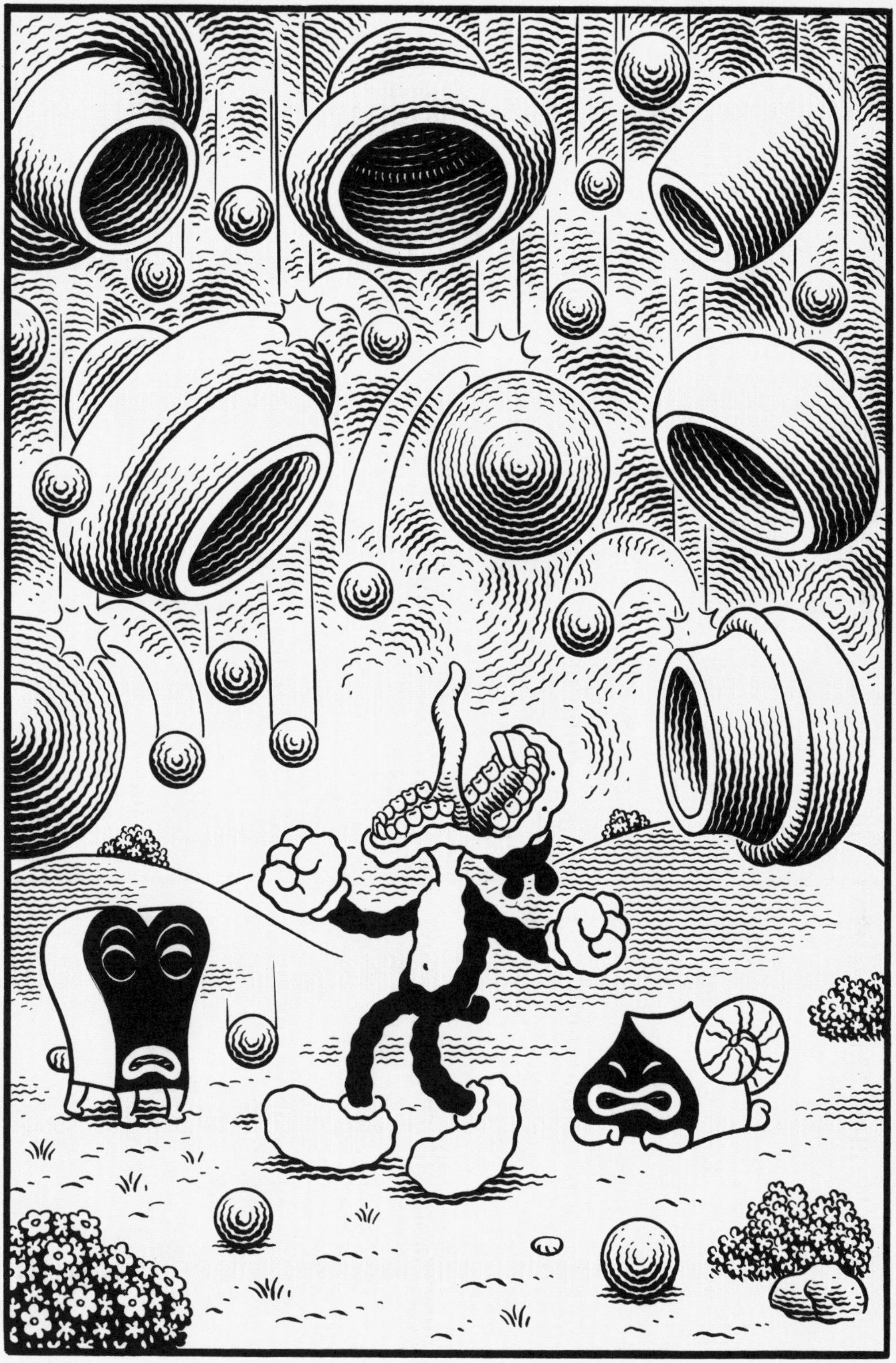

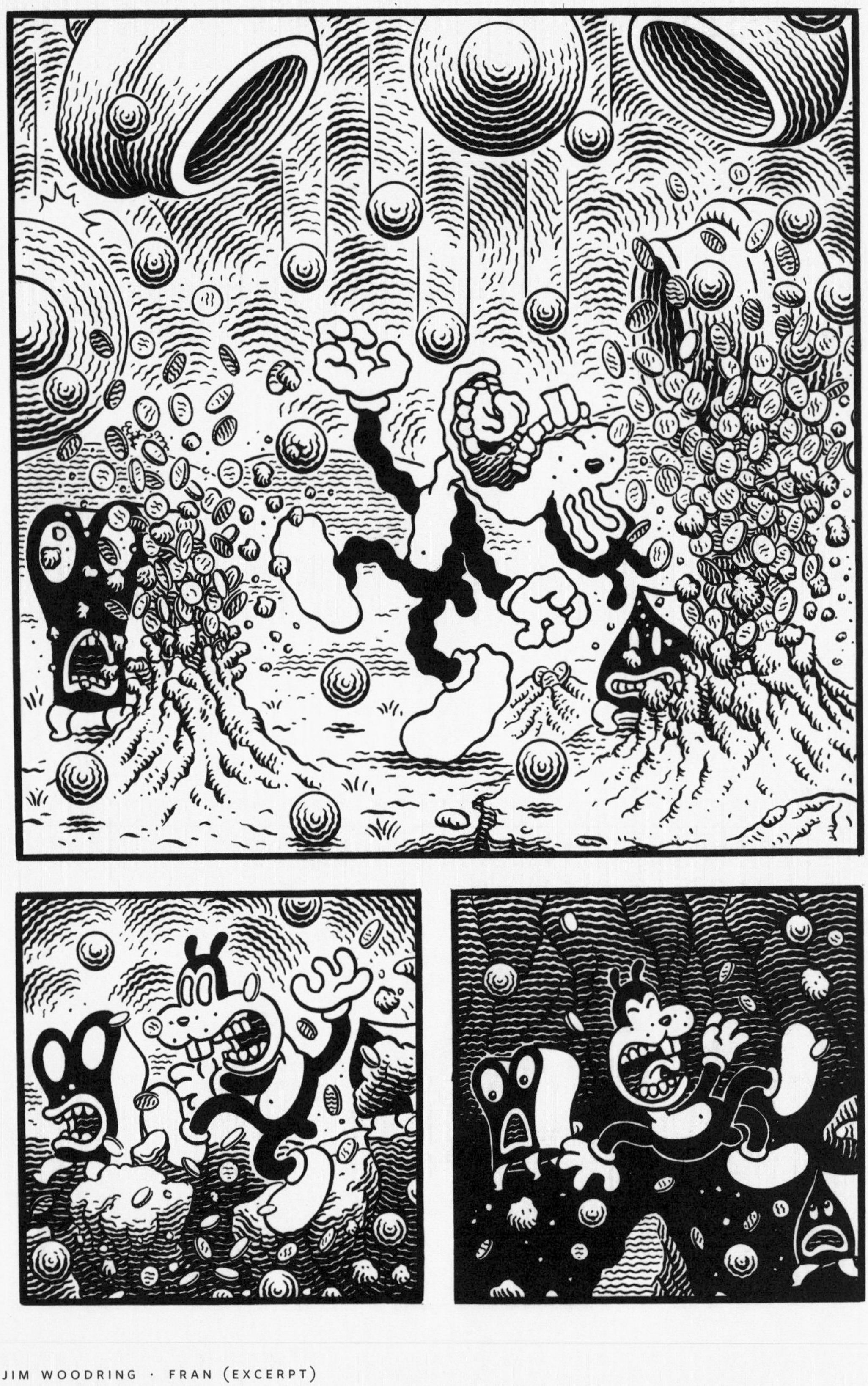

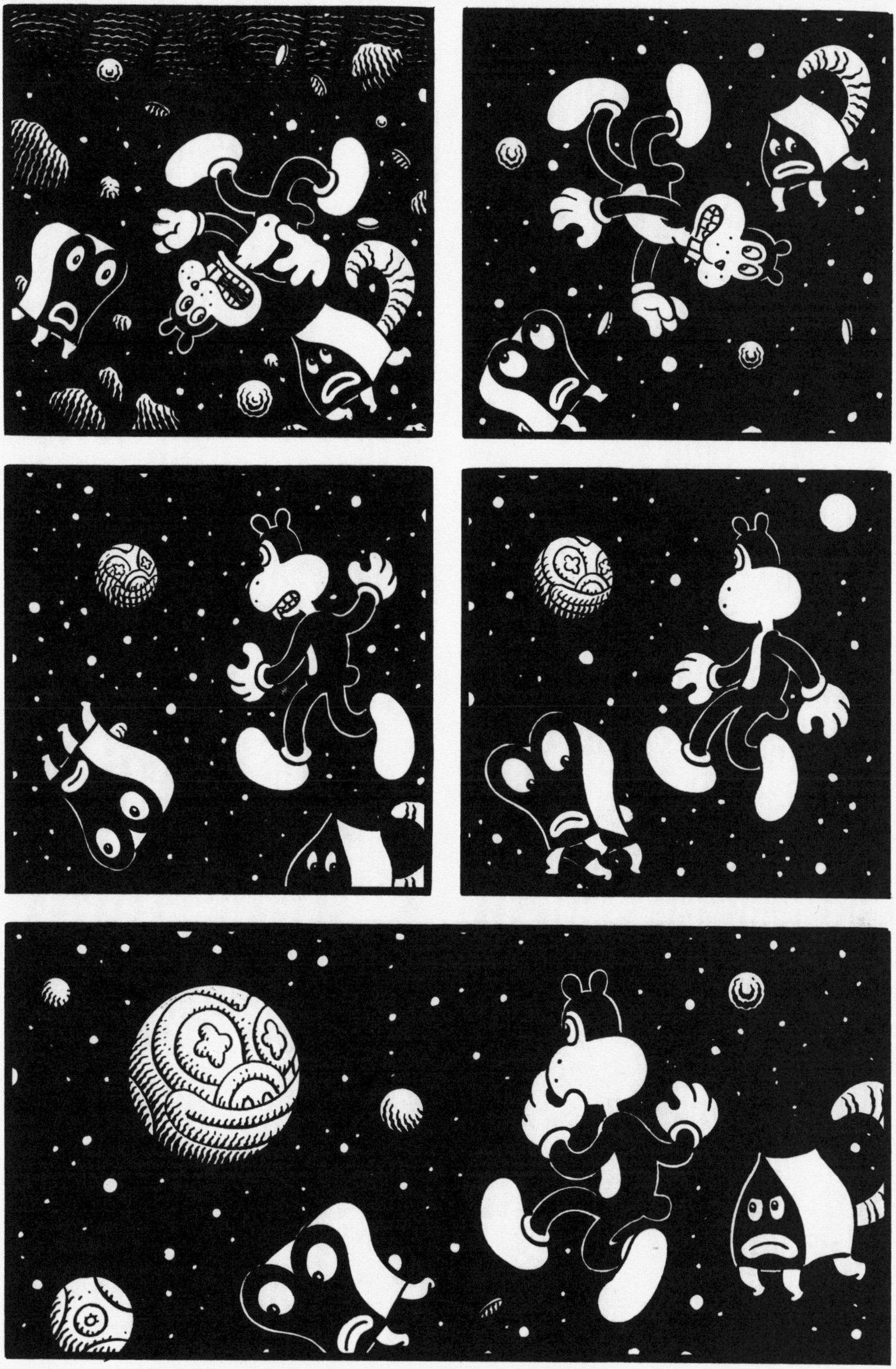

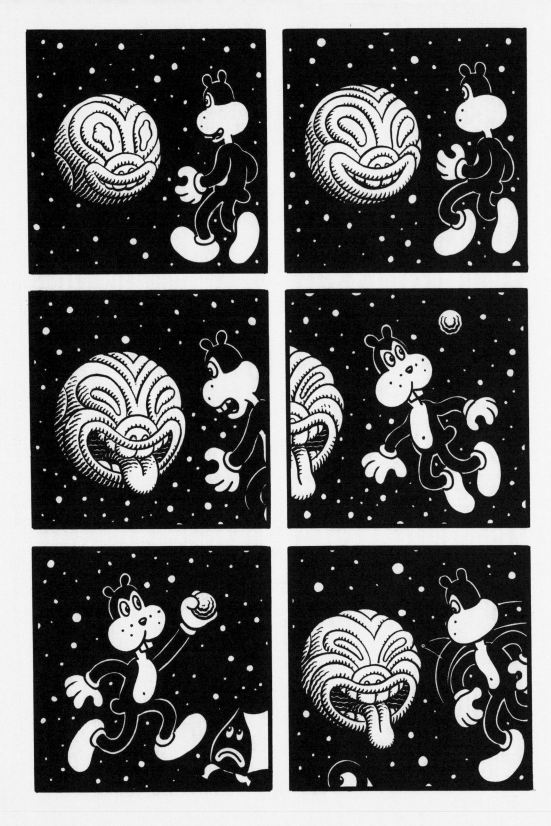

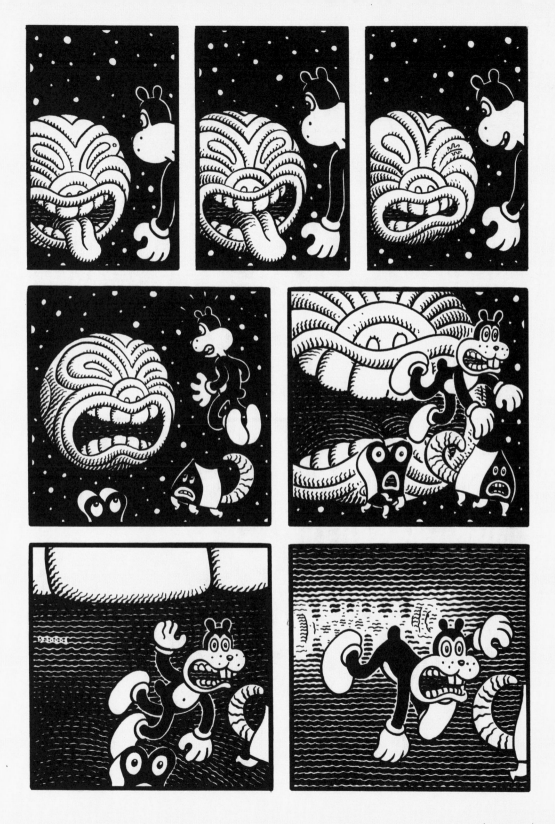

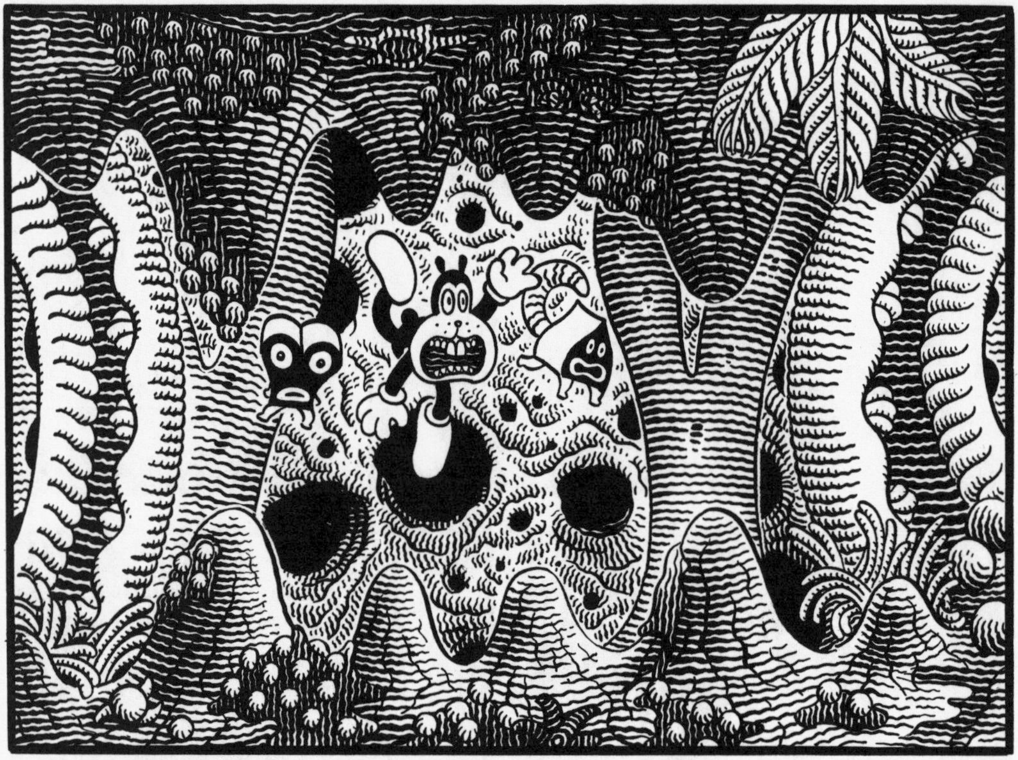

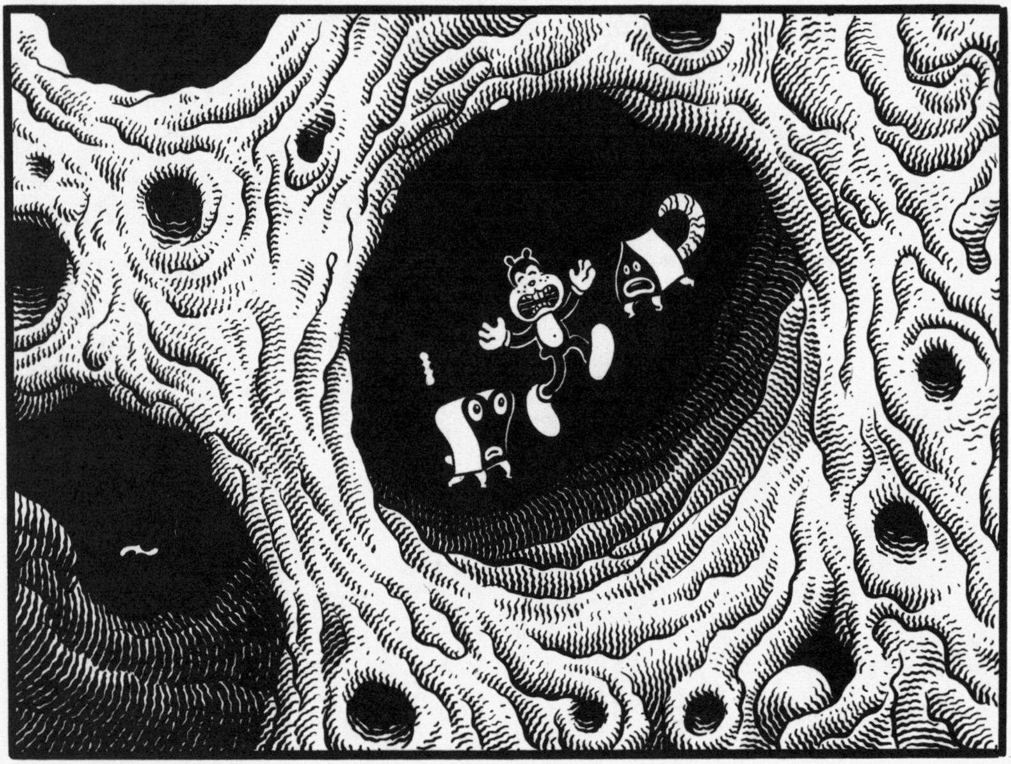

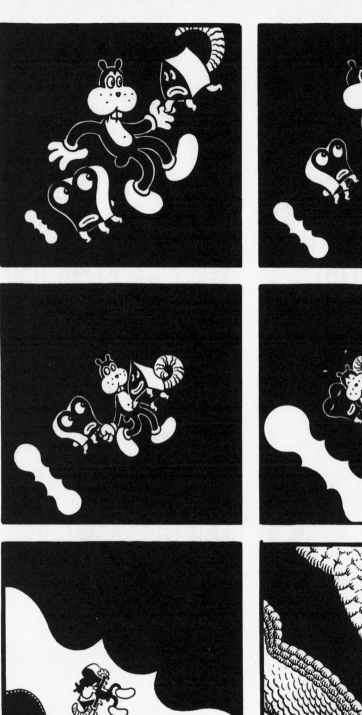

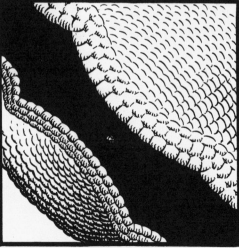

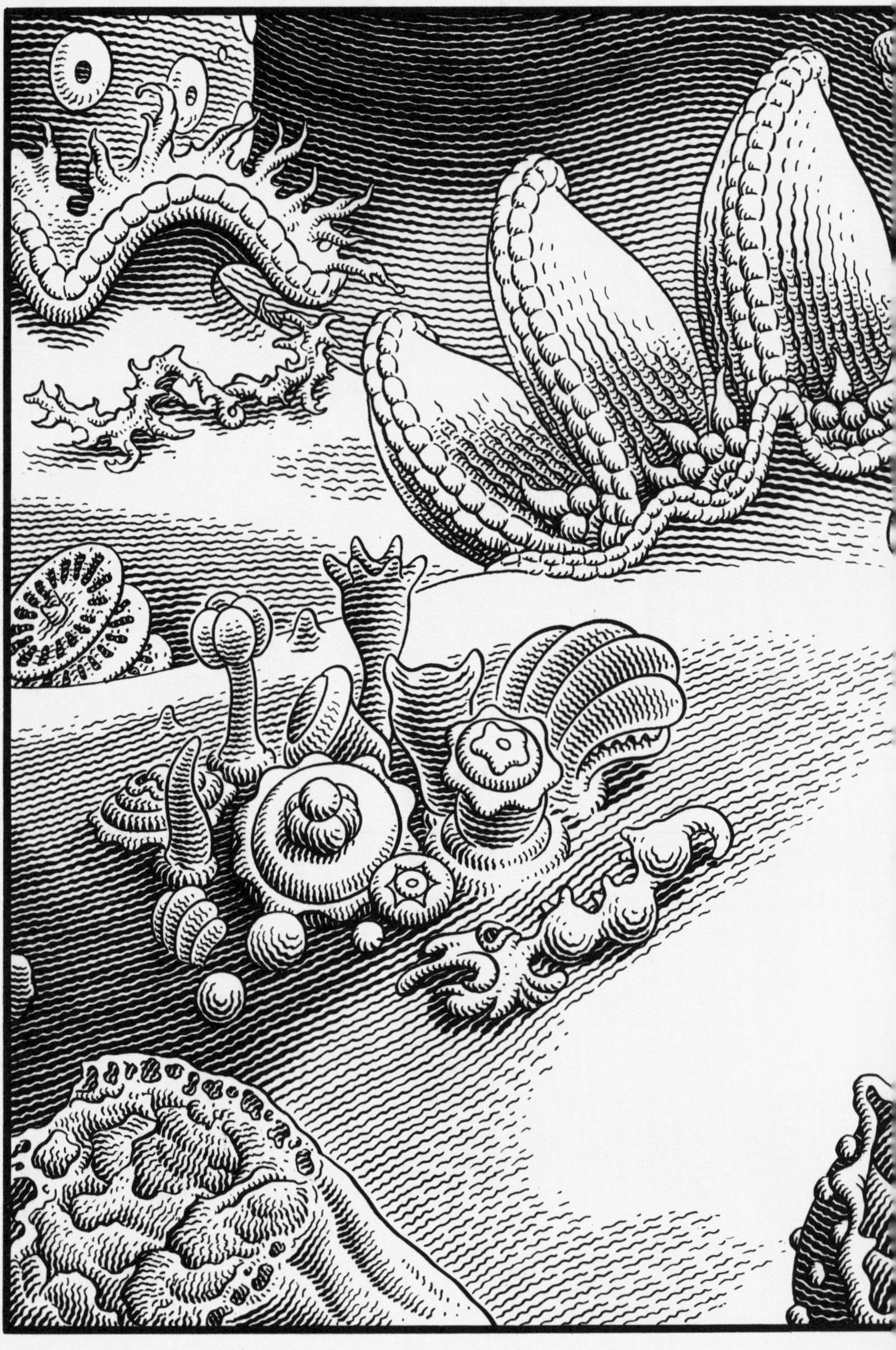

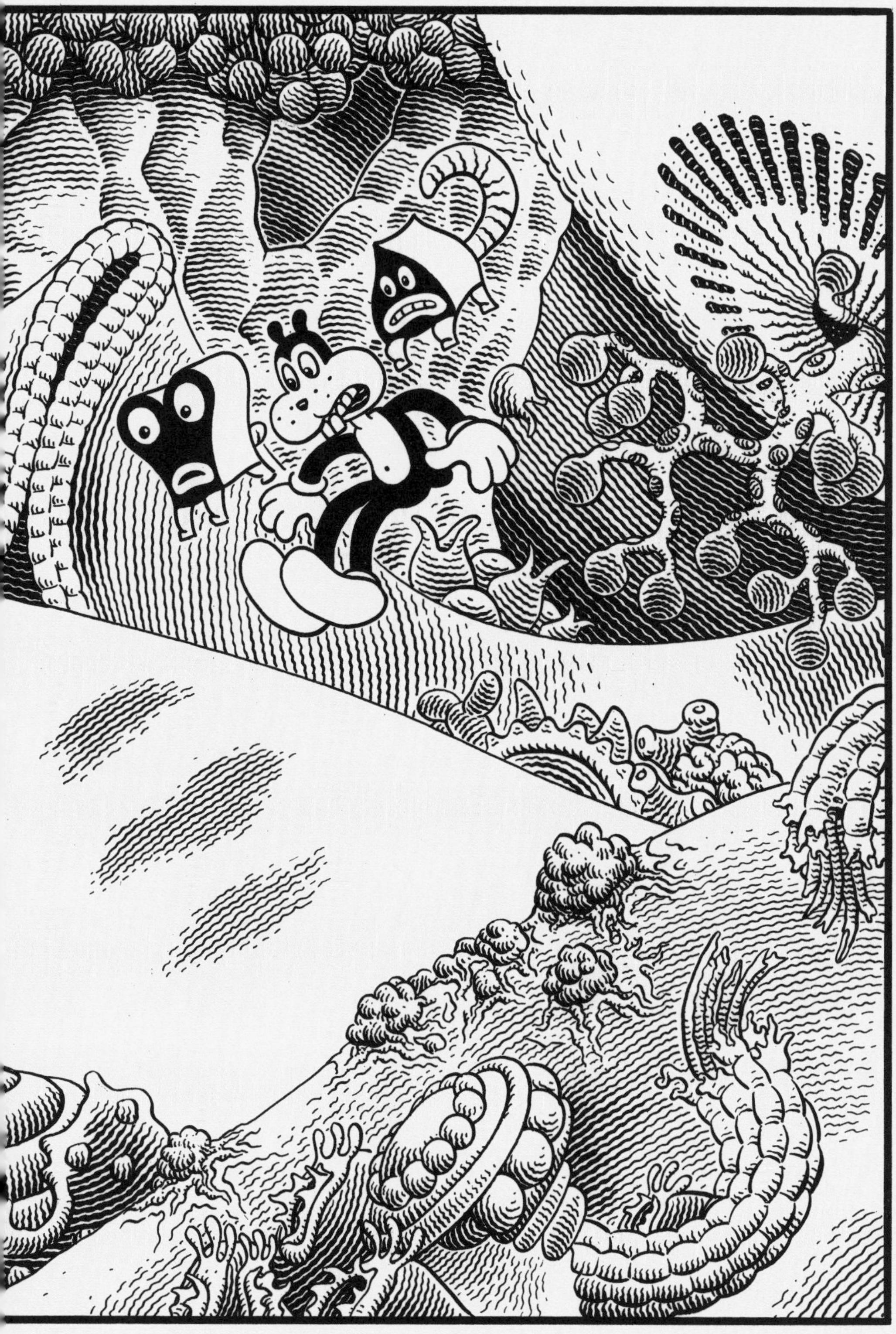

14-AN IMPERFECT PACIFIST

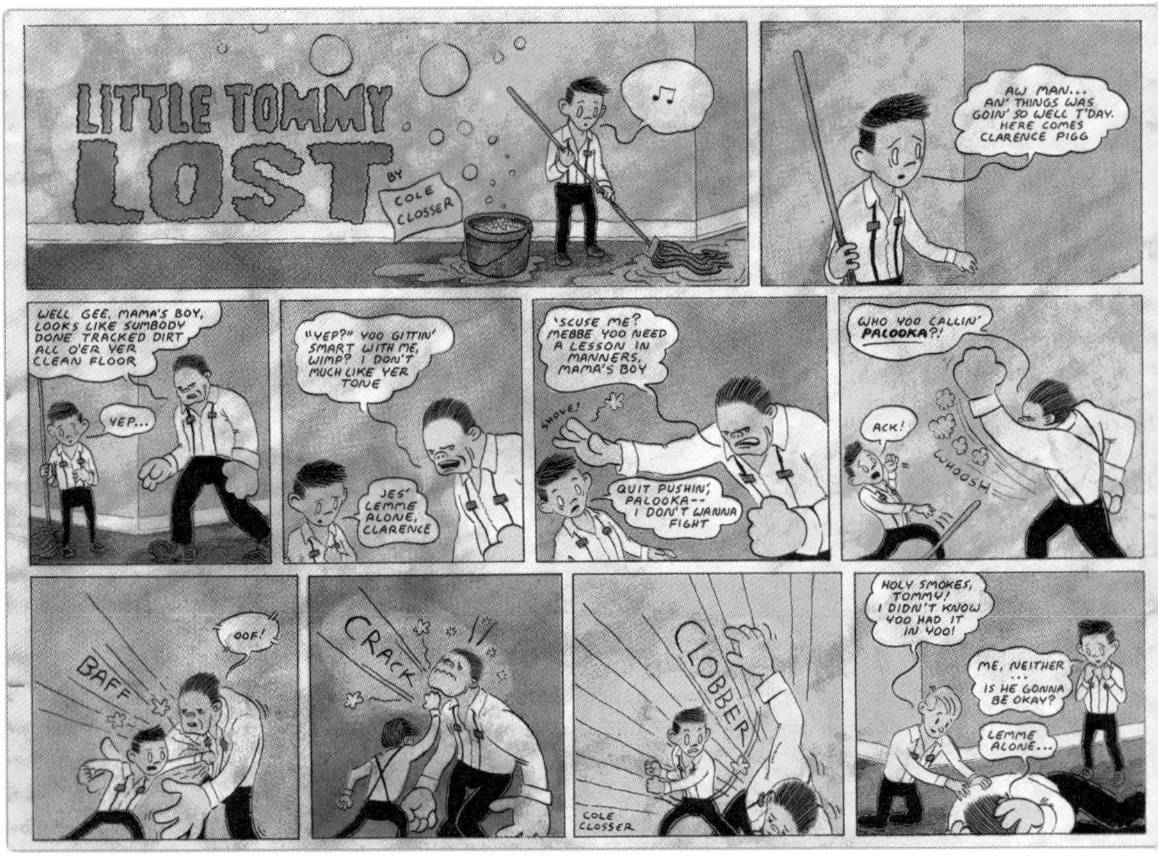
LITTLE TOMMY LOST
BY COLE CLOSSER
♫
AW MAN... AN' THINGS WAS GOIN' SO WELL T'DAY. HERE COMES CLARENCE PIGG
WELL GEE, MAMA'S BOY, LOOKS LIKE SUMBODY DONE TRACKED DIRT ALL O'ER YER CLEAN FLOOR
YEP...
"YEP?" YOO GITTIN' SMART WITH ME, WIMP? I DON'T MUCH LIKE YER TONE
JES' LEMME ALONE, CLARENCE
'SCUSE ME? MEBBE YOO NEED A LESSON IN MANNERS, MAMA'S BOY
SHOVE!
QUIT PUSHIN', PALOOKA-- I DON'T WANNA FIGHT
WHO YOO CALLIN' PALOOKA?!
ACK!
WHOOSH
BAFF
OOF!
CRACK
CLOBBER
COLE CLOSSER
HOLY SMOKES, TOMMY! I DIDN'T KNOW YOO HAD IT IN YOO!
ME, NEITHER ... IS HE GONNA BE OKAY?
LEMME ALONE...

15–STRENGTH IN NUMBERS

LITTLE TOMMY LOST
YOO BOYS SHOULDA BEEN THERE! I NEVER SEEN NUTHIN' LIKE IT IN MY WHOLE LIFE! OL' TOMMY SHORE SHOWED PIGG WHO'S BOSS! THREE PUNCHES AN' DOWN HE WENT! MAN OH MAN-- WHAT A FIGHTER!
GOOD ON YA, FELLA
HERE, HERE, PAL
I'M HEADIN' TO BED, GUYS. TH' FACT'RY WORE ME OUT T'DAY
LOOK, FELLAS-- THERE'S TH' OL' PUNCHIN' BAG NOW!
HEY, CLARENCE! HOW'S THAT JAW FEELIN'?
THAT'S QUITE A SHINER YOO GOT THERE, BIG GUY-- YA OUGHTTA PUT SOME ICE ON IT!
AW LET 'IM ALONE
TOMMY MAY HAVE WHIPPED HIM, BUT WHEN OUR LIL' BUDDY AIN'T 'ROUND, I'M ONE-HUNDR'D-PER-CENT TERRIFIED O' THAT GREAT BIG GO-RILLA!
AND HOW
HERE, HERE
COLE CLOSSER 9/28

16–AGREEMENTS, SECRETS, AND MAPS

LITTLE TOMMY LOST
NO!-- YOU WILL LISTEN TO ME!
MR. GREAVES IS SHORE GIVIN' TH' BUSINESS TO WHOEVER'S ON TH' OTHER END O' THAT PHONE
NEED I REMIND YOU THAT WE HAVE A BINDING AGREEMENT, CROMWELL? I WILL NOT BE THREATENED, DECEIVED, OR OTHERWISE TRIFLED WITH!
IT AIN'T POLITE TO EAVESDROP-- BUT HE'S HOLLERIN' SO LOUD THAT I GUESS I DON'T GOT MUCH CHOICE
THESE ARE DELICATE MATTERS AND THEY MUST NOT BE HURRIED, MY DEAR OLD FRIEND. ALL THINGS WILL COME TO EACH OF US IN DUE TIME. YOU WOULD BE WISE TO REMEMBER THAT I AM THE ONLY ONE WITH THE MAP, CROMWELL. WITHOUT ME, YOU HAVE NOTHING
NOW, JES' WHAT IN TH' HECK DO YOO S'POSE THAT CROOKED OLD BIRD IS UP TO?
COLE CLOSSER 9/29

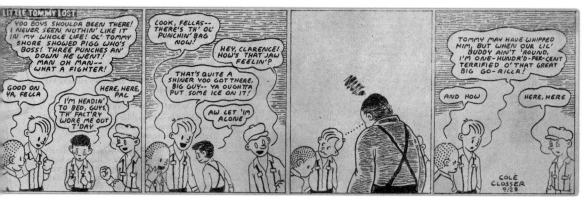

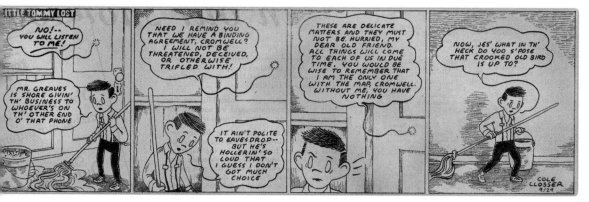

17–SOLITARY TOMMY

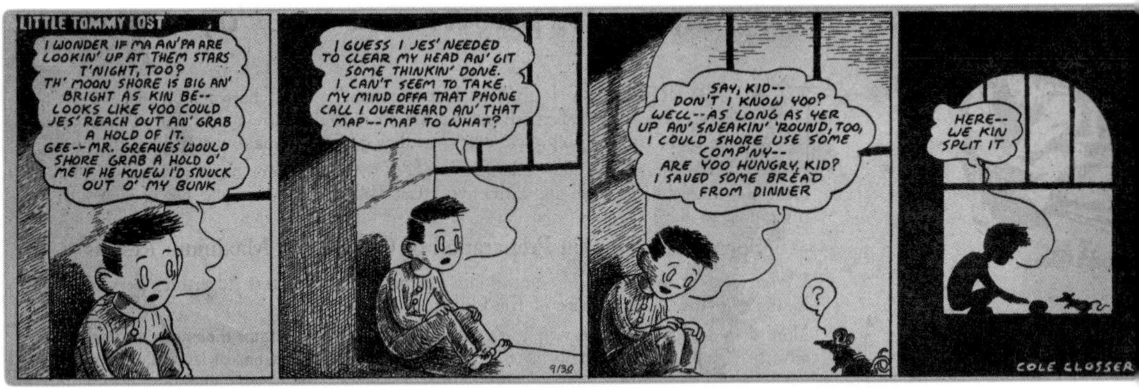
LITTLE TOMMY LOST
I WONDER IF MA AN' PA ARE LOOKIN' UP AT THEM STARS T'NIGHT, TOO? TH' MOON SHORE IS BIG AN' BRIGHT AS KIN BE-- LOOKS LIKE YOO COULD JES' REACH OUT AN' GRAB A HOLD OF IT. GEE--MR. GREAVES WOULD SHORE GRAB A HOLD O' ME IF HE KNEW I'D SNUCK OUT O' MY BUNK
I GUESS I JES' NEEDED TO CLEAR MY HEAD AN' GIT SOME THINKIN' DONE. I CAN'T SEEM TO TAKE MY MIND OFFA THAT PHONE CALL I OVERHEARD AN' THAT MAP--MAP TO WHAT?
9/30
SAY, KID-- DON'T I KNOW YOO? WELL--AS LONG AS YER UP AN' SNEAKIN' 'ROUND, TOO, I COULD SHORE USE SOME COMP'NY-- ARE YOO HUNGRY, KID? I SAVED SOME BREAD FROM DINNER
?
HERE-- WE KIN SPLIT IT
COLE CLOSSER

18–REMATCH

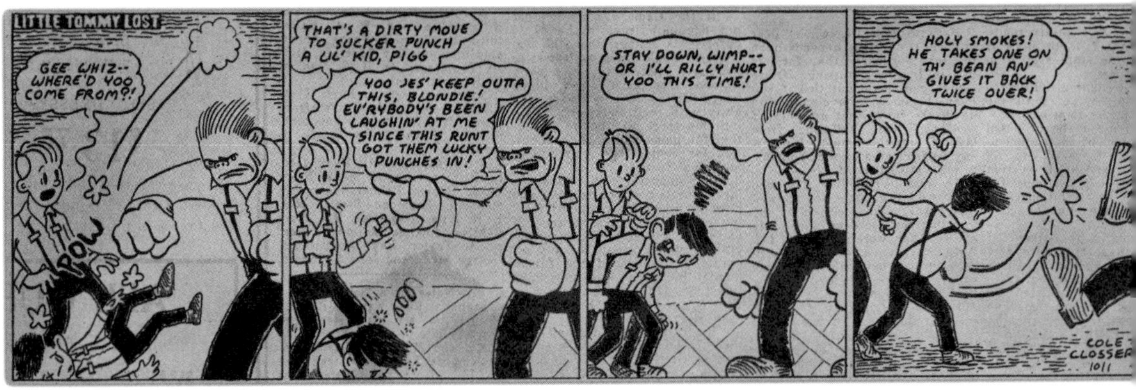
LITTLE TOMMY LOST
GEE WHIZ-- WHERE'D YOO COME FROM?!
POW
THAT'S A DIRTY MOVE TO SUCKER PUNCH A LIL' KID, PIGG
YOO JES' KEEP OUTTA THIS, BLONDIE! EV'RYBODY'S BEEN LAUGHIN' AT ME SINCE THIS RUNT GOT THEM LUCKY PUNCHES IN!
STAY DOWN, WIMP-- OR I'LL RILLY HURT YOO THIS TIME!
HOLY SMOKES! HE TAKES ONE ON TH' BEAN AN' GIVES IT BACK TWICE OVER!
COLE CLOSSER 10/1

19—INTRODUCTIONS AND EXITS

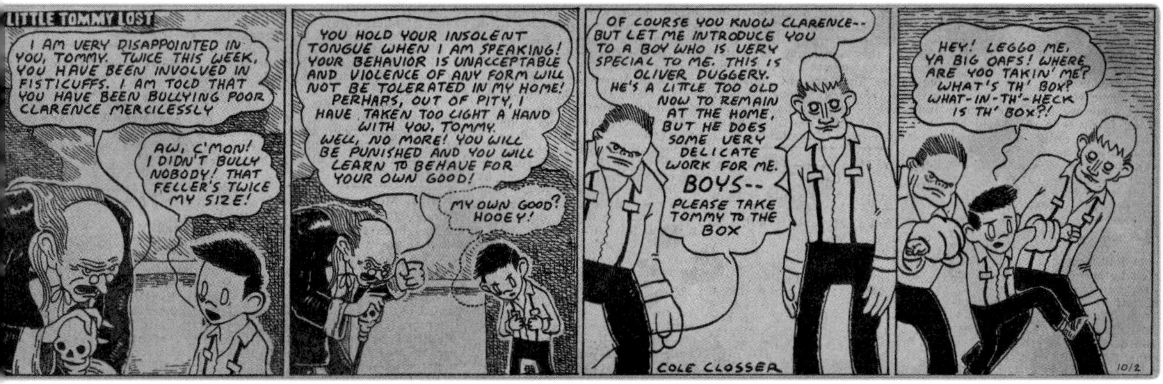
LITTLE TOMMY LOST
I AM VERY DISAPPOINTED IN YOU, TOMMY. TWICE THIS WEEK, YOU HAVE BEEN INVOLVED IN FISTICUFFS. I AM TOLD THAT YOU HAVE BEEN BULLYING POOR CLARENCE MERCILESSLY
AW, C'MON! I DIDN'T BULLY NOBODY! THAT FELLER'S TWICE MY SIZE!
YOU HOLD YOUR INSOLENT TONGUE WHEN I AM SPEAKING! YOUR BEHAVIOR IS UNACCEPTABLE AND VIOLENCE OF ANY FORM WILL NOT BE TOLERATED IN MY HOME! PERHAPS, OUT OF PITY, I HAVE TAKEN TOO LIGHT A HAND WITH YOU, TOMMY. WELL, NO MORE! YOU WILL BE PUNISHED AND YOU WILL LEARN TO BEHAVE FOR YOUR OWN GOOD!
MY OWN GOOD? HOOEY!
OF COURSE YOU KNOW CLARENCE-- BUT LET ME INTRODUCE YOU TO A BOY WHO IS VERY SPECIAL TO ME. THIS IS OLIVER DUGGERY. HE'S A LITTLE TOO OLD NOW TO REMAIN AT THE HOME, BUT HE DOES SOME VERY DELICATE WORK FOR ME. BOYS-- PLEASE TAKE TOMMY TO THE BOX
COLE CLOSSER
HEY! LEGGO ME, YA BIG OAFS! WHERE ARE YOO TAKIN' ME? WHAT'S TH' BOX? WHAT-IN-TH'-HECK IS TH' BOX?!
10/2

20—A NIGHT IN THE BOX

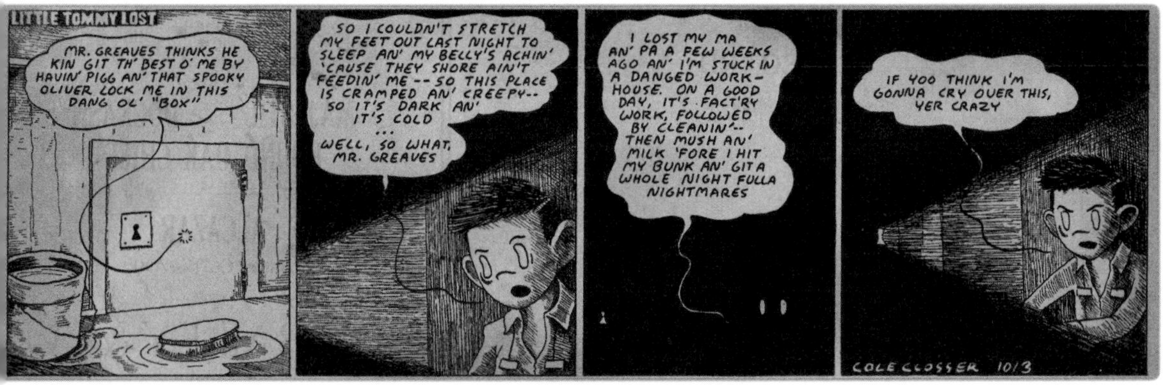
LITTLE TOMMY LOST
MR. GREAVES THINKS HE KIN GIT TH' BEST O' ME BY HAVIN' PIGG AN' THAT SPOOKY OLIVER LOCK ME IN THIS DANG OL' "BOX"
SO I COULDN'T STRETCH MY FEET OUT LAST NIGHT TO SLEEP AN' MY BELLY'S ACHIN' 'CAUSE THEY SHORE AIN'T FEEDIN' ME -- SO THIS PLACE IS CRAMPED AN' CREEPY-- SO IT'S DARK AN' IT'S COLD ... WELL, SO WHAT, MR. GREAVES
I LOST MY MA AN' PA A FEW WEEKS AGO AN' I'M STUCK IN A DANGED WORK-HOUSE. ON A GOOD DAY, IT'S FACT'RY WORK, FOLLOWED BY CLEANIN'-- THEN MUSH AN' MILK 'FORE I HIT MY BUNK AN' GIT A WHOLE NIGHT FULLA NIGHTMARES
IF YOO THINK I'M GONNA CRY OVER THIS, YER CRAZY
COLE CLOSSER 10/3

21– VISITING HOURS

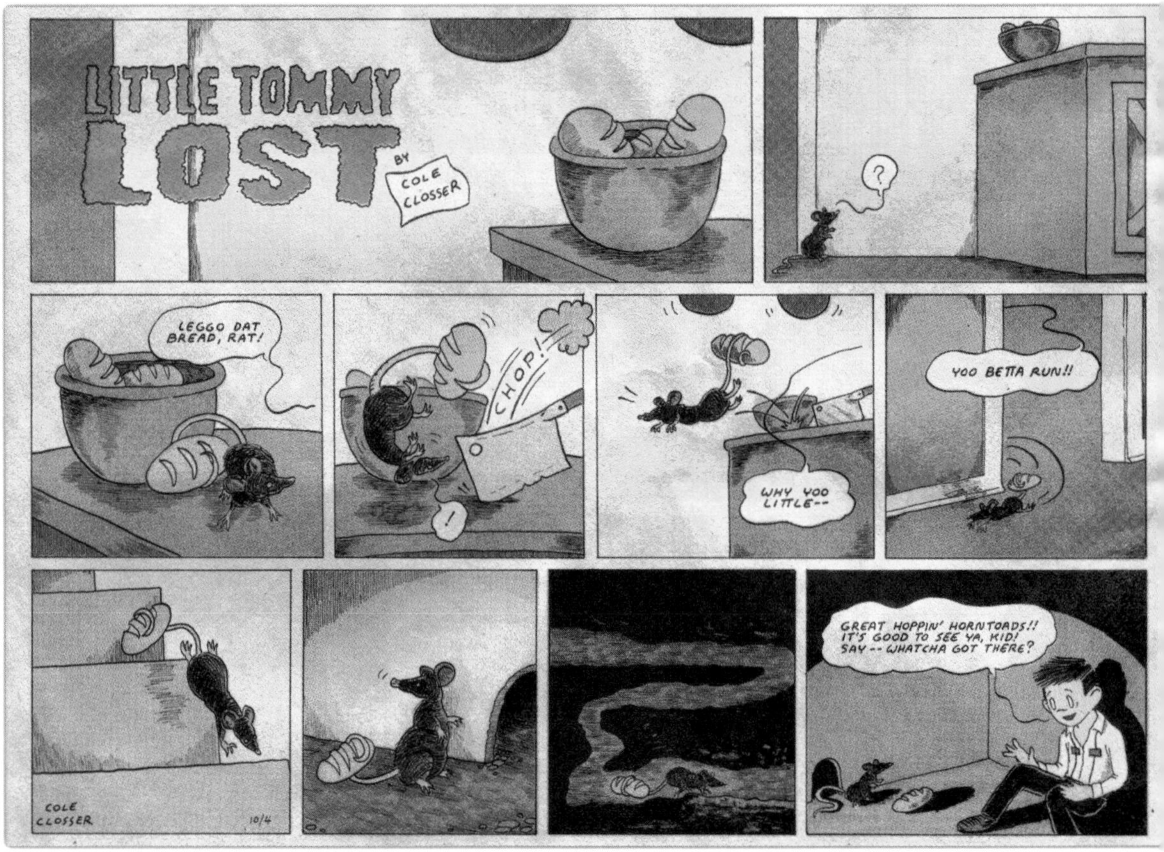

22–KEYS AND BONES

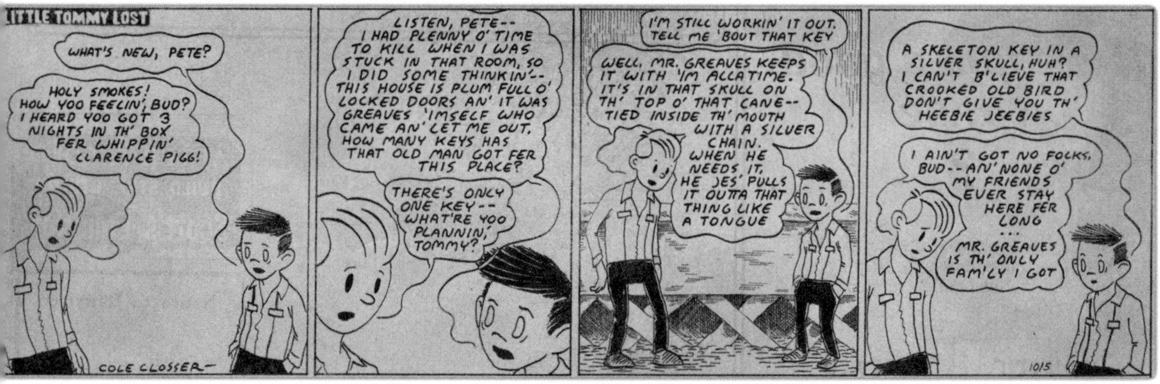
LITTLE TOMMY LOST
WHAT'S NEW, PETE?
HOLY SMOKES! HOW YOO FEELIN', BUD? I HEARD YOO GOT 3 NIGHTS IN TH' BOX FER WHIPPIN' CLARENCE PIGG!
COLE CLOSSER
LISTEN, PETE-- I HAD PLENNY O' TIME TO KILL WHEN I WAS STUCK IN THAT ROOM, SO I DID SOME THINKIN'-- THIS HOUSE IS PLUM FULL O' LOCKED DOORS AN' IT WAS GREAVES 'IMSELF WHO CAME AN' LET ME OUT. HOW MANY KEYS HAS THAT OLD MAN GOT FER THIS PLACE?
THERE'S ONLY ONE KEY-- WHAT'RE YOO PLANNIN', TOMMY?
I'M STILL WORKIN' IT OUT. TELL ME 'BOUT THAT KEY
WELL, MR. GREAVES KEEPS IT WITH 'IM ALLATIME. IT'S IN THAT SKULL ON TH' TOP O' THAT CANE-- TIED INSIDE TH' MOUTH WITH A SILVER CHAIN. WHEN HE NEEDS IT, HE JES' PULLS IT OUTTA THAT THING LIKE A TONGUE
A SKELETON KEY IN A SILVER SKULL, HUH? I CAN'T B'LIEVE THAT CROOKED OLD BIRD DON'T GIVE YOU TH' HEEBIE JEEBIES
I AIN'T GOT NO FOLKS, BUD-- AN' NONE O' MY FRIENDS EVER STAY HERE FER LONG ... MR. GREAVES IS TH' ONLY FAM'LY I GOT
10/5

23–TOMMY HAS A SHADOW

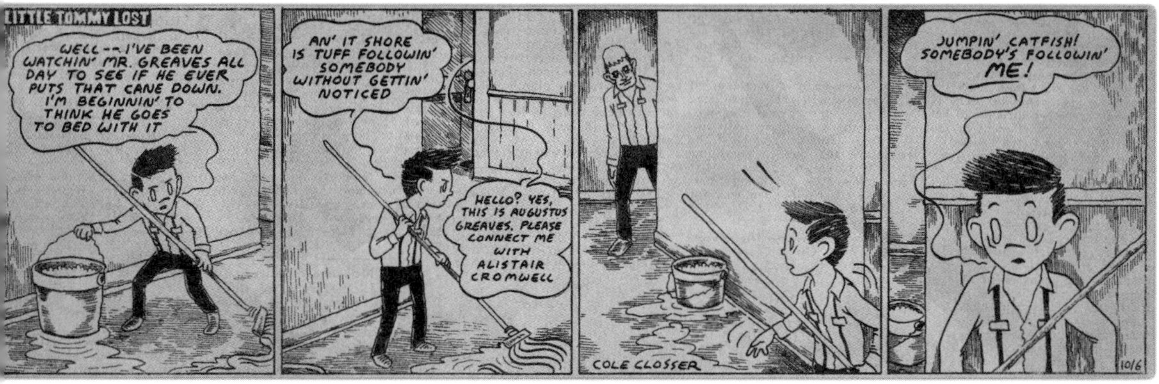
LITTLE TOMMY LOST
WELL-- I'VE BEEN WATCHIN' MR. GREAVES ALL DAY TO SEE IF HE EVER PUTS THAT CANE DOWN. I'M BEGINNIN' TO THINK HE GOES TO BED WITH IT
AN' IT SHORE IS TUFF FOLLOWIN' SOMEBODY WITHOUT GETTIN' NOTICED
HELLO? YES, THIS IS AUGUSTUS GREAVES. PLEASE CONNECT ME WITH ALISTAIR CROMWELL
COLE CLOSSER
JUMPIN' CATFISH! SOMEBODY'S FOLLOWIN' ME!
10/6

24–DIGGING

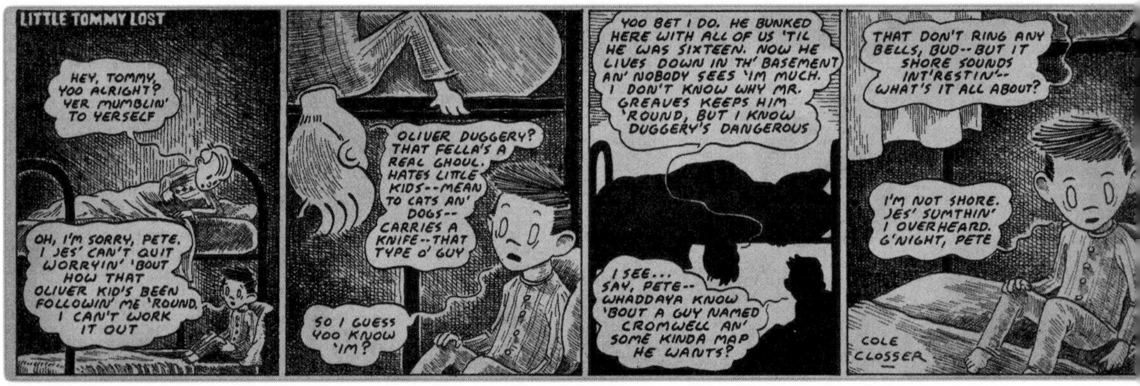

LITTLE TOMMY LOST
HEY, TOMMY, YOO ALRIGHT? YER MUMBLIN' TO YERSELF
OH, I'M SORRY, PETE. I JES' CAN'T QUIT WORRYIN' 'BOUT HOW THAT OLIVER KID'S BEEN FOLLOWIN' ME 'ROUND. I CAN'T WORK IT OUT
OLIVER DUGGERY? THAT FELLA'S A REAL GHOUL. HATES LITTLE KIDS--MEAN TO CATS AN' DOGS--CARRIES A KNIFE--THAT TYPE O' GUY
SO I GUESS YOO KNOW 'IM?
YOO BET I DO. HE BUNKED HERE WITH ALL OF US 'TIL HE WAS SIXTEEN. NOW HE LIVES DOWN IN TH' BASEMENT AN' NOBODY SEES 'IM MUCH. I DON'T KNOW WHY MR. GREAVES KEEPS HIM 'ROUND, BUT I KNOW DUGGERY'S DANGEROUS
I SEE... SAY, PETE--WHADDAYA KNOW 'BOUT A GUY NAMED CROMWELL AN' SOME KINDA MAP HE WANTS?
THAT DON'T RING ANY BELLS, BUD--BUT IT SHORE SOUNDS INT'RESTIN'--WHAT'S IT ALL ABOUT?
I'M NOT SHORE. JES' SUMTHIN' I OVERHEARD. G'NIGHT, PETE
COLE CLOSSER

25–POOR CLARENCE

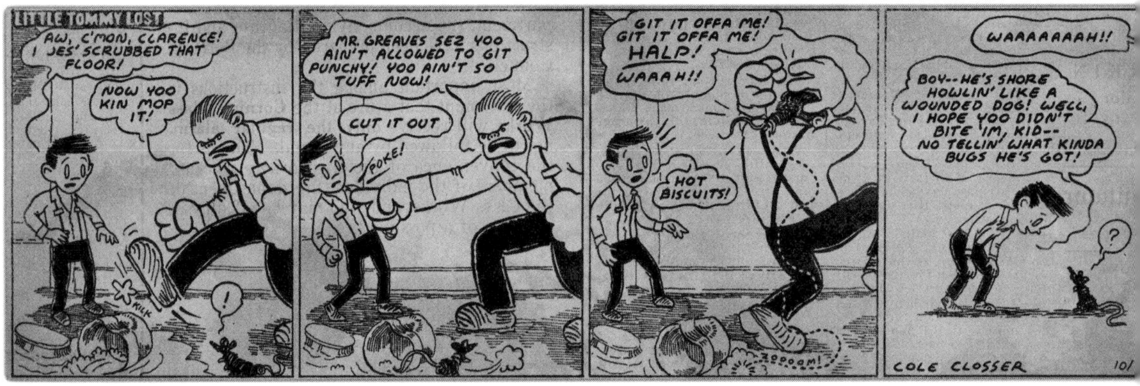

LITTLE TOMMY LOST
AW, C'MON, CLARENCE! I JES' SCRUBBED THAT FLOOR!
NOW YOO KIN MOP IT!
!
MR. GREAVES SEZ YOO AIN'T ALLOWED TO GIT PUNCHY! YOO AIN'T SO TUFF NOW!
CUT IT OUT
POKE!
GIT IT OFFA ME! GIT IT OFFA ME! HALP! WAAAH!!
HOT BISCUITS!
ZOOOOM!
WAAAAAAAH!!
BOY--HE'S SHORE HOWLIN' LIKE A WOUNDED DOG! WELL I HOPE YOO DIDN'T BITE 'IM, KID--NO TELLIN' WHAT KINDA BUGS HE'S GOT!
?
COLE CLOSSER
101

26—THINKING OF HOME

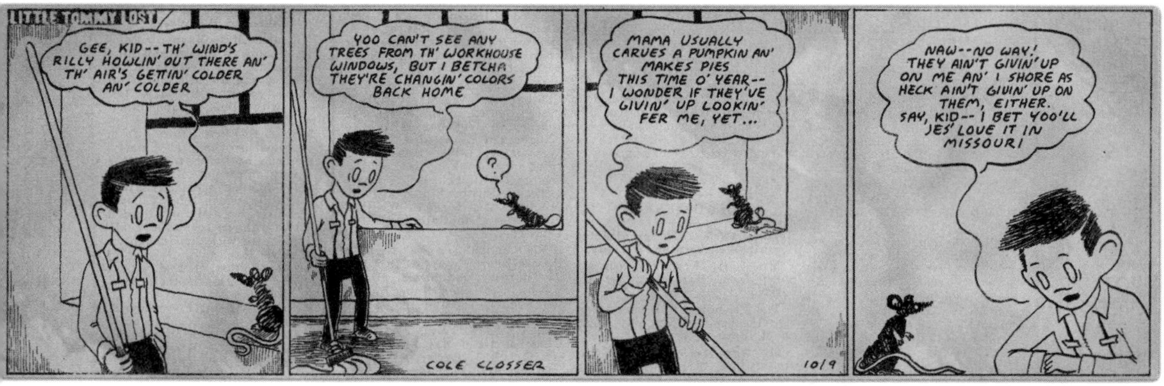
LITTLE TOMMY LOST
GEE, KID--TH' WIND'S RILLY HOWLIN' OUT THERE AN' TH' AIR'S GETTIN' COLDER AN' COLDER
YOO CAN'T SEE ANY TREES FROM TH' WORKHOUSE WINDOWS, BUT I BETCHA THEY'RE CHANGIN' COLORS BACK HOME
?
COLE CLOSSER
MAMA USUALLY CARVES A PUMPKIN AN' MAKES PIES THIS TIME O' YEAR-- I WONDER IF THEY'VE GIVIN' UP LOOKIN' FER ME, YET...
10/9
NAW--NO WAY! THEY AIN'T GIVIN' UP ON ME AN' I SHORE AS HECK AIN'T GIVIN' UP ON THEM, EITHER. SAY, KID-- I BET YOO'LL JES' LOVE IT IN MISSOURI

27—SILVER TEETH, SILVER TONGUE

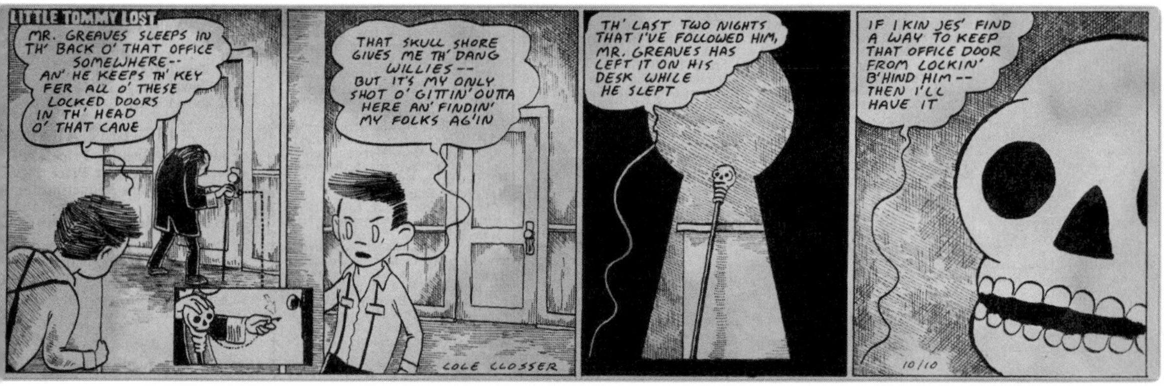
LITTLE TOMMY LOST
MR. GREAVES SLEEPS IN TH' BACK O' THAT OFFICE SOMEWHERE-- AN' HE KEEPS TH' KEY FER ALL O' THESE LOCKED DOORS IN TH' HEAD O' THAT CANE
THAT SKULL SHORE GIVES ME TH' DANG WILLIES-- BUT IT'S MY ONLY SHOT O' GITTIN' OUTTA HERE AN' FINDIN' MY FOLKS AG'IN
COLE CLOSSER
TH' LAST TWO NIGHTS THAT I'VE FOLLOWED HIM, MR. GREAVES HAS LEFT IT ON HIS DESK WHILE HE SLEPT
IF I KIN JES' FIND A WAY TO KEEP THAT OFFICE DOOR FROM LOCKIN' B'HIND HIM-- THEN I'LL HAVE IT
10/10

28–*PREMONITION*

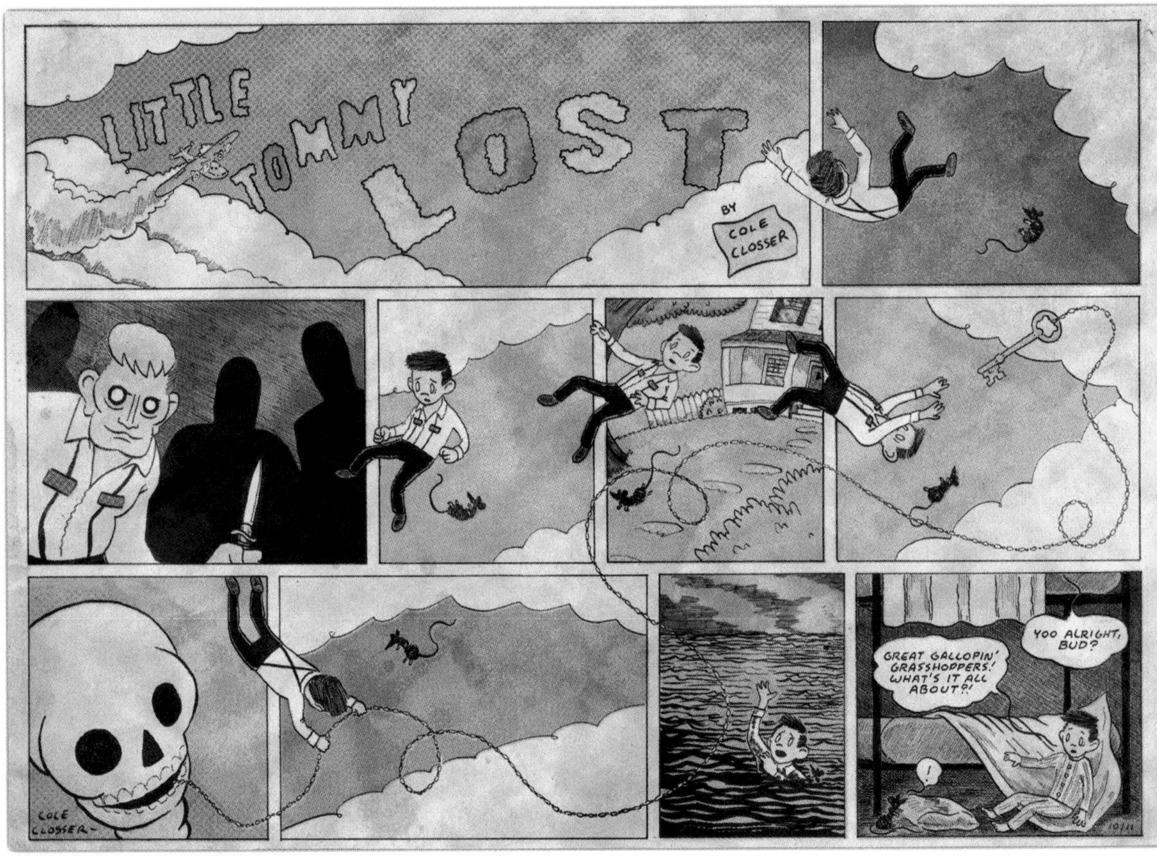
LITTLE TOMMY LOST
BY COLE CLOSSER
COLE CLOSSER
GREAT GALLOPIN' GRASSHOPPERS! WHAT'S IT ALL ABOUT?!
YOO ALRIGHT, BUD?
!

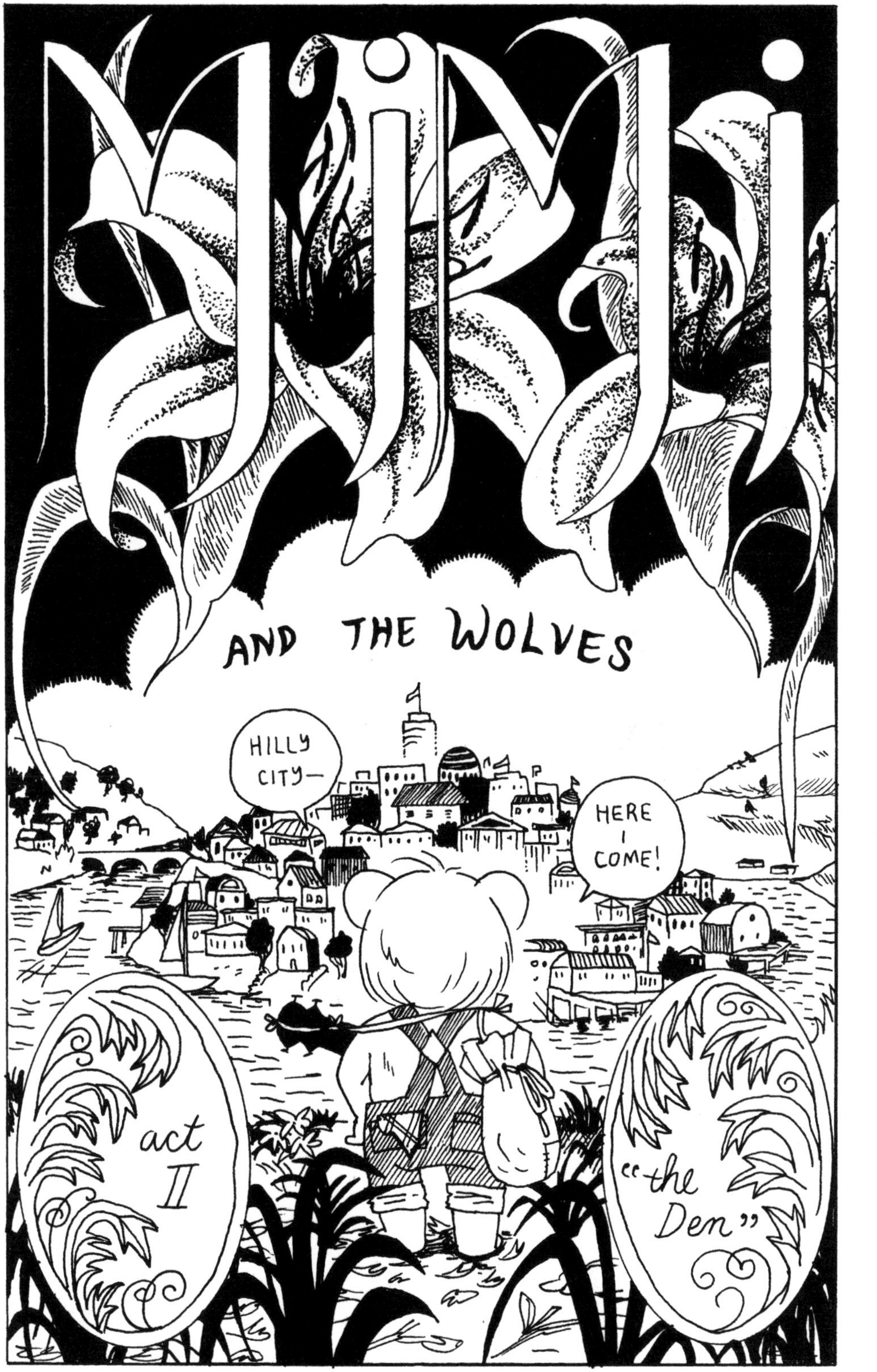
MIMI
AND THE WOLVES
HILLY CITY—
HERE I COME!
act II
"the Den"

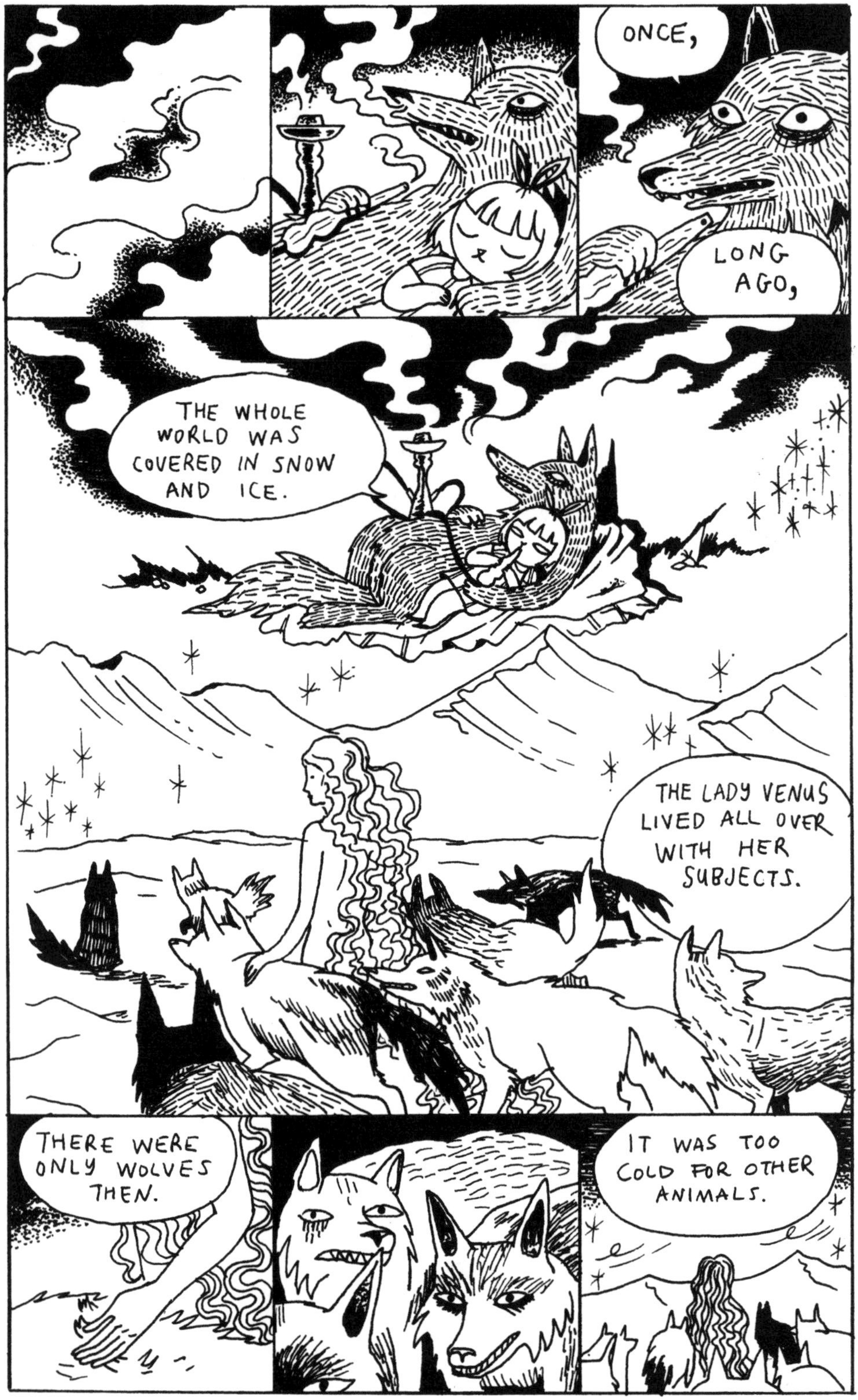
ONCE,
LONG AGO,
THE WHOLE WORLD WAS COVERED IN SNOW AND ICE.
THE LADY VENUS LIVED ALL OVER WITH HER SUBJECTS.
THERE WERE ONLY WOLVES THEN.
IT WAS TOO COLD FOR OTHER ANIMALS.

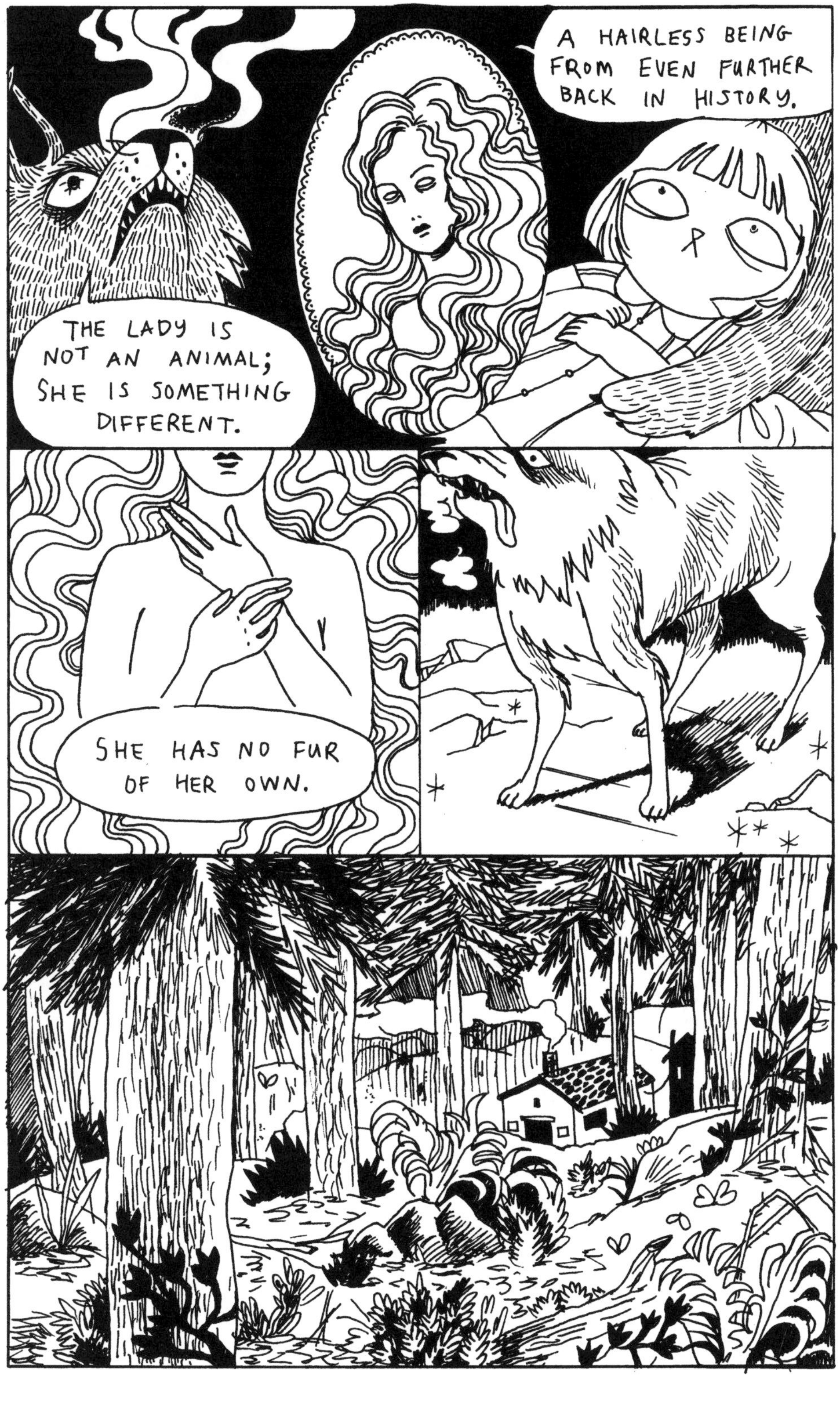

THE LADY IS NOT AN ANIMAL; SHE IS SOMETHING DIFFERENT.
A HAIRLESS BEING FROM EVEN FURTHER BACK IN HISTORY.
SHE HAS NO FUR OF HER OWN.

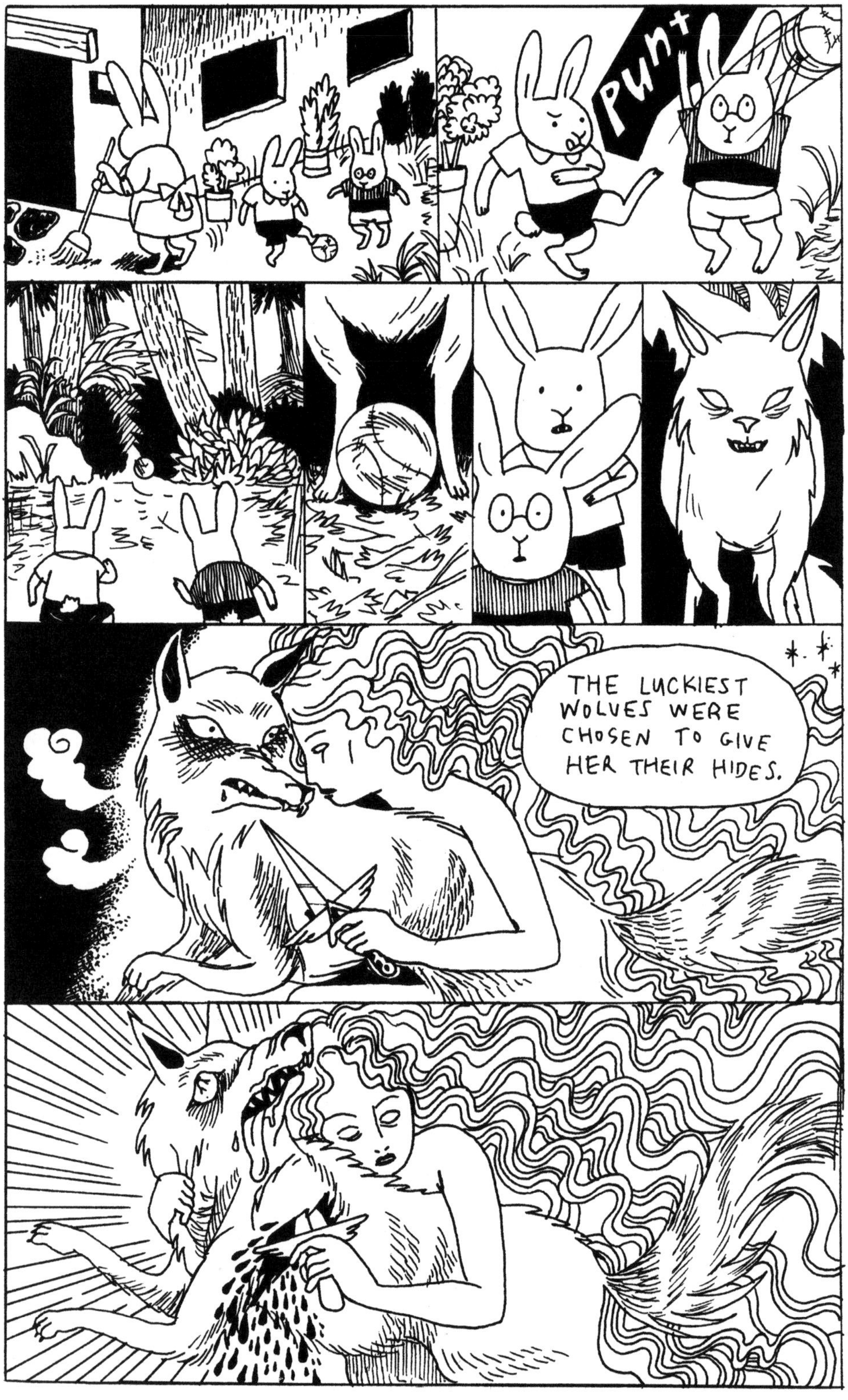
PUNT
THE LUCKIEST WOLVES WERE CHOSEN TO GIVE HER THEIR HIDES.

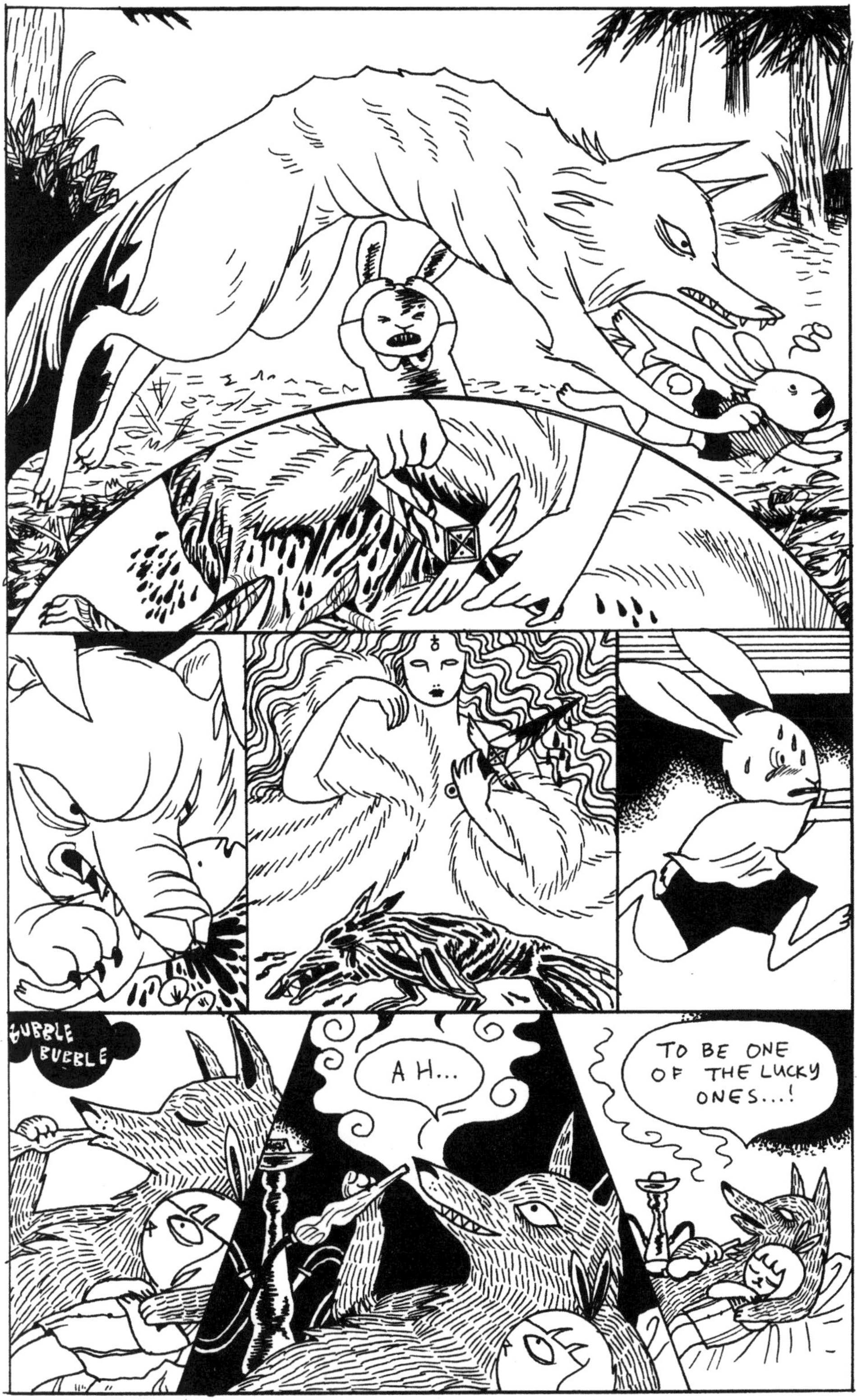
BUBBLE BUBBLE
AH...
TO BE ONE OF THE LUCKY ONES...!

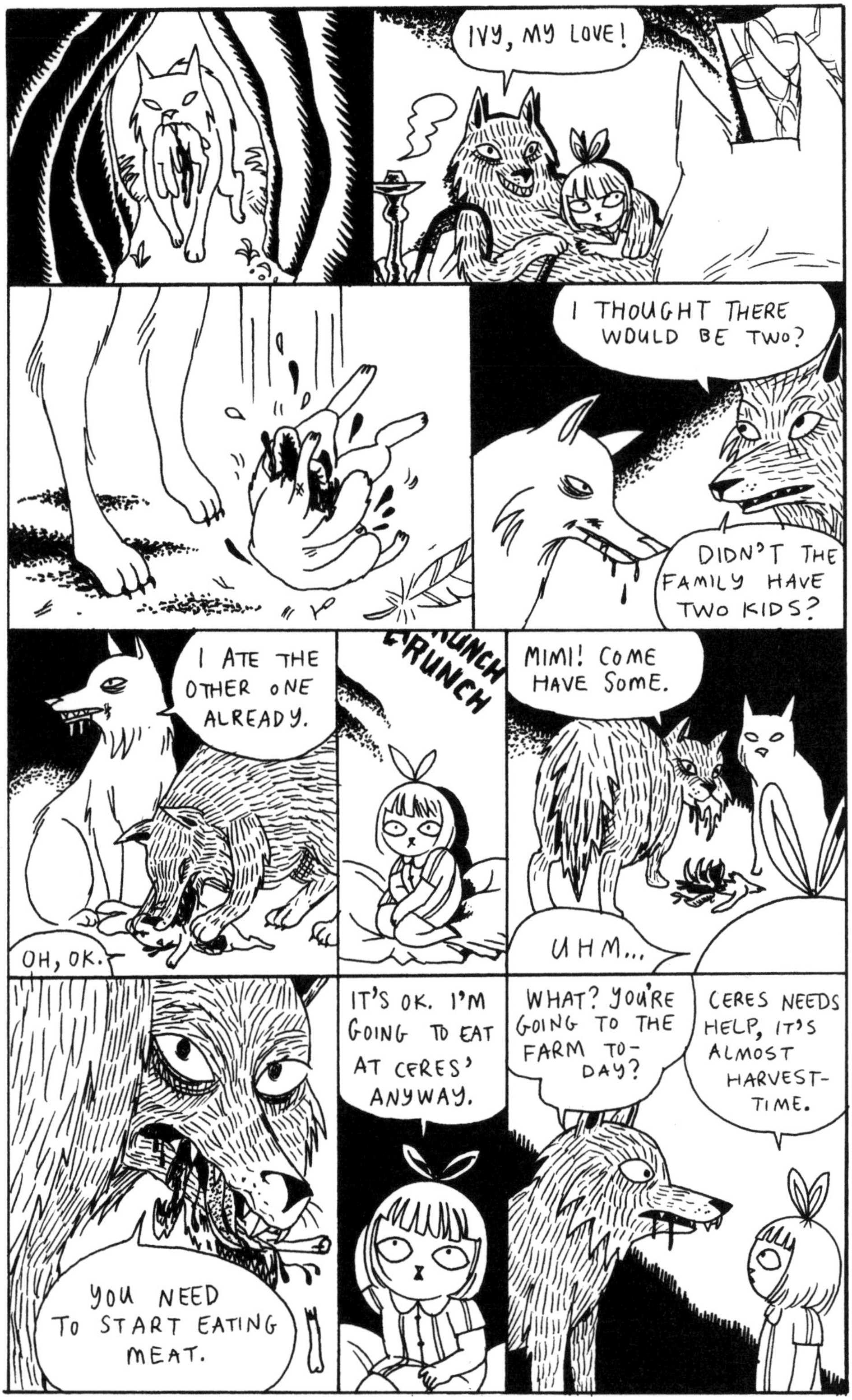
IVY, MY LOVE!
I THOUGHT THERE WOULD BE TWO?
DIDN'T THE FAMILY HAVE TWO KIDS?
I ATE THE OTHER ONE ALREADY.
OH, OK.
CRUNCH CRUNCH
MIMI! COME HAVE SOME.
UHM...
YOU NEED TO START EATING MEAT.
IT'S OK. I'M GOING TO EAT AT CERES' ANYWAY.
WHAT? YOU'RE GOING TO THE FARM TO-DAY?
CERES NEEDS HELP, IT'S ALMOST HARVEST-TIME.

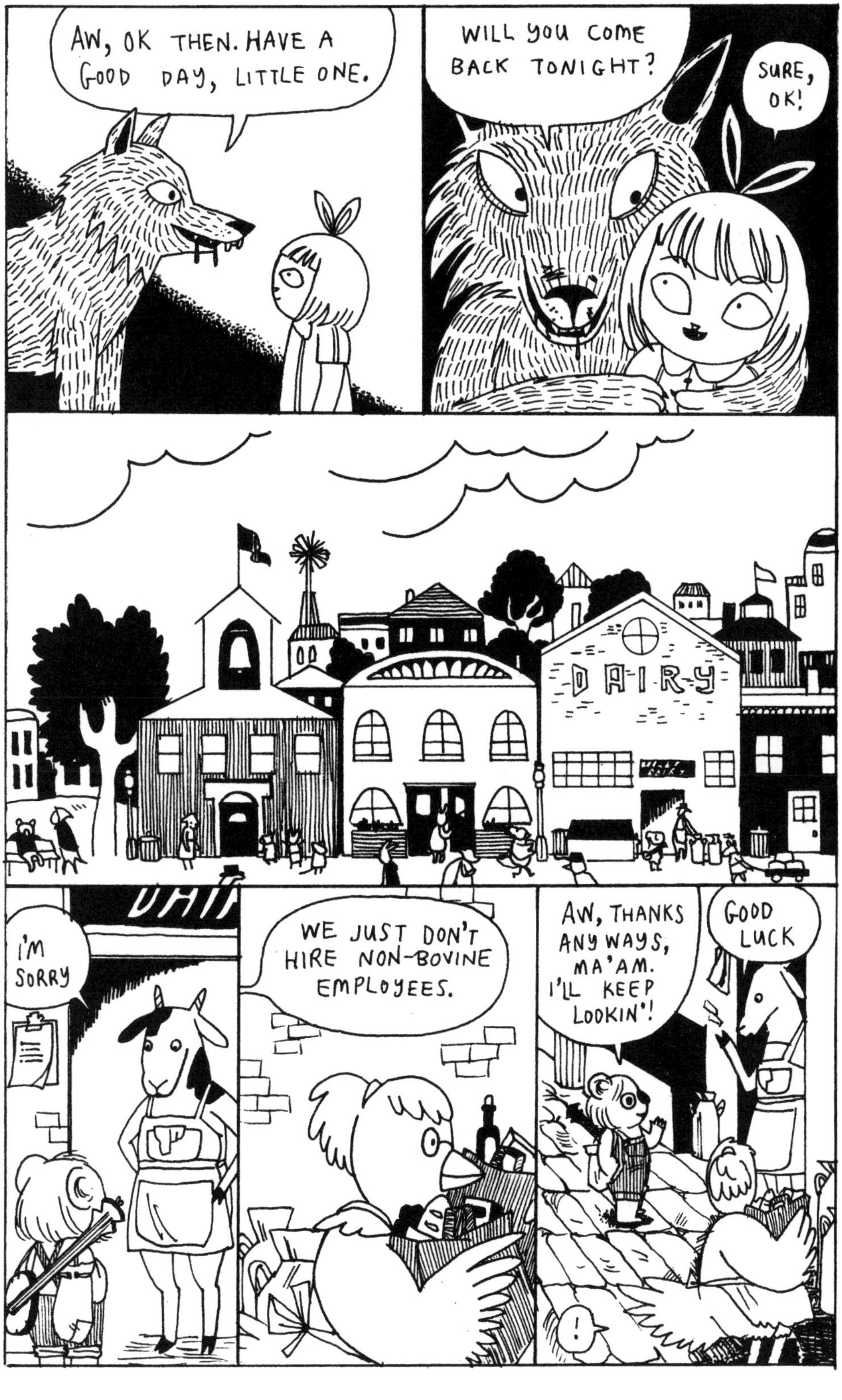
AW, OK THEN. HAVE A GOOD DAY, LITTLE ONE.
WILL YOU COME BACK TONIGHT?
SURE, OK!
DAIRY
I'M SORRY
WE JUST DON'T HIRE NON-BOVINE EMPLOYEES.
AW, THANKS ANYWAYS, MA'AM. I'LL KEEP LOOKIN'!
GOOD LUCK
!

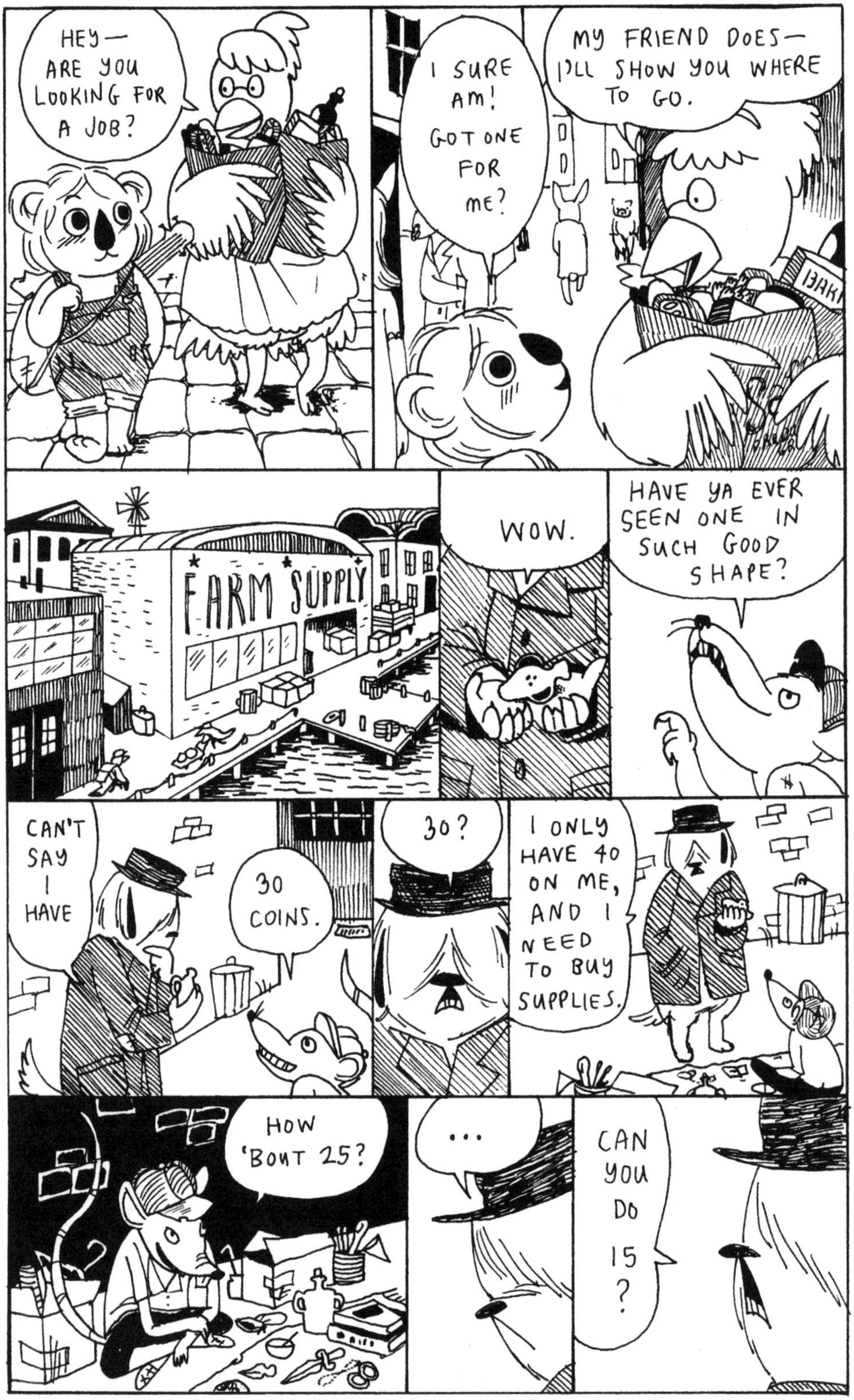
HEY— ARE YOU LOOKING FOR A JOB?
I SURE AM! GOT ONE FOR ME?
MY FRIEND DOES— I'LL SHOW YOU WHERE TO GO.
FARM SUPPLY
WOW.
HAVE YA EVER SEEN ONE IN SUCH GOOD SHAPE?
CAN'T SAY I HAVE
30 COINS.
30?
I ONLY HAVE 40 ON ME, AND I NEED TO BUY SUPPLIES.
HOW 'BOUT 25?
...
CAN YOU DO 15?

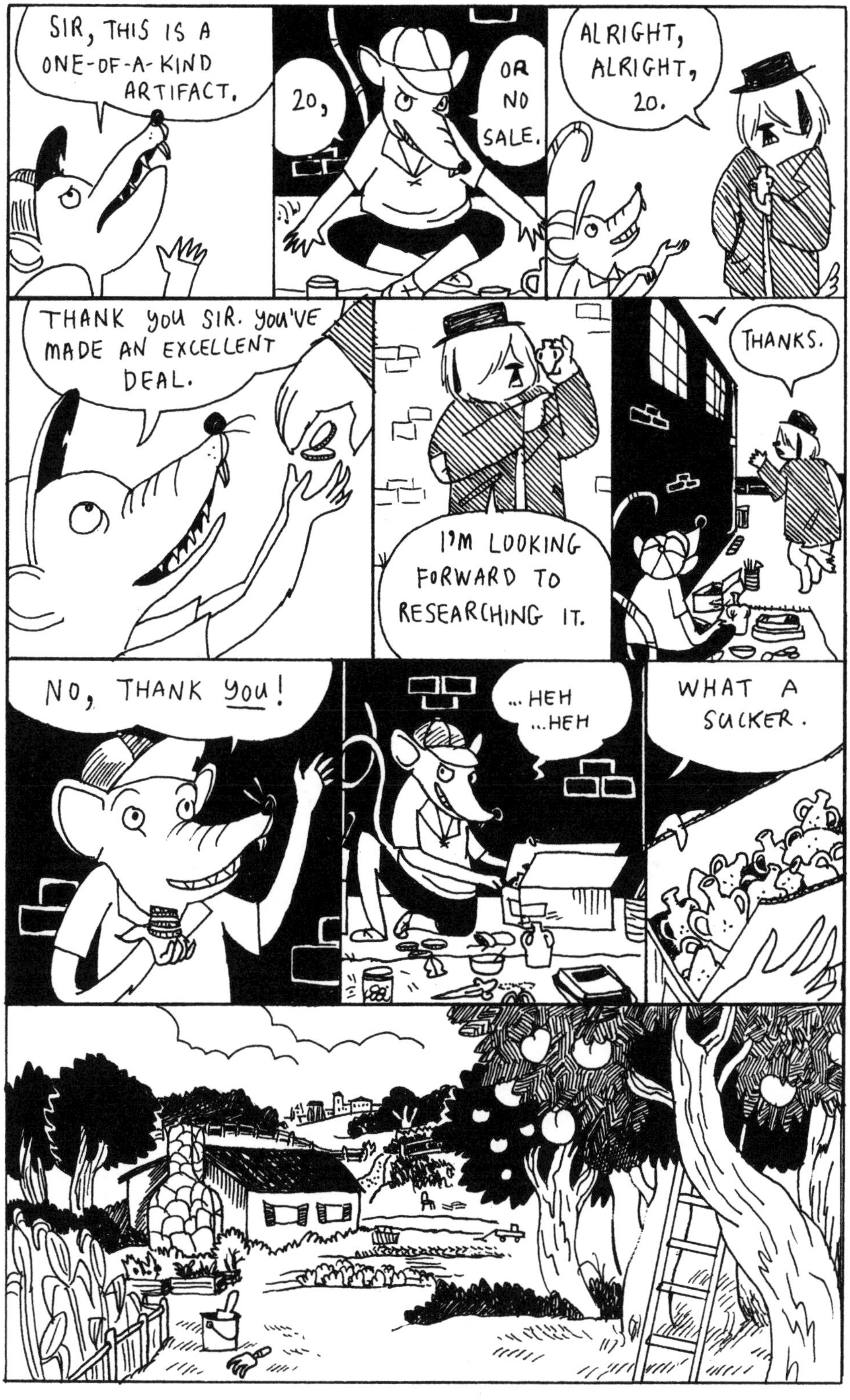
SIR, THIS IS A ONE-OF-A-KIND ARTIFACT.
20,
OR NO SALE.
ALRIGHT, ALRIGHT, 20.
THANK YOU SIR. YOU'VE MADE AN EXCELLENT DEAL.
I'M LOOKING FORWARD TO RESEARCHING IT.
THANKS.
NO, THANK YOU!
...HEH ...HEH
WHAT A SUCKER.

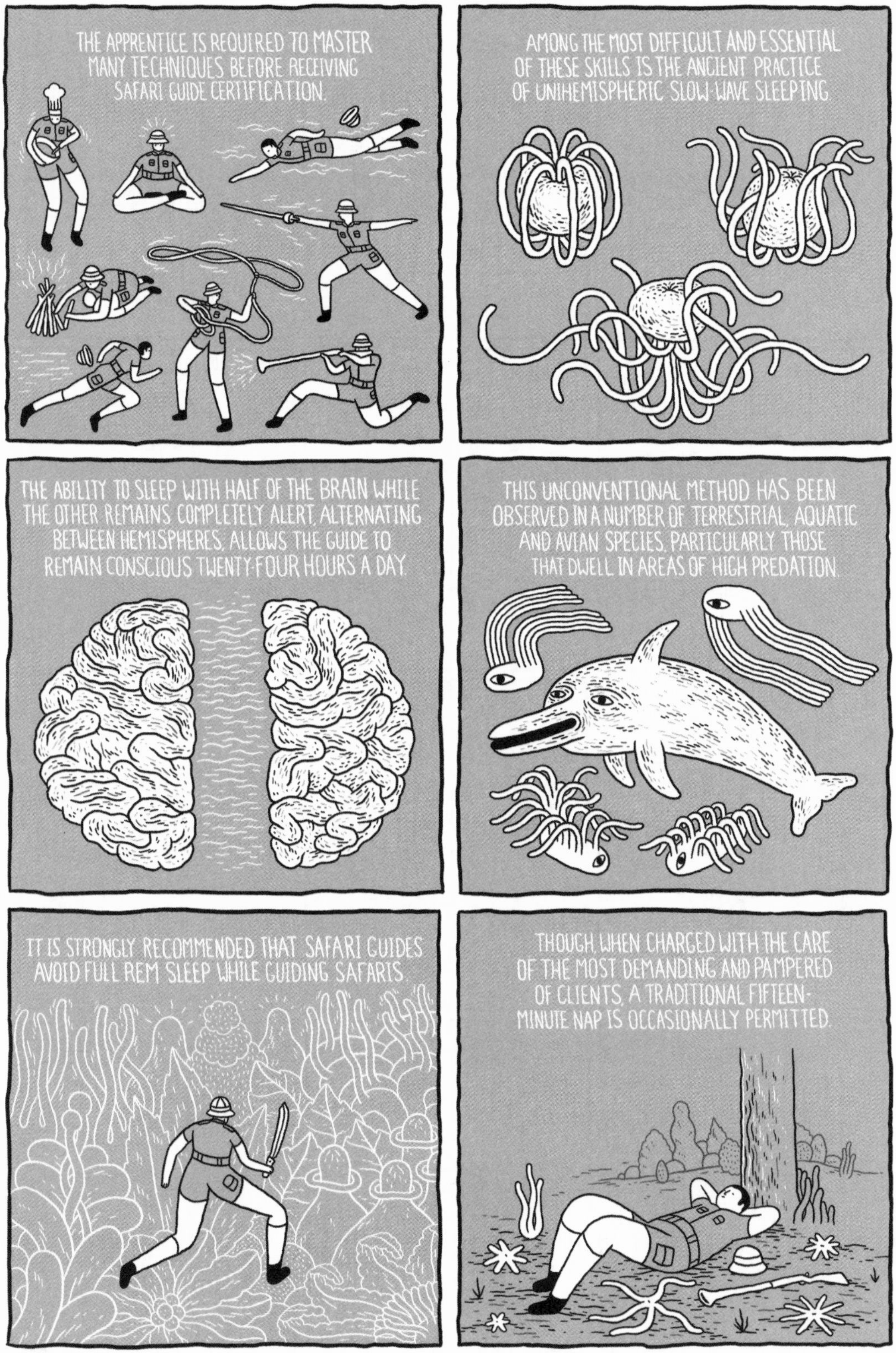
THE APPRENTICE IS REQUIRED TO MASTER MANY TECHNIQUES BEFORE RECEIVING SAFARI GUIDE CERTIFICATION.
AMONG THE MOST DIFFICULT AND ESSENTIAL OF THESE SKILLS IS THE ANCIENT PRACTICE OF UNIHEMISPHERIC SLOW-WAVE SLEEPING.
THE ABILITY TO SLEEP WITH HALF OF THE BRAIN WHILE THE OTHER REMAINS COMPLETELY ALERT, ALTERNATING BETWEEN HEMISPHERES, ALLOWS THE GUIDE TO REMAIN CONSCIOUS TWENTY-FOUR HOURS A DAY.
THIS UNCONVENTIONAL METHOD HAS BEEN OBSERVED IN A NUMBER OF TERRESTRIAL, AQUATIC AND AVIAN SPECIES, PARTICULARLY THOSE THAT DWELL IN AREAS OF HIGH PREDATION.
IT IS STRONGLY RECOMMENDED THAT SAFARI GUIDES AVOID FULL REM SLEEP WHILE GUIDING SAFARIS.
THOUGH, WHEN CHARGED WITH THE CARE OF THE MOST DEMANDING AND PAMPERED OF CLIENTS, A TRADITIONAL FIFTEEN-MINUTE NAP IS OCCASIONALLY PERMITTED.

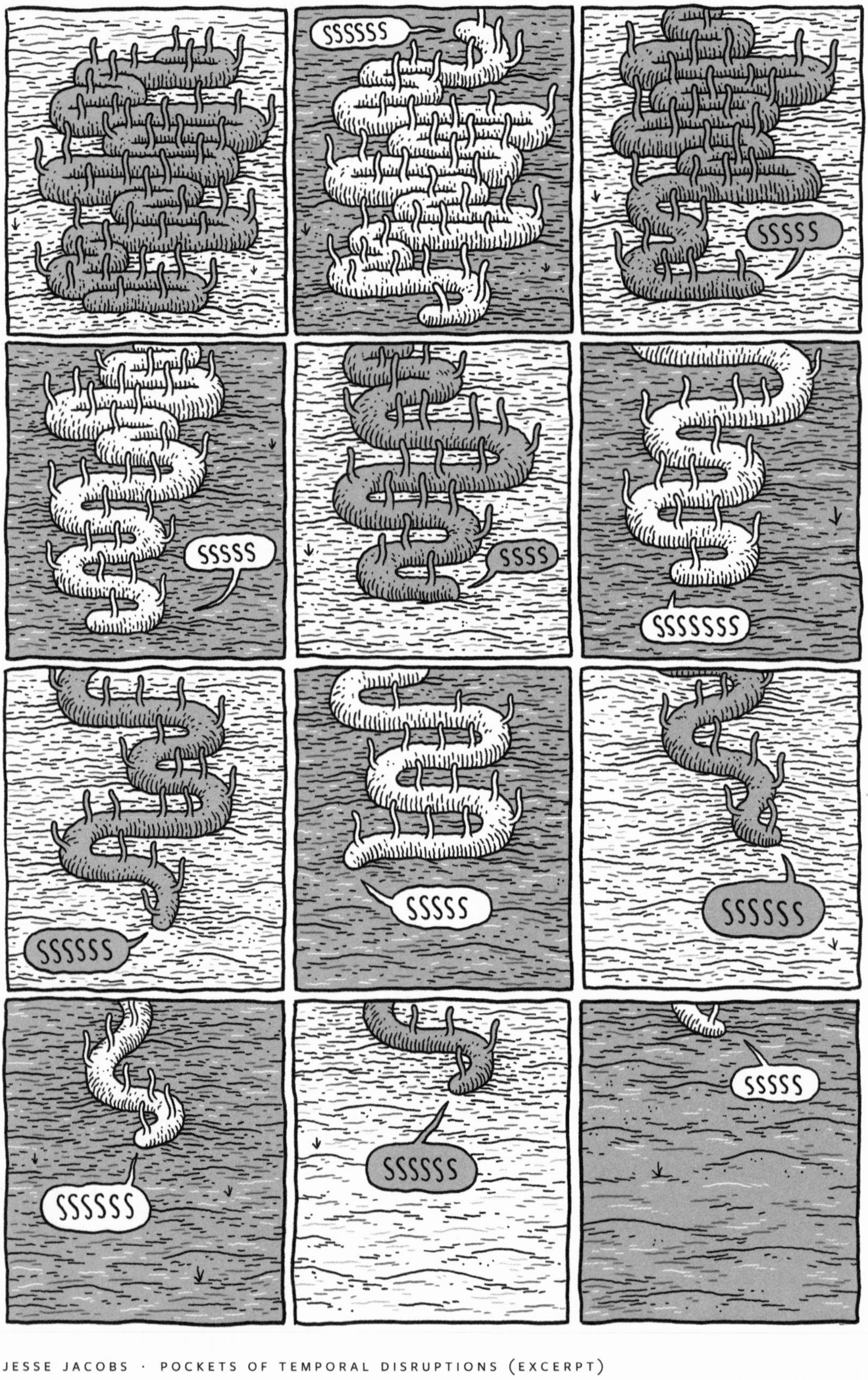
SSSSSS
SSSSS
SSSSS
SSSS
SSSSSSS
SSSSSS
SSSSS
SSSSSS
SSSSSS
SSSSSS
SSSSS

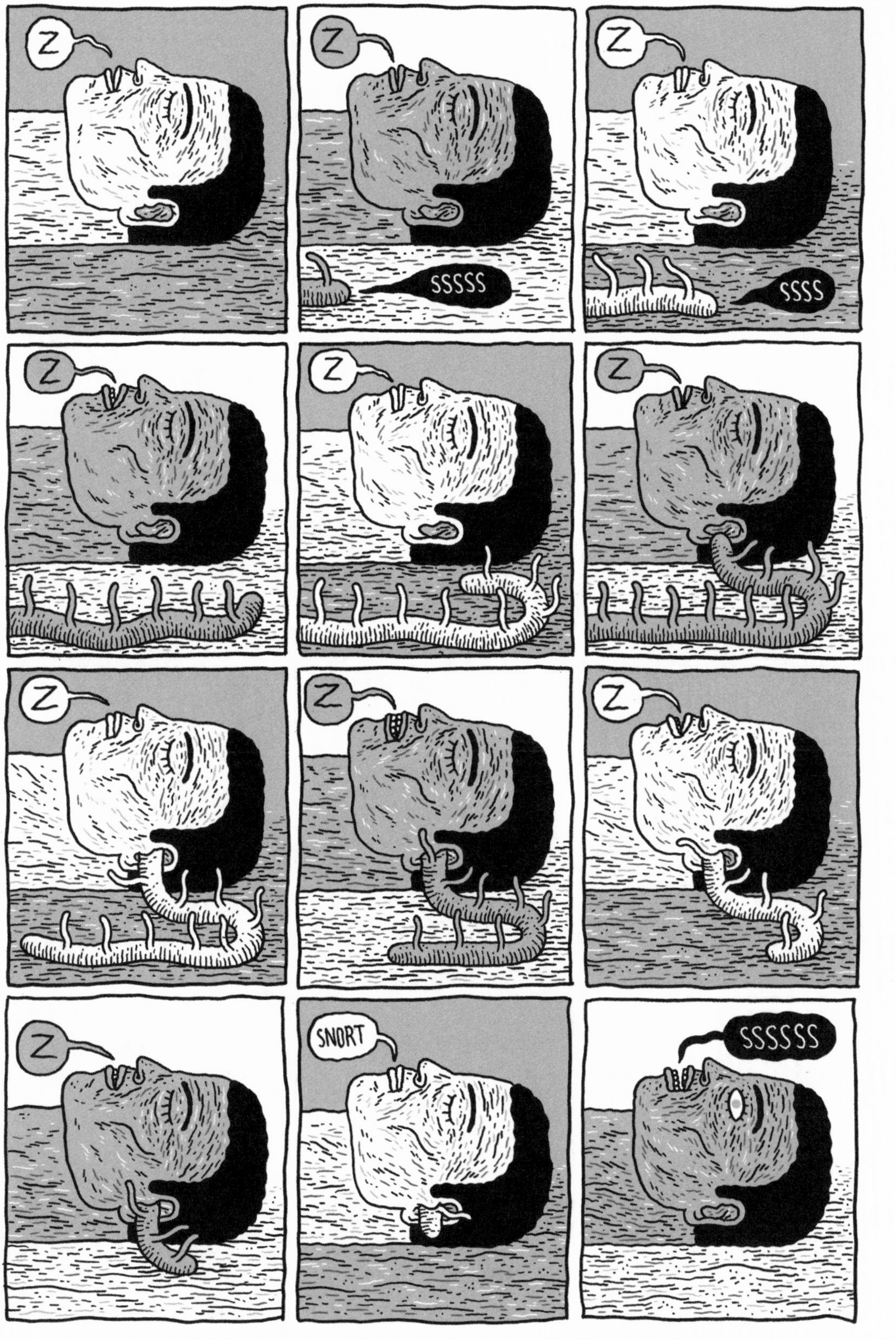
Z
Z
SSSSS
Z
SSSS
Z
Z
Z
Z
Z
Z
Z
SNORT
SSSSSS

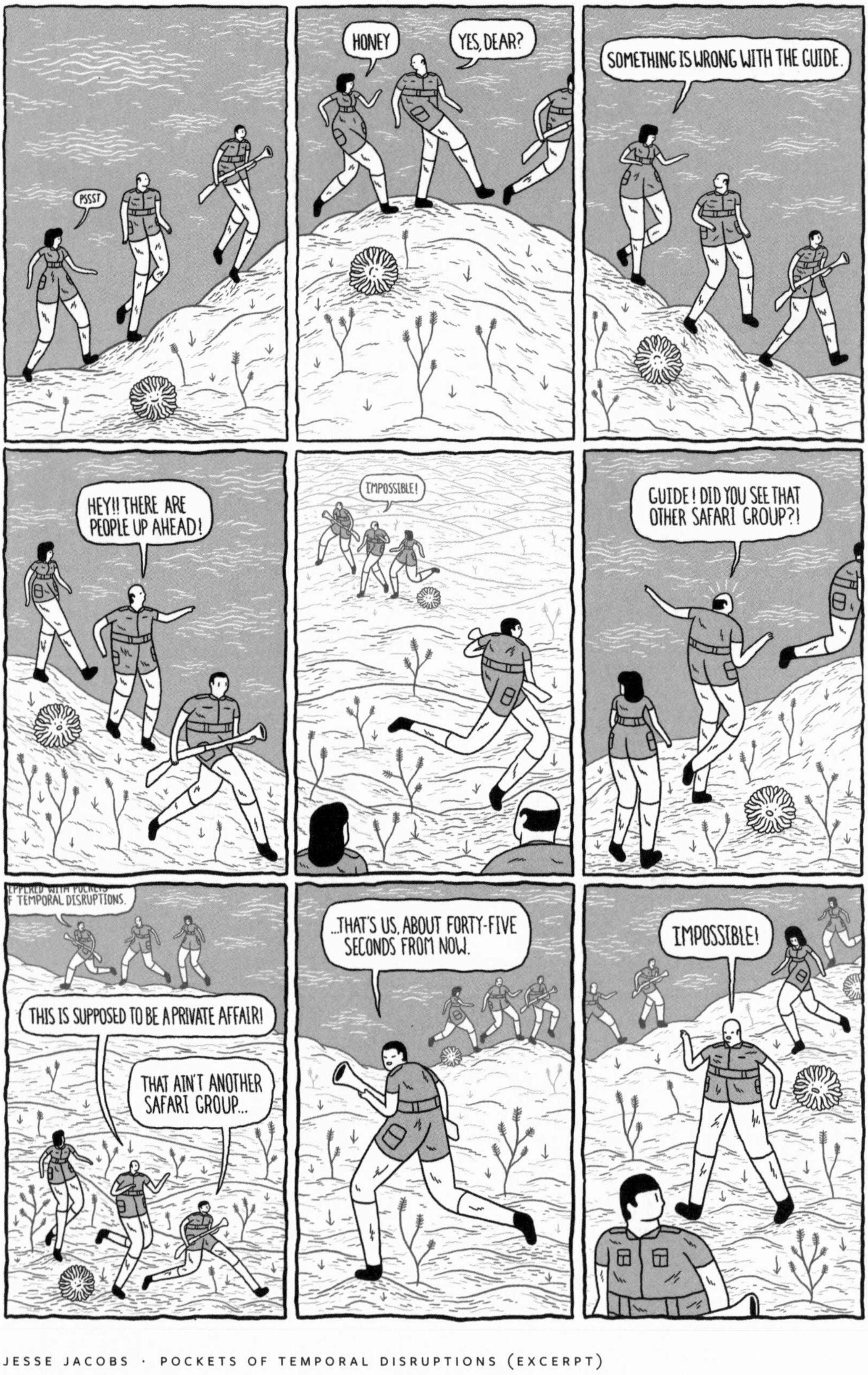
PSSST
HONEY
YES, DEAR?
SOMETHING IS WRONG WITH THE GUIDE.
HEY!! THERE ARE PEOPLE UP AHEAD!
IMPOSSIBLE!
GUIDE! DID YOU SEE THAT OTHER SAFARI GROUP?!
TEMPORAL DISRUPTIONS.
THIS IS SUPPOSED TO BE A PRIVATE AFFAIR!
THAT AIN'T ANOTHER SAFARI GROUP...
...THAT'S US, ABOUT FORTY-FIVE SECONDS FROM NOW.
IMPOSSIBLE!

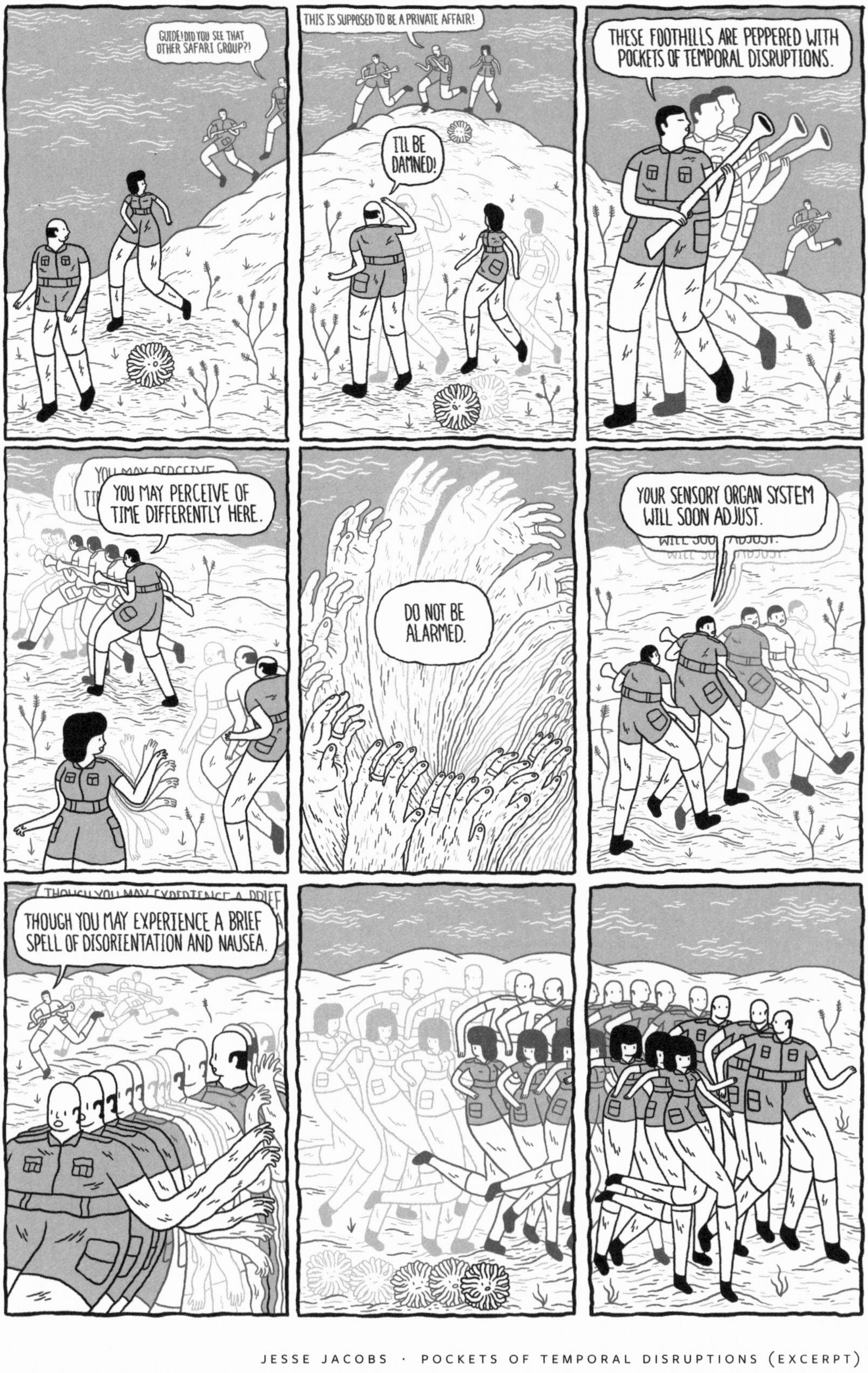

GUIDE! DID YOU SEE THAT OTHER SAFARI GROUP?!
THIS IS SUPPOSED TO BE A PRIVATE AFFAIR!
I'LL BE DAMNED!
THESE FOOTHILLS ARE PEPPERED WITH POCKETS OF TEMPORAL DISRUPTIONS.
YOU MAY PERCEIVE OF TIME DIFFERENTLY HERE.
DO NOT BE ALARMED.
YOUR SENSORY ORGAN SYSTEM WILL SOON ADJUST.
THOUGH YOU MAY EXPERIENCE A BRIEF SPELL OF DISORIENTATION AND NAUSEA.

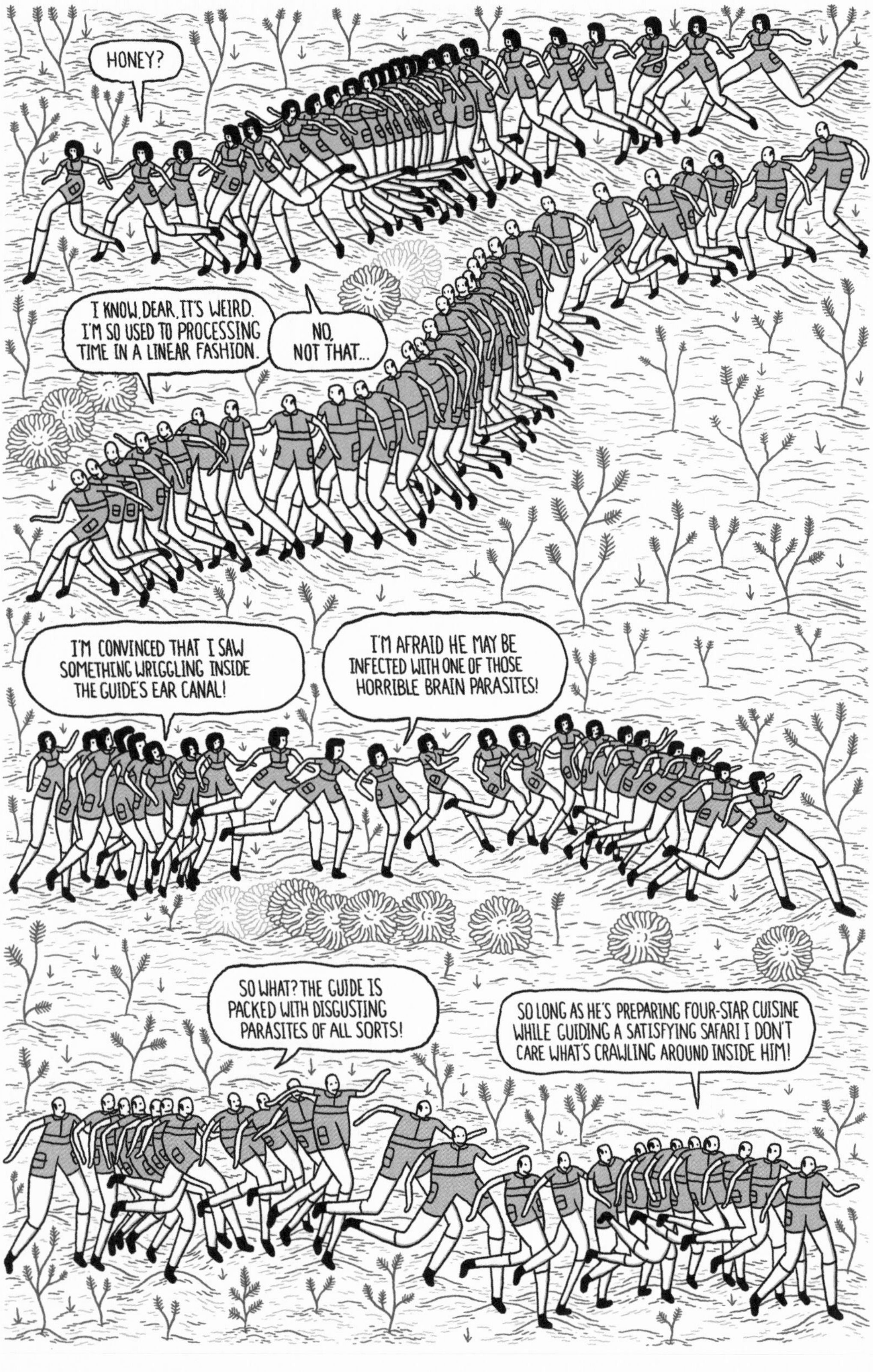
HONEY?
I KNOW, DEAR, IT'S WEIRD. I'M SO USED TO PROCESSING TIME IN A LINEAR FASHION.
NO, NOT THAT...
I'M CONVINCED THAT I SAW SOMETHING WRIGGLING INSIDE THE GUIDE'S EAR CANAL!
I'M AFRAID HE MAY BE INFECTED WITH ONE OF THOSE HORRIBLE BRAIN PARASITES!
SO WHAT? THE GUIDE IS PACKED WITH DISGUSTING PARASITES OF ALL SORTS!
SO LONG AS HE'S PREPARING FOUR-STAR CUISINE WHILE GUIDING A SATISFYING SAFARI I DON'T CARE WHAT'S CRAWLING AROUND INSIDE HIM!

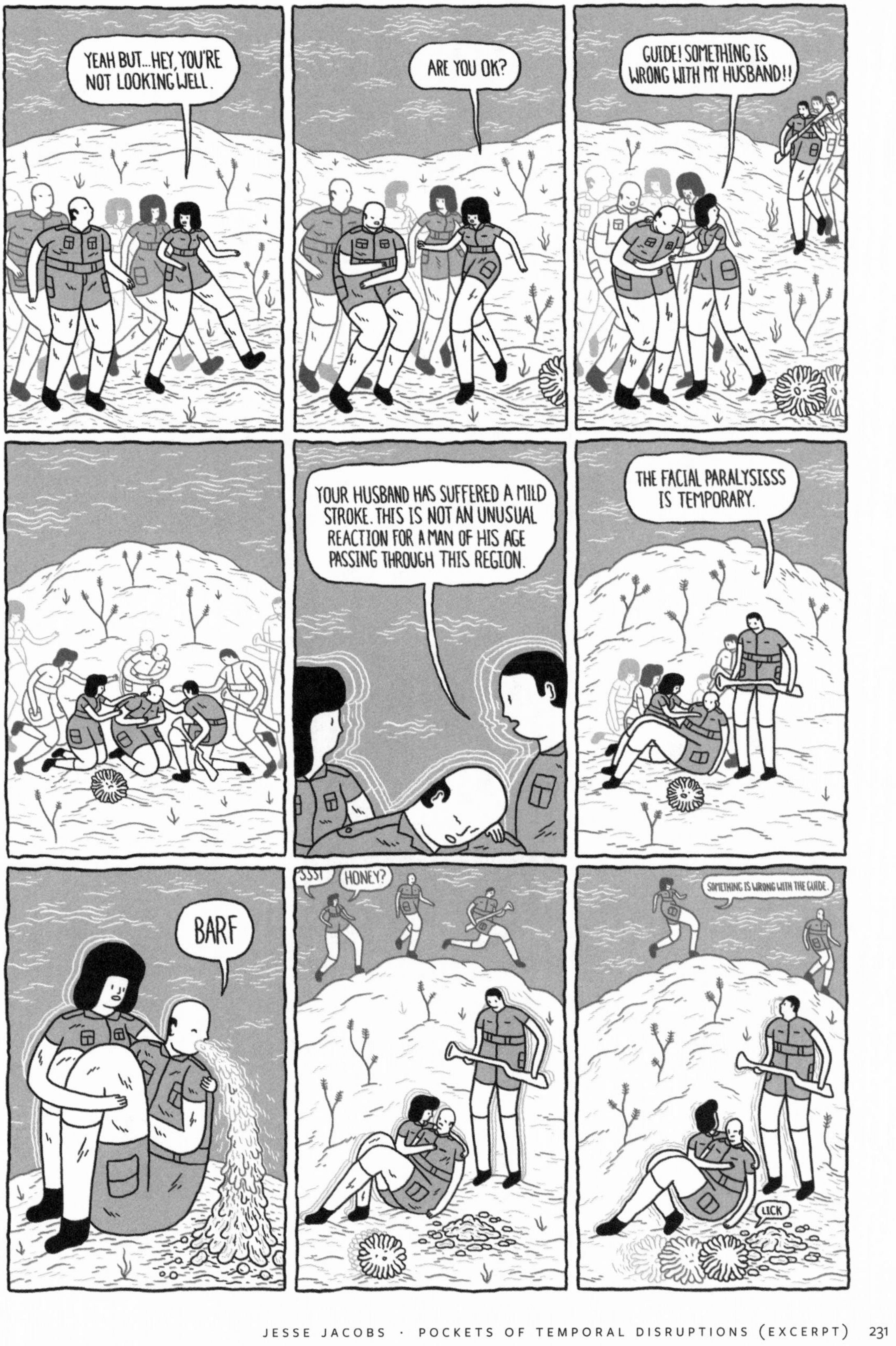
YEAH BUT... HEY, YOU'RE NOT LOOKING WELL.
ARE YOU OK?
GUIDE! SOMETHING IS WRONG WITH MY HUSBAND!!
YOUR HUSBAND HAS SUFFERED A MILD STROKE. THIS IS NOT AN UNUSUAL REACTION FOR A MAN OF HIS AGE PASSING THROUGH THIS REGION.
THE FACIAL PARALYSISSS IS TEMPORARY.
BARF
SSST
HONEY?
SOMETHING IS WRONG WITH THE GUIDE.
LICK

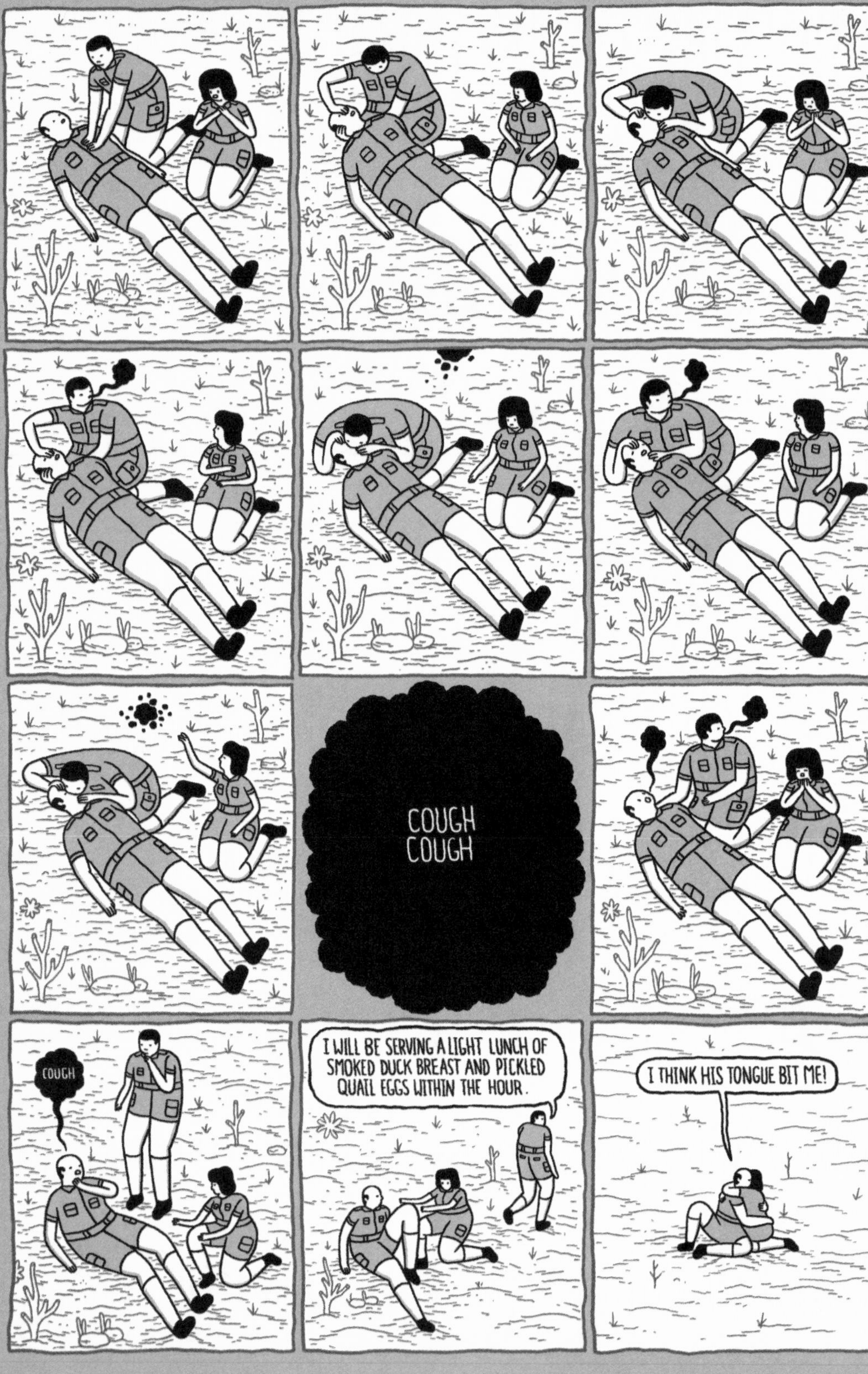
COUGH
COUGH
COUGH
I WILL BE SERVING A LIGHT LUNCH OF SMOKED DUCK BREAST AND PICKLED QUAIL EGGS WITHIN THE HOUR.
I THINK HIS TONGUE BIT ME!

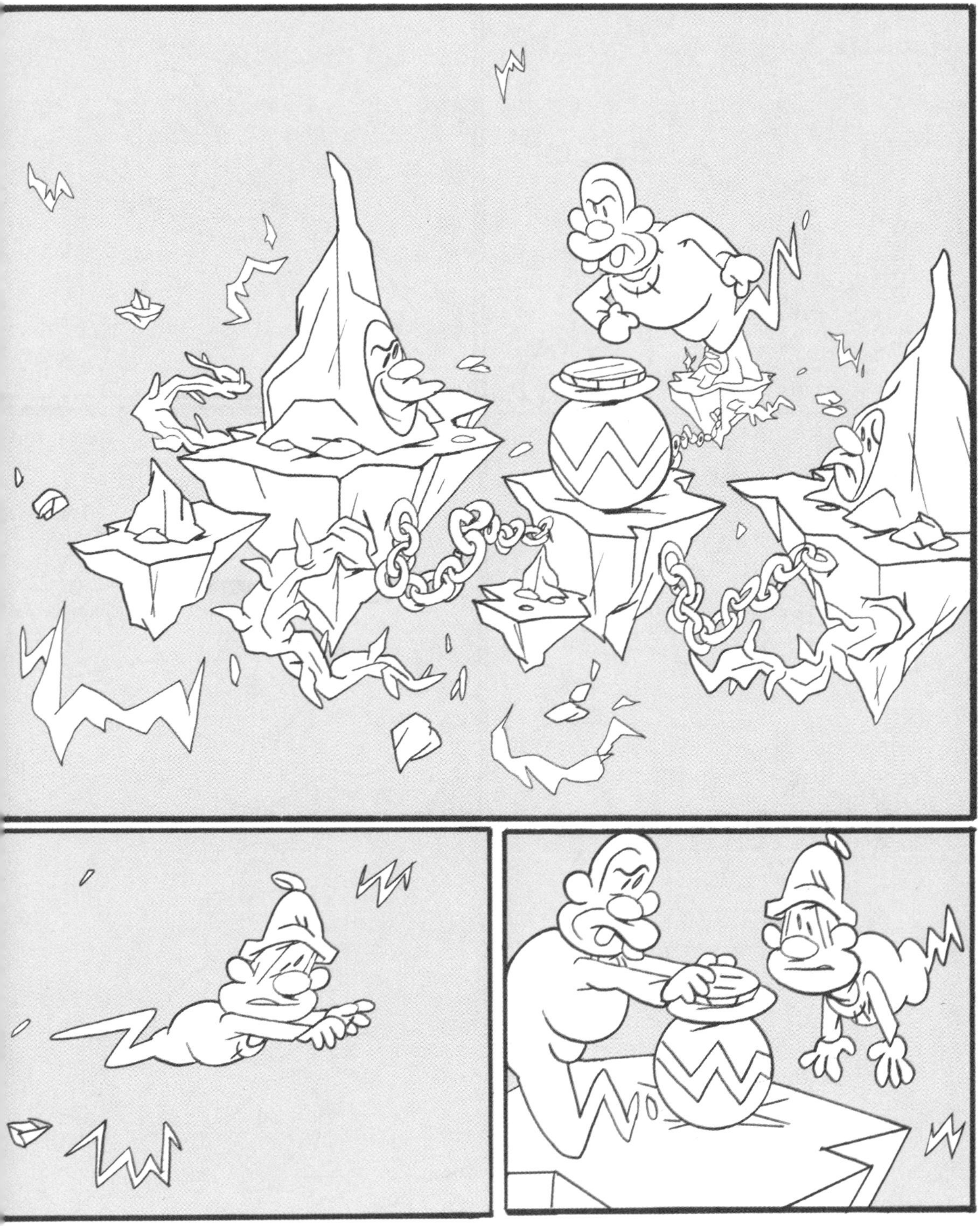

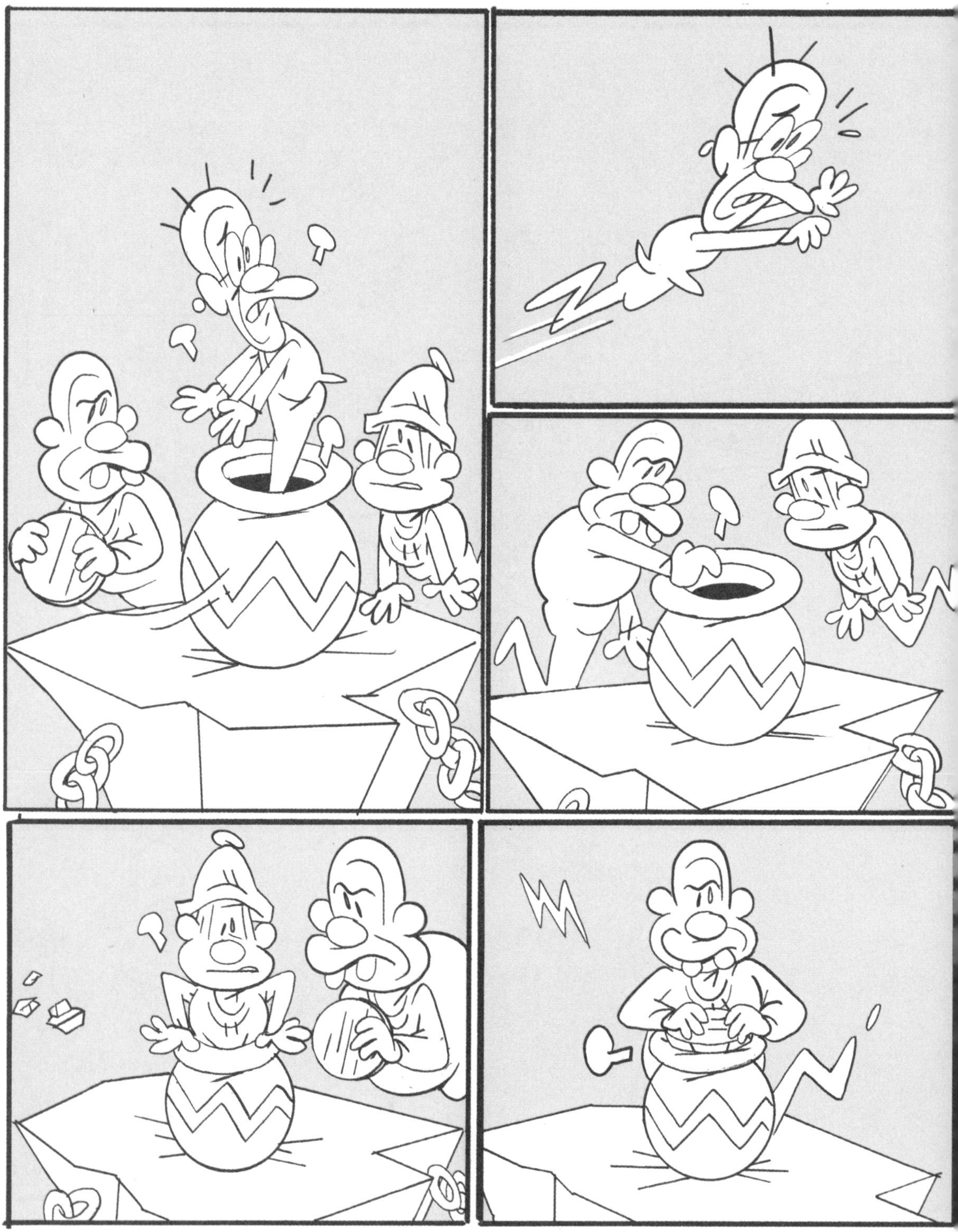

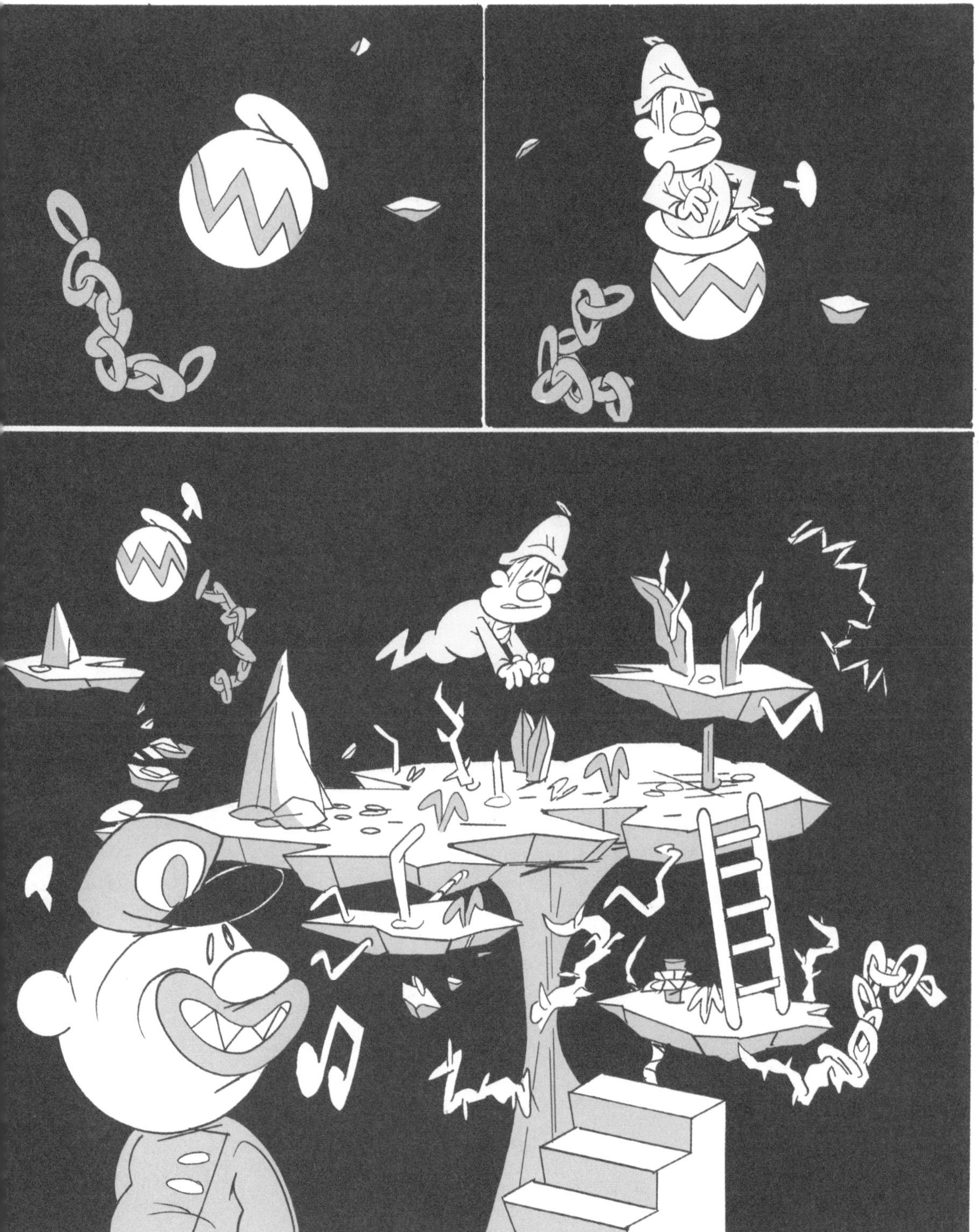

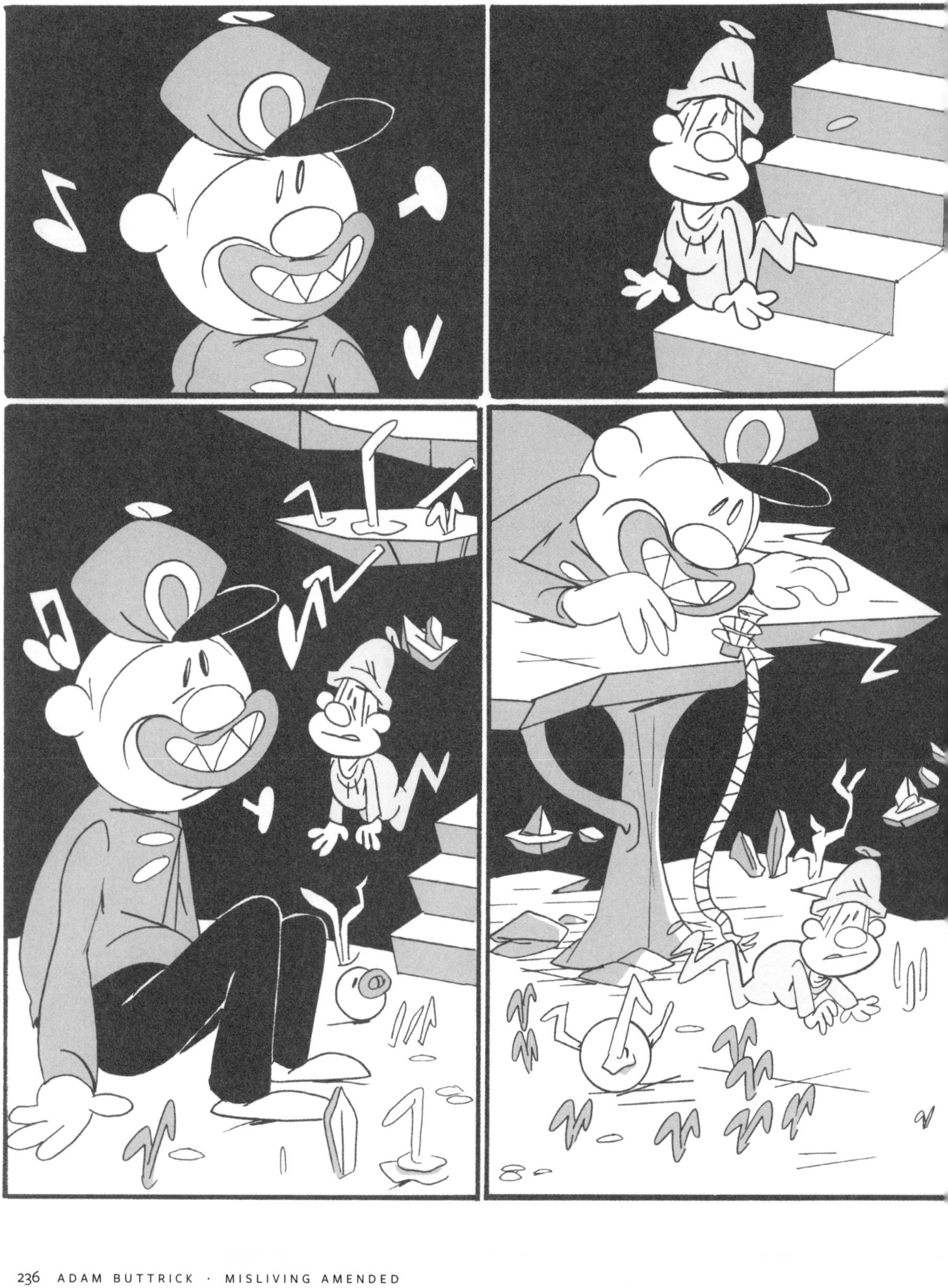

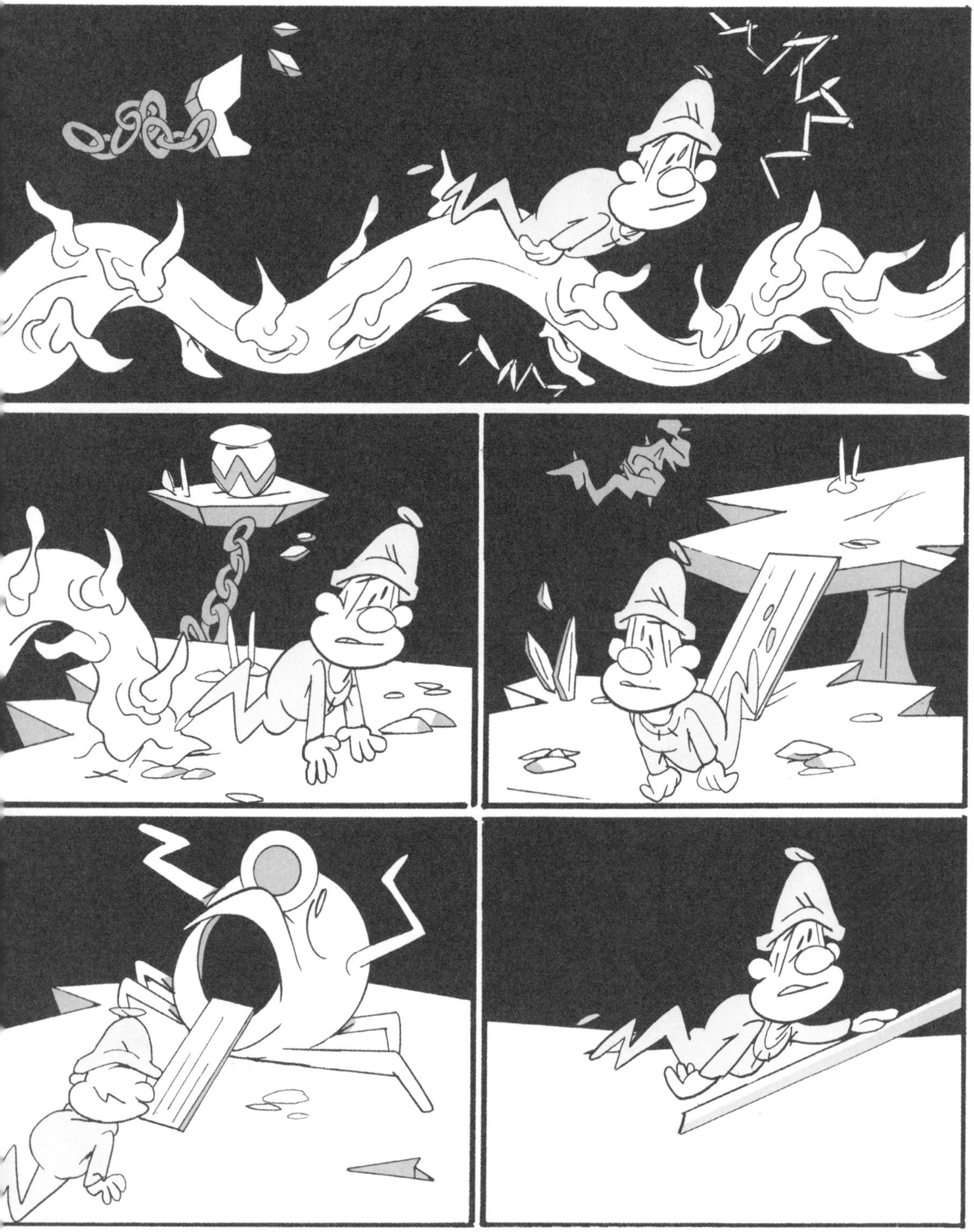

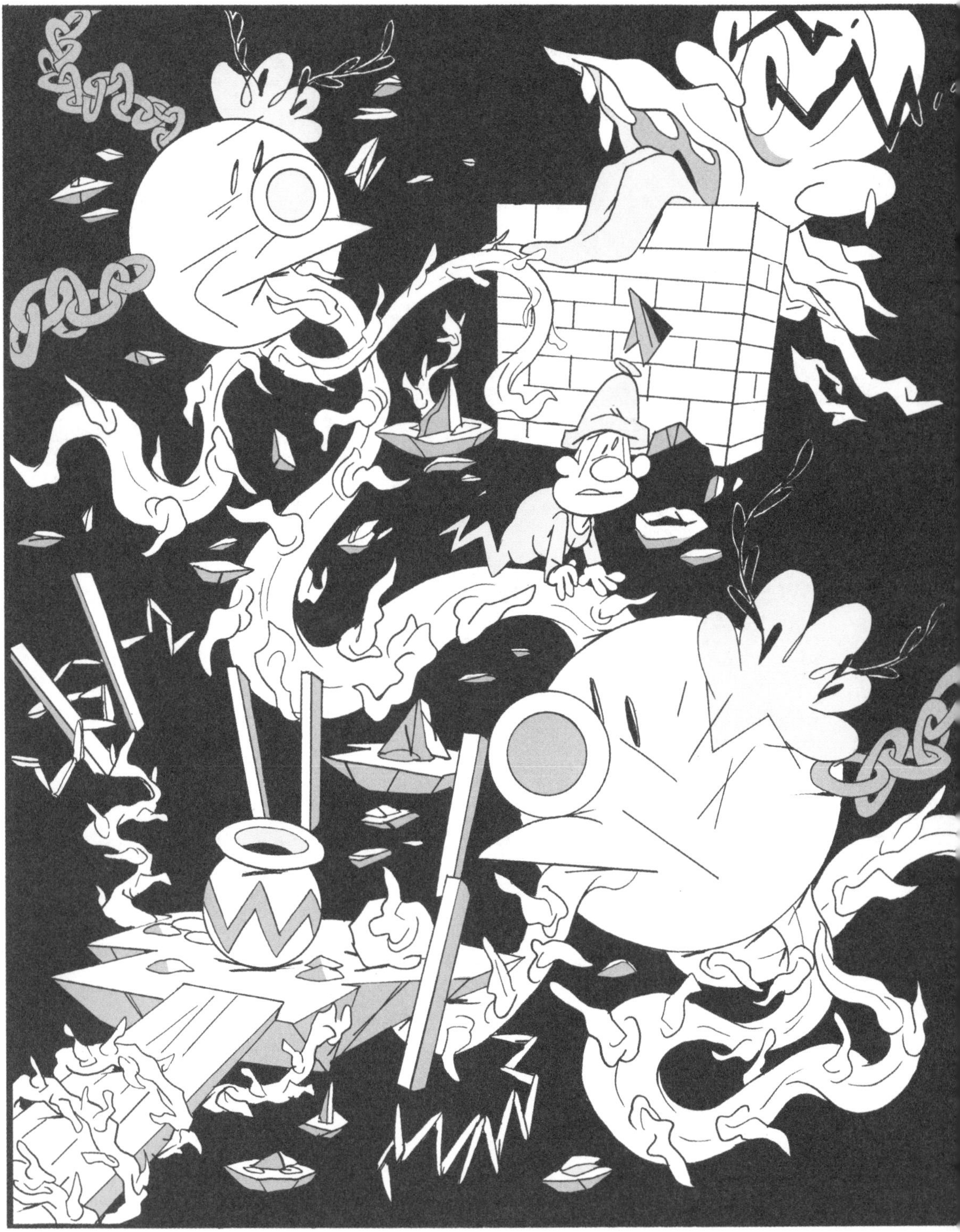

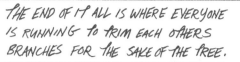

THE END OF IT ALL IS WHERE EVERYONE IS RUNNING TO TRIM EACH OTHERS BRANCHES FOR THE SAKE OF THE TREE.

IT IS AS EASY TO KISS AS IT IS TO LIE OR WHISPER. GIVE A MOUTH A STORY TO STOP ITS BODY'S FEET

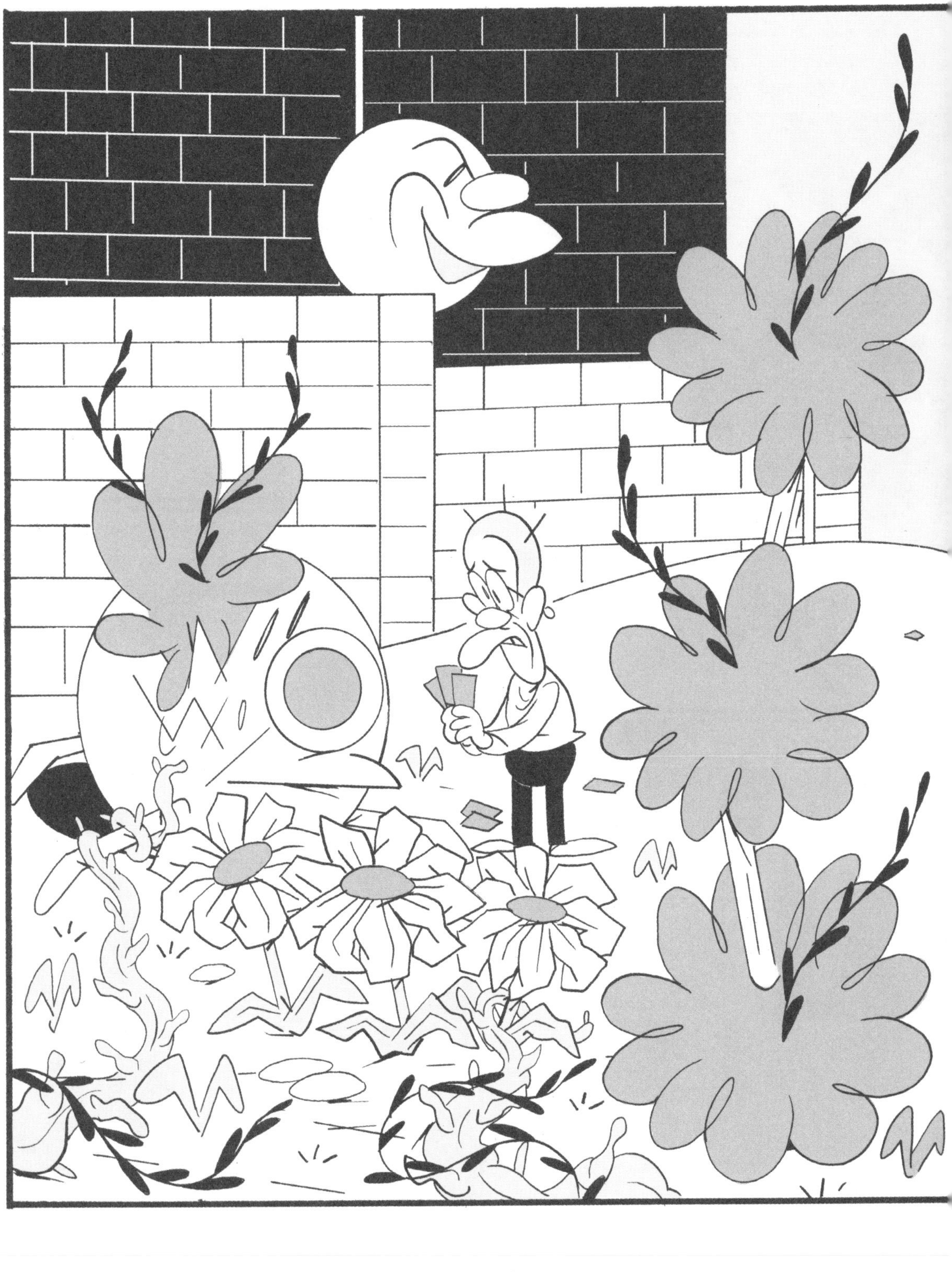

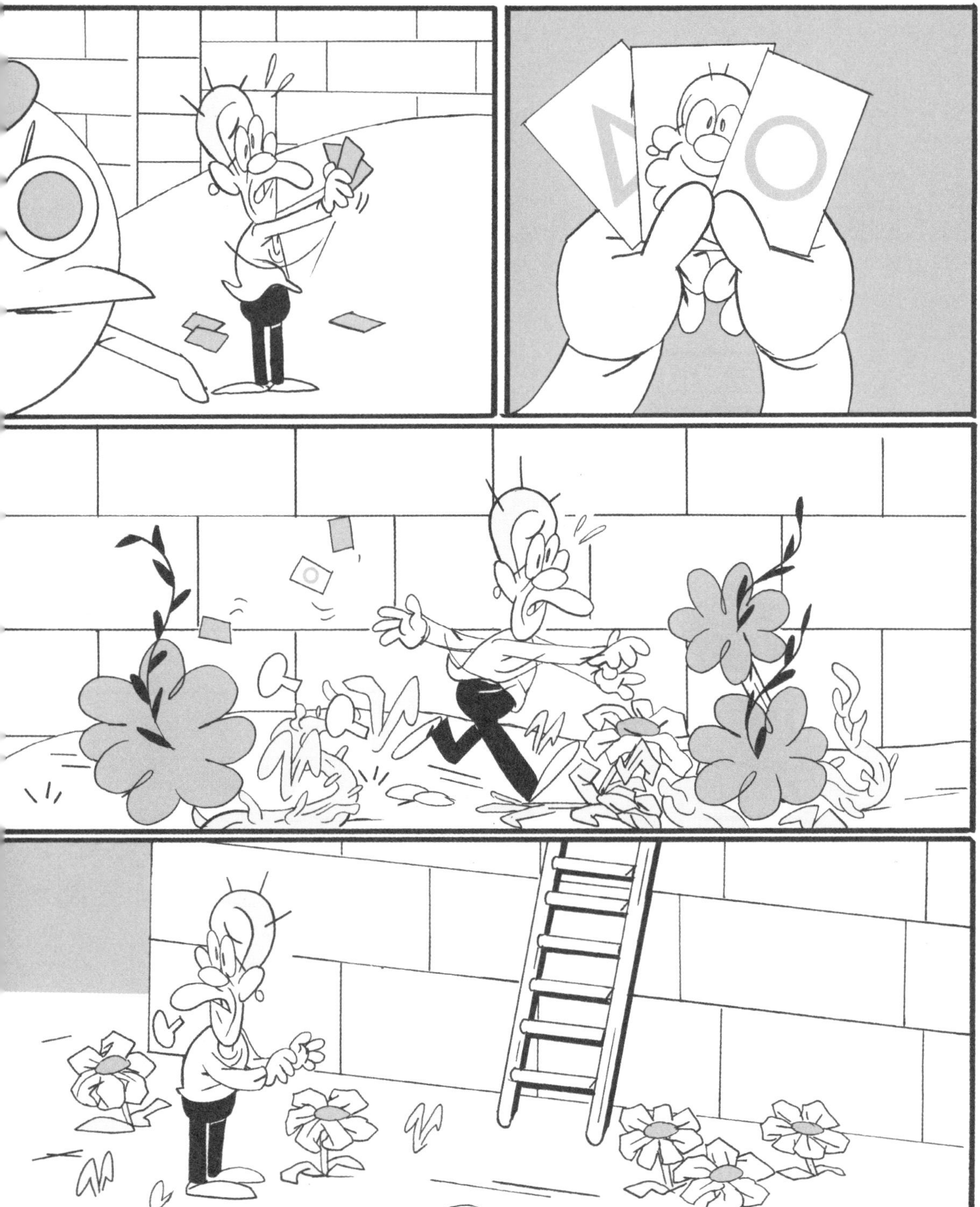

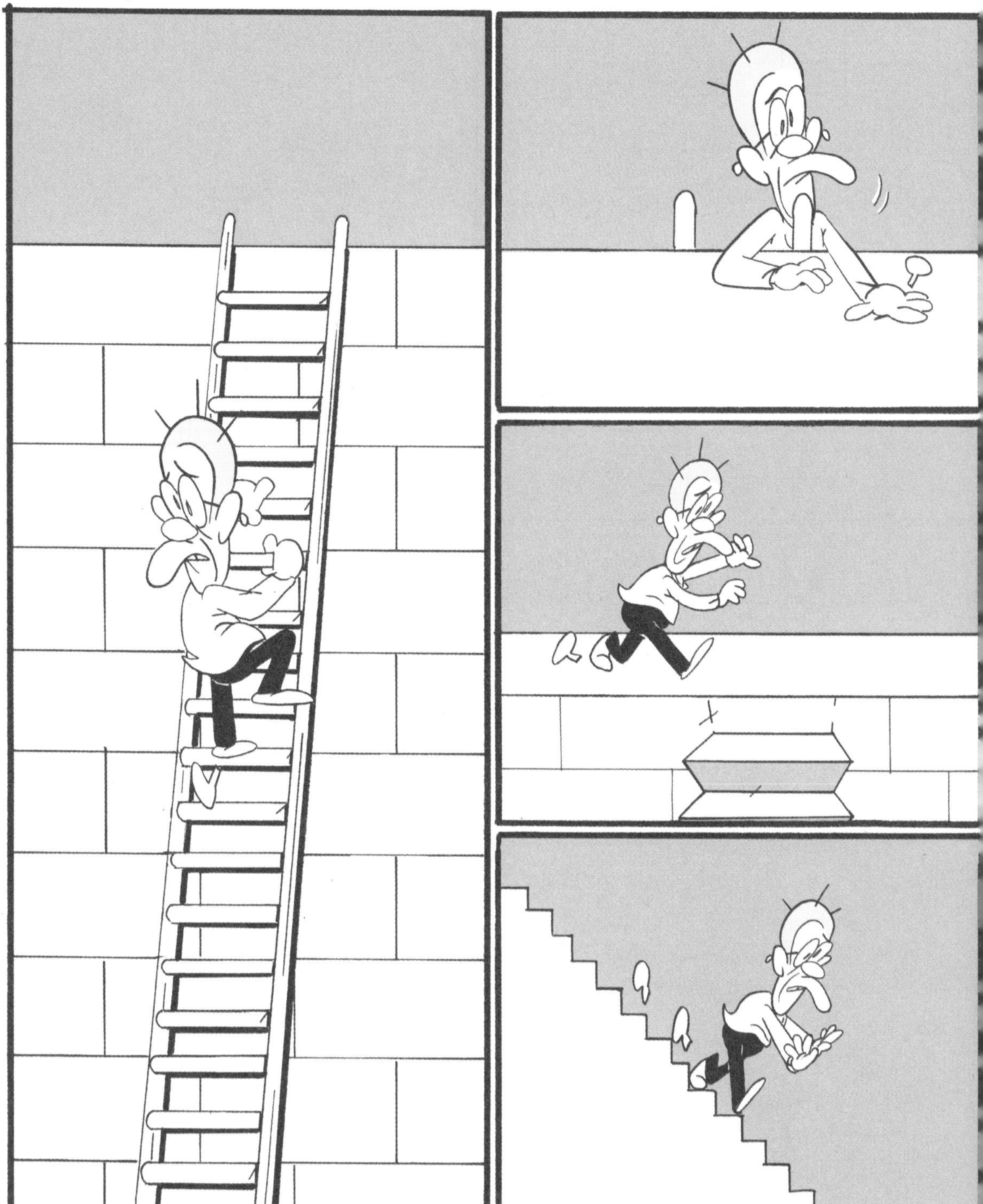

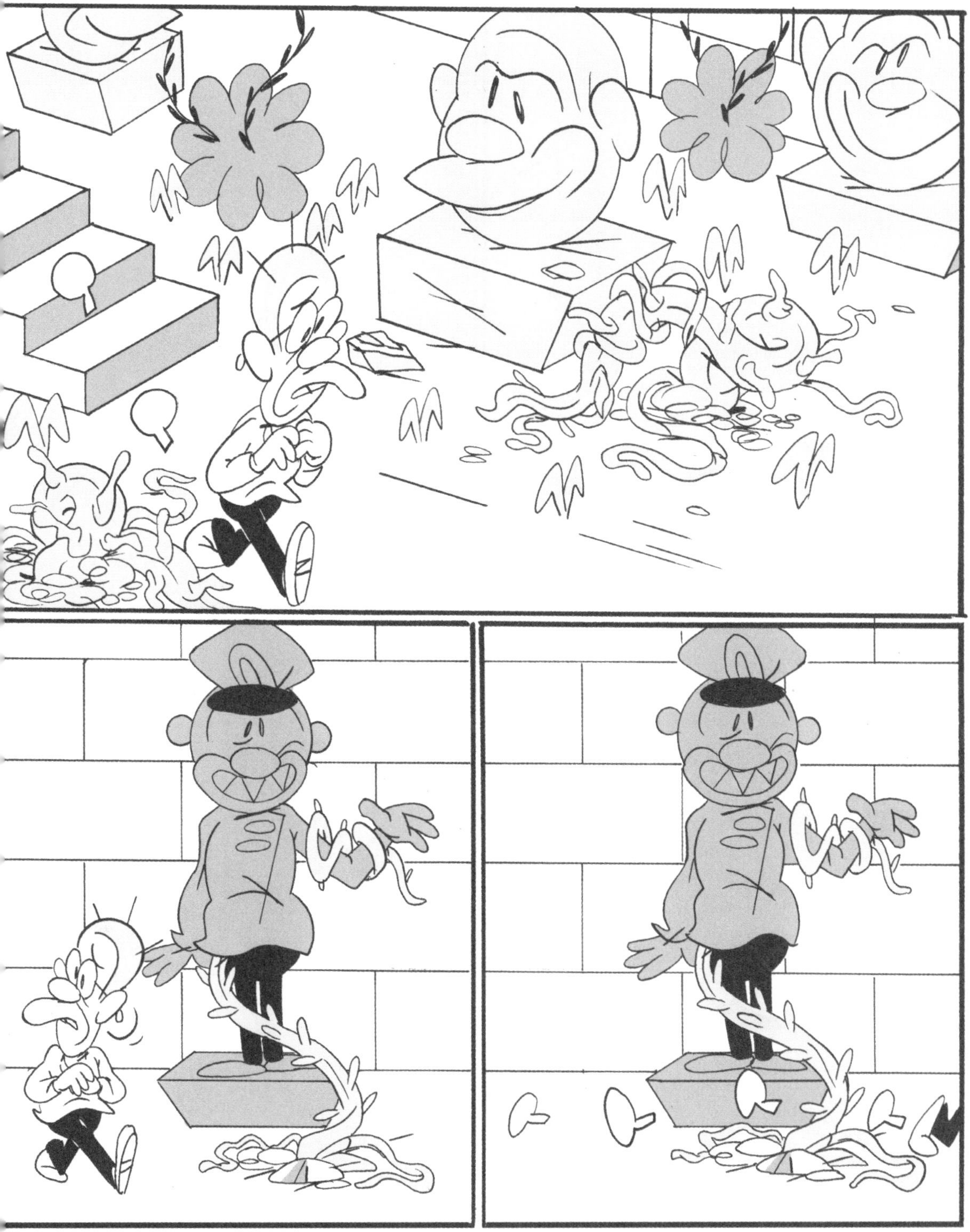

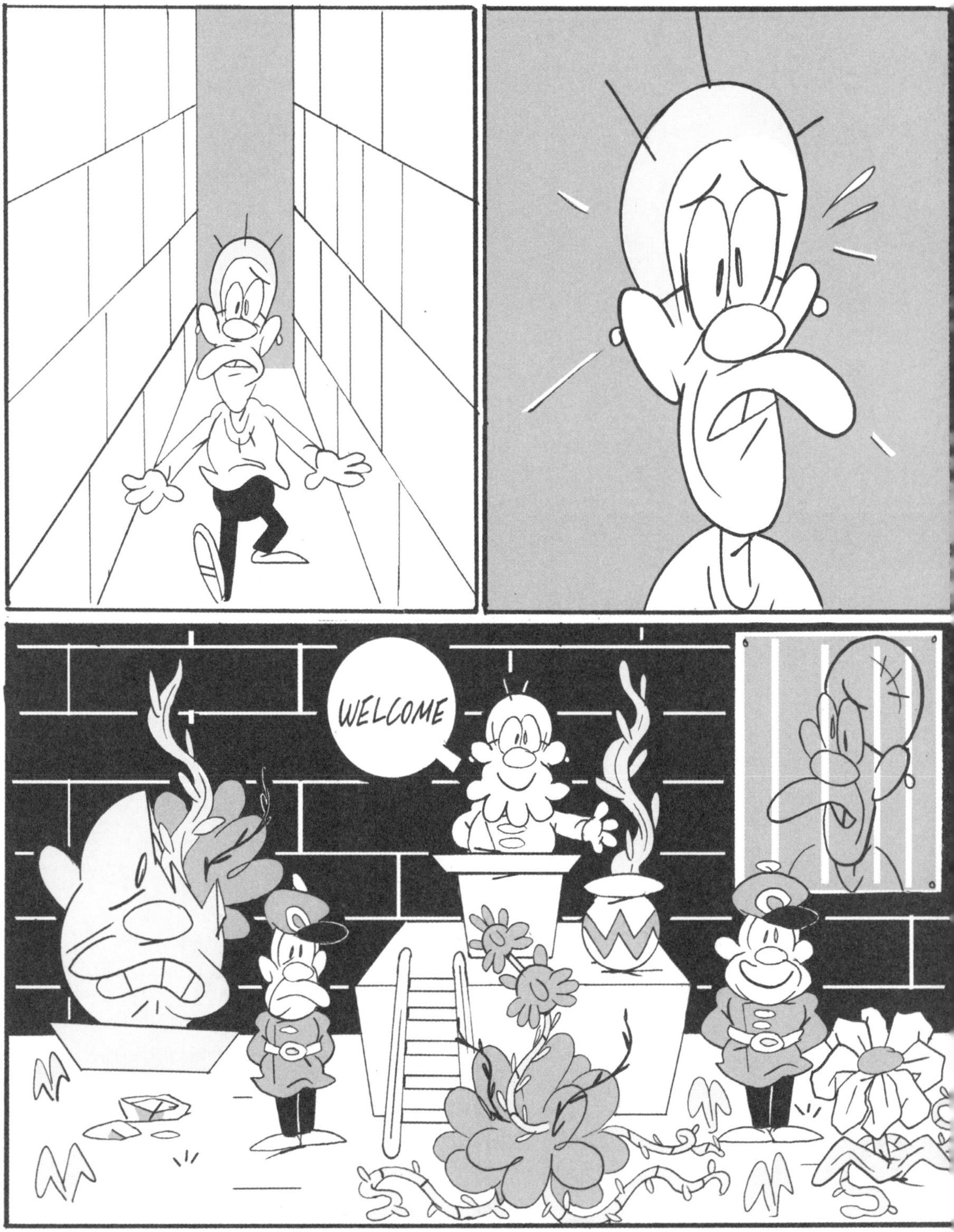
WELCOME

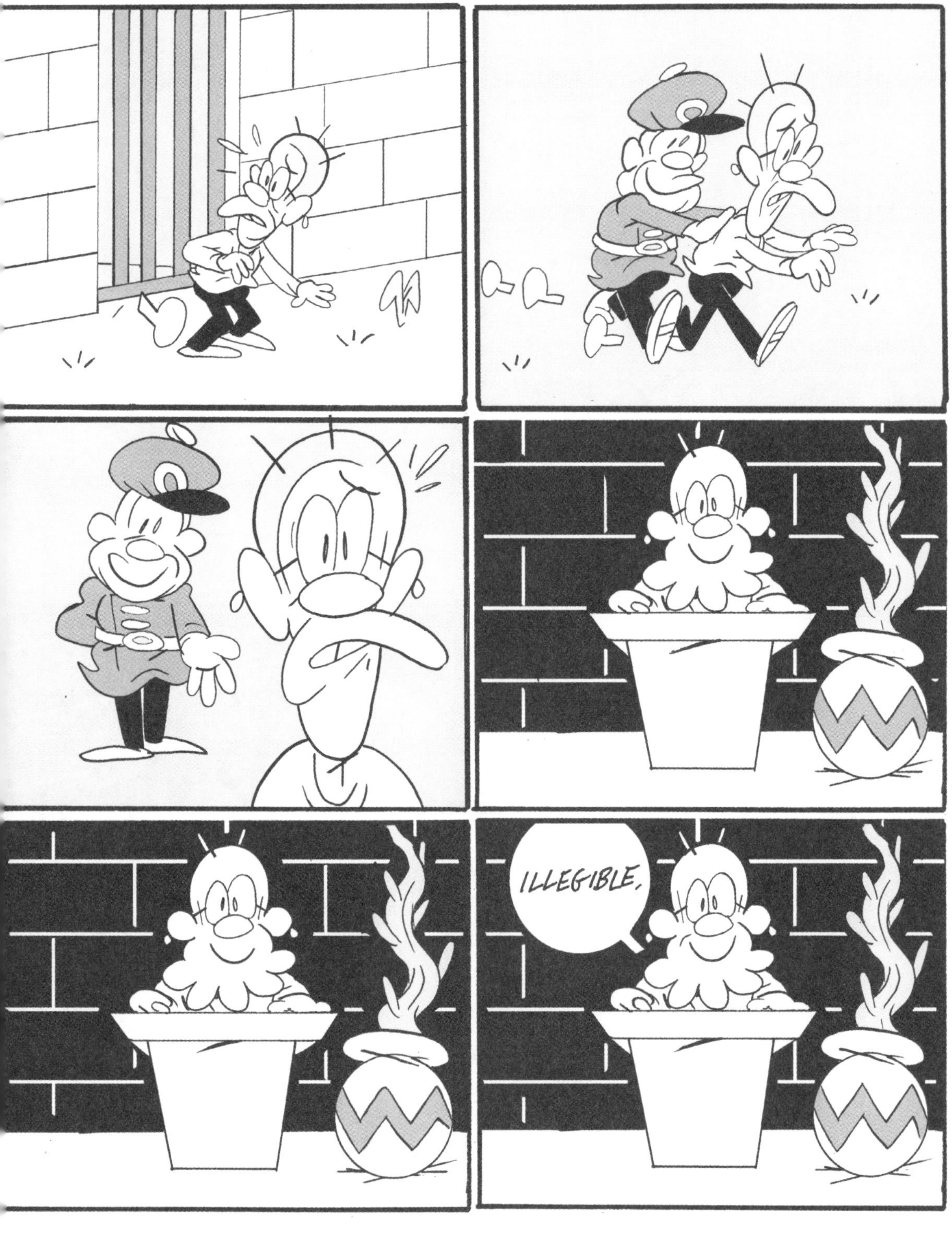
ILLEGIBLE.

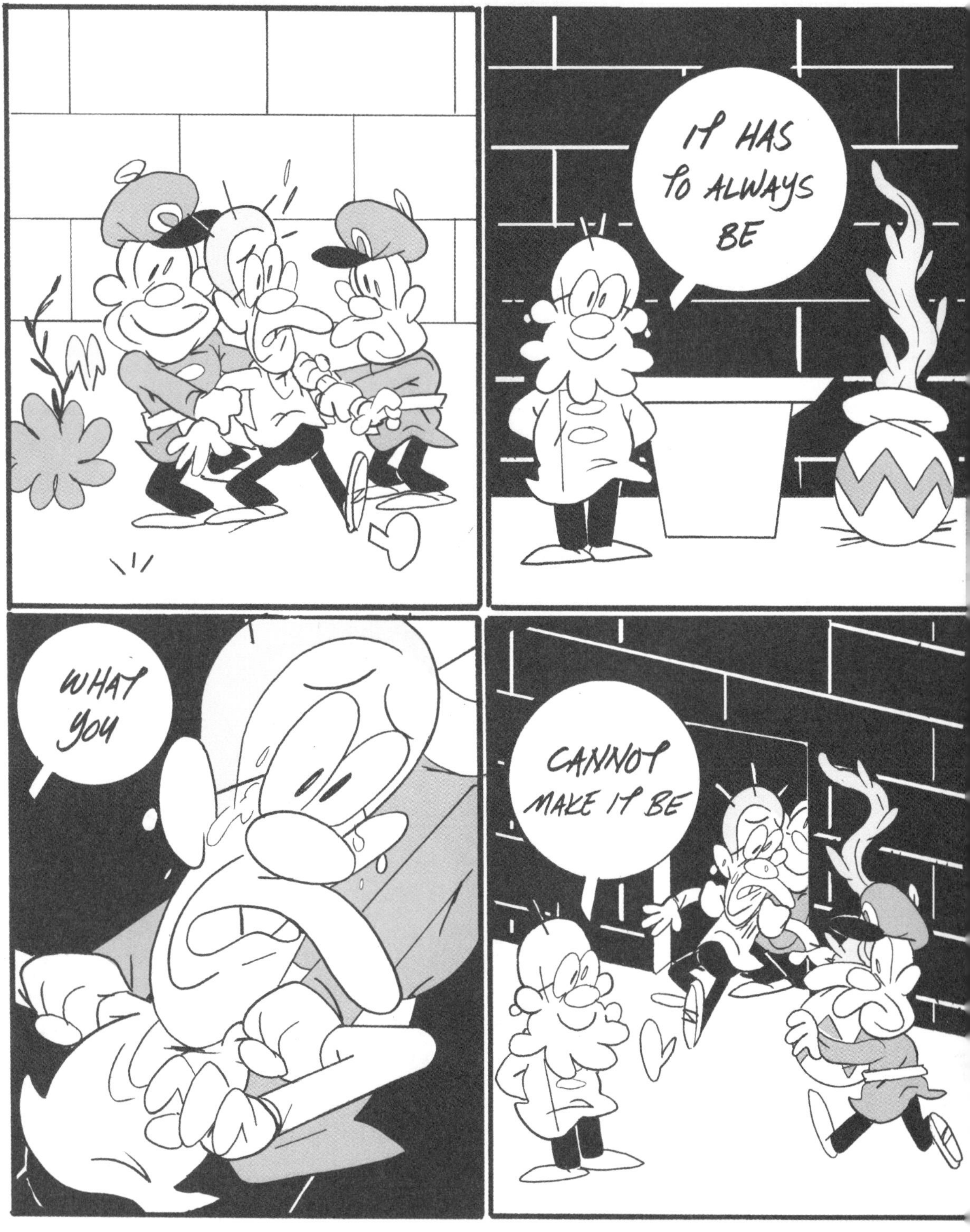
IT HAS TO ALWAYS BE
WHAT YOU
CANNOT MAKE IT BE

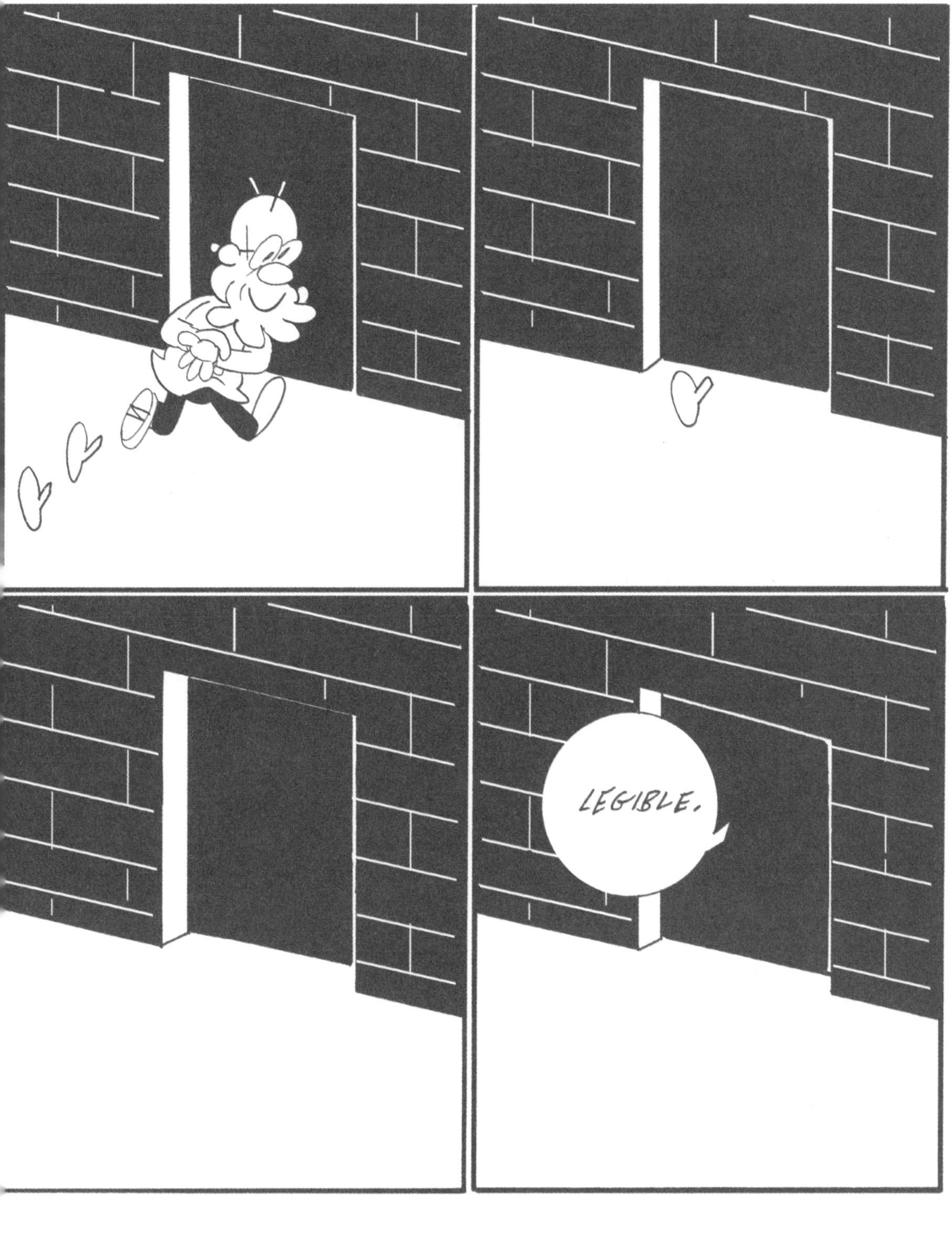
LEGIBLE.

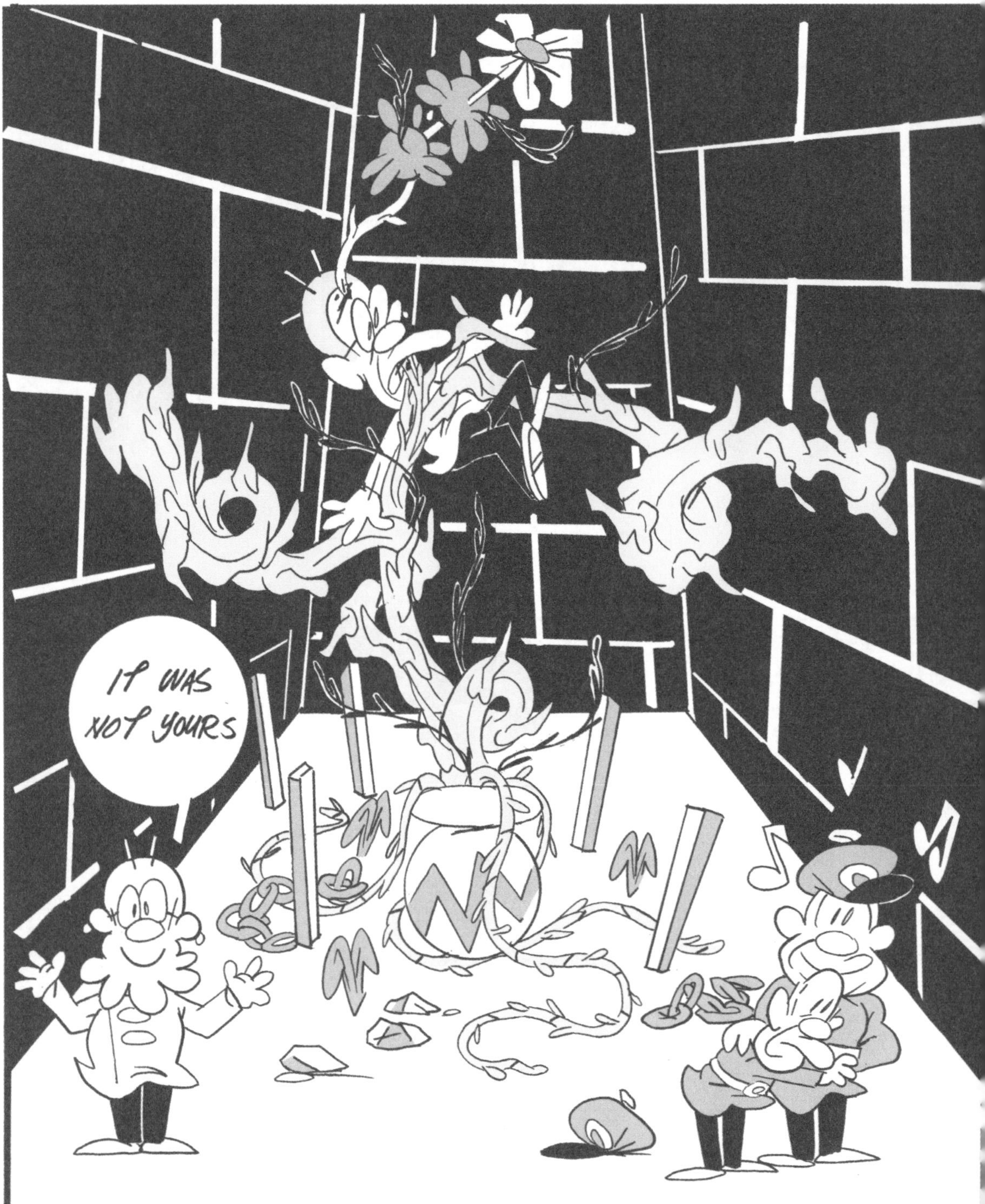
IT WAS NOT YOURS

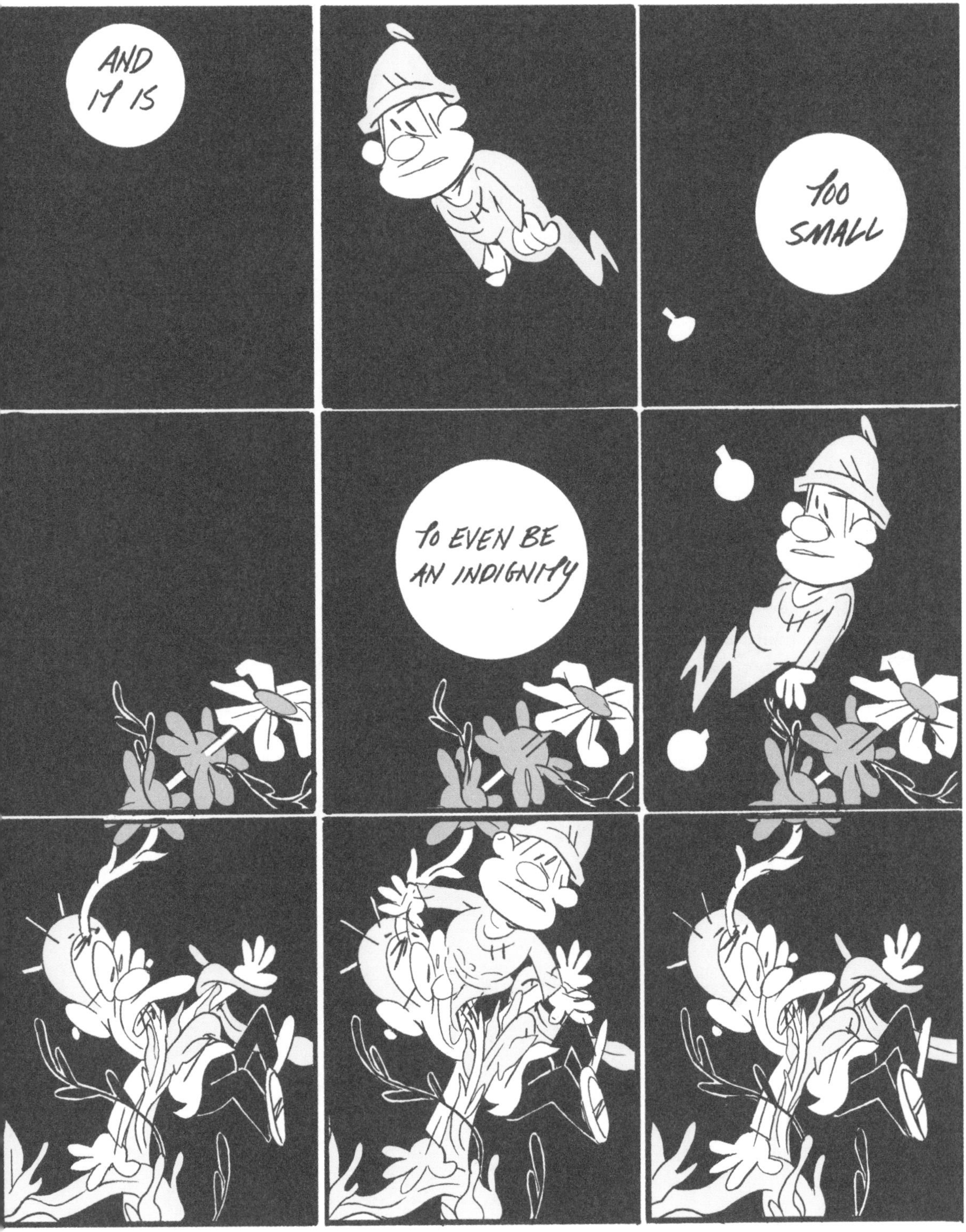
AND IT IS
TOO SMALL
TO EVEN BE AN INDIGNITY

CHAPTER EIGHT
Raging Her-Moans

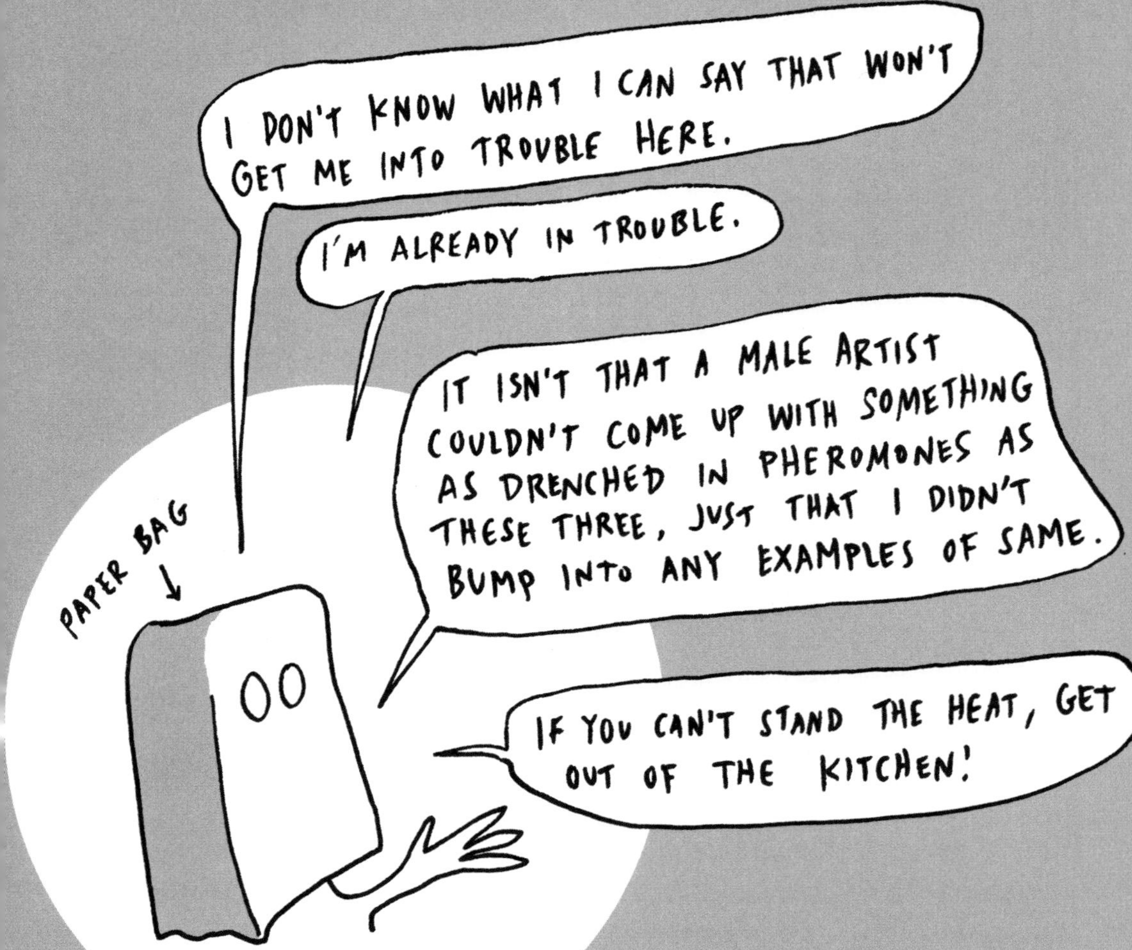
I DON'T KNOW WHAT I CAN SAY THAT WON'T GET ME INTO TROUBLE HERE.
I'M ALREADY IN TROUBLE.
IT ISN'T THAT A MALE ARTIST COULDN'T COME UP WITH SOMETHING AS DRENCHED IN PHEROMONES AS THESE THREE, JUST THAT I DIDN'T BUMP INTO ANY EXAMPLES OF SAME.
PAPER BAG
IF YOU CAN'T STAND THE HEAT, GET OUT OF THE KITCHEN!

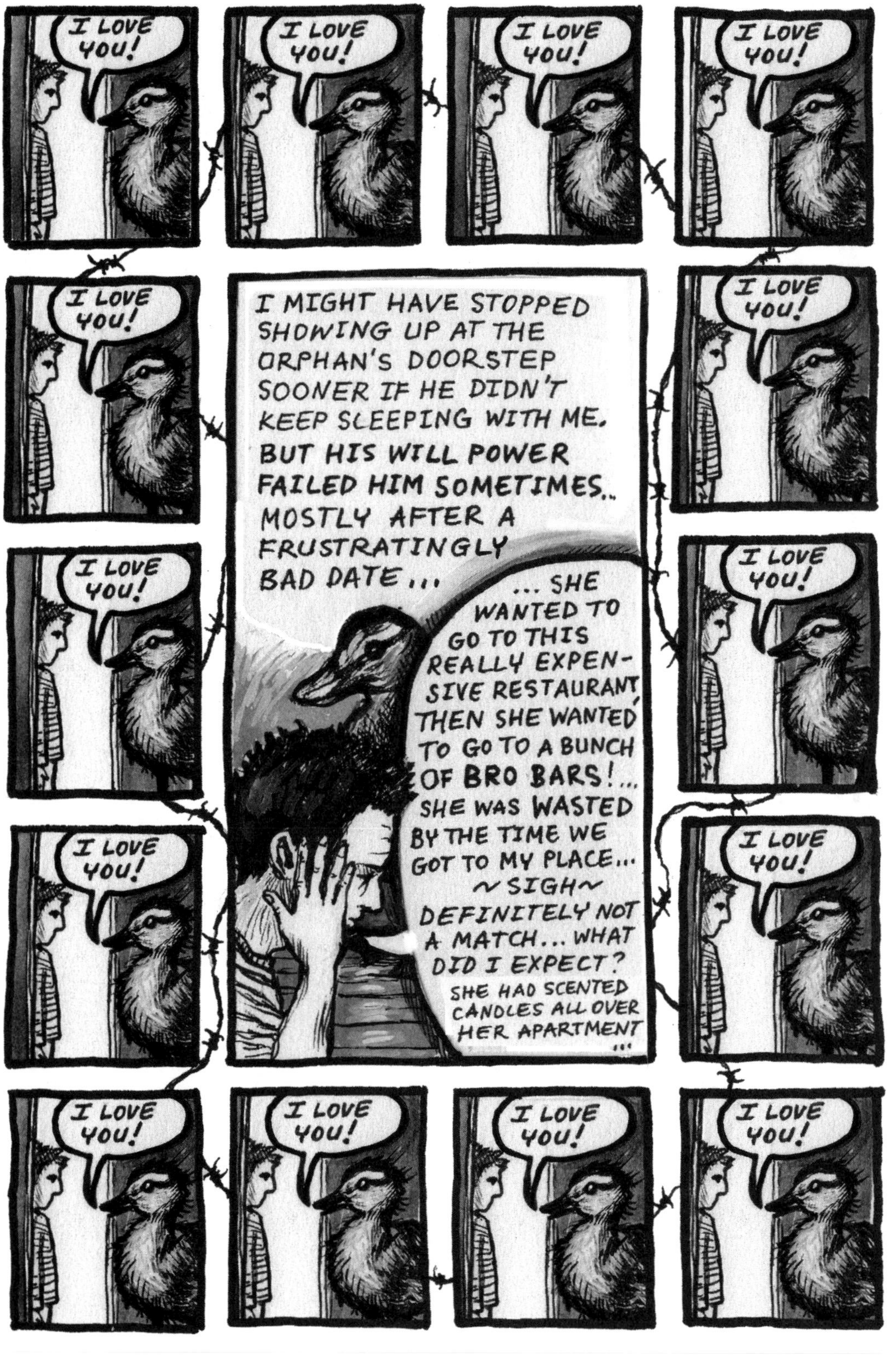
I LOVE YOU!
I LOVE YOU!
I LOVE YOU!
I LOVE YOU!
I LOVE YOU!
I MIGHT HAVE STOPPED SHOWING UP AT THE ORPHAN'S DOORSTEP SOONER IF HE DIDN'T KEEP SLEEPING WITH ME. BUT HIS WILL POWER FAILED HIM SOMETIMES... MOSTLY AFTER A FRUSTRATINGLY BAD DATE...
... SHE WANTED TO GO TO THIS REALLY EXPENSIVE RESTAURANT, THEN SHE WANTED TO GO TO A BUNCH OF BRO BARS!... SHE WAS WASTED BY THE TIME WE GOT TO MY PLACE... ~SIGH~ DEFINITELY NOT A MATCH... WHAT DID I EXPECT? SHE HAD SCENTED CANDLES ALL OVER HER APARTMENT ...
I LOVE YOU!
I LOVE YOU!
I LOVE YOU!
I LOVE YOU!
I LOVE YOU!
I LOVE YOU!
I LOVE YOU!
I LOVE YOU!
I LOVE YOU!

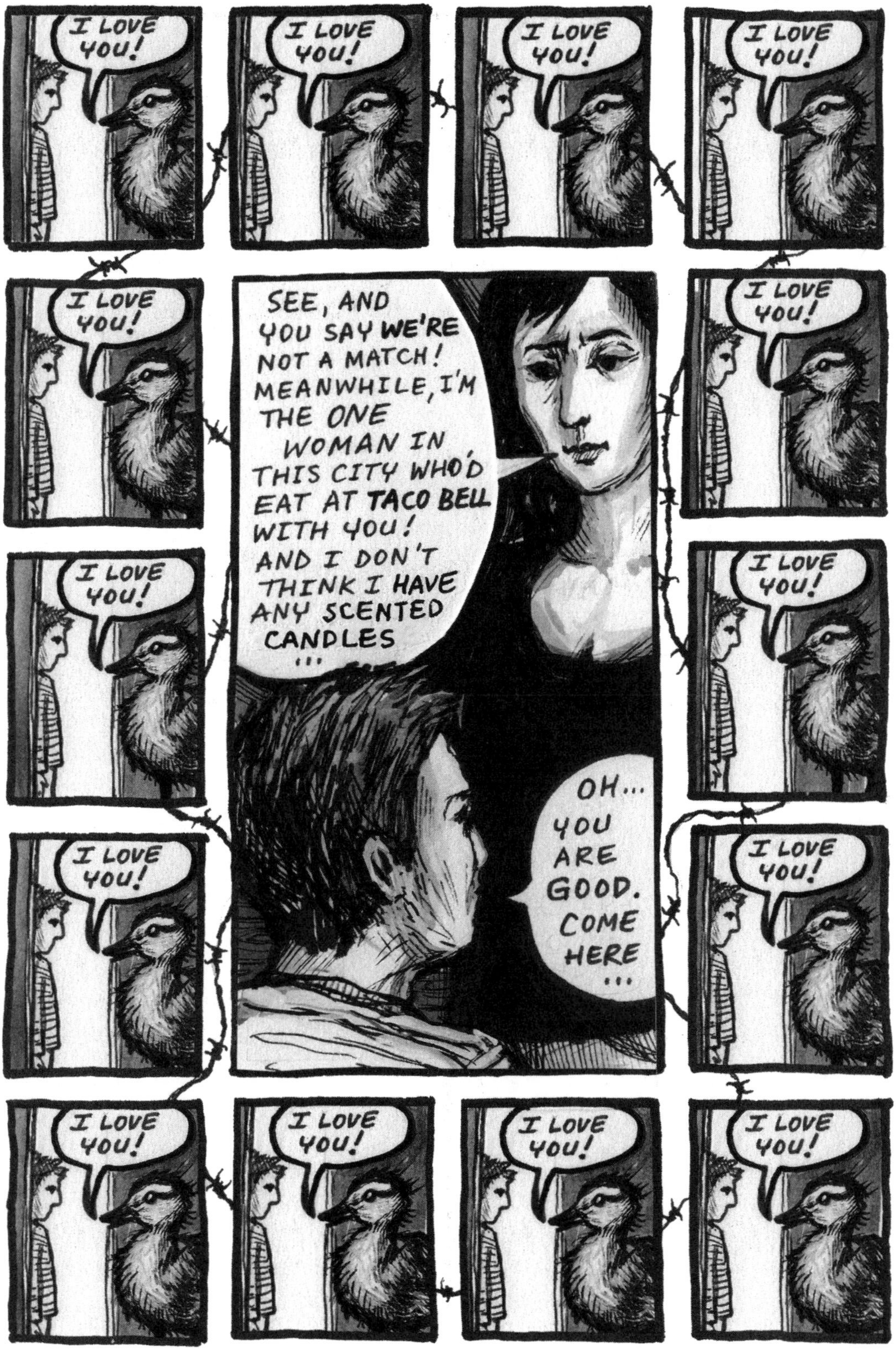
I LOVE YOU!
I LOVE YOU!
I LOVE YOU!
I LOVE YOU!
I LOVE YOU!
SEE, AND YOU SAY WE'RE NOT A MATCH! MEANWHILE, I'M THE ONE WOMAN IN THIS CITY WHO'D EAT AT TACO BELL WITH YOU! AND I DON'T THINK I HAVE ANY SCENTED CANDLES ...
I LOVE YOU!
I LOVE YOU!
I LOVE YOU!
OH... YOU ARE GOOD. COME HERE ...
I LOVE YOU!
I LOVE YOU!
I LOVE YOU!
I LOVE YOU!
I LOVE YOU!
I LOVE YOU!
I LOVE YOU!

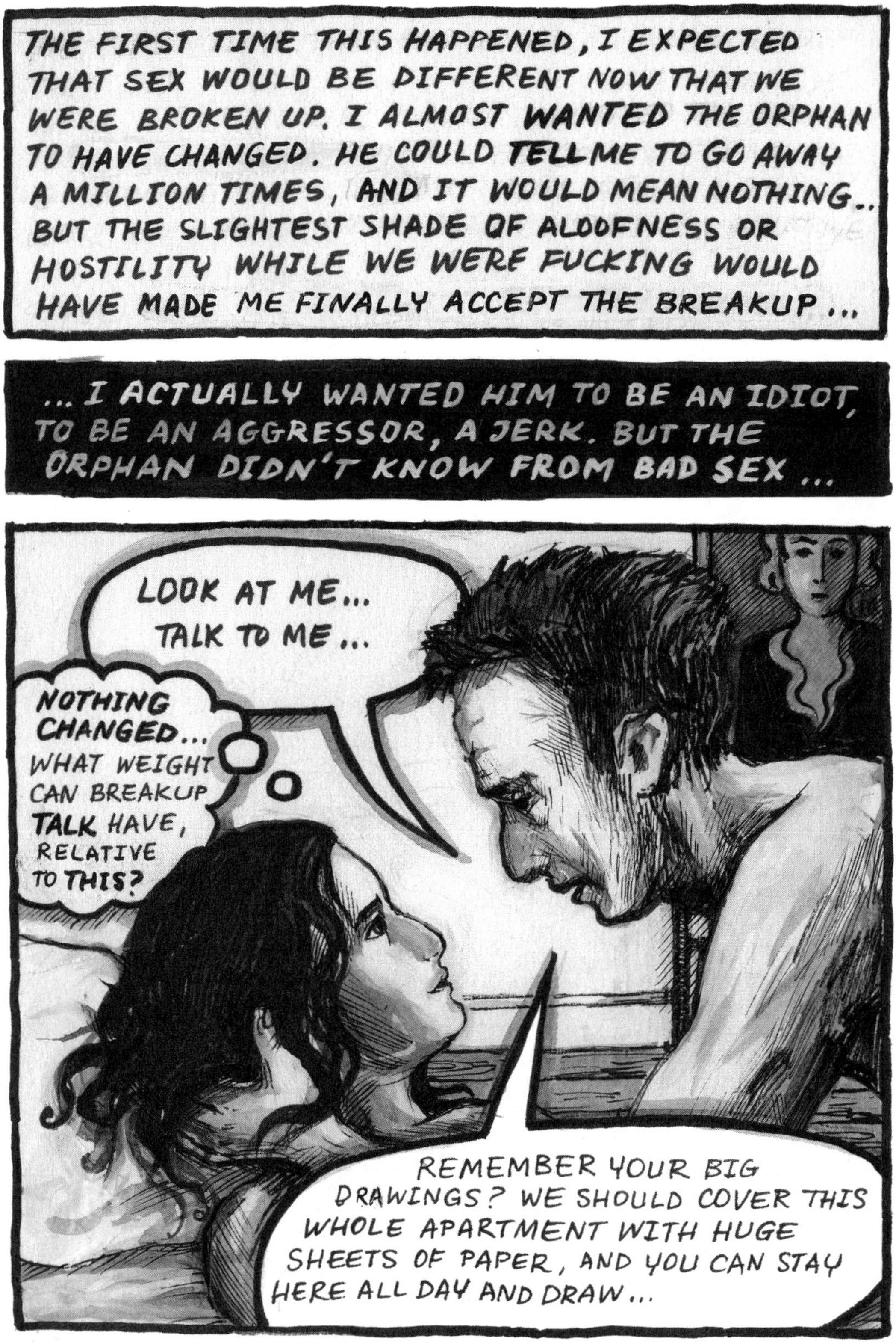
THE FIRST TIME THIS HAPPENED, I EXPECTED THAT SEX WOULD BE DIFFERENT NOW THAT WE WERE BROKEN UP. I ALMOST WANTED THE ORPHAN TO HAVE CHANGED. HE COULD TELL ME TO GO AWAY A MILLION TIMES, AND IT WOULD MEAN NOTHING.. BUT THE SLIGHTEST SHADE OF ALOOFNESS OR HOSTILITY WHILE WE WERE FUCKING WOULD HAVE MADE ME FINALLY ACCEPT THE BREAKUP...
...I ACTUALLY WANTED HIM TO BE AN IDIOT, TO BE AN AGGRESSOR, A JERK. BUT THE ORPHAN DIDN'T KNOW FROM BAD SEX...
LOOK AT ME... TALK TO ME...
NOTHING CHANGED... WHAT WEIGHT CAN BREAKUP TALK HAVE, RELATIVE TO THIS?
REMEMBER YOUR BIG DRAWINGS? WE SHOULD COVER THIS WHOLE APARTMENT WITH HUGE SHEETS OF PAPER, AND YOU CAN STAY HERE ALL DAY AND DRAW...

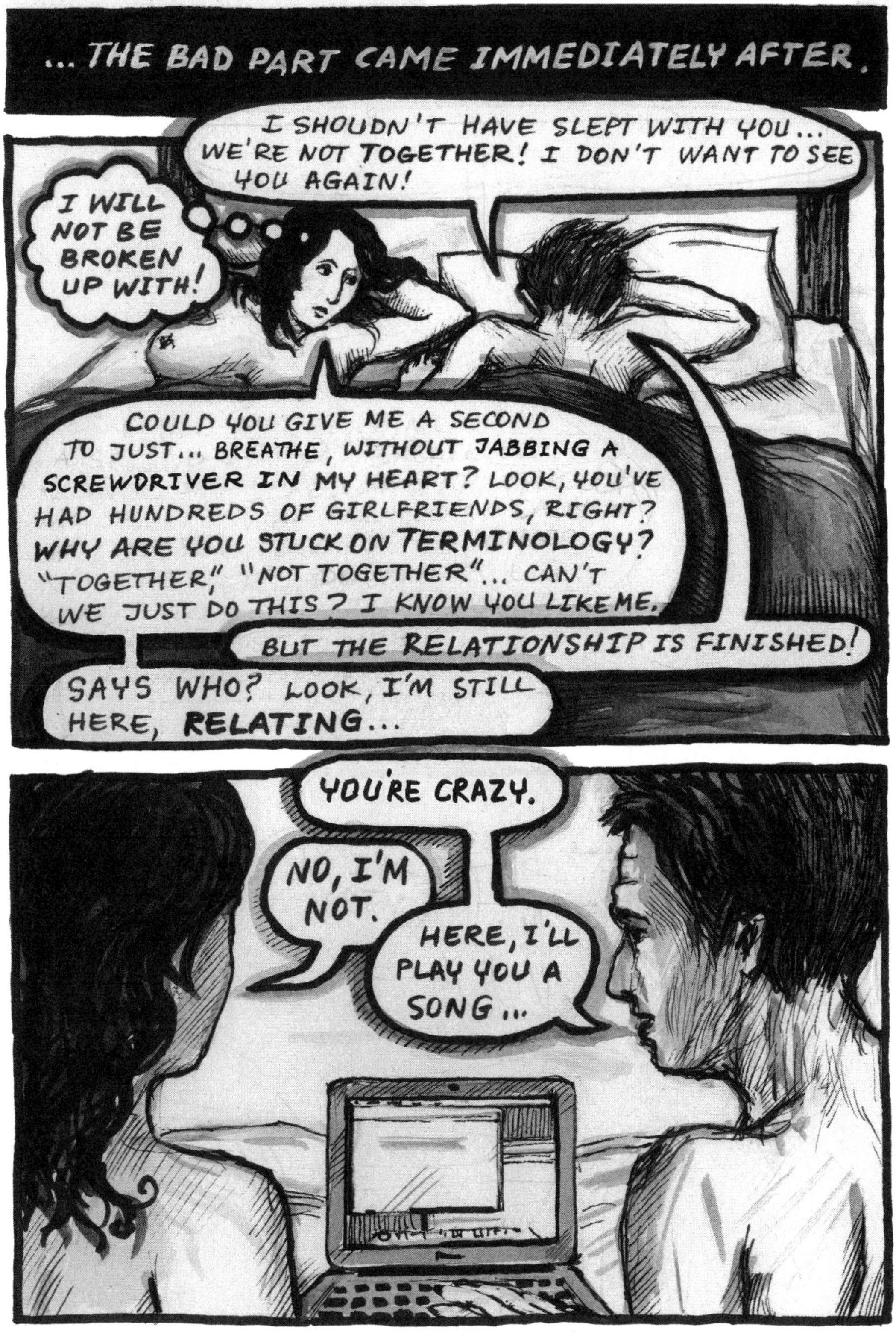

... THE BAD PART CAME IMMEDIATELY AFTER.
I SHOUDN'T HAVE SLEPT WITH YOU... WE'RE NOT TOGETHER! I DON'T WANT TO SEE YOU AGAIN!
I WILL NOT BE BROKEN UP WITH!
COULD YOU GIVE ME A SECOND TO JUST... BREATHE, WITHOUT JABBING A SCREWDRIVER IN MY HEART? LOOK, YOU'VE HAD HUNDREDS OF GIRLFRIENDS, RIGHT? WHY ARE YOU STUCK ON TERMINOLOGY? "TOGETHER," "NOT TOGETHER"... CAN'T WE JUST DO THIS? I KNOW YOU LIKE ME.
BUT THE RELATIONSHIP IS FINISHED!
SAYS WHO? LOOK, I'M STILL HERE, RELATING...
YOU'RE CRAZY.
NO, I'M NOT.
HERE, I'LL PLAY YOU A SONG...

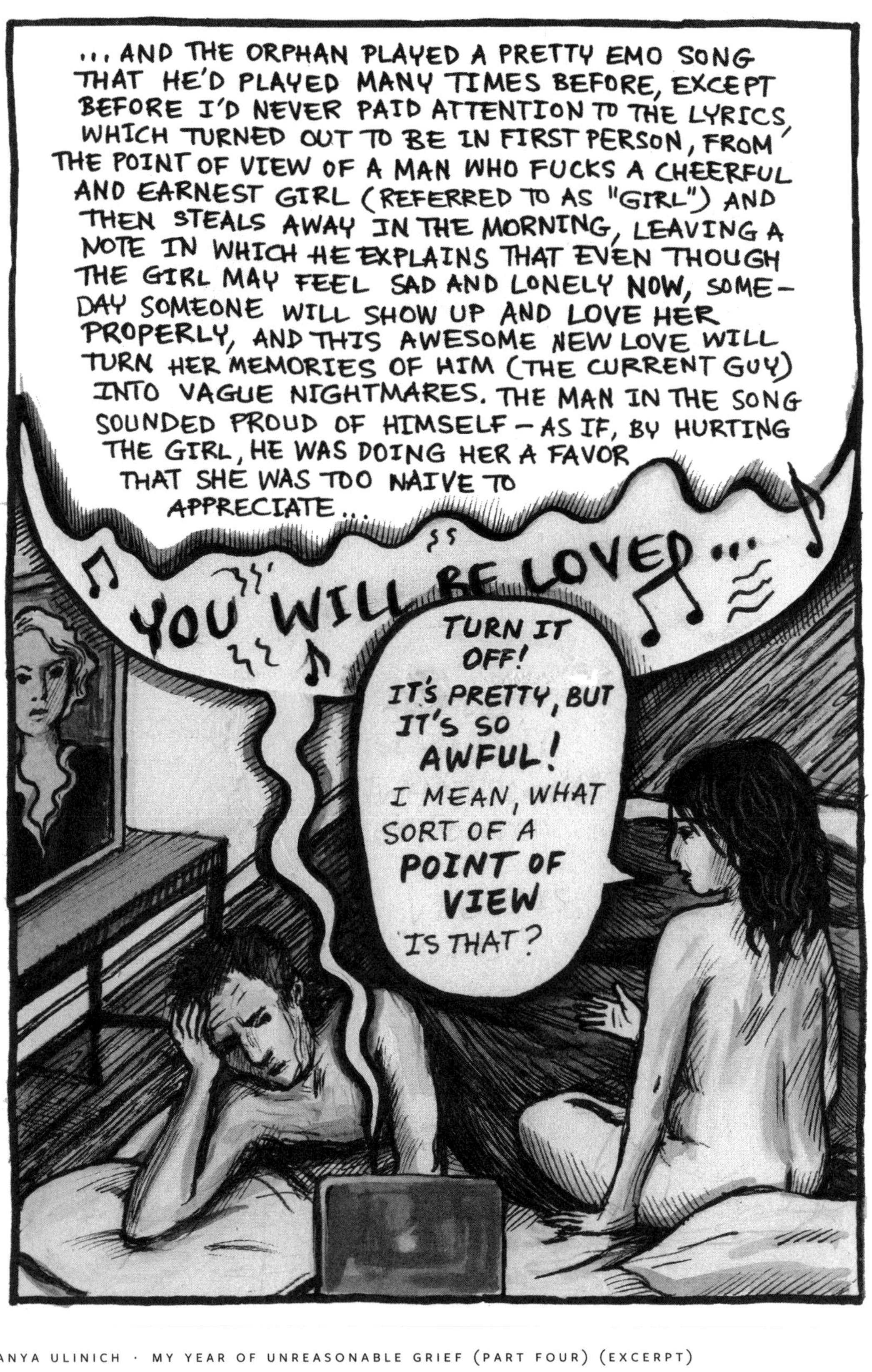
...AND THE ORPHAN PLAYED A PRETTY EMO SONG THAT HE'D PLAYED MANY TIMES BEFORE, EXCEPT BEFORE I'D NEVER PAID ATTENTION TO THE LYRICS, WHICH TURNED OUT TO BE IN FIRST PERSON, FROM THE POINT OF VIEW OF A MAN WHO FUCKS A CHEERFUL AND EARNEST GIRL (REFERRED TO AS "GIRL") AND THEN STEALS AWAY IN THE MORNING, LEAVING A NOTE IN WHICH HE EXPLAINS THAT EVEN THOUGH THE GIRL MAY FEEL SAD AND LONELY NOW, SOMEDAY SOMEONE WILL SHOW UP AND LOVE HER PROPERLY, AND THIS AWESOME NEW LOVE WILL TURN HER MEMORIES OF HIM (THE CURRENT GUY) INTO VAGUE NIGHTMARES. THE MAN IN THE SONG SOUNDED PROUD OF HIMSELF — AS IF, BY HURTING THE GIRL, HE WAS DOING HER A FAVOR THAT SHE WAS TOO NAIVE TO APPRECIATE...
YOU WILL BE LOVED...
TURN IT OFF! IT'S PRETTY, BUT IT'S SO AWFUL! I MEAN, WHAT SORT OF A POINT OF VIEW IS THAT?

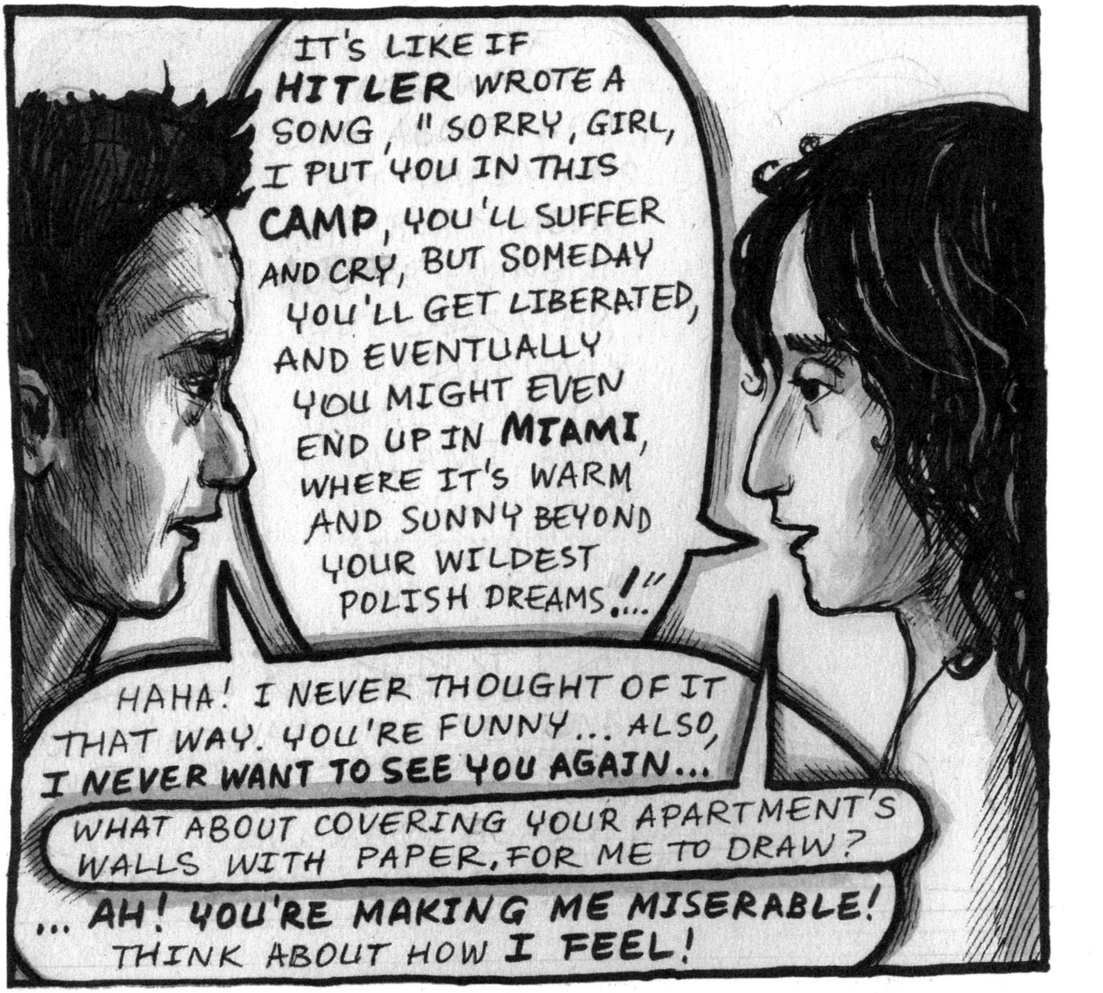
IT'S LIKE IF HITLER WROTE A SONG, "SORRY, GIRL, I PUT YOU IN THIS CAMP, YOU'LL SUFFER AND CRY, BUT SOMEDAY YOU'LL GET LIBERATED, AND EVENTUALLY YOU MIGHT EVEN END UP IN MIAMI, WHERE IT'S WARM AND SUNNY BEYOND YOUR WILDEST POLISH DREAMS!"...
HAHA! I NEVER THOUGHT OF IT THAT WAY. YOU'RE FUNNY... ALSO, I NEVER WANT TO SEE YOU AGAIN...
WHAT ABOUT COVERING YOUR APARTMENT'S WALLS WITH PAPER, FOR ME TO DRAW?
... AH! YOU'RE MAKING ME MISERABLE! THINK ABOUT HOW I FEEL!

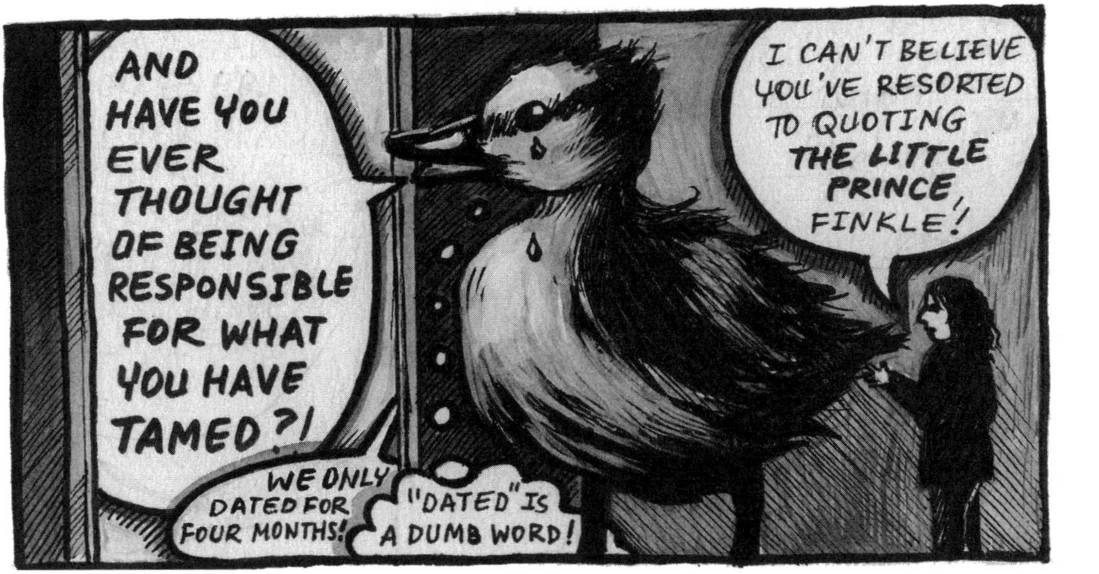
AND HAVE YOU EVER THOUGHT OF BEING RESPONSIBLE FOR WHAT YOU HAVE TAMED?!
I CAN'T BELIEVE YOU'VE RESORTED TO QUOTING THE LITTLE PRINCE, FINKLE!
WE ONLY DATED FOR FOUR MONTHS!
"DATED" IS A DUMB WORD!

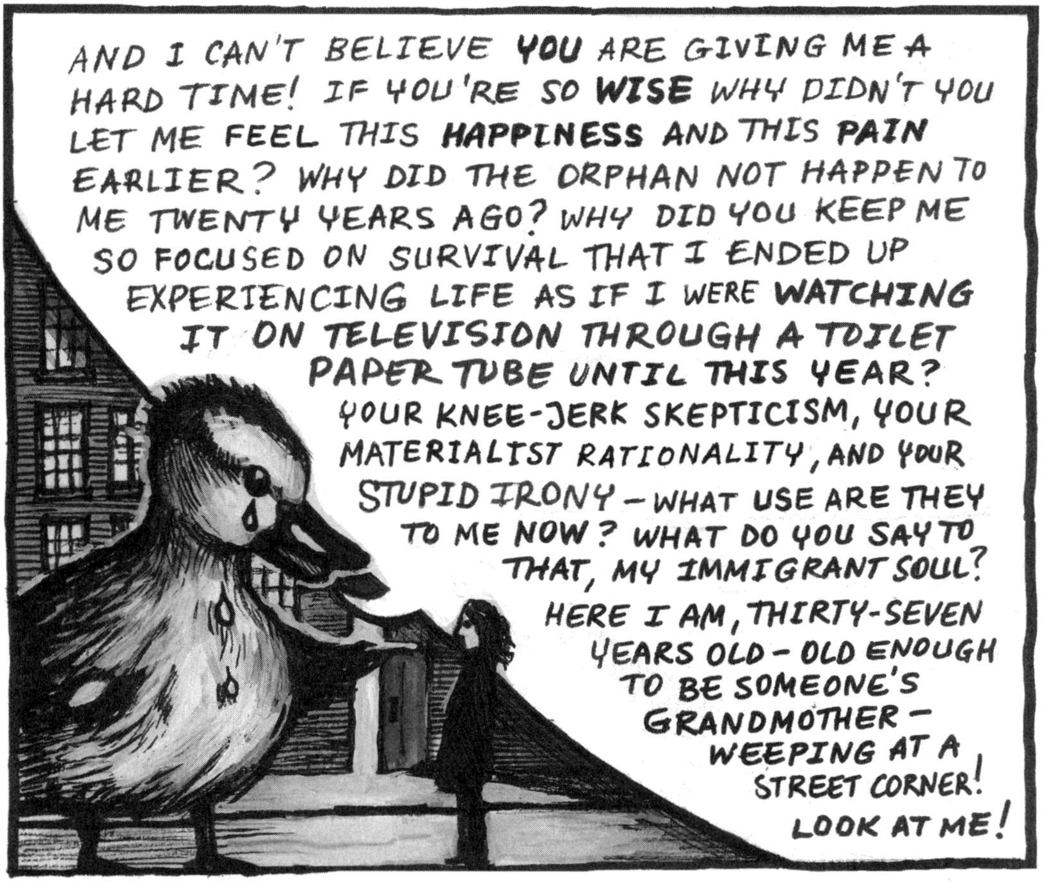
AND I CAN'T BELIEVE YOU ARE GIVING ME A HARD TIME! IF YOU'RE SO WISE WHY DIDN'T YOU LET ME FEEL THIS HAPPINESS AND THIS PAIN EARLIER? WHY DID THE ORPHAN NOT HAPPEN TO ME TWENTY YEARS AGO? WHY DID YOU KEEP ME SO FOCUSED ON SURVIVAL THAT I ENDED UP EXPERIENCING LIFE AS IF I WERE WATCHING IT ON TELEVISION THROUGH A TOILET PAPER TUBE UNTIL THIS YEAR?
YOUR KNEE-JERK SKEPTICISM, YOUR MATERIALIST RATIONALITY, AND YOUR STUPID IRONY – WHAT USE ARE THEY TO ME NOW? WHAT DO YOU SAY TO THAT, MY IMMIGRANT SOUL?
HERE I AM, THIRTY-SEVEN YEARS OLD – OLD ENOUGH TO BE SOMEONE'S GRANDMOTHER – WEEPING AT A STREET CORNER!
LOOK AT ME!

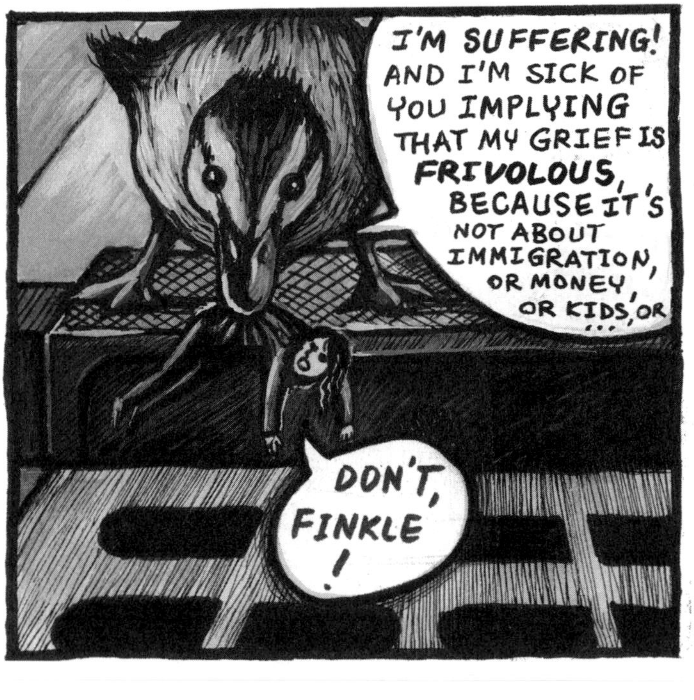
I'M SUFFERING! AND I'M SICK OF YOU IMPLYING THAT MY GRIEF IS FRIVOLOUS, BECAUSE IT'S NOT ABOUT IMMIGRATION, OR MONEY, OR KIDS, OR ...
DON'T, FINKLE!

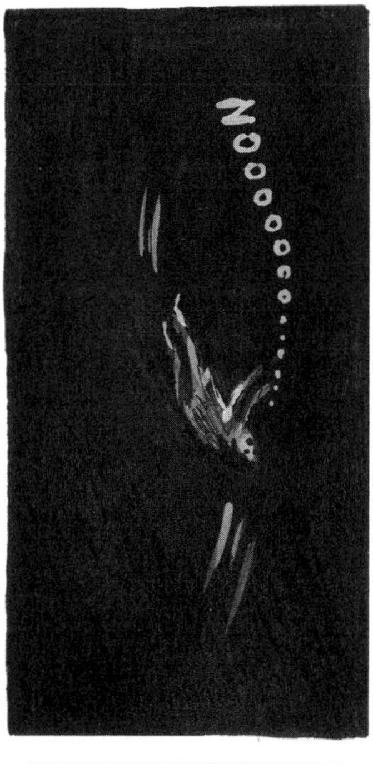
NOOOOOOOO.......

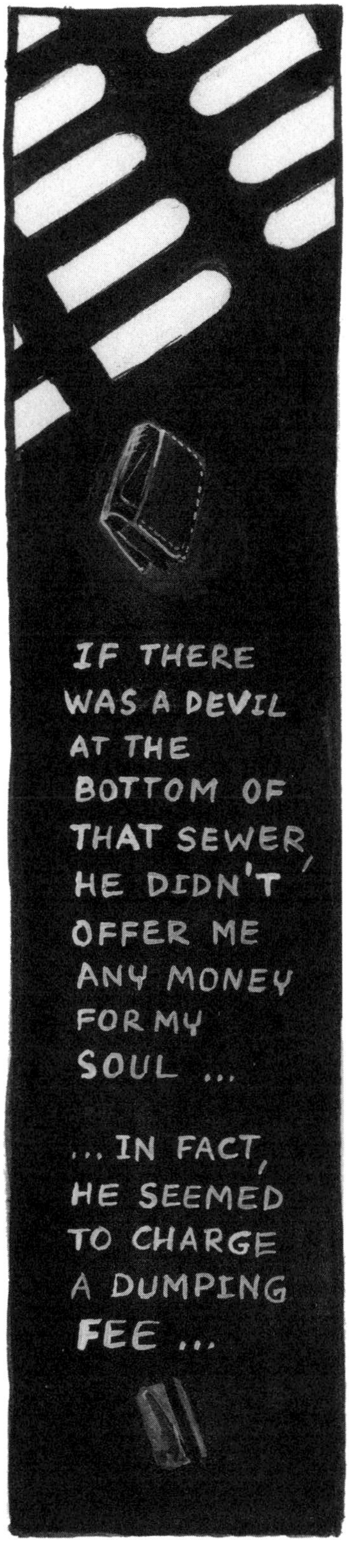
IF THERE WAS A DEVIL AT THE BOTTOM OF THAT SEWER, HE DIDN'T OFFER ME ANY MONEY FOR MY SOUL ...
... IN FACT, HE SEEMED TO CHARGE A DUMPING FEE ...

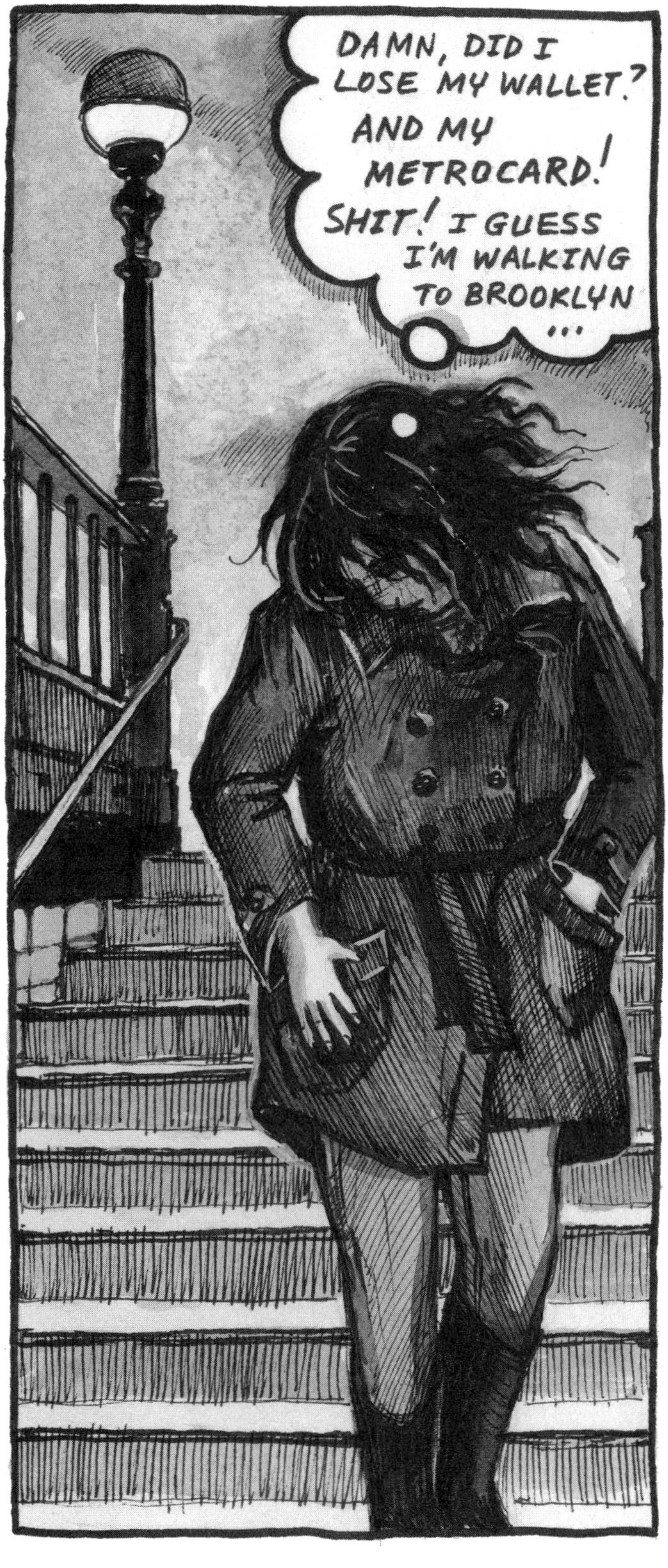
DAMN, DID I LOSE MY WALLET? AND MY METROCARD! SHIT! I GUESS I'M WALKING TO BROOKLYN ...

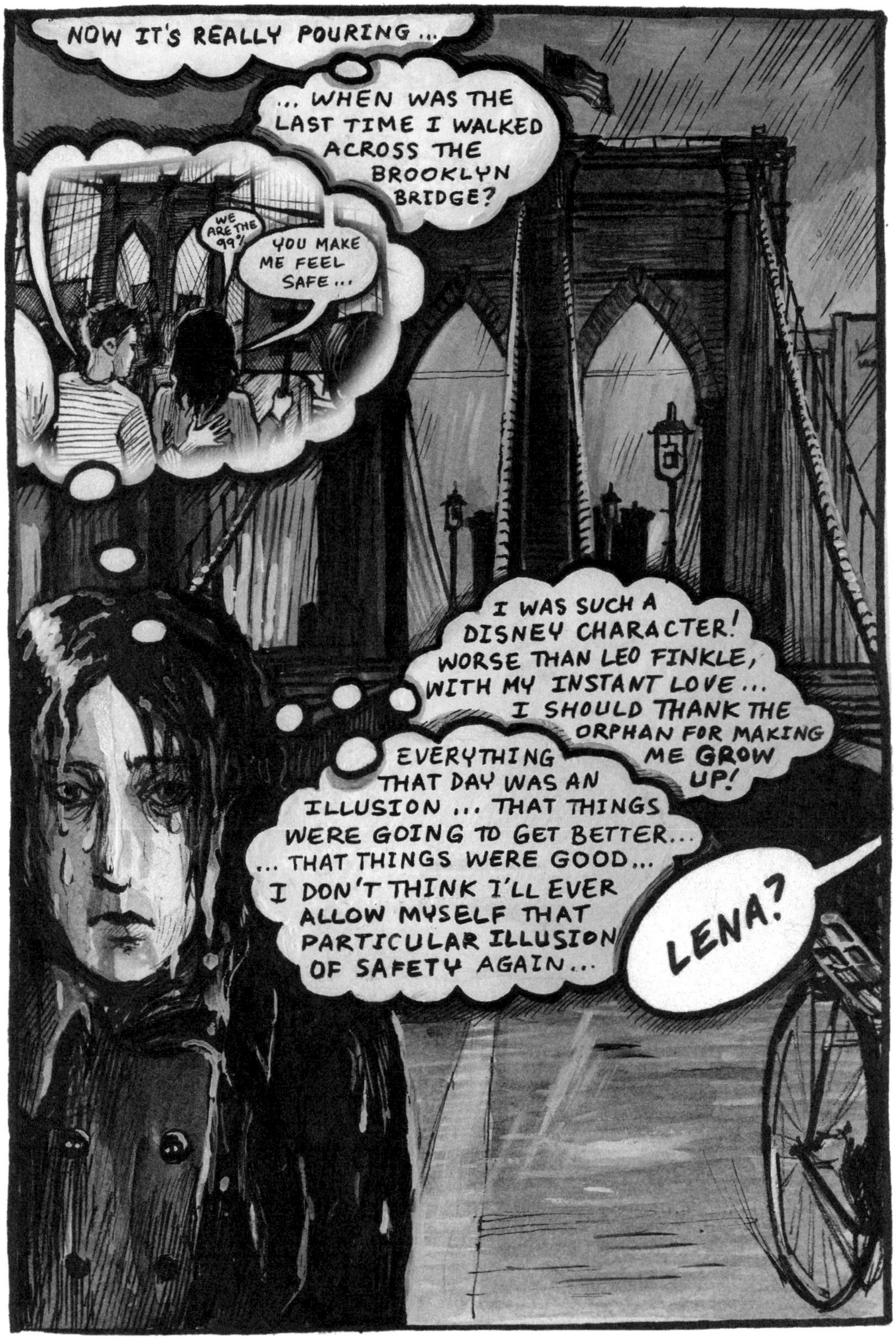
NOW IT'S REALLY POURING ...
... WHEN WAS THE LAST TIME I WALKED ACROSS THE BROOKLYN BRIDGE?
WE ARE THE 99%
YOU MAKE ME FEEL SAFE ...
I WAS SUCH A DISNEY CHARACTER! WORSE THAN LEO FINKLE, WITH MY INSTANT LOVE ... I SHOULD THANK THE ORPHAN FOR MAKING ME GROW UP!
EVERYTHING THAT DAY WAS AN ILLUSION ... THAT THINGS WERE GOING TO GET BETTER... ... THAT THINGS WERE GOOD... I DON'T THINK I'LL EVER ALLOW MYSELF THAT PARTICULAR ILLUSION OF SAFETY AGAIN...
LENA?

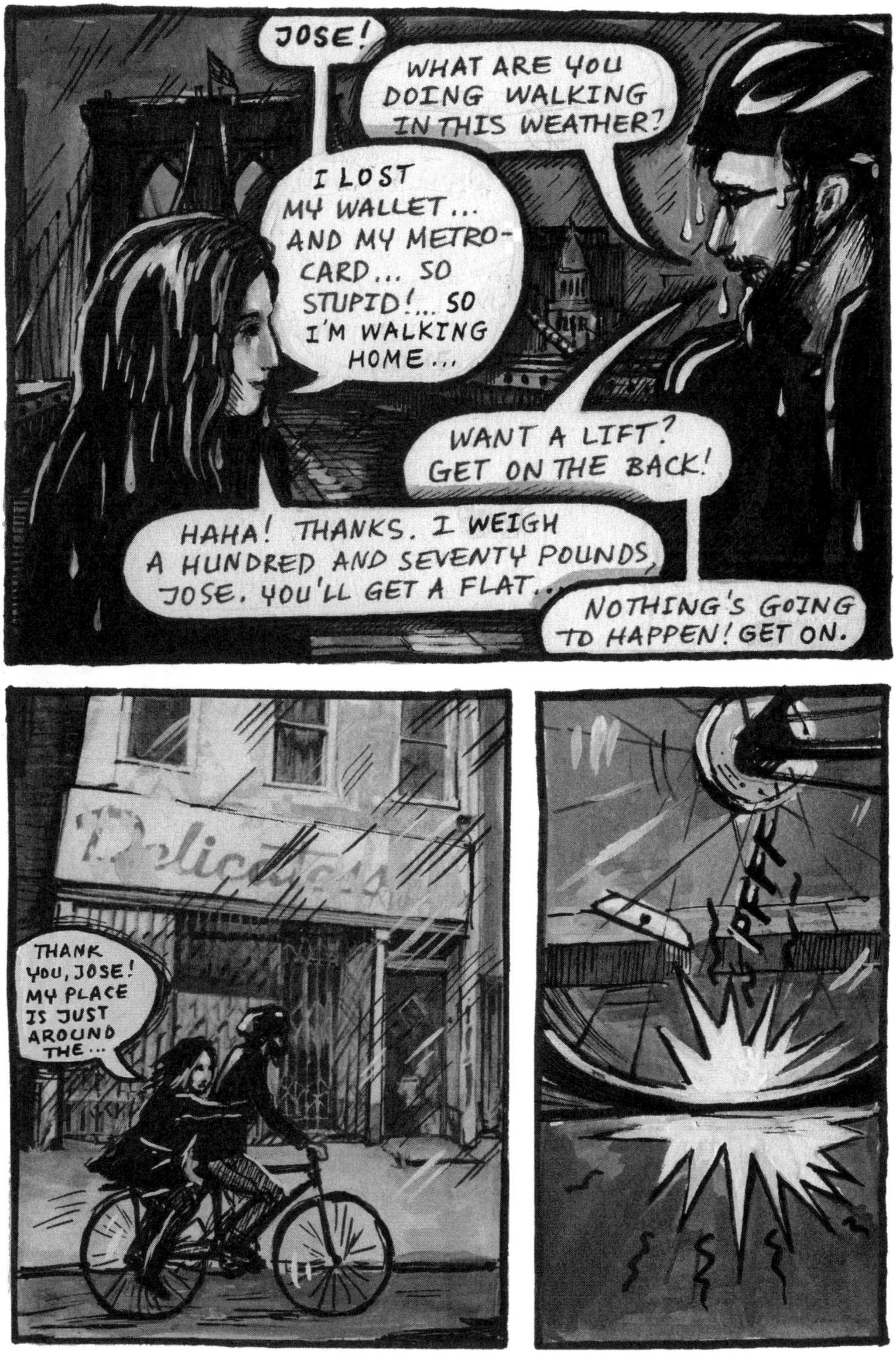
JOSE!
WHAT ARE YOU DOING WALKING IN THIS WEATHER?
I LOST MY WALLET... AND MY METRO-CARD... SO STUPID!... SO I'M WALKING HOME...
WANT A LIFT? GET ON THE BACK!
HAHA! THANKS. I WEIGH A HUNDRED AND SEVENTY POUNDS, JOSE. YOU'LL GET A FLAT...
NOTHING'S GOING TO HAPPEN! GET ON.
THANK YOU, JOSE! MY PLACE IS JUST AROUND THE...
PFFF

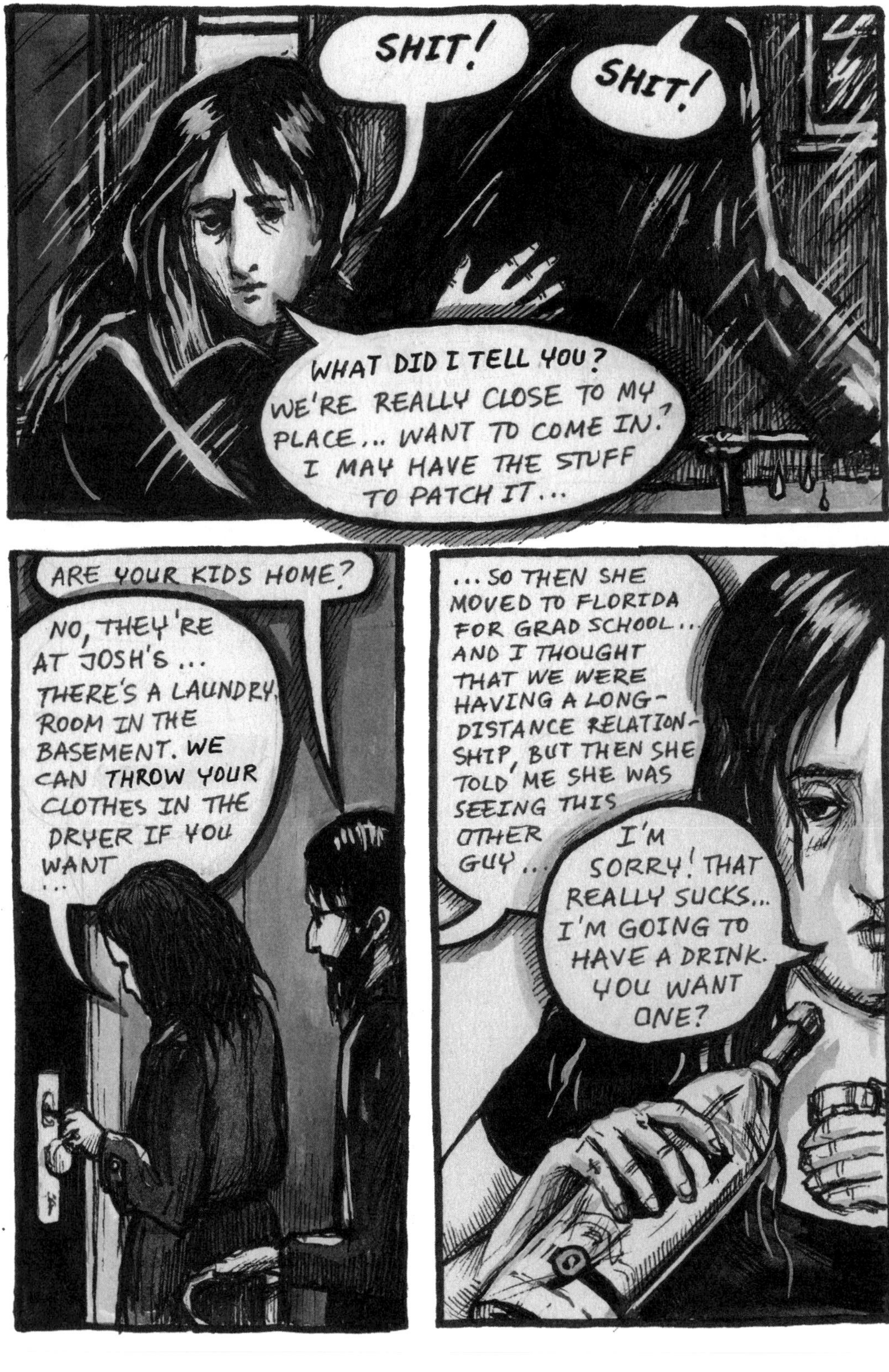
SHIT!
SHIT!
WHAT DID I TELL YOU? WE'RE REALLY CLOSE TO MY PLACE... WANT TO COME IN? I MAY HAVE THE STUFF TO PATCH IT...
ARE YOUR KIDS HOME?
NO, THEY'RE AT JOSH'S... THERE'S A LAUNDRY ROOM IN THE BASEMENT. WE CAN THROW YOUR CLOTHES IN THE DRYER IF YOU WANT...
...SO THEN SHE MOVED TO FLORIDA FOR GRAD SCHOOL... AND I THOUGHT THAT WE WERE HAVING A LONG-DISTANCE RELATIONSHIP, BUT THEN SHE TOLD ME SHE WAS SEEING THIS OTHER GUY...
I'M SORRY! THAT REALLY SUCKS... I'M GOING TO HAVE A DRINK. YOU WANT ONE?

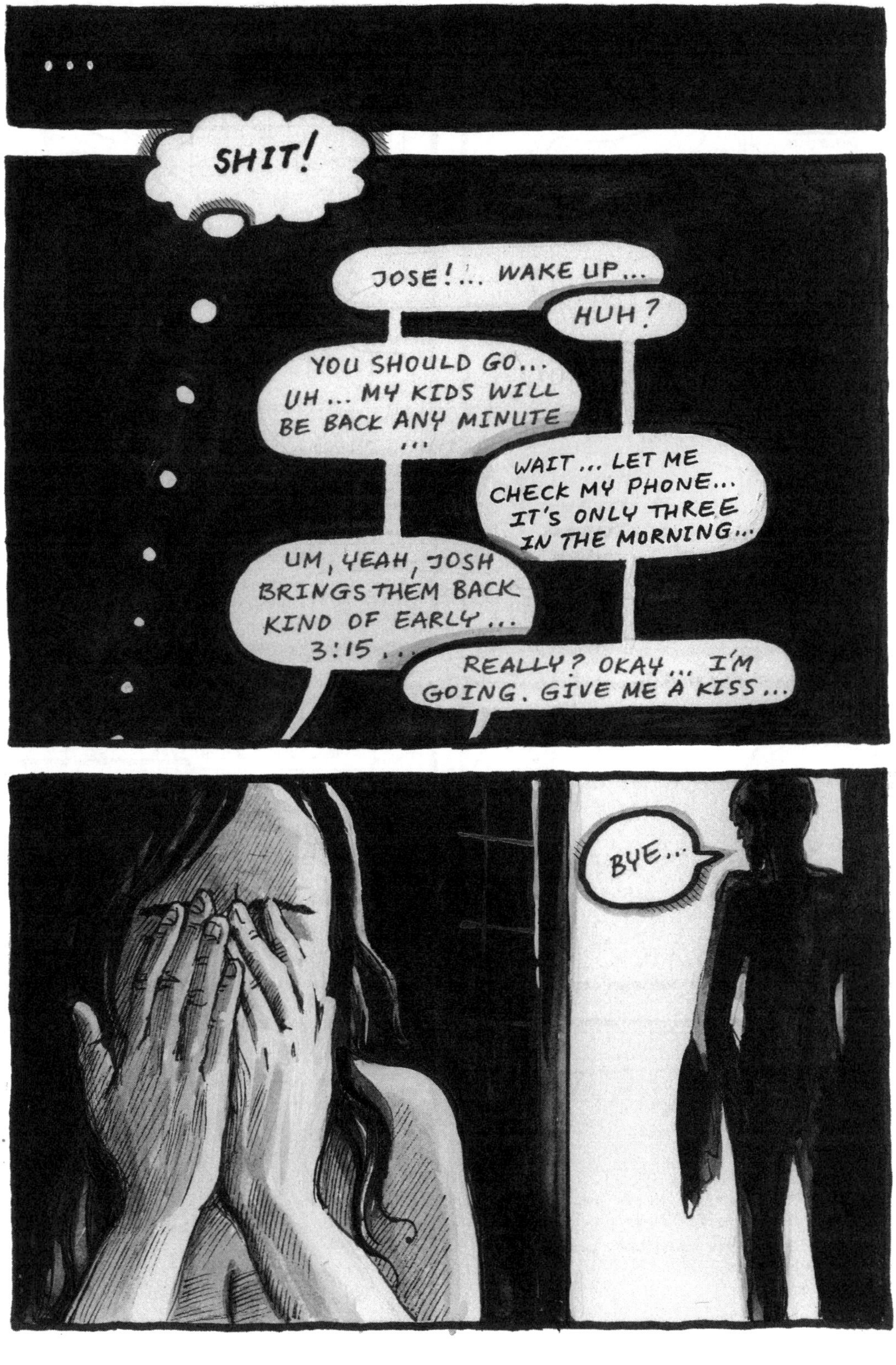
...
SHIT!
JOSE!... WAKE UP...
HUH?
YOU SHOULD GO... UH... MY KIDS WILL BE BACK ANY MINUTE ...
WAIT... LET ME CHECK MY PHONE... IT'S ONLY THREE IN THE MORNING...
UM, YEAH, JOSH BRINGS THEM BACK KIND OF EARLY... 3:15...
REALLY? OKAY... I'M GOING. GIVE ME A KISS...
BYE...

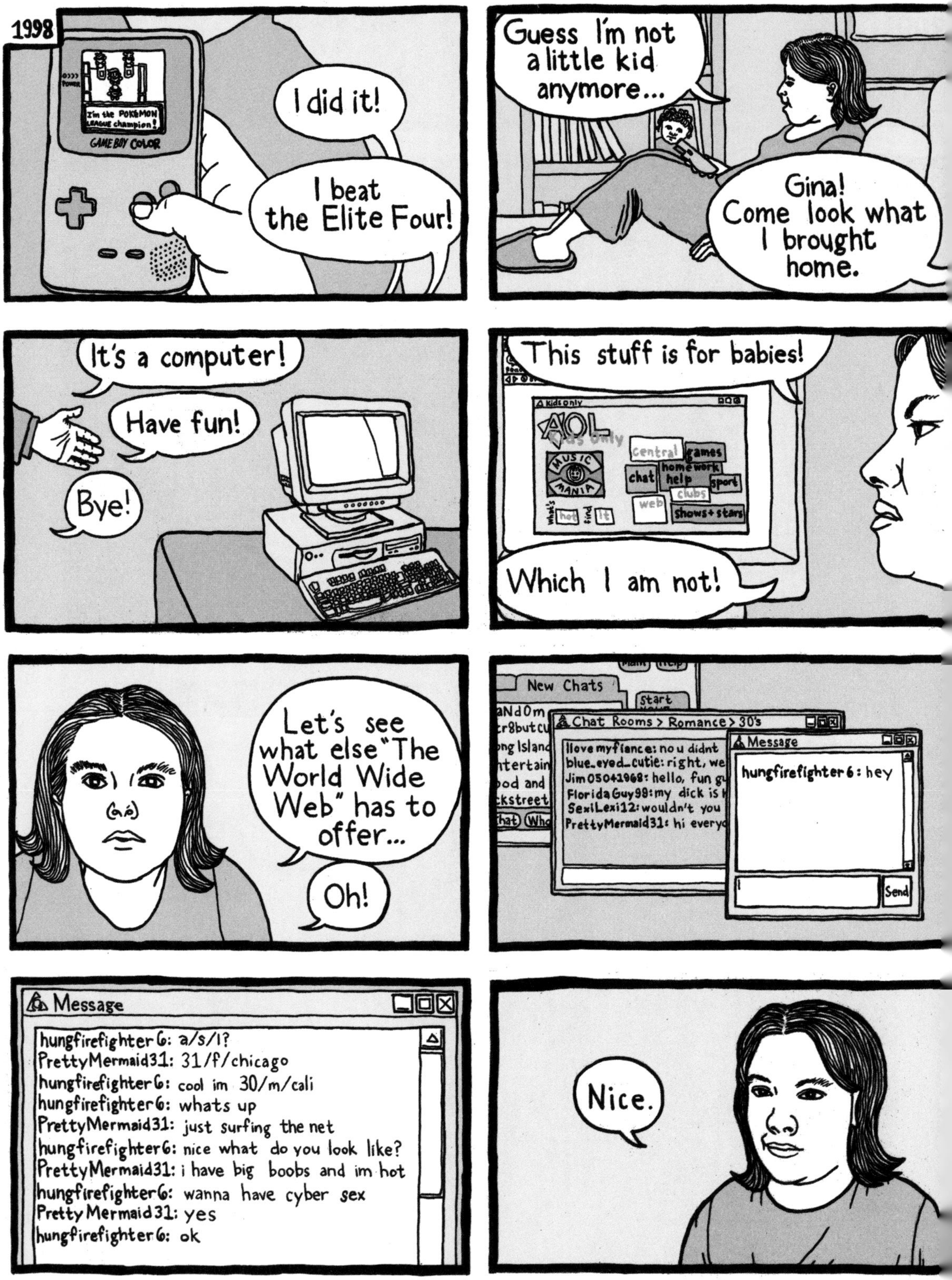
1998
I'm the POKéMON LEAGUE champion!
GAME BOY COLOR
I did it!
I beat the Elite Four!
Guess I'm not a little kid anymore...
Gina! Come look what I brought home.
It's a computer!
Have fun!
Bye!
This stuff is for babies!
Kids only
AOL
central
games
chat
homework help
sport
clubs
web
shows+stars
what's hot
find it
Which I am not!
Let's see what else "The World Wide Web" has to offer...
Oh!
New Chats
Chat Rooms > Romance > 30's
Ilove myfiance: no u didnt
blue_eyed_cutie: right, we
Jim05041968: hello, fun gu
FloridaGuy98: my dick is
SexiLexi12: wouldn't you
PrettyMermaid31: hi everyo
Message
hungfirefighter6: hey
Send
Message
hungfirefighter6: a/s/l?
PrettyMermaid31: 31/f/chicago
hungfirefighter6: cool im 30/m/cali
hungfirefighter6: whats up
PrettyMermaid31: just surfing the net
hungfirefighter6: nice what do you look like?
PrettyMermaid31: i have big boobs and im hot
hungfirefighter6: wanna have cyber sex
PrettyMermaid31: yes
hungfirefighter6: ok
Nice.

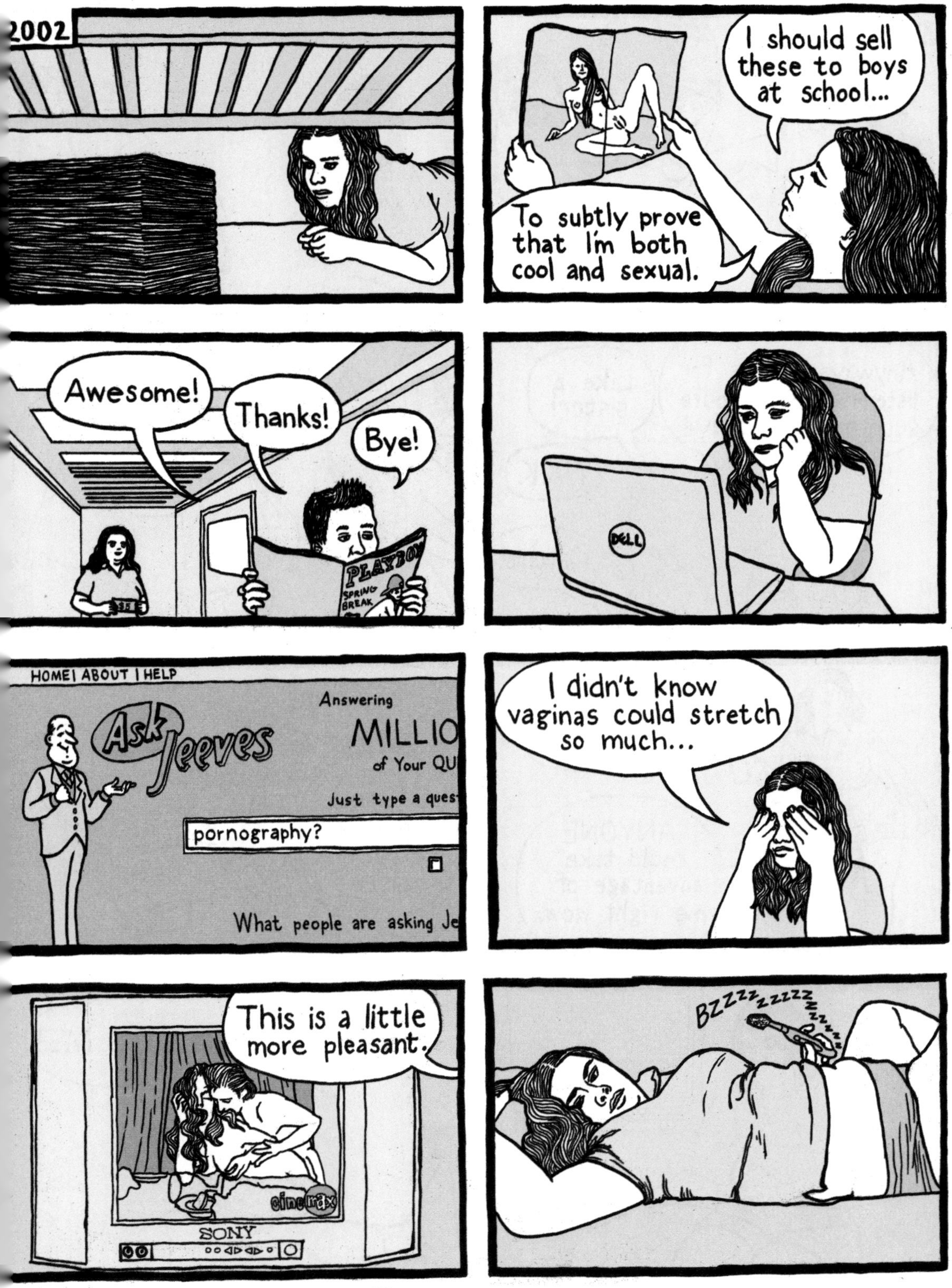
2002
I should sell these to boys at school...
To subtly prove that I'm both cool and sexual.
PLAYBOY SPRING BREAK
Awesome!
Thanks!
Bye!
DELL
HOME | ABOUT | HELP
Ask Jeeves
Answering MILLIO of Your QU
Just type a quest
pornography?
What people are asking Je
I didn't know vaginas could stretch so much...
This is a little more pleasant.
cinemax
SONY
BZZZZZZZZZZZZZZ

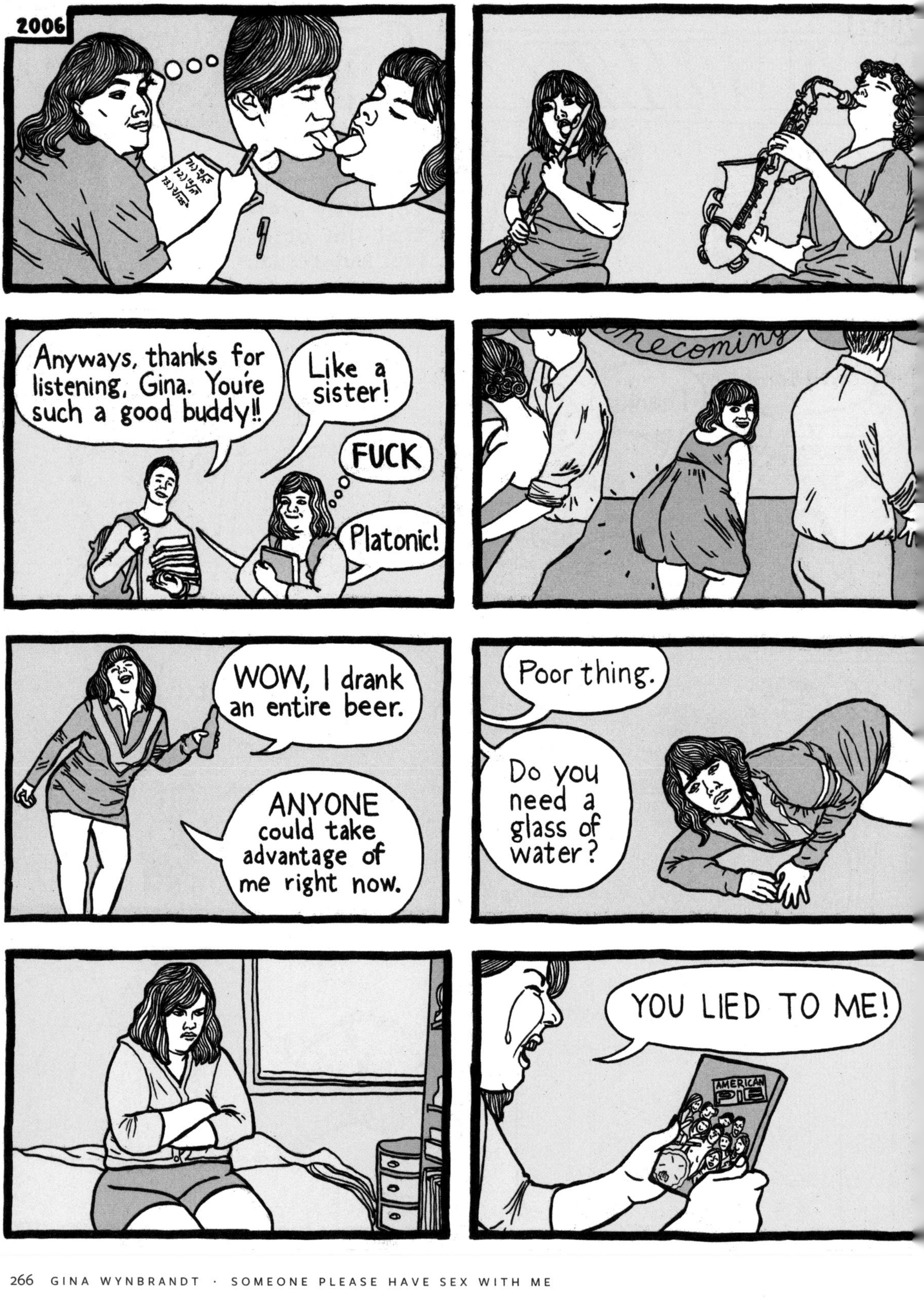
2006
Anyways, thanks for listening, Gina. You're such a good buddy!!
Like a sister!
FUCK
Platonic!
WOW, I drank an entire beer.
ANYONE could take advantage of me right now.
Poor thing.
Do you need a glass of water?
YOU LIED TO ME!
AMERICAN PIE

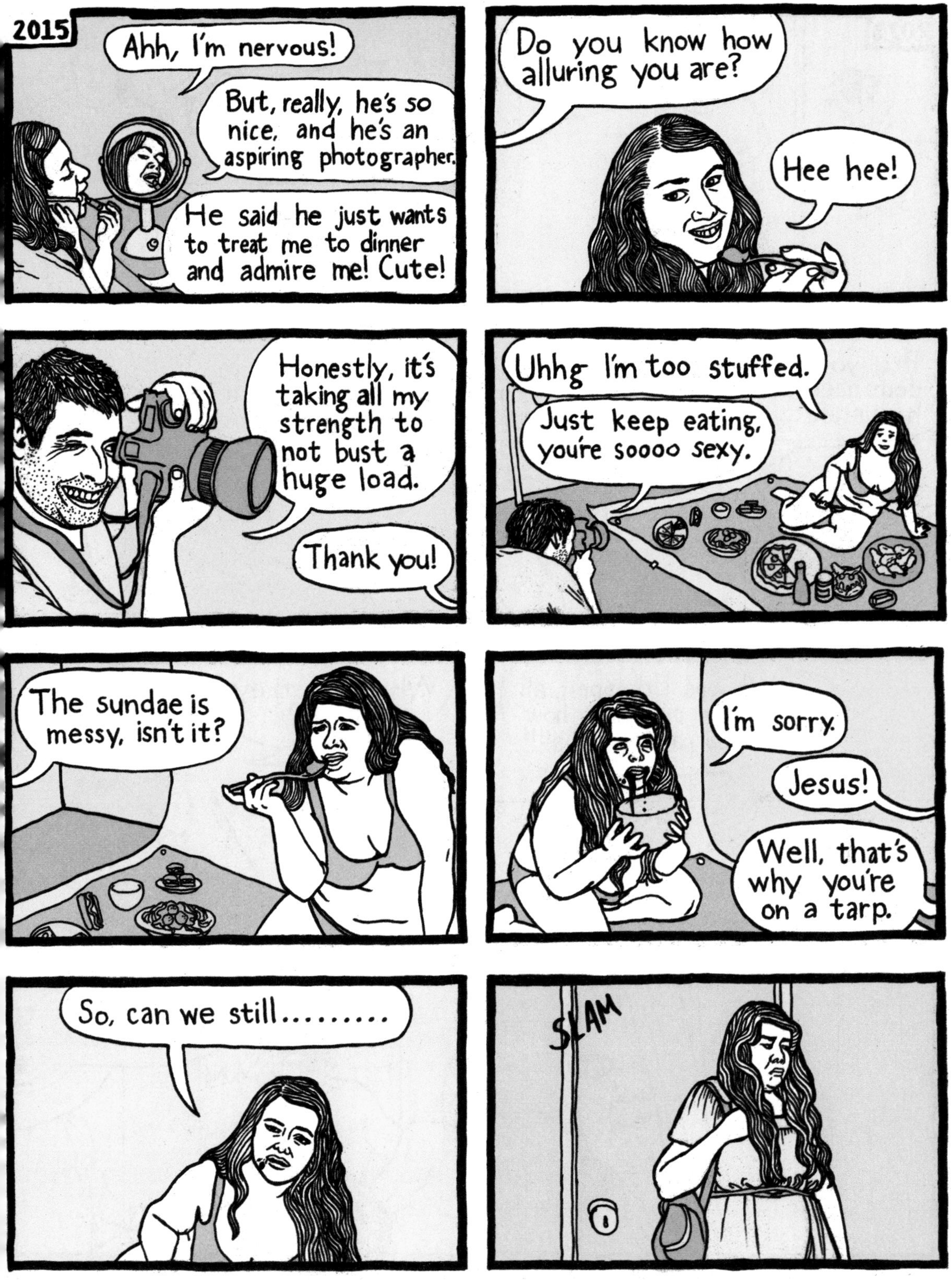
2015
Ahh, I'm nervous!
But, really, he's so nice, and he's an aspiring photographer.
He said he just wants to treat me to dinner and admire me! Cute!
Do you know how alluring you are?
Hee hee!
Honestly, it's taking all my strength to not bust a huge load.
Thank you!
Uhhg I'm too stuffed.
Just keep eating, you're soooo sexy.
The sundae is messy, isn't it?
I'm sorry.
Jesus!
Well, that's why you're on a tarp.
So, can we still.........
SLAM

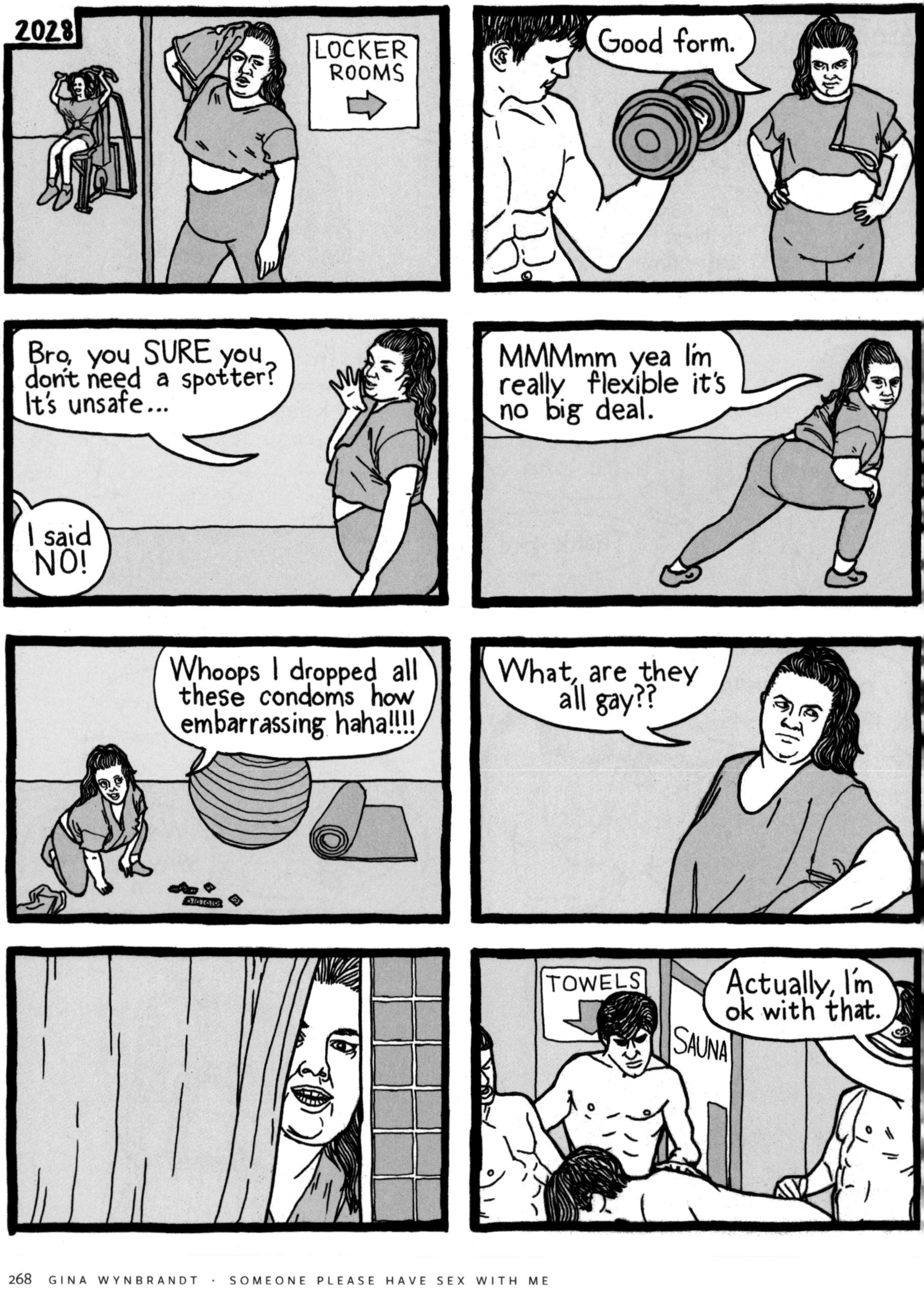
2028
LOCKER ROOMS
Good form.
Bro, you SURE you don't need a spotter? It's unsafe...
I said NO!
MMMmm yea I'm really flexible it's no big deal.
Whoops I dropped all these condoms how embarrassing haha!!!!
What, are they all gay??
TOWELS
SAUNA
Actually, I'm ok with that.

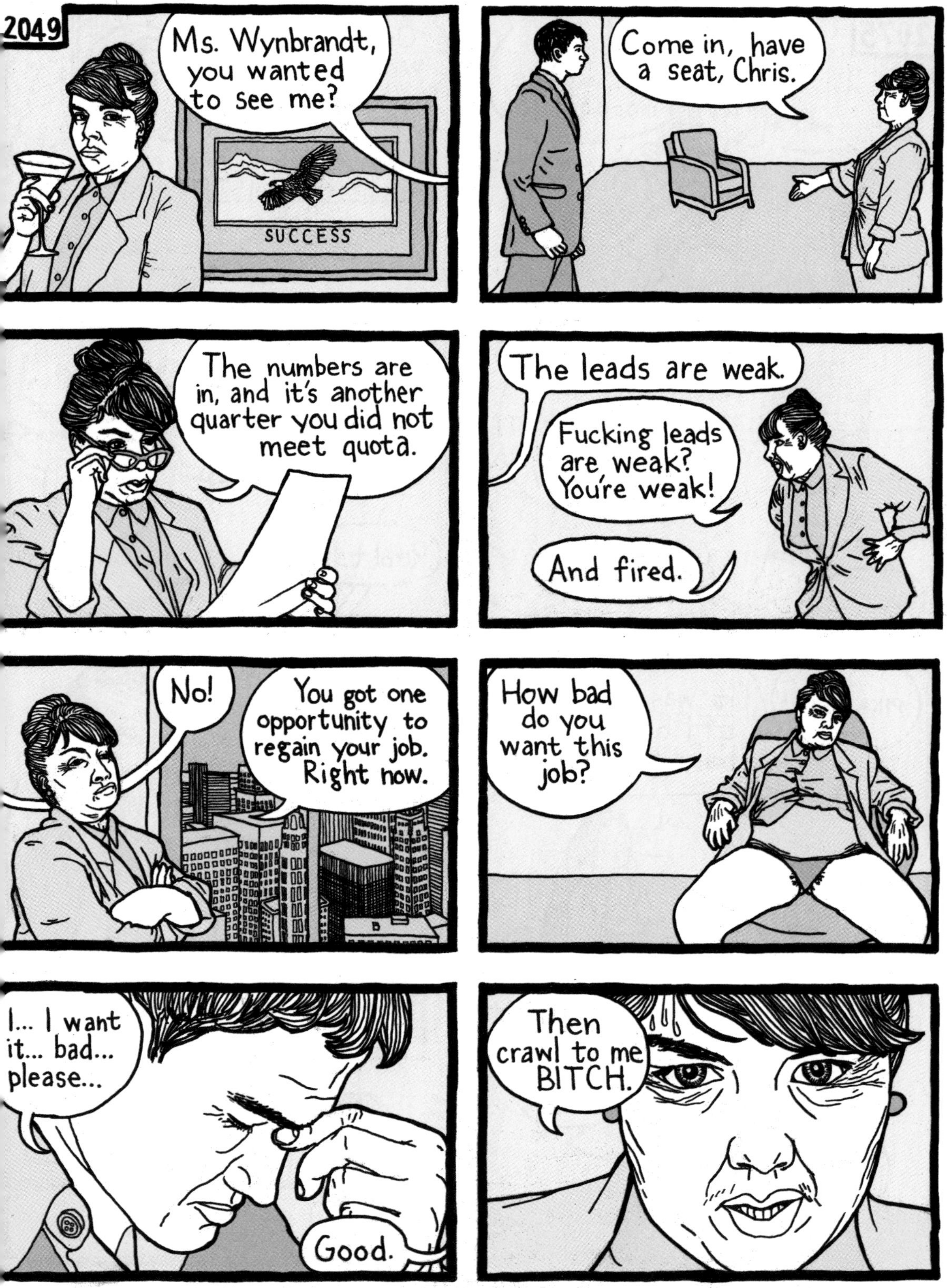
2049
Ms. Wynbrandt, you wanted to see me?
SUCCESS
Come in, have a seat, Chris.
The numbers are in, and it's another quarter you did not meet quota.
The leads are weak.
Fucking leads are weak? You're weak!
And fired.
No!
You got one opportunity to regain your job. Right now.
How bad do you want this job?
I... I want it... bad... please...
Good.
Then crawl to me BITCH.

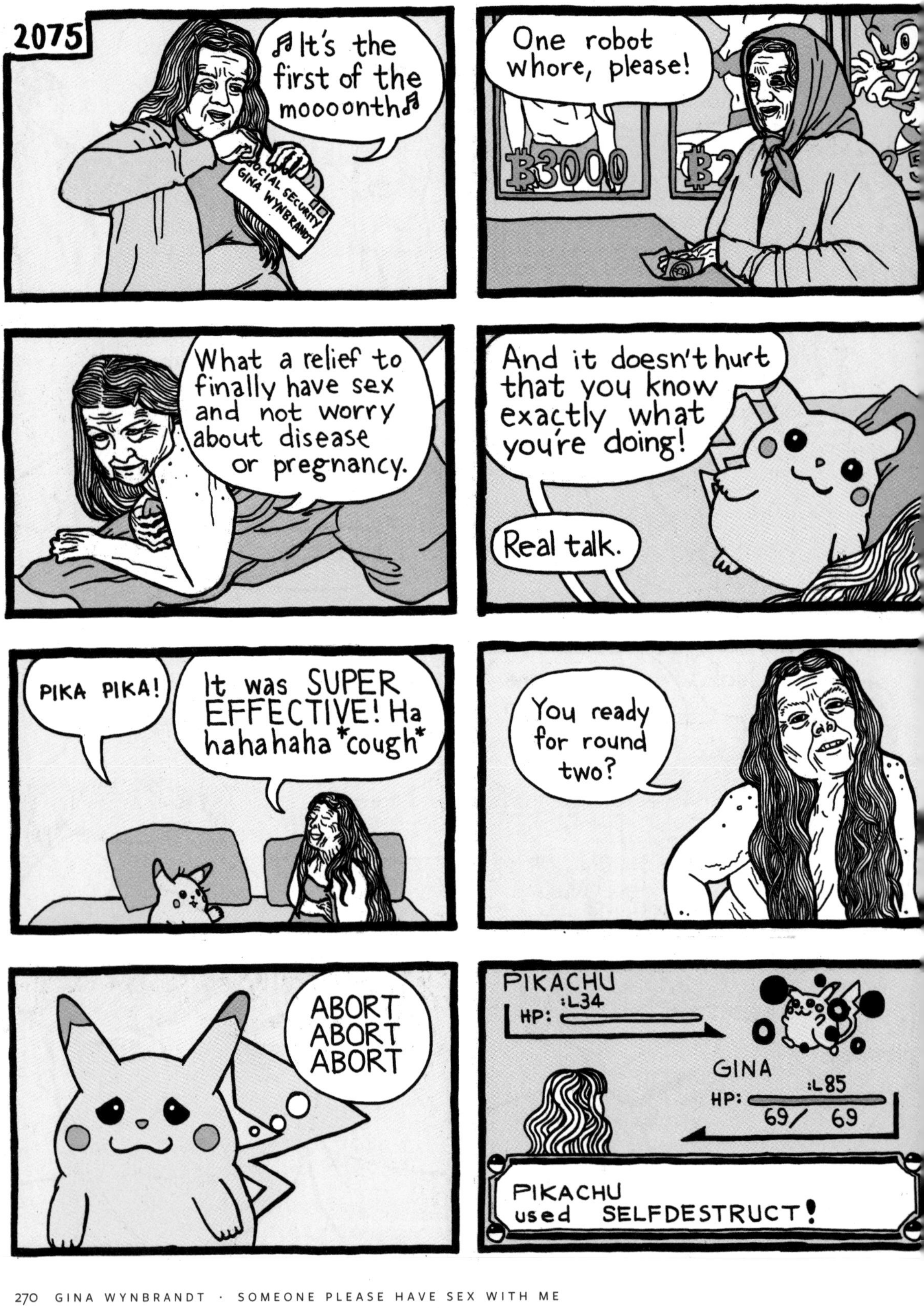
2075
♫It's the first of the moooonth♫
SOCIAL SECURITY GINA WYNBRANDT
One robot whore, please!
฿3000
What a relief to finally have sex and not worry about disease or pregnancy.
And it doesn't hurt that you know exactly what you're doing!
Real talk.
PIKA PIKA!
It was SUPER EFFECTIVE! Ha hahahaha *cough*
You ready for round two?
ABORT ABORT ABORT
PIKACHU
:L34
HP:
GINA
:L85
HP:
69/ 69
PIKACHU used SELFDESTRUCT!

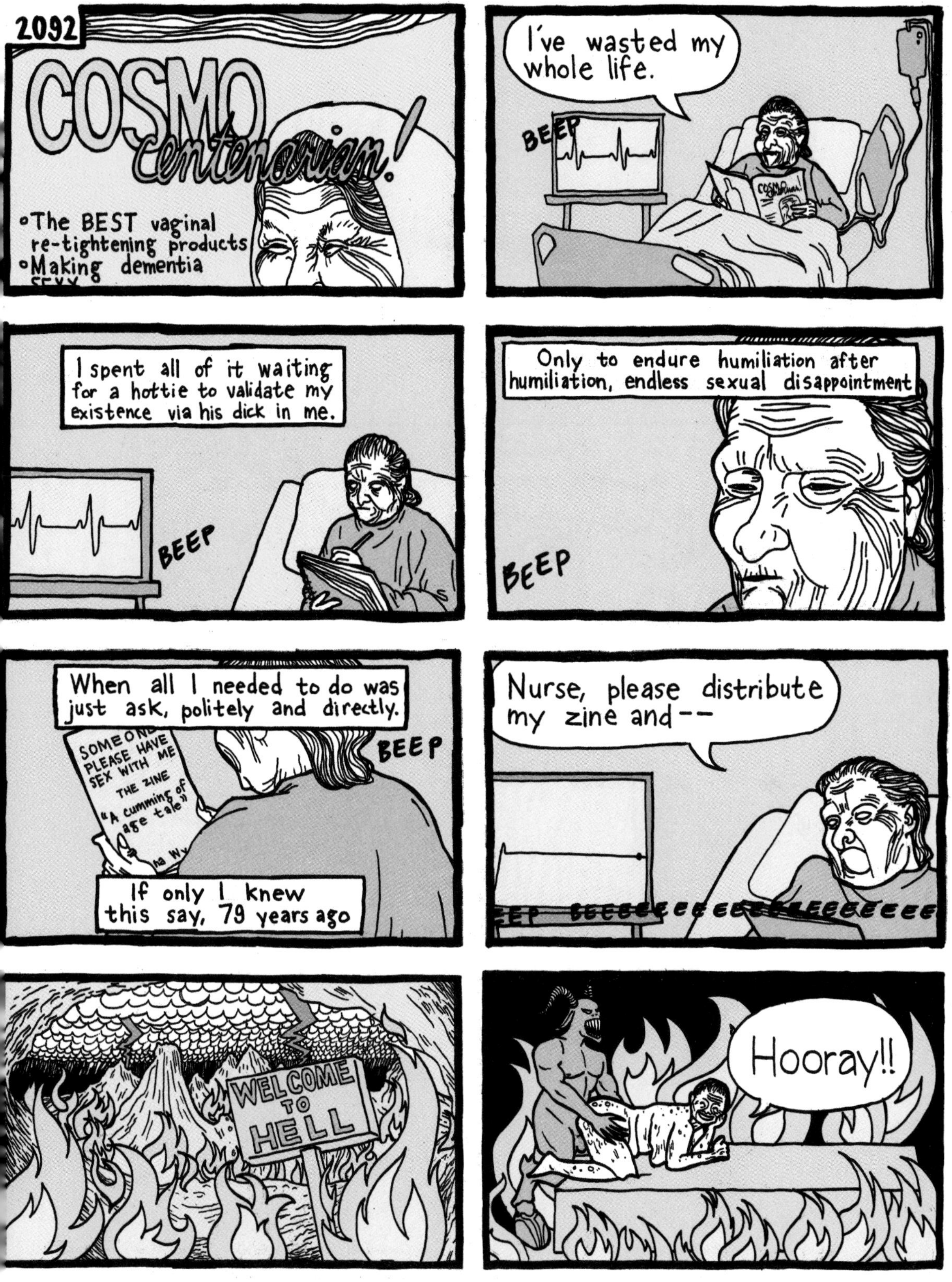
2092
COSMO centenarian!
•The BEST vaginal re-tightening products
•Making dementia
I've wasted my whole life.
BEEP
COSMO
I spent all of it waiting for a hottie to validate my existence via his dick in me.
BEEP
Only to endure humiliation after humiliation, endless sexual disappointment
BEEP
When all I needed to do was just ask, politely and directly.
SOMEONE PLEASE HAVE SEX WITH ME
THE ZINE
"A cumming of age tale"
BEEP
If only I knew this say, 79 years ago
Nurse, please distribute my zine and--
BEEEEEEEEEEEEEEEEEEEEE
WELCOME TO HELL
Hooray!!

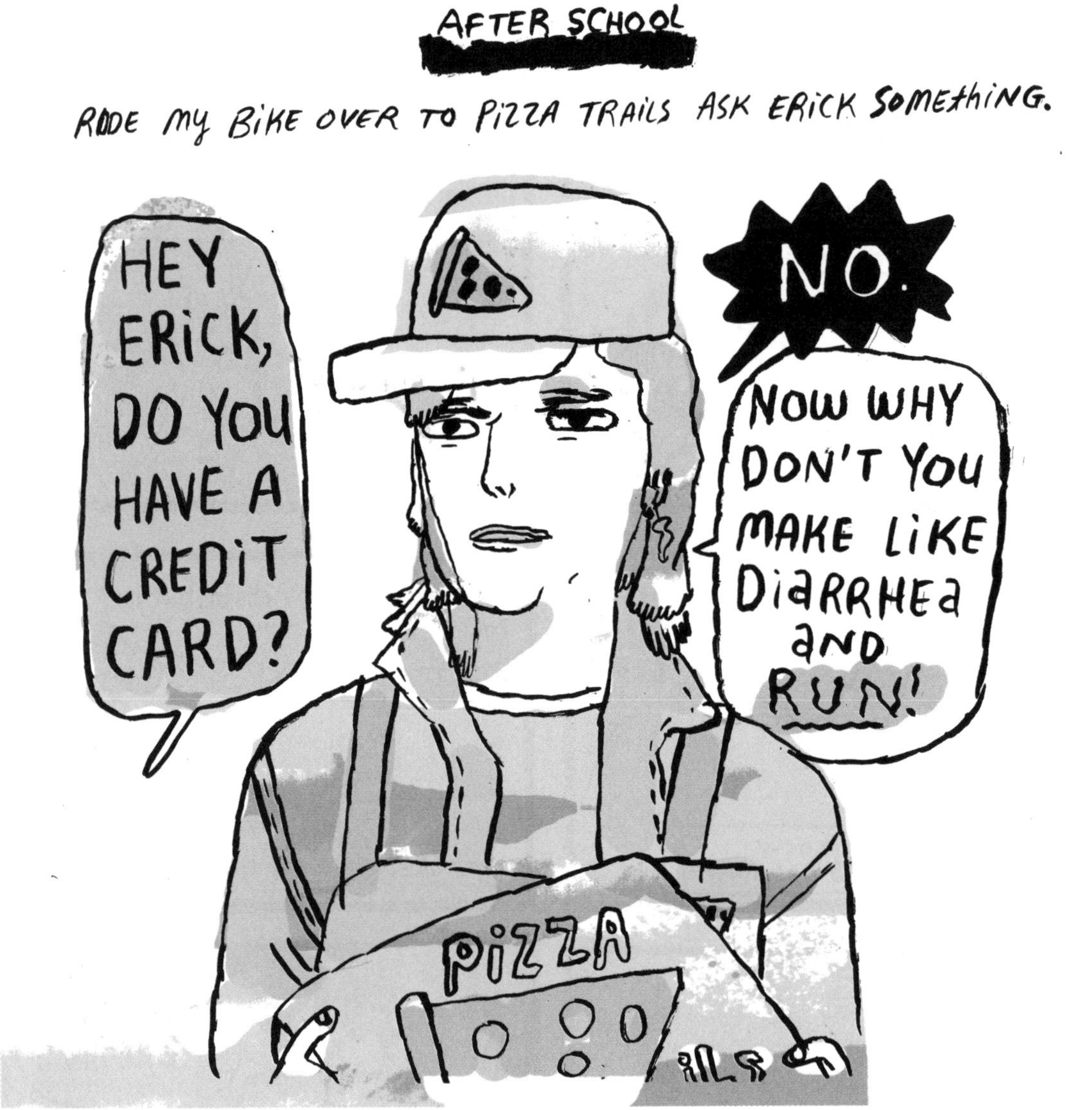
AFTER SCHOOL
RODE MY BIKE OVER TO PIZZA TRAILS ASK ERICK SOMETHING.
HEY ERICK, DO YOU HAVE A CREDIT CARD?
NO.
NOW WHY DON'T YOU MAKE LIKE DIARRHEA AND RUN!
PIZZA

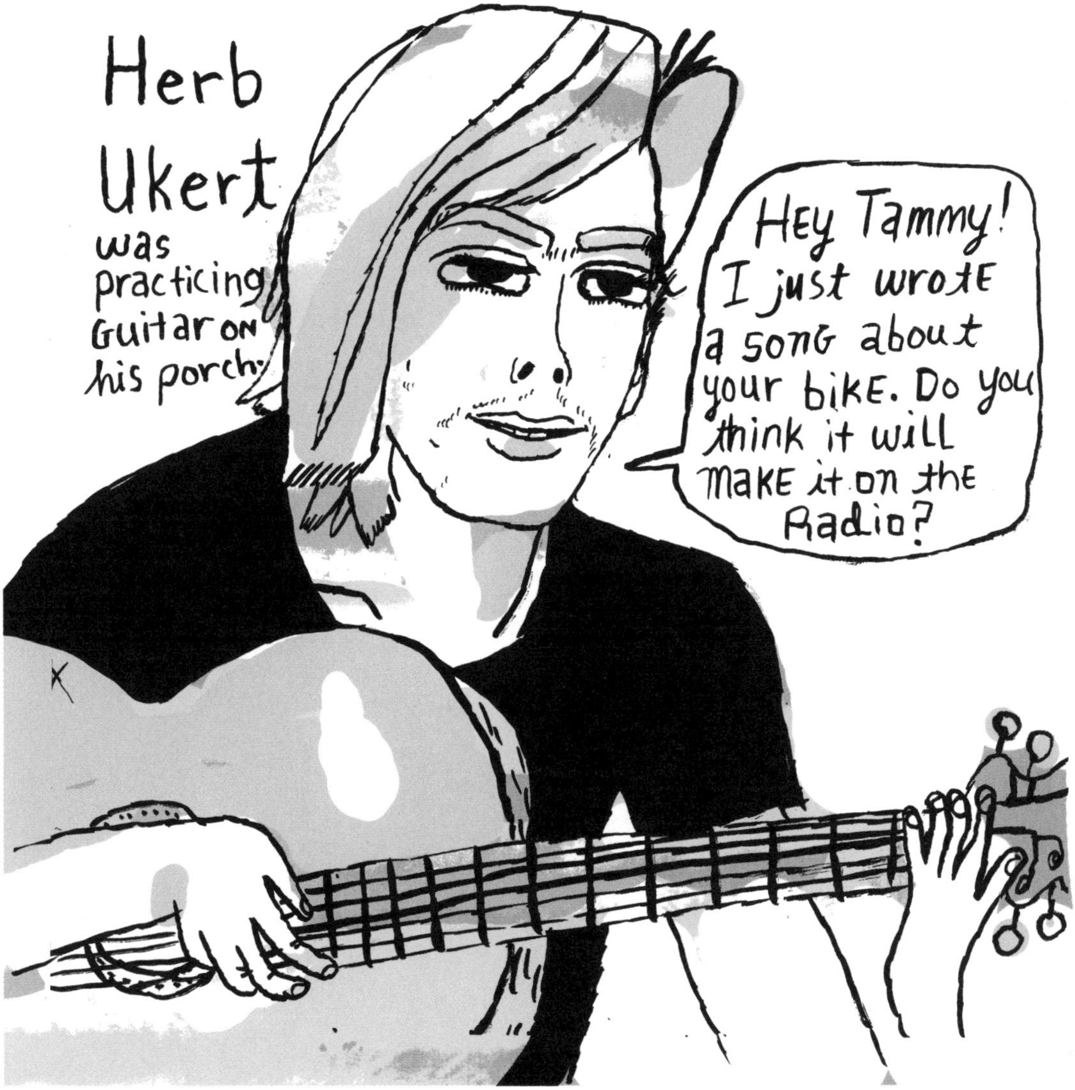
Herb Ukert was practicing Guitar on his porch.
Hey Tammy! I just wrote a song about your bike. Do you think it will make it on the Radio?

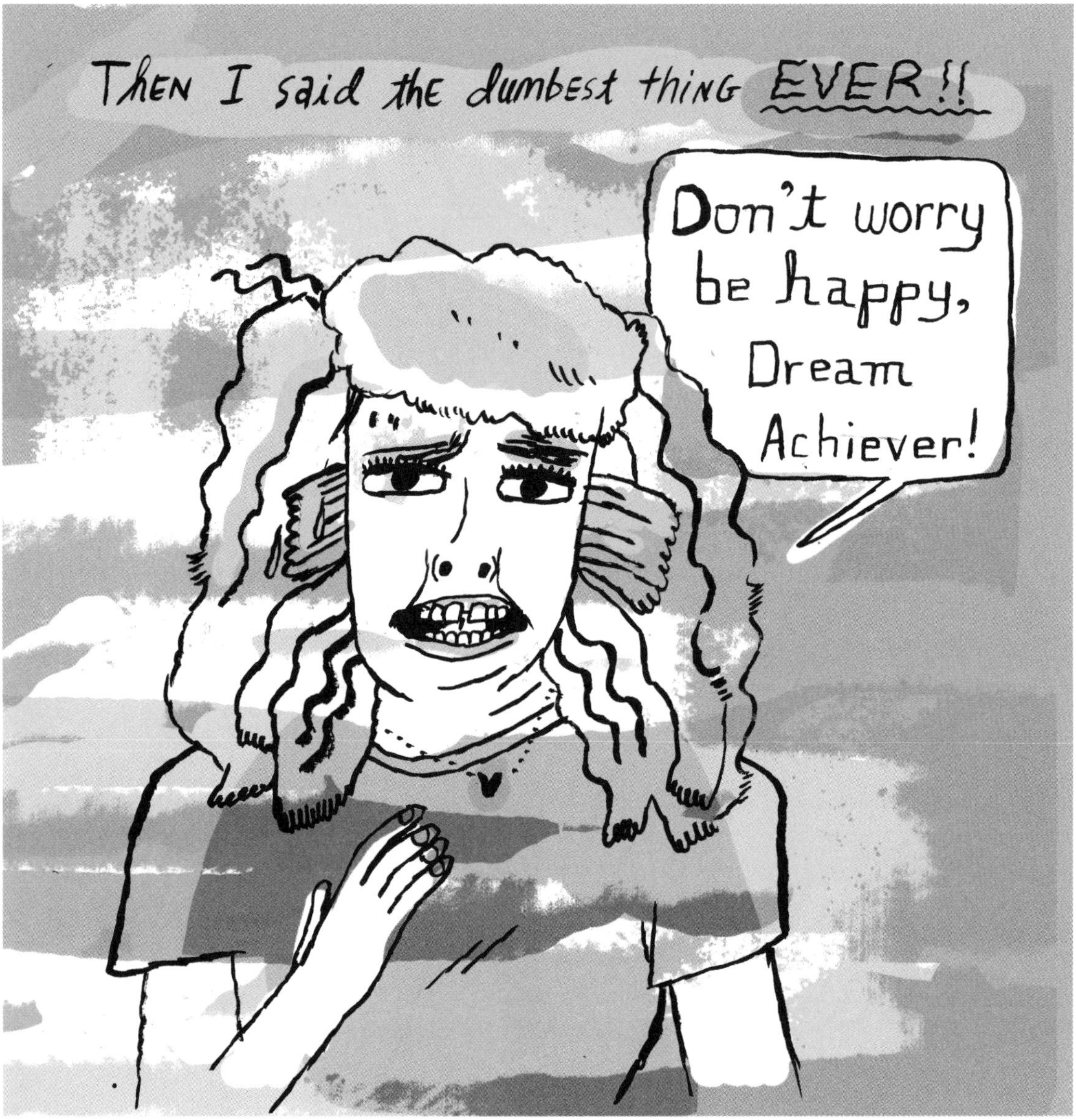
Then I said the dumbest thing EVER!!
Don't worry be happy, Dream Achiever!

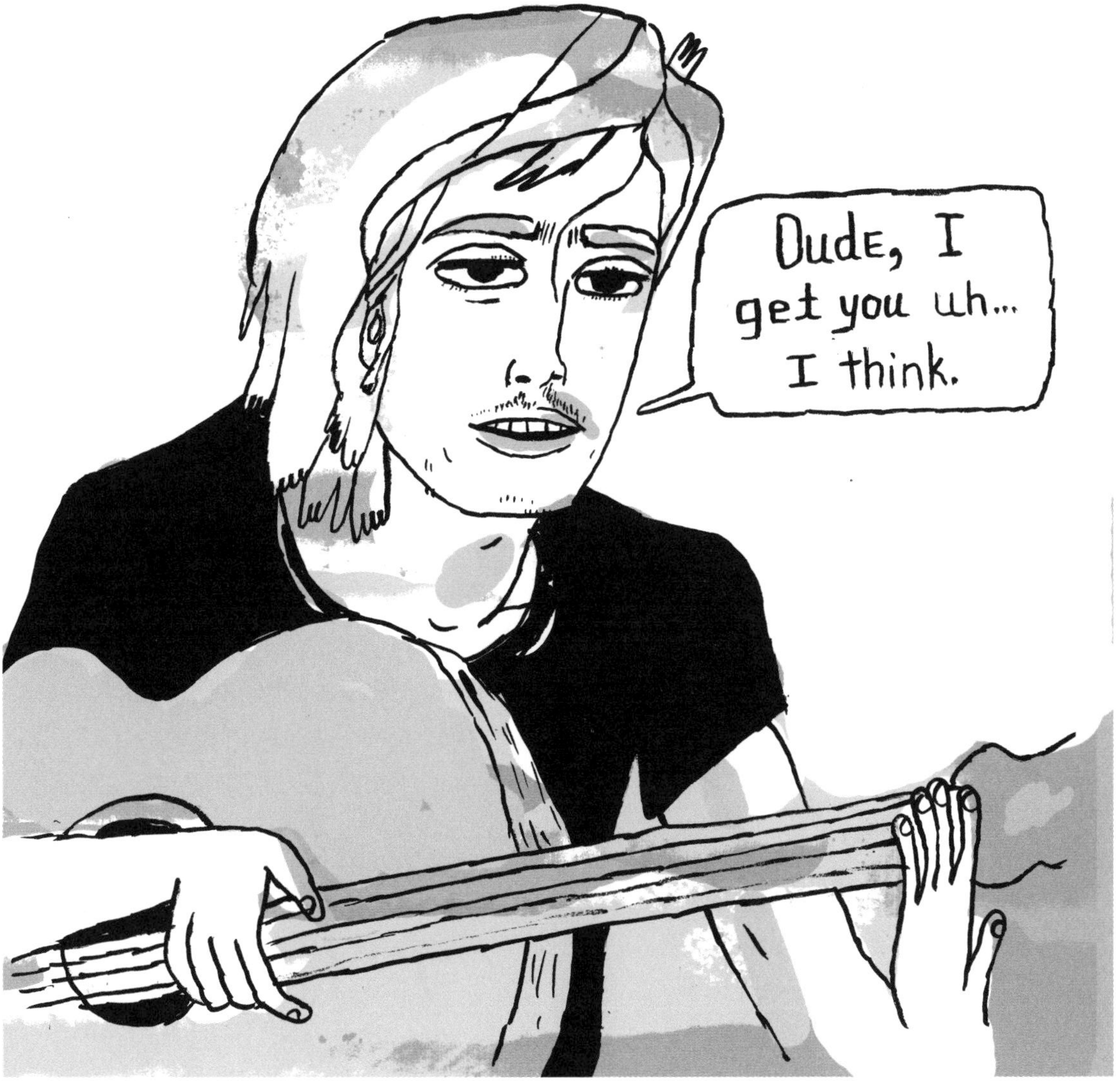
Dude, I get you uh... I think.

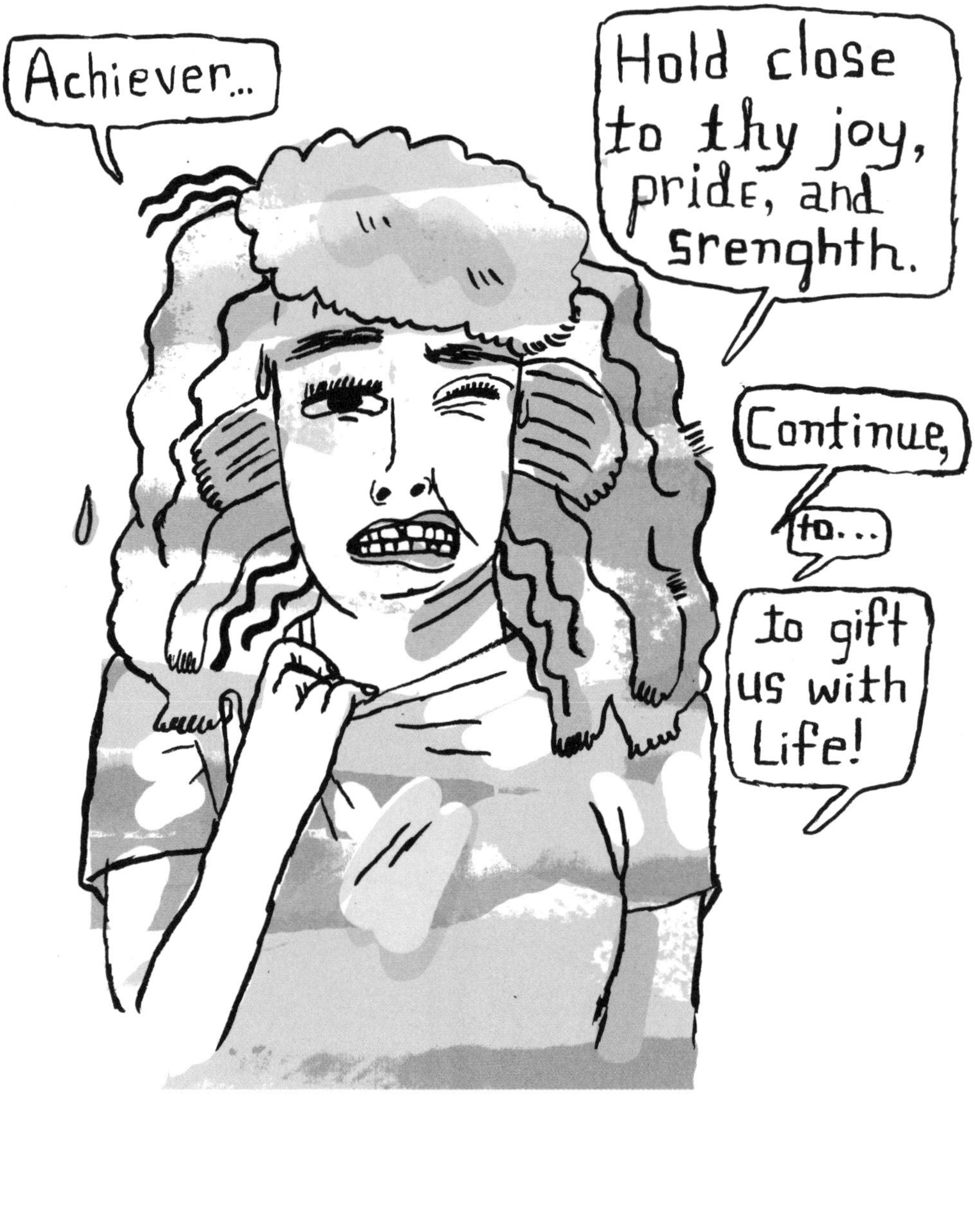
Achiever...
Hold close to thy joy, pride, and srenghth.
Continue,
to...
to gift us with Life!

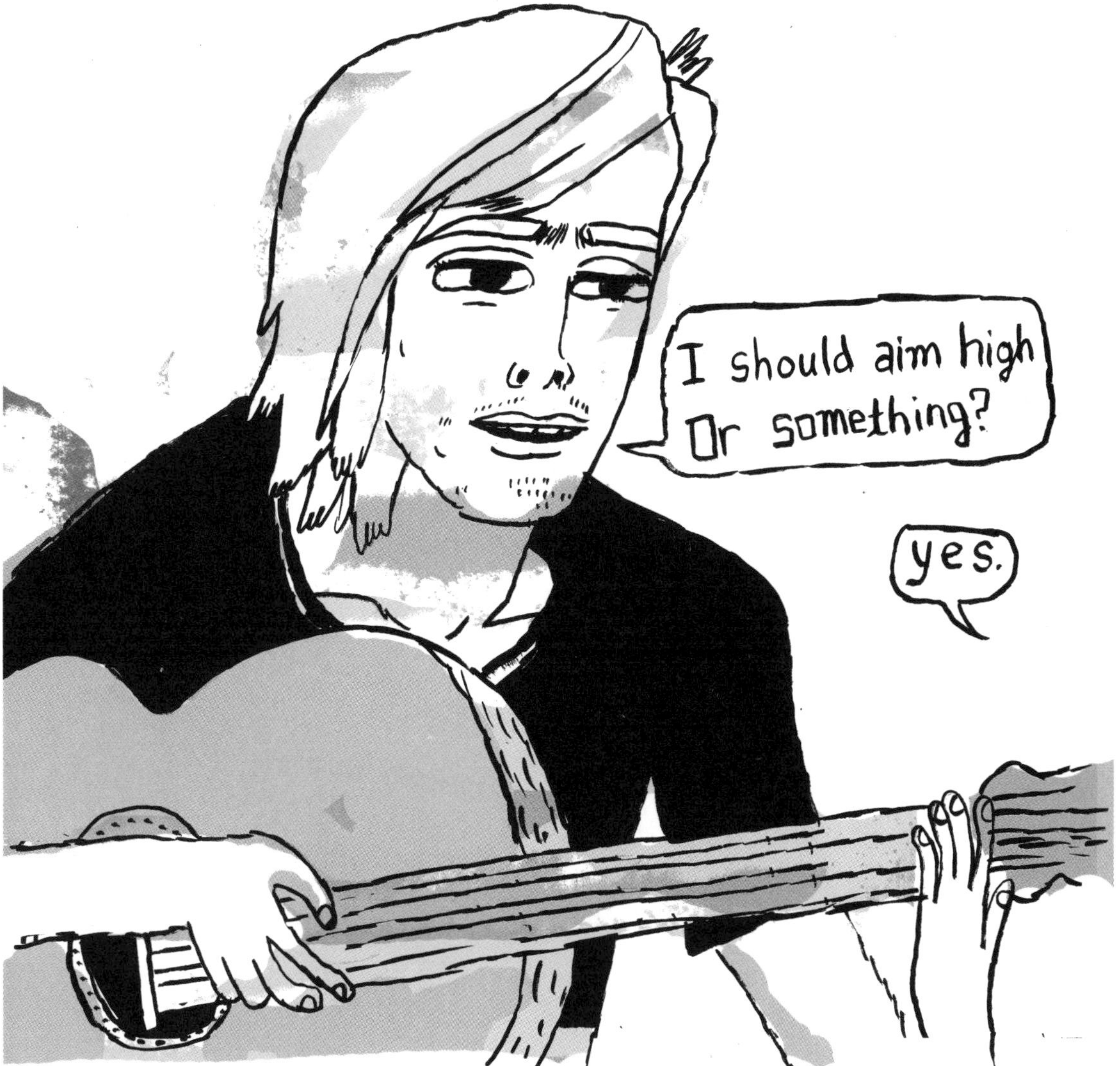
I should aim high
Or something?
yes.

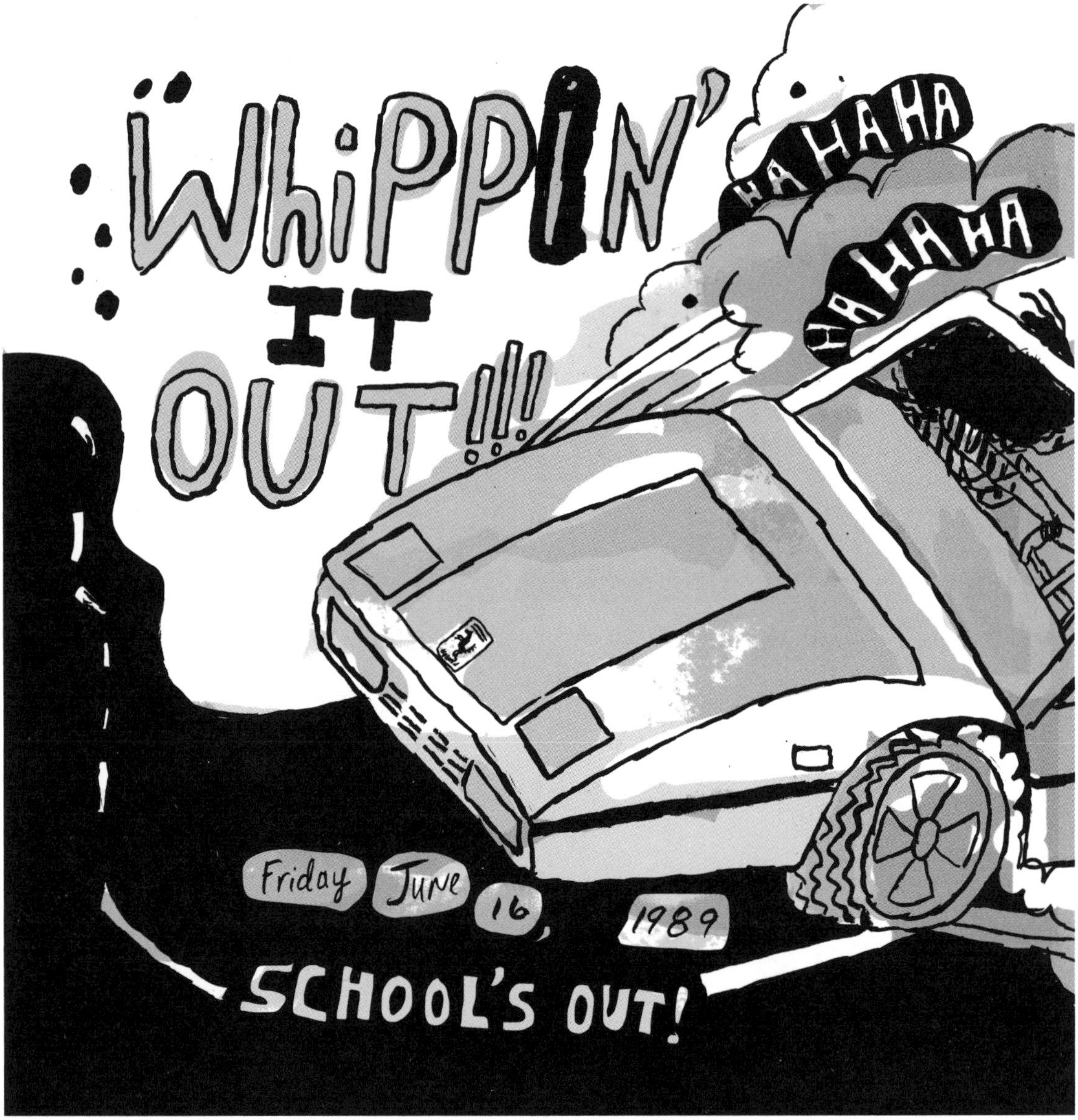
WHIPPIN' IT OUT!!!
HA HA HA HA
HA HA HA HA
Friday June 16, 1989
SCHOOL'S OUT!

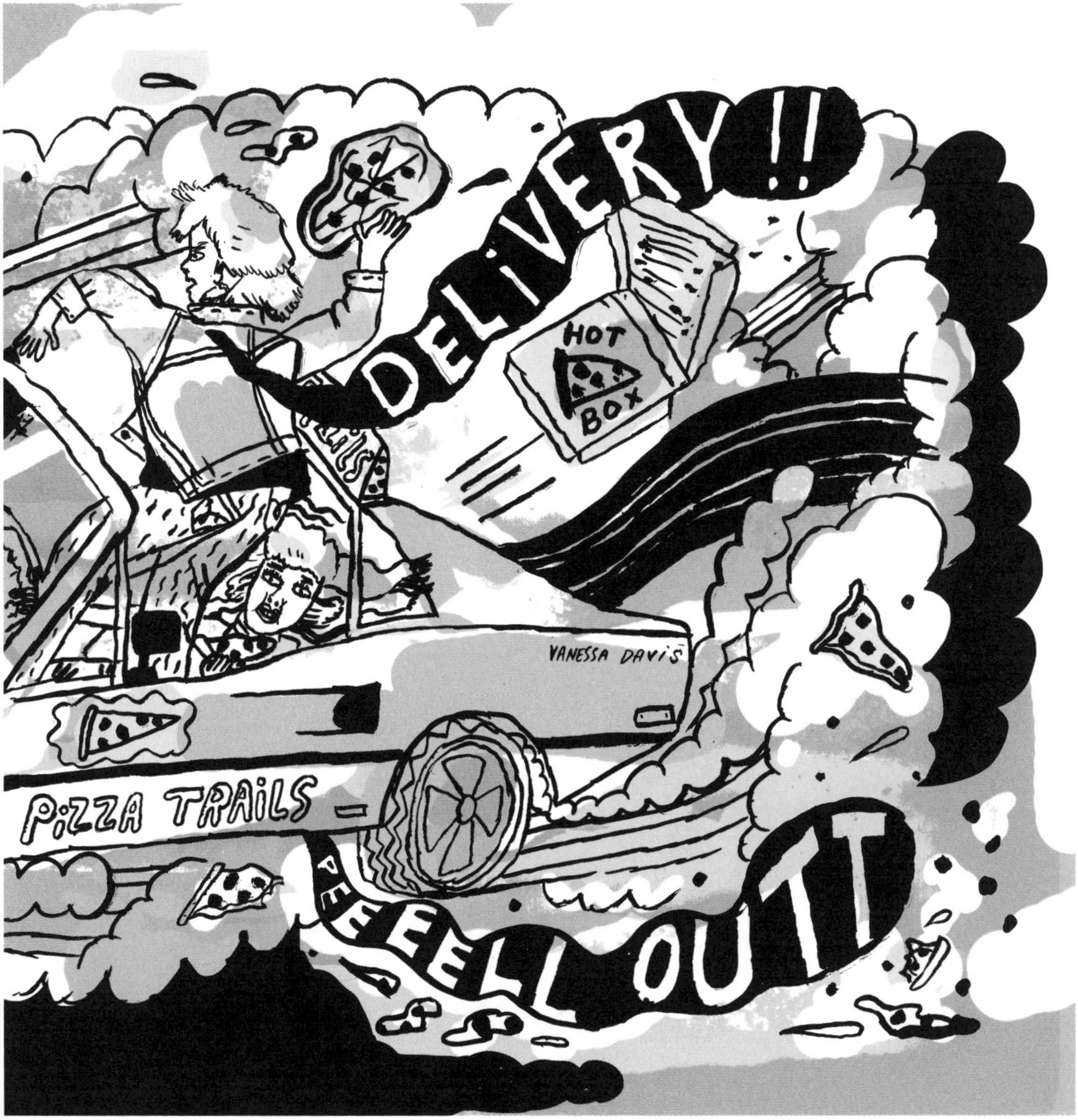
DELIVERY!!
HOT BOX
VANESSA DAVIS
PIZZA TRAILS
PEEEELL OUTT

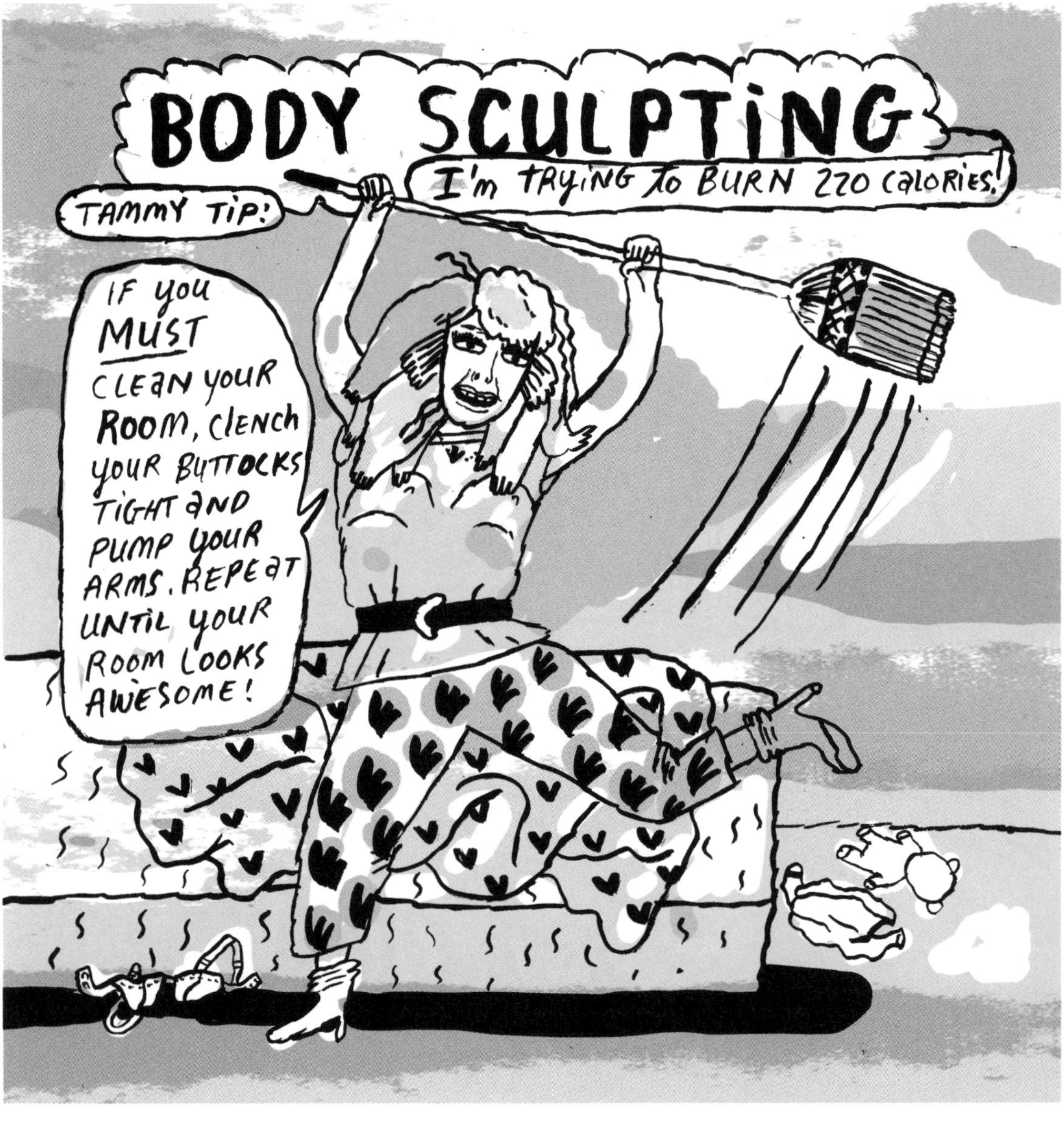
BODY SCULPTING
I'm TRYING to BURN 220 calories!
TAMMY TIP!
IF you MUST CLEAN your ROOM, clench your BUTTOCKS TIGHT and PUMP your ARMS. REPEAT UNTIL your ROOM LOOKS AWESOME!

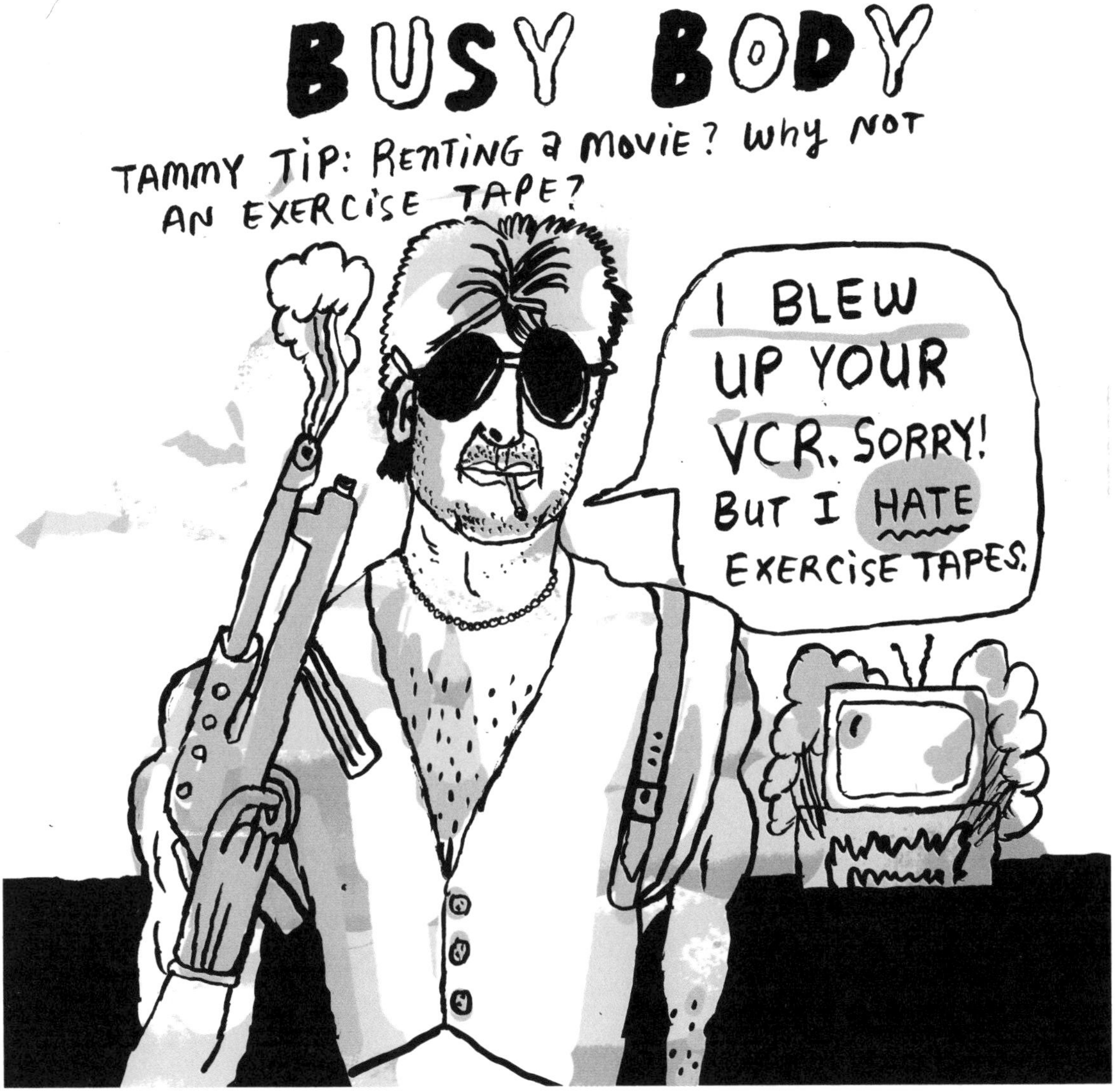
BUSY BODY
TAMMY TIP: RENTING a MOVIE? WHY NOT AN EXERCISE TAPE?
I BLEW UP YOUR VCR. SORRY! BUT I HATE EXERCISE TAPES.

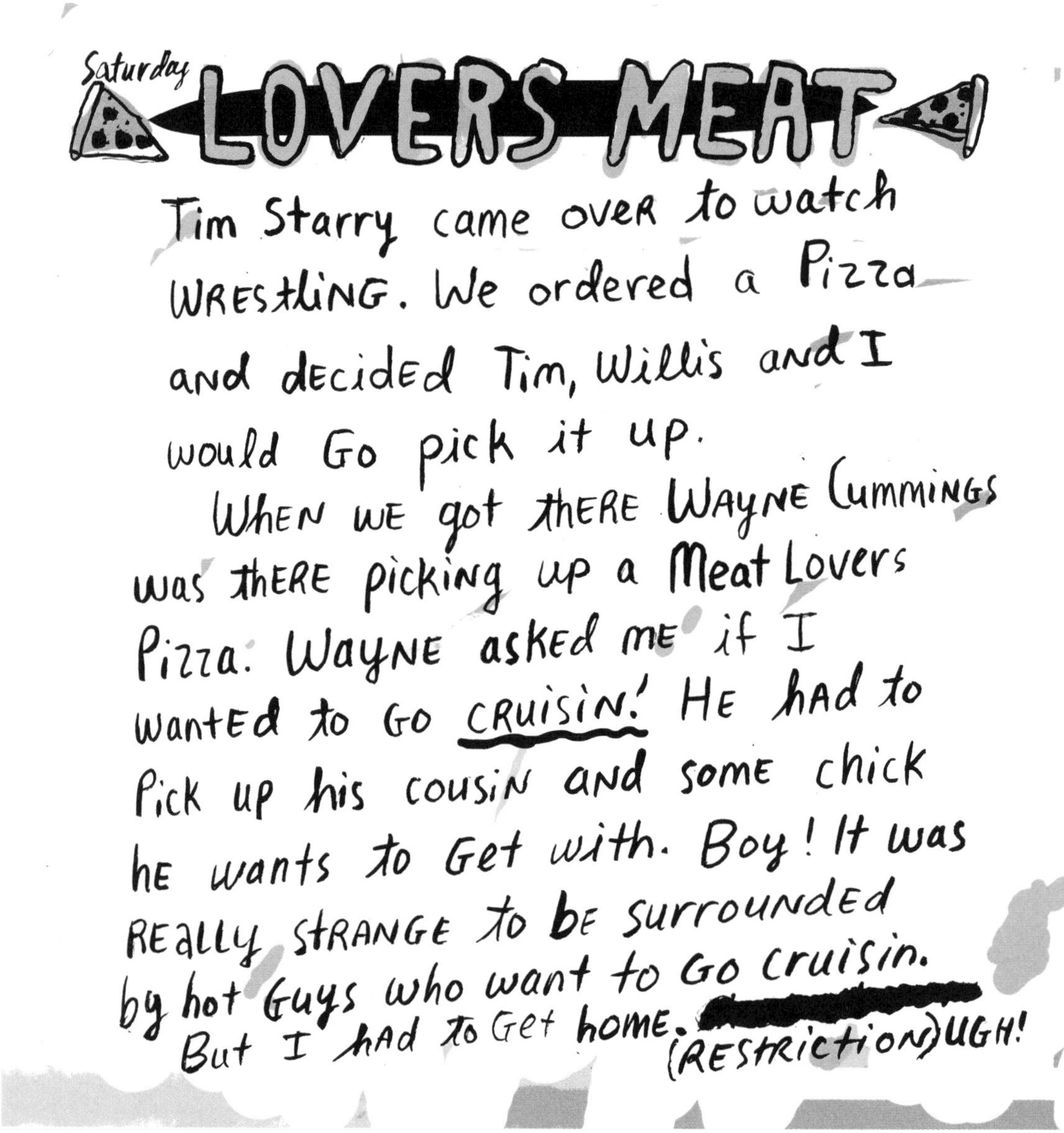
Saturday
LOVERS MEAT
Tim Starry came over to watch WRESTLING. We ordered a Pizza and decided Tim, Willis and I would Go pick it up.
When we got there Wayne Cummings was there picking up a Meat Lovers Pizza. Wayne asked me if I wanted to Go CRUISIN! He had to Pick up his cousin and some chick he wants to Get with. Boy! It was REALLY STRANGE to be surrounded by hot Guys who want to Go cruisin.
But I had to Get home. [redacted] (RESTRICTION) UGH!

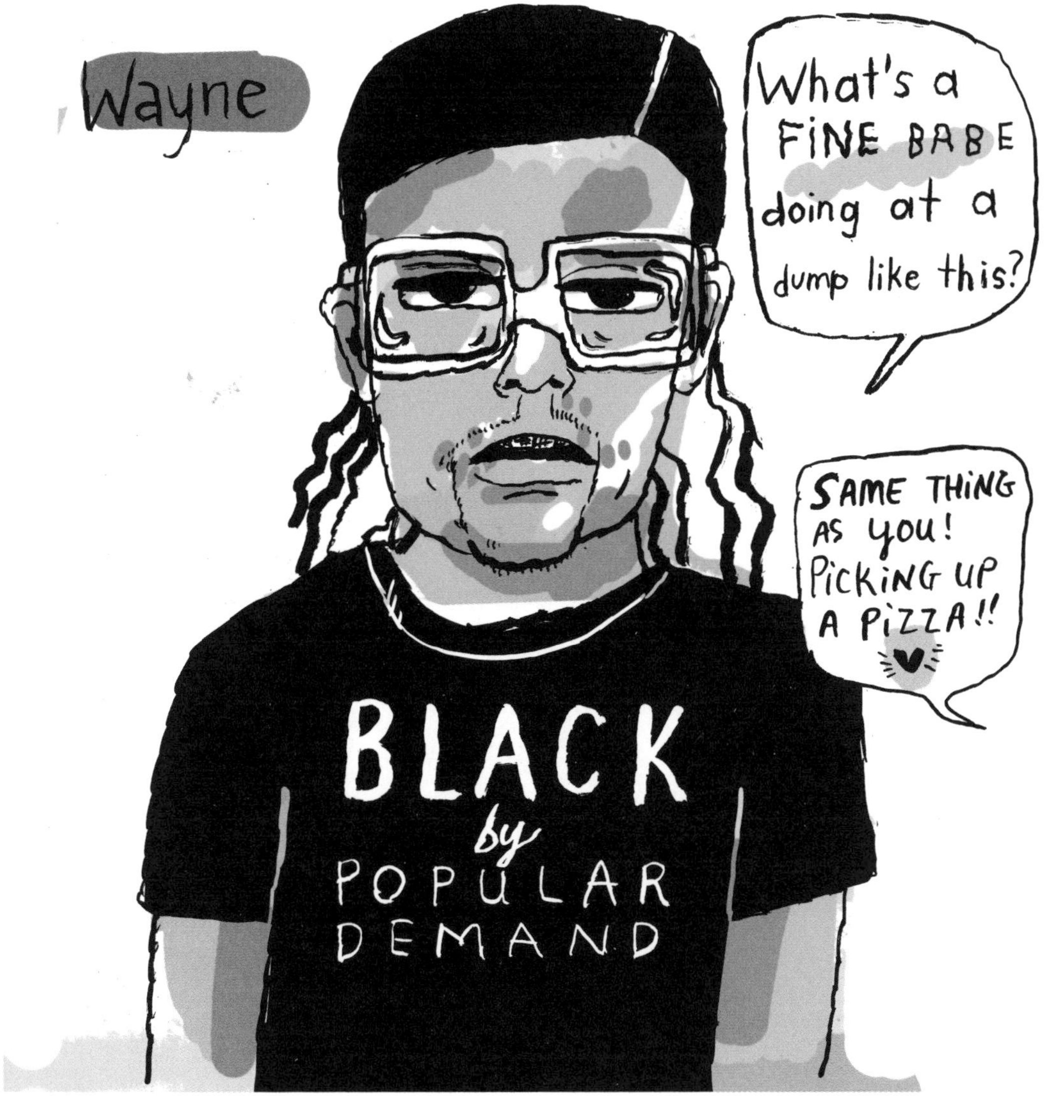
Wayne
What's a FINE BABE doing at a dump like this?
SAME THING AS YOU! PICKING UP A PIZZA!!
BLACK by POPULAR DEMAND

CHAPTER NINE

The Way We Live Now

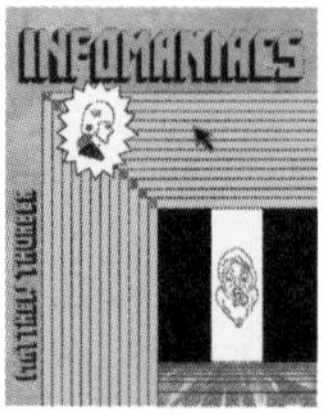
INFOMANIACS

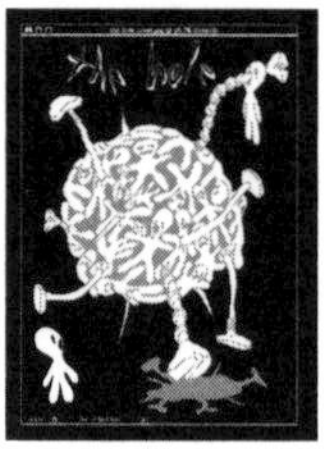
the hole

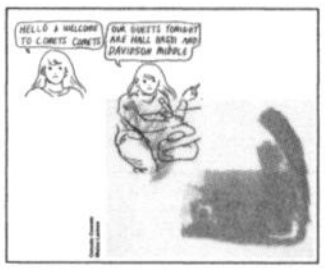

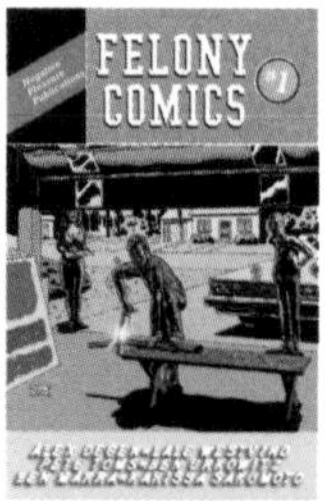
FELONY COMICS
#1

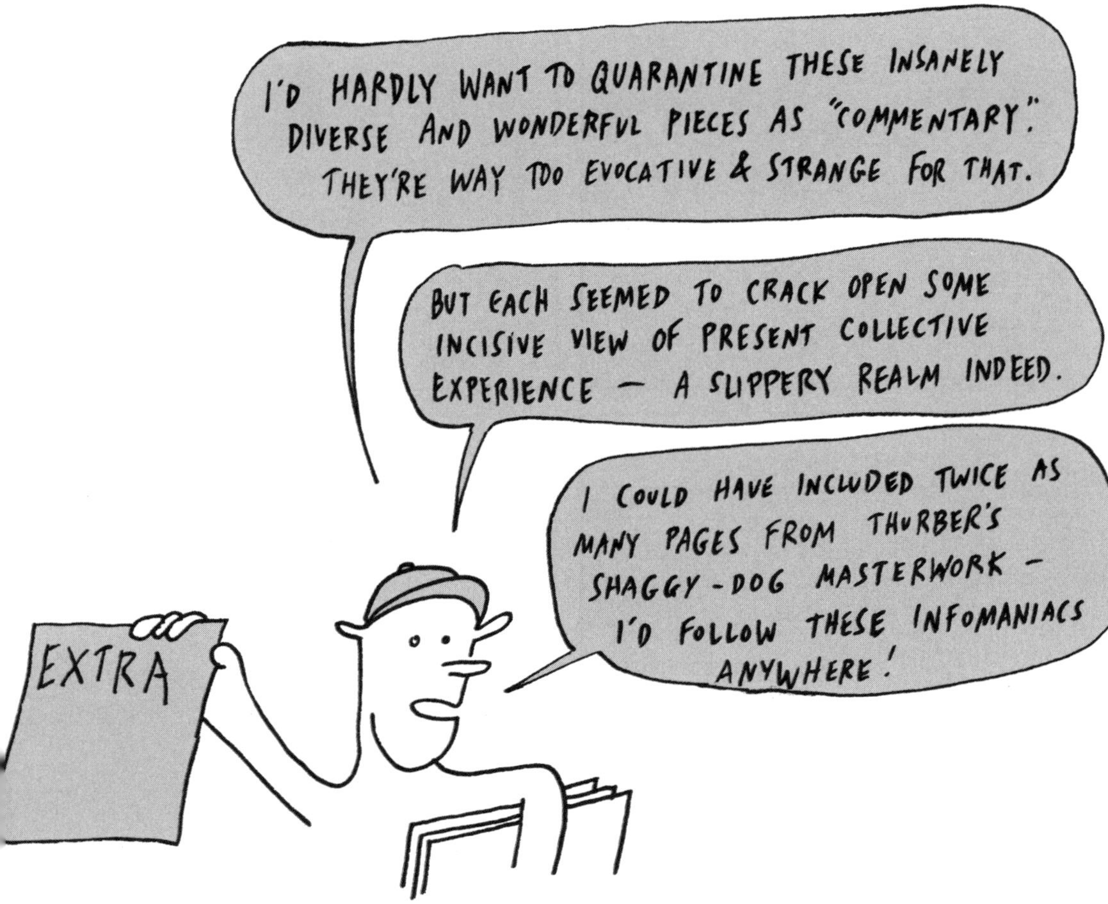
I'D HARDLY WANT TO QUARANTINE THESE INSANELY DIVERSE AND WONDERFUL PIECES AS "COMMENTARY." THEY'RE WAY TOO EVOCATIVE & STRANGE FOR THAT.
BUT EACH SEEMED TO CRACK OPEN SOME INCISIVE VIEW OF PRESENT COLLECTIVE EXPERIENCE — A SLIPPERY REALM INDEED.
I COULD HAVE INCLUDED TWICE AS MANY PAGES FROM THURBER'S SHAGGY-DOG MASTERWORK — I'D FOLLOW THESE INFOMANIACS ANYWHERE!
EXTRA

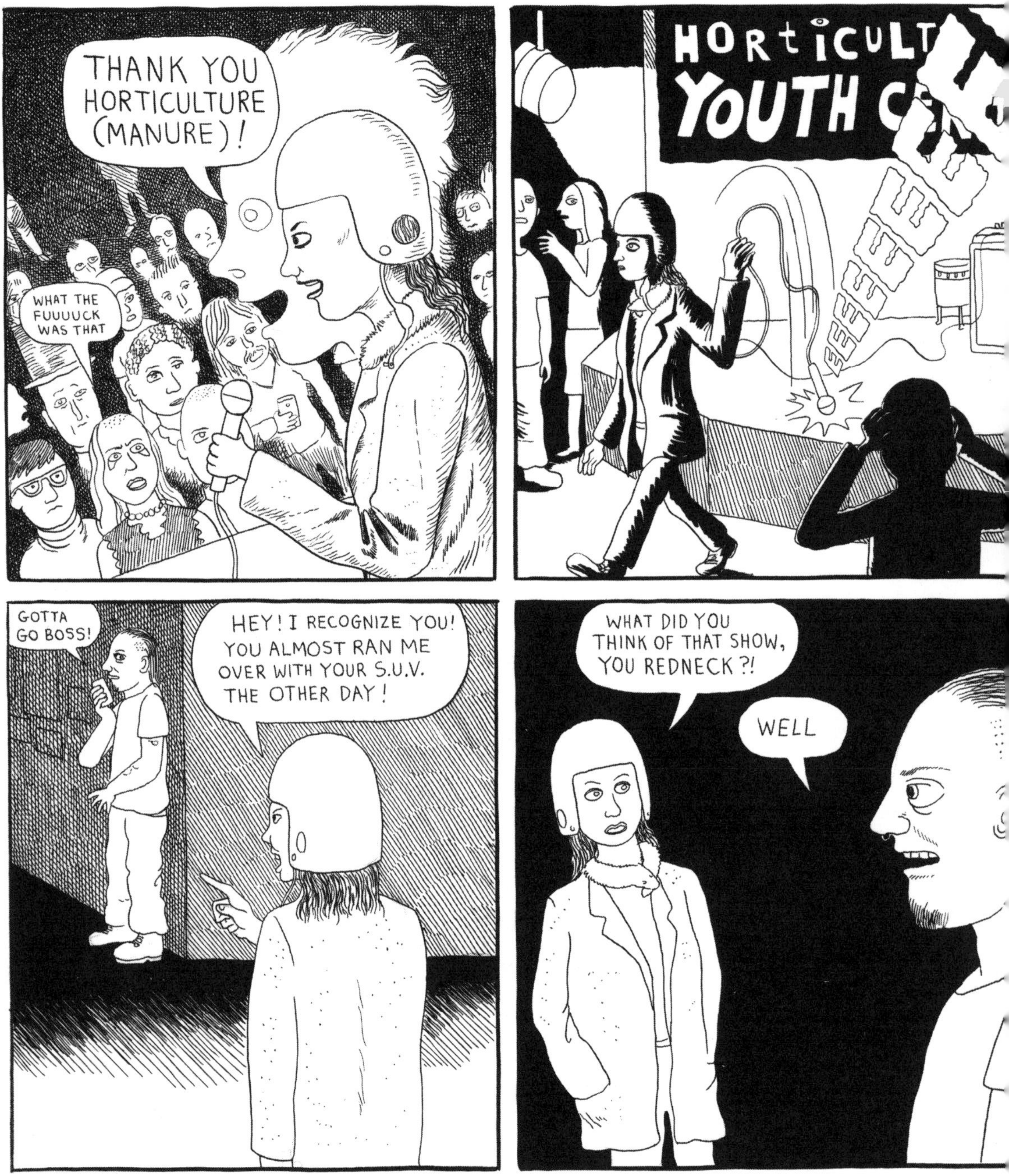
THANK YOU HORTICULTURE (MANURE)!
WHAT THE FUUUUCK WAS THAT
HORtiCULT
YOUTH C
GOTTA GO BOSS!
HEY! I RECOGNIZE YOU! YOU ALMOST RAN ME OVER WITH YOUR S.U.V. THE OTHER DAY!
WHAT DID YOU THINK OF THAT SHOW, YOU REDNECK?!
WELL

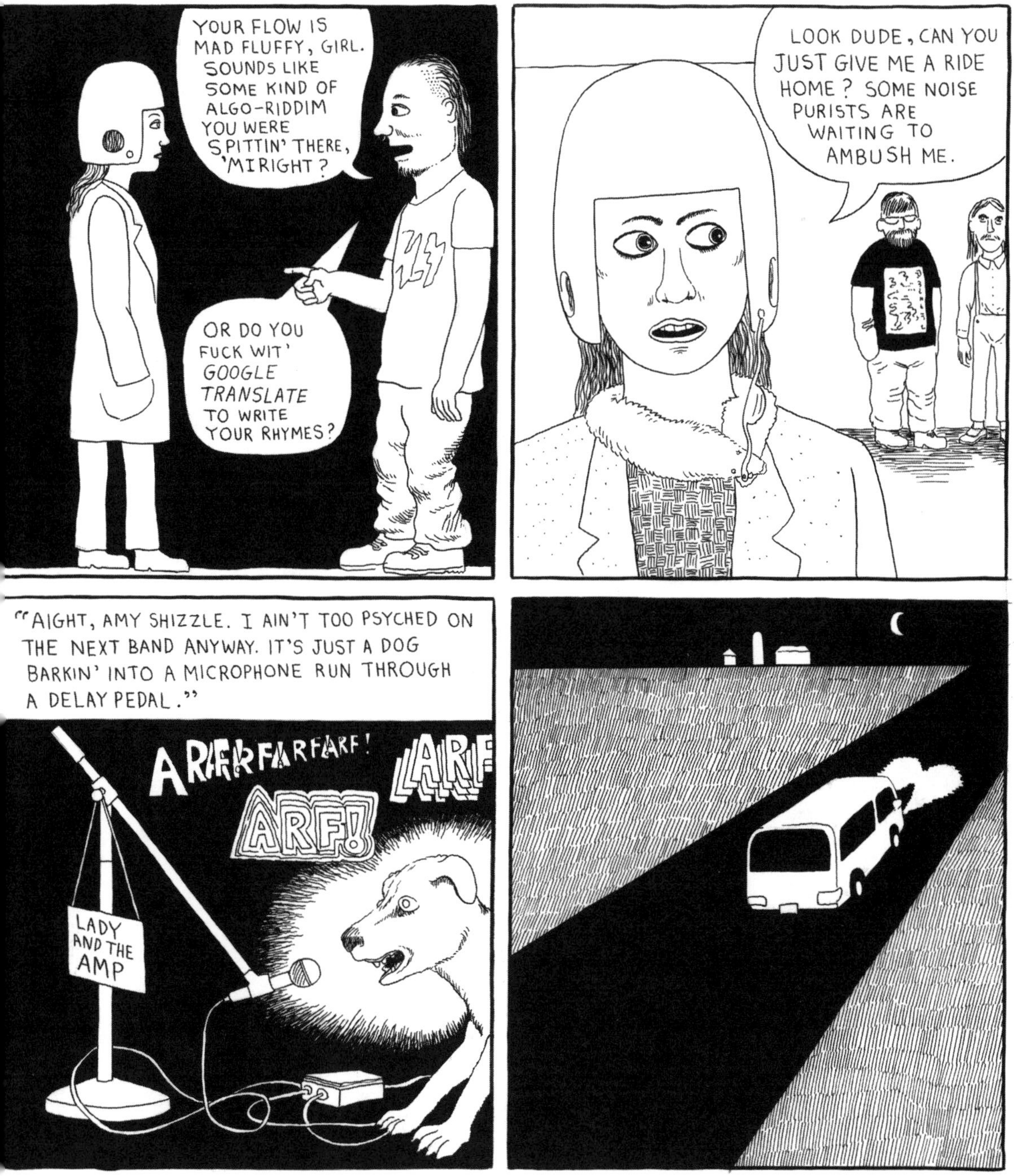
YOUR FLOW IS MAD FLUFFY, GIRL. SOUNDS LIKE SOME KIND OF ALGO-RIDDIM YOU WERE SPITTIN' THERE, 'MIRIGHT?
OR DO YOU FUCK WIT' GOOGLE TRANSLATE TO WRITE YOUR RHYMES?
LOOK DUDE, CAN YOU JUST GIVE ME A RIDE HOME? SOME NOISE PURISTS ARE WAITING TO AMBUSH ME.
"AIGHT, AMY SHIZZLE. I AIN'T TOO PSYCHED ON THE NEXT BAND ANYWAY. IT'S JUST A DOG BARKIN' INTO A MICROPHONE RUN THROUGH A DELAY PEDAL."
ARFARFARFARF!
ARF!
LADY AND THE AMP

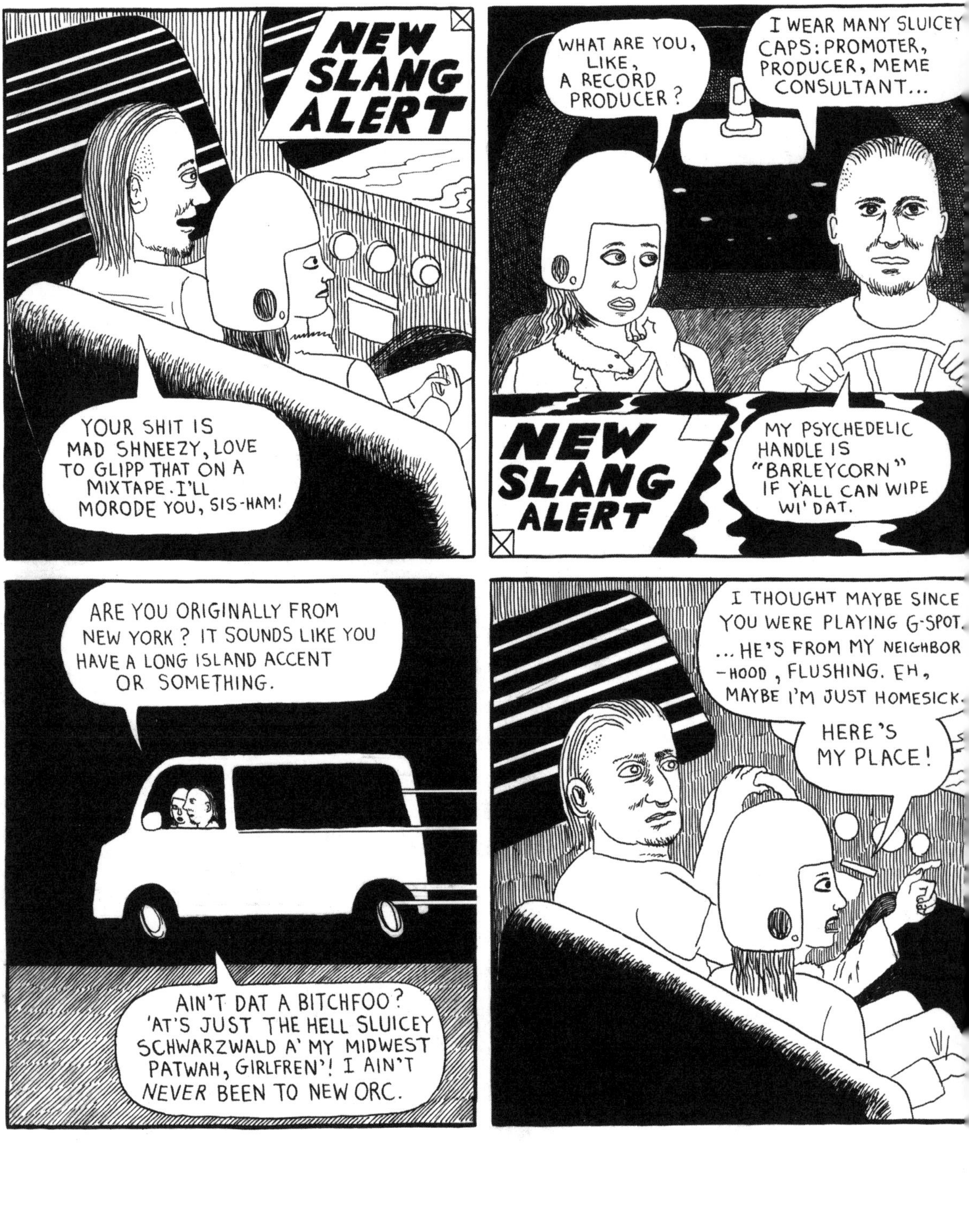
NEW SLANG ALERT
YOUR SHIT IS MAD SHNEEZY, LOVE TO GLIPP THAT ON A MIXTAPE. I'LL MORODE YOU, SIS-HAM!
WHAT ARE YOU, LIKE, A RECORD PRODUCER?
I WEAR MANY SLUICEY CAPS: PROMOTER, PRODUCER, MEME CONSULTANT...
NEW SLANG ALERT
MY PSYCHEDELIC HANDLE IS "BARLEYCORN" IF Y'ALL CAN WIPE WI' DAT.
ARE YOU ORIGINALLY FROM NEW YORK? IT SOUNDS LIKE YOU HAVE A LONG ISLAND ACCENT OR SOMETHING.
AIN'T DAT A BITCHFOO? 'AT'S JUST THE HELL SLUICEY SCHWARZWALD A' MY MIDWEST PATWAH, GIRLFREN'! I AIN'T *NEVER* BEEN TO NEW ORC.
I THOUGHT MAYBE SINCE YOU WERE PLAYING G-SPOT. ... HE'S FROM MY NEIGHBOR-HOOD, FLUSHING. EH, MAYBE I'M JUST HOMESICK.
HERE'S MY PLACE!

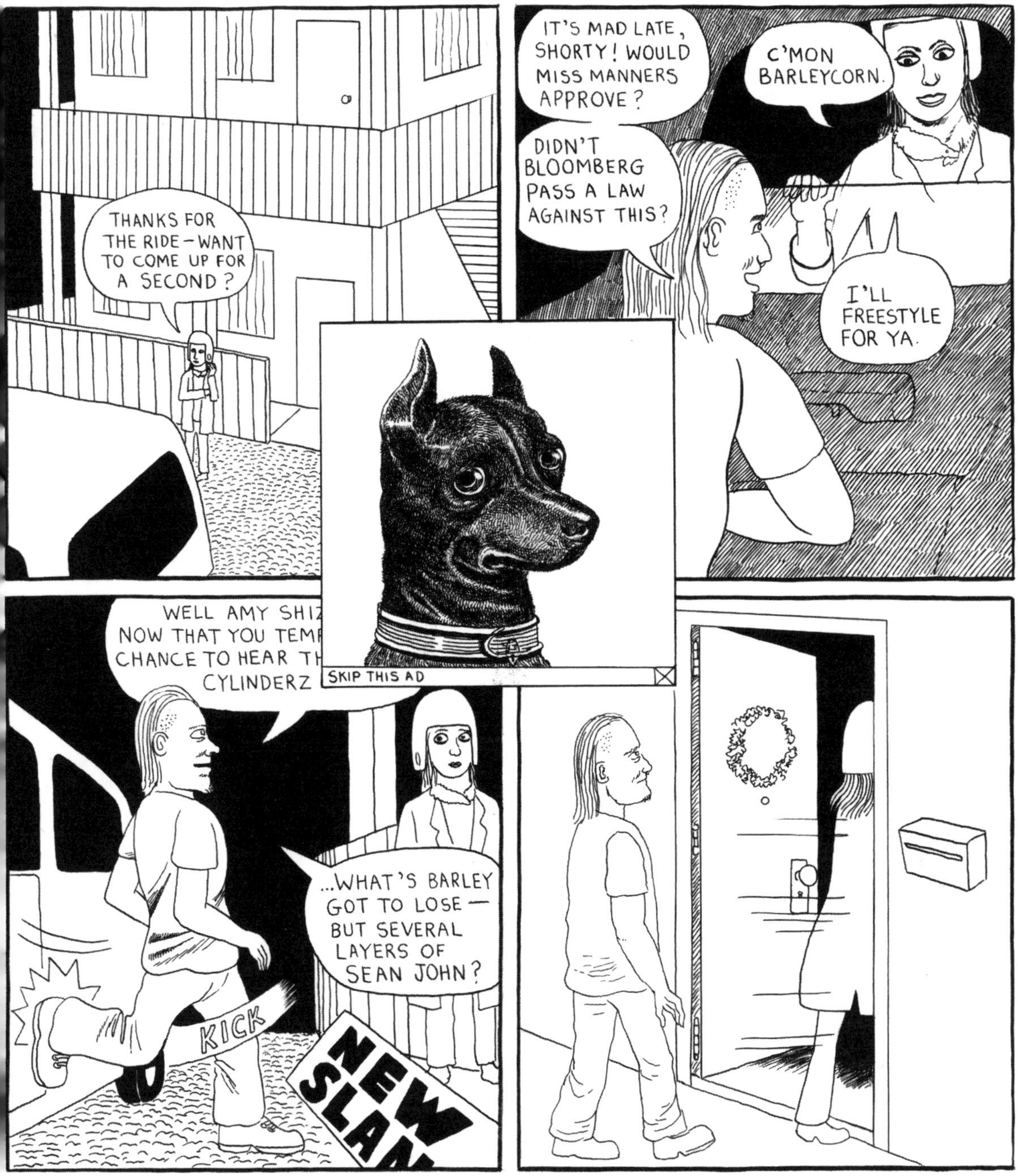

THANKS FOR THE RIDE—WANT TO COME UP FOR A SECOND?
IT'S MAD LATE, SHORTY! WOULD MISS MANNERS APPROVE?
DIDN'T BLOOMBERG PASS A LAW AGAINST THIS?
C'MON BARLEYCORN.
I'LL FREESTYLE FOR YA.
SKIP THIS AD
WELL AMY SHIZ
NOW THAT YOU TEMP
CHANCE TO HEAR TH
CYLINDERZ
...WHAT'S BARLEY GOT TO LOSE— BUT SEVERAL LAYERS OF SEAN JOHN?
KICK
NEW
SLAN

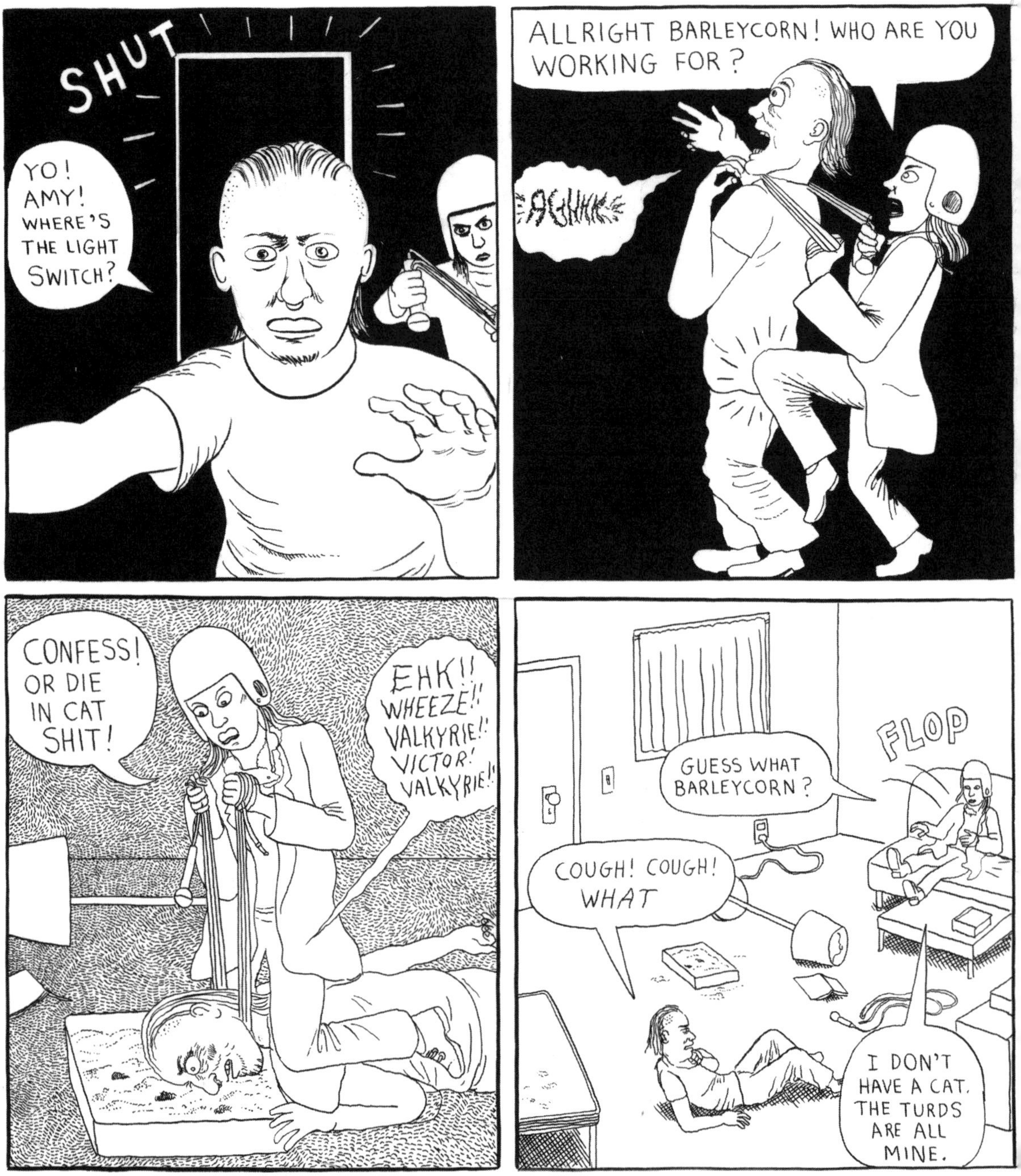
SHUT
YO! AMY! WHERE'S THE LIGHT SWITCH?
ALLRIGHT BARLEYCORN! WHO ARE YOU WORKING FOR?
CONFESS! OR DIE IN CAT SHIT!
EHK!! WHEEZE!! VALKYRIE!! VICTOR! VALKYRIE!!
FLOP
GUESS WHAT BARLEYCORN?
COUGH! COUGH! WHAT
I DON'T HAVE A CAT. THE TURDS ARE ALL MINE.

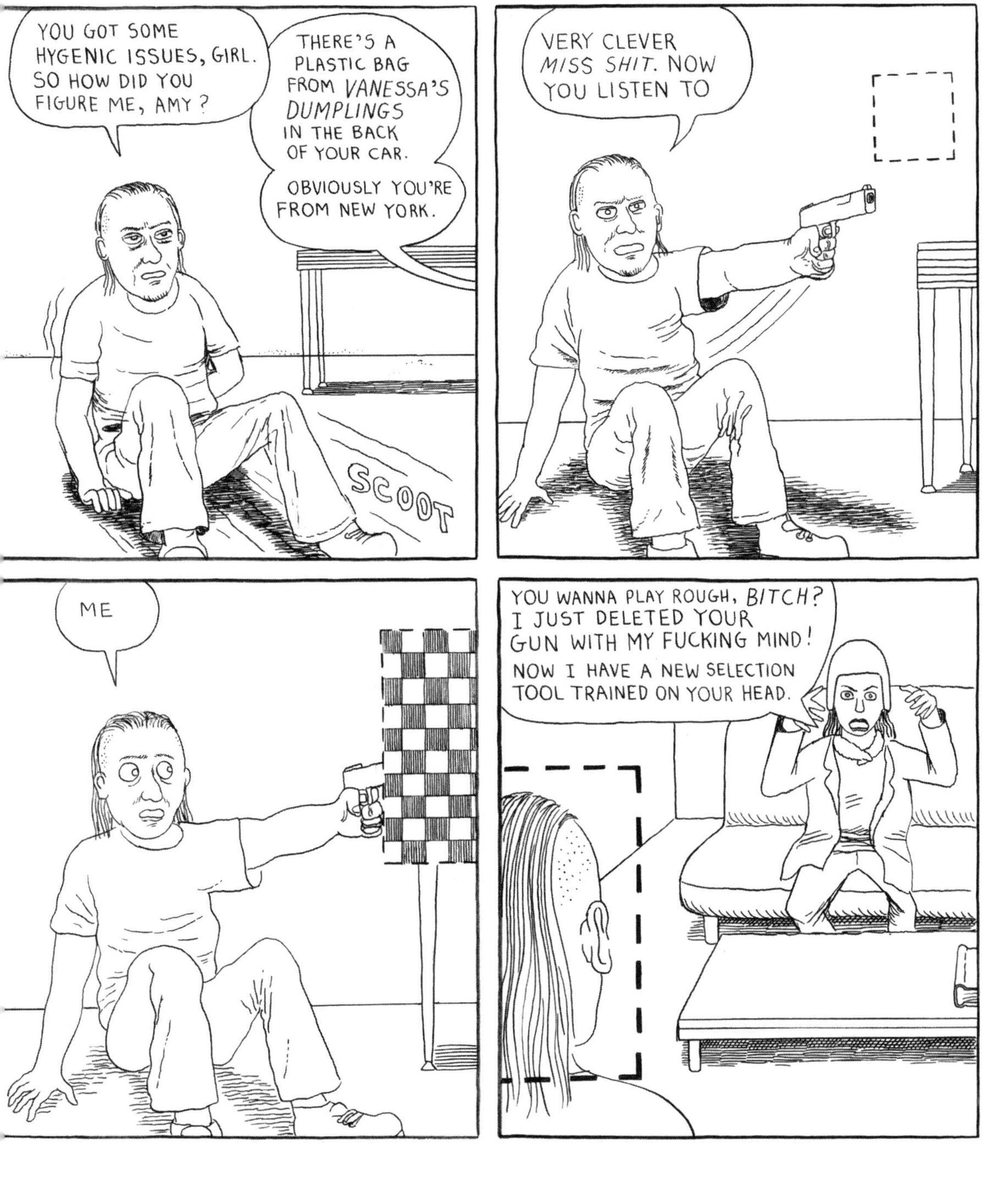
YOU GOT SOME HYGENIC ISSUES, GIRL. SO HOW DID YOU FIGURE ME, AMY?
THERE'S A PLASTIC BAG FROM VANESSA'S DUMPLINGS IN THE BACK OF YOUR CAR.
OBVIOUSLY YOU'RE FROM NEW YORK.
SCOOT
VERY CLEVER MISS SHIT. NOW YOU LISTEN TO
ME
YOU WANNA PLAY ROUGH, BITCH? I JUST DELETED YOUR GUN WITH MY FUCKING MIND!
NOW I HAVE A NEW SELECTION TOOL TRAINED ON YOUR HEAD.

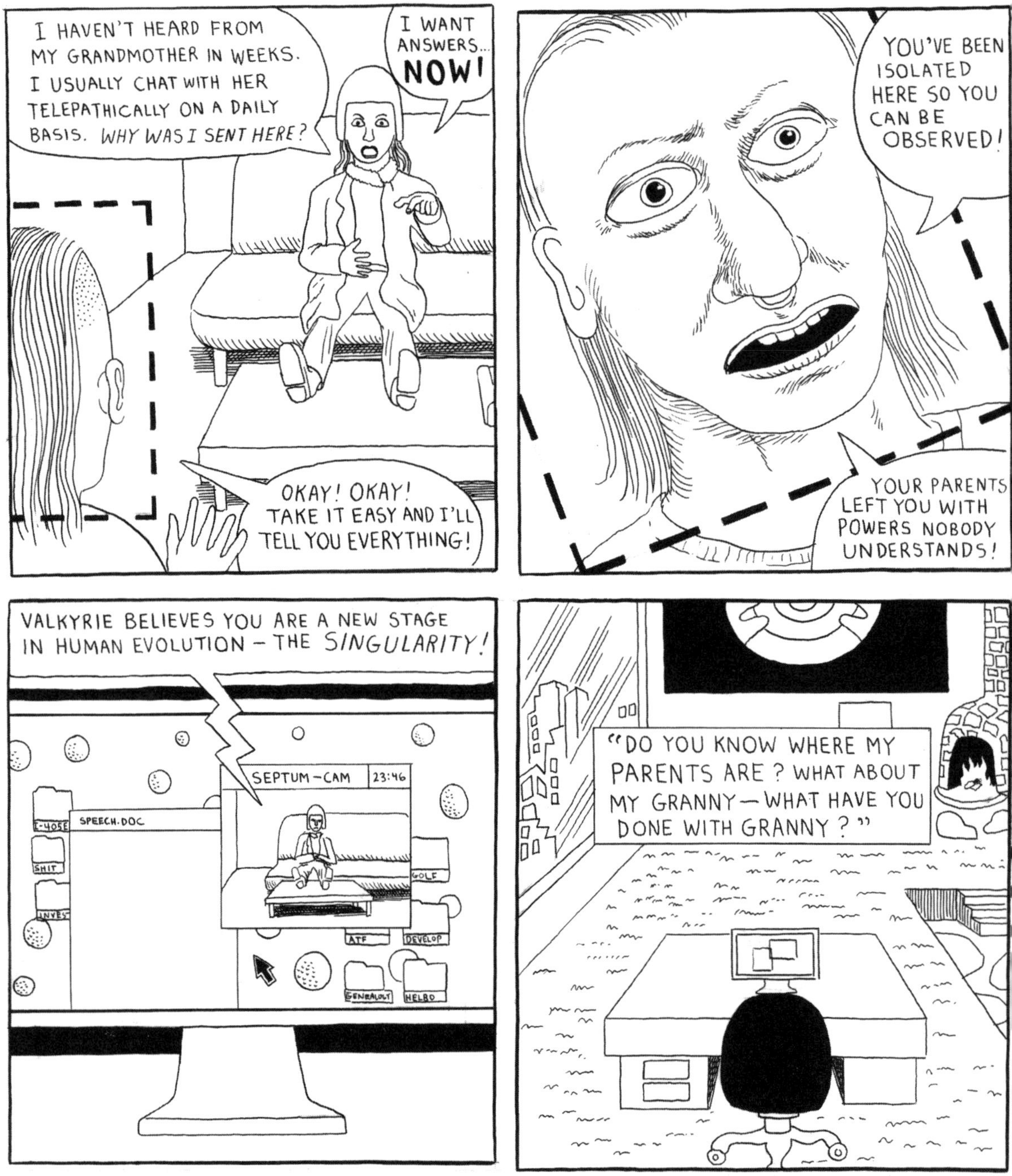

I HAVEN'T HEARD FROM MY GRANDMOTHER IN WEEKS. I USUALLY CHAT WITH HER TELEPATHICALLY ON A DAILY BASIS. *WHY WAS I SENT HERE?*
I WANT ANSWERS... **NOW!**
OKAY! OKAY! TAKE IT EASY AND I'LL TELL YOU EVERYTHING!
YOU'VE BEEN ISOLATED HERE SO YOU CAN BE OBSERVED!
YOUR PARENTS LEFT YOU WITH POWERS NOBODY UNDERSTANDS!
VALKYRIE BELIEVES YOU ARE A NEW STAGE IN HUMAN EVOLUTION — THE *SINGULARITY!*
SEPTUM-CAM
23:46
SPEECH.DOC
SHIT
GOLF
ATF
DEVELOP
"DO YOU KNOW WHERE MY PARENTS ARE? WHAT ABOUT MY GRANNY— WHAT HAVE YOU DONE WITH GRANNY?"

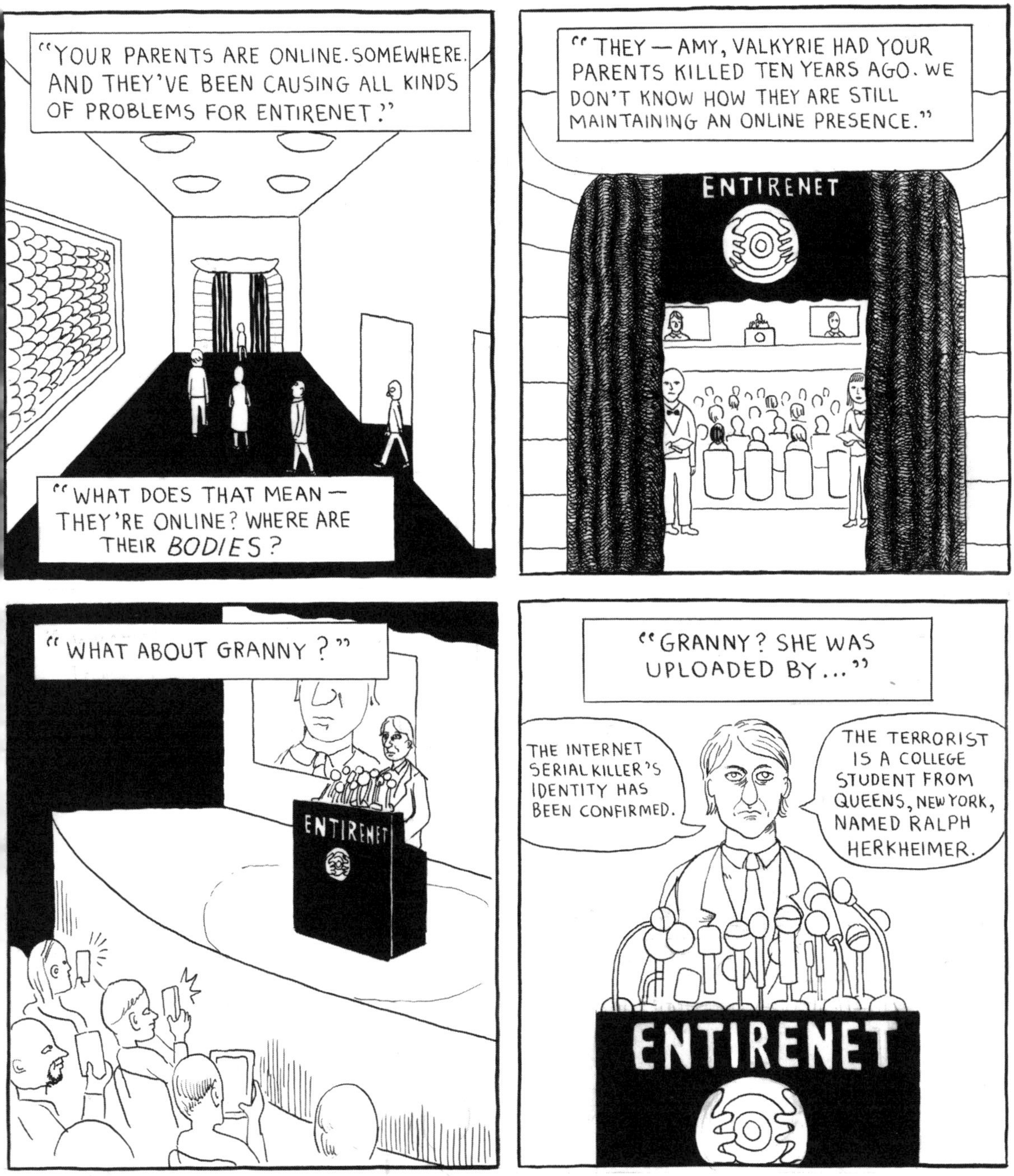
"YOUR PARENTS ARE ONLINE. SOMEWHERE. AND THEY'VE BEEN CAUSING ALL KINDS OF PROBLEMS FOR ENTIRENET."
"WHAT DOES THAT MEAN — THEY'RE ONLINE? WHERE ARE THEIR *BODIES*?
"THEY — AMY, VALKYRIE HAD YOUR PARENTS KILLED TEN YEARS AGO. WE DON'T KNOW HOW THEY ARE STILL MAINTAINING AN ONLINE PRESENCE."
ENTIRENET
"WHAT ABOUT GRANNY?"
ENTIRENET
"GRANNY? SHE WAS UPLOADED BY..."
THE INTERNET SERIAL KILLER'S IDENTITY HAS BEEN CONFIRMED.
THE TERRORIST IS A COLLEGE STUDENT FROM QUEENS, NEW YORK, NAMED RALPH HERKHEIMER.
ENTIRENET

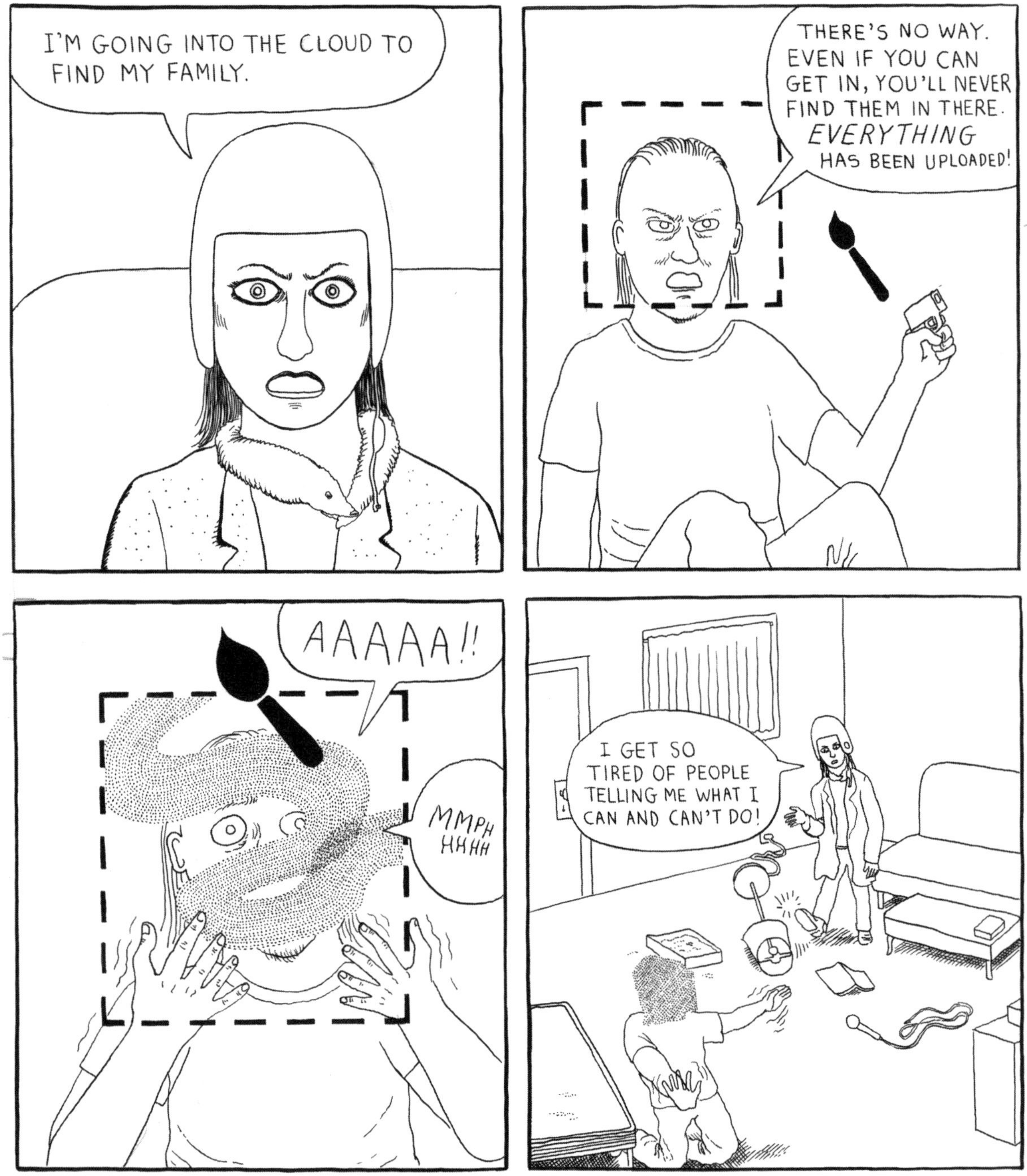
I'M GOING INTO THE CLOUD TO FIND MY FAMILY.
THERE'S NO WAY. EVEN IF YOU CAN GET IN, YOU'LL NEVER FIND THEM IN THERE. EVERYTHING HAS BEEN UPLOADED!
AAAAA!!
MMPHHHHH
I GET SO TIRED OF PEOPLE TELLING ME WHAT I CAN AND CAN'T DO!

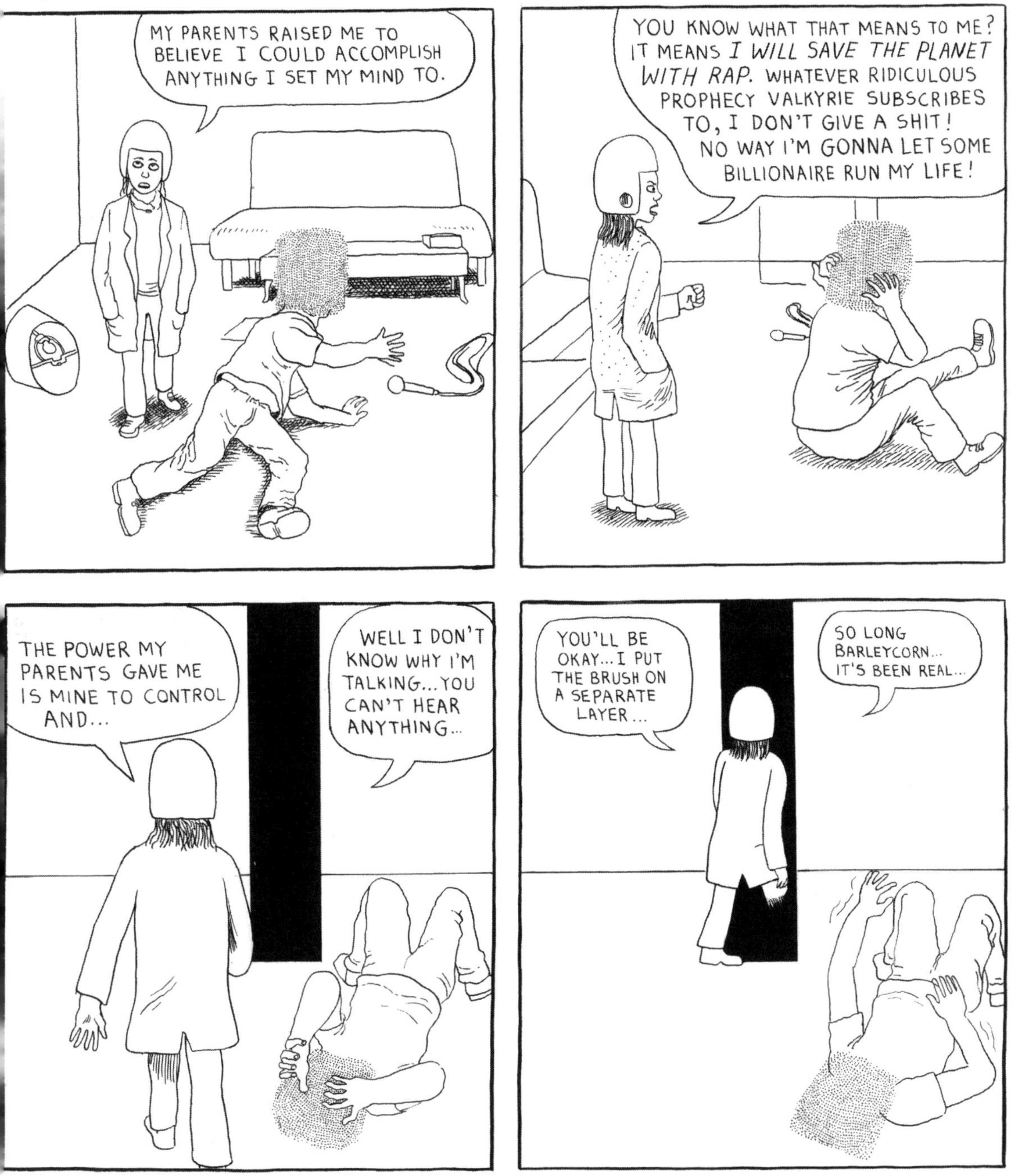
MY PARENTS RAISED ME TO BELIEVE I COULD ACCOMPLISH ANYTHING I SET MY MIND TO.
YOU KNOW WHAT THAT MEANS TO ME? IT MEANS *I WILL SAVE THE PLANET WITH RAP.* WHATEVER RIDICULOUS PROPHECY VALKYRIE SUBSCRIBES TO, I DON'T GIVE A SHIT! NO WAY I'M GONNA LET SOME BILLIONAIRE RUN MY LIFE!
THE POWER MY PARENTS GAVE ME IS MINE TO CONTROL AND...
WELL I DON'T KNOW WHY I'M TALKING... YOU CAN'T HEAR ANYTHING...
YOU'LL BE OKAY... I PUT THE BRUSH ON A SEPARATE LAYER...
SO LONG BARLEYCORN... IT'S BEEN REAL...

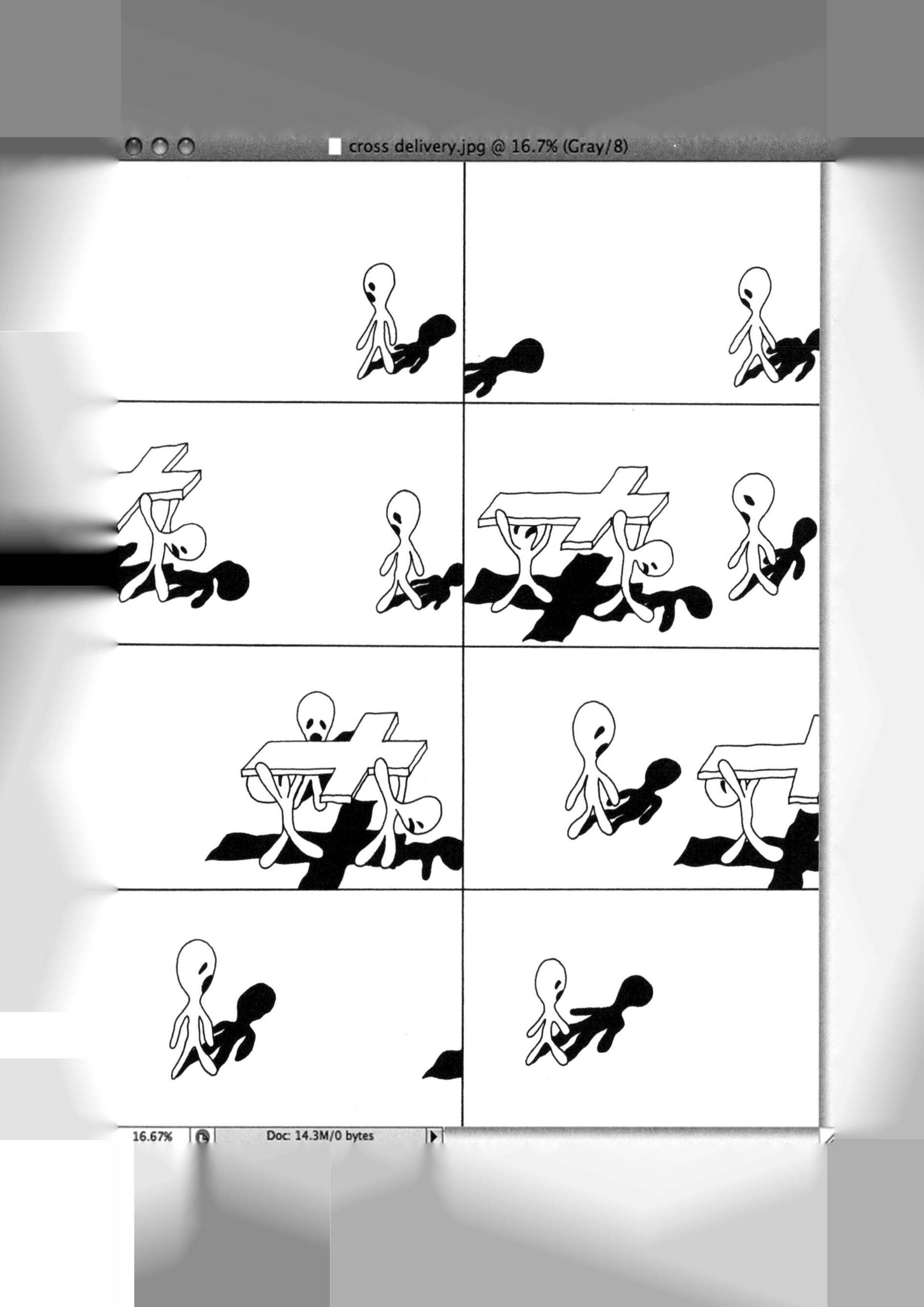
cross delivery.jpg @ 16.7% (Gray/8)
16.67%
Doc: 14.3M/0 bytes

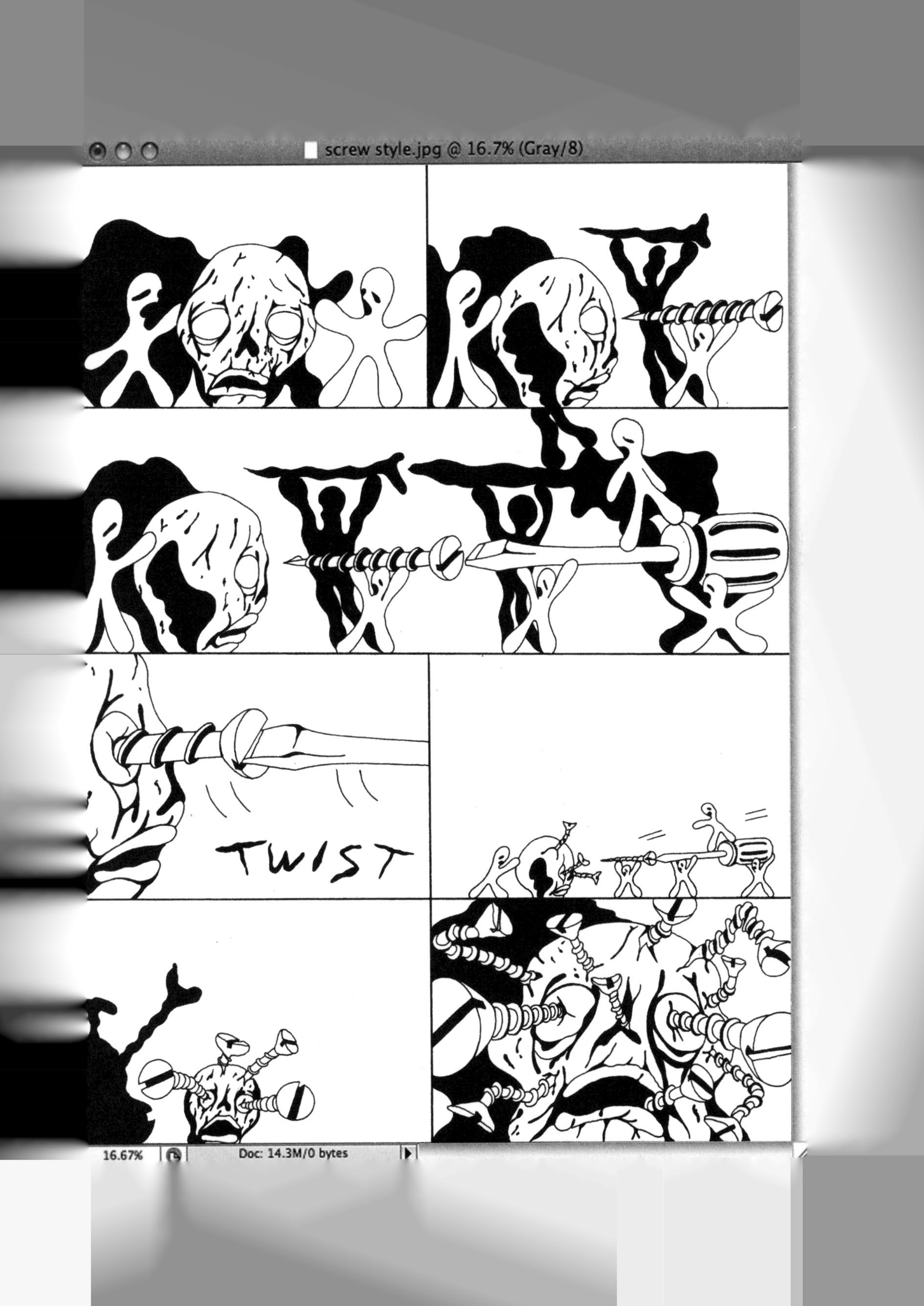
screw style.jpg @ 16.7% (Gray/8)
TWIST
16.67%
Doc: 14.3M/0 bytes

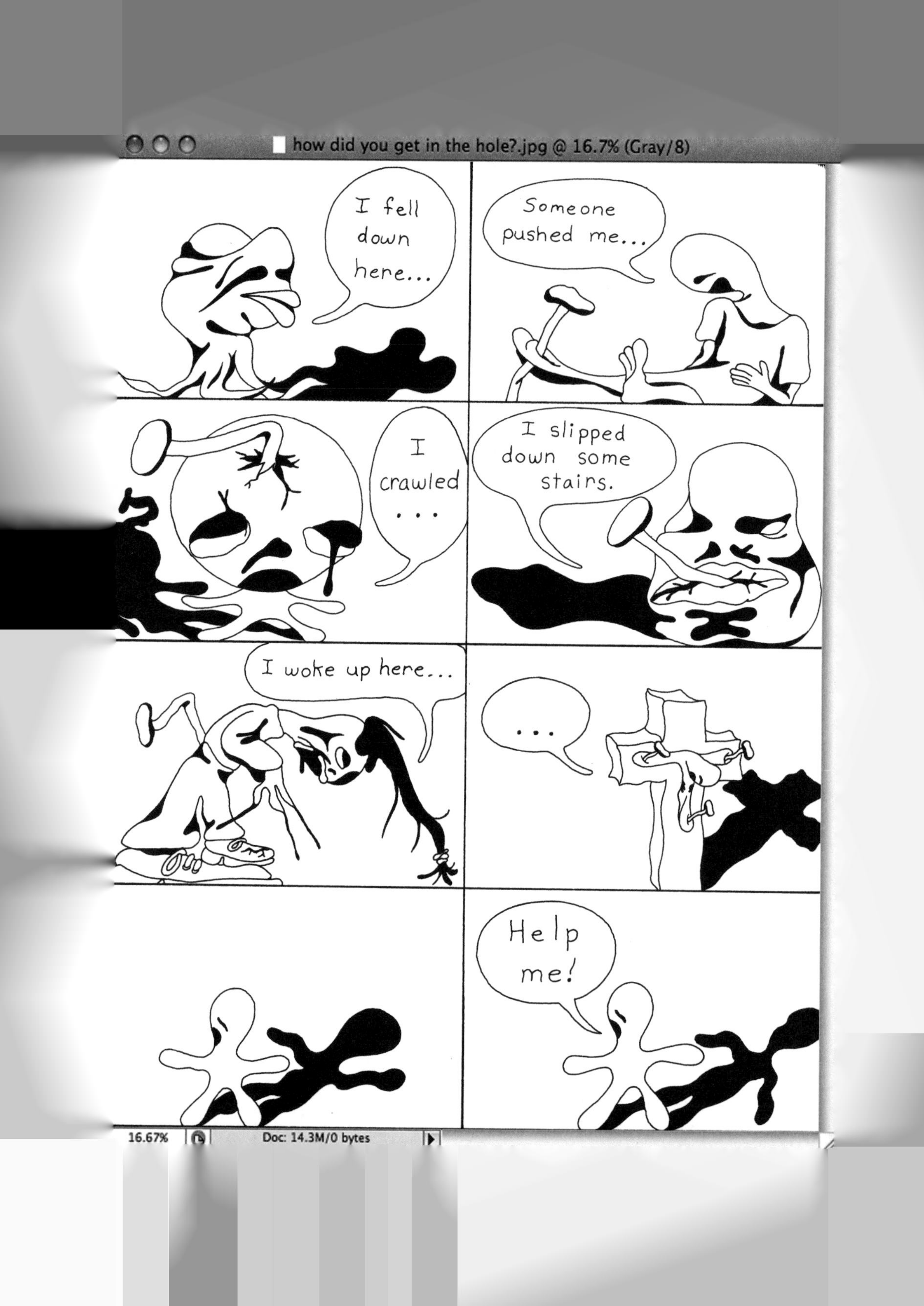
how did you get in the hole?.jpg @ 16.7% (Gray/8)
I fell down here...
Someone pushed me...
I crawled ...
I slipped down some stairs.
I woke up here...
...
Help me!
16.67%
Doc: 14.3M/0 bytes

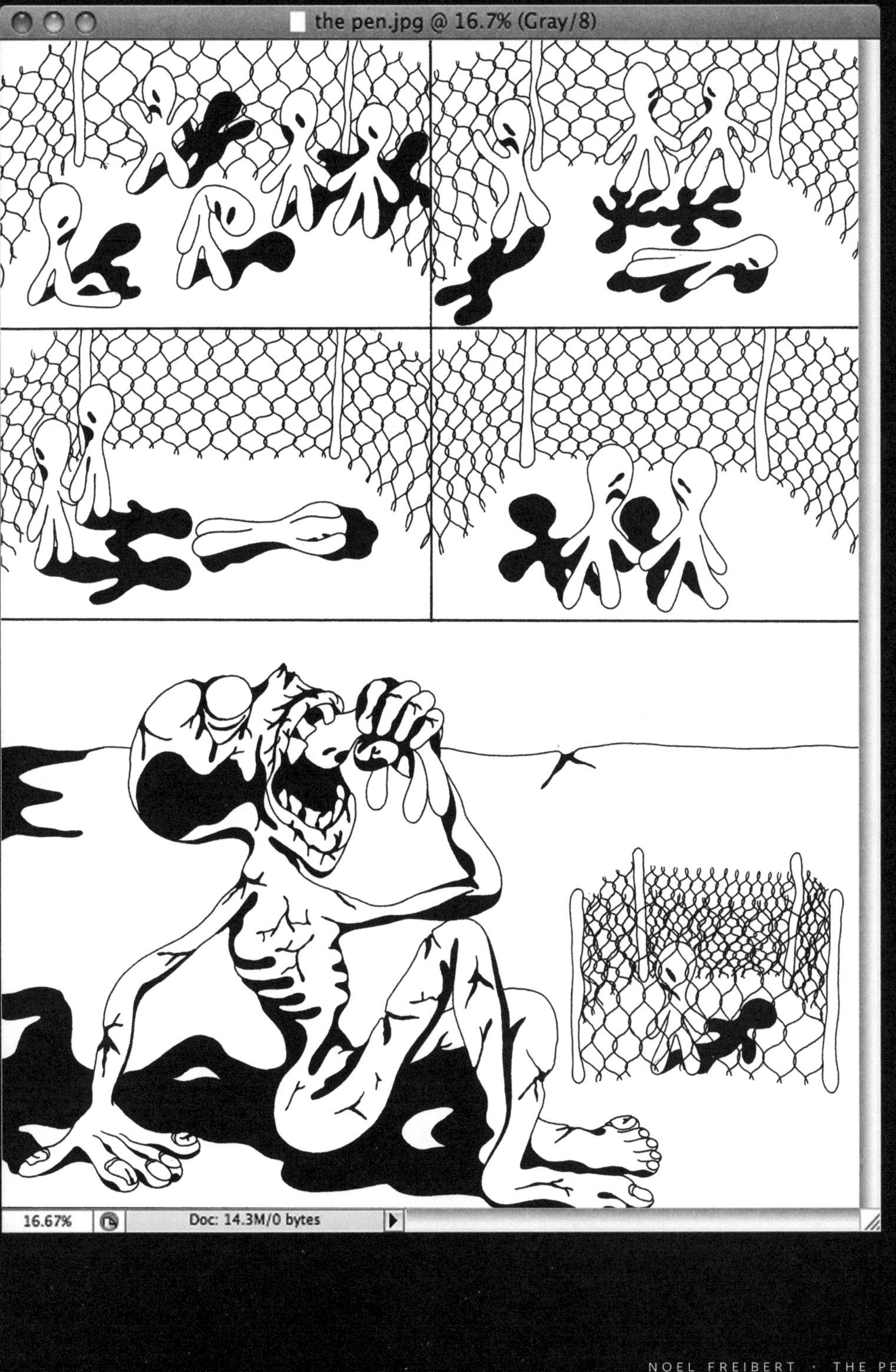
the pen.jpg @ 16.7% (Gray/8)
16.67%
Doc: 14.3M/0 bytes

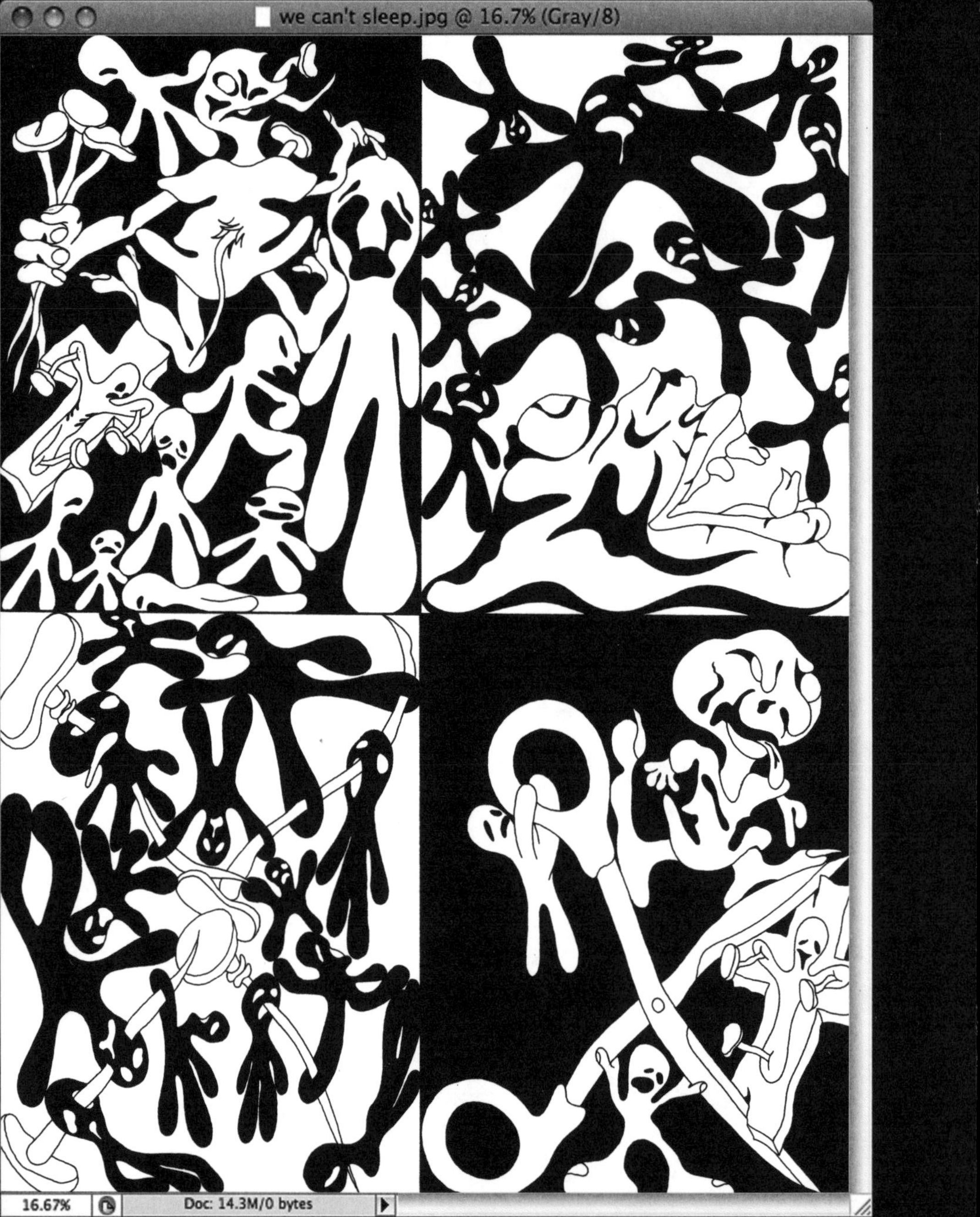
we can't sleep.jpg @ 16.7% (Gray/8)
16.67%
Doc: 14.3M/0 bytes

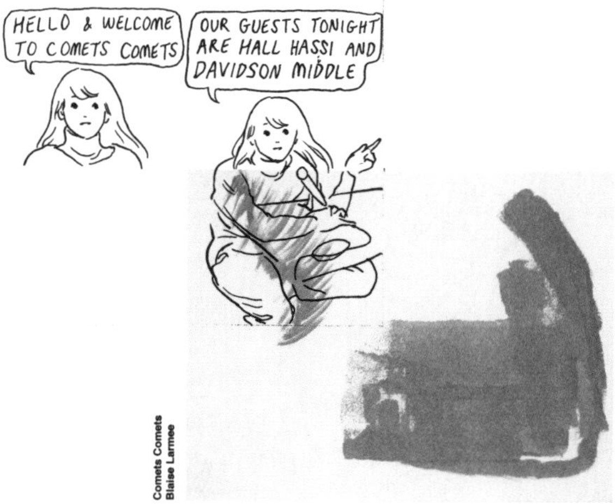
HELLO & WELCOME TO COMETS COMETS
OUR GUESTS TONIGHT ARE HALL HASSI AND DAVIDSON MIDDLE
Comets Comets
Blaise Larmee

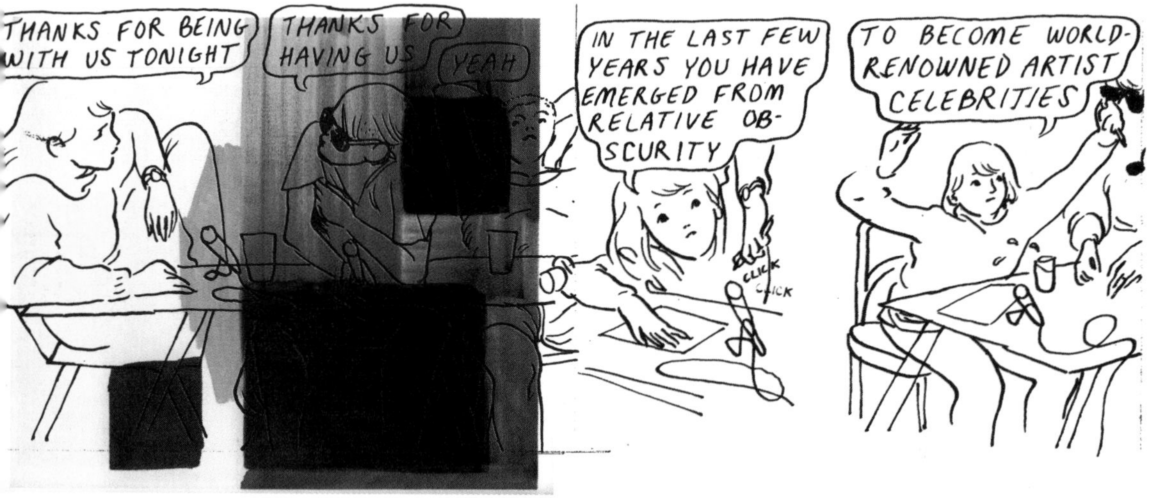
THANKS FOR BEING WITH US TONIGHT
THANKS FOR HAVING US
YEAH
IN THE LAST FEW YEARS YOU HAVE EMERGED FROM RELATIVE OB-SCURITY
CLICK
CLICK
TO BECOME WORLD-RENOWNED ARTIST CELEBRITIES

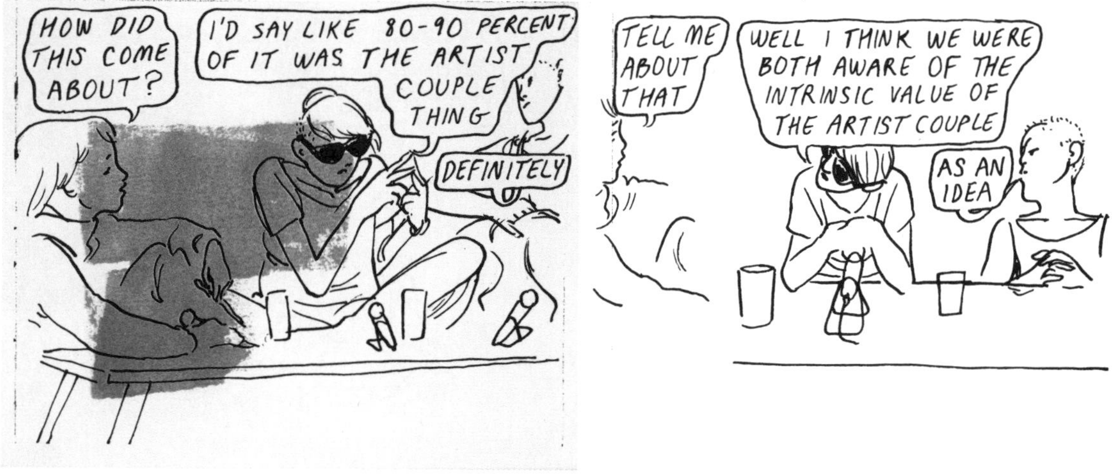
HOW DID THIS COME ABOUT?
I'D SAY LIKE 80-90 PERCENT OF IT WAS THE ARTIST COUPLE THING
DEFINITELY
TELL ME ABOUT THAT
WELL I THINK WE WERE BOTH AWARE OF THE INTRINSIC VALUE OF THE ARTIST COUPLE
AS AN IDEA

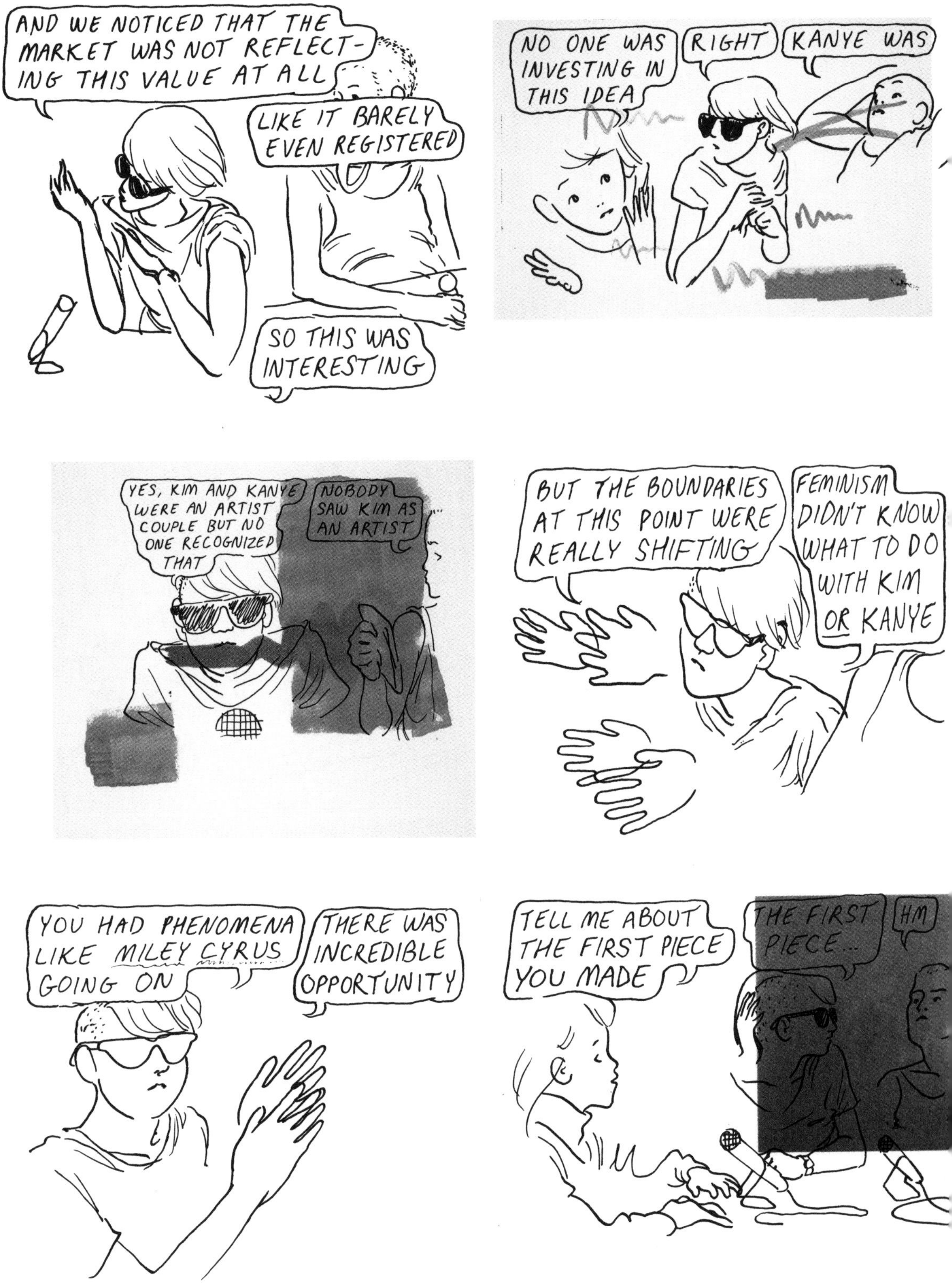
AND WE NOTICED THAT THE MARKET WAS NOT REFLECTING THIS VALUE AT ALL
LIKE IT BARELY EVEN REGISTERED
SO THIS WAS INTERESTING
NO ONE WAS INVESTING IN THIS IDEA
RIGHT
KANYE WAS
YES, KIM AND KANYE WERE AN ARTIST COUPLE BUT NO ONE RECOGNIZED THAT
NOBODY SAW KIM AS AN ARTIST
BUT THE BOUNDARIES AT THIS POINT WERE REALLY SHIFTING
FEMINISM DIDN'T KNOW WHAT TO DO WITH KIM OR KANYE
YOU HAD PHENOMENA LIKE MILEY CYRUS GOING ON
THERE WAS INCREDIBLE OPPORTUNITY
TELL ME ABOUT THE FIRST PIECE YOU MADE
THE FIRST PIECE...
HM

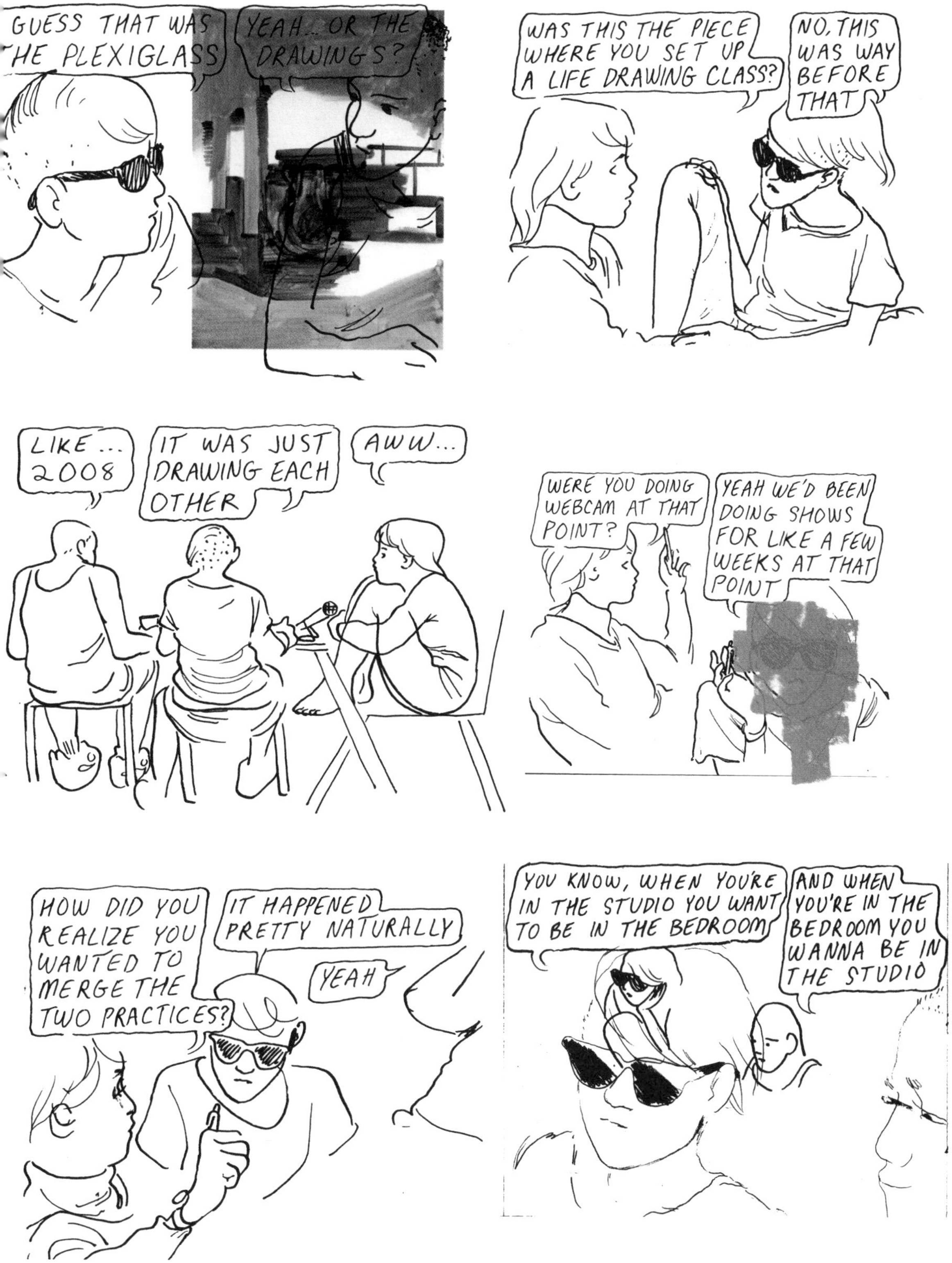

GUESS THAT WAS THE PLEXIGLASS
YEAH... OR THE DRAWINGS?
WAS THIS THE PIECE WHERE YOU SET UP A LIFE DRAWING CLASS?
NO, THIS WAS WAY BEFORE THAT
LIKE... 2008
IT WAS JUST DRAWING EACH OTHER
AWW...
WERE YOU DOING WEBCAM AT THAT POINT?
YEAH WE'D BEEN DOING SHOWS FOR LIKE A FEW WEEKS AT THAT POINT
HOW DID YOU REALIZE YOU WANTED TO MERGE THE TWO PRACTICES?
IT HAPPENED PRETTY NATURALLY
YEAH
YOU KNOW, WHEN YOU'RE IN THE STUDIO YOU WANT TO BE IN THE BEDROOM
AND WHEN YOU'RE IN THE BEDROOM YOU WANNA BE IN THE STUDIO

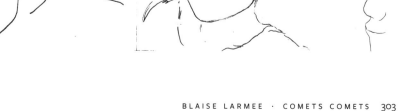

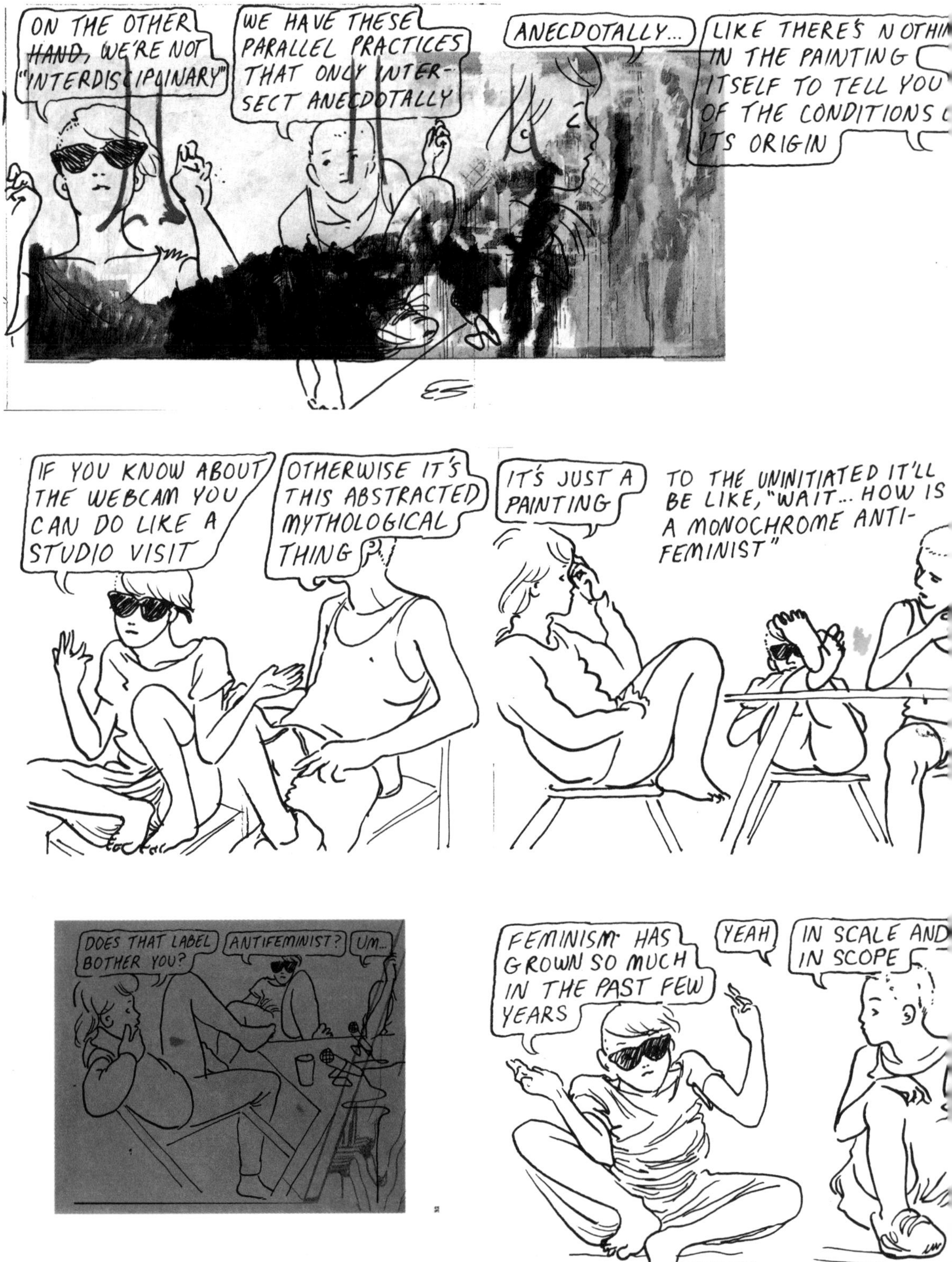
ON THE OTHER HAND, WE'RE NOT "INTERDISCIPLINARY"
WE HAVE THESE PARALLEL PRACTICES THAT ONLY INTERSECT ANECDOTALLY
ANECDOTALLY...
LIKE THERE'S NOTHIN IN THE PAINTING ITSELF TO TELL YOU OF THE CONDITIONS ITS ORIGIN
IF YOU KNOW ABOUT THE WEBCAM YOU CAN DO LIKE A STUDIO VISIT
OTHERWISE IT'S THIS ABSTRACTED MYTHOLOGICAL THING
IT'S JUST A PAINTING
TO THE UNINITIATED IT'LL BE LIKE, "WAIT... HOW IS A MONOCHROME ANTI-FEMINIST"
DOES THAT LABEL BOTHER YOU?
ANTIFEMINIST?
UM...
FEMINISM HAS GROWN SO MUCH IN THE PAST FEW YEARS
YEAH
IN SCALE AND IN SCOPE

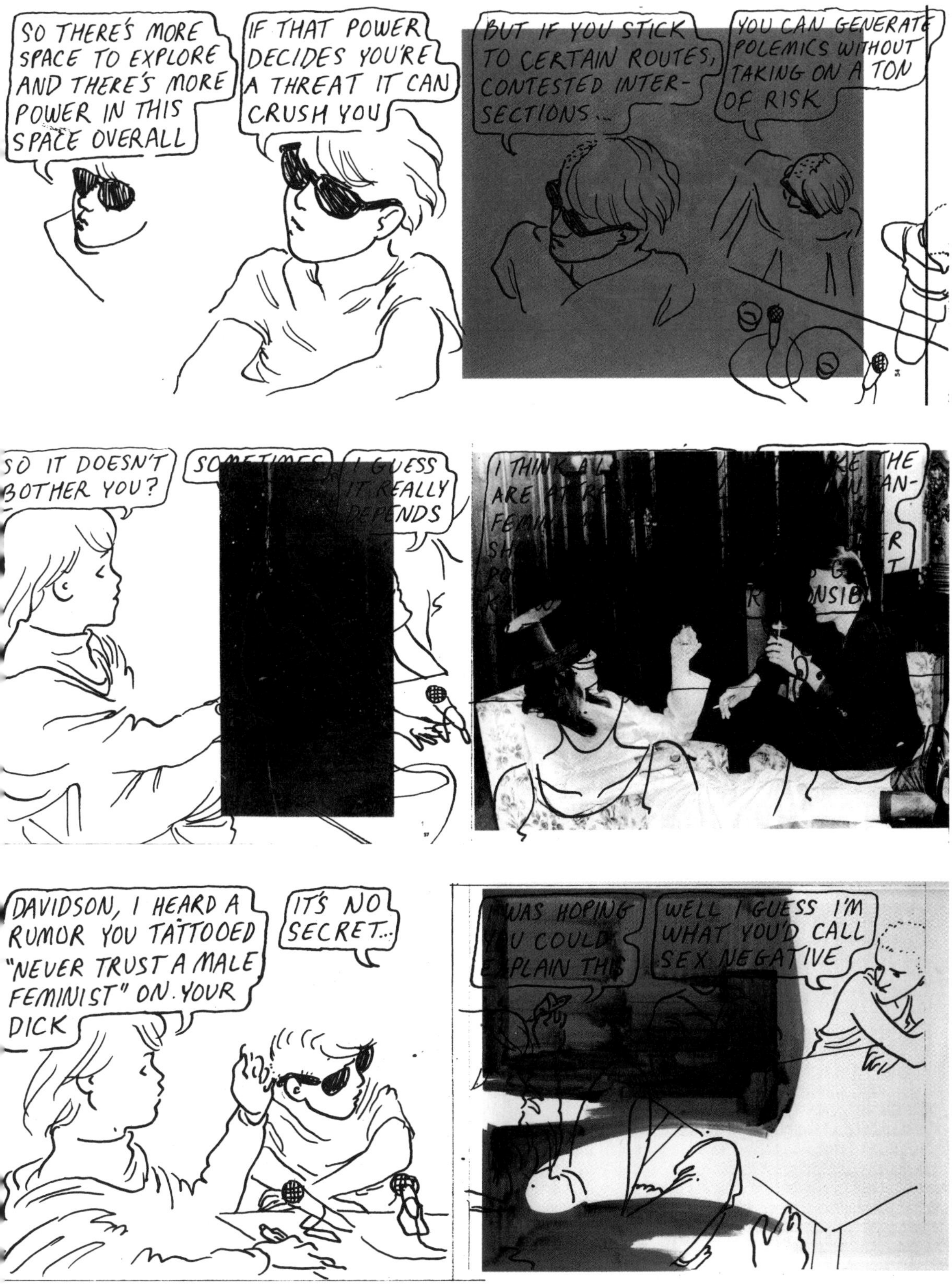
SO THERE'S MORE SPACE TO EXPLORE AND THERE'S MORE POWER IN THIS SPACE OVERALL
IF THAT POWER DECIDES YOU'RE A THREAT IT CAN CRUSH YOU
BUT IF YOU STICK TO CERTAIN ROUTES, CONTESTED INTER-SECTIONS...
YOU CAN GENERATE POLEMICS WITHOUT TAKING ON A TON OF RISK
SO IT DOESN'T BOTHER YOU?
SO[redacted]
[redacted]UESS [redacted]EALLY [redacted]ENDS
[redacted]
DAVIDSON, I HEARD A RUMOR YOU TATTOOED "NEVER TRUST A MALE FEMINIST" ON YOUR DICK
IT'S NO SECRET...
I WAS HOPING YOU COULD EXPLAIN THIS
WELL I GUESS I'M WHAT YOU'D CALL SEX NEGATIVE

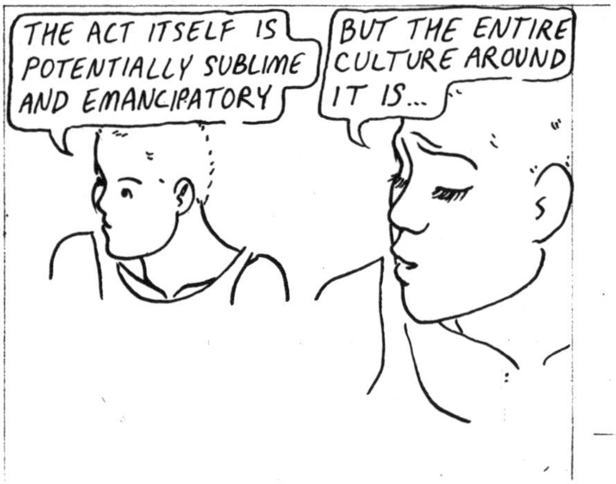
THE ACT ITSELF IS POTENTIALLY SUBLIME AND EMANCIPATORY
BUT THE ENTIRE CULTURE AROUND IT IS...

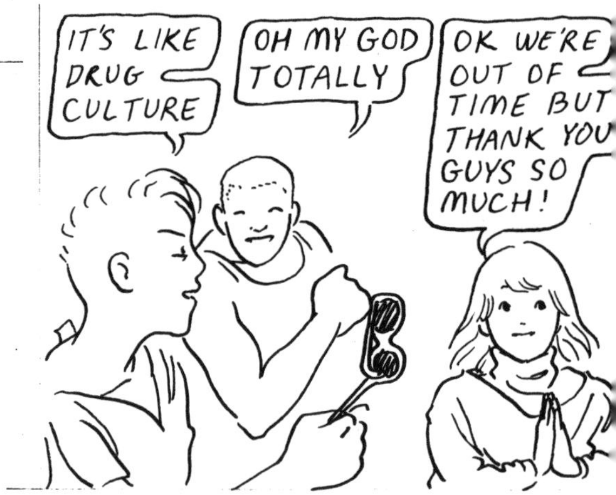
IT'S LIKE DRUG CULTURE
OH MY GOD TOTALLY
OK WE'RE OUT OF TIME BUT THANK YOU GUYS SO MUCH!

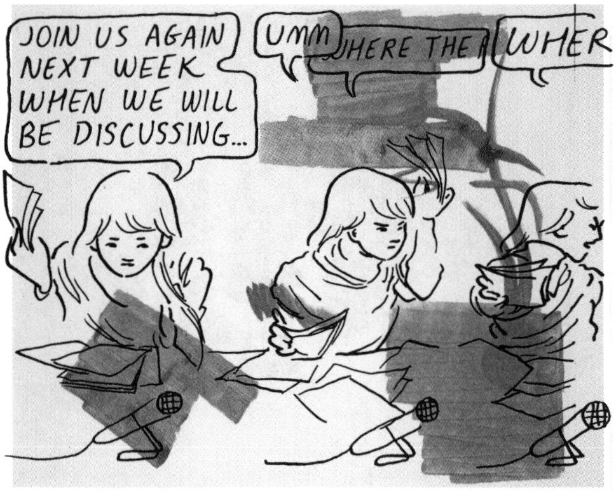
JOIN US AGAIN NEXT WEEK WHEN WE WILL BE DISCUSSING...
UMM
WHERE THE
WHER

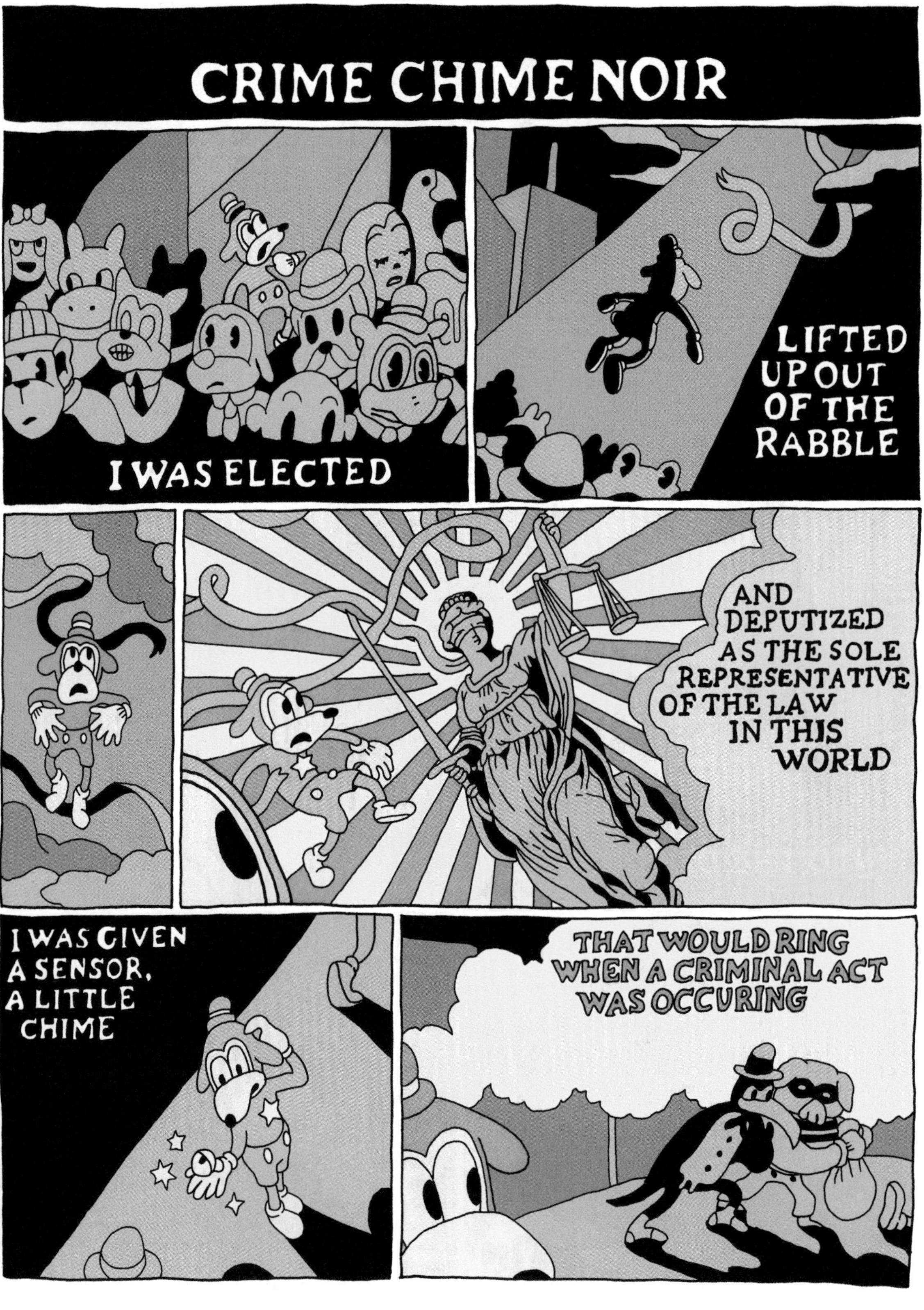
CRIME CHIME NOIR
I WAS ELECTED
LIFTED UP OUT OF THE RABBLE
AND DEPUTIZED AS THE SOLE REPRESENTATIVE OF THE LAW IN THIS WORLD
I WAS GIVEN A SENSOR, A LITTLE CHIME
THAT WOULD RING WHEN A CRIMINAL ACT WAS OCCURING

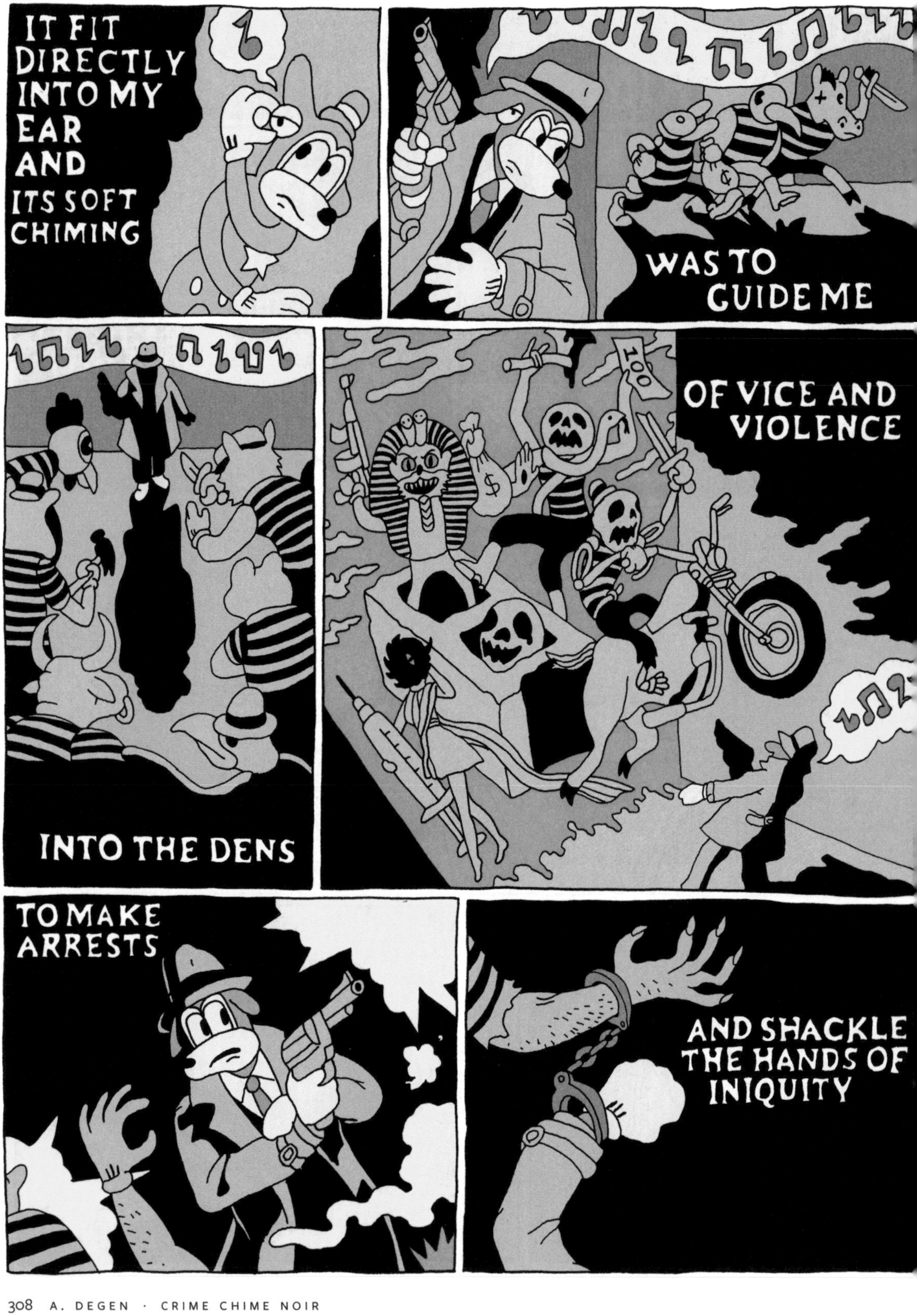
IT FIT DIRECTLY INTO MY EAR AND ITS SOFT CHIMING
WAS TO GUIDE ME
INTO THE DENS
OF VICE AND VIOLENCE
100
TO MAKE ARRESTS
AND SHACKLE THE HANDS OF INIQUITY

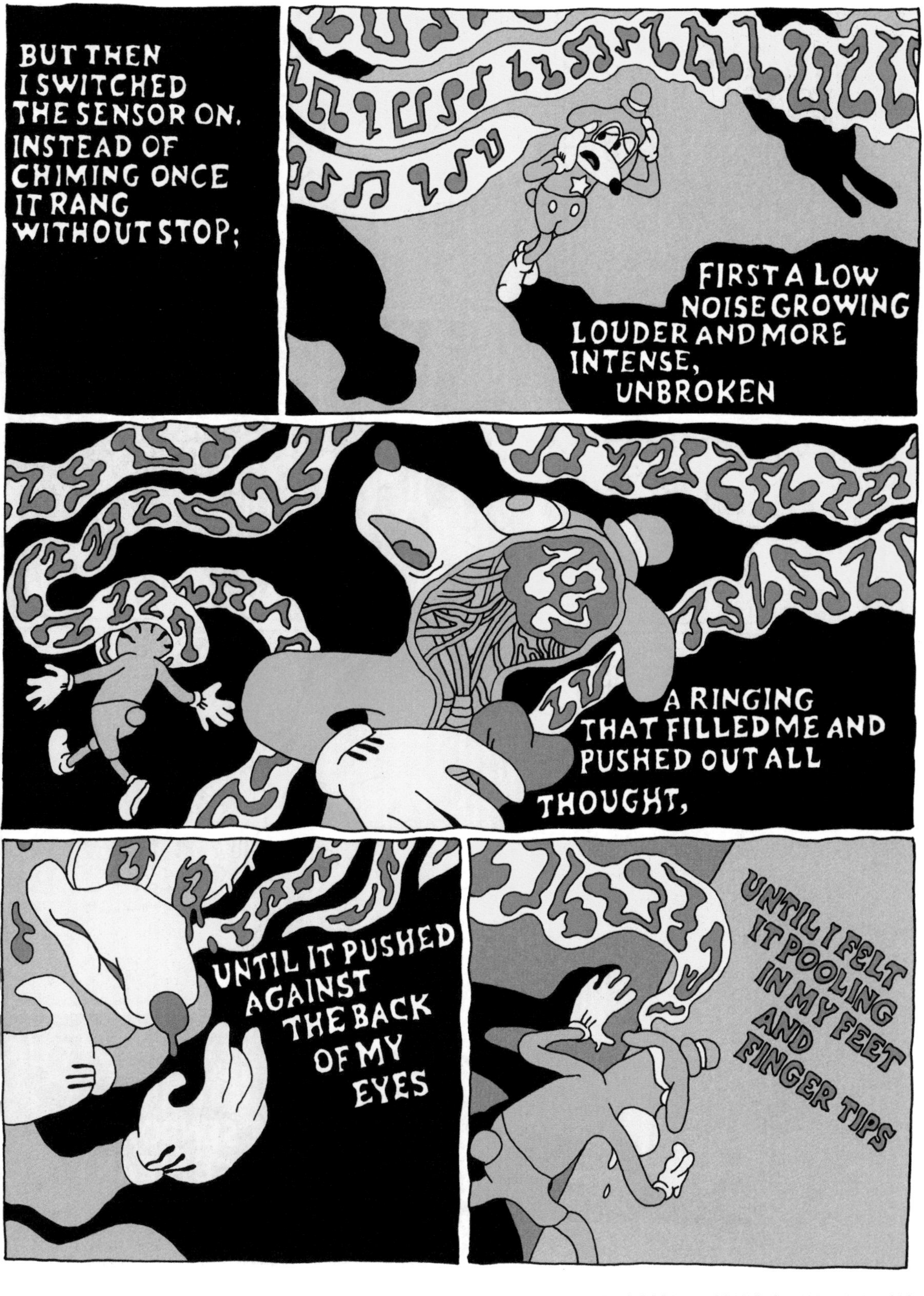
BUT THEN I SWITCHED THE SENSOR ON. INSTEAD OF CHIMING ONCE IT RANG WITHOUT STOP;
FIRST A LOW NOISE GROWING LOUDER AND MORE INTENSE, UNBROKEN
A RINGING THAT FILLED ME AND PUSHED OUT ALL THOUGHT,
UNTIL IT PUSHED AGAINST THE BACK OF MY EYES
UNTIL I FELT IT POOLING IN MY FEET AND FINGER TIPS

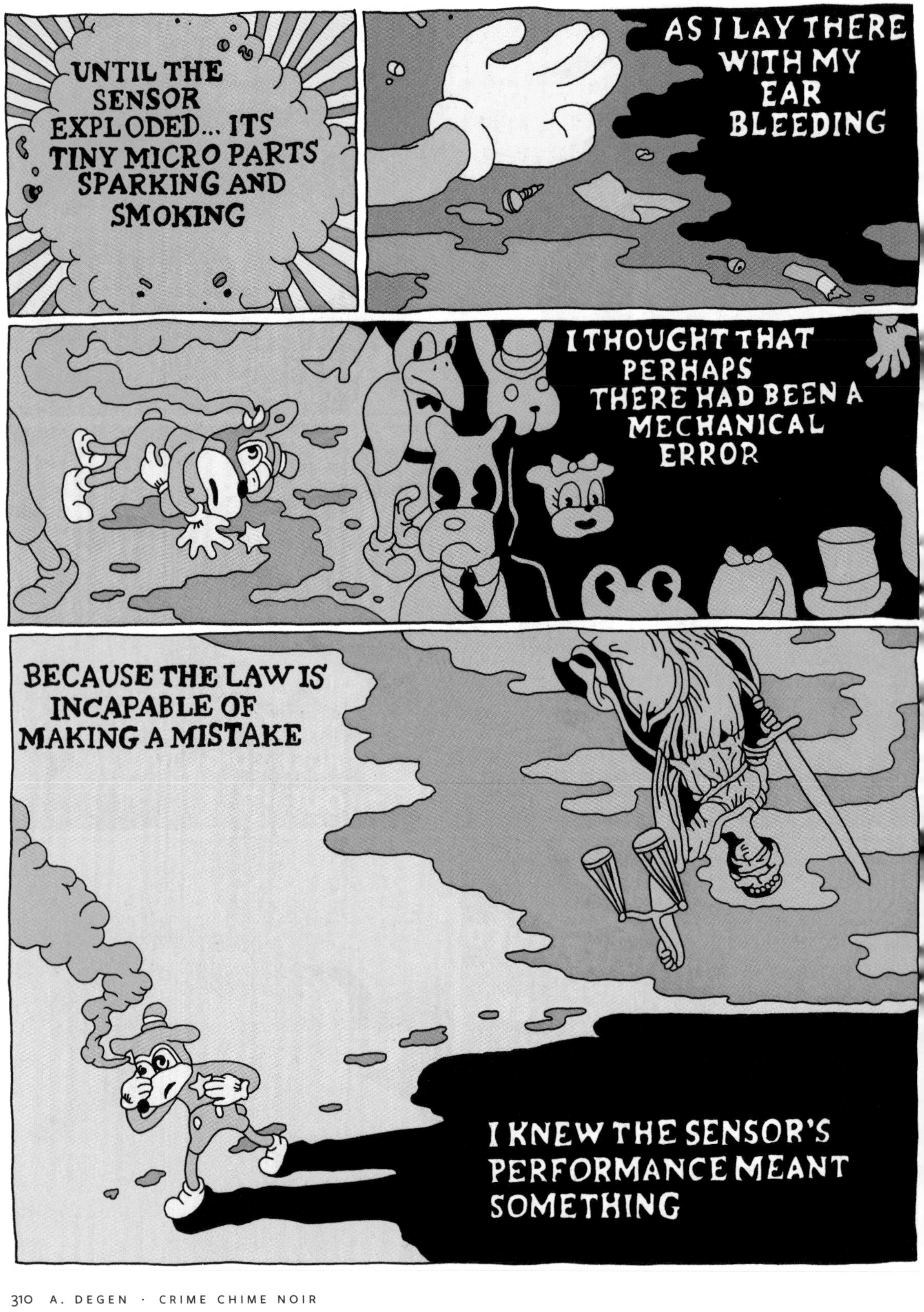
UNTIL THE SENSOR EXPLODED... ITS TINY MICRO PARTS SPARKING AND SMOKING
AS I LAY THERE WITH MY EAR BLEEDING
I THOUGHT THAT PERHAPS THERE HAD BEEN A MECHANICAL ERROR
BECAUSE THE LAW IS INCAPABLE OF MAKING A MISTAKE
I KNEW THE SENSOR'S PERFORMANCE MEANT SOMETHING

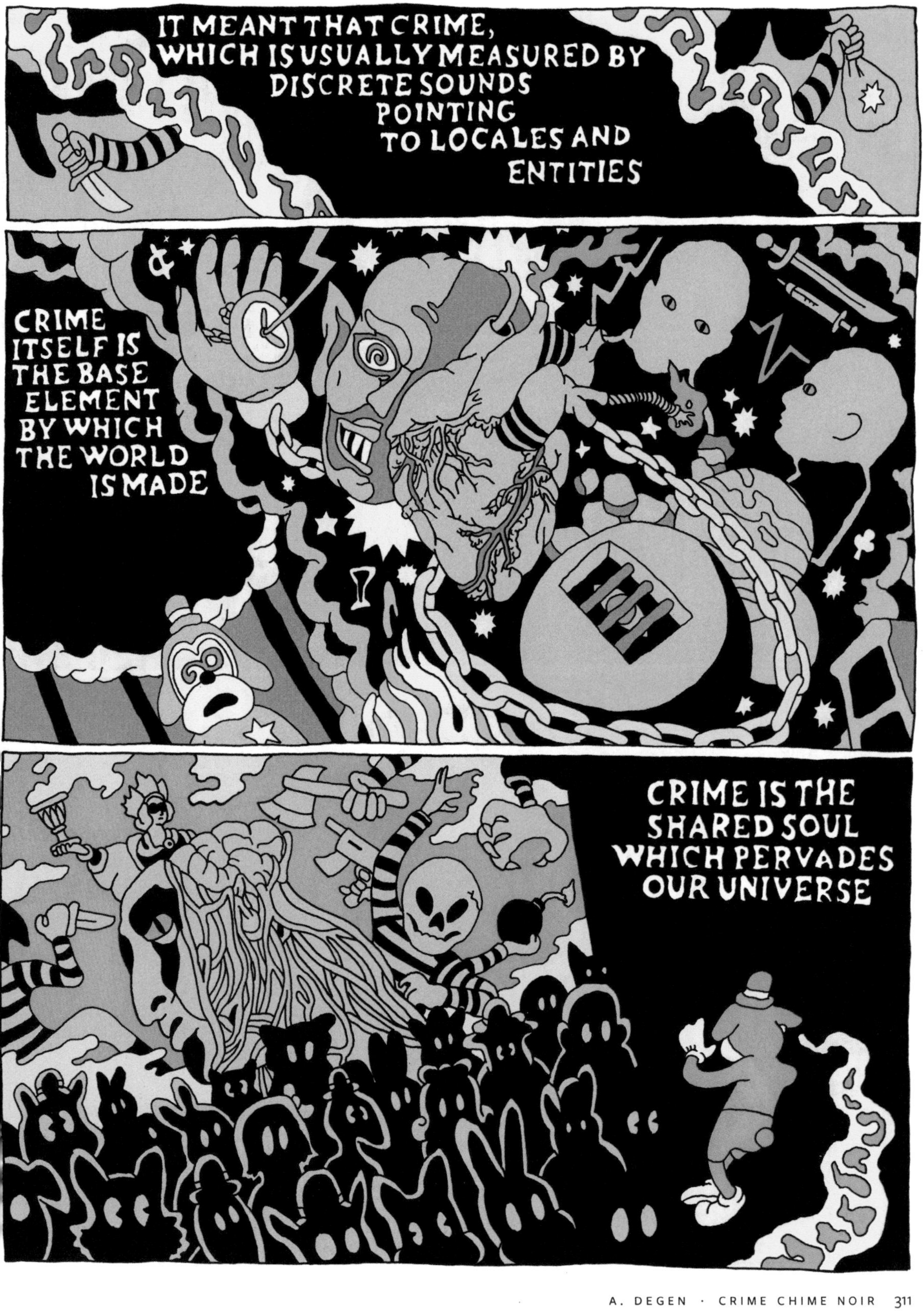
IT MEANT THAT CRIME, WHICH IS USUALLY MEASURED BY DISCRETE SOUNDS POINTING TO LOCALES AND ENTITIES
CRIME ITSELF IS THE BASE ELEMENT BY WHICH THE WORLD IS MADE
CRIME IS THE SHARED SOUL WHICH PERVADES OUR UNIVERSE

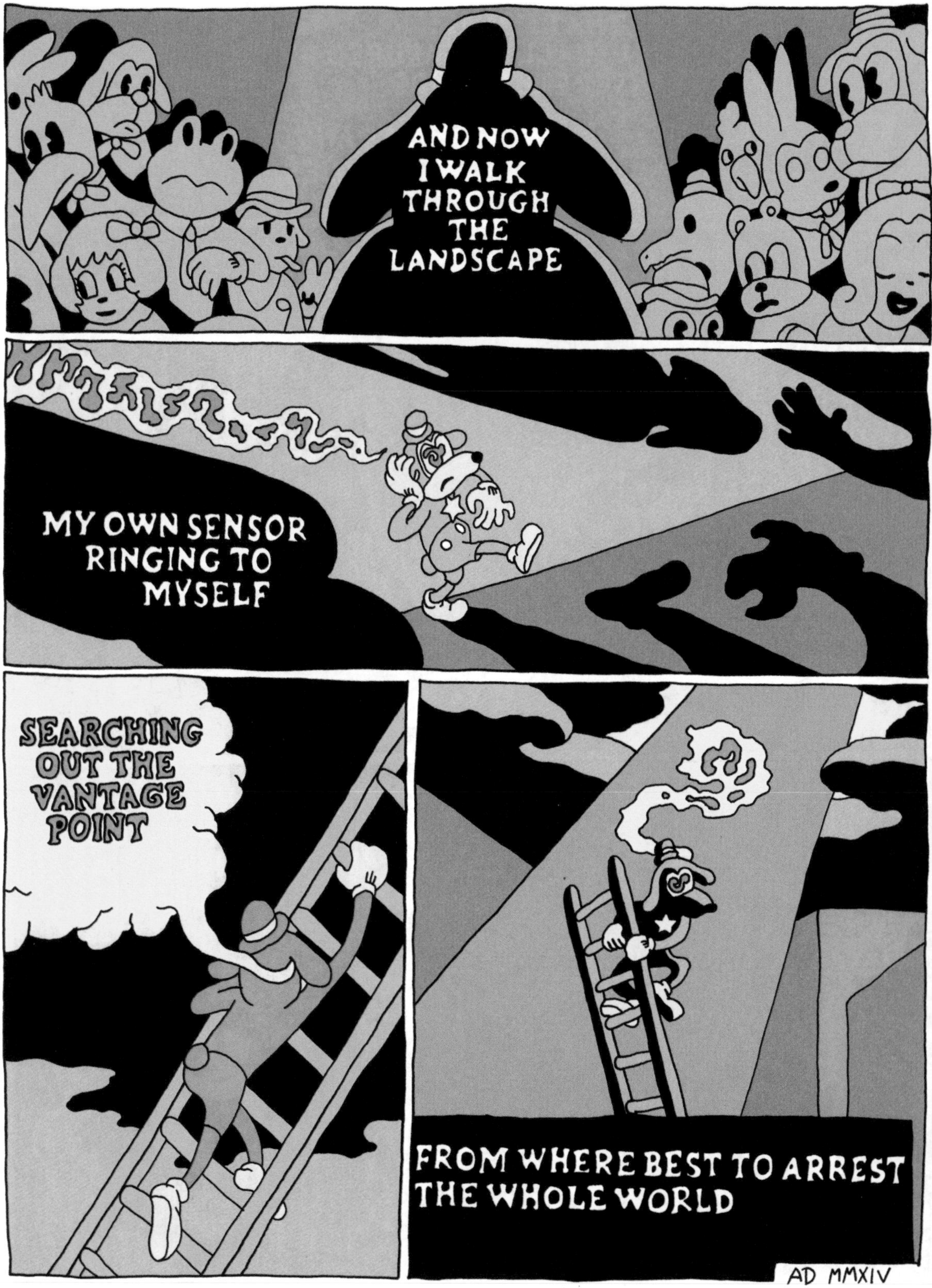
AND NOW I WALK THROUGH THE LANDSCAPE
MY OWN SENSOR RINGING TO MYSELF
SEARCHING OUT THE VANTAGE POINT
FROM WHERE BEST TO ARREST THE WHOLE WORLD
AD MMXIV

CHAPTER TEN
Brainworms

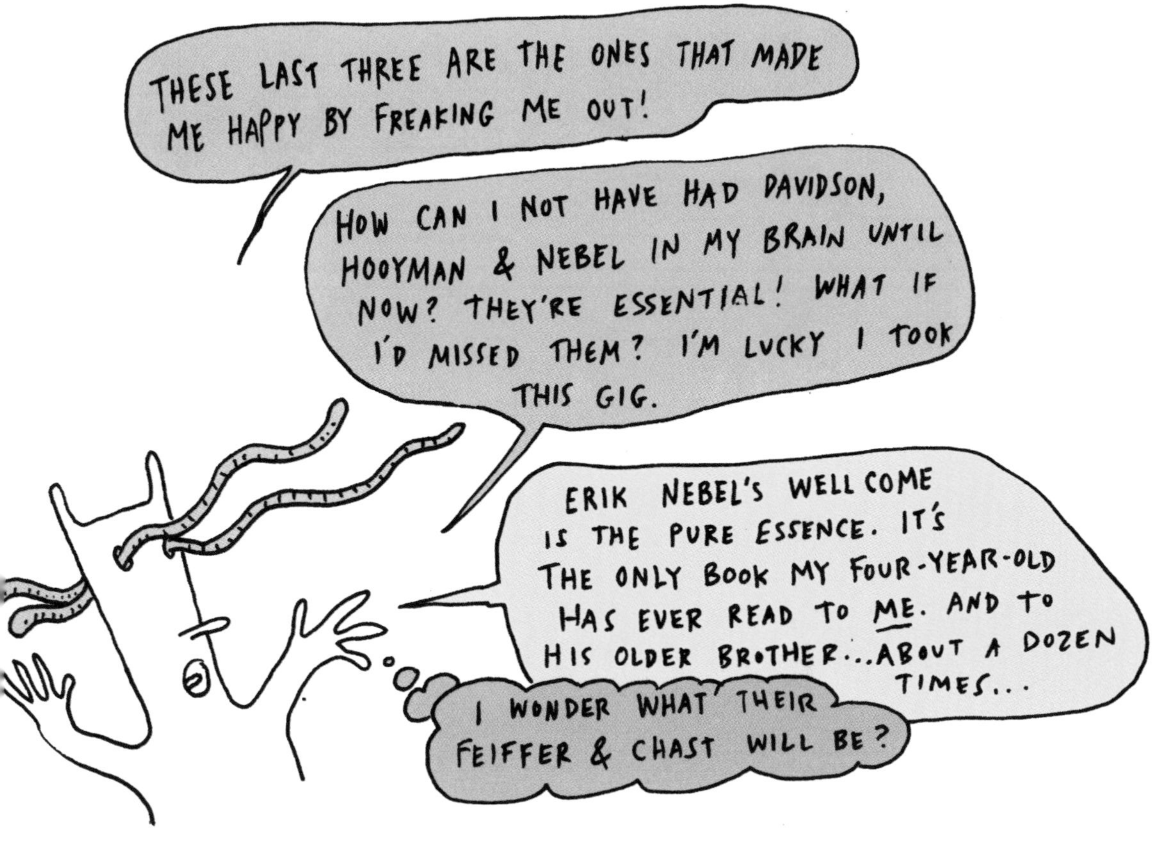

THESE LAST THREE ARE THE ONES THAT MADE ME HAPPY BY FREAKING ME OUT!
HOW CAN I NOT HAVE HAD DAVIDSON, HOOYMAN & NEBEL IN MY BRAIN UNTIL NOW? THEY'RE ESSENTIAL! WHAT IF I'D MISSED THEM? I'M LUCKY I TOOK THIS GIG.
ERIK NEBEL'S WELL COME IS THE PURE ESSENCE. IT'S THE ONLY BOOK MY FOUR-YEAR-OLD HAS EVER READ TO ME. AND TO HIS OLDER BROTHER...ABOUT A DOZEN TIMES...
I WONDER WHAT THEIR FEIFFER & CHAST WILL BE?

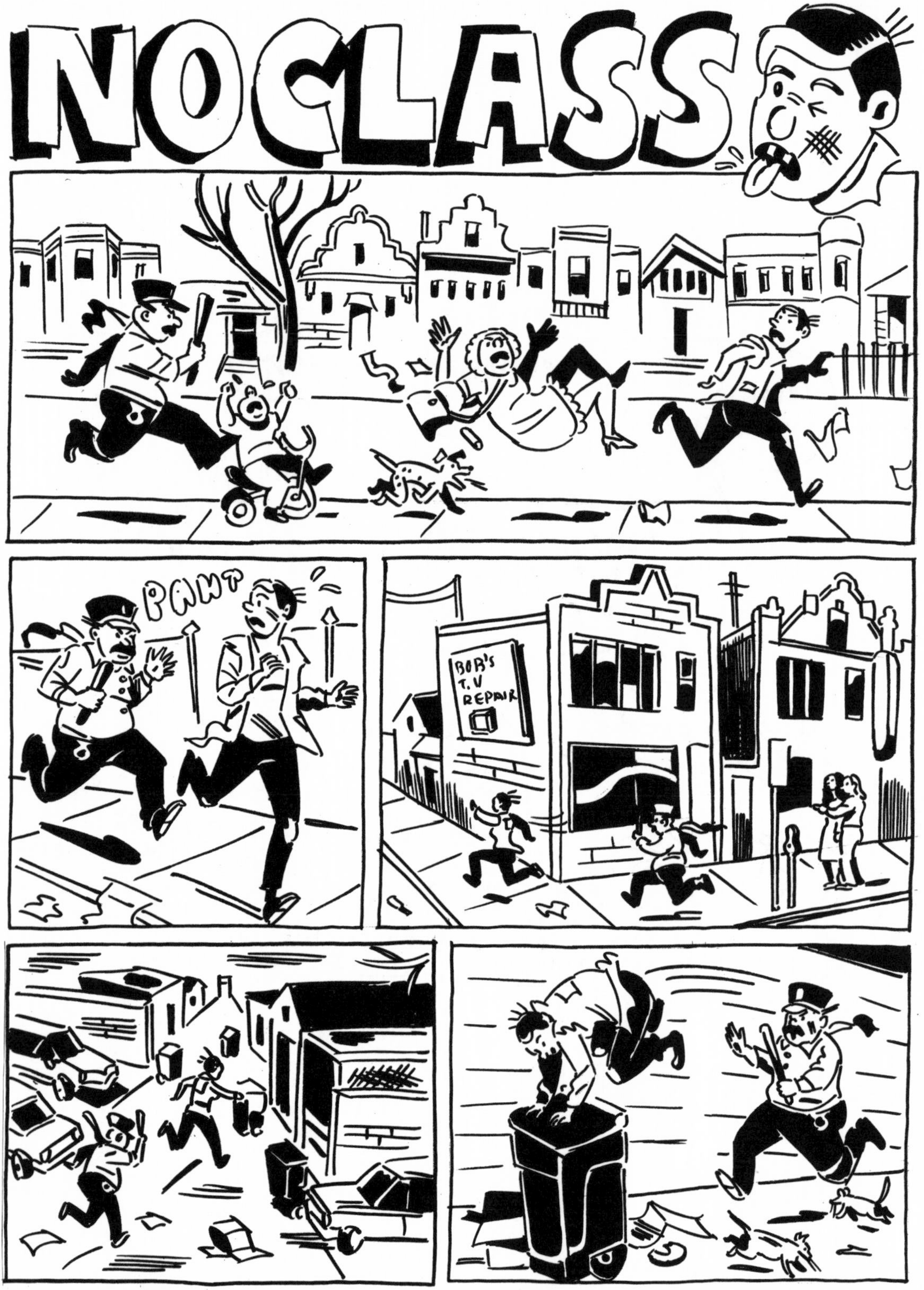
NOCLASS
PANT
BOB'S T.V REPAIR

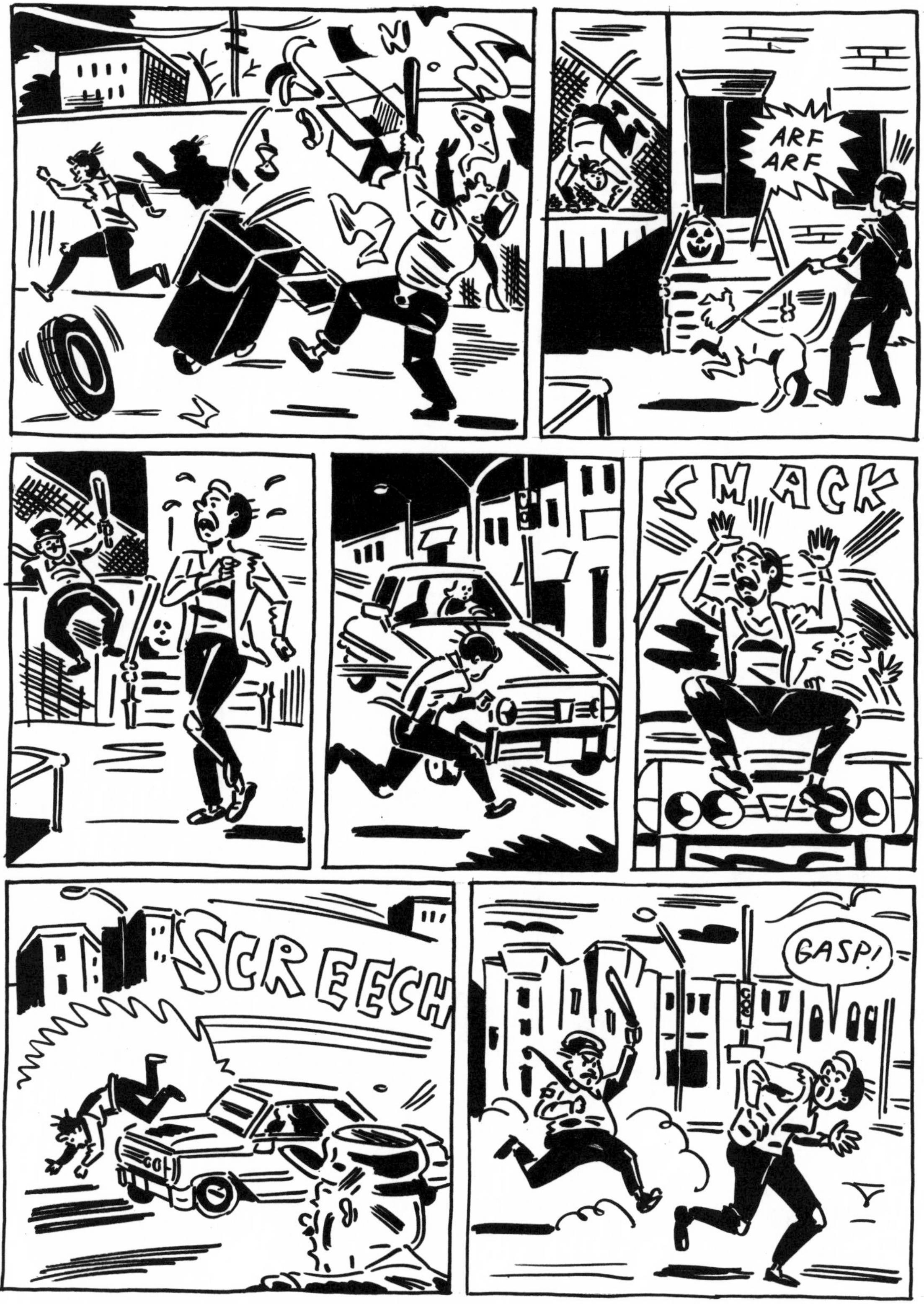
ARF
ARF
SMACK
SCREECH
GASP!

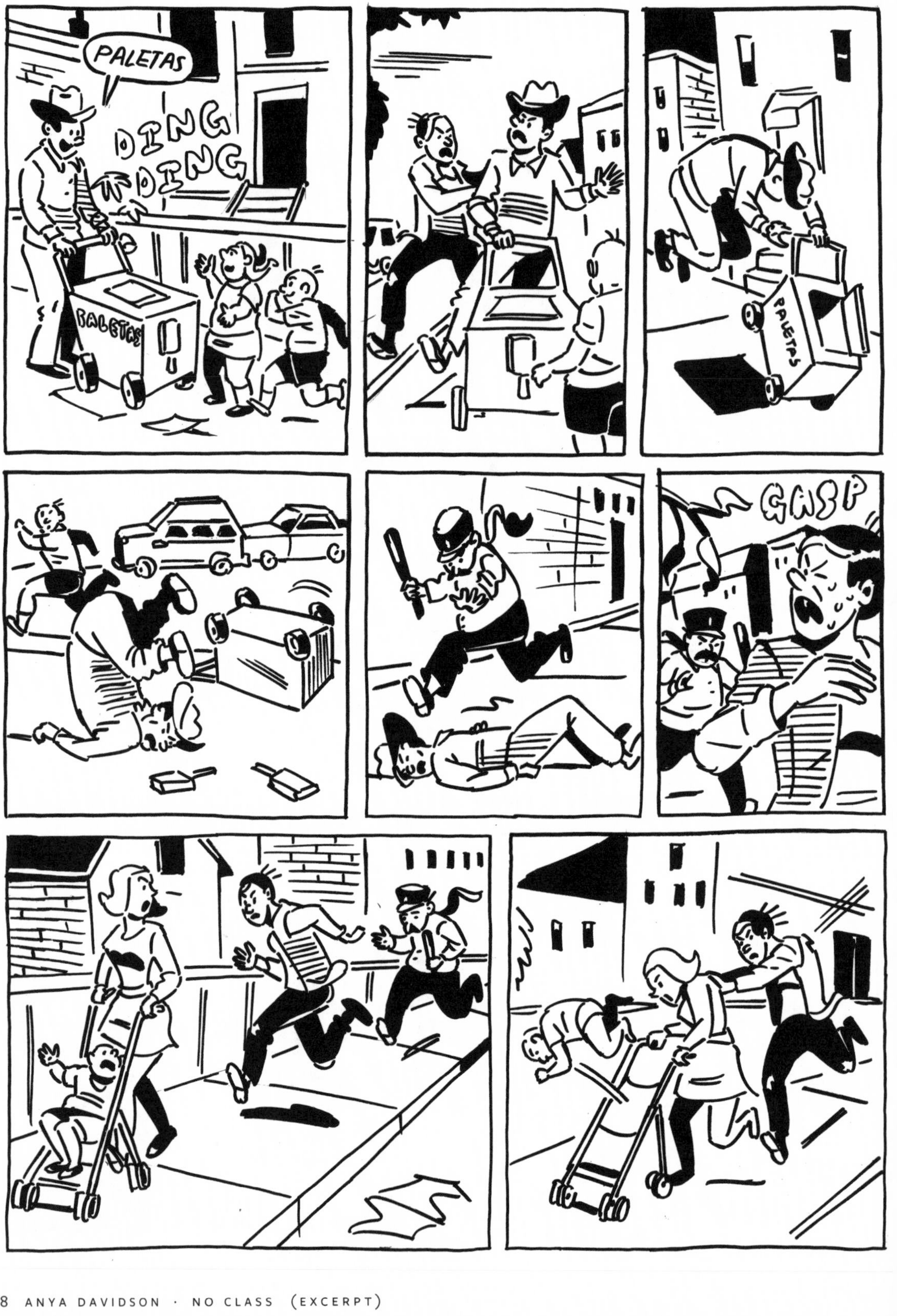
PALETAS
DING DING
PALETAS
PALETAS
GASP

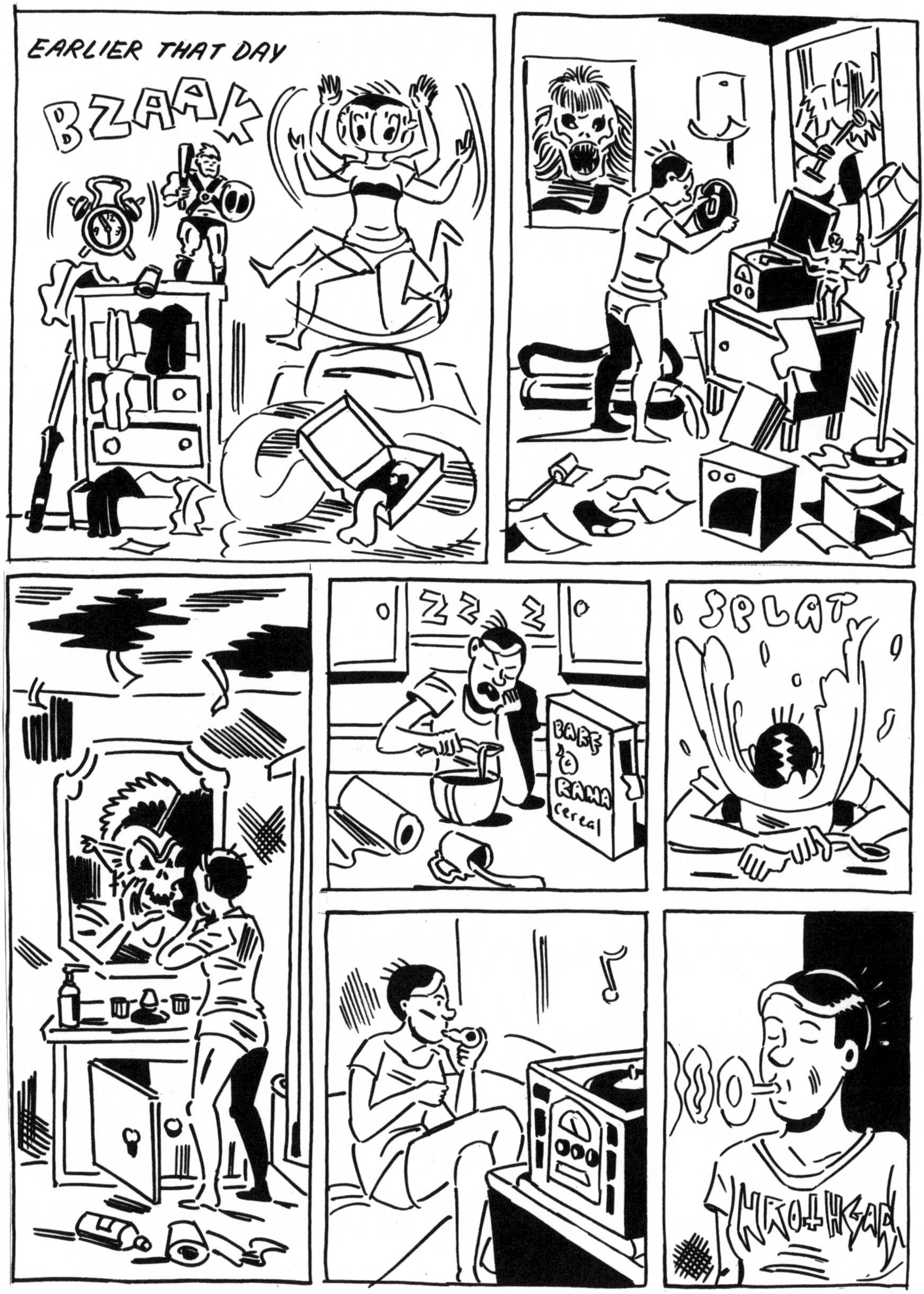
EARLIER THAT DAY
BZAAK
ZZZ
BARF O RAMA cereal
SPLAT
HROTHGAR

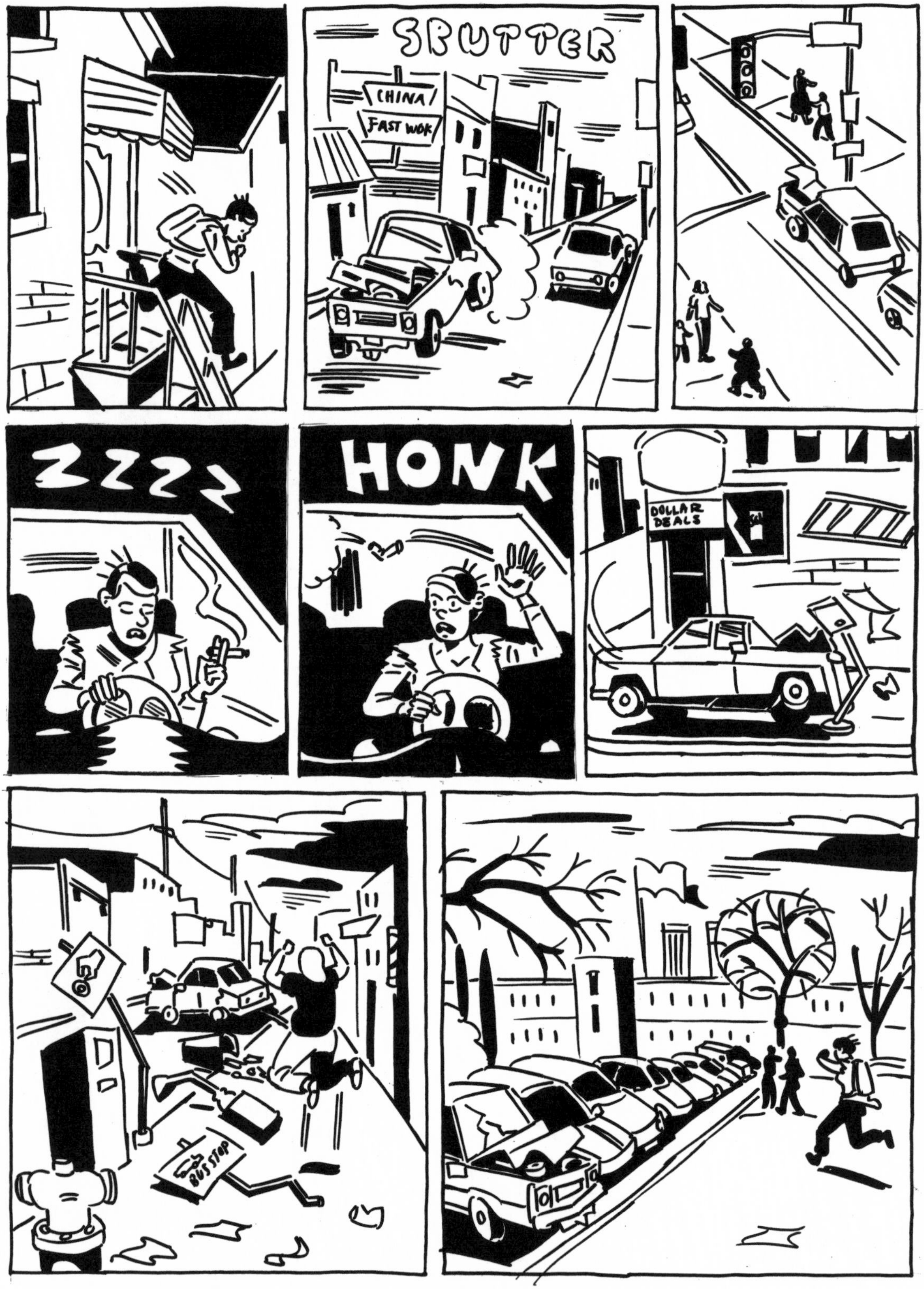
SPUTTER
CHINA
FAST WOK
ZZZZ
HONK
DOLLAR DEALS
BUS STOP

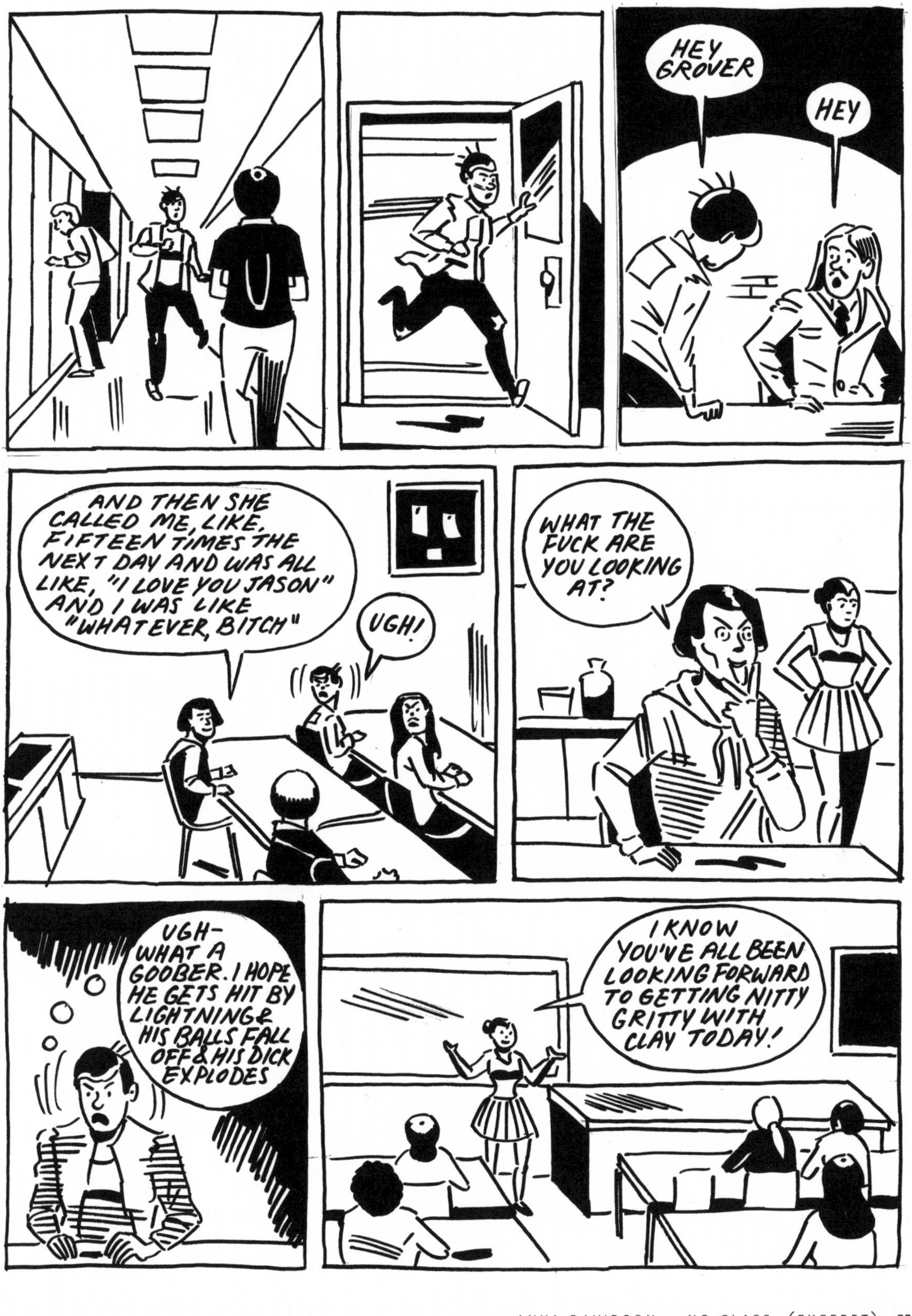
HEY GROVER
HEY
AND THEN SHE CALLED ME, LIKE, FIFTEEN TIMES THE NEXT DAY AND WAS ALL LIKE, "I LOVE YOU JASON" AND I WAS LIKE "WHATEVER, BITCH"
UGH!
WHAT THE FUCK ARE YOU LOOKING AT?
UGH- WHAT A GOOBER. I HOPE HE GETS HIT BY LIGHTNING & HIS BALLS FALL OFF & HIS DICK EXPLODES
I KNOW YOU'VE ALL BEEN LOOKING FORWARD TO GETTING NITTY GRITTY WITH CLAY TODAY!

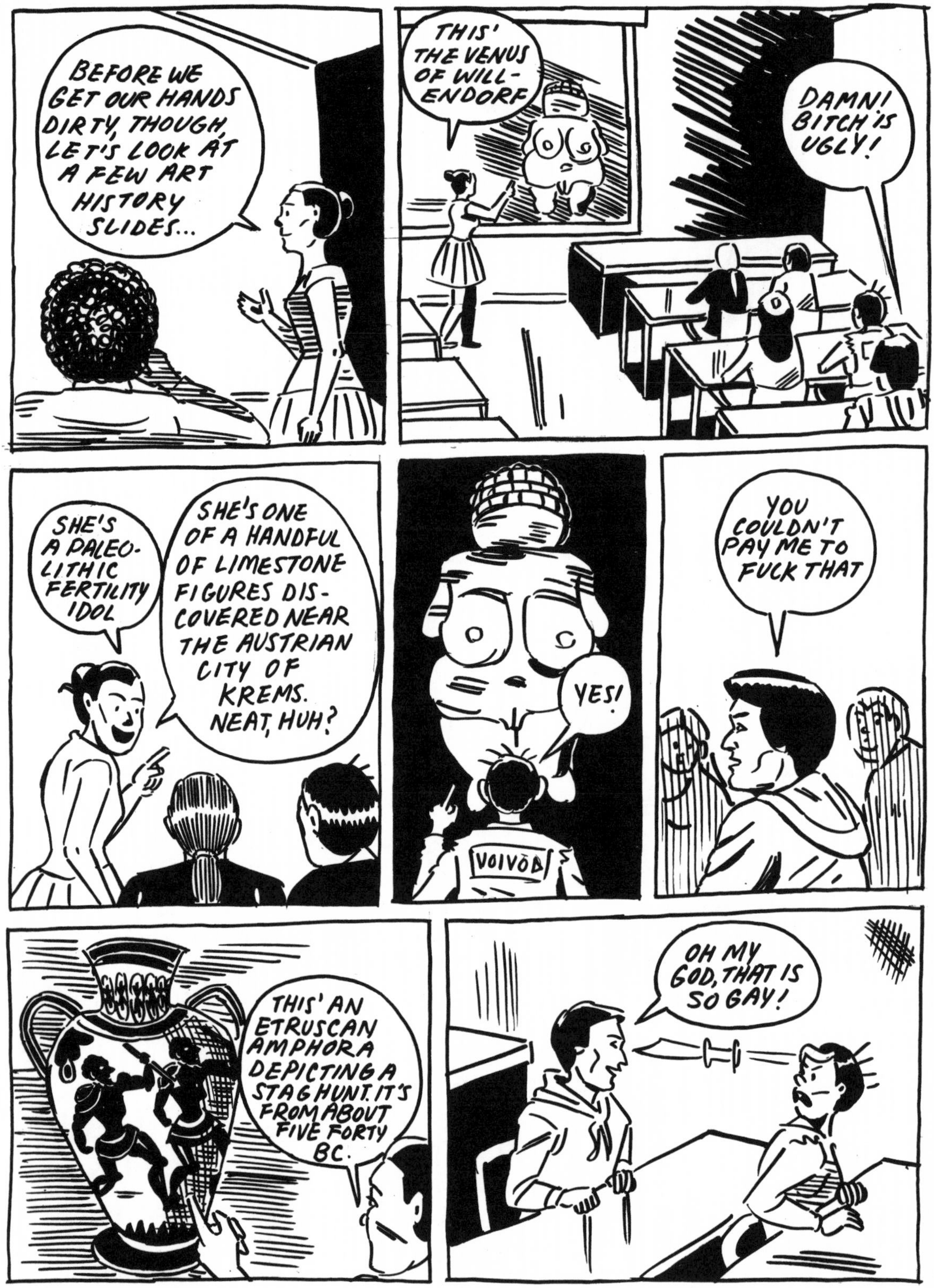
BEFORE WE GET OUR HANDS DIRTY, THOUGH, LET'S LOOK AT A FEW ART HISTORY SLIDES...
THIS' THE VENUS OF WILL-ENDORF
DAMN! BITCH IS UGLY!
SHE'S A PALEO-LITHIC FERTILITY IDOL
SHE'S ONE OF A HANDFUL OF LIMESTONE FIGURES DIS-COVERED NEAR THE AUSTRIAN CITY OF KREMS. NEAT, HUH?
YES!
VOIVOD
YOU COULDN'T PAY ME TO FUCK THAT
THIS' AN ETRUSCAN AMPHORA DEPICTING A STAG HUNT. IT'S FROM ABOUT FIVE FORTY BC.
OH MY GOD, THAT IS SO GAY!

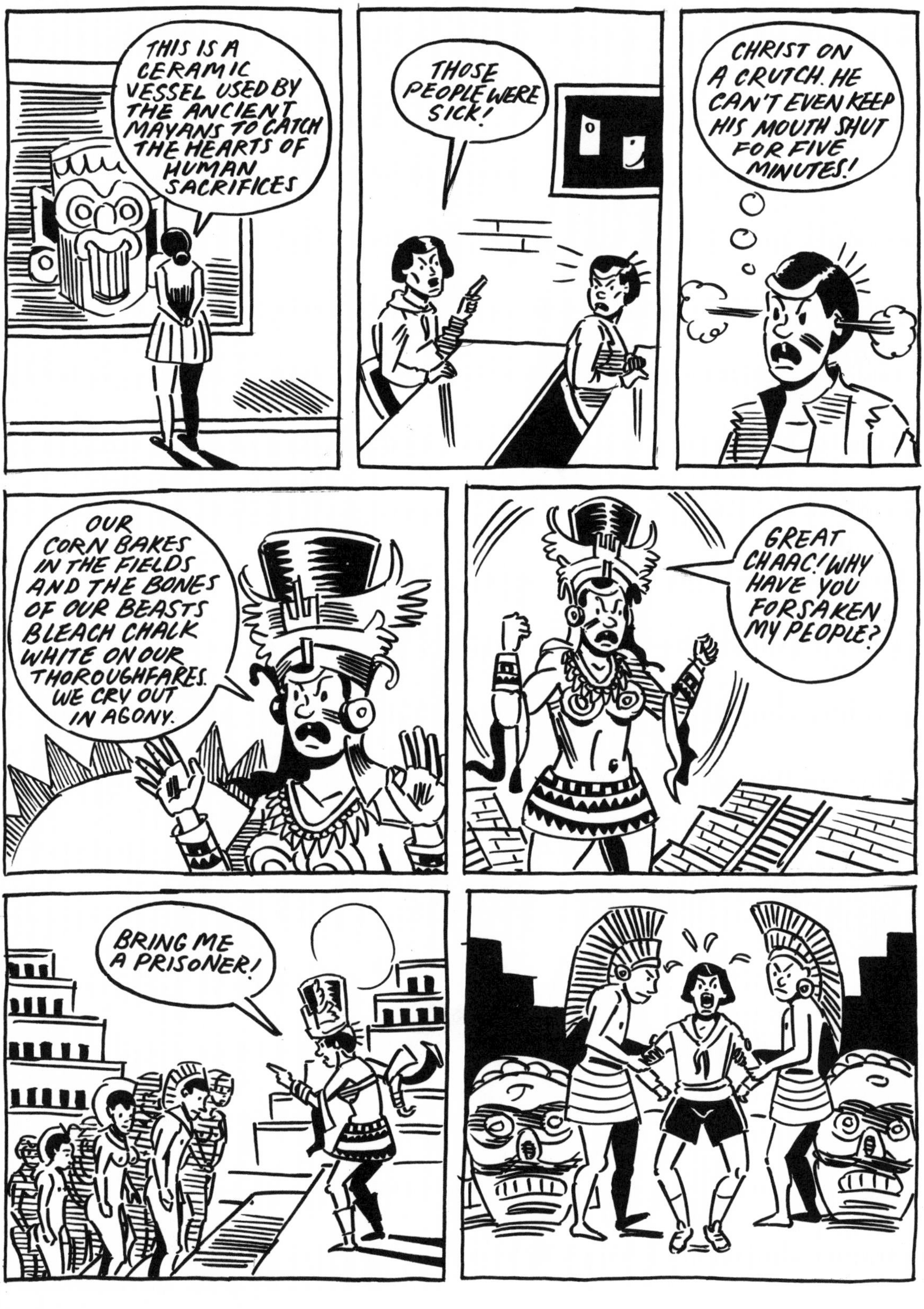
THIS IS A CERAMIC VESSEL USED BY THE ANCIENT MAYANS TO CATCH THE HEARTS OF HUMAN SACRIFICES
THOSE PEOPLE WERE SICK!
CHRIST ON A CRUTCH. HE CAN'T EVEN KEEP HIS MOUTH SHUT FOR FIVE MINUTES!
OUR CORN BAKES IN THE FIELDS AND THE BONES OF OUR BEASTS BLEACH CHALK WHITE ON OUR THOROUGHFARES. WE CRY OUT IN AGONY.
GREAT CHAAC! WHY HAVE YOU FORSAKEN MY PEOPLE?
BRING ME A PRISONER!

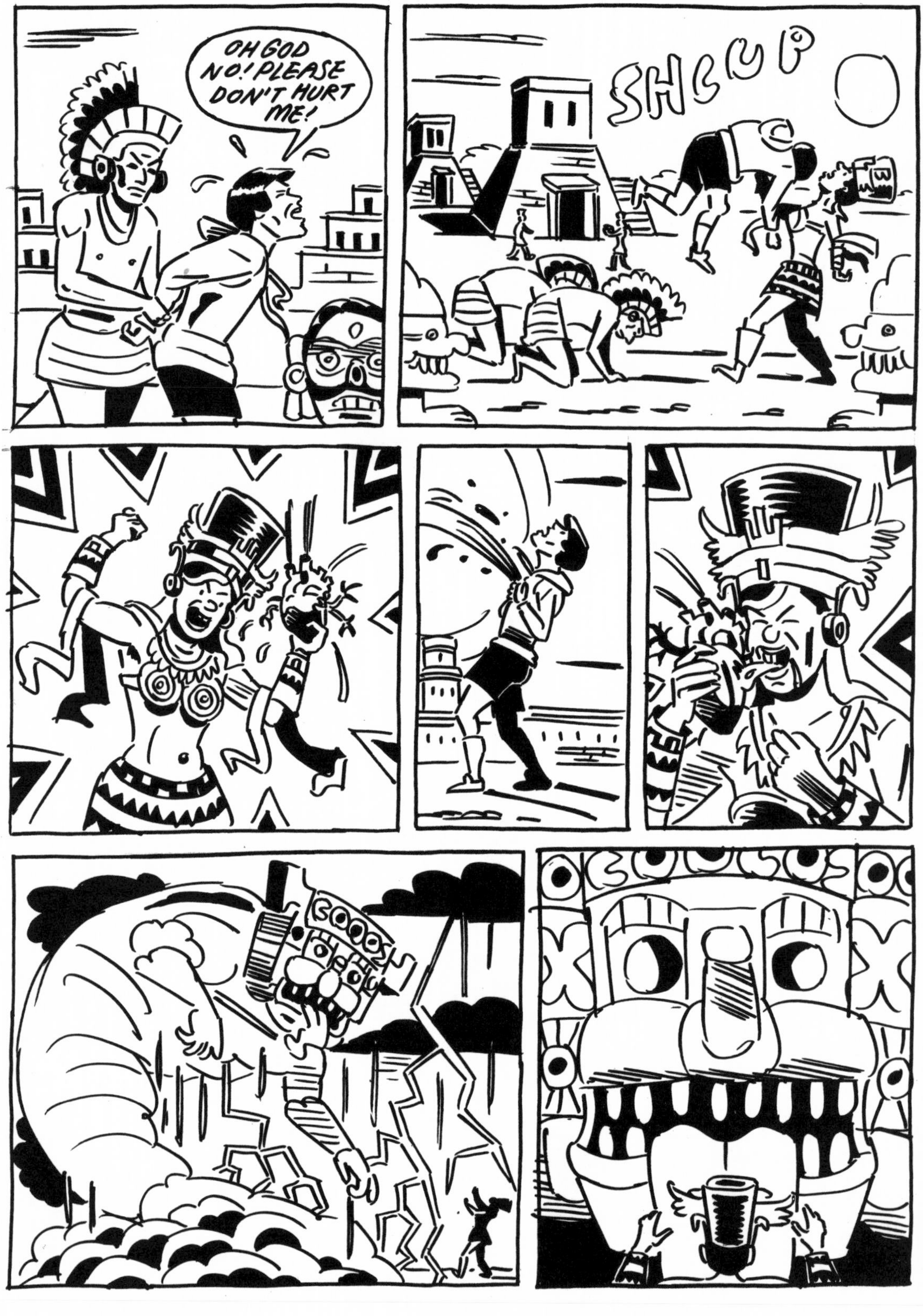
OH GOD NO! PLEASE DON'T HURT ME!
SHLUP

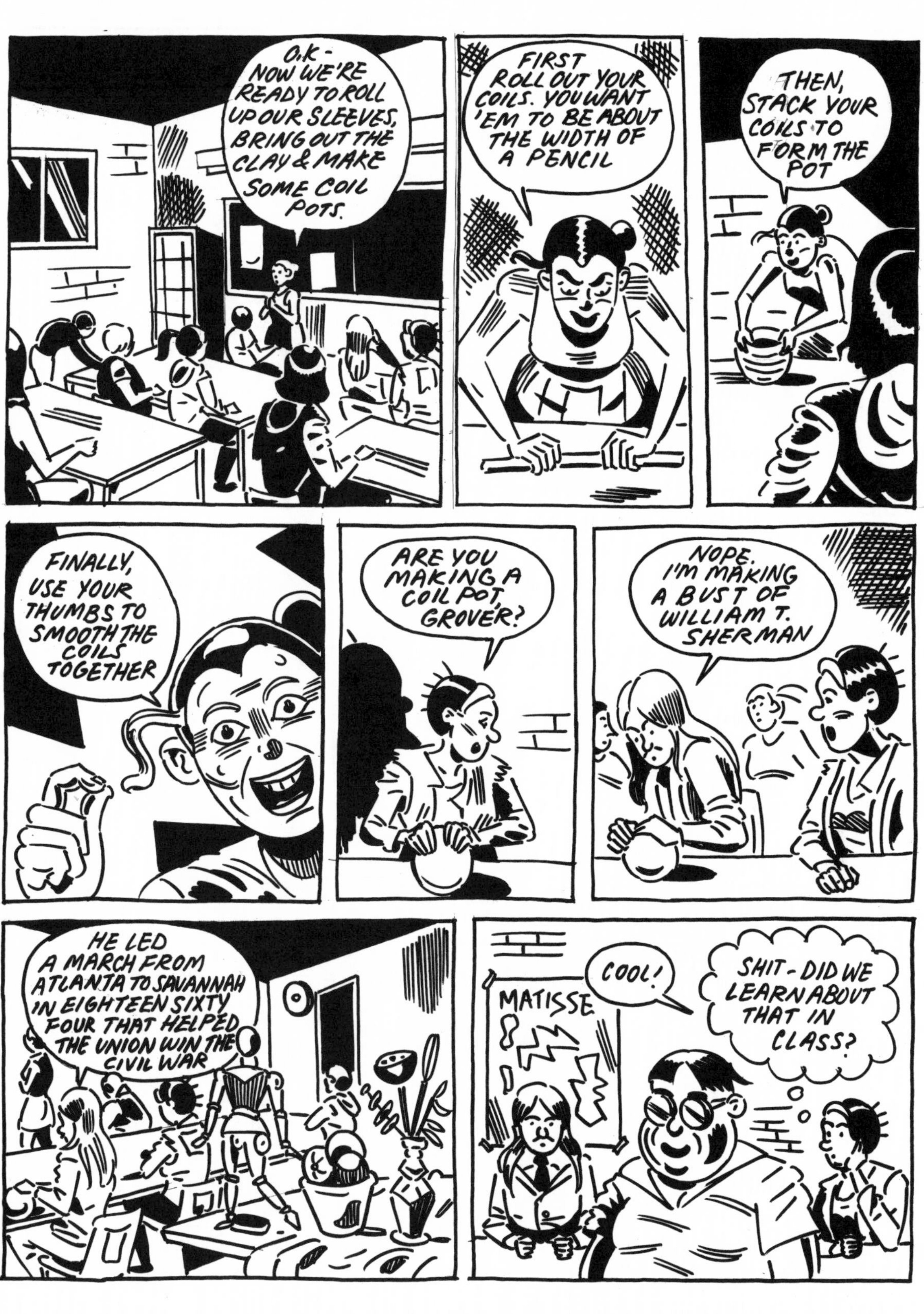
O.K - NOW WE'RE READY TO ROLL UP OUR SLEEVES, BRING OUT THE CLAY & MAKE SOME COIL POTS.
FIRST ROLL OUT YOUR COILS. YOU WANT 'EM TO BE ABOUT THE WIDTH OF A PENCIL
THEN, STACK YOUR COILS TO FORM THE POT
FINALLY, USE YOUR THUMBS TO SMOOTH THE COILS TOGETHER
ARE YOU MAKING A COIL POT, GROVER?
NOPE. I'M MAKING A BUST OF WILLIAM T. SHERMAN
HE LED A MARCH FROM ATLANTA TO SAVANNAH IN EIGHTEEN SIXTY FOUR THAT HELPED THE UNION WIN THE CIVIL WAR
MATISSE
COOL!
SHIT - DID WE LEARN ABOUT THAT IN CLASS?

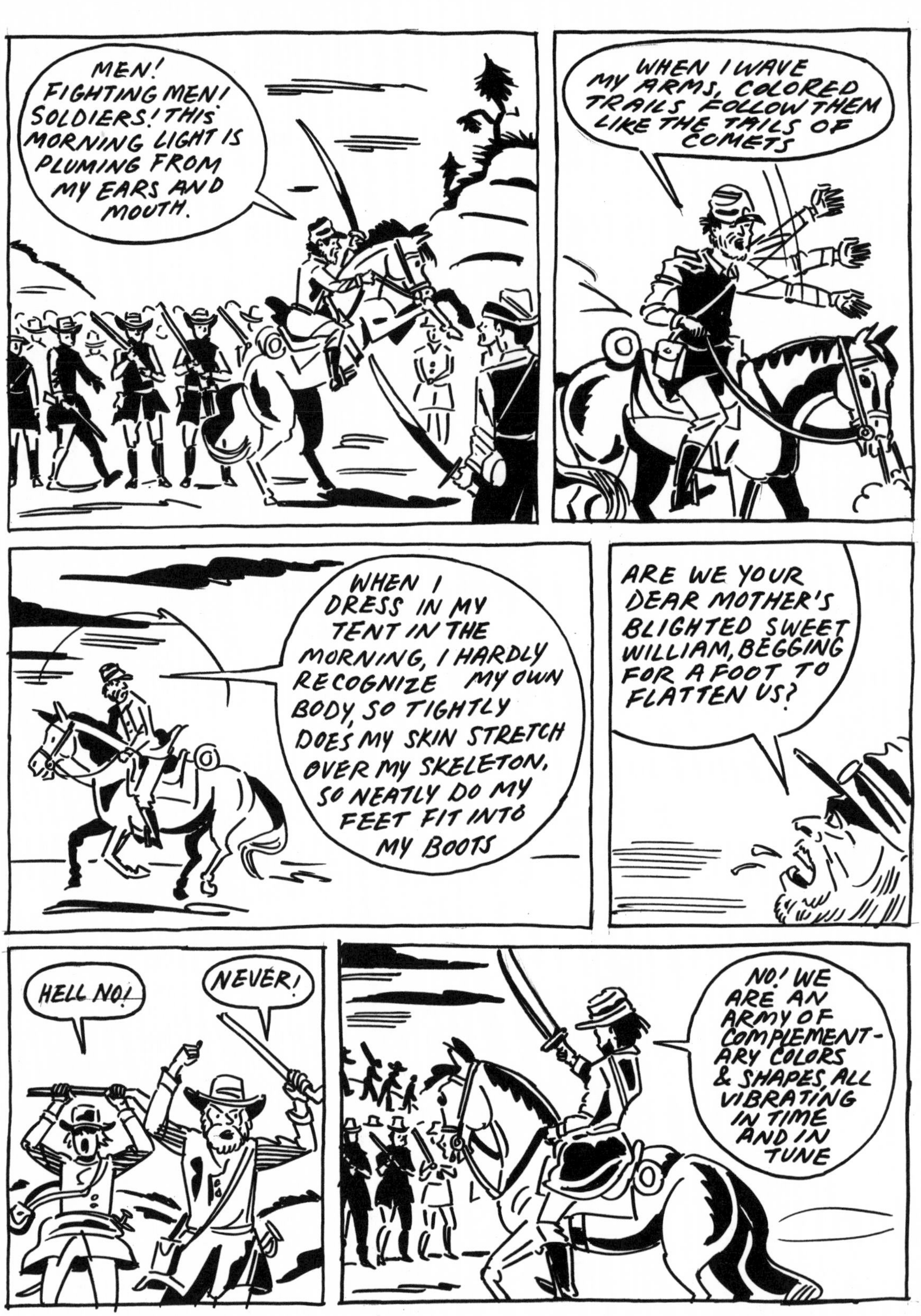
MEN! FIGHTING MEN! SOLDIERS! THIS MORNING LIGHT IS PLUMING FROM MY EARS AND MOUTH.
WHEN I WAVE MY ARMS, COLORED TRAILS FOLLOW THEM LIKE THE TAILS OF COMETS
WHEN I DRESS IN MY TENT IN THE MORNING, I HARDLY RECOGNIZE MY OWN BODY, SO TIGHTLY DOES MY SKIN STRETCH OVER MY SKELETON, SO NEATLY DO MY FEET FIT INTO MY BOOTS
ARE WE YOUR DEAR MOTHER'S BLIGHTED SWEET WILLIAM, BEGGING FOR A FOOT TO FLATTEN US?
HELL NO!
NEVER!
NO! WE ARE AN ARMY OF COMPLEMENT-ARY COLORS & SHAPES, ALL VIBRATING IN TIME AND IN TUNE

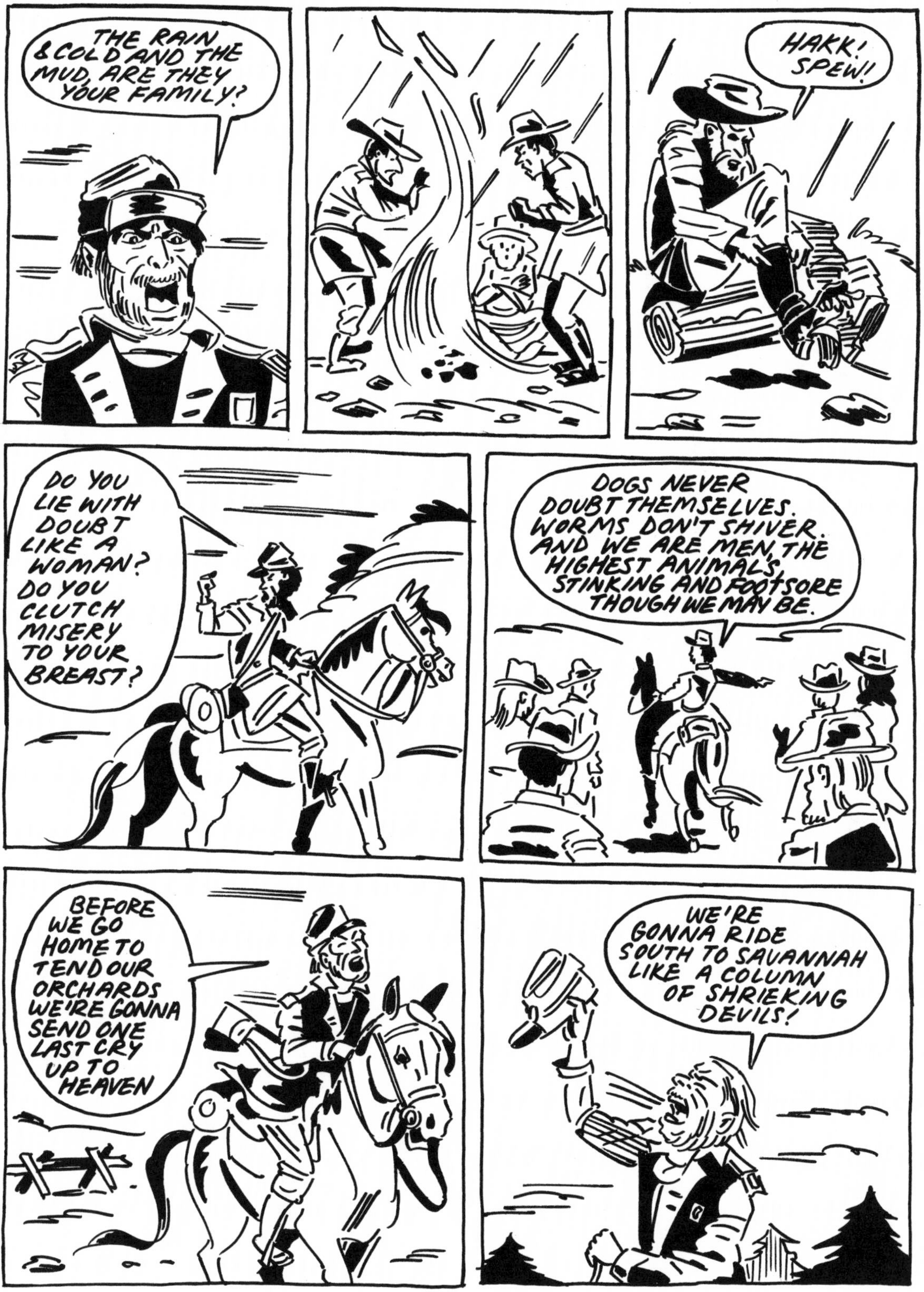
THE RAIN & COLD AND THE MUD, ARE THEY YOUR FAMILY?
HAKK! SPEW!
DO YOU LIE WITH DOUBT LIKE A WOMAN? DO YOU CLUTCH MISERY TO YOUR BREAST?
DOGS NEVER DOUBT THEMSELVES. WORMS DON'T SHIVER. AND WE ARE MEN, THE HIGHEST ANIMALS, STINKING AND FOOTSORE THOUGH WE MAY BE.
BEFORE WE GO HOME TO TEND OUR ORCHARDS WE'RE GONNA SEND ONE LAST CRY UP TO HEAVEN
WE'RE GONNA RIDE SOUTH TO SAVANNAH LIKE A COLUMN OF SHRIEKING DEVILS!

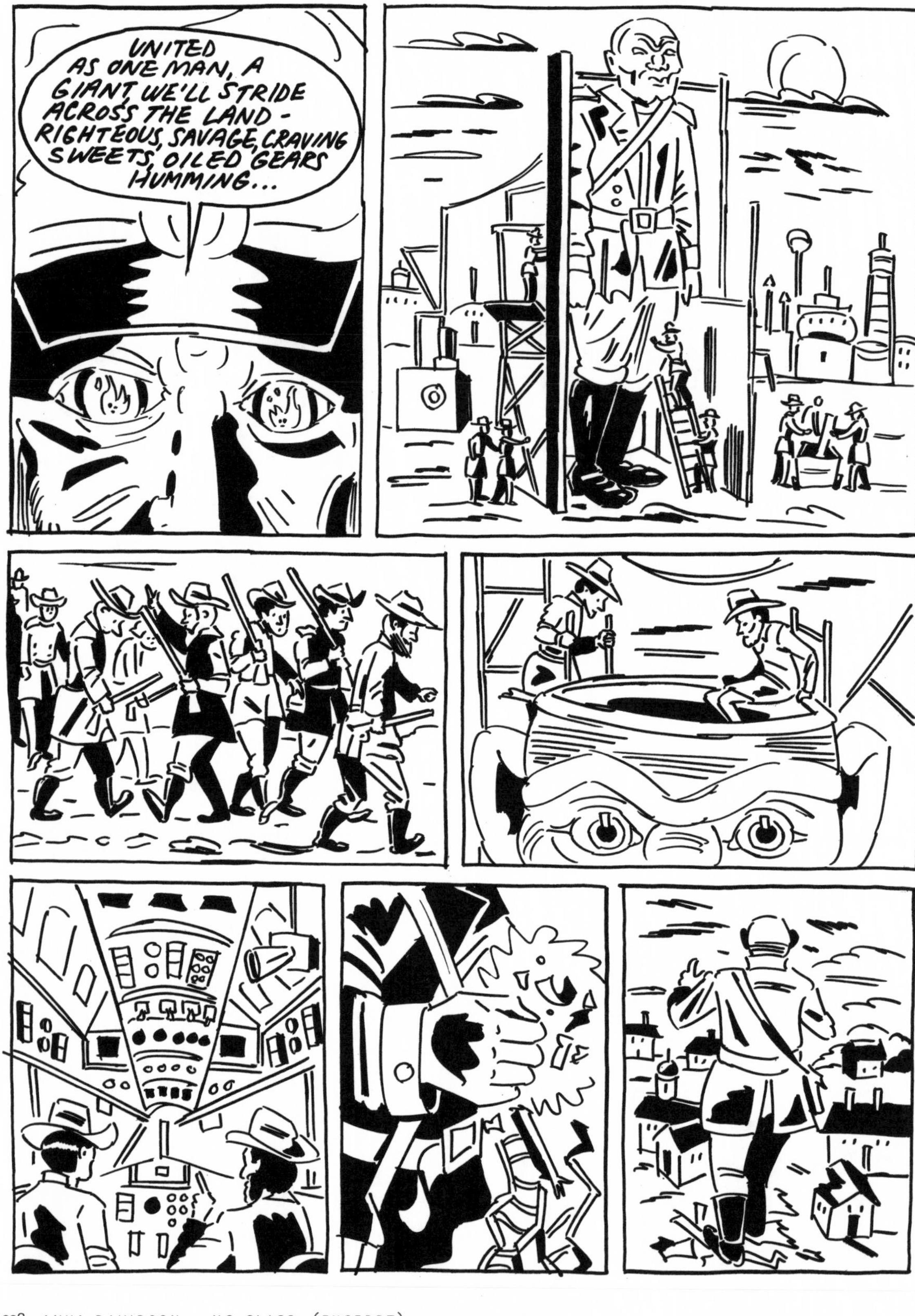
UNITED AS ONE MAN, A GIANT, WE'LL STRIDE ACROSS THE LAND - RIGHTEOUS, SAVAGE, CRAVING SWEETS, OILED GEARS HUMMING...

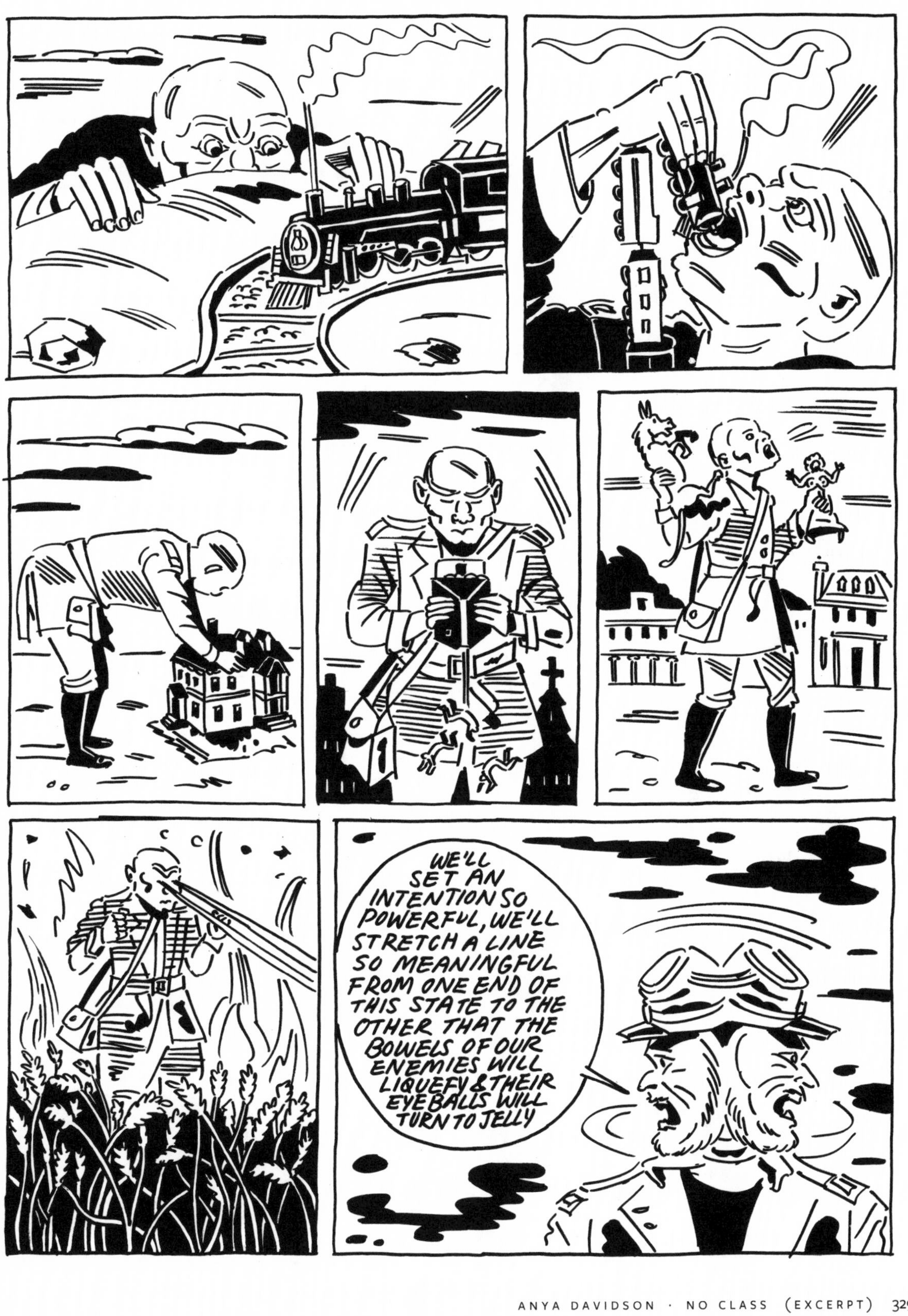
WE'LL SET AN INTENTION SO POWERFUL, WE'LL STRETCH A LINE SO MEANINGFUL FROM ONE END OF THIS STATE TO THE OTHER THAT THE BOWELS OF OUR ENEMIES WILL LIQUEFY & THEIR EYEBALLS WILL TURN TO JELLY

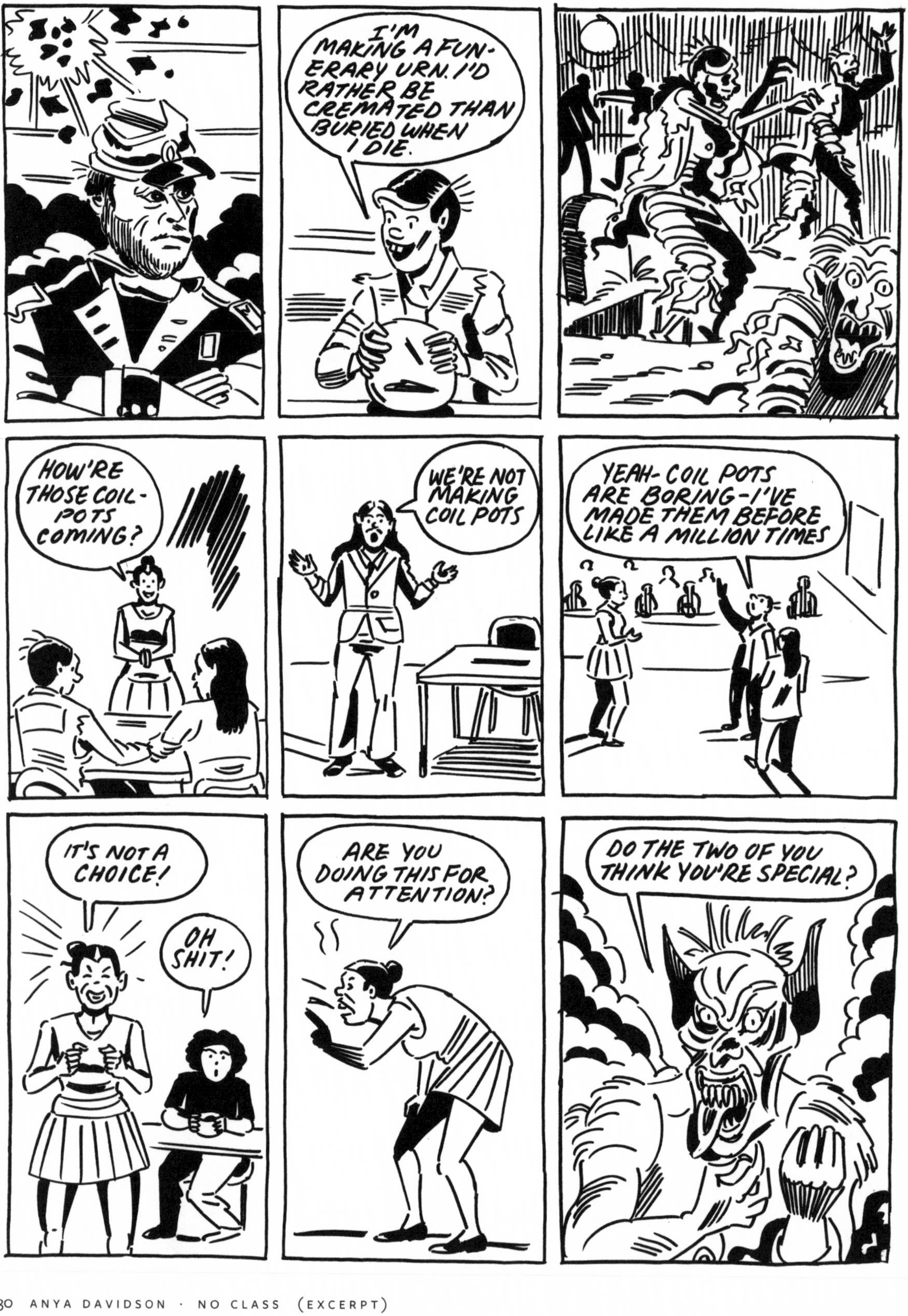

I'M MAKING A FUNERARY URN. I'D RATHER BE CREMATED THAN BURIED WHEN I DIE.
HOW'RE THOSE COIL-POTS COMING?
WE'RE NOT MAKING COIL POTS
YEAH- COIL POTS ARE BORING- I'VE MADE THEM BEFORE LIKE A MILLION TIMES
IT'S NOT A CHOICE!
OH SHIT!
ARE YOU DOING THIS FOR ATTENTION?
DO THE TWO OF YOU THINK YOU'RE SPECIAL?

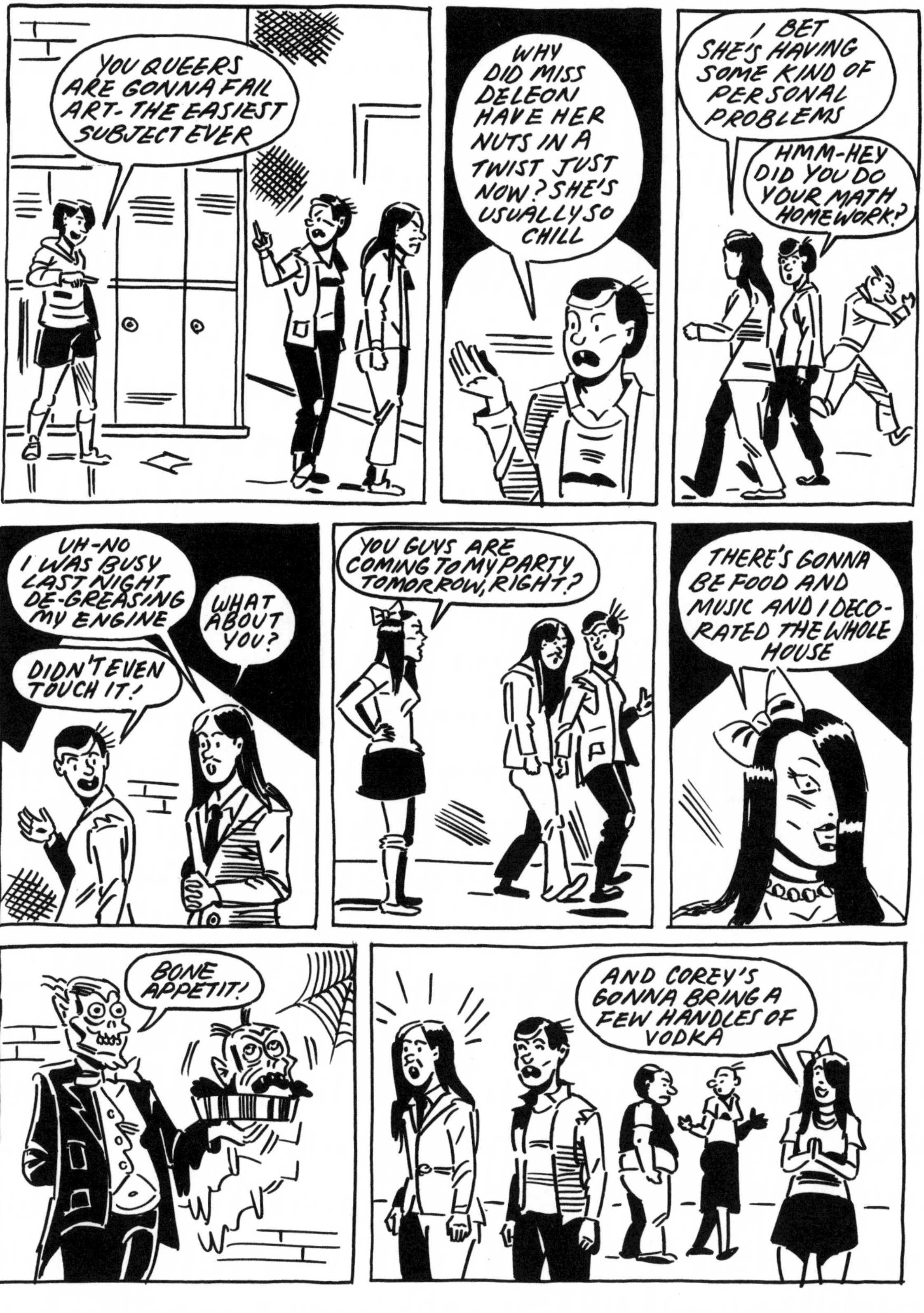
YOU QUEERS ARE GONNA FAIL ART- THE EASIEST SUBJECT EVER
WHY DID MISS DELEON HAVE HER NUTS IN A TWIST JUST NOW? SHE'S USUALLY SO CHILL
I BET SHE'S HAVING SOME KIND OF PERSONAL PROBLEMS
HMM-HEY DID YOU DO YOUR MATH HOMEWORK?
UH-NO I WAS BUSY LAST NIGHT DE-GREASING MY ENGINE
WHAT ABOUT YOU?
DIDN'T EVEN TOUCH IT!
YOU GUYS ARE COMING TO MY PARTY TOMORROW, RIGHT?
THERE'S GONNA BE FOOD AND MUSIC AND I DECORATED THE WHOLE HOUSE
BONE APPETIT!
AND COREY'S GONNA BRING A FEW HANDLES OF VODKA

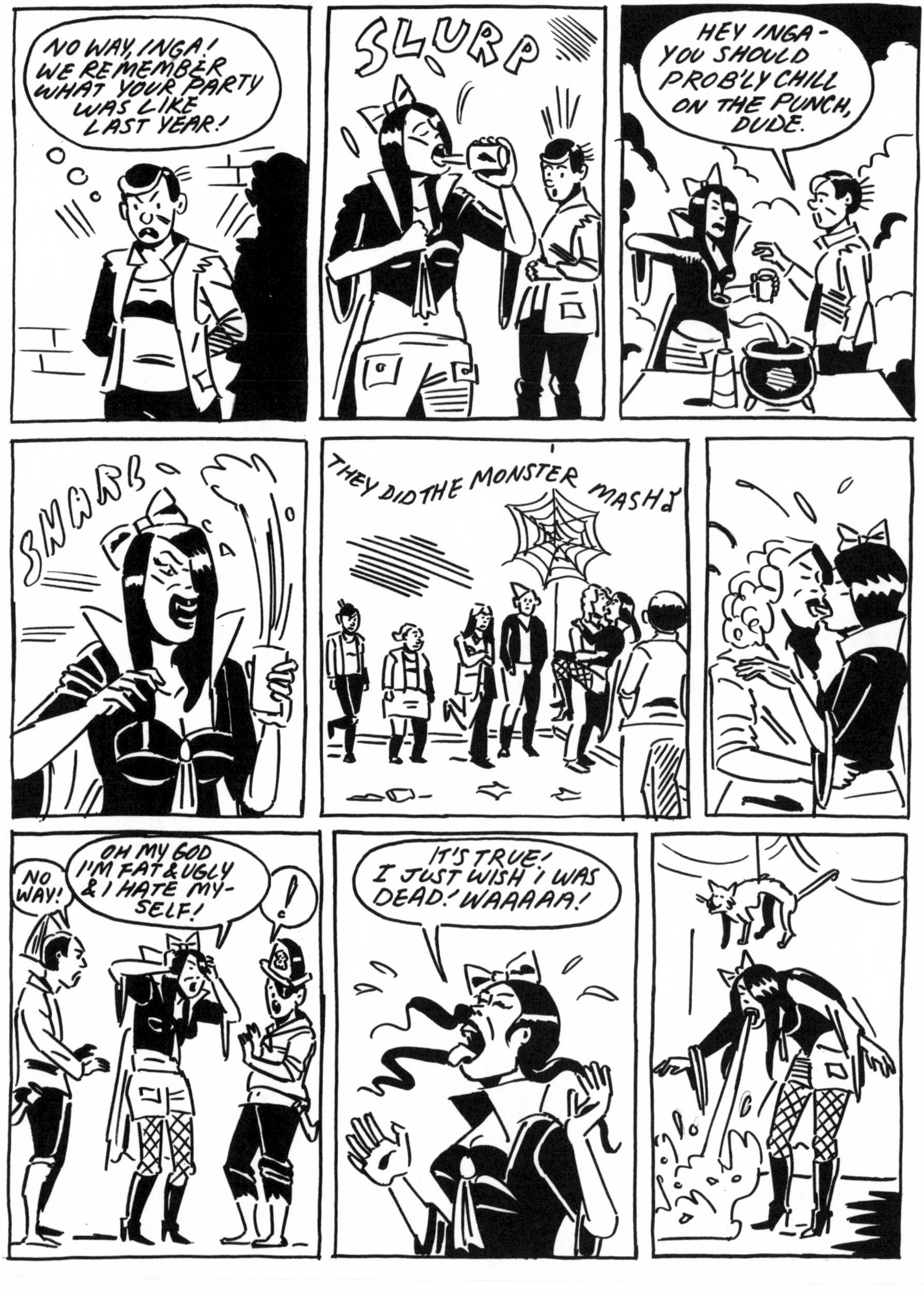

NO WAY, INGA! WE REMEMBER WHAT YOUR PARTY WAS LIKE LAST YEAR!
SLURP
HEY INGA- YOU SHOULD PROB'LY CHILL ON THE PUNCH, DUDE.
THEY DID THE MONSTER MASH♪
NO WAY!
OH MY GOD I'M FAT & UGLY & I HATE MY-SELF!
!
IT'S TRUE! I JUST WISH I WAS DEAD! WAAAAA!

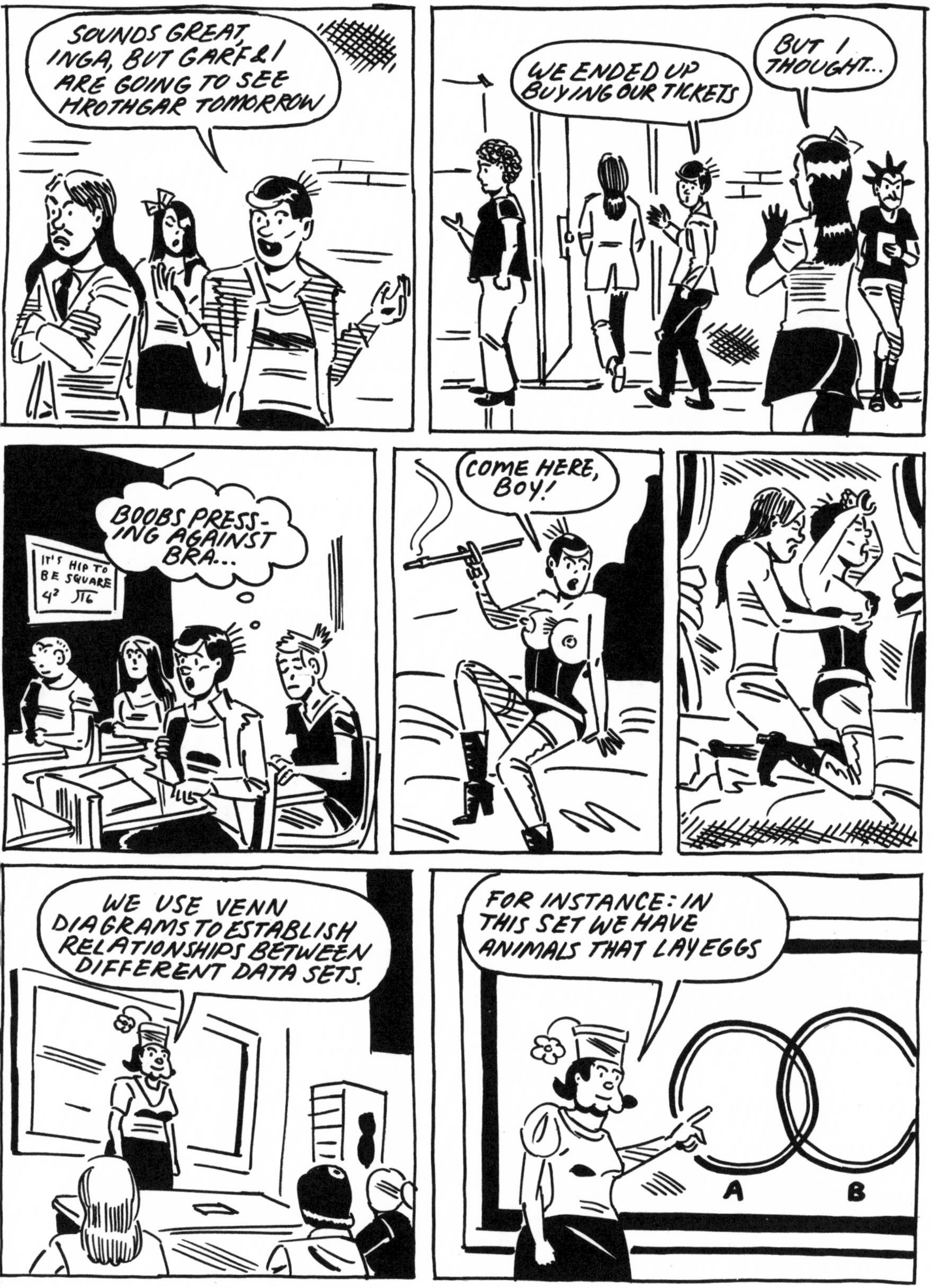
SOUNDS GREAT, INGA, BUT GARF & I ARE GOING TO SEE HROTHGAR TOMORROW
WE ENDED UP BUYING OUR TICKETS
BUT I THOUGHT...
BOOBS PRESSING AGAINST BRA...
IT'S HIP TO BE SQUARE
4² √16
COME HERE, BOY!
WE USE VENN DIAGRAMS TO ESTABLISH RELATIONSHIPS BETWEEN DIFFERENT DATA SETS.
FOR INSTANCE: IN THIS SET WE HAVE ANIMALS THAT LAY EGGS
A
B

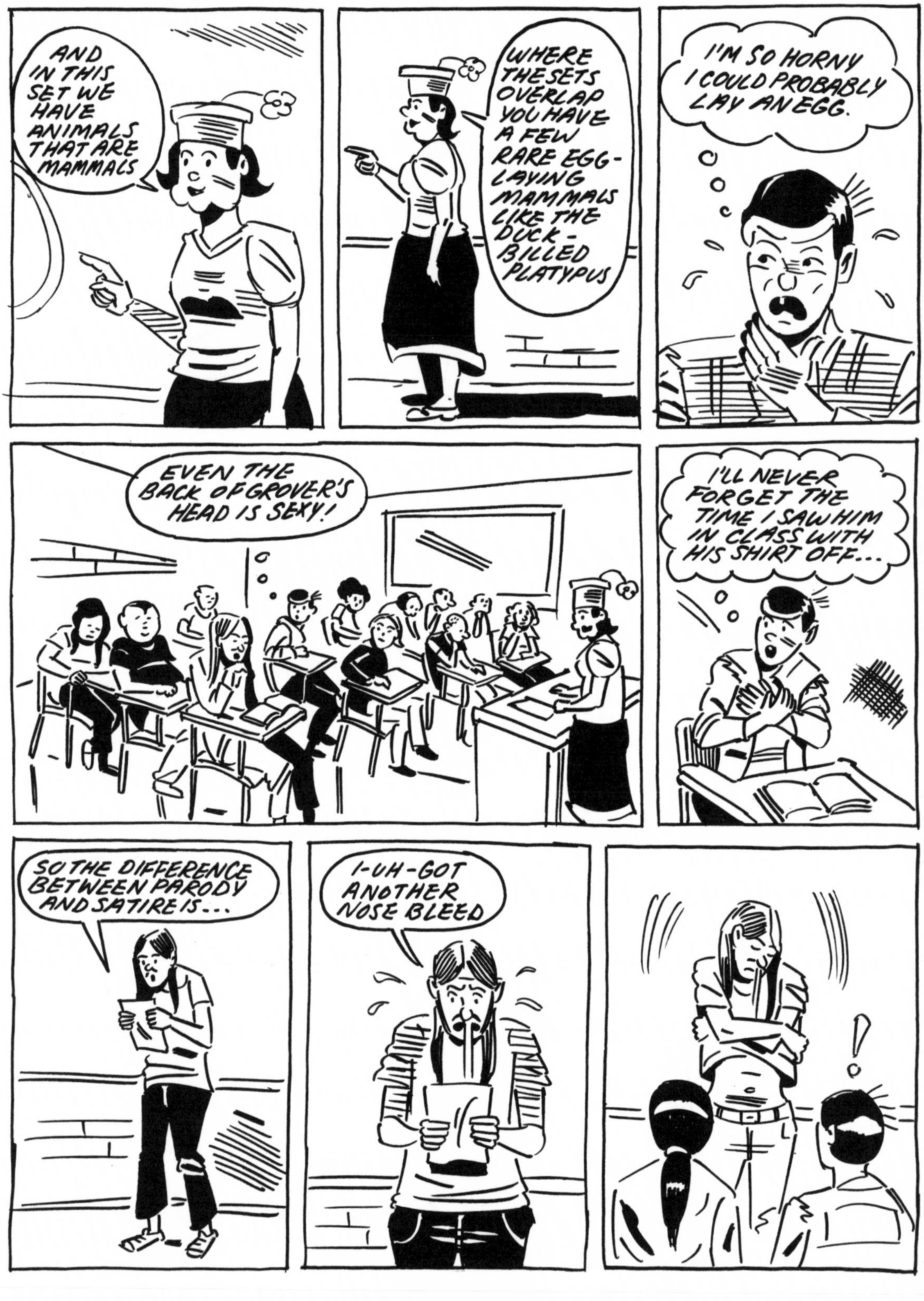
AND IN THIS SET WE HAVE ANIMALS THAT ARE MAMMALS
WHERE THE SETS OVERLAP YOU HAVE A FEW RARE EGG-LAYING MAMMALS LIKE THE DUCK-BILLED PLATYPUS
I'M SO HORNY I COULD PROBABLY LAY AN EGG.
EVEN THE BACK OF GROVER'S HEAD IS SEXY!
I'LL NEVER FORGET THE TIME I SAW HIM IN CLASS WITH HIS SHIRT OFF...
SO THE DIFFERENCE BETWEEN PARODY AND SATIRE IS...
I-UH-GOT ANOTHER NOSE BLEED
!

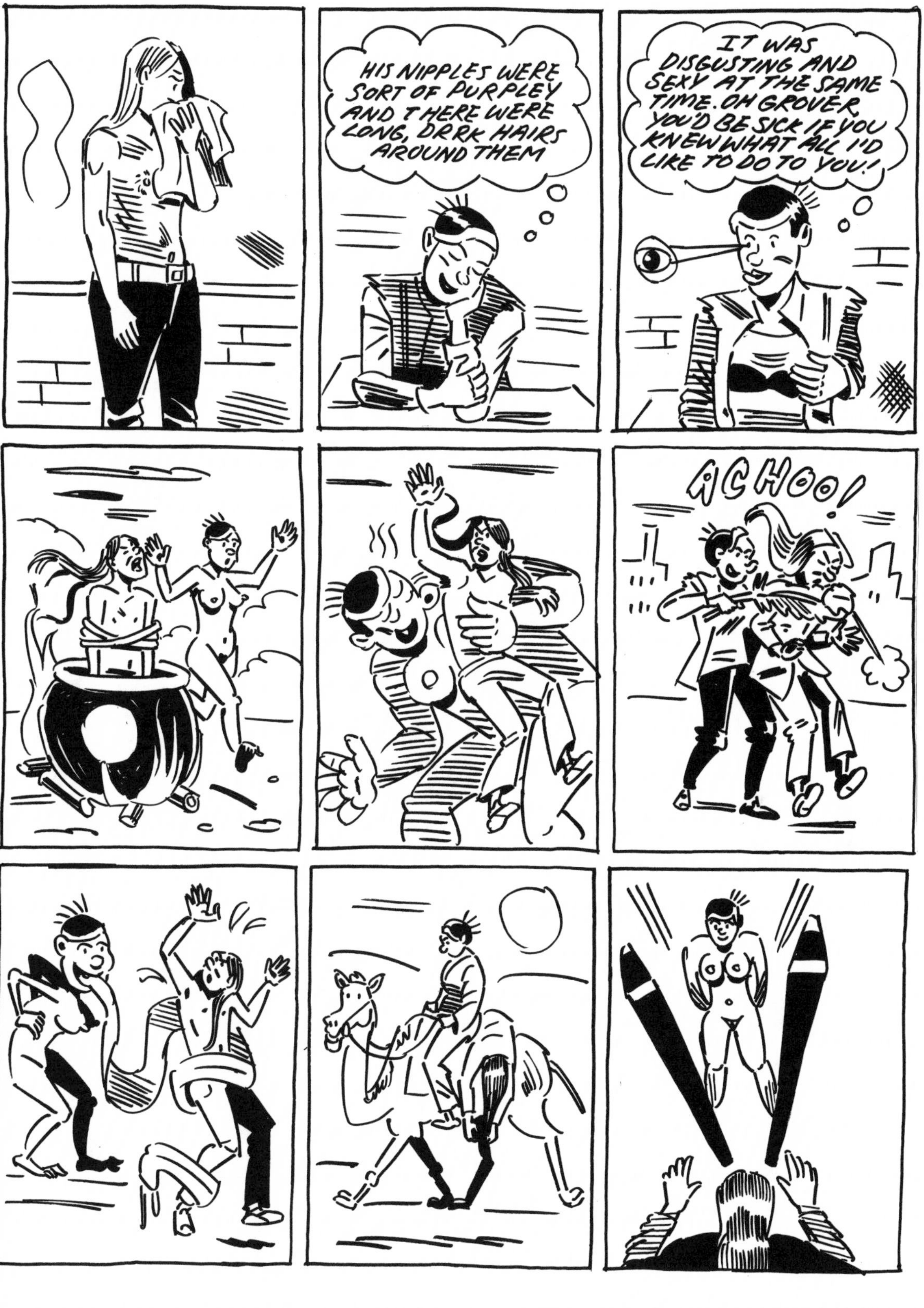
HIS NIPPLES WERE SORT OF PURPLEY AND THERE WERE LONG, DRRK HAIRS AROUND THEM
IT WAS DISGUSTING AND SEXY AT THE SAME TIME. OH GROVER, YOU'D BE SICK IF YOU KNEW WHAT ALL I'D LIKE TO DO TO YOU!
ACHOO!

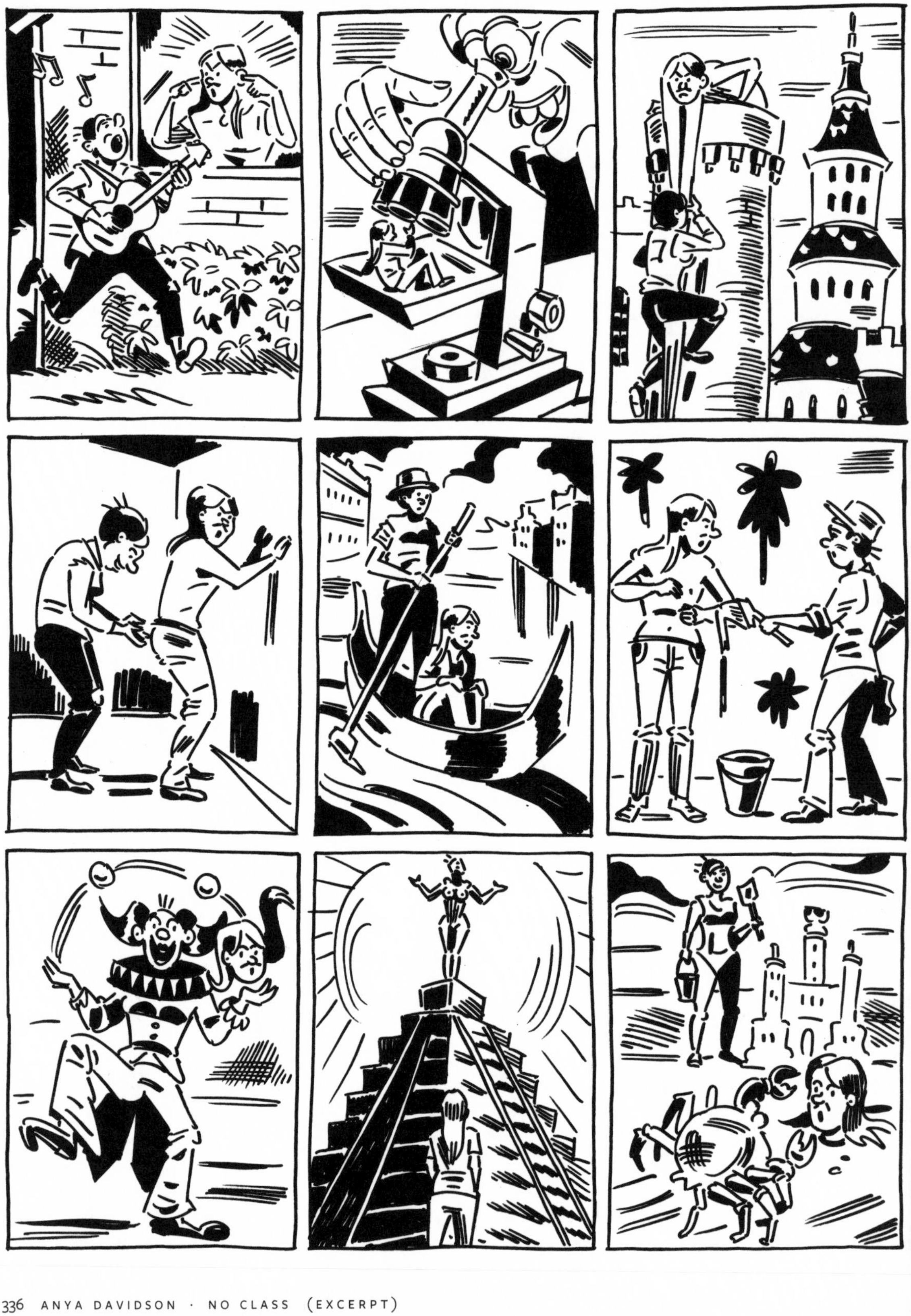

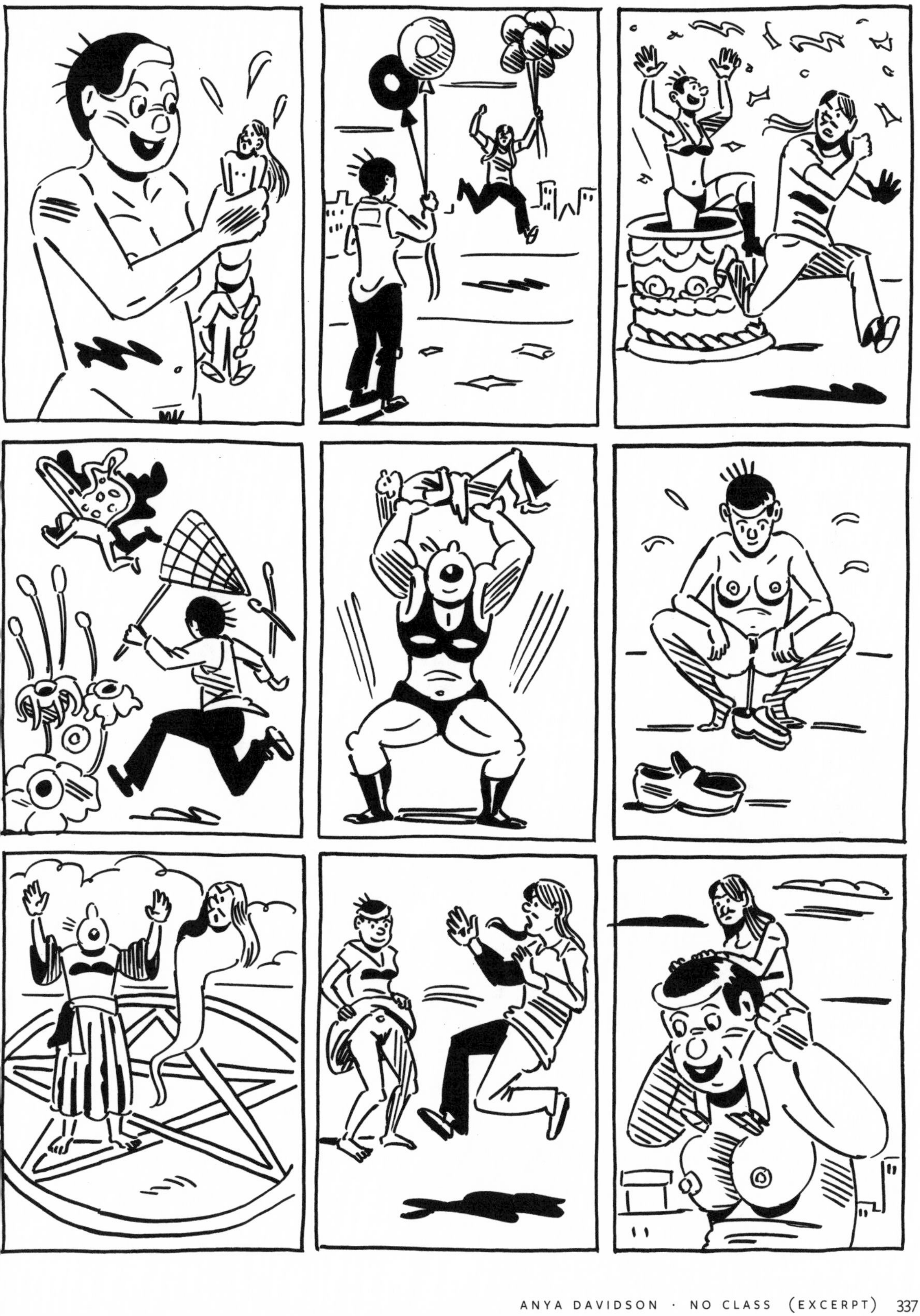

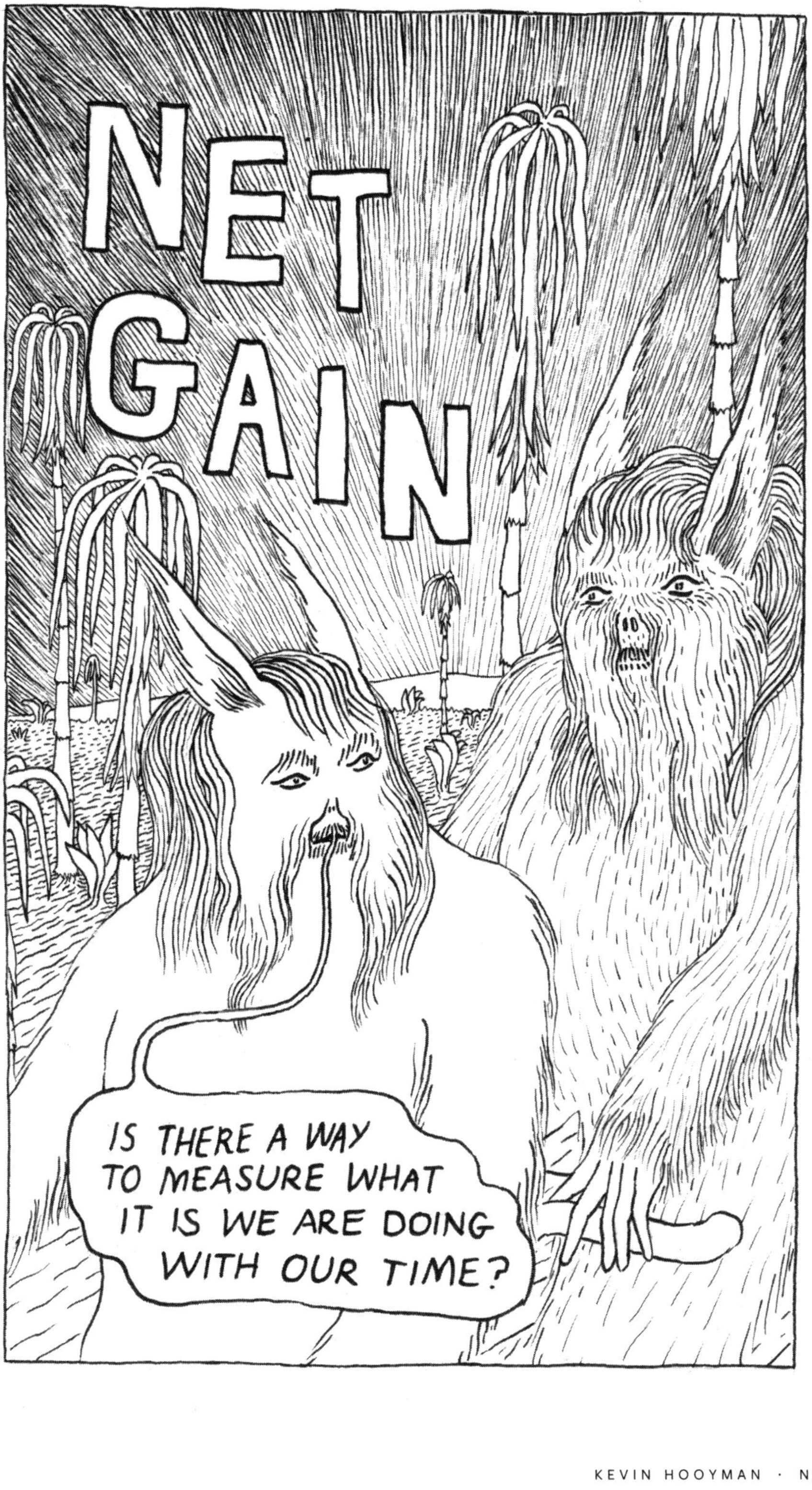
NET GAIN
IS THERE A WAY TO MEASURE WHAT IT IS WE ARE DOING WITH OUR TIME?

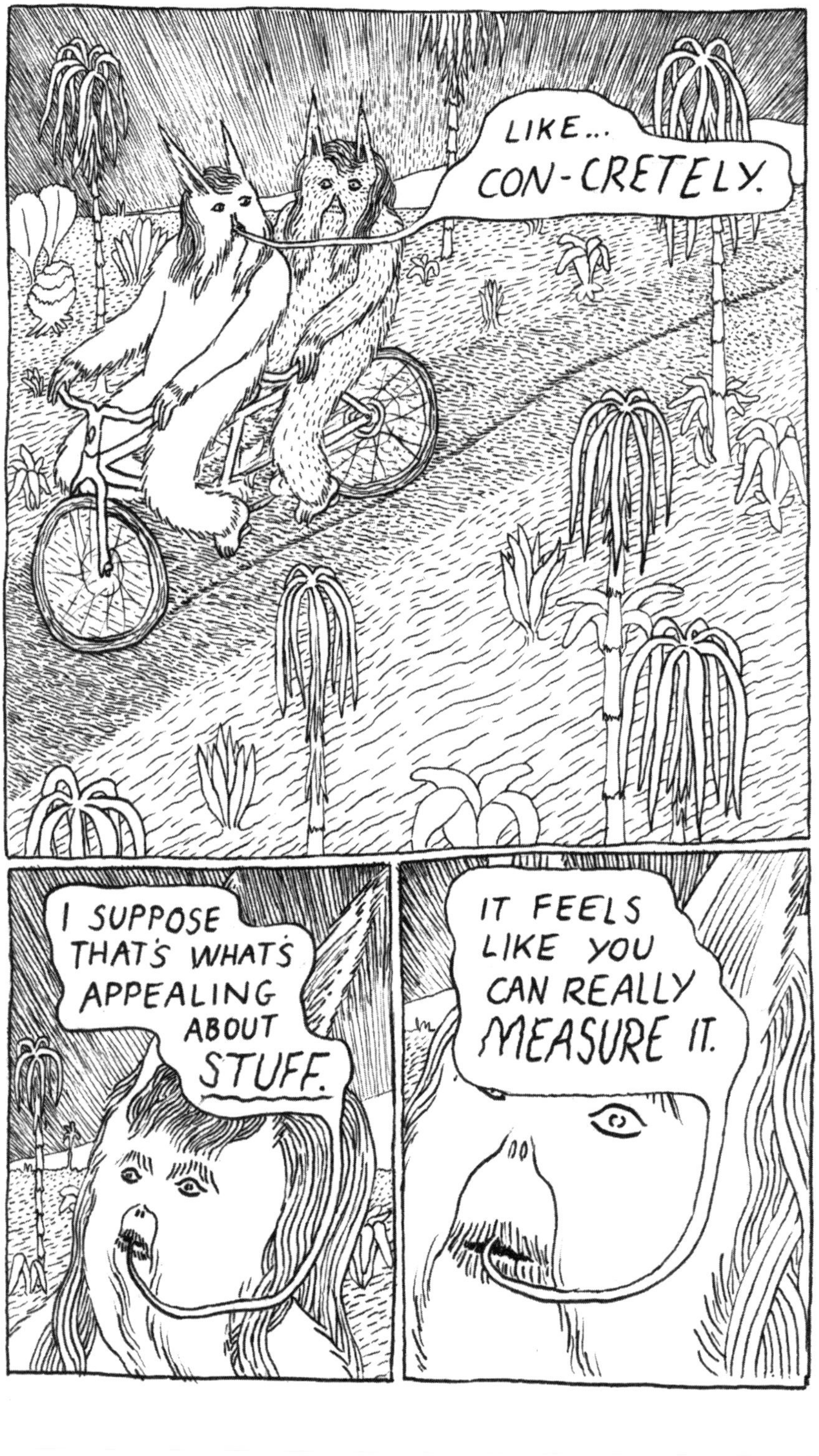
LIKE... CON-CRETELY.
I SUPPOSE THAT'S WHAT'S APPEALING ABOUT STUFF.
IT FEELS LIKE YOU CAN REALLY MEASURE IT.

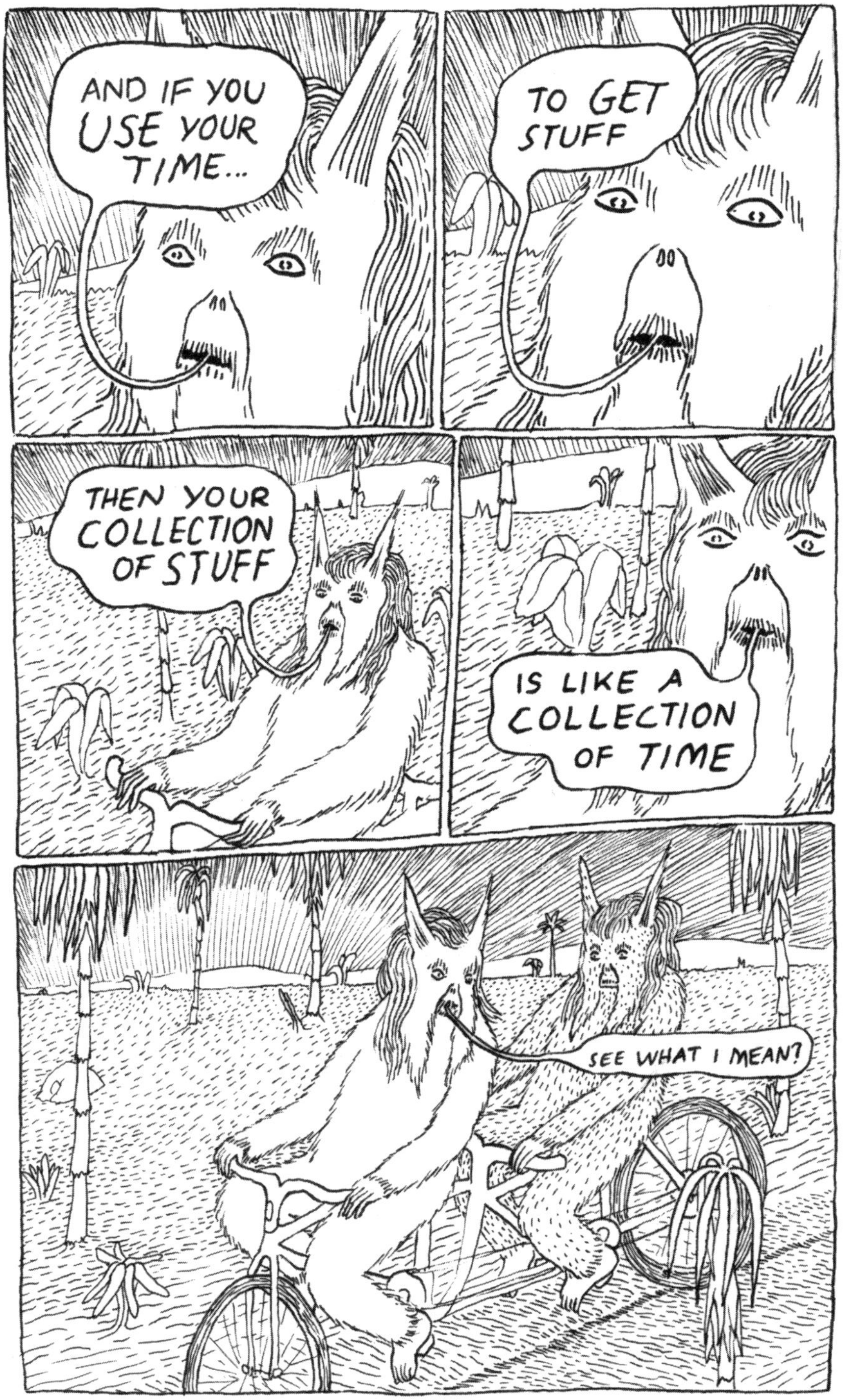
AND IF YOU USE YOUR TIME...
TO GET STUFF
THEN YOUR COLLECTION OF STUFF
IS LIKE A COLLECTION OF TIME
SEE WHAT I MEAN?

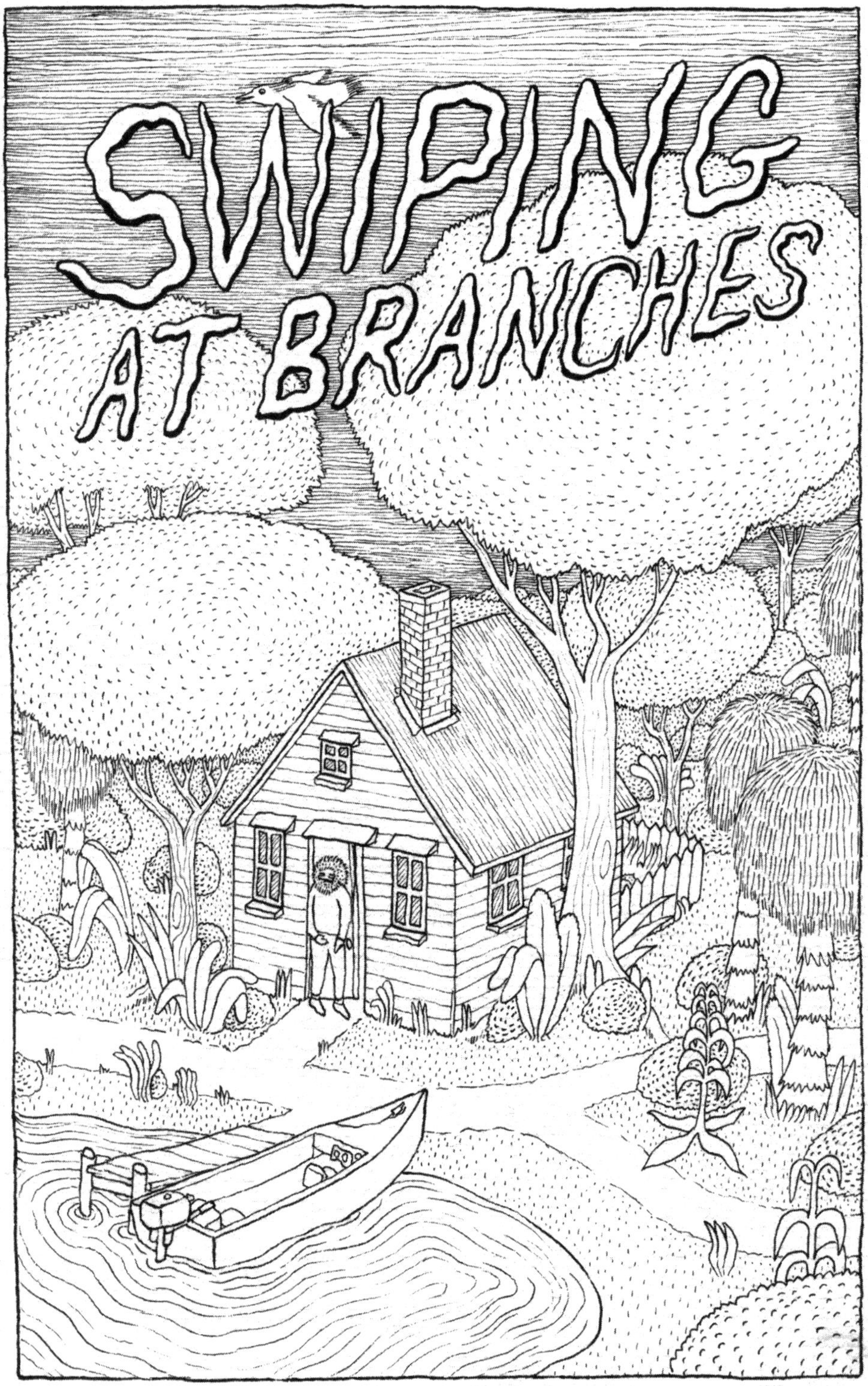
SWIPING AT BRANCHES

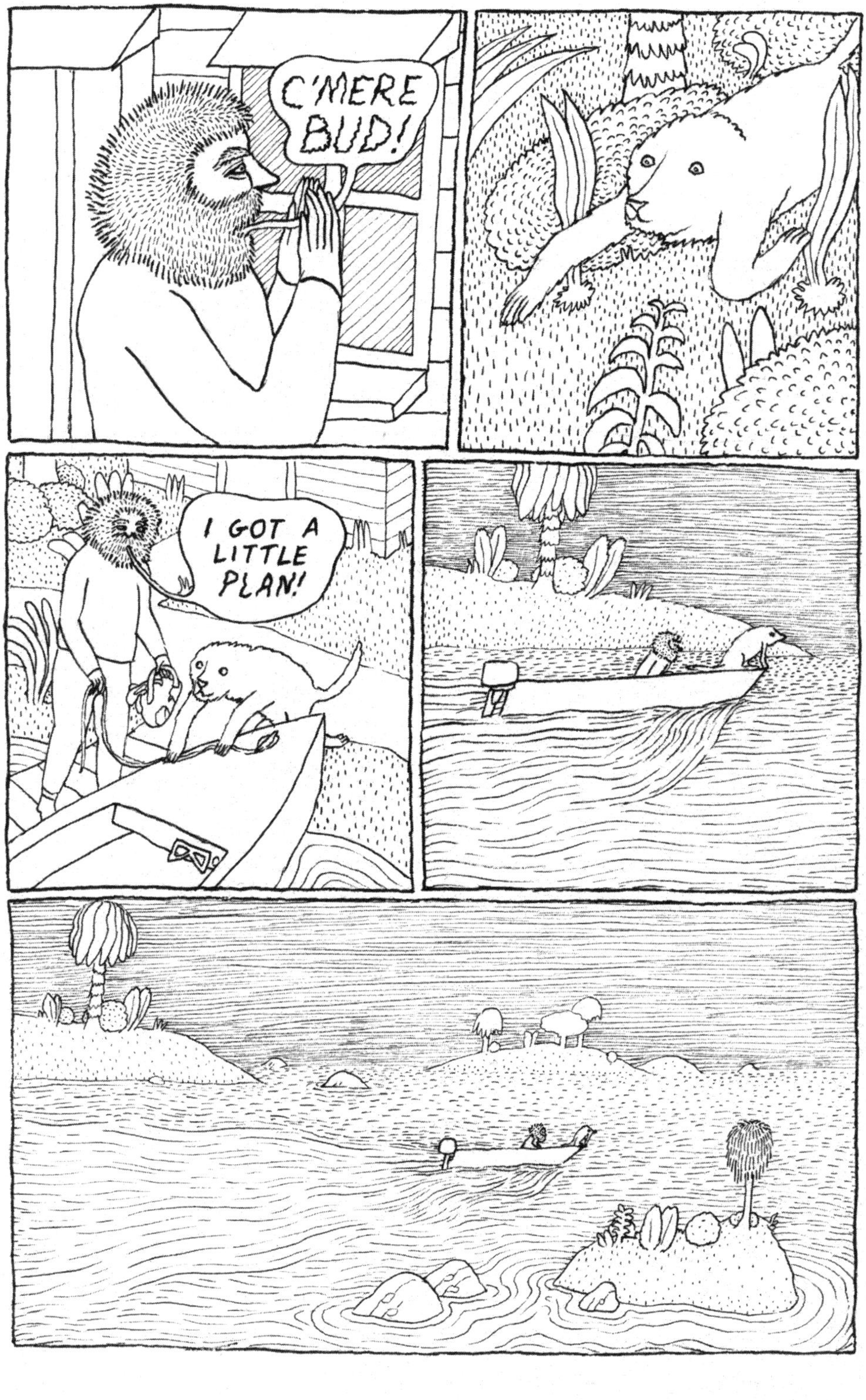
C'MERE BUD!
I GOT A LITTLE PLAN!

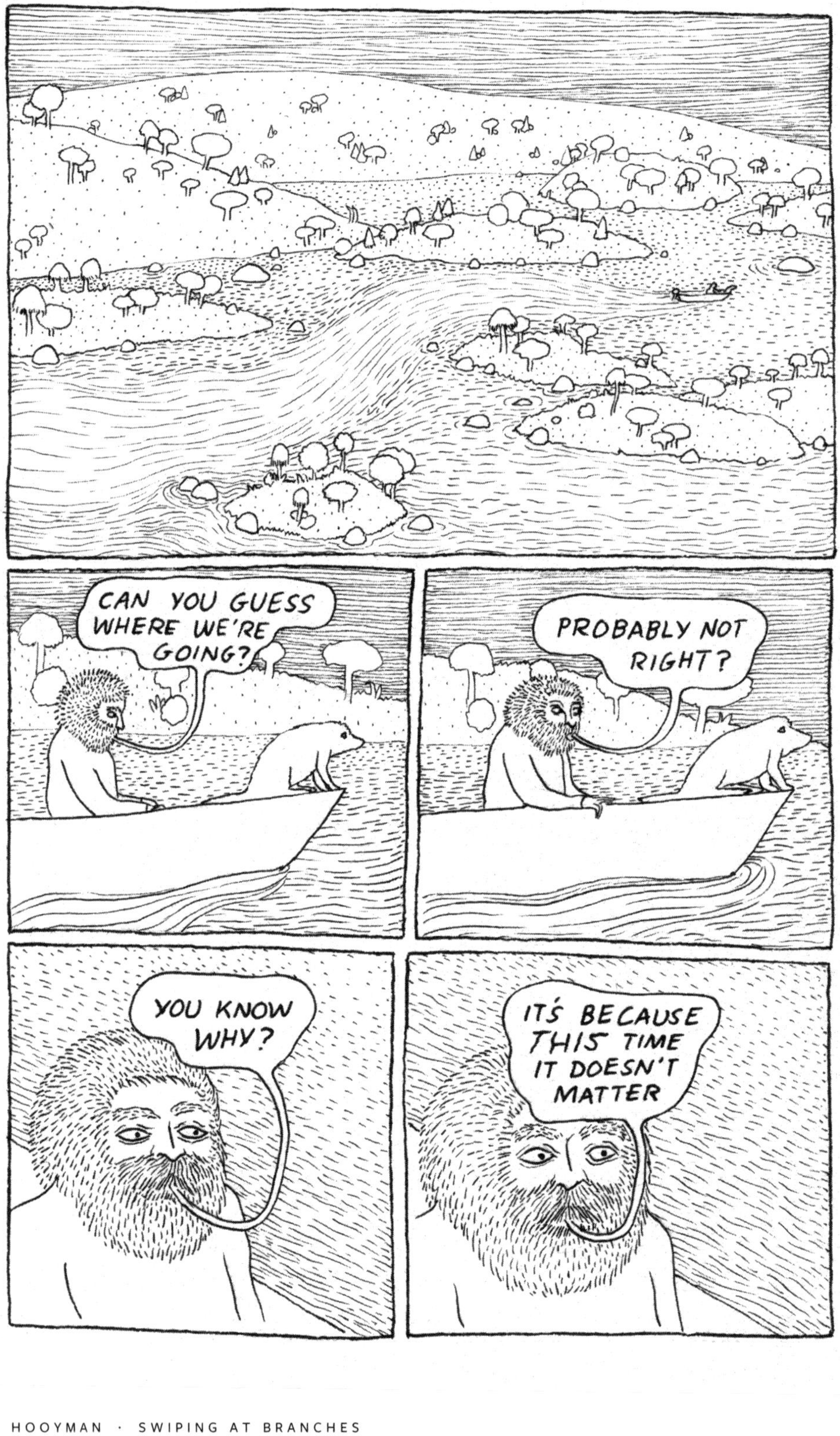
CAN YOU GUESS WHERE WE'RE GOING?
PROBABLY NOT RIGHT?
YOU KNOW WHY?
IT'S BECAUSE THIS TIME IT DOESN'T MATTER

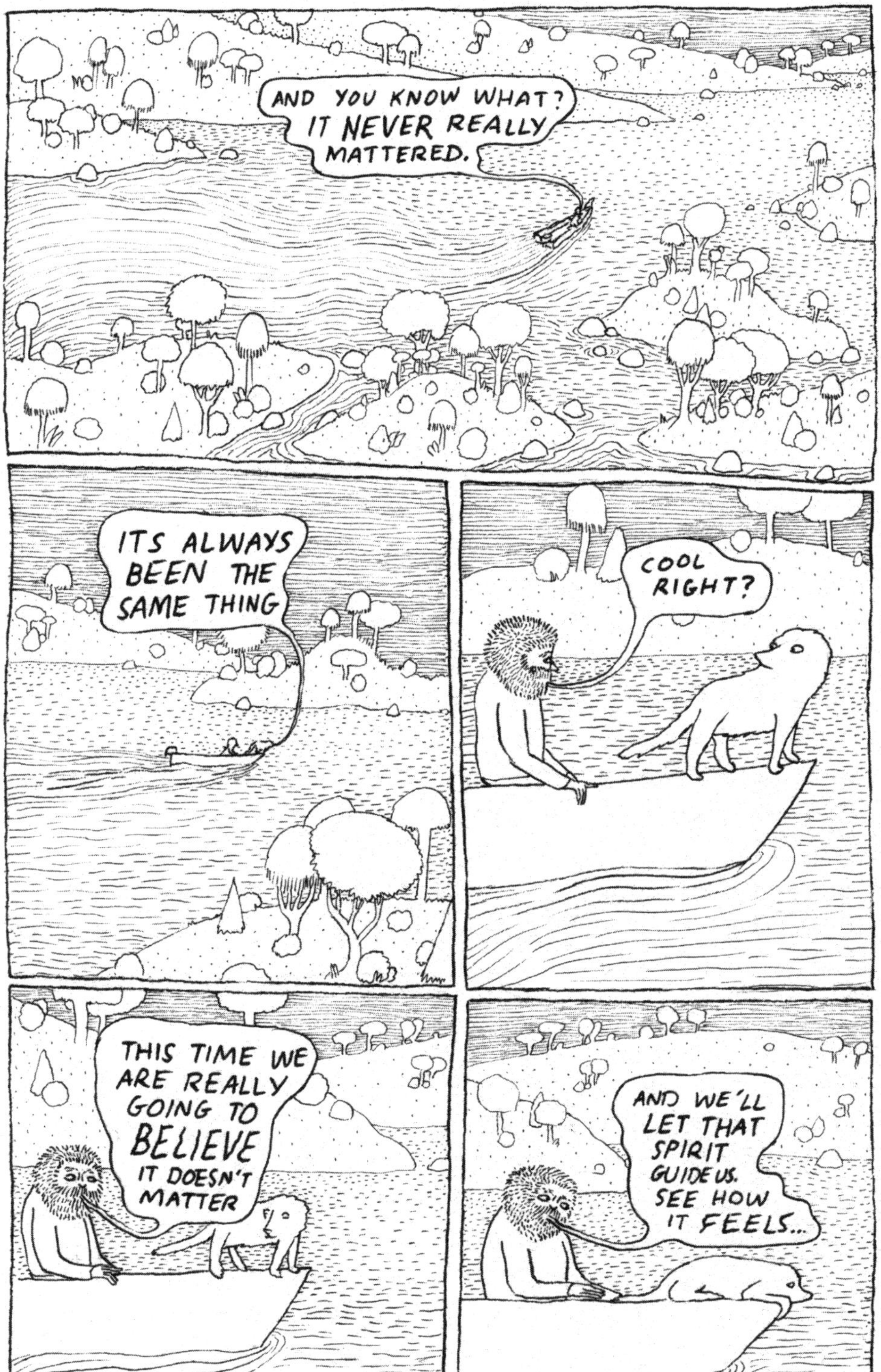
AND YOU KNOW WHAT? IT NEVER REALLY MATTERED.
ITS ALWAYS BEEN THE SAME THING
COOL RIGHT?
THIS TIME WE ARE REALLY GOING TO BELIEVE IT DOESN'T MATTER
AND WE'LL LET THAT SPIRIT GUIDE US. SEE HOW IT FEELS...

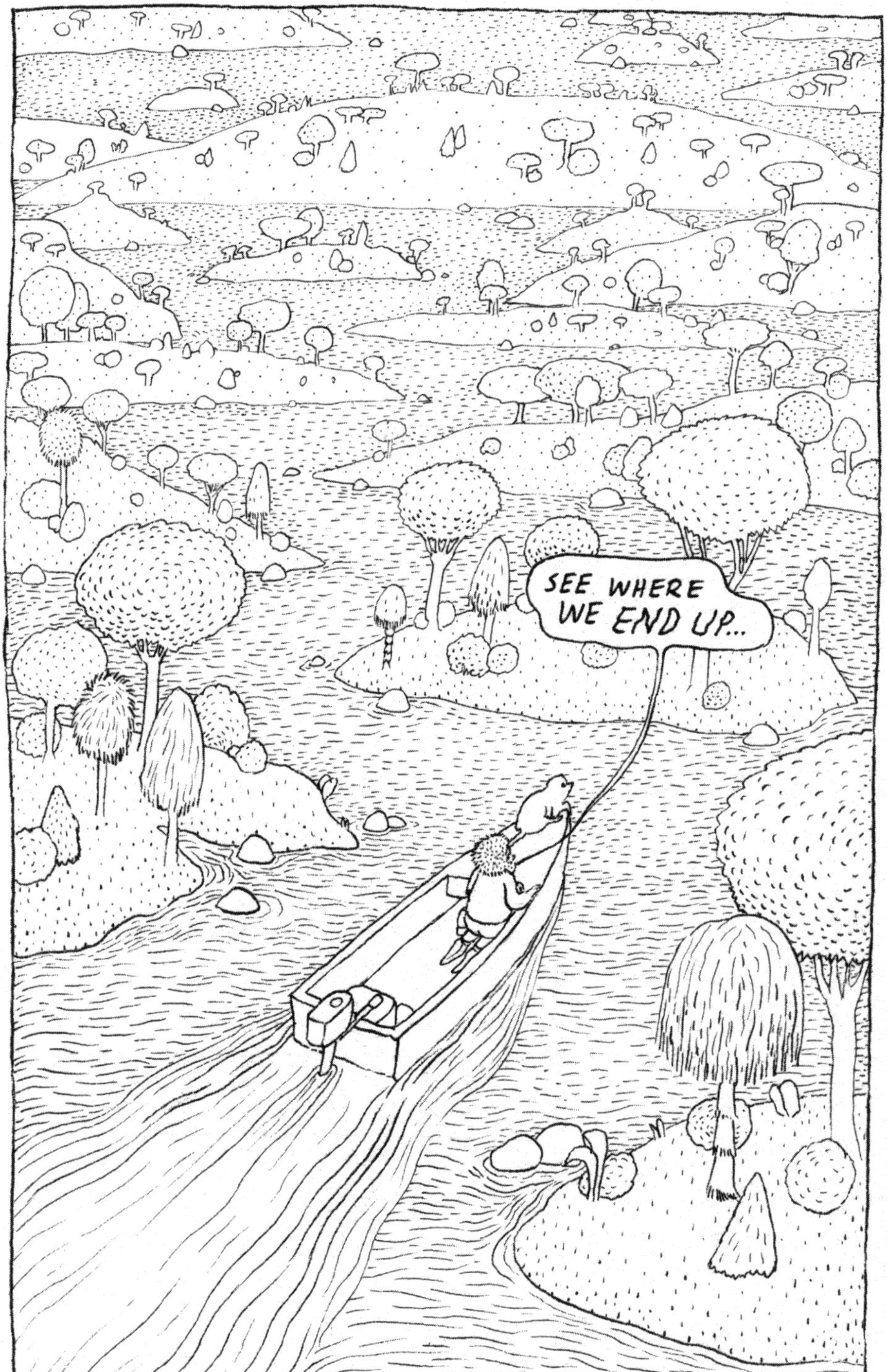
SEE WHERE WE END UP...

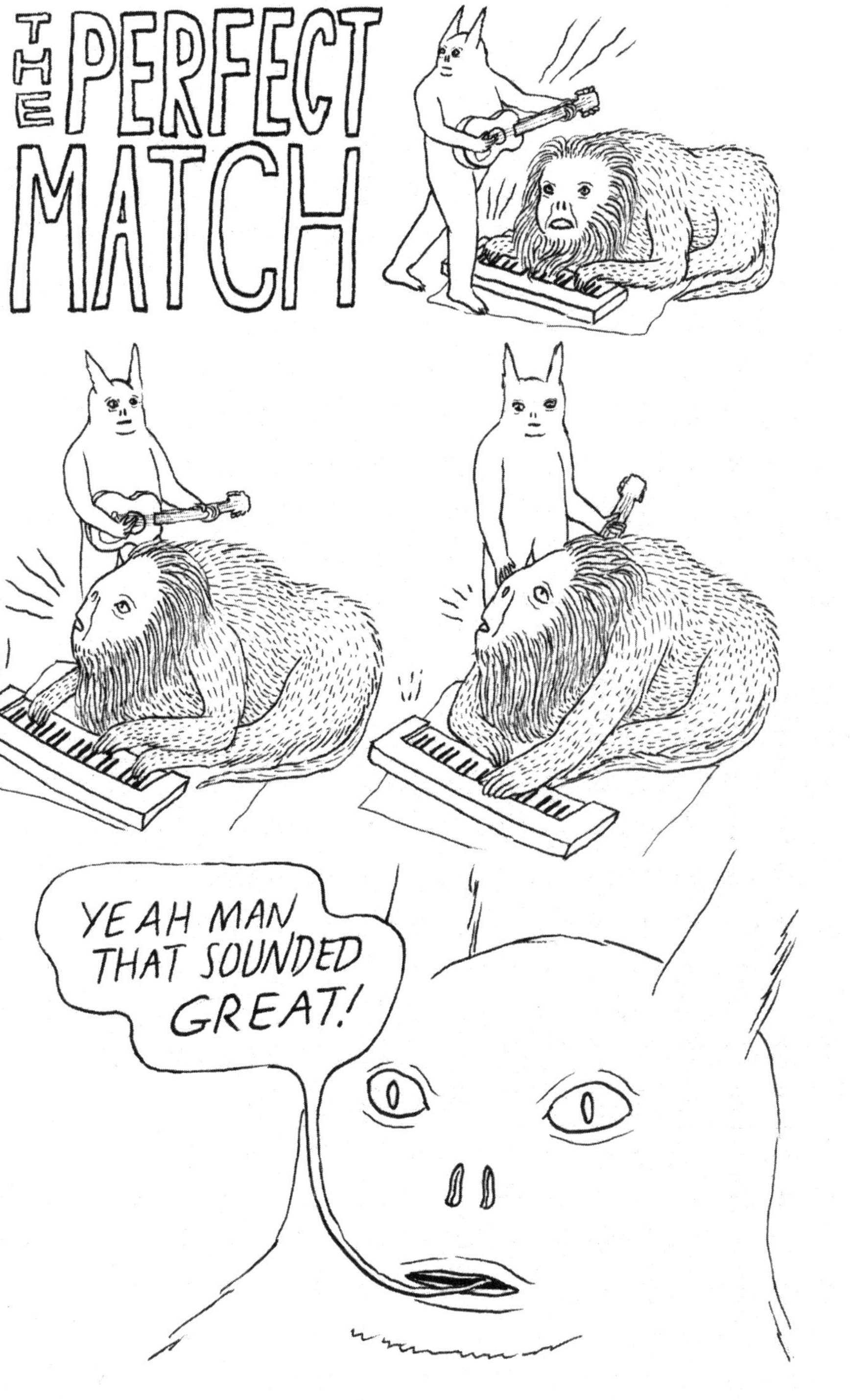
THE PERFECT MATCH
YEAH MAN THAT SOUNDED GREAT!

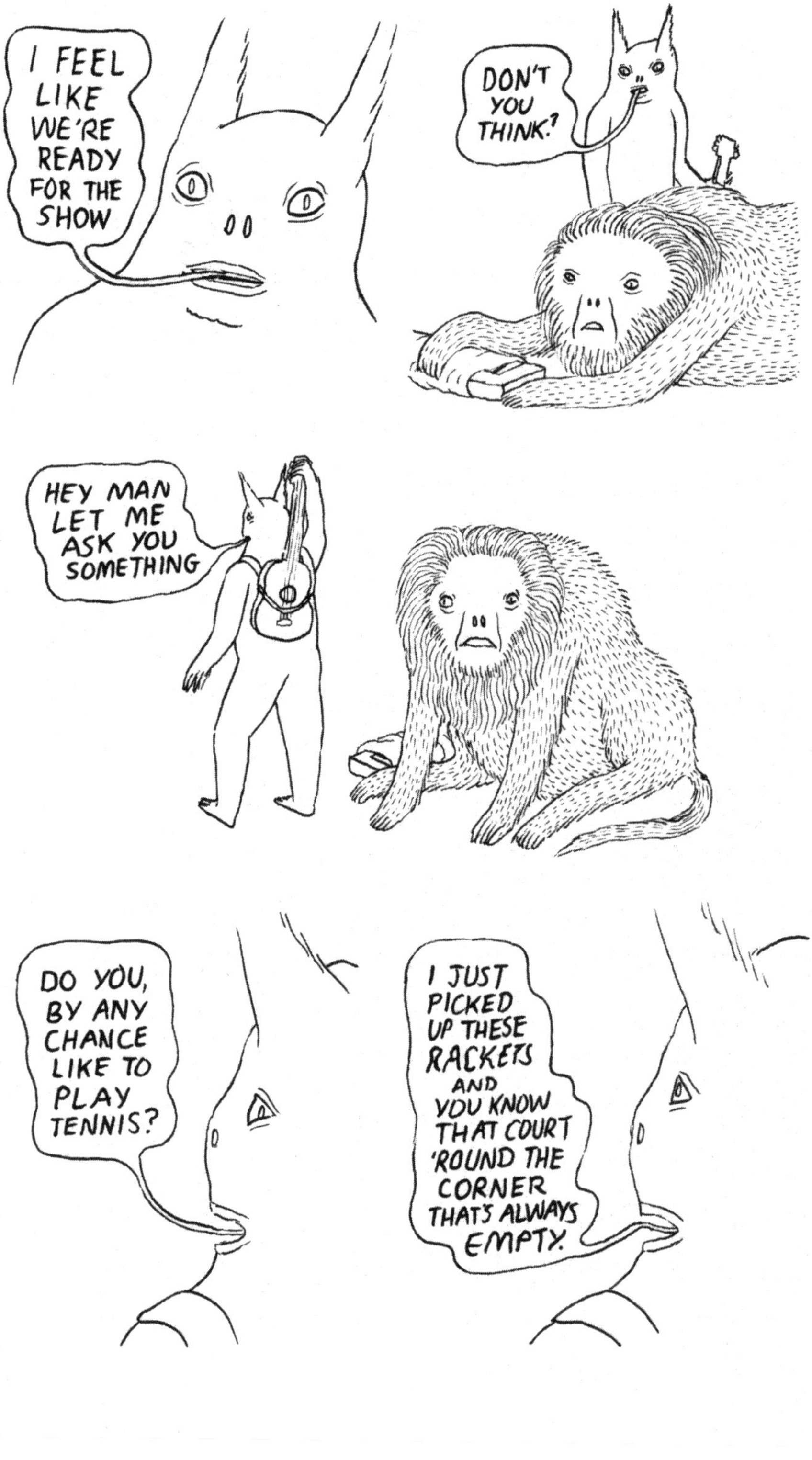
I FEEL LIKE WE'RE READY FOR THE SHOW
DON'T YOU THINK?
HEY MAN LET ME ASK YOU SOMETHING
DO YOU, BY ANY CHANCE LIKE TO PLAY TENNIS?
I JUST PICKED UP THESE RACKETS AND YOU KNOW THAT COURT 'ROUND THE CORNER THAT'S ALWAYS EMPTY.

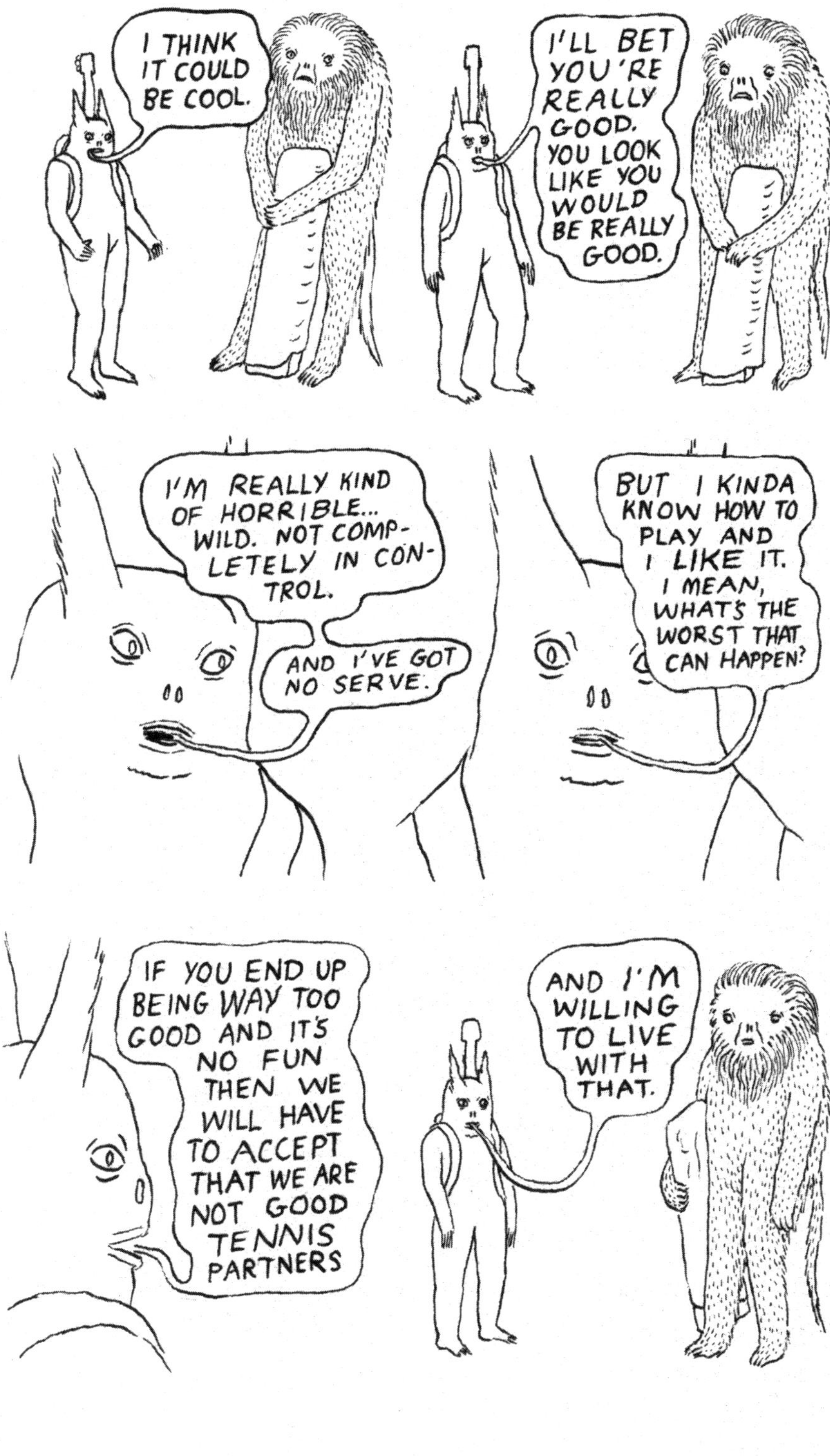
I THINK IT COULD BE COOL.
I'LL BET YOU'RE REALLY GOOD. YOU LOOK LIKE YOU WOULD BE REALLY GOOD.
I'M REALLY KIND OF HORRIBLE... WILD. NOT COMP-LETELY IN CON-TROL.
AND I'VE GOT NO SERVE.
BUT I KINDA KNOW HOW TO PLAY AND I LIKE IT. I MEAN, WHAT'S THE WORST THAT CAN HAPPEN?
IF YOU END UP BEING WAY TOO GOOD AND IT'S NO FUN THEN WE WILL HAVE TO ACCEPT THAT WE ARE NOT GOOD TENNIS PARTNERS
AND I'M WILLING TO LIVE WITH THAT.

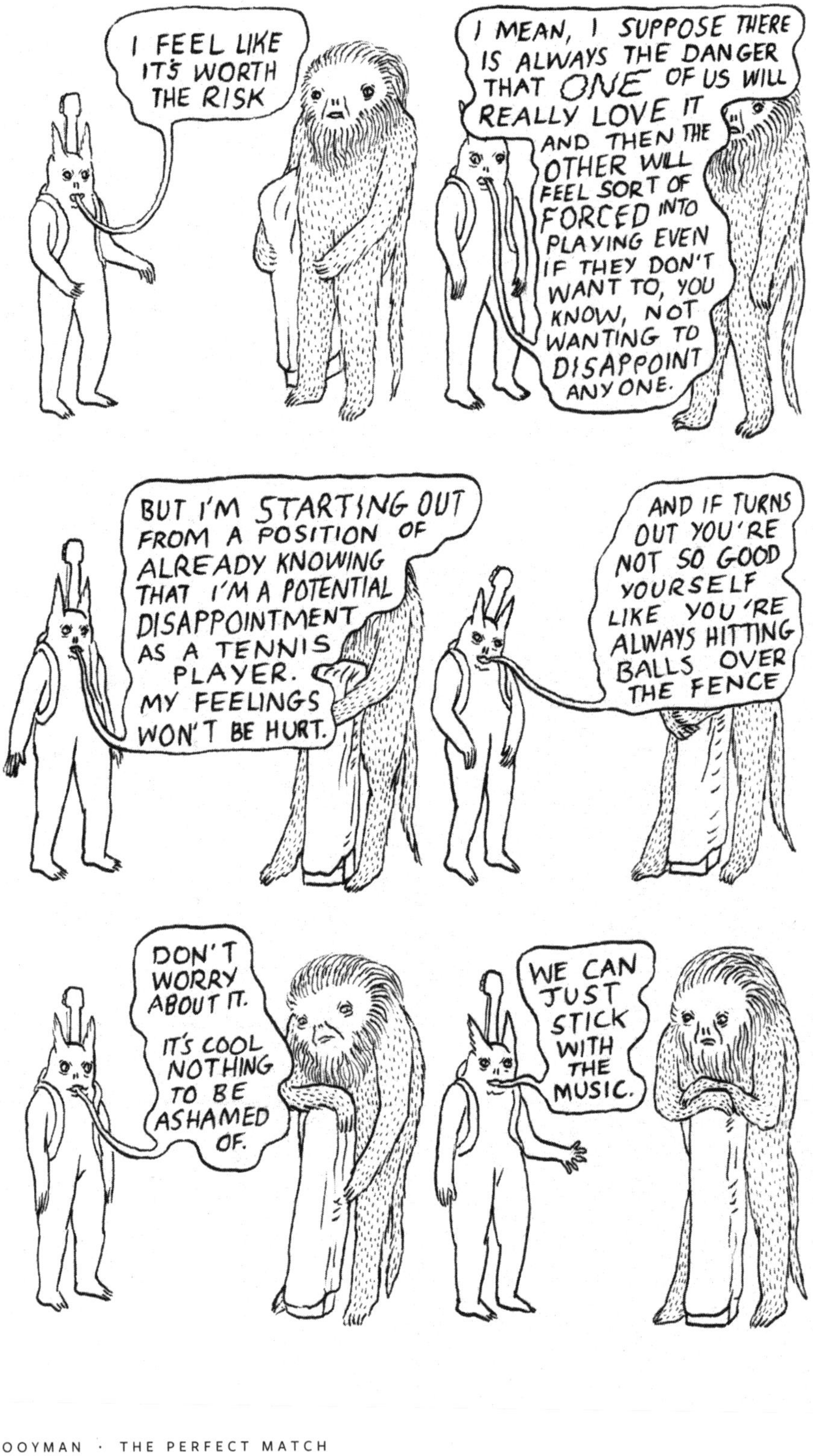
I FEEL LIKE IT'S WORTH THE RISK
I MEAN, I SUPPOSE THERE IS ALWAYS THE DANGER THAT ONE OF US WILL REALLY LOVE IT AND THEN THE OTHER WILL FEEL SORT OF FORCED INTO PLAYING EVEN IF THEY DON'T WANT TO, YOU KNOW, NOT WANTING TO DISAPPOINT ANYONE.
BUT I'M STARTING OUT FROM A POSITION OF ALREADY KNOWING THAT I'M A POTENTIAL DISAPPOINTMENT AS A TENNIS PLAYER. MY FEELINGS WON'T BE HURT.
AND IF TURNS OUT YOU'RE NOT SO GOOD YOURSELF LIKE YOU'RE ALWAYS HITTING BALLS OVER THE FENCE
DON'T WORRY ABOUT IT.
IT'S COOL NOTHING TO BE ASHAMED OF.
WE CAN JUST STICK WITH THE MUSIC.

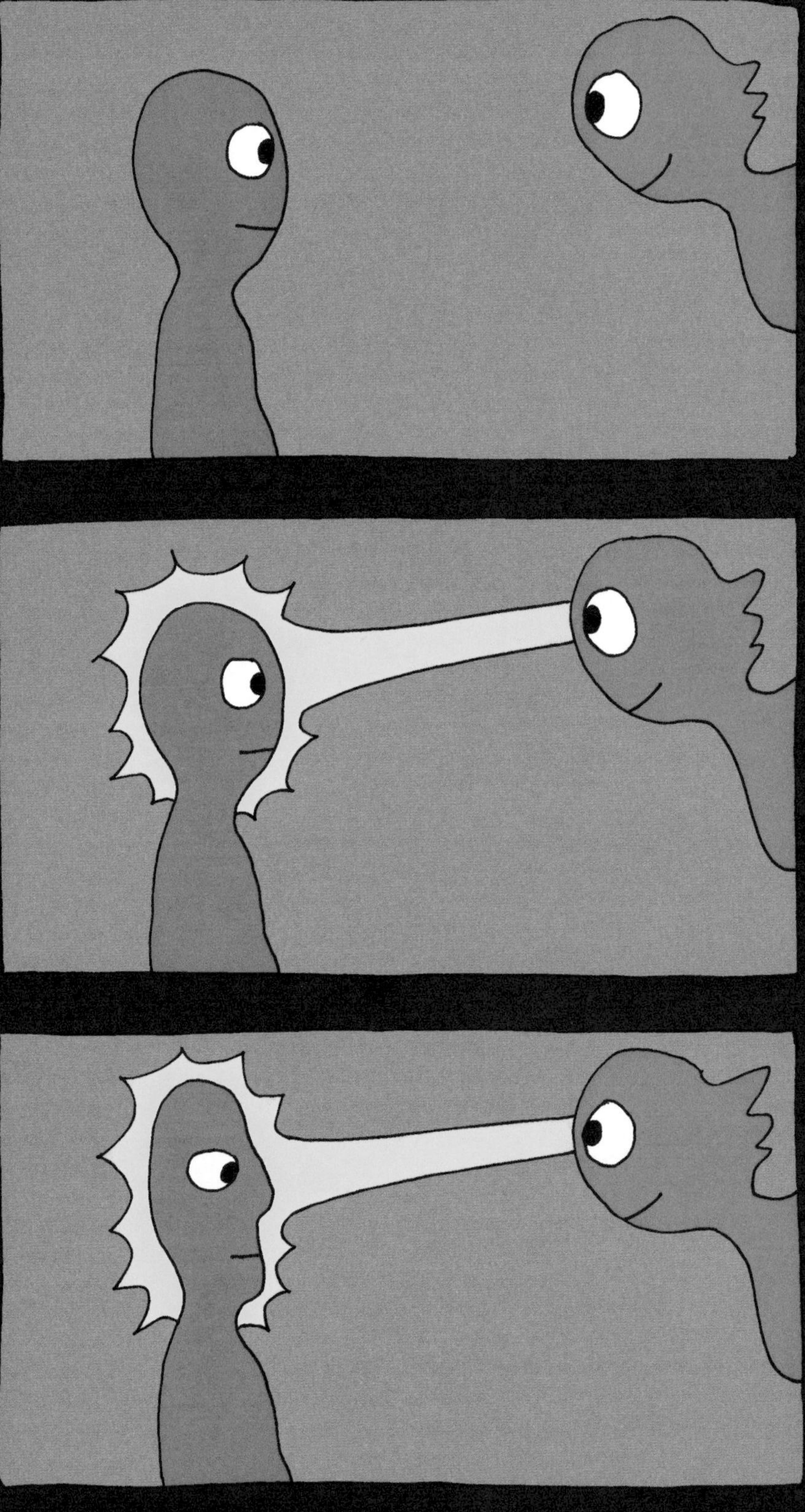

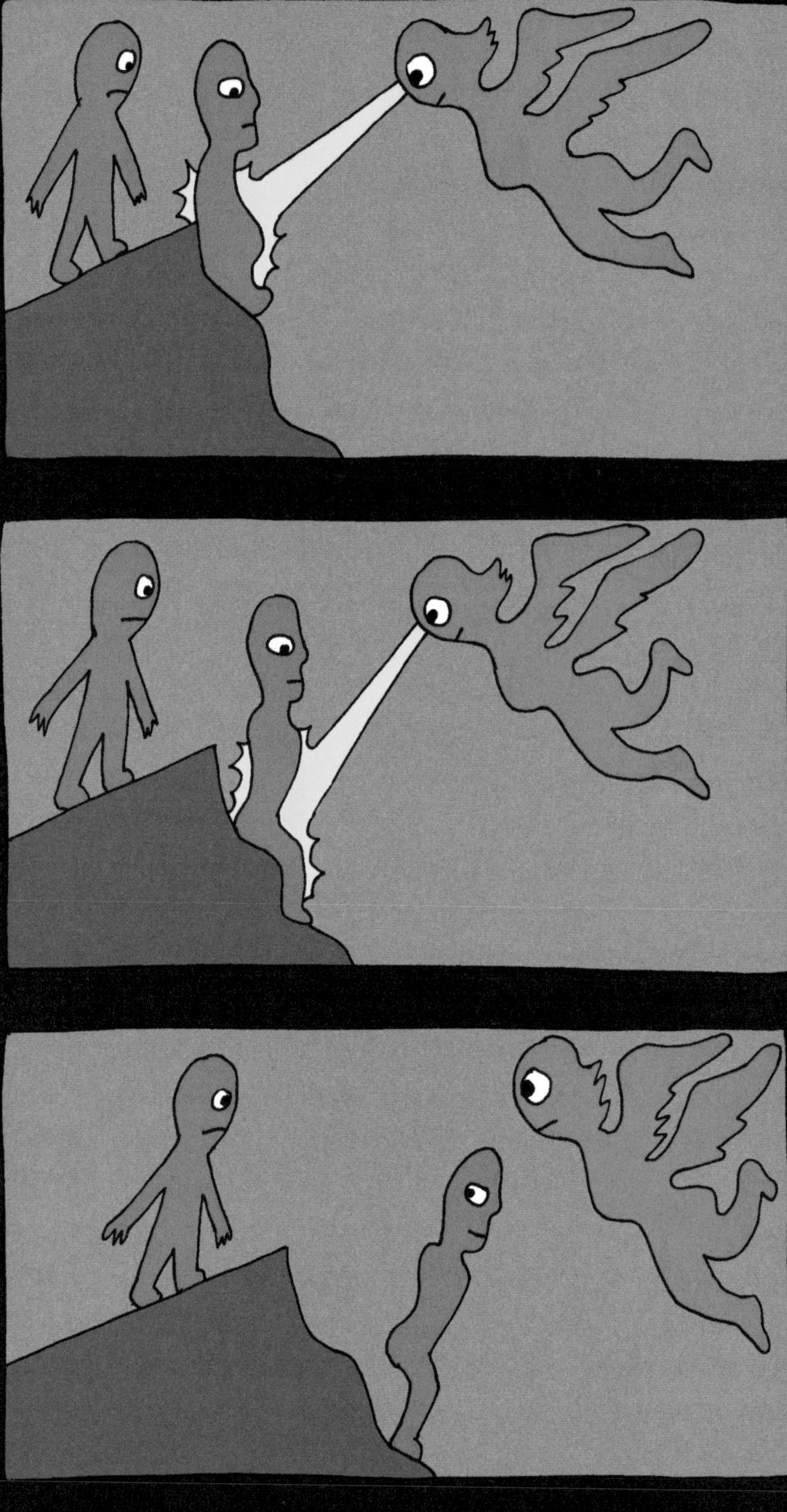

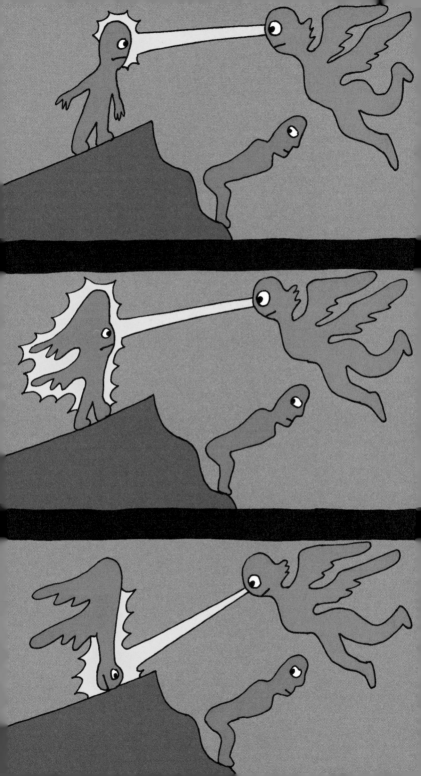

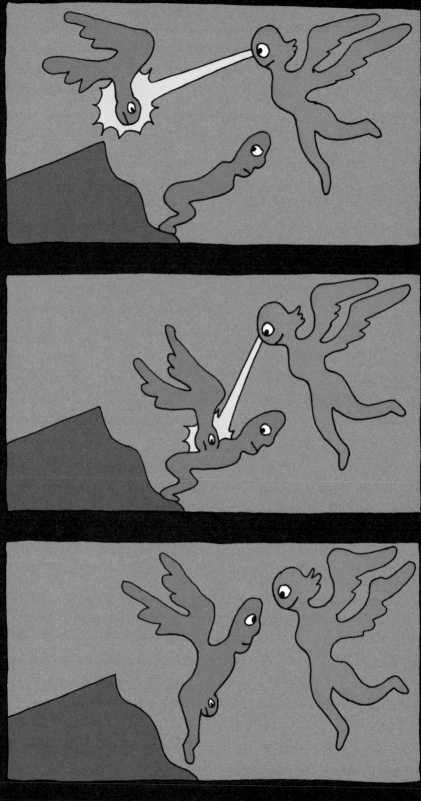

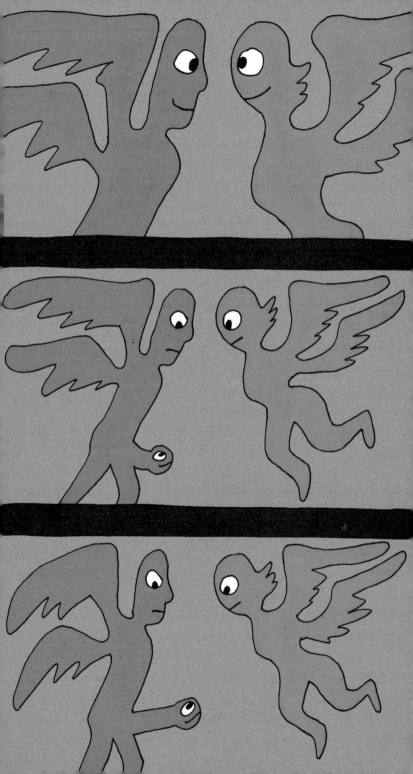

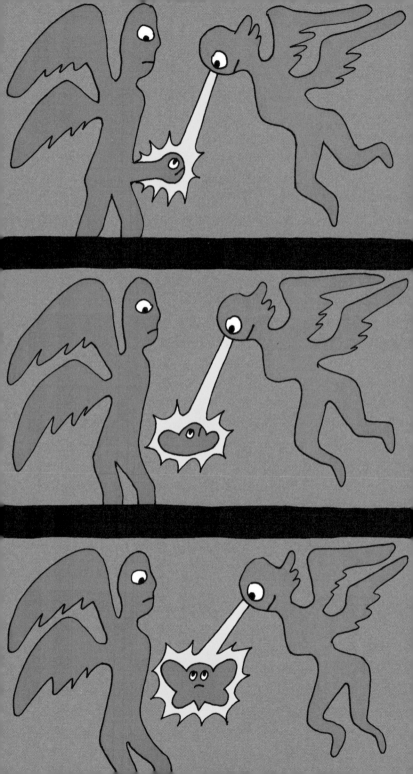

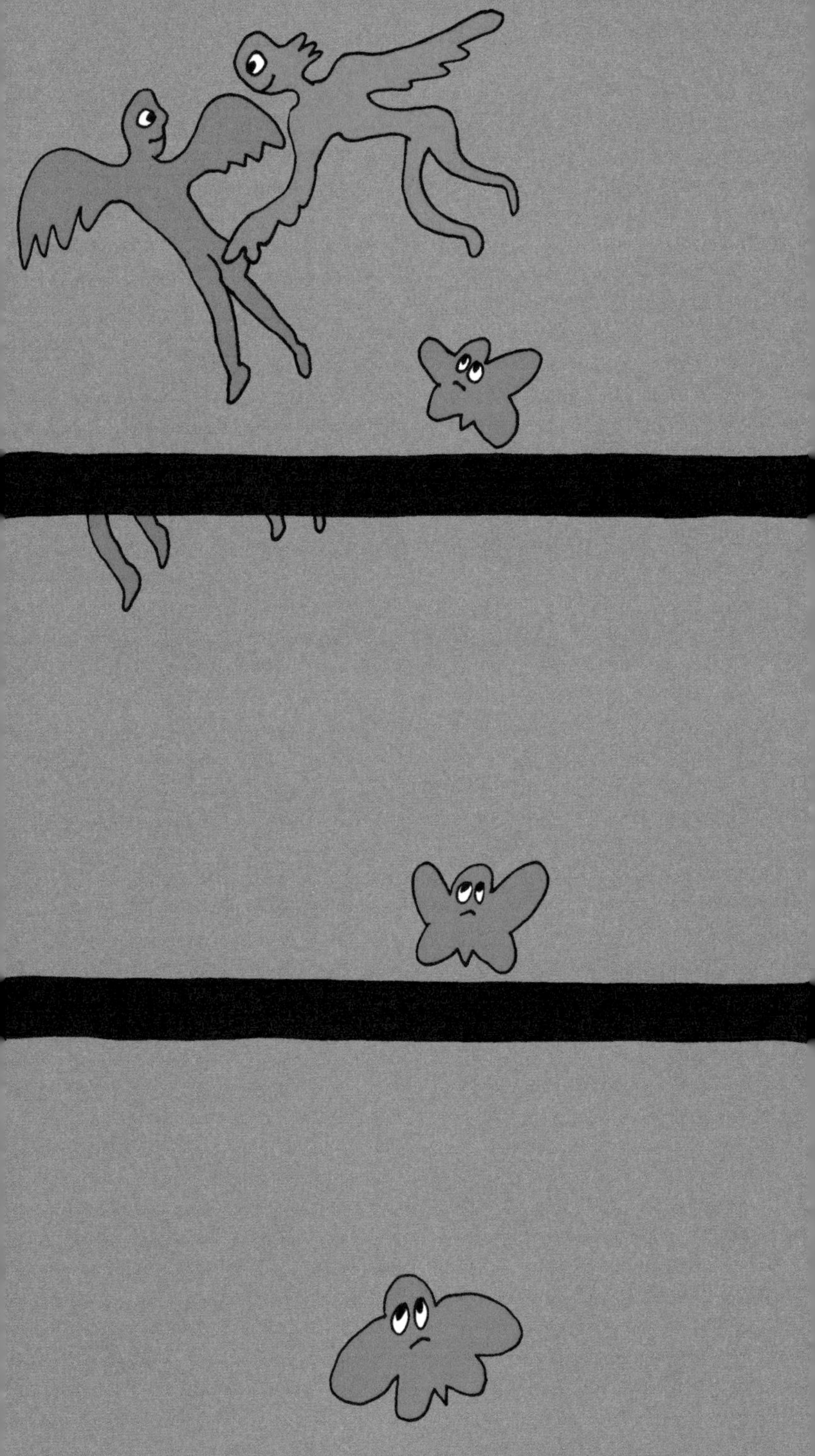

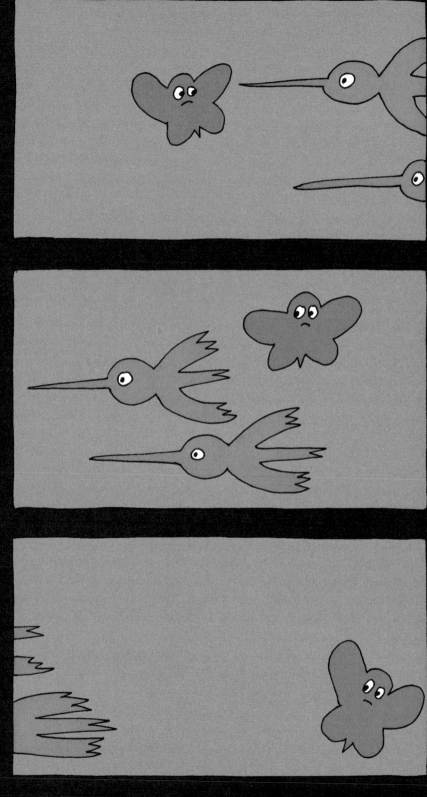

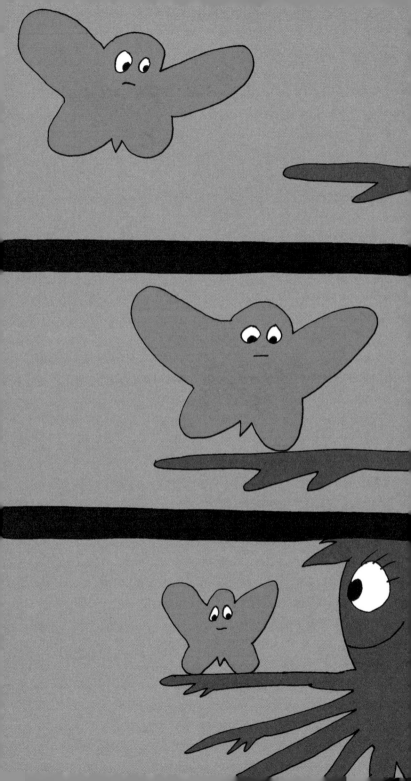

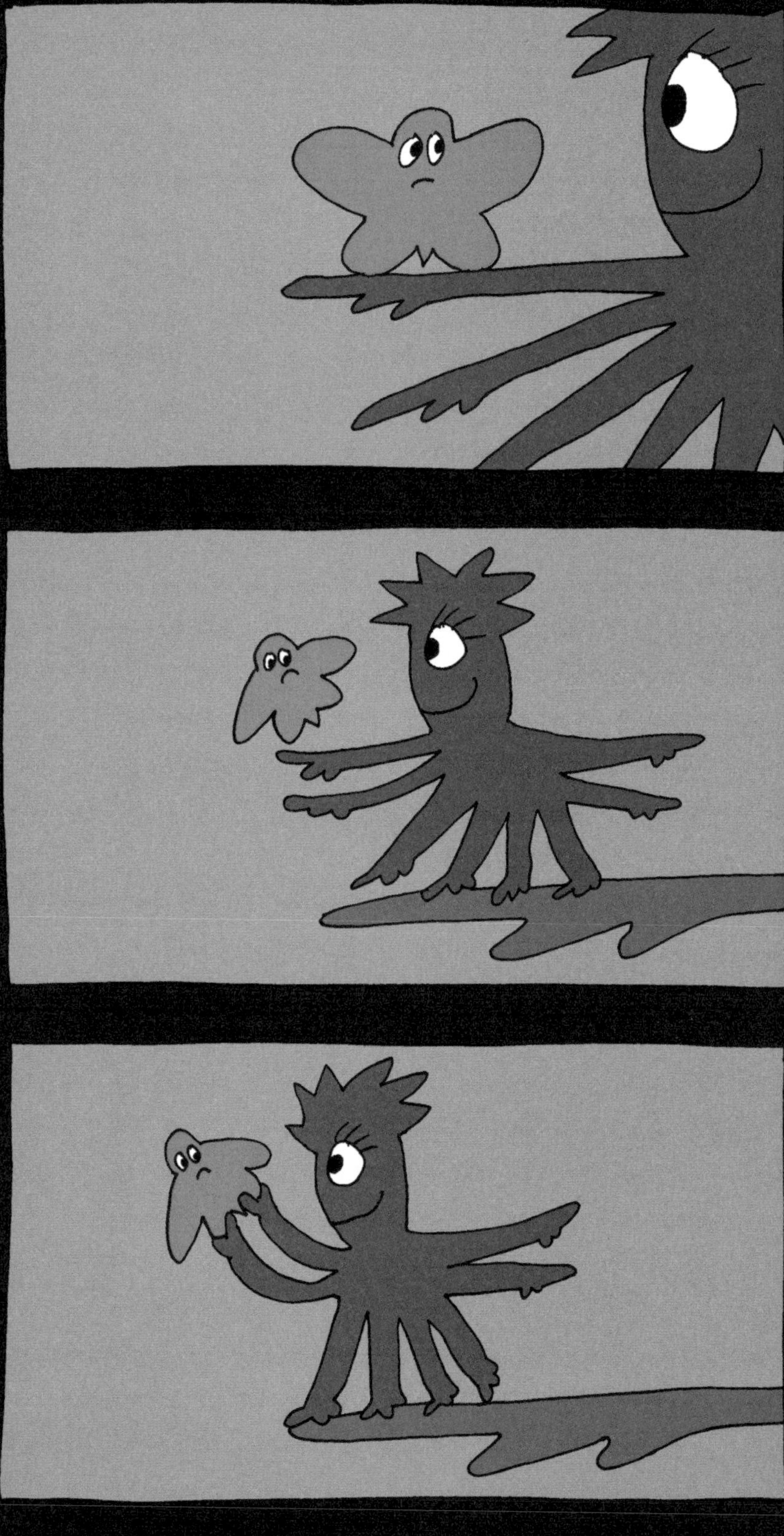

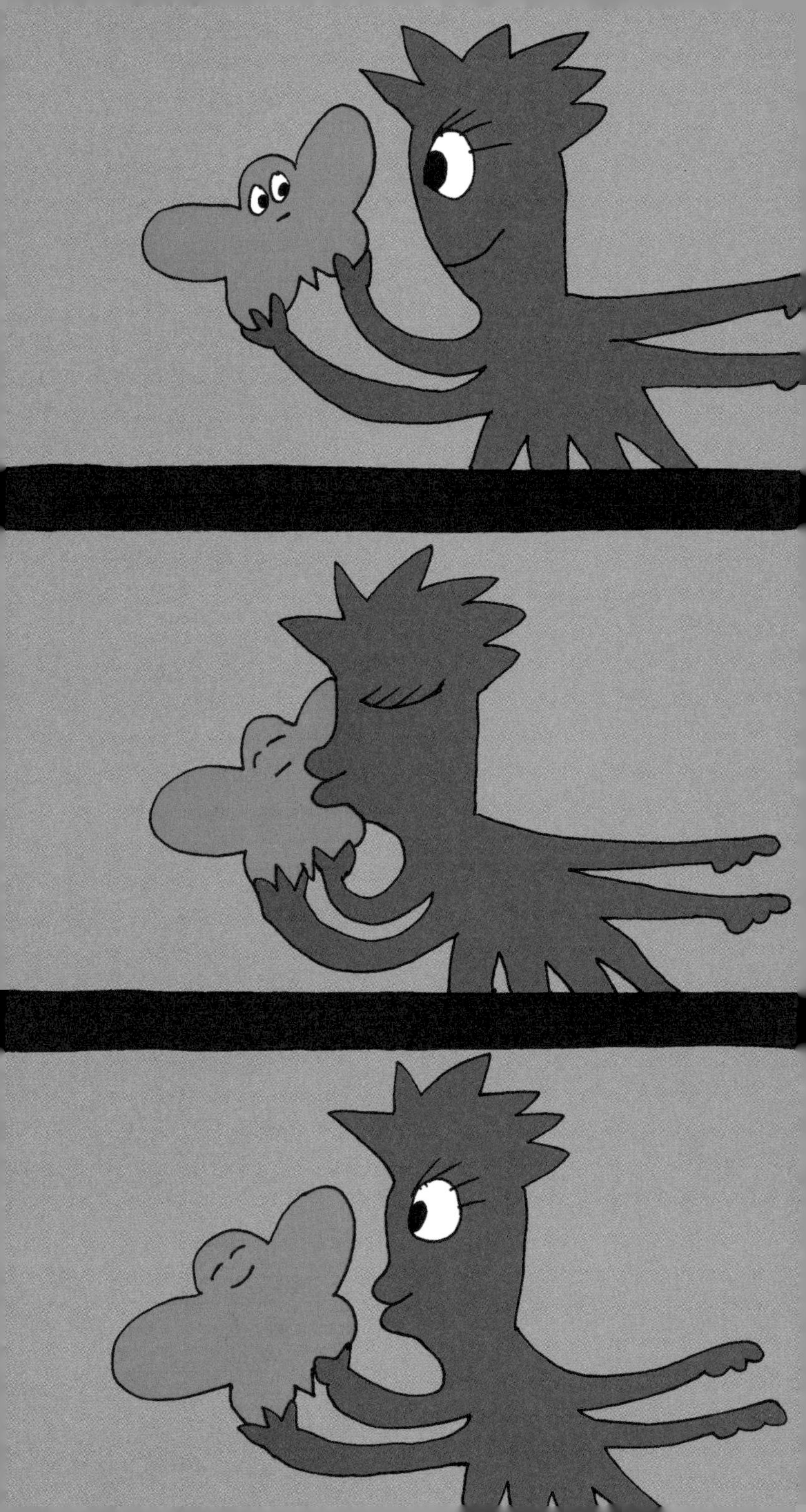

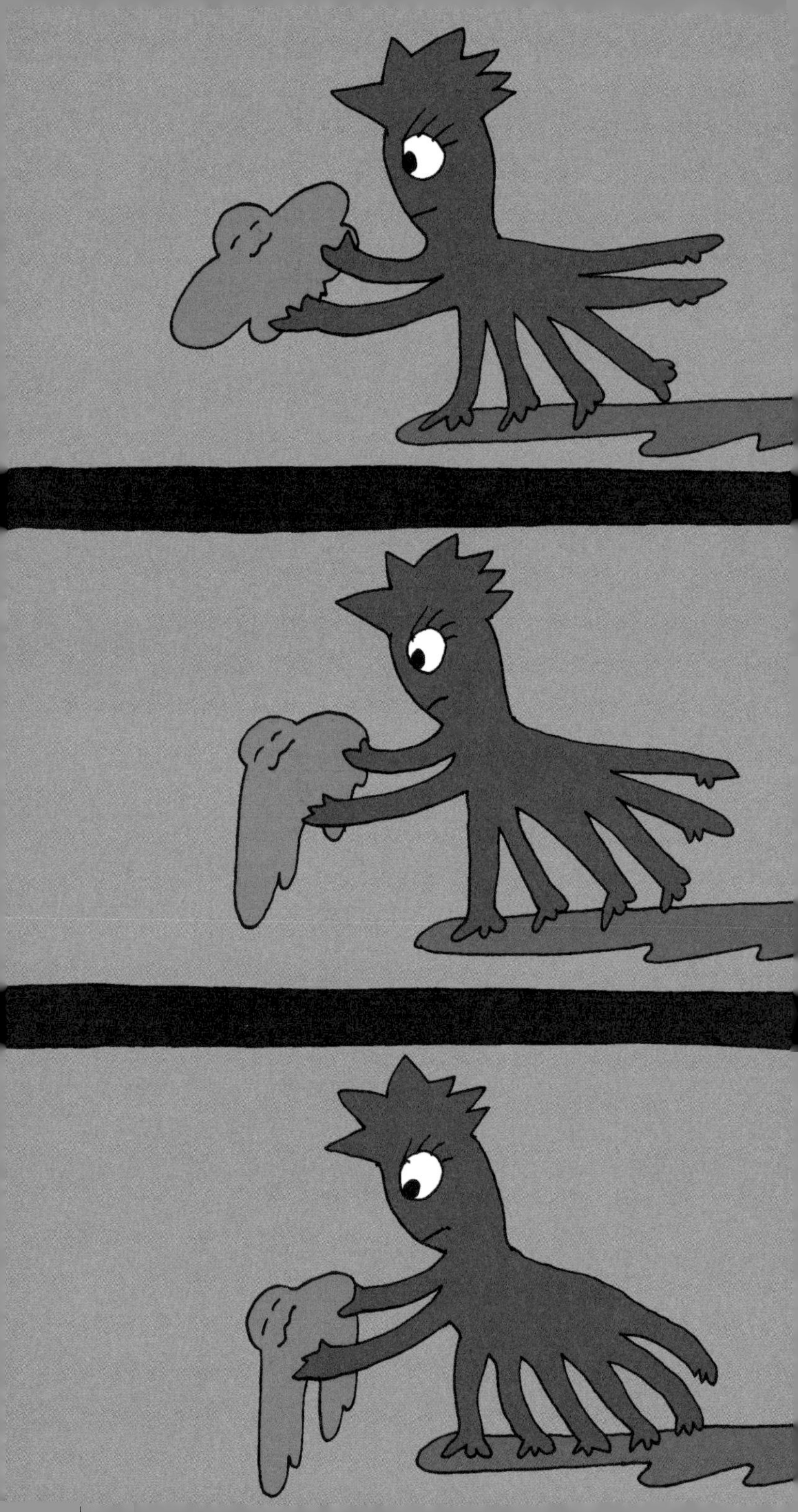

Contributors' Notes

Alabaster is a cartoonist, illustrator, printmaker, and crafter who lives in a little yellow-brick house on the Brooklyn/Queens border. **www.ala-bas-ter.tumblr.com**

▪ This story is an excerpt from the second book in a series, of which there will eventually be six. The author is self-publishing each book in two editions: one that is entirely handmade and one that is manufactured by machine.

Rosaire Appel: I'm an ex–fiction writer, a graphic artist exploring the betweens of reading/looking/listening. I make books (commercially printed, handmade, and recycled), ink drawings, and digital drawings. My subject is, basically, visual language. Using a combination of abstract comics and asemic writing, I develop sequences that remain open to interpretation, thus keeping the relationship between the viewer and the work active rather than passive. **www.rosaireappel.com**

▪ "briefly, before dawn" / an abstract comic. This is hand drawn on the computer using a stylus. "Briefly" refers to the thinness of the intervals between frames, marking time in what might otherwise be a continuous expanse. "Before dawn" acknowledges the muted tones and forms composited through tenuous lighting. The structure is rational; the narrative can only be approached subliminally.

Alternative writer, artist, and creator **Peter Bagge** is best known for the '90s comic series *Hate*, featuring the semi-autobiographical antihero Buddy Bradley, whose adventures have been collected in two volumes: *Buddy Does Seattle* and *Buddy Does Jersey,* both from Fantagraphics.

Bagge has also created three graphic novels: *Apocalypse Nerd* (Dark Horse), *Other Lives* (DC/Vertigo), and *Reset* (Dark Horse). A collection of the journalistic strips Bagge has done for *Reason* magazine has been published in a book entitled *Everyone Is Stupid Except For Me* (Fantagraphics).

Most recently, Bagge has written and drawn a full-length biographical comic, *Woman Rebel: The Margaret Sanger Story* (Drawn and Quarterly). **www.peterbagge.com**

▪ My reasons for doing a biography on Margaret Sanger are many: I'm fascinated by her time period in general, and I strongly believe her cause was a most worthy one—one that she greatly succeeded in, to the betterment of *all* of our lives. She also led a very wild, contentious, and *active* life—one that I thought lent itself surprisingly well to the comic book medium. And finally, I hoped to help clear up some of the many bits of misinformation floating around about her. Her reputation has been greatly and unjustly damaged in this Internet, sound-bite information age, sadly.

Josh Bayer was born in Buffalo, New York, and raised in Columbus, Ohio. His work deals with interpreting his influences, his own past, and the world around him through the prism of the comic book. He lives in Harlem, New York, at the time of this writing. **www.joshbayer.com**

▪ In the process of making comics is a place where I can be totally sincere. It's a place where I have freedom and can breathe clearly. In a world where almost every other decision of our day-to-day existence is compromised, it's something to hold dear.

Gabrielle Bell is the author of five books, including *The Voyeurs* and *Truth Is Fragmentary*. The title story of her book *Cecil and Jordan in New York* has been adapted for the film anthology *Tokyo!* by Michel Gondry, which she also cowrote. She lives in Beacon, New York. **www.gabriellebell.com**

▪ *The Colombia Diaries* is a collection of Gabrielle Bell's experiences traveling in Medellín and Bogotá, Colombia. Because she is very lazy, and yet so narcissistic she cannot bear to have an experience without having it intimately described and broadcasted all over the world via the Internet, she created me, a nameless fictional character, to act as her beleaguered servant and narrator. Having these adventures (or nonadventures) described in the third person allows even an insignificant story such as hers to be told with some level of professionalism, and, if I may humbly say so myself, insight.

Mat Brinkman: Non-comic drawing is my preference but since at least junior high school I have infrequently drawn comics with (in order) *Chainsaw Sam, Kap Trap, Oaf / Teratoid Heights,* and *Multiforce*, with one-offs here and there. **manifestedfestering.blogspot.com**

▪ "Cretin" has been brewing for some time and these are the only comics I have planned as it will be five issues (one every six months approximately). The scale of the drawings will change in future issues out of self-preservation.

Andy Burkholder is the author of *Absolute Loneliness by John S.* and *Qviet*. He lives in Chicago. **www.andyburkholder.com**

▪ This comic is about a mind moving too fast to articulate its thoughts. The narrator cannot communicate the intimacy of what he feels. He is trying to describe an ideal to a reader who is that ideal. It's impossible for the speaker to communicate what his ideal means and impossible for both the fictional reader and actual reader to know. The fictional reader might as well be a corpse.

Adam Buttrick is a cartoonist born in Grand Rapids, Michigan, in 1984. **www.adambuttrick.com**

▪ *Misliving Amended* was a comic book. The format allows for an expression that is complete while still open, questions that remain unanswered. Is this whole a part of something? Should it exist or be embarrassed? Nothing closed is worth our time. Comic books are open.

Roz Chast is a cartoonist at *The New Yorker*. *Can't We Talk About Something More Pleasant?*, her first graphic memoir, is about her parents' last decade, and her trying to take care of them when they were no longer able to care for themselves. **www.rozchast.com**

▪ This excerpt takes place during the final chapters of my mother's life. She didn't have Alzheimer's disease, and I don't think she had senile dementia. I'm not sure what was going on, except that her brain was not functioning in the way it had in the previous months. When I visited her in the Place (my name for the "assisted living" place she was in), we would be talking about my kids or current events or whatever, and then suddenly she would segue into a story that was really off the wall. Then she'd veer back into lucidity. It was very strange. Sometimes I could see the origins of these stories. For instance, she knew that I had a dream of having an apartment in Manhattan and several of her recurrent stories involved her giving me an apartment in Manhattan. Another genre involved Katie, my father's mother, with whom she had had a terrible relationship. These stories were generally about Katie coming after her in some way. And there were stories that I thought were somehow connected to her bonding with her live-in Jamaican aide and companion. But then there were others, like the swordfish-in-the-heart story. I couldn't figure that one out.

Cole Closser is a Missouri cartoonist and a graduate of the MFA program at the Center for Cartoon Studies in White River Junction, Vermont. His graphic novel *Little Tommy Lost* was named one of the ten best graphic novels of 2013 by the *A.V. Club* (an *Onion* website), and nominated for a Will Eisner Comic Industry Award in the category of Best Publication Design at the 2014 San Diego Comic-Con. Cole currently lives in the Ozarks and teaches drawing at Missouri State University and Drury University. Cole likes cats. **www.coleclosser.com**

▪ *Little Tommy Lost* is the story of a child separated from his parents on a trip to the big city, who unknowingly sets out on a great adventure as he searches for a way home. Reminiscent of the newspaper strips and lushly illustrated Sunday comics of the early twentieth century, Cole Closser's work is steeped in cartooning history, but filled with an unparalleled sense of the new.

Farel Dalrymple is the cartoonist behind *The Wrenchies* (First Second Books, 2014) and *Delusional* (Adhouse, 2013). Farel was also the artist on *Omega the Unknown* (Marvel Comics, 2010), with writer Jonathan Lethem. *Pop Gun War* (Dark Horse, 2000), Farel's first graphic novel, was a Xeric Grant recipient and received a gold medal from the Society of Illustrators. Farel is cofounder of the anthology *Meathaus* and creator of the Eisner-nominated webcomic *It Will All Hurt* for Study Group Comics. He currently resides in Oregon, working on a *Pop Gun War* sequel and illustrating *The Earfarmer* with writer Chris Stevens. **www.popgunwar.com**

▪ This sequence from *The Wrenchies* is the start of the "quest" section of the book. From chapter to chapter, I changed the storytelling style and the art a bit. This chapter and the "Hollis" chapter are both told through the character Hollis talking to the reader by way of his childhood idea of "God." My goal with *The Wrenchies* was to make an exciting existential fantasy story filled with some things from popular culture I grew up with, along with some slower poetic interludes, some fun experimental comic stuff, and some provocative subtext.

Anya Davidson was born in Sarasota, Florida, in 1983. She graduated with a BFA from the School of the Art Institute of Chicago in 2004. She is a cartoonist, musician, teaching artist, and printmaker whose work appeared in many 'zines and anthologies, including *Kramers Ergot*, before her debut graphic novel, *School Spirits*, was published by PictureBox Inc. Her current project, the Ignatz Award–nominated comic *Band for Life*, will be available in print from Fantagraphics Books in the not-too-distant future. She lives and shreds in Chicago. **www.anyadavidson.com**

▪ *School Spirits* is my first full-length graphic novel. The story centers around teenage friends, Oola and Garf, two girls who love heavy metal and are struggling to define their role in society. The fabric between imagination and reality is porous in the alternate universe they inhabit, and I was excited to illustrate their interior monologues and power fantasies, and to explore notions of gender and female friendship. The book is divided into several chapters, the longest of which is called "No Class." The 22-page excerpt that appears in this anthology is taken from that chapter.

Eleanor Davis is a cartoonist and illustrator. She lives in Athens, Georgia, and is from Tucson, Arizona. She is married to Drew Weing, who is also a cartoonist. Her book of short comics for adults, *How to Be Happy,* is available now from Fantagraphics Books. **www.doing-fine.com**

▪ I like Jennifer and Matt, the two main characters in "No Tears, No Sorrow," very much. They had accidentally hardened their hearts, and after their hearts unhardened neither of them knew what to do. I like to think that they'll meet again someday, in the doubly unreal world of unwritten fiction, and that they fall in love. For this reason it feels like a happy story to me.

A. Degen was born in 1981 in Brooklyn, New York, and is the author of *Areacc, Junior Detective Files, Softxray/mindhunters,* and *Mighty Star.* **adactivity.tumblr.com**

▪ This comic first appeared in *Felony Comics,* a crime-themed comics anthology from Negative Pleasure. When given the writing prompt "crime," I thought of the precode EC crime and suspense comics, which I love for their art and design, but hate for their hypocritical ham-fisted moralizing. Thinking about that, I decided to make a comic about judgment, morality, and zealotry. I drew the characters as Fleischer cartoons to reference that precode era and protect the identity of the innocent. The text of this comic is based on a dream I had on December 16, 2012.

Ben Duncan is an artist from the prairies living in and around the Vancouver, British Columbia, area. He grew up much like most children, that is to say making potions in large jars consisting of sun-battered dead snails and his and his brother's urine. **occasionalheadbunts.com**

▪ *Blane Throttle* is a 40-or-so-page document of life in a "purgatorial bog." Viewers and inhabitants of the bog encounter Blane, a would-be guide but mostly some sort of curious, deranged entity with a penchant for erratic and often abusive behavior. Sucking in air allows him to inflate his balloon-like head and cover ground, hopping from island to island. The story depicted in these selected pages focuses on two pilots in the bog crashing into and being subsequently absorbed by a cloud ghoul. *Blane Throttle* was originally made for the Study Group Comics website during 2013.

Jules Feiffer is a cartoonist, playwright, children's book author, and illustrator. He is a member of the American Academy of Arts and Letters, the American Academy of Arts and Sciences, and the Dramatist Guild Council. Abrams has just published *Out of Line: The Art of Jules Feiffer*, and Liveright will publish the second volume of the *Kill My Mother* trilogy in 2016. He lives in East Hampton, New York.

▪ *Kill My Mother* came into being as an odd and happy mix of boyhood dreams and old man reality. My earliest ambition as a boy cartoonist was to emulate my heroes Milton Caniff (*Terry and the Pirates*) and Will Eisner (*The Spirit*). My dream was to be an adventure strip cartoonist. But, hard as I worked at it, I didn't have the chops: my attempt at realistic drawing was unconvincing, and my skill with a brush was abysmal. So I gave it up and remade myself into a loose-lined satirist, drawing cartoons and writing plays. And lived a happy life doing both in the big city.

Then along came age. I couldn't hear much anymore, which is a deterrent at play rehearsals, and I couldn't walk much anymore, which made me useless in the city. So I moved to the East End of Long Island, which nicely sidestepped my physical infirmities, and I began work on a graphic novel that would combine in literary comic book form the disparate skills that I took turns at in the city: cartoons, kids' books, and plays. Again returning to boyhood, I aped the noir thriller style that I devoured as a teenager: books and stories by Cain, Hammett, and Chandler, and their movie adaptations by Huston, Hawks, and Wilder. And whaddayaknow, I discovered at age 80 that with a variety of the new pen-brush markers available, I could master the realistic drawing style that had eluded me for 75 years. This is the stuff that dreams are made of.

Here's looking at you, kid.

Noel Freibert (born in 1985) currently resides in Baltimore, Maryland. He is the editor of *Weird* magazine and creator of the forthcoming graphic novel *Old Ground*. His work has been shown internationally and is featured in the book collections of the Museum of Modern Art, New York, and the Baltimore Museum of Art. In 2014 he was named Best Comics Artist of Baltimore by the *City Paper*. **wweeiirrdd.tumblr.com**

• I developed "the hole" during the unusually harsh Baltimore winter of 2014. One of the prominent ideas going into the book was to have two blank black pages for every page of comics content. This literally buried the comics within the pages of the book and destroyed any potential that the printed comics spread might have achieved. The pages within "the hole" appear as screenshots taken from a computer but are accessed through print. In the end, the work is unlike reading a comic on paper or on a screen; it exists somewhere else.

Julia Gfrörer was born in 1982 in Concord, New Hampshire. Her work has appeared in *Thickness*, *Vice*, *Arthur*, and *Study Group Magazine*, and her graphic novel *Black Is the Color* was published by Fantagraphics Books in 2013. Her name rhymes with despair, and her heart is black as jet. **www.thorazos.net**

• *Palm Ash* uses tropes of early Christian martyrdom—tamed lions, bloodthirsty pagans, a surreptitiously scratched ichthys, a clandestine baptism—to illustrate the pain of watching helplessly when people you love are in danger, the willingness to endure or inflict pain when you believe it serves your ideals, and the desire (efficacious or not) to intervene in the pain of others. It was inspired by unearthing Daniel P. Mannix's wonderfully lurid *Those About to Die* at a church thrift store, and by a time I was forced to witness the abuse of a loved one.

Kevin Hooyman was born in 1974 in Two Harbors, Minnesota, and raised in Seattle, Washington. He has been self-publishing books of drawing and writing since 1998. **www.kevinhooyman.com**

• *Conditions on the Ground* is a 32-page monthly comic printed on a Risograph in my studio. The first issue came out in May 2013 and a collection of issues 1 through 10 will be published by Floating World Books later this year.

Jesse Jacobs works as an artist from his home in London, Ontario, Canada. His major books include *Safari Honeymoon* (Koyama Press, 2014), *By This Shall You Know Him* (Koyama Press, 2012), and *Even the Giants* (AdHouse Books, 2011). Jacobs's work has been translated into German by Rotopol Press and French by Éditions Tanibis. His comics and drawings have appeared in *Le Monde diplomatique*, *The Walrus*, and *Canadian Notes and Queries*. He has exhibited work throughout Canada, Japan, the United States, Europe, and Russia. **onemillionmouths.tumblr.com; www.jessejacobs.ca**

• *Safari Honeymoon* is a story about a newly wedded couple celebrating their union with a vacation to a very distant and exotic landscape. Their luxury getaway quickly reveals itself to be far more dangerous and strange than the brochure had described. Luckily, they are joined by their very capable guide, who uses his many abilities to provide the couple with safety, gourmet food, and big game. Within this unimaginable backdrop, teeming and crowded with all sorts of poisonous plants and sinister creatures, the pair discovers what it means to be in love.

Megan Kelso completed her BA at The Evergreen State College in Olympia, Washington, in 1991, where she studied history, following a brief stint at art school. Inspired by the explosion of 'zines, bands, and DIY art projects, she published the *Girlhero* minicomic which ran for six issues, made possible with funding from the Xeric Foundation. The comic was compiled into a book published by Highwater Books, titled *Queen of the Black Black*. Kelso received two Ignatz awards for her graphic novel *Artichoke Tales*. In 2007, she was invited by the *New York Times Magazine* to serialize her "Watergate Sue" comic as part of their weekly Funny Pages feature. Kelso is currently at work on her third collection of short stories. **megangirlhero.blogspot.com**

▪ "The Good Witch, 1947" is an excerpt from a longer story in progress called *The Good Witch*. I got the idea for this story from thinking about my grandmother's experience of motherhood. She was a single divorcee who struggled to raise two children in the exceedingly conformist world of post-WWII, small-town America.

Blaise Larmee (born in 1985) is the author of *Young Lions* (2010), which garnered Larmee a Xeric grant and an Ignatz nomination, and *3 Books* (2015), an omnibus published by 2d Cloud that comprises the following: "Nudes" (2012-2013), a series of drawings most recently published as a 'zine by Studio Collective, "Amateurs" (2013), a photobook originally published by 白石デザイン・オフィス, and "Ice Cream Kisses" (2014), a catalogue of paintings. Larmee is a former fellow of the Center for Cartoon Studies. His work has appeared in *The Lifted Brow, Torrent,* and *Sonatina*. Gaze Books is his publishing operation. **www.blaiselarmee.com**

▪ The idea of an individual changing society is so abstract and mythological it borders on the imaginary, and I work closer to the imaginary than you're supposed to, I think, as an artist, and it's really almost a childlike idea to think you have agency, and it's embarrassing to express that notion of agency, but I feel like I am this illustration of a person who has no role in society, who was trained to be a manager of managers but has no prospects aside from a vaguely defined massive social arena, where I'm occupied but not employed, and I'm concerned with meta structures but I can't understand the most basic societal structures, where I emerge from a lifetime of school and, not knowing what to do, continue to behave as if I'm in school.

Erik Nebel is a genderqueer cartoonist from Chicago who has found a home in Portland, Oregon. Erik's love affair with comics began at the age of 4 and continues today at the age of 44. Their work has been featured at various comics shows in Portland including Gridlords, The Projects, and Comics Underground. Nebel's most recent book of comics, *Well Come*, was published by Yeti Press in 2014. Their next major project is an autobiographical novel, planned for release in 2017. **eriknebel.tumblr.com**

▪ "I will post one page of comics every day for the rest of my life." That was my goal when I started putting my comics on Tumblr in 2012. It's been a good way to force myself to be productive. Also, I've become part of a community of an amazing bunch of people from all around the world who are fans of my work. Whenever I sit down to draw a comic, I'm not sure what will come out of my pen, but somehow each day, something strange, stirring, and startling ends up on the page.

Anders Nilsen is a cartoonist, illustrator, artist, and occasional curator based in Minneapolis. He is the author of *Rage of Poseidon, Big Questions, The End,* and *Poetry Is Useless,* among other works. He has received three Ignatz awards as well as the Lynd Ward Graphic Novel prize, and his work has been translated into several languages overseas. His drawing and painting have been shown internationally. **www.andersbrekhusnilsen.com**

▪ "Prometheus" is one of seven short stories from *Rage of Poseidon,* all of which retell stories from Greek myths and the Bible and bring them into the present day. The book had its origins when a novelist friend asked me to do a reading with him in 2011. Having often been dissatisfied with the way my comics work as slide readings, I decided to try adapting a group of short proselike pieces from my sketchbooks. So the story reprinted here was originally conceived as larger-than-life-scale single images accompanied by the spoken word.

Born in Montreal in 1959, **Diane Obomsawin** spent the first twenty years of her life in France. After studying graphic design, she returned to Canada in 1983 and turned her attention to painting, comics, and animation. *Here and There*, an autobiographical film about the artist's rootless child-hood, has garnered numerous prestigious distinctions. Over the years, Obomsawin has developed a unique style, achieving a balance between humor and seriousness, naiveté and gravitas, realism and poetry. She has published two books with Drawn and Quarterly: her first, *Kaspar*, is about the life of Kaspar Hauser; her second, *On Loving Women,* is about women's coming out experiences. **www.dianeobomsawin.com**

▪ *On Loving Women* is a collection of stories about first love and sexual identity. In this book I share friends' and lovers' personal accounts of coming into their queerness or first finding love with another woman.

Raymond Pettibon's work embraces a wide spectrum of American "high" and "low" culture, from the deviations of marginal youth to art history, literature, sports, religion, politics, and sexual-ity. Taking their points of departure in the Southern California punk-rock culture of the late 1970s and 1980s and the "do-it-yourself" aesthetic of album covers, comics, concert flyers, and fanzines that characterized the movement, his drawings have come to occupy their own genre of potent and dynamic artistic commentary.

Born in 1957 in Tucson, Arizona, Pettibon graduated with a degree in economics from the Uni-versity of California, Los Angeles, in 1977. His work has been represented by David Zwirner since 1995. **www.raypettibon.com**

▪ These works were first shown as part of *To Wit*, Pettibon's ninth solo exhibition at David Zwirner, New York, in 2013. They also appeared in the accompanying publication, *Raymond Pet-tibon: To Wit.*

The exhibition's title, "To Wit," conveys Pettibon's longstanding interest in the way language moves through its many registers: formal and highfalutin', literary, lyrical, and spoken. "To wit" is at once Shakespearean, legal, and tweetable. It is also a dedication to Wit, the broad principle of learning and humor that pervades this work.

Ed Piskor cut his teeth drawing *American Splendor* strips for Harvey Pekar. They went on to create two graphic novels together, *Macedonia* (2005, Villard), and *The Beats* (2007, Hill and Wang). Piskor then went on to create his own comics, the first being *Wizzywig* (2012, Top Shelf). He now does *Hip Hop Family Tree* full-time, published by Fantagraphics. **www.edpiskor.com**

▪ *Hip Hop Family Tree* is basically my thesis statement on the marriage between comics and hip hop, hidden beneath a pretty strict, linear history of rap music. The excerpts chosen have some panels that are brightly colored and different-looking than the rest of the narrative. These panels, complete with computer font lettering as opposed to the others containing hand lettering, are meant to be projections forward in time to a more modern era, and I chose to replicate more con-temporary production values to pull the reader out of the past for a moment or two.

After making xeroxed minicomics throughout the 1990s, **Ron Regé, Jr.**'s first book, *Skibber Bee~Bye*, was published in 2000. His most recent book, *The Cartoon Utopia*, came out in 2012. His work has also appeared in *The Best American Comics 2014, 2009*, and *2007*. He lives in Los Angeles. **ronregejr.tumblr.com**

▪ *The Pitchfork Review* didn't ask for any particular sort of comic when inviting me to contribute to their inaugural issue. Since they are a music magazine, I decided to use the opportunity to make something about the esoteric nature of music and sound. I'd done some stuff about the topic in my book *The Cartoon Utopia*, but felt there were more things I wanted to present. Reading about the ideas of early thinkers can be really fun. Music seems to be as magical and mysterious to us today as it was to Pythagoras and his followers.

Joe Sacco: I am mostly known for my journalism in comics form. I'm the author of *Palestine, Safe Area Gorazde, The Fixer, Footnotes in Gaza*, and *Journalism*, among other titles. My most recent book is *Bumf*, which has nothing at all to do with journalism and expresses my actionable contempt for authority in all its forms. I would rather be drawing than doing just about anything else.

▪ The excerpt is from a long, foldout, wordless illustration depicting the one day in the First World War—the first day of the Battle of the Somme. On July 1, 1916, the British army suffered almost 60,000 casualties, about half of the soldiers who went into the attack. I have long been fascinated with that battle and that day in particular.

David Sandlin was born in Belfast, Northern Ireland, in 1956. He currently lives in New York and teaches printmaking, book arts, and illustration at the School of Visual Arts. He has exhibited extensively in the U.S., Europe, Japan, and Australia and has been published in *The Best American Comics 2012* and *2009*, *The New Yorker, Raw,* and other publications. He has received fellowships and grants from the Guggenheim Foundation, the New York Public Library's Cullman Center for Scholars and Writers, the New York Foundation of the Arts, the Swann Foundation for Caricature and Cartoon, and other institutions. **www.davidsandlin.com**

▪ As the United States transitions to a post-empire psyche, its historical/mythological landscape will change with it. David Sandlin's latest narrative series, *76 Manifestations of American Destiny* (*Volume 1*), published by Sinland Press, represents American heroes and villains of fact and fiction and iconic occurrences and folktales in this fresh context. Loosely based on the nineteenth-century ukiyo-e master Taiso Yoshitoshi's *One Hundred Aspects of the Moon,* Sandlin replaces Samurai warriors, geisha murderesses, and haiku with depictions of U.S. political leaders, war battles, tabloid sex scandals, and country songs in a panorama of American history and legend.

R. Sikoryak is the author of *Masterpiece Comics* (Drawn and Quarterly), "Where Classics and Cartoons Collide." He's drawn for the *New York Times, The New Yorker, The Daily Show with Jon Stewart, The Onion, MAD, SpongeBob Comics, The Graphic Canon,* and others. He's also the host of the live comics–performance series Carousel. **www.rsikoryak.com**

▪ The astute reader may notice that Just Justine shares many positive qualities with a famous Amazon champion who immigrated to the United States. That extraordinary female was featured in comic pamphlets originally authored by William Moulton Marston and rendered by Harry George Peter in the 1940s. Like the Marquis de Sade's eighteenth-century protagonist, the Amazon was famous for regularly enduring bondage by ropes, chains, lassos, or handcuffs with honor and grace. Of course, there are two significant differences: Just Justine favors a Gallic rooster on her bodice and fleurs-de-lis on her shorts.

Matthew Thurber makes narrative work in many disciplines: comic books, musical theater, performance. He is the author of the graphic novels *1-800-MICE* (2011) and *INFOMANIACS* (2013), a cofounder of Tomato House Gallery and of the Potlatch, I Gather books-on-tape label. *Ambergris*, his ongoing multimedia performance project, often employs precinematic animation devices such as paper scrolls and has played at venues such as the Hammer Museum and the Fumetto Festival in Switzerland. His full-length play *Mining the Moon* was produced at the Brick Theater in July 2014. He lives in Brooklyn. **www.matthewthurber.com**

▪ *INFOMANIACS* was originally a serialized webcomic about the psychic repercussions of the Internet. The increasing daily intrusion of the Internet into everyday life, and the questions it raised about identity, addiction, privacy, and government control, manifested in a fast-paced, comedic spy story, influenced by John Le Carré and the "epic comedy" films of the '70s. The obsession with "The Singularity" in techno-futurist circles was parodied in a mad scramble to find the last human brain on earth to have never seen the Internet. As I was making this comic, the Edward Snowden and Chelsea Manning cases broke, real-life spy stories beside which my absurd fiction paled in comparison.

Anya Ulinich grew up in Moscow and immigrated to Arizona when she was seventeen. She holds an MFA in visual arts from the University of California, Davis. Her first novel, *Petropolis*, was published by Viking in 2007, and has since been translated into ten languages. Her graphic novel, *Lena Finkle's Magic Barrel*, was published by Penguin this year and named one of the Notable Books of 2014 by the *New York Times Book Review*. Ulinich's short stories and essays have appeared in the *New York Times*, *Newsweek*, *Zoetrope: All-Story*, *n+1*, *PEN America Journal*, and the *Jewish Daily Forward*. She has taught writing at the New School, NYU, and Gotham Writer's Workshop. **www.anyaulinichbooks.com**

▪ The pages excerpted here come from my graphic novel, *Lena Finkle's Magic Barrel*, which was published by Penguin in 2014. The protagonist, Lena Finkle, is a divorced New Yorker in her thirties who searches for love, meaning, and identity while raising her two teenage daughters. This excerpt is about heartbreak, and is pretty dark. The book as a whole is both dark and funny.

Henriette Valium: I was born in 1959 and raised in Repentigny, a typical French suburban town east of Montréal. I think as far as I know I've always drawn things. The white page has naturally been to me the cheapest and easiest way to express myself. Then high school in the '70s and later I went to college in art. Looking back on those years, it was for me a pure waste of time, essentially boozing and partying. You can't learn to be an artist. Beside paintings, I do also a few music collages on my computer. I have a hate and love relationship with comics, and no artistic goal at all. I think comics attracts all the losers and immature teenagers like myself, moving constantly between five and fifteen, stuck in an adult world they will never understand. For me drawing is more like an obsessive-compulsive disorder sickness, or a matter of basic survival if you want. If I stop painting and drawing, I will simply jump off the next bridge. **www.henriettevalium.com**

▪ These ten pages called "Lâcher de Chiens" are the opening story of my next comic book that I'm working on now. This story is made out of a real event. Back in 2005, a new guy in the neighborhood one Sunday morning let his two dogs out in the lane when my little kids were playing, so I've been really really mad at him. A year later, their mother kicks my ass out of the house with the cops, so I blended the two events to make a story. After that I ended up north of town near the highway in a building full of divorced losers like me, so from this comes the name of the book "Le Palais des Champions" (the palace of champions), sixty pages all in color. Will be ready in 2015 (I hope).

Esther Pearl Watson has a BFA from Art Center College of Design and an MFA from CalArts. Her illustrations have appeared in many magazines and newspapers. *Unlovable* has appeared in *Bust* magazine since 2004 and is loosely based on a diary dated from the 1980s that Esther found in a gas station bathroom in 1997. **www.estherpearlwatson.com; www.funchicken.com**

▪ Summer vacation is here and Tammy Pierce is back with more sometimes ordinary, often humiliating, occasionally poignant, and usually hilarious exploits! Her hopes, dreams, agonies, and defeats are brought to vivid, comedic life by Watson's lovingly grotesque drawings, filled with all the '80s essentials—too much mascara, leg warmers with heels, and huge hair, etc.—as well as timeless teen concerns like acne, dandruff, and the opposite sex (or same sex, in some cases).

Jim Woodring was born in Los Angeles in 1952. His first successful work was the self-published autojournal *JIM*, which documented his tumultuous, vision-haunted inner life. His metaphysical *Frank* comics, which present a model of Woodring's view of reality in scary, funny animal fables, have won numerous awards. Woodring works in pen and ink, watercolor, oil, charcoal, and other media to concretely convey his elusive, slippery ideas. He lives in Seattle and on **www.jimwoodring.com**

▪ In 2011's *Congress of the Animals,* I took my main character, Frank, out of his familiar world—the Unifactor—to give him a change of air and some romance. That book ended with Frank immersed in domestic bliss with his newly acquired inamorata Fran. Unexpectedly and unfortunately, Fran was a stultifying influence on him. Frank had always awakened early in the morning hungry for adventure and he generally found some. With Fran's appearance he began to sleep in. The Unifactor wasn't having it. The excerpt in these pages shows the dissolution of that relationship as orchestrated by Fran, who it turns out is something more than she first appeared to be.

Gina Wynbrandt was born in Chicago in 1990. She writes comics about personal humiliations, sexual disappointment, and popular culture. Her favorite food is ice cream. **www.ginawynbrandt.com**

▪ *Someone Please Have Sex wth Me* is my sexual autobiography. I like to make people laugh through self-deprecation, and I'm a chronic oversharer, so this was a fun comic to make. It's also an official plea for someone to have sex with me, which sadly has not been taken seriously.

Notable Comics

from September 1, 2013, to August 31, 2014

Selected by Bill Kartalopoulos

CHRISTOPHER ADAMS
Yule Log.

SAM ALDEN
Anime. *It Never Happened Again.*

T. EDWARD BAK
Island of Memory.

TAYLOR-RUTH BALDWIN
Hanging Rock Comics.
thisishangingrockcomics.tumblr.com

KATE BEATON
Ducks. *beatonna.tumblr.com/post
/81993262830/here-is-a-sketch-comic-i-made
-called-ducks-in*

DREW BECKMEYER
Everything Unseen #4: Parts 8 & 9.

BRIAN BLOMERTH
Hypermaze.

ANNA BONGIOVANNI
Out of Hollow Water.

STEVE BRODNER
Tonkin Ghosts. *www.latimes.com/opinion/op-ed
/la-oe-tonkin-gulf-incident-20140801-photogallery
.html*

ELIJAH BRUBAKER
Reich #11.

JULIEN CECCALDI
Coquelicot Moment. *Mould Map #3.*

SEYMOUR CHWAST
A Connecticut Yankee in King Arthur's Court.

CHRIS CILLA
The Debt and the Damages. *Rotland Dreadfuls*
#8.

MAX CLOTFELTER
Shame Train. *Despair*, vol. 2.

DAVE COLLIER
Downtown Sugar Shack. *Descant 164.*

JORDAN CRANE
Untitled. *Monster 2013*, vol. 3.

DAME DARCY
Voyage of the Temptress.
damedarcy.com/web-comix

GEOFF DARROW
Shaolin Cowboy #1–4.

CLAUDIA DÁVILA
Like a Sparrow. *Taddle Creek #33.*

MIKE DAWSON
Angie Bongiolatti.

ANDY DOUGLAS DAY
Miss Hennipin.

JULIE DELPORTE
Everywhere Antennas.

KRYSTAL DIFRONZO
Saint's Love.

STEVE DITKO
#9 Teen and #20.

SARAH DRAKE
Tipu's Tiger.

NICK DRNASO
The Grassy Knoll.

DENNIS EICHHORN AND VARIOUS
Real Good Stuff #1 & 2.

INÉS ESTRADA
CS.

C.F.
Untitled. *Mould Map #3.*

EDIE FAKE
Night Taps. *Believed Behavior*, Season One.

SOPHIE FRANZ
Untitled. *Barrio Mothers.*

RENÉE FRENCH
Hagelbarger and That Nightmare Goat.

GG
Semi-Vivi. *ohgigue.tumblr.com/post/95116930421
/semi-vivi-by-gg-made-for-the-comics-workbook*

SOPHIE GOLDSTEIN
Mother. *Pitchfork Review #1.*

CARLOS GONZALEZ
Test Tube #1 & 2.

V. A. GRAHAM & J. A. EISENHOWER
Scaffold #3.

JOHN HANKIEWICZ
The Intermission Festival. *Ink Brick* #1.

GILBERT HERNANDEZ
Maria M.: Book One.

JAIME HERNANDEZ
Stories in *Love and Rockets: New Stories* #6.

CATHY G. JOHNSON
Rabbit. *Happiness* #4

BEN KATCHOR
Comics from *Metropolis Magazine.*

KEREN KATZ
A Small Fire in the National Library. *Fire Theater.*

AIDAN KOCH
Configurations. *www.aidankoch.com/index.php?/special-project/configurations*

ALINE KOMINKSY-CRUMB
Of What Use Is an Old Bunch? *Critical Inquiry*, Spring 2014.

PATRICK KYLE
New Comics #3.

JESSE LUCAS
Cash. *jesselucas.com/tagged/cash/chrono*

NICK MAANDAG
Facility Integrity.

MELISSA MENDES
Joey.

DREW MILLER
Orbiter's Prism.

CORRINE MUCHA
Get Over It!

KRIS MUKAI
Commuter.

ROMAN MURADOV
Picnic Ruined.

JASON MURPHY
Me Nut Nut Nut #2.

JONNY NEGRON
Bitch of a Bitch. *www.vice.com/read/bitch-of-a-bitch*

MARÉ ODOMO
Internet Comics #2.

JASON OVERBY
Permission Phase. *abstractcomics.blogspot.com/2014/02/permission-phase.html*

JOHN PHAM
Epoxy #4.

DAVID PLUNKERT
Heroical #1.

JOHN PORCELLINO
King-Cat #74.

PROLE.INFO
Abolish Work.

JESSE REKLAW
Lessoned. *Couch Tag.*

KEILER ROBERTS
Powdered Milk #13.

YUMI SAKUGAWA
Never Forgets.

RICHARD SALA
Violenzia.

FRANK SANTORO
Pompeii.

DARYL SEITCHICK
Missy #1 & 2.

SETH
Palookaville #21.

DASH SHAW
Cosplayers #1 & 2.

JASON SHIGA
Demon: Chapters 1–4. *www.shigabooks.com*

CAITLIN SKAALRUD
Houses of the Holy: Part One.

JORDAN SPEER
QCHQ.

CONOR STECHSCHULTE
The Dormitory.

SASHA STEINBERG
Body Language. *Suspect Device* #4.

A. K. SUMMERS
Pregnant Butch.

IAN SUNDAHL
Irrational Logic. *Social Discipline*, vol. 7.

JILLIAN TAMAKI AND MARIKO TAMAKI
This One Summer.

WHIT TAYLOR
The Anthropologists.

CRAIG THOMPSON
Azzolino's Story Without End. *Fairy Tale Comics.*

SETH TOBOCMAN
Edith in Flames. *World War 3 Illustrated* #45.

PETE TOMS
In Post. *ifeelawesome.net/inpost*

BENJAMIN URKOWITZ
The Facts. *Felony Comics #1.*

MALACHI WARD
Ritual 3: Vile Decay.

CHRIS WARE
Possession. *The New Yorker*, June 9 & 16, 2014.

MATT WEINECKE
Your media guide to the differences between #Ferguson and #pumpkinfest. *twitter.com /MattTW/status/523833164758675456/photo/1*

LAUREN WEINSTEIN
Carriers. *nautil.us/blog/carriers-a-webcomic-on -health-luck-and-life*

STEVEN WEISSMAN
Barrack Hussein Obama. *whatthingsdo.com /single-panel/top-secret/#6674*

LALE WESTVIND
Now and Here.

JESS WHEELOCK
Untitled. *Puppyteeth #4.*

ERIC KOSTIUK WILLIAMS
Hungry Bottom Comics #3.

SOPHIE YANOW
War of Streets and Houses.

MICKEY ZACCHILLI
RAV #9.

CREDITS

"briefly, before dawn" by Rosaire Appel. First published in *Central Booking Magazine,* Volume IV, Issue III. Copyright © 2014 by Rosaire Appel. Reprinted by permission of Rosaire Appel.

"Woman Rebel: The Margaret Sanger Story" (excerpt) by Peter Bagge. First published in *Women Rebel: The Margaret Sanger Story.* Copyright © 2014 by Peter Bagge. Reprinted by permission of Drawn & Quarterly.

"Theth" (excerpt) by Josh Bayer. First published in *Theth, Retrofit Giant Size Annual.* Copyright © 2014 by Josh Bayer. Reprinted by permission of Josh Bayer.

"The Colombia Diaries, Sept 14–16" by Gabrielle Bell. First published in *Truth Is Fragmentary.* Copyright © 2014 by Gabrielle Bell. Reprinted by permission of Gabrielle Bell.

"Cretin Keep On Creep'n Creek" by Mat Brinkman. First published in *UDWFG,* vol.1. Copyright © 2014 by Mat Brinkman. Reprinted by permission of Mat Brinkman.

"Pretty Smart" by Andy Burkholder. First published in *Believed Behavior Season One.* Copyright © 2014 by Andrew Burkholder. Reprinted by permission of Andrew Burkholder.

"Misliving Amended" by Adam Buttrick. First published in *Misliving Amended.* Copyright © 2014 by Adam Buttrick. Reprinted by permission of Adam Buttrick.

"Can't We Talk About Something More Pleasant?" (excerpt) by Roz Chast. First published in *Can't We Talk About Something More Pleasant?* by Roz Chast. Copyright © 2014 by Roz Chast. Reprinted by permission of Bloomsbury Publishing Inc.

"Little Tommy Lost: Book One" (excerpt) by Cole Closser. First published in *Little Tommy Lost: Book One,* Koyama Press. Copyright © 2014 by Cole Closser. Reprinted by permission of Cole Closser and Koyama Press.

"The Wrenchies" (excerpt) by Farel Dalrymple. First published in THE WRENCHIES, pp. 190–199. From *The Wrenchies* © 2014 by Farel Dalrymple. Reprinted by permission of First Second, an imprint of Roaring Brook Press, a division of Holtzbrinck Publishing Holdings Limited Partnership. All Rights Reserved.

"No Class" (excerpt) by Anya Davidson. First published in *School Spirits.* Copyright © 2014 by Anya Davidson. Reprinted by permission of PictureBox, Inc.

"No Tears, No Sorrow" by Eleanor Davis. First published in *How to Be Happy.* Copyright © 2014 by Eleanor Davis. Reprinted by permission of Eleanor Davis.

"Crime Chime Noir" by A. Degen. First published in *Felony Comics #1.* Copyright © 2014 by A. Degen. Reprinted by permission of A. Degen.

"Blane Throttle" (excerpt) by Ben Duncan. First published on the Study Group Comics website. Copyright © 2014 by Ben Duncan. Reprinted by permission of Ben Duncan.

"Kill My Mother" (excerpt) by Jules Feiffer. First published in *Kill My Mother: A Graphic Novel* by Jules Feiffer. Copyright © 2014 by B. Mergendeiler Corp. Used by permission of Liveright Publishing Corporation.

"Cross Delivery," "Screw Style," "How did you get in the hole?," "The Pen," and "We Can't Sleep" by Noel Freibert. First published in *the hole.* Copyright © 2014 by Noel Freibert. Reprinted by permission of Noel Freibert.

"Palm Ash" by Julia Gfrörer. First published in *Palm Ash.* Copyright © 2014 by Julia Gfrorer. Reprinted by permission of Julia Gfrörer.

"Lâcher de Chiens" by Henriette Valium. First published in *Descant 164.* Copyright © 2014 by Henriette Valium (Patrick Henley). Reprinted by permission of Henriette Valium (Patrick Henley).

Image of Jonathan Lethem by Paul Hornschemeier. Copyright © 2014 by Paul Hornschemeier. Reprinted with permission.

Front cover:
Raymond Pettibon
Untitled, 2015
Colored pencil, ink, and gouache on paper
8 x 7⅛ inches (20.3 x 18.1 cm)
Courtesy the artist and David Zwirner, New York

Back cover:
Raymond Pettibon
No Title (Zip!...), 2015
Graphite and ink on paper
5¼ x 9 inches (13.3 x 22.9 cm)
Courtesy the artist and David Zwirner, New York

THE BEST AMERICAN SERIES®

FIRST, BEST, AND BEST-SELLING

The Best American series is the premier annual showcase for the country's finest short fiction and nonfiction. Each volume's series editor selects notable works from hundreds of magazines, journals, and websites. A special guest editor, a leading writer in the field, then chooses the best twenty or so pieces to publish. This unique system has made the Best American series the most respected — and most popular — of its kind.

Look for these best-selling titles in the Best American series:

The Best American Comics

The Best American Essays

The Best American Infographics

The Best American Mystery Stories

The Best American Nonrequired Reading

The Best American Science and Nature Writing

The Best American Science Fiction and Fantasy

The Best American Short Stories

The Best American Sports Writing

The Best American Travel Writing

Available in print and e-book wherever books are sold.
Visit our website: *www.hmhco.com/popular-reading/general-interest-books/by-category/best-american*

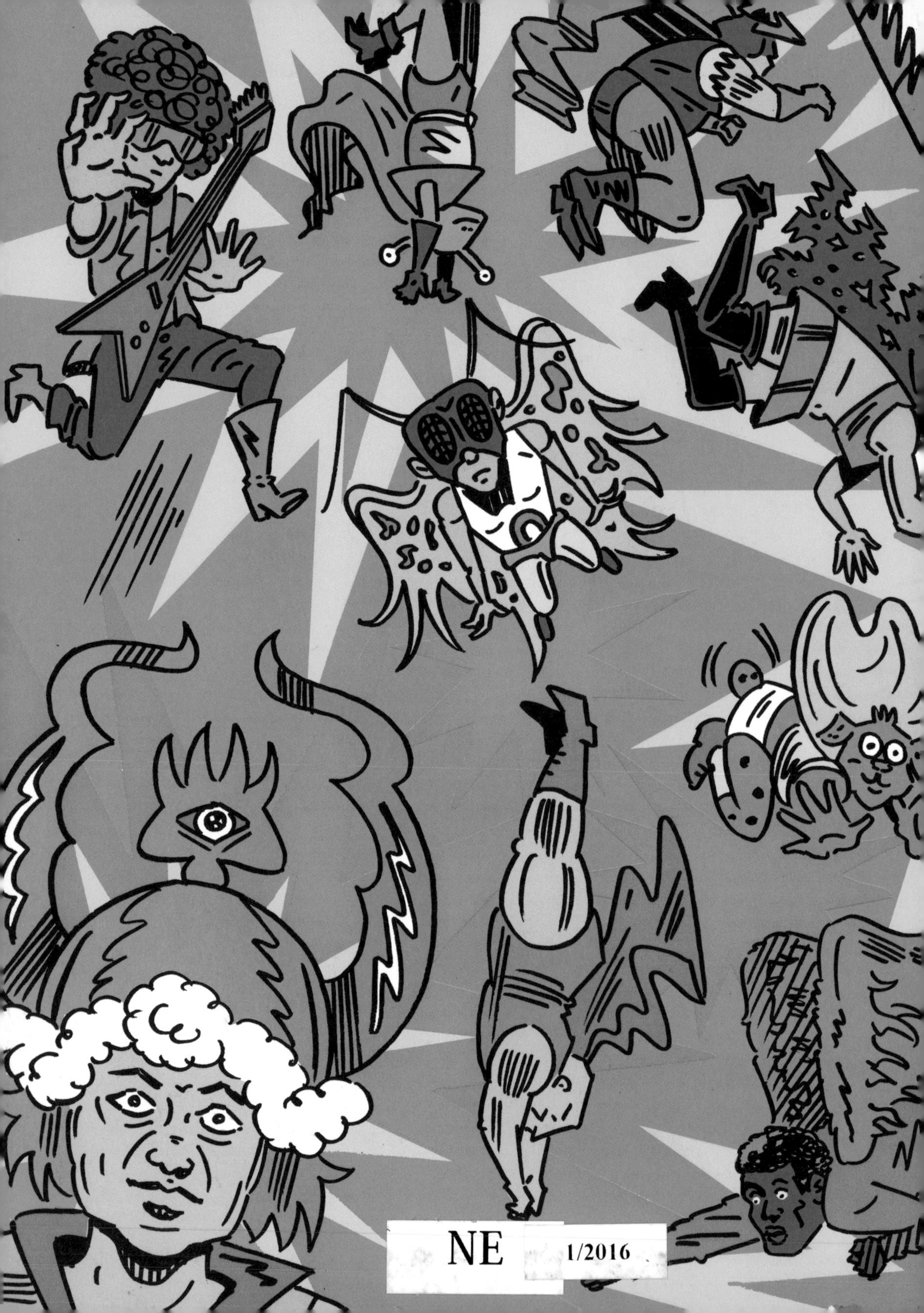